Competition Law and Policy in Digital Markets

Competition Law and Policy in Digital Markets

A Comparative Analysis of the EU and China

MARIA IOANNIDOU
Reader in Competition Law, Centre for Commercial Law Studies and Department of Law, Queen Mary University of London, UK

BINGWAN XIONG
Professor of Law, School of Law, Renmin University of China, China

OXFORD
UNIVERSITY PRESS

OXFORD
UNIVERSITY PRESS

Great Clarendon Street, Oxford, OX2 6DP,
United Kingdom

Oxford University Press is a department of the University of Oxford.
It furthers the University's objective of excellence in research, scholarship,
and education by publishing worldwide. Oxford is a registered trade mark of
Oxford University Press in the UK and in certain other countries

Published in the United States of America by Oxford University Press
198 Madison Avenue, New York, NY 10016, United States of America

British Library Cataloguing in Publication Data
Data available

Library of Congress Control Number: 2024948868

ISBN 9780192843388

DOI: 10.1093/9780191925955.001.0001

Printed and bound by
CPI Group (UK) Ltd, Croydon, CR0 4YY

MIX
Paper | Supporting
responsible forestry
FSC® C013604
FSC
www.fsc.org

The manufacturer's authorised representative in the EU for product safety is
Oxford University Press España S.A. of El Parque Empresarial San Fernando de Henares,
Avenida de Castilla, 2 – 28830 Madrid (www.oup.es/en or
product.safety@oup.com). OUP España S.A. also acts as importer into Spain
of products made by the manufacturer.

Acknowledgements

This book is the culmination of a long intellectual journey, which started at the end of 2018, first as a general idea discussed during the lunch break on the side of the Inaugural Summit on 'Digital Economy and the Rule of Law for Future Generations' organized by Renmin University Institute of Law and Technology in Beijing. As is often the case with book projects, maybe the more so with joint endeavours, what started as an ambitious project with the best intentions to be completed in a couple of years took longer to come to fruition.

The book's subject matter, exploring competition law enforcement in the digital economy, has evolved exponentially since 2018, not only in Europe and China but also in literally every major competition law jurisdiction around the globe. The ever-growing developments in this field rendered its completion challenging, though admittedly very rewarding.

Apart from the existing challenges in framing the scope of the book, during this time, a lot has happened for the authors both personally and professionally. There are numerous people at Queen Mary University of London (QMUL), the Hellenic Competition Commission (HCC), Renmin Law School, National Development and Reform Commission (NDRC), and the National Data Bureau to which the authors are indebted for their mentorship and support. Without their friendship, continuous discussions and inspiration of ideas and arguments, this book would not have come into being. The authors are grateful to each and every one of them.

In particular, there are so many people at both QMUL and the HCC that Maria would like to thank. At QMUL, colleagues have provided a supportive intellectual environment with whom various ideas were discussed throughout this project. In particular, special thanks are due to Ioannis Kokkoris for support and Eyad Dabbah for constantly providing a collegiate environment in her competition law endeavours. The transition from academic life to being a Commissioner Rapporteur and Member of the Board at the HCC between 2019 and 2022, during which a large part of this book project was drafted, was made much easier due to the support of Maria's colleagues at the authority. Ioannis Lianos, with his forward-looking and inspiring approach to competition law, made the transition from academia to agency enforcement much easier. Marianna Rantou and Kelly Benetatou have been the colleagues everyone would wish for. The HCC Directorate-General for Competition comprises amazing people, and Maria is forever grateful to each of them, especially teams that have worked on anything related to boats, from the first case on ferry routes to the last case on tug services. Throughout Maria's academic and regulatory journey, Vasiliki Brisimi has been a source of inspiration and knowledge, but most of all a great friend. Part of the research for this project has been presented in various fora over the years and has benefited from insights and comments of many colleagues.

Bingwan, on his part, is, first of all, enormously grateful to the superb colleagues in the Institute of Law and Technology at Renmin University, the Research Centre for Civil and Commercial Law and the Foreign-Related Legal Consulting Service Centre. Their great passion for and dedication to the next generation of rule of law in the digital era around the globe greatly encouraged him to jump into the field of competition law, a challenging field for a scholar whose previous scholarship was mainly on civil law. Nevertheless, the seven-year intellectual journey has proved to be extraordinarily fulfilling and rewarding, to see how the scholarship of civil law could chemically react with that of competition law. Bingwan is certainly deeply indebted to Maria, not only for her strong leadership in the conception and implementation of this joint project but also, even more importantly, for her infinite patience to wait for his sections. Wei Han, another key intellectual companion throughout this project, was always ready to help navigate through hard questions that cropped up during this long journey, be it of policies, of cases, or of general theories. Jingmeng Cai, Li Chen, Feng Deng, Jiangqiu Ge, Yanbei Meng, Shitong Qiao, Liming Wang, Dong Yang, and Jun Ye were inspirational in working on several key parts of this project. Special thanks are also due to Fuqian Deng and Qiqin Qian, two remarkable research assistants whose extensive and high-quality research assistance in almost all stages of this monograph are inseparable from its completion. Thanks are given to Qian Guo, Xinmiao Lai, Bo Liu, Junlan Lv, Menguing Sun, Mingze Wang, Yi Shen, Shuyun Yi, and many others who have provided precious assistance in literature review, policy collection, case briefing, text translation, and proofreading. Yongwei Chen's contribution to the preparation of the book proposal was also valuable and worthy of particular credit. Bingwan is also grateful to the generous support from the National Natural Science Foundation of China on the research project of Theory and Institutional Design of Public Data Open Utilization and Authorized Operation (NO.72342010).

Max Kaltenmeier, Xinmiao Lai, and Enzo Rebelo provided valuable assistance in the final editing stage. Charlotte Kershaw at OUP has been consistently supportive throughout the publication process and always accommodating with the time frame. Maria and Bingwan are thankful to them for rendering the publication process very seamless.

Foremost, Maria and Bingwan would like to thank their families for their constant and unwavering support throughout this project and beyond. Constants define them and the things they do in life. On her part, Maria owes huge thanks to Charilaos, Anna, and Odysseas for making everything (including completing this monograph) so much more meaningful and rewarding. Bingwan, on his part, is extremely grateful to Yan, who made huge efforts throughout this project in taking good care of Shangyu and Shangyuan. The lovely smiles of Shangyu and Shangyuan have also given constant vigour to move the projects forward. All of them have contributed immensely to the completion of this project.

Contents

PART B. COMPETITION LAW AND DIGITAL MARKETS IN THE EU

PART C. COMPETITION LAW AND DIGITAL MARKETS IN CHINA

PART D. COMPARATIVE ASSESSMENT: NORMATIVE CONCLUSIONS

Figures

Tables

Table of Cases and Decisions

EUROPEAN COURT OF JUSTICE

GENERAL COURT

EUROPEAN COMMISSION DECISIONS

NATIONAL CASES

Belgium

China

Germany

United States

Table of Legislation

EUROPEAN UNION

Directives

Regulations

Guidelines

Notices

National Legislation and Regulation

China

Germany

Greece

United Kingdom

United States

Abbreviations

ACCC	Australian Competition and Consumer Commission
ACM	Authority for Consumers and Markets (Netherlands)
ACR	automatic content recognition
AdC	Autorité de la Concurrence (France)
AEC test	'as-efficient-competitor' test
AFA	anti-fragmentation agreements
AFC	AdSense for Content
AFS	AdSense for Search
AFSh	AdSense for Shopping
AG	Advocate General
AGCM	Italian Competition Authority
AI	artificial intelligence
AICOA	American Innovation and Choice Online Act
AML	Anti-Monopoly Law (China)
AdMob	AdSense for Mobile Applications
AMR	Administration for Market Regulation (China)
API	application programming interface
APPA	across-platform parity agreement
ARC	Act against Restraints of Competition (Germany)
ATT	App Tracking Transparency
AV	audio-visual
AWS	Amazon Web Services
B2B	business to business
B2C	business to consumer
BDS	BeiDou Satellite
BEREC	Body of European Regulators for Electronic Communications
BKA	Bundeskartellamt (Germany)
BRICS	Brazil, Russia, India, China, South Africa
C2C	consumer to consumer
CAC	Cyberspace Administration of China
CAT	Competition Appeals Tribunal (UK)
CBIT	China Banking and Insurance Information Technology
CCCS	Competition and Consumer Commission
CCPC	Competition and Consumer Protection Commission
CD	Commission Decision
CEO	chief executive officer
CEIBS	China–Europe International Business School
CESifo	Institute for Economic Studies–Institute for Economic Research
CJEU	Court of Justice of the European Union (EU)

CMA	Competition and Markets Authority (UK)
CMC	China Music Corporation
CNIL	National Commission on Informatics and Liberty
CNKI	China National Knowledge Infrastructure
CNMC	Comisión Nacional de los Mercados y la Competencia (Spanish Competition Authority)
CNNIC	China Internet Information Center
CPC	Communist Party of China
CPI	Competition Policy International
CPI	consumer price index
CPO	collective proceedings order
CPS	core platform service
CRM	customer relation management (software)
CSS	comparison shopping service
CTR	click-through rate
DAU	daily active users
DFA	DoubleClick for Advertisers
DFP	DoubleClick for Publishers
DGA	Data Governance Act
DMA	Digital Markets Act (EU)
DMCC	Digital Markets, Competition and Consumer Bill/Act 2024
DoJ	Department of Justice (US)
DSA	Digital Service Act (EU)
DSP	demand-side platform
EC	European Community
ECN	European Competition Network
EDPS	European Data Protection Supervisor (EU)
EEA	European Economic Area (EU)
EGEL	Economy Energy, E(Gas and Electricity) Ltd
EPC	European Publishers Council
EU HMG	EU Horizontal Merger Guidelines
EUMR	European Union Merger Regulation (EU)
FASB	Financial Accounting Standards Board
FBA	Fulfilment by Amazon
FCO	Federal Cartel Office (Germany)
FMP	Facebook Marketing Partners
FRAND	fair, reasonable, and non-discriminatory
FTC	Federal Trade Commission (US)
GAFAM	Google Apple Facebook Amazon Microsoft
GC	General Court of the Court of Justice of the European Union (EU)
GDPR	General Data Protection Regulation (EU)
GE	General Electric
GEMA	Gas and Electricity Markets Authority (UK)
GFA	Google Ad Manager for Advertisers
GFP	Google for Publishers
GIF	graphics interchange format

GMS	Google Mobile Services
GPU	graphic processing unit
GSA	Google services agreements
HBER	Horizontal Block Exemptions Regulation (EU)
HCC	Hellenic Competition Commission
HMG	Horizontal Mergers Guidelines (EU)
HMT	hypothetical monopoly test
HRG	Horizontal Co-operation Agreements Guidelines (EU)
HRS	Hotel Reservation Service
IAAS	infrastructure as a service
IAB	Interactive Advertising Bureau
IAP	in-app purchase
ICN	International Competition Network
ICO	Information Commissioner's Office (UK)
IDE	integrated development environments
IFR	Interchange Fee Regulation
IHG	InterContinental Hotels Group
IM	instant messaging
IoT	Internet of Things
IP	intellectual property
IPO	initial public offering
KOL	key opinion leader
M&A	merger and acquisition
MAU	monthly active users
MADA	mobile application distribution agreements
MAG	Merger Assessment Guidelines (UK)
MAP	minimum advertised prices
MFCC	most-favoured-customer clauses
MFN	most-favoured-nation clauses
MIIT	Ministry of Industry and Information Technology
MLS	multiple listing systems
MNO	mobile network operator
MOFCOM	Ministry of Commerce of the People's Republic of China
MS	Member State
NASDAQ	National Association of Securities Dealers Automated Quotations
NCA	national competition authority
NCT	New Competition Tool
NDRC	National Development and Reform Commission (China)
NFC	near-field communication
NHMG	Non-Horizontal Merger Guidelines (EU)
NIICS	number-independent interpersonal communications services
NPC	National People's Congress
nyd	not yet decided
OECD	Organisation for Economic Co- operation and Development
OEM	original equipment manufacturers
Ofgem	Office of Gas and Electricity Markets (UK)

OFT	Office of Fair Trading (UK)
OIS	online intermediation service
OS	operating system
OTA	online travel agents
P2B Regulation	Platform-to-Business Regulation (EU)
PaaS	platform as a service
PCW	price comparison websites
PIPL	Personal Information Protection Law (China)
PKU	Peking University
PMFN	platform most favoured nation
PRC	People's Republic of China
PSD2	Second Payment Services Directive
PSN	professional social network
R&D	research and development
RHG	Revised Horizontal Guidelines
RPM	resale price maintenance
RSA	revenue-share agreements
RVC	robot vacuum cleaner
SaaS	software as a service
SAIC	State Administration for Industry and Commerce (China)
SAMR	State Administration for Market Regulation (China)
SDS	selective distribution system
SEP	standard essential patent
SLC	substantial-lessening-of-competition test
SME	small and medium-sized enterprises
SO	Statement of Objections (EU)
SPC	Supreme People's Court of the People's Republic of China
SN	social networking
SOE	state-owned enterprise
SSNDQ	small but significant non-transitory decrease in quality
SSNIP	small but significant non-transitory increase in price
SSP	supply-side platform
SVOD	subscription-based video on demand
SWD	Staff Working Document of the European Commission (EU)
TEU	Treaty on European Union
TFEU	Treaty on the Functioning of the European Union (EU)
TME	Tencent Music Group
USACM	US Association for Computational Mechanics
VBER	Vertical Block Exemption Regulation (EU)
VIE	variable interest entity
VR	virtual reality
VRG	Guidelines on Vertical Restraints (EU)
VSTS	Visual Studio Teams Services
WLM	Windows Live Messenger
WMP	Windows Media Player

PART A

THE CONTEXT: CHARACTERISTICS OF DIGITAL MARKETS AND COMPETITION LAW IMPLICATIONS

1
Introduction

I. Scope

Technological developments in big data, data analytics, powerful algorithms, and machine learning have transformed markets and brought numerous benefits to consumers and businesses. A variety of different platforms, apps, and new business models have significantly reduced prices and expanded consumers' choices. At the same time, the ongoing digital revolution has created new challenges and risks for competition law enforcers. And as has been accurately highlighted, 'any change, even a change for the better, is always accompanied by drawbacks and discomforts'.[1] Such a digital transformation has resulted in unprecedented levels of market concentration, with a handful of digital giants controlling the provision of many goods and services. Tech firms including Google,[2] Amazon, Facebook,[3] Apple, and Microsoft dominate the globe. To be precise, they dominate the globe with the exception of China, a market with its very own digital giants' equivalents. Interestingly, Big Tech companies in the Western world have their home-grown Chinese counterparts, and often the history behind these behemoths is intertwined. Google, for example, has grown exponentially from a search engine based on the ingenious algorithm PageRank to an ecosystem offering a constellation of online services to consumers and businesses. PageRank, though, was influenced by another algorithm which aimed at crawling, indexing, and ranking pages online called RankDex.[4] RankDex was developed by Robin Li in 1996, who then established the search engine Baidu in 2000. Amazon was established as an online bookstore in 1997. Since then, it has grown exponentially to dominate online commerce. Alibaba, founded by Jack Ma in 1998, has prevented the expansion of Amazon in China.

China has its own home-grown digital giants and has recently stepped up competition law enforcement and regulatory uptakes. At the same time, the structure of digital markets depicts significant similarities. For example, with respect to digital

[1] A Bennett, *The Great Adventure* (Stagedoor, 2014).

[2] Since October 2015, Google has been a wholly owned subsidiary of Alphabet Inc. It is Alphabet's largest subsidiary and the umbrella company for its Internet interests. See Fortune, 'Alphabet in Fortune Rankings' <https://fortune.com/company/alphabet> (accessed 6 June 2024).

[3] Facebook signalled its metaverse ambition and rebranded as Meta in October 2021. Facebook remains Meta's flagship product. See Meta, 'About Meta' <https://about.meta.com/company-info> (accessed 13 June 2024). References to Meta and Facebook in this book are used interchangeably.

[4] Rankdex, 'About Meta and Facebook' <http://www.rankdex.com/about.html> (accessed 3 October 2023).

Competition Law and Policy in Digital Markets. Maria Ioannidou and Bingwan Xiong, Oxford University Press.
 DOI: 10.1093/9780191925955.003.0001

advertising in 2019, with 40 per cent of global e-commerce value being concentrated in China,[5] the global revenue was concentrated in both US and Chinese firms, with Google, Facebook, and Alibaba in the top three, followed by Amazon, Baidu, and Tencent.[6] These digital behemoths have built their business models based on the unprecedented data aggregation. Policymakers even speak, somewhat rhetorically, of 'data monopolisation'.[7] In essence, both jurisdictions studied in this book—the European Union (EU) and China—are called on to address the same problems involving different players. At the same time, one should acknowledge China's importance for Western digital giants and vice versa. For example, in 2021, around 40 per cent of Amazon's top sellers were based in China,[8] whereas one of these Chinese companies (Anker) has thrived on Amazon Marketplace, building a USD 2 billion phone accessory business.[9]

The rise of such digital ecosystems has challenged the ability of competition law to adequately capture new conduct. The term 'ecosystem' connotes the 'various aspects of a platform's activities and services which interrelate and often complement or connect to a core service' and is characterized by 'the presence of complementarities and interdependencies between economic activities'.[10] Many jurisdictions around the world, like the EU and China, have listed competition law enforcement as a tool to better regulate and facilitate the development of their own digital markets. At the same time, and acknowledging the respective limits of competition law enforcement, they have also been considering, and have adopted, complementary regulations.

The EU and China have established loose forms of competition cooperation since 2003, even before the enactment of the Chinese Anti-Monopoly Law on 1 August 2008.[11] More recently, in 2019, the EU Directorate-General (DG) for Competition and the State Administration for Market Regulation (SAMR) signed the Terms of Reference of the EU–China Competition Policy Dialogue with the

[5] B Evans, 'Tech in 2020: Standing on the Shoulders of Giants' (February 2020) <https://static1.squarespace.com/static/50363cf324ac8e905e7df861/t/5ed23bd3bdbbdb299cb6aa9f/1590836452410/2020+Benedict+Evans+Shoulders+of+Giants.pdf>, slide 105 (accessed 6 June 2024).

[6] J Enberg, 'Global Digital Ad Spending 2019: Digital Accounts for Half of Total Media Ad Spending Worldwide' (EMarketer, 28 March 2019) <https://www.emarketer.com/content/global-digital-ad-spending-2019> (accessed 6 June 2024).

[7] UK House of Lords Select Committee on Artificial Intelligence, 'AI in the UK: Ready, Willing and Able?'(Report of Session 2017–2019, 16 April 2018), para 129.

[8] B Evans, 'The New Gatekeepers' (presentation, December 2023) <https://www.ben-evans.com/presentations>, slide 41 (accessed 28 September 2023).

[9] *Ibid*, slide 42.

[10] Competition and Markets Authority (CMA), 'Online Platforms and Digital Advertising' (Market Study—Final Report) (Digital Platforms Report, 1 July 2020) Appendix E: Ecosystems of Google and Facebook <https://assets.publishing.service.gov.uk/media/5fe49531d3bf7f089e48dec9/Appendix_E_Ecosystems_v.2_WEB.pdf> (accessed 18 August 2023), paras 1 and 2. For a discussion, see Chapter 2, section IV.1.

[11] European Commission (EU), 'Bilateral Relations with Peoples' Republic of China' <https://competition-policy.ec.europa.eu/international-relations/bilateral-relations/china_en> (accessed 28 September 2023).

aim of engaging in an exchange of views on their respective experience with competition law enforcement.[12] The EU and China also regularly engage in policy dialogue with respect to the challenges posed by the digital economy. For example, the two parties recently held the second EU–China High-Level Digital Dialogue,[13] where they discussed issues pertaining to platform regulation, data, and artificial intelligence (AI).[14] Taking stock of the changing market dynamics, this book provides a critical comparative analysis of the application of competition law in digital markets in the EU and China, focusing on both published decisions and procedural or informal institutional arrangements. It offers a thoughtful account of legal doctrines, policies, and practices relevant to competition enforcement and regulation in both jurisdictions.

The book will, first, identify and map the economic characteristics of digital markets and the challenges they raise for competition law enforcement and, second, present the decisional practice to date and critically evaluate various proposals to tackle such challenges. It will provide a taxonomy of possible competition law problems and discuss 'novel' types of anticompetitive conduct at the intersection of consumer, data protection, and competition laws. The book will also identify 'gap cases', querying whether competition laws can act as a gap filler or whether other regulatory tools are better suited to address such problems. The book examines these questions in two key competition law jurisdictions, examining the similarities and divergent approaches in an attempt to contribute to a more transparent debate between competition law enforcers in the EU and China. While acknowledging the broader political tensions between the two jurisdictions,[15] the focus of this book is narrower, specifically addressing competition law enforcement.

With a focus on key competition law cases in digital markets, the analysis discusses the approach in the EU and China in a comparative and normative manner. The critical exposition of the current practices, both official decisions and soft regulatory interventions, support the two normative claims. First, this book calls

[12] European Commission (EU), 'Terms of Reference of the EU China Competition Policy Dialogue' (2019) <https://competition-policy.ec.europa.eu/system/files/2021-06/China-EU_competition-policy-dialogue_terms-of-reference_en.pdf> (accessed 6 June 2024).

[13] European Commission (EU), 'EU–China: Commission and China Hold Second High-Level Digital Dialogue' (press release, 18 September 2023) <https://ec.europa.eu/commission/presscorner/detail/en/ip_23_4488> (accessed 6 June 2024).

[14] *Ibid.* See also European Commission (EU), Competition Cooperation—EU–Asia Partnership, 'Competition Weeks' <https://competitioncooperation.eu/competition-weeks>; European Commission (EU), '21st EU–China Competition Week (19, 26–28 April 2021) <https://competitioncooperation.eu/21st-eu-china-competition-week-2> (both accessed 6 June 2024)

[15] See, e.g. European Commission (EU), 'Speech by President von der Leyen on EU–China Relations to the Mercator Institute for China Studies and the European Policy Centre' (30 March 2023) <https://ec.europa.eu/commission/presscorner/detail/en/speech_23_2063> (accessed 6 June 2024). With respect to the wider debate on the future of Europe, see E Letta, 'Much More Than a Market' (April 2024) <http://much-more-than-a-market-report-by-enrico-letta.pdf>; Emmanuel Macron, 'Europe—It Can Die. A New Paradigm at the Sorbonne' (Groupe d'Études Géopolitiques, Sorbonne 2 speech, 25 April 2024) <https://geopolitique.eu/en/2024/04/26/macron-europe-it-can-die-a-new-paradigm-at-the-sorbonne> (accessed 13 May 2024).

for an 'integrative' approach to competition law enforcement, with data protection and consumer protection considerations informing competition law analysis. Given the prevalence of data-driven business models and a handful of powerful players, which have emerged as unavoidable trading partners, the book argues that public-interest considerations, such as privacy and fairness, which are traditionally found in data protection and consumer law, have a role to play in the substantive application of competition law in digital markets.

The second normative claim pertains to the comparative analysis of competition law enforcement and competition agencies and courts as institutions. It maintains that, given the influence of EU competition law on the Chinese Anti-Monopoly Law, there is an argument to be made in favour of a more regular dialogue and cross-fertilization of ideas. In addition, it would be interesting and timely to decipher how two key competition law jurisdictions apply their respective competition laws against different digital giants and the potential impact of such application in the evolution of digital markets. And whereas technology has bestowed a digital component to the growing majority of markets, the scope of this book is narrower and discusses developments in those sectors that have attracted considerable competition law and regulatory scrutiny, including search engines, operating systems (OS), adverting technology (AdTech), marketplaces, web browsers, and social networks.[16] The scope of inquiry allows for drawing important comparative insights based on the markets and ecosystems covered, the main players, and the respective problems. In terms of scope, we focus on competition law tools, namely provisions prohibiting anticompetitive agreements and abuse of market power as well as regulating merger transactions, and their respective applications in the digital era. With respect to Chinese competition law, we also cover administrative monopolies.

II. Digital Markets and the Main Players in the EU

GAFAM (Google, Amazon, Facebook, Apple, and Microsoft) (or FAANG (Facebook, Amazon, Apple, Netflix, and Google) or, more recently, MAMAA (Meta, Apple, Microsoft, Amazon, and Alphabet) and GAMMA (Google, Amazon, Microsoft, Meta, and Apple))[17] companies are the most powerful companies in the

[16] See e.g. CMA, 'Mobile Ecosystems (Statement of Scope)' (15 June 2021), para 33 referring to the Digital Markets Taskforce advice to the government on the Digital Markets Unit's priorities regarding Strategic Market Status assessments in the following sectors: online marketplaces, app stores, social networks, web browsers, online search engines, operating systems, and cloud computing services.

[17] See M Quirroz Gutierrez, 'Not FAANG But MAMAA: Jim Cramer Reveals New Acronym for the 5 Largest Tech Giants' (29 October 2021) <https://fortune.com/2021/10/29/faang-mamaa-jim-cramer-tech-facebook-meta> (accessed 22 February 2023). GAMMA stands for Google, Amazon, Microsoft, Meta, and Apple. See CMA, 'AI Foundation Models—Update Paper' (11 April 2024).

world, claiming the top spots on the National Association of Securities Dealers Automated Quotations (NASDAQ) by market capitalization.[18] These companies have at least doubled their valuation in the period 2014–2019,[19] though recently they have exhibited some signs of stagnation.[20] Meta, for example, laid off more than 11,000 employees in November 2022, accounting for a 13 per cent reduction in its workforce,[21] and it has announced plans to further reduce its workforce.[22] Such layoffs appear to be common across the tech industry, yet one needs to keep in mind that they may subsequently be followed by *en masse* hiring.[23] This was particularly seen during the COVID-19 pandemic, where it was reported that Big Tech companies increased their headcount.[24]

This section first provides a brief exposition of the Big Tech platform companies, (their respective evolution and business models) that have attracted EU Commission and Member States' competition law enforcement scrutiny, namely Google (Alphabet), Amazon, Facebook (Meta), Apple, and Microsoft. Each of these powerful platforms serves as an example of the respective business model that built its respective ecosystem around specific services and then ventured out into other markets. Hence, the following presentation of GAFAM presents the historic evolution and expansion of these firms. The discussion provides a concise first presentation of GAFAM's offerings, which should serve as an introduction to the analysis in subsequent chapters of this book.

II.1 Google

Scott Galloway famously pronounced that 'Google is the new god', since everyone now resorts to Google for every possible question they have.[25] Google

[18] NASDAQ, 'Market Activity China' <https://www.nasdaq.com/market-activity/stocks/screener?exchange=NASDAQ&sortname=marketcap&sorttype=1> (accessed 6 June 2024).

[19] Statista, 'Digital Economy Compass—2019', 112.

[20] M Field, 'Technology Intelligence' (*The Telegraph*, 26 October 2022).

[21] See e.g. C Criddle and H Murphy, 'Meta Cuts 11,000 Staff in Largest Cull in Company's History' (*Financial Times*, 9 November 2022) <https://www.ft.com/content/348068b1-24d9-434b-9ae7-6599027bf84f> (accessed 13 June 2024).

[22] H Murphy and C Criddle, 'Meta Axes Further 10,000 Jobs in Fresh Round of Cuts' (*Financial Times*, 14 March 2023) <https://www.ft.com/content/57d43e90-f23e-48c4-8f62-2b6981e136e4> (accessed 6 June 2024).

[23] Evans, 'The New Gatekeepers' (n8), slides 13–15, highlighting that after having laid off 11,000 people, it subsequently hired 15,000 people.

[24] C Duffy, 'How Big Tech's Pandemic Bubble Burst' (CNN Business, 22 January 2023) <https://edition.cnn.com/2023/01/22/tech/big-tech-pandemic-hiring-layoffs/index.html> (accessed 13 June 2024). On the COVID-19 pandemic boosting Big Tech's growth, see United Nations Conference on Trade and Development (UNCTAD), 'Global Competition Law and Policy Approaches to Digital Markets' (2024), 1.

[25] J Koetsier, 'Galloway: Google Is God, Apple Is Sex, Facebook Is Love, And Amazon Is . . . Death?" (Forbes, 10 May 2017) <https://www.forbes.com/sites/johnkoetsier/2017/05/10/galloway-google-is-god-apple-is-sex-facebook-is-love-and-amazon-is-death> (accessed 6 June 2024).

was characterized as the pioneer of big data and targeted advertising long before Facebook.[26] It was founded in 1998 by Larry Page and Sergey Brin, both of whom were PhD students at Stanford University in California at the time. Google went public via an initial public offering (IPO) in 2004. In the original founders' letter, Page and Brin claimed that 'Google is not a conventional company [and it does] not intend to become one'.[27] Indeed, it is a company that has shaped the world like few others. Since 2 October 2015, Google has been a wholly owned subsidiary of Alphabet Inc, which comprises a collection of businesses, the largest of which is Google. According to Alphabet's 10-K Securities and Exchange Commission (SEC) filing, Alphabet reports its activities related to Google as two segments: Google Services and Google Cloud, whereas all non-Google businesses are collectively reported as Other Bets (which include earlier-stage technologies further afield from their core Google business).[28]

In the company's own words, 'Google Services' core products and platforms include Android, Chrome, Gmail, Google Drive, Google Maps, Google Photos, Google Play, Search, and YouTube, each with broad and growing adoption by users around the world'.[29] Google's portfolio of products and services allude straight to its ad-funded business model based on the offering of such 'free' (without a monetary exchange) products and their monetization through its online advertising services.

Google Search, Google's general search engine, laid the foundations of what is today known as the Google ecosystem. What distinguished Google Search[30] from other search engines in the late 1990s (such as Alta Vista) is that while the latter returned results that mentioned the search term many times, Brin and Page, inspired by the logic of academic citations, developed the algorithm PageRank as a new method 'for computing a ranking of every web page based on the graph of the web'.[31] PageRank takes into account not only the number of links into a website

[26] R Foroohar, *Don't Be Evil—The Case against Big Tech* (Penguin, 2019), 5.

[27] US Securities and Exchange Commission (SEC), 'Alphabet Inc's FORM 10-K' (Commission File No 001-37580) (31 December 2020), Part I, Item 1, Business <https://www.sec.gov/Archives/edgar/data/1652044/000165204421000010/goog-20201231.htm#id55be7992b374e1a9a2bc48887ddbb3f_16> (accessed 6 June 2024).

[28]

> Alphabet is mostly a collection of companies, the largest of which, of course, is Google. This newer Google is a bit slimmed down, with the companies that are pretty far afield of our main internet products contained in Alphabet instead. What do we mean by far afield? Good examples are our health efforts: Life Sciences (that works on the glucose-sensing contact lens), and Calico (focused on longevity). Fundamentally, we believe this allows us more management scale, as we can run things independently that aren't very related.

See Alphabet Investor Relations, 'G Is for Google' <https://abc.xyz/#> (accessed 3 October 2023).

[29] SEC, 'Alphabet Inc's Form 10-K' (n27), 6.

[30] Or BackRub, as the project was initially dubbed.

[31] S Brin and L Page, 'The PageRank Citation Ranking: Bringing Order to the Web' <http://ilpubs.stanford.edu:8090/422/1/1999-66.pdf>; John Battelle, 'The Birth of Google' (WIRED, 8 January 2005) <https://www.wired.com/2005/08/battelle> (both accessed 6 June 2024).

but also the number of links into each of the linking websites. At the beginning, Brin and Paged opposed the ad-funded business model for their search engine,[32] yet eventually, in a bid to generate revenue, they decided that 'advertising doesn't have to be evil[33]—if it's actually useful and relevant'.[34] As we shall see with respect to the enforcement actions against Google, to what extent this remains the case is questionable.[35]

Google Search tops the list of the most popular search engines outside China.[36] In the years that have followed, Google has grown exponentially from a search engine with a revenue model based on licensing search technology to an ad-funded ecosystem offering a wide range of (usually) complementary and interdependent products to consumers, as well as its advertising and non-advertising business customers.[37] Google is active in many consumer-facing markets; search and web browsing (Google Search and Chrome); specialized search (e.g. Google Shopping and Google Travel); OS (Android, Chrome OS, Wear OS); devices (e.g. Google Home smart speaker and Google Pixel Smartphone); G Suite and productivity (Gmail, Calendar, Google Translate); Streaming (Google Play and YouTube); and Navigation (e.g. Google Maps and Waze).[38]

Google is also the main player (alongside Facebook) in digital advertising, with a variety of different products catering for the needs of publishers and advertisers,[39] amongst which are its platforms Google Ads (formerly AdWords) and Google AdSense, which have attracted the scrutiny of the European Commission.[40]

[32] S Brin and L Page, 'The Anatomy of a Large-Scale Hypertextual Web Search Engine' (1998) 30 Computer Networks 107:

> Currently, the predominant business model for commercial search engines is advertising. The goals of the advertising business model do not always correspond to providing quality search to users [. . .] we expect that advertising funded search engines will be inherently biased towards the advertisers and away from the needs of the consumers. Since it is very difficult even for experts to evaluate search engines, search engine bias is particularly insidious.

[33] Google's moto since 2000 summarizing the company's values. See Alphabet Investor Relations, 'Google Code of Conduct' <https://abc.xyz/investor/google-code-of-conduct/> (accessed 6 June 2024).

[34] A Fisher, 'Google Was Not a Normal Place: Brin, Page, and Mayer on the Accidental Birth of the Company That Changed Everything' (Vanity Fair, 10 July 2018) <https://www.vanityfair.com/news/2018/07/valley-of-genius-excerpt-google> (accessed 6 June 2024) (excerpt from his book, *Valley of Genius: The Uncensored History of Silicon Valley—as Told by the Hackers, Founders, and Freaks Who Made It Boom* (Twelve 2014) quote attributed to Douglas Edwards, Google employee number 59).

[35] See Chapter 5, section II.3. An example here of a search engine that was allegedly of superior quality but eventually failed due to Google's tactics is Neeva. See M Stoller, 'The First Big Antitrust Trial of the Century Is About to Start' (BIG, 6 August 2023) <https://www.thebignewsletter.com/p/how-a-google-antitrust-case-could> (accessed 3 October 2023).

[36] In China, Baidu tops the list. See Statista (n19), 199.

[37] CMA, 'Online Platforms and Digital Advertising' (n10), Appendix E, paras 16–24.

[38] *Ibid*, para 17 and figure E.1. See also *Google Android* (Case AT.40099) Commission Decision, C(2018) 4761 final (Brussels, 18 July 2018), paras 105–111.

[39] CMA 'Online Platforms and Digital Advertising' (n10), Appendix E, para 42.

[40] *Google Search (AdSense)* (Case AT.40411) Commission Decision, C(2019) 2173; European Commission (EU), 'Commission Sends Statement of Objections to Google over Abusive Practices in Online Advertising Technology' (press release, 14 June 2023) <https://ec.europa.eu/commission/

Its revenues come mainly from online advertising, either as a seller of advertising space on its own websites or as an intermediary between advertisers and publishers (websites and ads). As early as 2002, Google claimed publicly that it was the 'world's largest ad network',[41] and (reportedly) it collects more data than any other company.[42]

II.2 Amazon

Amazon was founded by Jeff Bezos in 1994 as an online book retailer with the ambition to become the largest bookstore in the world. Amazon's exponential growth surpassed its founder's ambition. The company launched its IPO in 1997.[43] The following year, Amazon started to expand beyond the online book retailing, and in 2005, it ventured into cloud computing with the Amazon Web Service (AWS) emerging as a key player in this field. In 2011, Amazon launched Amazon Music and Amazon Video. Yet, at the beginning, and for quite some time, Amazon was suffering losses, and even in 2000, the company was yet to make a profit. Still, its stock price would rise.[44]

Amazon is now a leader in online retail, entertainment, devices (e.g. Fire Tablet, Fire TV, Echo, and Ring) and web services.[45] Quantitative evidence suggests that Amazon is the first online shop in 'the most relevant' EU e-commerce markets.[46] In the company's own words,

> [w]e seek to be Earth's most *customer-centric company*. We are guided by four principles: customer obsession rather than competitor focus, passion for

presscorner/detail/en/ip_23_3207> (accessed 6 June 2024). On these cases, see Chapter 5, section II.3 below. On Google's business model, see also *Google Android* (n38), paras 105 et seq.

[41] *Google Search (AdSense)* (n40), para 265.

[42] Statista (n19), 32, based on the analysis of 144 million websites in more than 20 countries, Google has 64.4 per cent of tracked websites, followed by Facebook with 28.8 per cent. See also Privacy International, 'Personal Data and Competition: Mapping Perspectives, Identifying Challenges and Enhancing Engagement for Competition Regulators and Civil Society' (Report, April 2022), 13:

> [o]n the webpages PI analysed Google was the most prevalent third-party tracker and Google's advertising services DoubleClick and AdSense were used by most of these webpages. 70.39% of the webpages used DoubleClick. Other Google products such as Google Analytics, Google Tag Manager and Google Fonts are also widely used. 87.8% of webpages in France had a Google tracker, 84.09% in Germany and 92.16% in the UK.

[43] In 1997, Amazon reached its millionth customer, with Jeff Bezos hand delivering the books ordered in Japan, with all of Amazon's employees signing the Amazon box. See WIRED, 'The Merchant King: Jeff Bezos' (1 August 2005) <https://www.wired.com/2005/08/1997> (accessed 3 October 2023).

[44] L Khan, 'Amazon's Antitrust Paradox' (2017) 127 Yale Law Journal 710, 712.

[45] SEC, 'Amazon's Form 8-K' (Commission File No 000-22513) (28 October 2021) <https://d18rn0p25nwr6d.cloudfront.net/CIK-0001018724/105ca2e5-1440-4fb5-815f-44f87165ee9a.pdf> (accessed 6 June 2024).

[46] Statista (n19), 137.

invention, commitment to operational excellence, and *long-term thinking.* In each of our segments, we serve our primary customer sets, consisting of consumers, sellers, developers, enterprises, and content creators. In addition, we provide services, such as advertising to sellers, vendors, publishers, authors, and others, through programs such as sponsored ads, display, and video advertising.[47]

II.3 Facebook

Facebook's core service is social networks,[48] as a distinct subcategory of social media.[49] It was founded by Mark Zuckerberg and a group of other Harvard students in October 2003, originally as FaceMash, changing its name to Facebook in February 2004, and incorporating in the summer of 2004. The company launched its IPO in 2012. Facebook's ecosystem now comprises (apart from Facebook) Instagram and WhatsApp and generates its total revenue from selling advertising space.[50] Facebook has also invested in virtual and augmented-reality services with Facebook Reality Labs and Oculus Quest. In October 2021, Facebook's parent company, Facebook Inc, was rebranded as Meta. In its founder's words about Meta's futuristic (and, for others dystopic, vision),

> [f]rom now on, we will be metaverse-first, not Facebook-first. That means that over time you won't need a Facebook account to use our other services. [...] the word 'meta' comes from the Greek word meaning 'beyond'. [. . .] [I]t symbolizes that there is always more to build, and there is always a next chapter to the

[47] SEC, 'Amazon's Form 10-K' (Commission File No 000-22513) (31 December 2020) <https://d18rn0p25nwr6d.cloudfront.net/CIK-0001018724/336d8745-ea82-40a5-9acc-1a89df23d0f3.pdf> (accessed 6 June 2024).

[48] In *Facebook/WhatsApp*, the Commission noted that '[w]hile there is no established definition, social networking services can be generally described as services which enable users to connect, share, communicate and express themselves online or through a mobile app'. See *Facebook/WhatsApp* (Case M.7217) Commission Decision, C(2014) 7239, para 46.

[49] Social media is indeed a blurry concept. See CMA, 'Online Platforms and Digital Advertising' (n10), 54. Social media platforms can be generally defined as

> online services that allow users to participate in social networking, communicate with other users, and share and consume content generated by other users (including professional publishers). Social media platforms generally display content for consumption as linear 'feeds', curated by algorithms or displayed chronologically. Examples include Facebook, Instagram and Snapchat. Platforms may also offer additional functions, including instant messaging services.

As the Bundeskartellamt noted in its Facebook decision, the demand for social networks is fundamentally different from that of other social media, since the primary purpose of the latter lies in connecting users and exchange content and opinions on a daily basis. See Bundeskartellamt, 'Bundeskartellamt Prohibits Facebook from Combining User Data from Different Sources' (press release, 7 February 2019) <https://www.bundeskartellamt.de/SharedDocs/Meldung/EN/Pressemitteilungen/2019/07_02_2019_Facebook.html> (accessed 6 June 2024).

[50] SEC, 'Facebook's Form 10-K' (Commission File No 001-35551) (31 December 2020) <https://d18rn0p25nwr6d.cloudfront.net/CIK-0001326801/4dd7fa7f-1a51-4ed9-b9df-7f42cc3321eb.pdf> (accessed 6 June 2024).

> story. Ours is a story that started in a dorm room and grew beyond anything we imagined; into a family of apps that people use to connect with one another, to find their voice, and to start businesses, communities, and movements that have changed the world.[51]

Facebook's growth of its user base has been exponential; what started as a university social network in 2004 had 1.84 billion on average daily active users (DAUs) as of December 2020, with an increase of 11 per cent year-on-year.[52] Just like Google, Facebook has built its own ecosystem around its core consumer-facing service of social media.[53] Facebook is active in social media (Facebook, Instagram, WhatsApp, Messenger); retail (Facebook shops and Marketplace); streaming (Facebook Watch and Facebook Gaming App); and devices (Portal and Oculus).[54]

II.4 Apple

Apple was founded by Steve Jobs, Steve Wozniak, and Ronald Wayne in 1976 and was incorporated by Jobs and Wozniak in 1977 in Cupertino, California. Apple went public in 1980. At its inception, Apple was a computer manufacturer. The company's meteoric rise coincided with Steve Jobs' return in 1997 and the launching of design products, starting with the iMac. In 2001, Apple launched the iPod music player,[55] and in 2003, the iTunes Music Store. In 2007, Apple started its iOS range of products: first with the iPhone in 2007, then the iPod Touch and the iPad in 2010.

The company, which started as a computer manufacturer, now produces a wide range of products, from personal computers and tablets to smartphones and wearables and accessories, such as AirPods, Apple TV, and Apple Watch, and sells various related services.[56] Its services comprise advertising, AppleCare, Cloud Services, and the provision of digital content primarily through the AppStore. Its services also include Apple Music, Apple News+, and Apple TV+, amongst others. Finally, the company offers payment services, including Apple Card and Apple Pay.

[51] Meta, 'Founder's Letter' (28 October 2021) <https://about.fb.com/news/2021/10/founders-letter> (accessed 3 October 2023).

[52] SEC, 'Facebook's Form 10-K' (n50), 52.

[53] CMA, 'Online Platforms and Digital Advertising' (n10), 56.

[54] See also *ibid*, Appendix E.

[55] WIRED, '2002: What They Were Thinking' <https://www.wired.com/2005/08/2002> (accessed 6 June 2024).

[56] SEC, 'Apple's Form 10-K' (Commission File No 001-36743) (25 September 2021) <https://d18rn0p25nwr6d.cloudfront.net/CIK-0000320193/42ede86f-6518-450f-bc88-60211bf39c6d.pdf> (accessed 6 June 2024).

II.5 Microsoft

Microsoft was founded by Bill Gates and Paul Allen in 1975 and has revolutionized and popularized personal computers. Today, Microsoft is the world's largest software company, with its most popular products including Microsoft Windows OS, the Microsoft Office suite, and the Internet Explorer web browser. Microsoft also produces very popular hardware products such as the Microsoft Surface touchscreen personal computer and the Xbox series of video game consoles.[57] The company is also a leader in cloud technology and services,[58] as well as communication and customer relationship management software.[59]

III. Digital Markets and the Main Players in China

As with the above analysis on the main EU players in the digital economy, this section briefly presents their counterparts in China. The focus is on those companies that have already attracted competition law scrutiny.

III.1 Alibaba Group

Alibaba Group Holdings Limited was founded on 28 June 1999 by Jack Ma and specialized in e-commerce and online retail. Later on, its business expanded to fintech, cloud computing, and entertainment. On 19 September 2014, Alibaba Group's IPO on the New York Stock Exchange raised USD 25 billion, making it one of the most valuable companies in the world.[60] Alibaba is one of the world's largest wholesale e-commerce platforms for global trade, whose three strategic areas include consumption, cloud, and globalization.[61]

Alibaba Group tops the list with some of the most popular platforms in the Chinese commerce sector, including the B2B marketplace site Alibaba.com, the famous B2C/C2C e-commerce platform Taobao, and Tmall. As for the local consumer services, Alibaba is the major shareholder of the delivery platform—Ele.me

[57] Fortune, 'Microsoft in Fortune Rankings' <https://fortune.com/company/microsoft> (accessed 6 June 2024).

[58] N Reith, '10 Biggest Software Companies' (Investopedia, updated 31 October 2023) <https://www.investopedia.com/articles/personal-finance/121714/worlds-top-10-software-companies.asp> (accessed 6 June 2024).

[59] See, e.g. *Microsoft/Nuance* (Case M.10290) Commission Decision, C(2021) 9923, para 2.

[60] LB Baker, J Toonkel, and R Vlastelica, 'Alibaba Surges 38 Percent on Massive Demand in Market Debut' (*Reuters*, 19 September 2014) <https://www.reuters.com/article/us-alibaba-ipo/alibaba-surges-38-percent-on-massive-demand-in-market-debut-idUSKBN0HD2CO20140919> (accessed 6 June 2024).

[61] See the official website of the Alibaba Group <https://www.alibabagroup.com/en-US/about-alibaba-businesses> (accessed 6 June 2024).

(a competitor of Meituan) and also owns Amap (a taxi and navigation service provider competing with Didi); both of these take up a considerable market share. In addition, the fintech platform Alipay and the cloud computing platform Alibaba Cloud also add value to Alibaba's multidimensional business landscape.

On 10 April 2021, Alibaba was fined by the SAMR for abuse of dominance.[62] According to the penalty decision, Alibaba had imposed 'either–or choice' requirements on merchants, preventing them from selling products on other competing platforms.[63] A fine of ¥18.23 billion (ca €2.37 billion) was imposed, far exceeding the USD 975 million (ca €126.6 million) penalty imposed on Qualcomm in 2015.[64]

III.2 Meituan

Meituan was founded by Wang Xing, the founder of the famous social network Renren.com, in March 2010, simulating the famous Groupon site from the United States. In 2015, Meituan merged with one of its most major competitors, Dianping, and became the biggest online-to offline (O2O) company in China. In 2018, Meituan was listed on the Main Board of the Stock Exchange of Hong Kong. Since its establishment, Meituan has advanced the digital upgrading of services and goods retail on both the supply and demand sides, including recommendations for shops and restaurants, group buying services, on-demand takeout delivery, and bike-sharing.

Meituan provides clients with deals and coupons for rebates and generates profits through commission for each deal. To illustrate, with the help of big data and a navigation system, Meituan's food delivery connects the online merchants with offline consumers. It focuses on providing food delivery services, allowing users to order food through mobile applications and then delivering the food to the destination. Meituan–Dianping enables customers to make group purchases at discounted prices using electronic coupons, which can be recuperated at the dealer's site or in designated areas. Moreover, the bike-sharing service makes it convenient for consumers to rent shared bicycles through smartphones, solving the 'last mile' transportation challenge.

[62] SAMR, '市场监管总局发布阿里巴巴集团控股有限公司在中国境内网络零售平台服务市场垄断案行政处罚决定书和行政指导书 [The SAMR Publishes the Decision of an Administrative Penalty and Administrative Guidance for the Case of Alibaba Holdings' Monopolistic Behaviours in the Market of Online Retail Platforms in China]' (10 April 2021) <https://www.samr.gov.cn/zt/qhfldzf/art/2021/art_74b2593fd32a432baf3dcbd163935167.html> (accessed 6 June 2024).

[63] SAMR, '国家市场监督管理总局行政处罚决定书（国市监处〔2021〕28号） [The SAMR Administrative Prohibition Decision [2021] No 28]' (10 April 2021) <https://www.samr.gov.cn/xw/zj/art/2023/art_4966dda92ab34c398615f5878c10c8f1.html> (accessed 7 November 2022).

[64] R Zhong, 'China Fines Alibaba $2.8 Billion in Landmark Antitrust Case' (*New York Times*, 9 April 2021) <https://www.nytimes.com/2021/04/09/technology/china-alibaba-monopoly-fine.html> (accessed 6 June 2024).

In the area of antitrust, the most noteworthy case concerning Meituan is the abuse of dominance on the takeout delivery platform. Meituan was fined over ¥3.4 billion (ca €0.44 million) for abuse of dominance on 8 October 2021.[65] According to the penalty decision released by the SAMR, Meituan had violated subparagraph 4, paragraph 1, Article 17 of the Anti-Monopoly Law (AML) by forcing the restaurants on its takeout platform to choose between competing platforms.[66] This case can be traced back to the aforementioned merger between Meituan and Dianping in 2015. At the time of the merger, the parties did not provide prior notification, and no regulatory measures were taken by the authorities.[67] Commentators have criticized the government for failing to take effective measures against this merger, which was evidently questionable under the framework of antitrust law.[68] By ruling that the Meituan–Dianping alliance stemming from the merger had abused its dominant position, the SAMR acknowledged, to some extent, that the merger from six years ago had had anticompetitive consequences.

On the other hand, Meituan seems to have fallen victim to an administrative monopoly in the bicycle-sharing business. To protect the interests of local companies or business affiliated to the public sector, multiple cities have employed restrictive policies to exclude national bike-sharing platforms like Meituan. The regulatory authorities have declared such measures in breach of the AML and have demanded their repeal.[69]

III.3 Tencent

Tencent was founded on 11 November 1998 by five co-founders, Ma Huateng, Zhang Zhidong, Xu Chenye, Chen Yidan, and Zeng Liqing. Tencent was listed on the Hong Kong Stock Exchange (HKEX) in 2005. On 5 September 2016, Tencent overtook China Mobile to become the most valuable public company in China.[70]

[65] Reuters, 'Chinese Delivery Giant Meituan Handed $527 Million Antitrust Fine' (8 October 2021) <https://www.reuters.com/article/china-regulation-meituan-idUSKBN2GY0U5> (accessed 6 June 2024).

[66] SAMR, '国家市场监督管理总局行政处罚决定书（国市监处罚〔2021〕74号）[The SAMR Administrative Prohibition Decision [2021] No 74]' (8 October 2021) <https://www.samr.gov.cn/xw/zj/art/2023/art_31910760066b4f69aa119a20dee250ad.html> (accessed 10 April 2024).

[67] G Shau, '按《反垄断法》拆分美团大众点评，或将恢复外卖平台市场有效竞争 [Research on Competition Law, Separating Meituan and Dazhong Dianping According to the Anti-Monopoly Law May Restore the Competition in Takeout Delivery Market]' (*Sina Weibo*, 18 August 2022) <https://weibo.com/ttarticle/p/show?id=2309404803639637311636> (accessed 6 June 2024).

[68] Retric, '美团牵手大众点评：一场事先张扬的合并案 [Meituan Holds Hands with Dazhong Dianping: Chronicle of a Merger Case Foretold]' (36KR, 8 October 2015) <https://36kr.com/p/1720945295361> (accessed 7 June 2024).

[69] M Liu and K Ma, '各地被要求破除垄断 共享单车市场迎变局 [Local Governments Demanded to Break Off Monopoly, the Bike-Sharing Business Facing Its Change]' (*China Daily*, 23 November 2022) <https://cnews.chinadaily.com.cn/a/202211/23/WS637d8014a3109bd995a518a6.html> (accessed 6 June 2024).

[70] F Wang, '腾讯市值首度超过中国移动 成亚洲市值最高公司 [Tencent's Market Value Exceeds China Mobile for the First Time and Becomes the Most Valuable Company in Asia]' (3 October

Its social network is the core service of Tencent, which even evolves into Tencent's distinct ecosystem. Services such as online video, gaming, and music streaming have expanded via Tencent's social networking platform QQ and WeChat. WeChat, in particular, is a free messaging and calling app that allows users to easily connect with others across countries. It offers features such as group chats and supports voice, photo, video, and text messages. As a supplementary function, WeChat Pay is widely used for daily transactions.

The most infamous monopoly case involving Tencent is the 2010 *Qihu v Tencent* case. After Tencent released the Tencent Computer Manager, a competing product to Qihu's 360 Computer Manager, Qihu published a program called 'Koukou [QQ] safeguard', claiming Tencent's social networking program QQ to be unsafe. In retaliation, Tencent publicly made QQ incompatible with Qihu's 360 Computer Manager, citing safety concerns.[71] The business war escalated, with both parties accusing each other of unfair competition for several rounds, and Qihu eventually sued Tencent for abusing its dominant position. This rivalry ended with the Supreme People's Court's (SPC's) ruling that while Qihu had violated competition law, Tencent QQ did not enjoy a dominant position.[72]

More recently, Tencent has faced antitrust concerns related to merger control. After 2020, the SAMR shifted to a stricter attitude towards monopoly regulation in the digital markets and imposed fines on companies for failing to make notifications of relevant mergers. Amongst these cases, Tencent stands out. For example, on 5 January 2022, the SAMR published thirteen decisions on failure-to-notify fines, with Tencent being held liable for six fines. In these cases, Tencent was found to be in violation of Article 21 of the AML for failing to notify relevant mergers. Although fines were imposed, the SAMR determined that these mergers had not harmed market competition and did not enjoin the transactions.[73]

2018) <https://web.archive.org/web/20181003101012/http://tech.163.com/16/0905/14/C075PMN400097U7R.html> (accessed 6 June 2024).

[71] Tencent, '致广大QQ用户的一封信 [A Letter to QQ Users]' (6 November 2010) <https://web.archive.org/web/20101106123940/http://im.qq.com/qq.shtml> (accessed 6 June 2024).

[72] J Li, '最高法终审《3Q大战》腾讯奇虎分别回应 [The Supreme People's Court Announces the Final Verdict on Tencent v. Qihu, with Tencent and Qihu Respond Respectively]' (4 March 2016) <https://web.archive.org/web/20160304072357/http://legal.people.com.cn/n/2014/0224/c42510-24450589.html> (accessed 6 June 2024); X Ma, '《3Q大战》4年长跑落幕：为互联网竞争树司法标杆 ["War between 3Q" Closes after the Four-Year March: Setting a Judicial Benchmark for Internet Competition]' (IFeng Finance, 16 October 2014) <https://finance.ifeng.com/a/20141016/13191381_0.shtml> (accessed 6 June 2024).

[73] J Fan, '新年首批13张反垄断罚单：横跨6年各罚50万，腾讯领9张 [The First 13 Anti-Monopoly Fines in the New Year: Over 6 Years, ¥500 Thousand Each Case, Tencent Responsible for 6]' (ThePaper.cn, 5 January 2022) <https://www.thepaper.cn/newsDetail_forward_16151802> (accessed 6 June 2024).

III.4 Didi

Didi was founded in 2012 by Cheng Wei, and its core business is e-hailing services. Currently, Didi holds the largest market share in the e-hailing service industry, making it the leading platform in this sector.[74] Didi launched its IPO in 2021 and became listed on the New York Stock Exchange (NYSE) but was forced to delist in 2022 due to regulatory pressure.[75] As one of the world's leading mobility technology platforms, Didi offers a wide range of traffic-friendly services, including ride hailing, taxi hailing, chauffeur services, hitchhiking, and other forms of shared mobility. It is dedicated to collaborating with policymakers, the taxi industry, the automotive industry, and communities to address transportation and environmental issues by utilizing big data, AI, and locally tailored smart mobility innovations.

On the one hand, Didi has faced antitrust controversies regarding merger control. In 2015, Didi and Kuaidi, the two leading players in China's e-hailing industry, merged to form Didi Kuaidi, which was valued at about USD 6 billion at that time, in an effort to head off Uber's expansion throughout China.[76] In 2016, Didi and Uber China, which owned the largest market share of China's online car-hailing sector, announced another merger. Both of these mergers raised concerns about potential antitrust issues.[77]

On the other hand, Didi's penetration into many regions is inhibited by the monopolistic behaviours of local governments. A number of local governments have taken measures to intervene and exclude e-hailing platforms to maintain social stability. Competition from e-hailing platforms was perceived by taxi drivers as a fundamental threat to their lifeblood, leading them to engage in collective protests.[78] It is widely recognized that stability is a paramount concern for the Chinese government, both at the central and local levels. Thus, city governments primarily concerned with social stability have employed multiple regulatory instruments,

[74] Foresight Industry Research Institute, '洞察2022：中国网约车行业竞争格局及市场份额 [Insight 2022: The Online Ride-Hailing Competition Landscape and Market Share in China, Tencent News]' (25 May 2022) <https://new.qq.com/rain/a/20220525A09Z2P00> (accessed 6 June 2024).

[75] Reuters, '滴滴启动纽交所退市并准备香港上市 [Didi Starts to Delist in NYSE and Prepares to Go Public in HKEX]' (3 December 2021) <https://www.zaobao.com.sg/realtime/china/story20211203-1219519> (accessed 6 June 2024).

[76] China Europe International Business School (CEIBS), 'Lessons from the Didi Dache and Kuaidi Dache Taxi-App Merger' (15 April 2015) <https://www.ceibs.edu/lessons-didi-dache-and-kuaidi-dache-taxi-app-merger>(accessed 2 February 2023).

[77] Pengpai News, '滴滴快的合并引发垄断质疑，商务部称未收到相关申报 [Didi Kuaidi Merger Raises Monopoly Questions, MOFCOM Claims No Relevant Notification Was Received]' (ThePaper.cn, 16 February 2015) <https://www.thepaper.cn/newsDetail_forward_1304327> (accessed 6 June 2024); DNA Web Team, 'China: Didi–Uber Merger Would Lead to Monopoly, Fare Hike?' (updated 2 August 2016) <https://www.dnaindia.com/world/report-china-didi-uber-merger-would-lead-to-monopoly-fare-hike-2240357> (accessed 2 February 2023).

[78] A Jacobs, 'Strikes by Taxi Drivers Spread across China' (*New York Times*, 14 January 2015) <https://www.nytimes.com/2015/01/15/world/asia/taxi-strikes-spread-across-china.html> (accessed 6 June 2024).

including a quota system,[79] requirements on e-hailing drivers,[80] and technical requirements on e-hailing vehicles,[81] to inhibit the development of e-hailing platforms. Nevertheless, there have been attempts by the central government to repeal these anticompetitive measures for the development of a unified market.[82]

III.5 Ctrip

Ctrip, founded in Shanghai in 1998 by its four founders—Liang Jianzhang, Fan Min, Ji Qi and Shen Nanpeng—went public on NASDAQ in 2003. Ctrip is a major player in the online travel agency (OTA) business, offering booking services for plane tickets and hotel rooms. Following mergers with its biggest competitors (Qunar, Yilong, and Tongcheng), Ctrip came to dominate over 60 per cent of the market share, solidifying its position as the undisputed leader in the market.[83]

Ctrip was involved in two types of antitrust issues. First, it was accused of discriminating against regular customers through the use of data and algorithms. Price discrimination is not illegal *per se*, as evidenced by frequent coupons or student discounts in everyday life. But discrimination performed by a dominant firm might violate Article 22 of the AML. Although there has not been any antitrust case on this issue yet, such behaviours have drawn widespread consumer criticism. Several litigations on price discrimination using big data have been filed, but they have primarily been argued as cases related to consumer law rather than antitrust violations.[84] Second, Ctrip was found to be in violation of antitrust regulations for

[79] For example, in 2016, the city of Lanzhou in Gansu province adopted such a system. See J Liu, '兰州拟限定网约车数量 专家争议政策合理性 [Lanzhou Planning to Limit the Number of E-Hailing Cars, Experts Dispute the Rationality of the Policy]' (CAIXIN, 16 August 2018) <https://china.caixin.com/2016-08-16/100978004.html> (accessed 17 July 2022).

[80] For example, Beijing and Shanghai require e-hailing drivers to hold a local hukou (permanent local residency). See J Yu, '上海出租车非沪籍司机或超三成 主管部门正研究适度放宽属地限制 [The Number of Non-Shanghainese Taxi Drivers May Exceed 30% in Shanghai, the Competent Authorities Studying to Moderately Relax Territorial Restrictions]' (24 June 2019) <https://finance.youth.cn/finance_gdxw/201906/t20190624_11990904.htm> (accessed 17 July 2022).

[81] For example, the city of Wuhan requires that the price of an e-hailing car should be no less than ¥120k. As explained by then Vice Director of Wuhan Traffic and Transportation Commission Sun Jiang, 'by stipulating that the price of the vehicle must be over ¥120k, we intend to encourage more high-end vehicles to enter the e-hailing market'. See Hubei Daily, '武汉网约车《新政》下周实施 车辆总价要求12万以上[Wuhan's New Policy on E-Hailing Cars Will Come into Force Next Week, Requiring the Price of the Car to Be More Than ¥120k]' (15 April 2017) <https://www.hubei.gov.cn/zxjy/rdhy/201704/t20170415_1764294.shtml> (accessed 6 June 2024).

[82] J Cai, 'The Sharing Economy and China's Antimonopoly Law: From the Didi Case to Regulatory Challenges' (2020) 28(1) Asia Pacific Law Review 159, 177–178.

[83] X Wu, '同程、艺龙合并，携程的资本收割机是如何炼成的？ [Tongcheng Merged with Yilong, How Was the Ctrip Capital Built?]' (iFeng Finance, 8 January 2018) <https://finance.ifeng.com/a/20180108/15914472_0.shtml> (accessed 6 June 2024).

[84] Pengpai News, '大数据杀熟，携程被判退一赔三！ [Price Discrimination Using Data, Ctrip Is Subject to Full Refund and a Three Times Damage]' (26 July 2021) <https://www.thepaper.cn/newsDetail_forward_13758311> (accessed 6 June 2024).

employing most-favoured-nation (MFN) clauses, which prohibit hotels on the platform from offering lower prices via other platforms or offline sales, according to the Hong Kong Competition Commission.[85] Ctrip had to make a commitment to terminate, revoke, waive, or otherwise cease to apply any MFN clauses and refrain from entering into or applying any obligations that would constitute such clauses.[86]

IV. Structure

After framing the scope of the book in the introduction (Chapter 1), Part A discusses the main technological, economic, and architectural characteristics of digital markets (Chapter 2) and the challenges they raise for competition law enforcement (Chapter 3). Chapter 2 outlines and discusses those characteristics of digital markets that are relevant to competition laws. Chapter 3 starts by discussing the aims of competition law and then—in light of these aims—identifies possible anticompetitive practices in digital markets and the risks they pose in terms of their enforcement. Part A sets the scene and serves to highlight the commonalities in terms of the risks and challenges troubling competition agencies in the EU and China. It also identifies the multiplicity of aims embraced by different competition law regimes with a focus on the resurgence of 'fairness' considerations in competition law rhetoric.

Having set out the context in relation to both the economic perspective of digital markets (Chapter 2), as well as the possible legal implications for competition law enforcement (Chapter 3), Part B then explores competition law enforcement in digital markets in the EU; this is followed by Part C, with a similar analysis in the Chinese context. Part B comprises three chapters on anticompetitive agreements, abuse of dominance, and mergers, respectively. Part C has a similar structure. Yet, in addition to the three topics covered in the previous part, it also contains a fourth chapter addressing China's competition law enforcement against administrative monopoly, which refers to governmental abuses of administrative power to eliminate or restrict market competition. The book provides a detailed overview of the relevant jurisprudence from Europe and China. Examples from other jurisdictions are also employed to aid the analysis, where relevant.

[85] Hong Kong Competition Commission, 'Notice Issued under Section 2 of Schedule 2 of the Competition Ordinance Regarding the Commission's Proposal to Accept Commitments in Online Travel Agents Case (EC/02NJ)', <https://www.compcomm.hk/en/enforcement/consultations/past_consultations/files/OTA_Notice_ENG.pdf> (accessed 6 June 2024).

[86] Hong Kong Competition Commission, 'Commitments Given by Trip International Travel (Hong Kong) Limited and Ctrip.com (Hong Kong) Limited to the Competition Commission Pursuant to Section 60 of the Competition Ordinance (Cap. 619)', para 3 <https://www.compcomm.hk/tc/enforcement/consultations/past_consultations/files/Proposed_Commitments_Ctrip_HK.pdf> (accessed 6 June 2024).

Part B includes three chapters that focus on the EU. Chapter 4 discusses the various issues pertaining to the application of Article 101 of the Treaty on the Functioning of the European Union (TFEU) in digital markets. Such issues include the notion of undertaking, algorithmic collusion, and concerted practices as well as vertical restraints. The discussion covers the relevant EU case law as well as selected cases from other jurisdictions. Chapter 5 then discusses the application of Article 102 TFEU. It covers both exploitative and exclusionary abuses. Key to digital markets is the emergence of a handful of players with a central role in their respective ecosystems. The cases against Big Tech, while covering different types of abuse and different business models, all raise similar questions with respect to the design of platform ecosystems and how the players at the core of these ecosystems can behave within the ecosystem and whether they can assume a central role therein. Chapter 6 examines the application of EU merger control to data-driven mergers and discusses the relevant cases.

Part C assesses the relevant Chinese cases in digital markets in four chapters. As the development of the digital markets is outpacing that of legislation, Chinese enforcers are applying soft regulatory methods to tackle monopoly issues in a way that fills the incompleteness of the formal enforcement of anti-monopoly laws. Considering the enforcers' avoidance of public anti-monopoly decisions, the limited number of anti-monopoly adjudications, and the under-developed legal reasoning in many of the published documents, this part pays special attention to soft regulatory interventions by anti-monopoly enforcers, such as, for example, the 'inquiry process', which in Chinese literally means 'to meet and talk' ('yue tan', 约谈) and makes reference to interviews with officials of these agencies as well as experts engaging in relevant deliberations. Chapter 7 explains the low levels of investigations into anticompetitive agreements in digital markets (including vertical agreements, horizontal agreements, and algorithmic agreements) and assesses the Chinese regulatory approach thereto. Special attention is paid to the enforcement against the business practice of the 'either–or choices' requirement for merchants, community group-buying business, and bike-sharing. The vague status of MFN clauses practised by Ctrip is also considered. Chapter 8 covers two types of exclusionary abuses in the online retail market and social network and media markets in China, where either–or choices and algorithmic-based anticompetitive behaviours are addressed in regard to platforms such as Alibaba Group, Meituan, Tencent, Sherpa, Ctrip, and Didi. In these high-profile cases, public enforcement investigations are carried out alongside a private enforcement mechanism, which is still a frontier area to be explored in China. This chapter largely centres on clarifying China's criteria for assessing anticompetitive effects, as well as the introduction of private enforcement and algorithm audit as a strong backup. Chapter 9 considers a series of merger cases in China's digital markets, including the markets of transport services, video broadcasting services, and food delivery services. China has undergone a shift of regulatory attitude towards merger control review, which will be especially illustrated with platforms operated under a variable interest entity (VIE) structure. China's reformulation of its notification threshold for merger initiatives and its inclusion of non-price factors in anticompetitive assessment are also covered in this chapter. Chapter 10 discusses the administrative monopoly in China's digital markets, a unique type of monopoly prohibited by China's' AML. When digital platforms—whose lack of physical presence has made it hard to control them from the regulator's perspective—enter into the sectors that are tightly regulated, such as offline taxi markets, the regulatory agencies tend to set heavy regulatory rules for them, which, in effect, restricts competition between new entrants and incumbent players. Chapter 10 analyses these cases in detail with information from interviewed officials, academics, and business practitioners. Moreover, this chapter explains how the decentralized regulatory powers had contributed to these administrative monopolies in China's digital markets and sheds light on how the state succeeded in tackling some of these types of anticompetitive practices.

Part D offers the comparative and normative implications of the preceding analysis. In globalized markets, policymakers, enforcers, and market players need to have regard for the objectives and regulatory tools of other jurisdictions. Chapter 11 identifies the more pertinent issues in the EU and China and offers comparative conclusions. It then critically reflects on the role of competition laws and policies in an era of globalized digital markets and the way forward.

2
Technological, Economic, and Architectural Characteristics of Digital Markets

I. Introduction

Attempting to provide an all-inclusive definition of digital markets and the digital economy is a difficult endeavour. Digital markets can be described, in a nutshell, as 'those where companies develop and apply *new technologies to existing businesses*, or *create brand new services using digital capabilities*'.[1] The digital economy, on the other hand, may be described as the economy 'in which industries [. . .] have *embedded digital technologies deep in their production processes* to boost economic performance'.[2] Furthermore, digital activities have been described as those 'where digital technologies are a "core component" of the products and services provided as part of that activity'.[3]

Such a wide definition of digital markets and the digital economy highlights the fact that they are ubiquitous and have truly transformed everyday life. It also underscores the importance of technology, which drives and shapes market developments, thereby shaping the very economic characteristics of such markets. In turn, such characteristics affect competition law enforcement and call for a reconceptualization of the existing legal tools and for complementing regulation to address the ensuing challenges. The various benefits of digital markets have been acknowledged in many policy reports,[4] which, at the same time, mainly allude

[1] Competition and Markets Authority (CMA), 'The CMA's Digital Markets Strategy: June 2019' (Policy paper, updated 9 February 2021) <https://www.gov.uk/government/publications/competitionandmarketsauthoritysdigitalmarketsstrategy/thecmasdigitalmarketsstrategy> (accessed 17 August 2023).

[2] Huawei and Oxford Economics, 'Digital Spillover: Measuring the True Impact of the Digital Economy' (2017) <https://www.huawei.com/minisite/gci/en/digital-spillover/files/gci_digital_spillover.pdf>, 3 (accessed 17 August 2023).

[3] CMA, 'Mobile Ecosystems' (Market Study Interim Report, 14 December 2021), para 63.

[4] See, e.g. European Commission (EU), 'Competition Policy for the Digital Era' (A report by Jacques Crémer, Yves-Alexandre de Montjoye, and Heike Schweitzer) (EU Experts Report, 2019), 12; Digital Competition Expert Panel, 'Unlocking Digital Competition' (Report prepared by J Furman, D Coyle, A Fletcher, D McAuley and P Marsden) (Furman Report, March 2019), paras 1.13–1.23; DN Cicilline, 'Investigation of Competition in Digital Markets—Majority Staff Report and Recommendations—Subcommittee on Antitrust, Commercial, and Administrative Law of the Committee on the Judiciary of the House of Representatives' (US Congress Cicilline Report, 2020), <https://www.govinfo.gov/content/pkg/CPRT-117HPRT47832/pdf/CPRT-117HPRT47832.pdf>, 2 (accessed 7 June 2024).

Competition Law and Policy in Digital Markets. Maria Ioannidou and Bingwan Xiong, Oxford University Press.
 DOI: 10.1093/9780191925955.003.0002

to potential problems and a lack of effective competition. In a nutshell, what is observed is that a handful of digital platforms have obtained entrenched market power in certain key markets due to *strong network effects*, control of valuable *data* flows, and *economies of scale*.[5]

This chapter maps out the *architectural as well as economic characteristics* and *digital technologies* that largely shape contemporary digital markets. The analysis starts by providing an overview of key digital technologies, since these technologies drive and shape the architecture and economic characteristics of digital markets. The analysis on digital technologies—given that they are omnipresent—is not comprehensive; rather, the focus is on selected technologies, such as data-fuelled algorithms powering artificial intelligence (AI), which have called for a rethinking of the competition law enforcement toolbox (section II). The discussion then moves on to discuss the main economic characteristics of digital platform markets, which include network effects, economies of scale, and large data accumulation—and have been collectively termed 'incumbency advantages' (section III).[6] Such characteristics, in turn, attribute and shape the architectural characteristics of ecosystem competition. As the discussion below highlights, references to digital markets may even now seem dated since competition assessment has moved beyond market boundaries to the analysis of ecosystem competition (section IV). Unavoidably, the characteristics of digital markets impact upon the assessment of market definition and market power (section V). Finally, this chapter briefly presents different platform business models by selecting certain key players that—as the subsequent chapters will reveal—have attracted competition and regulatory scrutiny (section VI).

II. Key Digital Technologies: Technological Characteristics

II.1 Introduction

The world is experiencing a technological revolution identified as the Fourth Industrial Revolution.[7] Moving from the mechanization of production through to the use of water and steam power (First Industrial Revolution), to mass production (Second Industrial Revolution) enabled by electric power, to the automation

[5] EU Experts Report (n4); Furman report (n4); US Congress Cicilline Report (n4). See also CMA, 'Response to the Government's Consultation "A New Pro-Competition Regime for Digital Markets"' (29 September 2021), para 4.

[6] CMA, 'Online Platforms and Digital Advertising' (Market Study—Final Report) (Digital Platforms Report, 1 July 2020), 5.

[7] K Schwab, 'The Fourth Industrial Revolution: What It Means, How to Respond' (World Economic Forum, 14 June 2016) <https://www.weforum.org/agenda/2016/01/the-fourth-industrial-revolution-what-it-means-and-how-to-respond> (accessed 17 August 2023). See also K Schwab, *The Fourth Industrial Revolution* (World Economic Forum, 2016).

of production (Third Industrial Revolution), we are now experiencing the Fourth Industrial Revolution. The latter has been hailed for its great promise, while highlighting the inherent perils of fast-pace technological advancements,[8] and is characterized by unprecedented speed in technological breakthroughs such as AI, machine learning and the Internet of Things (IoT), enabling mass digitization and interconnection.[9]

The Organisation for Economic Co-operation and Development (OECD) has identified *digitization* and *interconnection* as the two technological pillars driving digital transformation.[10] Digitization, defined as the '*conversion of an analogue signal conveying information (e.g. sound, image, printed text) to binary bits*', allows information to be stored as data[11] and fuels *datafication*, which can be defined as the third pillar driving digital transformation, allowing the extraction of value from large data sets,[12] which are stored and accessed online via cloud computing services.[13] A range of technological developments, sharing these technical pillars, is fuelling an unprecedented digital transformation.[14] These technologies include the IoT, big data analytics, machine learning as a component of AI, and blockchain.[15] The technological opportunities and capabilities are driving ever-expanding business models fuelled by considerations of large data accumulation.[16] Google, for example, has ventured from its original search engine business into other business sectors ranging from operating systems, hardware, and household technology to telecommunications infrastructure and autonomous vehicles.[17]

In this section, the aim is to map selected key digital technologies at the heart of digital markets, which allow the ever-expanding reach of incumbent players and have influenced the application of competition law and the perception with respect to its role in 'taming' digital transformation, when need be. Such technologies, apart from their transformative role with the inherent benefits and risks, also

[8] Schwab, 'The Fourth Industrial Revolution' (n7); Schwab, *The Fourth Industrial Revolution* (n7).

[9] Schwab, 'The Fourth Industrial Revolution' (n7); Schwab, *The Fourth Industrial Revolution* (n7).

[10] Organisation for Economic Co-operation and Development (OECD), 'Digital Economy Outlook 2017' (2017), 25.

[11] *Ibid.*

[12] M Lycett, '"Datafication": Making Sense of (Big) Data in a Complex World' (2013) 22 European Journal of Information Systems 381.

[13] Discussing cloud computing, see A Cunningham and C Reed, 'Caveat Consumer?—Consumer Protection & Cloud Computing Part 1—Issues of Definition in the Cloud' (2013) <https://papers.ssrn.com/sol3/papers.cfm?abstract_id=2202758> (accessed 19 December 2023).

[14] It has been noted that digital transformation is fuelled by the intersection of cloud computing, Big Data, the IoT, and AI. See T Siebel, *Digital Transformation: Survive and Thrive in an Era of Mass Extinction* (Rosetta Books, 2019), chapter 2.

[15] OECD, 'Digital Economy Outlook 2017' (n10).

[16] German Monopolies Commission (Monopolkommission), 'Competition Policy: Challenges of Digital Markets', Special Report No 68 (2015), 3.

[17] *Ibid.*

present a useful tool for competition authorities for the detection of anticompetitive practices.[18] In as much as digital technologies are omnipresent in our everyday lives, providing a detailed account of these technologies is beyond the scope of this book.[19] Here, we discuss AI as well as algorithms and data, as key AI enablers, and also the metaverse as an emerging digital space encapsulating various digital technologies.[20]

II.2 Artificial Intelligence

AI encompasses various technologies combining data, processing algorithms, and computing power.[21] More broadly, AI has been described as a diverse field falling at the intersection between philosophy, neuroscience, statistics, computer science, and robotics.[22] Policymakers and regulators around the world have highlighted its transformational potential and have been devising strategies to harness its benefits and minimize the ensuing risks,[23] with policymakers currently focusing on

[18] For an account of such efforts and respective tools, see Hellenic Competition Commission, 'Computational Competition Law and Economics: Issues, Prospects (Inception Report)' (26 January 2021); See also Stanford Law School, 'Stanford Computational Antitrust Project' <https://law.stanford.edu/codex-the-stanford-center-for-legal-informatics/computational-antitrust-project> (accessed 31 May 2024).

[19] For a taxonomy of digital technologies, see JR Røed Steen and Fafo Institute for Labour and Social Research, 'Key Technologies in the Digital Transformation: Towards a Social Science Taxonomy of Digital Technology', 13, where the authors distinguish between technological drivers (i.e. computing power, storage, and connectivity), universal to every digital technology; basic technologies that are universally applicable such as AI and platforms; and technology systems, such as the IoT and cyber-physical systems.

[20] Other digital technologies include blockchain, data analytics, AI, 3D printing, the IoT, Automation & Robotics, and cloud computing. See United Nations Conference on Trade and Development (UNCTAD), 'Digital Economy Report' (2019), 6–8.

[21] European Commission (EU), 'White Paper on Artificial Intelligence—a European Approach to Excellence and Trust', COM(2020) 65 final (Brussels, 19 February 2020), 2.

[22] Autorité de la Concurrence (AdC) and Bundeskartellamt, 'Algorithms and Competition' (November 2019), 10.

[23] See, e.g. European Commission (EU), 'Artificial Intelligence for Europe' COM(2018) 237 final (Brussels, 25 April 2018); European Commission (EU), 'White Paper on Artificial Intelligence' (n21); European Parliament (EU), 'Proposal for a Regulation of the European Parliament and of the Council Laying Down Harmonized Rules on Artificial Intelligence (Artificial Intelligence Act) and Amending Certain Union Legislative Acts', COM/2021/206 final (2021) (AI Act Proposal). On 9 December 2023, the EU Parliament and Council reached provisional agreement on the AI Act, with the EU becoming the first jurisdiction to enact dedicated legislation to regulate AI. See Council of the EU, 'Artificial Intelligence Act: Council and Parliament Strike a Deal on the First Rules for AI in the World' (Press release, 9 December 2023) <https://www.consilium.europa.eu/en/press/press-releases/2023/12/09/artificial-intelligence-act-council-and-parliament-strike-a-deal-on-the-first-worldwide-rules-for-ai> (accessed 7 June 2024). The AI Act passed on 13 March 2024. See European Parliament, 'Artificial Intelligence Act: MEPs Adopt Landmark Law' (Press release, 13 March 2024) <https://www.europarl.europa.eu/news/en/press-room/20240308IPR19015/artificial-intelligence-act-meps-adopt-landmark-law> (accessed 24 April 2024). See also UK House of Lords Select Committee on AI, 'AI in the UK: Ready, Willing and Able?' (Report of Session 2017–2019, 6 April 2018). On China's AI strategy, see J Ding, 'Deciphering China's AI Dream' (March 2018) <https://www.fhi.ox.ac.uk/wp-content/uploads/Deciphering_Chinas_AI-Dream.pdf> (accessed 17 August 2023).

generative AI and AI foundation models,[24] which can create new content (e.g. text, music, or videos) by relying on vast amounts of existing data. More broadly, the application of AI is present in many aspects of our everyday lives. We now have digital assistants (such as Siri and Alexa, as well as Xiao Du and Xiao Ai in China); a personalized shopping and search environment (through Amazon and Google, respectively as well as Taobao and Baidu in China); a tailored film and music environment (through Netflix and Spotify as well as Netease Music and QQ Music, for example, in China); and a personalized online environment via social media applications (such as Instagram and Twitter, as well as MicroBlog, WeChat, and Douyin in China). Similarly, AI is being used in various sectors such as health, agriculture, transport, finance, energy, education, and law. The list seems endless and ever growing.

A distinction needs to be drawn here between 'narrow' and 'general' AI. Defining AI presents a very difficult task, not least because it is impossible to come up with an all-inclusive and concise definition of intelligence; but also because of the interdisciplinary nature of AI, which brings together members of various disciplines such as computer scientists, engineers, neuroscientists, psychologists, lawyers, and philosophers. Artificial general intelligence is defined as the ability to perform akin to human intelligence, that is perform a wide range of tasks.[25] Narrow AI focuses on a set of predetermined tasks. Other ways to distinguish between the two is 'strong' and 'weak' AI,[26] though the lines between the two become increasingly blurred. Furthermore, based on their application scenarios, AI can be categorized as follows: on the one hand, 'everyday' AI, handling tasks such as searching or recommendations, which has already reached a stage of maturity; and on the other, 'professional' AI, employed in specialized areas such as finance and medicine, which still requires massive development.[27]

AI technologies are now omnipresent, with global revenues in AI applications expected to rise from USD 7 billion in 2018 to USD 90 billion in 2025, with investment rising from USD 12 billion in 2018 to USD 232 billion in 2025.The largest

[24] Department for Science, Innovation and Technology (UK), 'A Pro-Innovation Approach to AI Regulation', CP 815 (March 2023); Department for Science, Innovation and Technology (UK), 'Pro-Innovation Regulation of Technologies Review—Digital Technologies' (A report by Sir Patrick Vallance) (March 2023), 8; CMA, 'AI Foundation Models: Initial Review' (4 May 2023), para 7. A very famous example of such AI technology is ChatGPT. See CMA *ibid*, paras 8–9. See CMA, 'AI Foundation Models: Update Paper' (11 April 2024), para 9; CMA, 'AI Foundation Models: Initial Report—Technical Update Report' (16 April 2024). See also European Commission (EU), 'Commission Launches Calls for Contributions on Competition in Virtual Worlds and Generative AI' (Press release, 9 January 2024) <https://ec.europa.eu/commission/presscorner/detail/en/ip_24_85> (accessed 24 April 2024).

[25] General AI is amply encapsulated in Alan Turing's question from 1950, 'Can machines think?'. See A Turing, 'Computing and Machinery Intelligence' (1950) LIX(236) Mind 433.

[26] Big Innovation Centre, 'What Is AI?' (Report based on the 1st meeting of the All-Party Parliamentary Group on Artificial Intelligence, APPG AI) (2017).

[27] iResearch, 'AI Report' <https://report.iresearch.cn/report/202201/3925.shtml> (accessed 21 September 2023).

of such revenues (45 per cent) will be made in North America, followed by Asia and Europe with an estimated one-quarter each. China is one of the main players worldwide in the AI market and has plans to become the world leader by 2030,[28] while it presents itself as the country gaining the most from implementing AI.[29]

In China's commercial practice, 'everyday' AI with data analysis based on machine learning has been widely adopted, equipping platforms with a wealth of information on their competitors and customers. Such AI-based information is proven to be quite beneficial for platforms to reap profits as it allows them to generate a detailed description of each type of customer based on their behaviour and to predict their preferences. The most predominant case in point is ByteDance, a company surrounded by controversy. ByteDance launched the viral apps, Toutiao and Douyin, with its infamous algorithms, which feed customers with articles and videos tailored to their preference and create an 'informational cocoon', which has been widely criticized.[30] Actually, in China's digital markets, similar algorithms have been employed in almost every field, such as search platforms like Baidu and Dianping, streaming services like Youku, and online shopping sites like Taobao and JD. Moreover, take-out delivery services also stand out, optimizing their services with data accumulation and algorithmic analyses. As individual deliverymen perform their duties, the platforms record their regular routes and time usage to calculate shortcuts and the average time consumed on each order. Therefore, the suggested routes are shortened and the time constraint becomes stricter for future orders. Over time, the location information recorded by take-out platforms like Meituan or Eleme is even more comprehensive than apps concentrated on map services like Amap or Baidu. Scholars have defined such a process as 'digital taylorism', named after Frederick Winslow Taylor, who recorded details of workers' workflow for rigorous management.[31]

In addition, AI's function in algorithmic data processing manifests in price discrimination. Price discrimination is not illegal per se, as evidenced by frequent coupons or student discounts in everyday life. However, discrimination performed by a dominant firm might violate competition rules. In China, for example, several civil litigations on price discrimination exploiting big data have been filed by private actors from the perspective of contract or consumer law, but as further elaborated in Chapter 8, antitrust cases are still rather rare.[32]

[28] Statista, 'Digital Economy Compass—2019', 46.

[29] *Ibid*, 71.

[30] H Xiao, '算法责任：理论证成、全景画像与治理范式 [Algorithmic Responsibility: Theoretical Justification, Panoramic Portrait and Governance Paradigm]' (2022) 38(4) 管理世界 [Journal of Management World] 200, 200–201.

[31] See L Chen and Y Han, '责任自治与数字泰勒主义：外卖平台资本的双重管理策略研究 [Self-Governance and Digital Taylorism: A Study on the Due Management Strategy of Takeout Platform Capital]' in Tianfu WANG (ed), (2020) 清华社会学评论 [Tsinghua Sociological Review] (社会科学文献出版社[Social Science Academic Press]), 14.

[32] Beijing No 4 Intermediate People's Court, *Cai Wenzong v Beijing Jingdong Three Hundred and Sixty Degrees E-commerce Co, Ltd* [2022] (蔡文宗诉北京京东叁佰陆拾度电子商务有限公司信息网络买卖合同纠纷上诉案，(2022)京04民终601号) 10 January 2023；Changsha Furong District

II.3 Algorithms

II.3.1 Types of Algorithms

In simple terms, algorithms are a series of instructions aimed at solving a specific problem based on set parameters and the given input.[33] They transform inputs into outputs. In the literature, algorithms have been categorized according to different criteria, such as their respective tasks, their input parameters, and the method of learning.[34] As algorithms are literally everywhere and are used by businesses in a wide variety of different settings, any categorization based on the tasks they perform is prone to be incomplete. Common types of algorithms include scraping algorithms, which monitor and extract data aiding, for example, online retailers to observe their competitors; pricing algorithms, which track and possibly subsequently adjust prices; recommending algorithms, which offer a personalized online experience based on the accumulation of consumer data; ranking algorithms, which tailor the ranking of results to the individual's needs and thus present a subset of recommending/personalization algorithms; and matching algorithms, used to pair supply and demand.[35]

Algorithms can also be distinguished based on their level of sophistication, which is influenced by the different input parameters and methods of learning. 'Static'[36] or 'simple' adaptive algorithms[37] follow certain rules that remain unchanged to perform their respective tasks, for example matching competitors' lowest price.[38] Dynamic algorithms, on the other hand, are programmed to decide autonomously—based on learning data—the best way to achieve their objective.[39] In the case of dynamic algorithms, both the sequence of instructions and the outcome can change. Dynamic algorithms can rely on supervised learning, where the training data are coupled with correct outputs/labels; unsupervised learning,

People's Court, *Liu Quan v Beijing Sanfu Technology Co Ltd* [2018] (刘权诉北京三快科技有限公司侵权责任纠纷案，(2018) 湘0102民初13515号) 1 April 2019

[33] Monopolkommission, 'Algorithms and Collusion' (2018) <https://www.monopolkommission.de/images/HG22/Main_Report_XXII_Algorithms_and_Collusion.pdf>, 4 (accessed 14 February 2021). The CMA adopted the following definition: 'an algorithm is any well-defined computational procedure that takes some value, or set of values, as input and produces some value, or set of values as output'. See CMA, 'Pricing Algorithms', CMA 94 (8 October 2018), para 2.1 with reference to Cormen et al. (2001), *Introduction to Algorithms*. Algorithms can also be defined as 'a procedure that takes inputs and follows a series of well-defined steps to produce an output, and therefore can be implemented without the use of code'. See CMA, *ibid*, para 3.9.

[34] See the respective analysis in AdC and Bundeskartellamt (n22).

[35] *Ibid*.

[36] L Bernhardt and R Dewenter, 'Collusion by Code or Algorithmic Collusion? When Pricing Algorithms Take Over' (2020) 16 European Competition Journal 312, 315.

[37] E Ezrachi and M Stucke, 'Sustainable and Unchallenged Algorithmic Tacit Collusion' (2020) 17 Northwestern Journal of Technology and Intellectual Property 217, 241.

[38] See CMA, 'Pricing Algorithms' (n33), para 2.8.

[39] On machine learning algorithms, see *ibid*, para 2.12; G Rebala, A Ravi, and S Churiwala, *An Introduction to Machine Learning* (Springer, 2019), 19–22.

where no labels are provided; and re-enforcement learning, where no data set is provided and the algorithm learns through the interaction with a dynamic environment.[40] Q-learning algorithms present an example of reinforcement learning algorithms that learn from constant interaction with their environment in order to deliver an optimal pricing policy.[41]

II.3.2 Challenges: Collusion and Opacity in Decision Making

From a competition law perspective, the widespread use of algorithms increases monitoring and adapting and thereby arguably increases the risk of collusive outcomes. First, algorithms may allow better monitoring, collection, and processing of competitors' information in real time and thereby improve the detection and punishment of possible deviations. Second, they present powerful tools to signal the intention to collude and to further sustain parallel behaviour through, for example, allowing companies to follow a price leader and adapt accordingly. In these scenarios, algorithms are used as a tool to implement pre-existing anticompetitive agreements, thereby presenting an extension of human will. The more controversial issue is whether algorithms can autonomously lead to collusive outcomes and, if that is the case, whether competition law tools can be applicable in such situations.[42]

Another issue with respect to algorithms that may raise competition concerns is opacity in decision making.[43] For example, regulators have examined the potential of app store search algorithms to affect app rankings.[44] With respect to such rankings, developers have indicated that they do not have sufficient and clear information about how Apple's and Google's search algorithms determine the app ranking.[45]

The opacity and lack of transparency in algorithmic decision making raises broader ethical questions and highlights the need for increased transparency and accountability, which can only be tackled through a constellation of various regulatory tools, amongst which is the European Union Digital Markets Act (EU DMA).[46] In addition, in the EU, the 'right to explanation' for automated algorithmic

[40] CMA, 'Pricing Algorithms' (n33), para 2.12.

[41] *Ibid*, para 2.14. On Q-learning algorithms' potential to lead to collusion, see T Klein, 'Autonomous Algorithmic Collusion: Q-Learning under Sequential Pricing', Amsterdam Law School Legal Studies Research Paper No 2018-15 (2018).

[42] On the various scenarios of algorithmic collusion, see Chapter 4, section III.2.

[43] F Pascquale, *The Black Box Society* (Harvard UP, 2015).

[44] CMA, 'Mobile Ecosystems' (Interim Report) (n3), para 6.111, with references to the Australian Competition and Consumer Commission's (ACCC's) 'Digital Platform Services Inquiry—Interim Report No 4—General Online Retail Marketplaces' (March 2022) <https://www.accc.gov.au/system/files/DPB%20%20DPSI%20%20March%202022%20%20Full%20interim%20report%20%2031%20March%202022.pdf>, 89–91 (accessed 7 June 2024).

[45] CMA, 'Mobile Ecosystems' (Interim Report) (n3).

[46] See Regulation (EU) 2022/1925 of the European Parliament and of the Council of 14 September 2022 on contestable and fair markets in the digital sector and amending Directives (EU) 2019/1937 and (EU) 2020/1828, [2022] OJ L 265/1 (Digital Markets Act). On the DMA, see Chapter 3, section V.2.1.

decision making in the General Data Protection Regulation (GDPR) attempts to address such concerns, yet it is vague and rests upon judicial clarification.[47] It has been argued that the 'right to explanation' in the GDPR remains an empty shell and resembles a limited right to be informed.[48] Such a 'right to explanation' appears only in recital 71 of the GDPR and not in the binding provisions, yet it may be inferred through judicial interpretation by a combined interpretation of Article 15 (right of access) and Article 22 (right not to be subject to a decision based solely on automated decision making). The Commission Guidance on the GDPR does not mention a 'right to explanation' for automated decision making, only the 'right to object to processing and not to be subject to a decision based solely on automated processing'.[49] The Platform-to-Business Regulation also seeks to improve transparency with respect to ranking algorithms,[50] whereas the Digital Services Act (DSA) aims at improving the transparency and accountability of algorithmic decision making.[51] The DSA has been coined as an instrument protecting democracy in the EU, through requiring platforms to be transparent about how their algorithms work, and to be able to explain to users how their recommender systems choose which content to show and which ads to view.[52] Finally, the proposed AI Act seeks to improve the safety, security, and fundamental rights protection of AI systems.[53]

Explaining algorithmic decision making can be complex from a technical perspective. Self-learning algorithms learn from past experience.[54] For many machine-learning algorithms, the decisional process can be unpacked. However, for deep-learning algorithms—a subclass of machine-learning algorithms, which are a category of neural network-based algorithms relying on complex computation

[47] Regulation (EU) 2016/679 of the European Parliament and of the Council of 27 April 2016 on the protection of natural persons with regard to the processing of personal data and on the free movement of such data, and repealing Directive 95/46/EC, [2016] OJ L 119/1 (General Data Protection Regulation [GDPR]); British Academy and Royal Society, 'Data Management and Use: Governance in the 21st Century', 39.

[48] S Wachter, B Mittelstadt, and L Floridi, 'Why a Right to Explanation of Automated Decision-Making Does Not Exist in the General Data Protection Regulation' (2017) 7(2) International Data Privacy Law 76.

[49] European Commission (EU), 'Stronger Protection, New Opportunities—Commission Guidance on the Direct Application of the General Data Protection Regulation as of May 2018', COM(2018) 43 final (2018), 15.

[50] Regulation (EU) 2019/1150 of the European Parliament and of the Council of 20 June 2019 on promoting fairness and transparency for business users of online intermediation services, [2019] OJ L 186/57 (P2B Regulation), Article 5.

[51] Regulation (EU) 2022/2065 of the European Parliament and of the Council of 19 October 2022 on a single market for digital services and amending Directive 2000/31/EC, [2022] L 277/1 (Digital Services Act), Articles 14, 27, and 34 (amongst others).

[52] M Vestager, 'Algorithms and Democracy' (Speech, Algorithm Watch Online Policy Dialogue, 30 October 2020).

[53] AI Act Proposal (n23).

[54] OECD, 'Algorithms and Collusion—Note from the European Union' (21–23 June 2017), para 2.

over multiple features—the explanation of the respective decision-making process may be very complex and difficult to unpack.[55]

More worryingly, the widespread use of algorithms creates personalized online environments, leading two-thirds of people in the United States and one-fifth of people in Europe to be informed through social media; yet the opacity of algorithms conceals the way such personalized environments work and are formed.[56] Applying targeted advertising strategies to the political arena undermines democracy.[57] Our participation in digital markets as consumers directly affects our behaviour as citizens therein and in our societies in general, since the digital and the real worlds can no longer be discerned.

In a similar vein to the EU, since 2020, China has been advocating legislation in algorithmic regulation. For instance, the Implementation Outline for the Construction of a Rule of Law Society (2020–2025) proposes to regulate new technology applications such as algorithmic recommendations.[58] The Guidelines for Anti-Monopoly in the Field of Platform Economy (the 'Guidelines') explicitly include algorithm regulation; the Guiding Opinions on Strengthening Overall Governance of Internet Information Service Algorithms issued in September 2021 emphasized the need to 'complete algorithm security regulation mechanisms'.[59] The 14th Five-Year Plan for the Development of the Digital Economy issued at the end of 2021 points out that efforts will be made to accelerate the construction of the information network infrastructure and a national-level integrated big data centre system coordinating computing power, algorithms, data, and application resources.[60] More recently, in March 2022, the Cyberspace Administration of China (CAC) launched the QingLang Operation special action on algorithm regulation by carrying out onsite inspections on Internet enterprises.[61] The Regulations on the Administration of Algorithmic Recommendation

[55] A Gal, 'It's a Feature, Not a Bug: On Learning Algorithms and What They Teach Us', DAF/COMP/WD(2017)50 (OECD, 7 June 2017), para 12.

[56] M Vestager, 'A Healthy Democracy in a Social Media Age' (Democrazy—Democracy in Crisis?, 7 June 2017).

[57] *Ibid.*

[58] Central People's Government of the People's Republic of China, '中共中央印发《法治社会建设实施纲要（2020－2025年）》[Implementation Outline for the Construction of a Rule of Law Society (2020–2025)]' (7 December 2020) <https://www.gov.cn/zhengce/2020-12/07/content_5567791.htm> (accessed 27 September 2023).

[59] Office of the Central Cyberspace Affairs Commission, '关于印发《关于加强互联网信息服务算法综合治理的指导意见》的通知 [Guiding Opinions on Strengthening Overall Governance of Internet Information Service Algorithms]' (17 September 2021) <http://www.cac.gov.cn/2021-09/29/c_1634507915623047.html> (accessed 27 September 2023).

[60] State Council, '国务院关于印发《十四五》数字经济发展规划的通知 [14th Five-Year Plan for the Development of the Digital Economy]' (12 December 2021) <https://www.gov.cn/gongbao/content/2022/content_5671108.htm?eqid=c4653e630000247800000000464620cb> (accessed 27 September 2023).

[61] Office of the Central Cyberspace Affairs Commission, '关于开展"清朗2022年算法综合治理"专项行动的通知 [Notice on the QingLang Operation—2022 Algorithmic Comprehensive Management]' (8 April 2022) <http://www.cac.gov.cn/2022-04/08/c_1651028524542025.htm> (accessed 27 September 2023).

of Internet Information Service ('Algorithmic Recommendation Regulations') released in March 2022 are another step forward.[62] A preliminary legal system of algorithmic governance in China has been established.[63] Considering the potential role of algorithms in certain cases of abuse by digital platforms and China's active legislation and enforcement with respect to algorithms, algorithm regulation might serve as a supplementary method for the antitrust enforcement against platforms' abuse of market dominance.

The combination of algorithms and data has raised anticompetitive concerns, which have spurred the authorities into action; these actions include publishing regulations like the Manual on Antitrust for Platform Economy.[64] In China, a high-profile antitrust case involving algorithms and data in digital markets concerned the Alibaba Group. The Alibaba Group was fined 18.2 billion CNY for forcing its store owners to choose among competing platforms and penalizing store owners who operated on other platforms. One of the instruments employed by the Alibaba Group to enforce such unequal requirement was to move non-compliant store owners down the ranking by utilizing its search algorithms.[65] The SAMR decided that such behaviour constituted abuse of dominance, which will be discussed in detail in the section of 'either–or choice' in Chapter 8.

II.4 Data

As mentioned above, algorithms transform input (data) to outputs. In this vein, it has been accurately noted that '*the algorithm without data is blind. Data without algorithms is dumb*.'[66] Digital economy and AI technologies rely on ever-expanding troves of data.[67] This prevalence of data and algorithms in our modern society

[62] Central People's Government of the People's Republic of China, '互联网信息服务算法推荐管理规定 [Regulations on the Administration of Algorithmic Recommendation of Internet Information Service]' (1 March 2022) <https://www.gov.cn/zhengce/2022-11/26/content_5728941.htm> (accessed 27 September 2023).

[63] B Zou and Y Wang, '新反垄断法落地，平台监管如何着棋？ [How the New AML Tackles Platform Regulation?]' (财经杂志 [Caijing Magazine], 18 August 2022) <https://new.qq.com/rain/a/20220818A08J4900> (accessed 30 October 2022).

[64] Antimonopoly Commission of the State Council, '国务院反垄断委员会关于平台经济领域的反垄断指南（国反垄发〔2021〕1号）[Anti-Monopoly Guidelines on the Platform Economy]' (7 February 2021) <https://www.gov.cn/xinwen/2021-02/07/content_5585758.htm> (accessed 7 November 2022).

[65] State Administration for Market Regulation (SAMR), '国家市场监督管理总局行政处罚决定书（国市监处〔2021〕28号） [The SAMR Administrative Prohibition Decision [2021] No 28]' (10 April 2021) <https://www.samr.gov.cn/xw/zj/art/2023/art_4966dda92ab34c398615f5878c10c8f1.html> (accessed 7 November 2022).

[66] CNIL, 'How Can Humans Keep the Upper Hand? The Ethical Matters Raised by Algorithms and Artificial Intelligence' (December 2017), 18.

[67] See, e.g. European Commission (EU), 'Digital Single Market: Commission Welcomes European Parliament's Vote on New Rules for Sharing Public Sector Data' (4 April 2019) <http://europa.eu/rapid/press-release_STATEMENT-19-1935_en.htm> (accessed 20 August 2022).

has been encapsulated in the concept of 'dataism',[68] 'data capitalism',[69] or 'surveillance capitalism'.[70] Big data, similarly to algorithms, cannot be accurately captured in an all-inclusive definition.[71] Rather, they are described by their respective features since they depict unprecedented volume, variety, velocity, and value.[72] Since everything we do in our digital interconnected world leaves a digital trace, it is only natural that the amount of data keeps growing. It was reported that, in 2018, the total amount of data generated was 33 zettabytes. Data generation is predicted to grow exponentially to more than 2,100 zettabytes by 2035.[73] Linked to this is the evolution in data storage solutions, with cloud storage and blockchain being on the rise.[74]

There are different categories of data, each of which may call for a different degree of intervention. As acknowledged by the European Commission, the heterogeneity of data needs to be taken into account in discussions on whether and how to grant access to it. Data can be distinguished as volunteered, observed, or inferred data.[75] Such data is collected from the real world and should be distinguished from synthetic data, that is data with analytical value that are AI-generated.[76]

Volunteered data comprise data that are intentionally offered, such as (for example) posting on or liking a post on social media.[77] On the other hand, observed data are generated by our digital activity and comprise behavioural data that are automatically generated by such an activity, for example cookies tracking online activity. Inferred data is a combination of the other two categories, with the distinction between these categories not being clear cut.[78] Depending on how they are collected and used, they can be distinguished as anonymous individual-level data, non-anonymous individual-level data, aggregated data, or contextual data.[79] Non-anonymous individual-level data is any individual-level data (volunteered,

[68] Y Harari, *Homo Deus: A Brief History of Tomorrow* (Penguin, 2015); Y Harari, 'Yuval Noah Harari on Big Data, Google and the End of Free Will' (*Financial Times*, 26 August 2016) <https://www.ft.com/content/50bb4830-6a4c-11e6-ae5b-a7cc5dd5a28c> (accessed 20 August 2022).

[69] See, e.g. All-Party Parliamentary Group (APPG) AI, 'Ethics and Legal in AI: Data Capitalism' (26 June 2017).

[70] S Zuboff, *The Age of Surveillance Capitalism* (Profile Books 2019).

[71] CMA, 'Pricing Algorithms' (n33), para 2.21.

[72] See M Stucke and A Grunnes, *Big Data and Competition Policy* (OUP, 2016), para 2.03.

[73] Statista, 'Digital Economy Compass' (n28), 4. According to other estimates, about 2.5 exabytes are produced every day. See IT Media Consulting, 'Data Driven Economy—Market Trends and Policy Perspectives' (Executive Summary Research Report, 2017), 5. See also OECD, 'Big Data: Bringing Competition Policy to the Digital Era', DAF/COMP(2016)14 (2016).

[74] Statista, 'Digital Economy Compass' (n28).

[75] EU Experts Report (n4), 8.

[76] M Gal and O Lynskey, 'Synthetic Data: Legal Implications of the Data-Generation Revolution' (2024) 109(4) Iowa Law Review 1087.

[77] EU Experts Report (n4), 24.

[78] *Ibid*, 25.

[79] *Ibid*, 25.

observed, or inferred) that is used to cater to the needs of the person that generated the data. An example here is the use of a person's data on a social network to provide personalized advertising. In the case of anonymous individual-level data, the data is used anonymously for purposes other than the original purpose for which it was collected, for example to train machine-learning algorithms. Such data may benefit the individual in the long run through, for example, the suggestion of better recommendations. The third category, aggregated data, takes the anonymization process a step further and comprises standardized data that are irreversibly aggregated. Finally, contextual data are those not derived from individual level data.

Of particular importance in the digital economy is access to individual-level data since powerful platforms (e.g. search engines and social media) rely on targeted advertising.[80] Such data is also a key input to train machine-learning AI algorithms. Their collection and use, while enabling and fuelling AI-driven innovation, raise a constellation of ethical concerns, which regulators and policymakers have sought to address through the adoption of dedicated legal tools[81] and advocacy efforts.

II.5 Metaverse

The metaverse can be generally defined as a virtual, immersive environment where people interact through avatars.[82] In October 2021, the world's most powerful social network platform outside China changed its name to Meta in order to reflect the evolution in social connection.[83] This concept of metaverse clearly reflects

[80] Privacy International, 'Personal Data and Competition: Mapping Perspectives, Identifying Challenges and Enhancing Engagement for Competition Regulators and Civil Society' (Report, April 2022).

[81] See, e.g. GDPR (n47). See also the regulatory initiatives as part of the European Data Strategy: European Commission (EU), 'European Data Strategy' <https://commission.europa.eu/strategy-and-policy/priorities-2019-2024/europe-fit-digital-age/european-data-strategy_en> (accessed 18 August 2023). See notably, Regulation (EU) 2022/868 of the European Parliament and of the Council of 30 May 2022 on European data governance and amending Regulation (EU) 2018/1724, [2022] OJ L 152/1 (Data Governance Act); Regulation (EU) 2023/2854 of the European Parliament and of the Council of 13 December 2023 on harmonised rules on fair access to and use of data and amending Regulation (EU) 2017/2394 and Directive (EU) 2020/1828 (Data Act) [2023] OJ L 1/71. On the interplay between competition law and data, see M Ioannidou and D Mantzari (eds), *Research Handbook in Competition Law and Data Privacy* (Edward Elgar, 2024) < https://eur-lex.europa.eu/legal-content/EN/TXT/PDF/?uri=OJ:L_202302854&qid=1730801376936>.

[82] F Wenzel Bulst and S De Vinck, 'DG COMP: Understanding the Metaverse—a Competition Perspective" (17 October 2022) <https://eaccny.com/news/chapternews/dg-comp-understanding-the-metaverse-a-competition-perspective/#_ftn1> (accessed 11 April 2023). See also European Commission (EU), 'Commission Launches Calls for Contributions' (n24).

[83] Meta, 'About Facebook' <https://about.facebook.com/meta/#> (accessed 2 October 2024).

the development of virtual-reality (VR) technologies and the emergence and anticipated growth of virtual worlds. Virtual worlds are particularly popular in the gaming industry, though their potential transcends physical and virtual boundaries in multiple sectors, ranging from medicine to culture and from manufacturing to smart cities.[84] Yet, while it potentially reveals the future evolution, the development of the metaverse remains to be seen. Ultimately, its evolution depends on how consumers interact in such a virtual parallel universe and find value.[85] Monetization strategies of the metaverse will strongly rely on data accumulation and subsequent monetization through digital advertising.[86]

From a competition law perspective, and depending on the metaverse expansion, it is imperative that popular metaverses remain open so that users can easily port their data and activity between different ecosystems.[87] The impact of Big Tech acquisitions on the future evolution of the metaverse is on the radar of competition authorities. The US Federal Trade Commission (FTC), for example, sought a preliminary injunction to block the deal between Meta and Within in July 2022, arguing that such an acquisition would create a monopoly in the VR fitness app market.[88] Within is the developer of the very popular VR fitness app, Supernatural, which is available on Meta's Quest headsets. Interestingly, the deal was agreed in October 2021, only a day after Facebook's rebranding to Meta.[89] The FTC's action to block the merger was dismissed, and the agency decided not to pursue the case further.[90] Despite this outcome, in principle, the judge accepted the FTC's potential competition theory of harm in this case, namely that this transaction would lead to a substantial lessening of competition since it would have prevented competition from an independent Meta entry in the VR fitness market.[91] The FTC failed to submit the necessary evidence to substantiate such a proposition.[92]

[84] European Commission (EU), 'An EU Initiative on Virtual Worlds: A Head Start Towards the Next Technological Transition' (Call for evidence, 2023).

[85] M Jacobides, 'Thoughts about the World & Media—2021–22 Review' <https://www.jacobides.com/2021-22-review> (accessed 7 June 2024).

[86] Bulst and De Vinck (n82).

[87] *Ibid.*

[88] FTC, 'FTC Seeks to Block Virtual Reality Giant Meta's Acquisition of Popular App Creator Within' (Press release, 27 July 2022) <https://www.ftc.gov/news-events/news/press-releases/2022/07/ftc-seeks-block-virtual-reality-giant-metas-acquisition-popular-app-creator-within> (accessed 24 February 2023).

[89] K Paul and D Bartz, 'Meta Battles US Antitrust Agency over Future of Virtual Reality' (Reuters, 9 December 2022) <https://www.reuters.com/technology/meta-battles-us-antitrust-agency-over-future-virtual-reality-2022-12-08> (accessed 24 February 2023).

[90] FTC, 'Commission Order Returning Matter to Adjudication and Dismissing the Complaint' (24 February 2023) <https://www.ftc.gov/system/files/ftc_gov/pdf/d09411commorderdismisscomplaint.pdf> (accessed 24 February 2023).

[91] *FTC v Meta*, Order Denying Plaintiff's Motion for Preliminary Injunction (Case No 5:22-cv-04325-EJD) (31 January 2023), 39–40.

[92] *Ibid*, 59–60.

III. Economic Characteristics of Digital Markets: Platform Economics

III.1 Introduction

Digital markets are dominated by platforms, which have radically transformed not only the digital economy but also the economy and the world as a whole. Thus, the discussion of the economic characteristics of digital markets is, in effect, a discussion about the economics of platforms. Platforms have been described as digital intermediaries, which 'bring together or facilitate transactions between third parties on the Internet'.[93] Such a definition encompasses a specific category of platforms, namely transaction platforms. Yet, as the subsequent discussion will reveal, there are a multitude of different platforms. Some features are common to any platform, yet they may present important differences, depending on whether they are vertically integrated; their business model, as well as the provision of more platform services; and the development of ecosystems.[94] The EU Commission has highlighted the wide prevalence of platform intermediaries coupled with strong data-driven network effects, which may lead to the emergence of a handful of platforms as 'quasi gatekeepers'[95] or 'regulators'.[96] Equally, the Chinese regulators have noted the potential role of giant platforms as 'gatekeepers'. Article 58 of the Personal Information Protection Law of the People's Republic of China (PRC) (the 'PIPL') stipulates 'special obligations for the personal information processor that provides important Internet platform services involving a huge number of users and complicated business types'.[97] This provision is deemed to

[93] OECD, 'The Economic and Social Role of Internet Intermediaries' (April 2010), 9.

[94] Konkurrensverket, 'The Competition on Digital Platform Markets in Sweden—Summary' (2021), 6.

[95] European Commission (EU), 'Proposal for a Regulation of the European Parliament and of the Council on Promoting Fairness and Transparency for Business Users of Online Intermediation Services', COM(2018) 238 final (Brussels, 24 April 2018), 1.

[96] EU Experts Report (n4), 60. For a discussion, see N Dunne, 'Platforms as Regulators' (2021) 9 Journal of Accounting and Economics 244. For an earlier account, see K Boudreau and A Hagiu, 'Platform Rules: Multi-Sided Platforms as Regulators' in A Gawer (ed), *Platforms, Markets, and Innovation* (Edward Elgar 2009), 163.

[97] According to Article 58 of the PIPL,

> [a] personal information processor that provides important internet platform services involving a huge number of users and complicated business types shall perform the following obligations: (1) establishing and improving the personal information protection compliance system in accordance with the provisions of the state and establishing an independent organization mainly composed of external members to supervise the protection of personal information; (2) following the principles of openness, fairness, and justice, formulating platform rules, and clarifying the norms and obligations that product or service providers within the platform should meet when processing personal information; (3) stopping providing services for product or service providers within the platforms that process personal information in serious violation of laws and administrative regulations; and (4) regularly publishing social responsibility reports on personal information protection for public supervision.

create obligations for some large platforms serving as the personal information gatekeepers.[98] Compared to the gatekeeper regime that has emerged in Europe, the PIPL combines personal information protection and gatekeeper regulation.[99] Article 58 of the PIPL identifies the gatekeeper from a perspective of personal information processor, and the four obligations set out therein are mainly designed for personal information protection. In terms of the specific identification of gatekeepers under Article 58 of the PIPL, the 'Guidelines for the Classification and Rating of Internet Platforms (Draft for Public Consultation)'[100] and the 'Guidelines for the Implementation of Responsibility of Internet Platforms (Draft for Public Consultation)',[101] drafted by the SAMR in 2021, are considered to be of great value.[102] However, there is a difference between the objectives of the two guidelines and Article 58 of the PIPL. The former is to regulate the business activities of Internet platforms, whilst the latter is to unify multifaceted rules on consumer rights protection, anti-unfair competition, anti-monopoly, personal information protection, and regulation of Internet users and content, as well as intellectual property protection.

This section first discusses the various types of platforms and then delves into the platform-specific characteristics that often lead to concentrated markets.

III.2 Platforms: Presenting Various Categorizations

There has been an exponential growth of online platforms, with their respective activities covering 'online advertising platforms, marketplaces, search engines, social media and creative content outlets, application distribution platforms, communications services, payment systems, and platforms for the collaborative economy'.[103] Peer platforms act as intermediaries providing an online marketplace where sellers and consumers interact through various forms of Internet-empowered digital

National People's Congress of the People's Republic of China, 'Personal Information Protection Law of the People's Republic of China' (updated 29 December 2021) <http://en.npc.gov.cn.cdurl.cn/2021-12/29/c_694559_3.htm> (accessed 6 June 2024).

[98] X Cheng, '大型网络平台违反守门人义务的民事责任 [Civil Liability for Breach of Gatekeeper Obligations by Large Online Platforms]' (2023) 5 Science of Law (Journal of Northwest University of Political Science and Law) 1, 1–10.

[99] H Zhou, '《个人信息保护法》《守门人条款》解析 [Analysis of the "Gatekeeper Clause" of the Personal Information Protection Law]' (2022) 5 Science of Law (Journal of Northwest University of Political Science and Law) 41.

[100] SAMR, '互联网平台分类分级指南（征求意见稿) [Guidelines for Classification and Rating of Internet Platforms (Draft for Public Consultation)]' (29 October 2021) <https://news.cctv.com/2021/10/29/ARTI9KXeKHs4KPZU58VL7GVs211029.shtml> (accessed 7 June 2024).

[101] *Ibid.*

[102] Zhou (n99), 46–47.

[103] European Commission (EU), 'Online Platforms and the Digital Single Market Opportunities and Challenges for Europe', (Communication, 25 May 2016), 2.

communications.[104] Social media platforms (such as Facebook, Instagram, and Twitter) enable social interaction between users for free, while capitalizing on their expanding member basis on the advertising side. Search engines are also a type of platform; they can be divided into horizontal search engines, such as Google, which answer general queries, and vertical search engines that address specific queries, for example on hotel bookings or restaurants.[105] The German National Competition Authority (NCA) refers to 'audience providing platforms', which provide a 'free' service and are financed through advertising.[106] Another very accurate term, focusing on the business model of these platforms, is attention merchants, which refers to firms that strive to attract and sell to advertisers users' attention.[107]

Platforms may intermediate transactions between their two sides, and based on this criterion, they can be divided into *transaction* and *non-transaction* platforms. For example, Uber intermediates and allows the interaction between drivers and users. On the other hand, Facebook is a non-transaction platform since users do not enter into a transaction with advertisers. Depending on the power to control the interactions on the platform, there are also varying degrees of intermediation. For example, on the one hand, credit card networks intermediate between customers and merchants, yet they control a very small part of the interaction. On the other hand, Big Tech platforms have centralized control over a variety of interactions taking place on the platform.

Other authors rely on different platform characteristics and distinguish between advertising platforms, cloud platforms, industrial platforms, product platforms, and lean platforms. Advertising platforms such as Google and Facebook rely on the vast extraction and processing of users' data in exchange for advertising space. Cloud platforms such as AWS and Salesforce own and rent hardware, software, and digital development tools to other businesses. Industrial platforms, such as Predix by GE and MindSphere by Siemens, develop hardware and software, transforming manufacturing into internet-connected processes. Product platforms, such as Spotify, offer products and services in return for a subscription fee. Finally, lean platforms, such as Uber and Airbnb, usually own no assets.[108] Another distinction

[104] FTC, '"Sharing" Economy Issues Facing Platforms, Participants and Regulators', (FTC Staff Report, November 2016), 3; OECD, 'Protecting Consumers in Peer Platform Markets: Exploring the Issues' (2016), 7.

[105] Monopolkommission, 'Competition Policy' (n16), 6.

[106] Bundeskartellamt, 'Background Information on the Facebook Proceeding' (19 December 2017) <http://www.bundeskartellamt.de/SharedDocs/Publikation/EN/Diskussions_Hintergrundpapiere/2017/Hintergrundpapier_Facebook.pdf?__blob=publicationFile&v=6> (accessed 7 June 2024), which distinguishes between the market for social networks (Facebook), professional networks (LinkedIn, Xing), messaging services (WhatsApp, Snapchat), and other social media (YouTube/Twitter), though the German NCA acknowledges that they may be partly substitutable.

[107] T Wu, *The Attention Merchants: How Our Time and Attention Are Gathered and Sold* (Atlantic Books, 2017).

[108] N Srnicek, *Platform Capitalism* (Polity Press, 2016), 32.

here is between transaction, innovation, and hybrid platforms. Transaction platforms, as mentioned above, match buyers and sellers. Innovation platforms rely on a central actor's foundation facilitating innovation and one side comprises developers/complementors, whereas hybrid platforms are a combination of the latter two categories.[109]

Commentators have also drawn a distinction between platforms and aggregators.[110] Interpreting the concept of platforms linguistically, they adopt a functional approach to platforms as constructs enabling the provision of new products and services. Operating systems (OS) are listed as an example of platforms, since they allow developers to build and provide their apps. On the contrary, aggregators just aggregate and sort out existing information about products and services and cannot be used to operate something new besides the aggregation function. Examples listed as aggregators include Google Search, Facebook, Twitter, Uber, and Airbnb. The distinctive characteristic of aggregators is that the core to their business model is the filtering of relevant information and presentation to consumers in a way that presents the best choices. Unavoidably, such filtering limits consumer choice, and the latter should not be interpreted on its own as being anticompetitive.[111] Whereas the distinction between aggregators and platforms offers a lens for competition law analysis, in essence what is common to both is the intermediation function as well the 'winner-takes-all' characteristic. In that sense, aggregators are platforms.[112]

In effect, other commentators have proposed the distinction between two main groups of platforms, aggregators, and marketplaces.[113] In the former group, we find platforms such as search engines (e.g. Google Search and Microsoft Bing) and social media (e.g. Facebook and Twitter), which provide users with a valuable service at zero monetary price, while monetizing their services through advertising. Marketplaces, on the other hand, consist of platforms that match users and suppliers of goods and services, such as (for example) Uber and eBay.

[109] MA Cusumano, A Gawer, and DB Yoffie, *The Business of Platforms: Strategy in the Age of Digital Competition, Innovation, and Power* (HarperBusiness, 2019).

[110] T Schrepel, 'Platforms or Aggregators: Implications for Digital Antitrust Law' (2021) 12(1) Journal of European Competition Law & Practice 1.

[111] *Ibid.* On the concept of aggregators and the implications for antitrust law, see B Thompson, 'Aggregation Theory' (Stratechery, 21 July 2015) <https://stratechery.com/2015/aggregation-theory/https://stratechery.com/2015/aggregation-theory>; B Thompson, 'Antitrust and Aggregation' (Stratechery, 26 April 2016) <https://stratechery.com/2016/antitrust-and-aggregation>; B Thompson, 'Defining Aggregators' (Stratechery, 26 September 2017) <https://stratechery.com/2017/defining-aggregators> (all accessed 18 August 2023).

[112] In fact, B Thompson, who coined the theory, refers to aggregators as platforms, with certain distinct characteristics: (i) a direct relationship with users,; (ii) zero marginal costs, and (iii) a decrease in customer acquisition costs over time. See Thompson, 'Defining Aggregators' (n111).

[113] G Parker, G Petropoulos, and M Van Alstyne, 'Digital Platforms and Antitrust' (Working paper, 2020) <https://www.bruegel.org/working-paper/digital-platforms-and-antitrust> (accessed 18 August 2023).

The above analysis presented many different categorizations of platforms. Given the multiplicity of platforms, any attempted definition is prone to appear either too narrow or too wide.[114] Common to all, however, is the intermediation role and the reliance on data and algorithms.

III.3 Platforms: Economic Characteristics and Market Concentration

As the above discussion on the typology of digital platforms showcases, in general they depict certain characteristics that lead to market concentration.[115] Such characteristics include, in particular, their multi-sided nature, different direct and indirect network effects depending on the platform, the existence of economies of scale due to the lack of (or very low) variable costs they incur for the provision of digital goods and services, and data-related economies of scope. In addition, certain digital platforms, such as social networks or general search engines, offer their services at zero monetary prices, thereby influencing consumers' switching incentives, since competition takes place regarding parameters other than price, such as quality and innovation.[116]

Depending on the platform, network effects connoting that the value of participating in the platform increases with the number of users can be direct or indirect.[117] With direct network effects, the value of participating in the platform increases the more users that are participating on the same side of the platform. For example, Facebook users value their participation on the platform more when the number of connections and friends increases and the platform has a higher number of users. Indirect network effects connote the increase in value when the

[114] European Commission (EU), 'Synopsis Report on the Public Consultation on the Regulatory Environment for Platforms, Online Intermediaries and the Collaborative Economy' (2016), 6; European Parliament (EU), 'Motion for a European Parliament Resolution on Online Platforms and the Digital Single Market', 2016/2276(INI), Report A8-0204 (2017), para 6 <http://www.europarl.europa.eu/sides/getDoc.do?pubRef=-//EP//TEXT+REPORT+A8-2017-0204+0+DOC+XML+V0//EN> (accessed 18 August 2023).

[115] On the economic characteristics of platforms, see P Belleflamme and M Peitz, *The Economics of Platforms* (CUP, 2021).

[116] Furman Report (n4), paras 1.65 et seq; CMA, Digital Platforms Report (n6), 46; EU Experts Report (n4), chapter II; ACCC, 'Digital Platforms Inquiry—Final Report' (June 2019), 43 <https://www.accc.gov.au/system/files/Digital%20platforms%20inquiry%20%20final%20report.pdf> (accessed 7 June 2024); Stigler Committee on Digital Platforms, 'Final Report' (Stigler Report, 2019), 34–43 <https://www.sipotra.it/wpcontent/uploads/2020/02/StiglerCommitteeonDigitalPlatformsFinalReport.pdf> (accessed 7 June 2024). See also OECD, 'Digital Competition Policy: Are Ecosystems Different?—Note by Amelia Fletcher', DAF/COMP/WD(2020)96 (9 November 2020), paras 8–18.

[117] On multi-sided markets literature, see J Rochet and J Tirole, 'Platform Competition in Two-Sided Markets' (2003) 1 Journal of the European Economic Association 990–1029; J Rochet and J Tirole, 'Two-Sided Markets: A Progress Report" (2006) 37 Rand Journal of Economics 645; M Armstrong, 'Competition in Two-Sided Markets' (2006) 37 Rand Journal of Economics 668; D Evans and R Schmalensee, 'Markets with Two-Sided Platforms' (2008) 1 Issues in Competition Law and Policy (ABA Section of Antitrust Law), chapter 28.

number of users on the other side of the platform increases,[118] and give rise to a 'chicken-and-egg' problem since users will be willing to use a platform if the latter already has a large user base on the other side, and vice versa.[119] For example, the more users Facebook has, the more valuable it is for advertisers, and the more users of Android or iOS there are, the more valuable they are for app developers. For transaction platforms, indirect network effects are bidirectional in the sense that, for example, in credit card platforms, the higher the number of merchants the more valuable the platform is for cardholders and vice versa. On the contrary, for non-transaction platforms such as ad-funded social media platforms, the more users the platform has the more valuable it is for advertisers. However, a larger number of advertisers does not impact, or may even negatively impact, users.

Network effects may pose a barrier to expansion and entry, yet they can be mitigated through switching or multi-homing. However, consumer behaviour may reinforce entry barriers, since behavioural economics research has highlighted the power of defaults.[120] Network effects have been assessed by the Commission as an entry barrier to the market for online search advertising and online search advertising intermediation.[121] With respect to online search advertising, a potential entrant has to attract a large number of advertisers[122] and employ a general search service with sufficient reach and performance.[123] However, these two conditions are hard to meet, given Google's competitive advantage in online search advertising due to the strength of its general search engine.[124] With respect to online search advertising intermediation, a potential entrant needs to attract a large number of advertisers and publishers and build a portfolio of online search ads.[125] In *Microsoft*, the Commission took into account indirect network effects in assessing anticompetitive foreclosure. In particular, the Commission examined the effects of bundling WMP with Microsoft OS on content providers and software developers, and on certain adjacent markets.[126] According to the Commission, 'in view of the indirect network effects that obtain in the media player market, "the ubiquitous presence of the [Windows Media Player] code provides [that media player] with a significant competitive advantage, which is liable to have a harmful effect on the structure of competition in that market'.[127]

[118] For other examples of social media depicting direct and indirect network effects, see CMA, Digital Platforms Report (n6), paras 3.203 et seq.

[119] B Caillaud and B Jullien, 'Chicken & Egg: Competition among Intermediation Service Providers' (2003) 34(2) Rand Journal of Economics 309.

[120] Stigler Report (n116), 42–43; CMA, Digital Platforms Report (n6), 11.

[121] *Google Search (AdSense)* (Case AT.40411) Commission Decision, C(2019) 2173, paras 249, 293.

[122] *Ibid*, para 250.

[123] *Ibid*, para 251.

[124] *Ibid*, para 254.

[125] *Ibid*, para 294.

[126] *Microsoft* (Case COMP/C-3/37.792) Commission Decision, C(2004) 900, paras 879–899.

[127] Case T-201/04 *Microsoft v Commission*, ECLI:EU:T:2007:289, para 983 with reference to Commission Microsoft Decision (n126), para 878. See also para 1061:

Network effects have also been assessed in a number of merger cases in the digital economy, where the Commission engaged in a case-by-case assessment.[128] On the one hand, network effects may reinforce the market power of the incumbents and lead to market tipping,[129] whereas, depending on the case at hand, they may enable new entrants to scale up and challenge the incumbents.[130]

In fact, in the digital economy, markets may have already tipped in favour of the incumbent firms. Let's take the example of the social network services, with Facebook having emerged as the main player. The picture was different in its early days, with a number of social networks with new entrants emerging.[131] In digital markets, businesses focus on competition *for* the market and not competition *in* the market since, in such markets, there is a strong incumbency advantage limiting market contestability and preventing new entrants from challenging the incumbent, even if they can offer better-quality products or services.[132]

The importance of access to vast data sources is another factor leading to market concentration in the digital economy. Data powers predictions that match users' needs. As discussed in section II above, data feeding powerful algorithms is what fuels the digital economy. The more data a platform has, the better predictions it can make, thus offering better-quality products and services.[133] Such a data advantage may act as an entry barrier, since powerful platforms with a large base collect more data and such data allow them to improve their offerings, thereby enlarging their base to collect even more data. In *Google AdSense*, for example, the Commission treated users' data as an entry barrier to the market for online search advertising, since 'a potential entrant would have to invest significantly in order to

> [t]he Commission's theory is based on the fact that the market for streaming media players is characterised by significant indirect network effects or, to use the expression employed by Mr Gates, on the existence of a 'positive feedback loop'. That expression describes the phenomenon where, the greater the number of users of a given software platform, the more there will be invested in developing products compatible with that platform, which, in turn reinforces the popularity of that platform with users.

[128] See Chapter 6.

[129] See, e.g. *Microsoft/LinkedIn* (Case COMP/M.8124) Commission Decision, C(2016) 8404, paras 302, 339–340, 351–352.

[130] See, e.g. *Google/DoubleClick* (Case M.4731) European Commission Decision, C(2008) 927 final, paras 342, 344; *Microsoft/Skype* (Case COMP/M.6281) Commission Decision, C(2011) 7279, para 91.

[131] For an account of the emergence of social networks between 1997 and 2006, see D Boyd and N Ellison, 'Social Network Sites: Definition, History, and Scholarship' (2008) Journal of Computer Mediated Communication 210, 212. See also C Hughes, 'It's Time to Break Up Facebook' (Opinion) (*New York Times*, 9 May 2019) <https://www.nytimes.com/2019/05/09/opinion/sunday/chris-hughes-facebook-zuckerberg.html> (accessed 18 August 2023).

[132] E Argentesi et al, 'Merger Policy in Digital Markets: An Ex Post Assessment' (2020) 17 Journal of Competition Law and Economics 95, 105. On 'incumbency advantage', see G Biglaiser and J Crémer, 'The Value of Incumbency When Platforms Face Heterogeneous Customers' (2019) <https://www.tse-fr.eu/sites/default/files/TSE/documents/doc/wp/2016/wp_tse_630.pdf> (accessed 18 August 2023). See also E Calvano and M Polo, 'Market Power, Competition and Innovation in Digital Markets: A Survey' (2021) 54 Information Economics and Policy 1, 6.

[133] Calvano and Polo (n132).

gather user click data', since such data improve search quality.[134] Apart from data acting as an entry barrier, the vast data accumulation by powerful platforms, given consumers often present inertia in scrutinizing the terms under which they allow access to their data, may also exert a negative externality on other users with different privacy preferences.[135]

A final characteristic that merits discussion here and has been addressed in the EU Commission decisional practice, as the subsequent discussion will reveal, is the monetization strategy of a subset of platforms coined as 'attention platforms' or 'attention merchants'.[136] Such platforms, which include (for example) search or social media platforms, vie for human attention, offering their services at zero monetary prices, whereas they trade such attention on the advertising side. The application of competition law in this context faces many challenges with respect, in particular, to the appropriate market definition and assessment of market power, as section V will reveal.

IV. Architectural Characteristics of Digital Markets: From Platforms to Ecosystems

IV.1 Ecosystem Competition

Building on the characteristics of platforms discussed above, we now observe the emergence of digital ecosystems.[137] A concept developed three decades ago,[138] 'ecosystem' has provided an important analytical lens through which to understand competition in digital markets.[139] The strategic management literature was the first

[134] *Google AdSense* (n121), para 246.

[135] T Valletti, '"An Offer We Can't Refuse": How We Gave Away Our Data and Made Big Tech What It Is Today' (Pro Market, 18 January 2021) <https://www.promarket.org/2021/01/18/facebook-whats app-terms-of-service-ads-data-privacy> with reference to D Acemoglu et al, 'Too Much Data: Prices and Inefficiencies in Data Markets', National Bureau of Economic Research Working Paper 26296 (2019) <https://www.nber.org/system/files/working_papers/w26296/w26296.pdf> (both accessed 18 August 2023).

[136] T Wu, *The Attention Merchants: The Epic Scramble to Get Inside Our Heads* (Knopf 2016); T Wu, 'Blind Spot: The Attention Economy and the Law' (2019) 82 Antitrust Law Journal 771; Calvano and Polo (n132) 10.

[137] On the distinction, see M Jacobides, C Cernamo, and A Gawer, 'Distinguishing between Platforms and Ecosystems: Complementarities, Value Creation, and Coordination Mechanisms' (Working paper, 14 October 2020) <https://www.jacobides.com/_files/ugd/0b15b1_7e0678d2815541bb920c77ec4 1e4d305.pdf> (accessed 18 August 2023). For a comprehensive legal theory on digital ecosystems, see I Lianos, K Hendrik Eller, and Tobias Kleinschmitt, 'Towards a Legal Theory of Digital Ecosystems', University College London, Centre for Law, Economics and Society Research Paper Series No 2 (2024).

[138] JF Moore, 'Predators and Prey: A New Ecology of Competition' (1993) (May/June) Harvard Business Review <https://hbr.org/1993/05/predators-and-prey-a-new-ecology-of-competition> (accessed 18 August 2023).

[139] I Lianos, 'Competition Law for a Complex Economy' (2019) 50 International Review of Intellectual Property and Competition Law 643, 647, with further references to M Jacobides, C Cernamo, and A Gawer, 'Towards a Theory of Ecosystems' (2018) 39 Strategic Management Journal 2255.

to coin and expand on the concept of 'ecosystem', focusing on the ecosystem's role as the 'hub' ('lead firm' or 'ecosystem captain') of various inter-firm interactions on a platform ('ecosystem members').[140] There is a general consensus on the nature of ecosystems as *multilateral interdependent structures*,[141] distinguishing ecosystems as structure and ecosystems as co-evolution. The proponents of ecosystems as structure emphasize their role as a structure of multilateral interdependence,[142] whereas those that focus on ecosystems as co-evolution focus on co-evolution as a means to coordinate production.[143]

Digital ecosystems have been described as designating '*a complex set including a generic modular technology* (for example an algorithm) which can be used to supply different types of products or services, *and a platform* which uses the modular technology to produce *a set of services which it combines with other services offered by third parties (complementors) in such a way that the attractiveness of each service is enhanced by the offerings of the other services*' (emphasis added).[144] Thus, within such ecosystems, there is an observed leadership by one firm providing a platform on which other actors/system members, the complementors, align their business strategy and provide complementary goods and services.[145] Petit and Teece identify five characteristics of digital ecosystems, the 'five Cs' as they call them. The first is *cross-business competition* at three levels: between platforms, between a platform and its complementors, and between complementors. The second is *co-evolution* between the various members of the ecosystem. The third is the importance of *complementors* for the success of the ecosystem. The fourth is the simultaneous existence between competition and cooperation, *co-opetition*, between the various ecosystem members. Finally, the fifth is the ecosystem's leader providing a *conscious direction* that contributes to its success.[146]

Nowadays, the most powerful platforms have developed into multi-actor and multi-product ecosystems.[147] In general, the term 'ecosystem' encompasses all of a platform's activities that interrelate, complement, or connect to a core service. Hence,

[140] M Jacobides, C Cenrnanmo, and A Gawer, "'Towards a Theory of Ecosystems"' (2018n139) 39 Strategic Management Journal, 2255, 2258--2259 with further references.

[141] H Hou and Y Shi, 'Ecosystem-as-Structure and Ecosystem-as-Coevolution: A Constructive Examination' (2021) 100 Technovation 1, 2.

[142] *Ibid*, with further references to R Adner, 'Ecosystem as Structure: An Actionable Construct for Strategy' (2017) 43 Journal of Management 39, and Jacobides, Cernamo, and Gawer, 'Towards a Theory of Ecosystems' (n139).

[143] Hou and Shi (n141), with further references to J Moore, 'Business Ecosystems and the View from the Firm' (2006) 51 Antitrust Bulletin 31.

[144] F Jenny, 'Changing the Way We Think: Competition, Platforms and Ecosystems' (2021) 9 Journal of Accounting and Economics 1, 3.

[145] OECD, 'Taking Ecosystems Competition Seriously in the Digital Economy—Note by Nicolas Petit and David J. Teece' (Hearing on Competition Economics of Digital Ecosystems) DAF/COMP/WD(2020)90 (2 December 2020), para 10.

[146] *Ibid*, paras 11–21. Here, we note that the final C, conscious direction, endows the ecosystem leader with quasi-regulatory power, thereby raising issues with respect to potential competition law liability. For the analysis of the respective case law, see Chapter 5 below.

[147] Jacobides, Cernamo, and Gawer, 'Distinguishing between Platforms and Ecosystems' (n137); CMA, Digital Platforms Report (n6).

important to the development of ecosystems is the existence of complementary and interdependent relations between various services,[148] which, from a competition law perspective, may endow incumbents with increased power outside of the confines of a specific market. Taking Google and Facebook, for example, these platforms became so powerful by embarking on and strengthening their core service, and then leveraging their power into other markets.[149] Such digital ecosystems may even have been built through competitors' envelopment acquisitions.[150] Such acquisitions may take place in markets for complementary products or in unrelated markets in order to acquire valuable data sources.[151] The former may result in product tying and the latter in data tying.

The illustrations below depict GAFAM Big Tech's ecosystems, which build on and expand from a core service into interrelated and/or complementary services. Figures 2.1–2.5 below include some of the respective ecosystem services and are not inclusive. It is worth noting that every GAFAM is a digital conglomerate and is amongst the ten largest companies in the world by market valuation.[152]

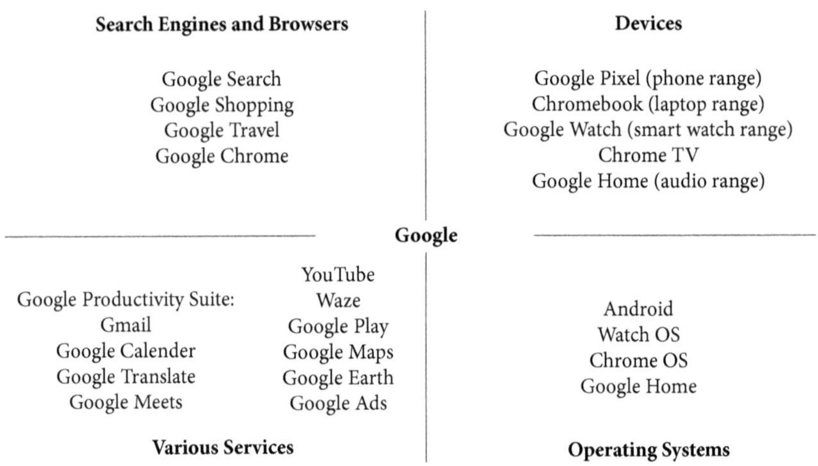

Figure 2.1 Google's Ecosystem

[148] CMA, 'Online Platforms and Digital Advertising' (Market Study—Final Report) (Digital Platforms Report, 1 July 2020) Appendix E: Ecosystems of Google and Facebook <https://assets.publishing.service.gov.uk/media/5fe49531d3bf7f089e48dec9/Appendix_E_Ecosystems_v.2_WEB.pdf> (accessed 18 August 2023).

[149] CMA, Digital Platforms Report (n6), para 2.36.

[150] Devising the theory, see T Eisenmann, G Parker, and M Van Alstyne, 'Platform Envelopment' (2011) 32 Strategic Management Journal 1270.

[151] D Condorelli and J Padilla, 'Harnessing Platform Envelopment in the Digital World' (2020) 16 Journal of Competition Law and Economics 143; D Condorelli and J Padilla, 'Data-Driven Envelopment with Privacy-Policy Tying' (Working paper, 2020) <https://papers.ssrn.com/sol3/papers.cfm?abstract_id=3504025> (accessed 18 August 2023).

[152] European Commission (EU), 'Evaluation of the Commission Notice on the Definition of Relevant Market for the Purposes of Community Competition Law of 9 December 1997', SWD(2021) 199 final (Staff working document, 12 July 2021), 13.

Figure 2.2 Amazon's Ecosystem

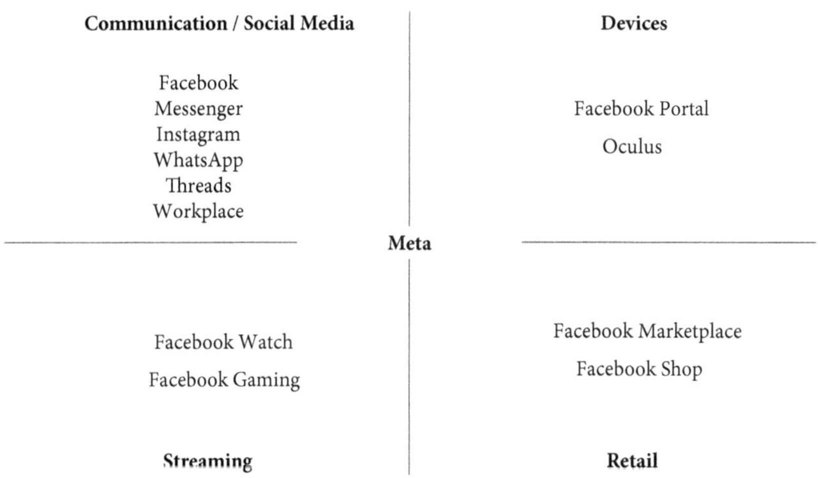

Figure 2.3 Meta's [Facebook] Ecosystem

Such digital ecosystems usually employ the business model the incumbents adopt in their core market.[153] Google's and Facebook' ecosystems are ad-centric, since the focus is on attracting consumers' attention and monetizing such attention through advertising. Other ecosystems, such as those of Apple or Microsoft,

[153] M Bourreau, 'Some Economics of Digital Ecosystems' (Hearing on Competition Economics of Digital Ecosystems), DAF/COMP/WD(2020)89 (13 November 2020), para 18.

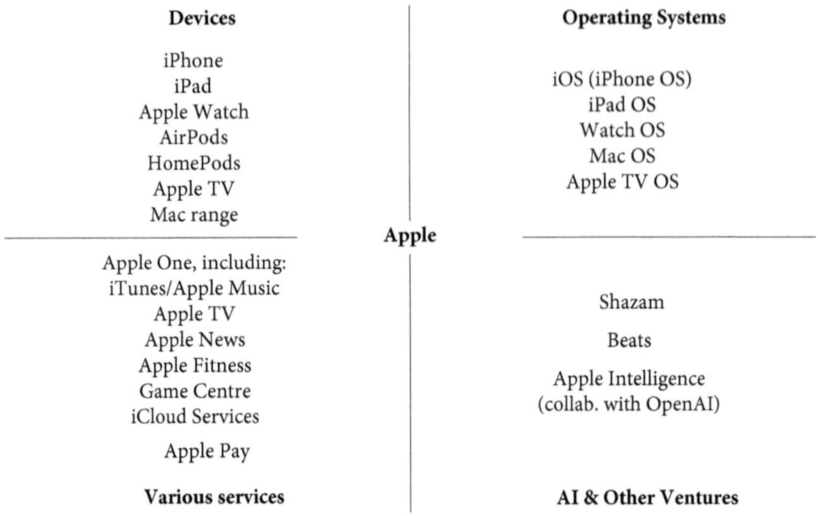

Figure 2.4 Apple's Ecosystem

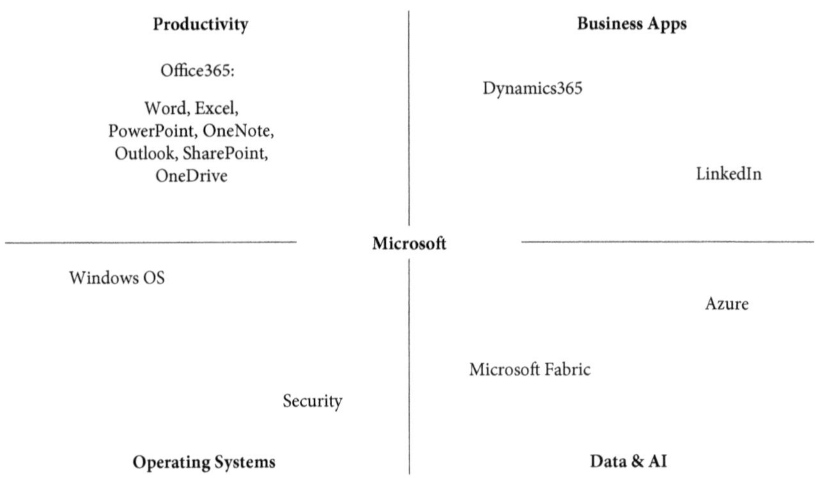

Figure 2.5 Microsoft's Ecosystem

are device- or service-centric, resting on their products' and services' modular design,[154] allowing these firms to expand their product lines and create consumption synergies and make revenues from their products or services.[155]

[154] A product has a modular design when it comprises modules that can interact through standardized interfaces. As opposed to an integrated design, in a modular design one can reuse components between different products and services within the same firm. See Bourreau (n153), para 9.

[155] Bourreau (n153), paras 19–20.

The problem that regulatory authorities, including competition authorities, are called on to tackle is the ability of the platform to influence complementors, which are orchestrated and managed by the platform.[156] Research has shown that platform orchestrators may compete against complementors by entering into their product spaces. Complementors' success, as well as the magnitude of their platform-specific investment, affect the platform's decision to enter a complementor's product space.[157] In addition, ecosystems' structural characteristics have led to a revival of conglomerate concerns.[158]

In China, we find its own home-grown ecosystems. A typical example is the Alibaba ecosystem. Since its establishment in 1999,[159] e-commerce has been Alibaba's core business. Subsequently, its vigorous development and expansion has spawned new opportunities for a wide range of areas such as payment services, data management services, and entertainment services. Figure 2.6 demonstrates its current commercial map.

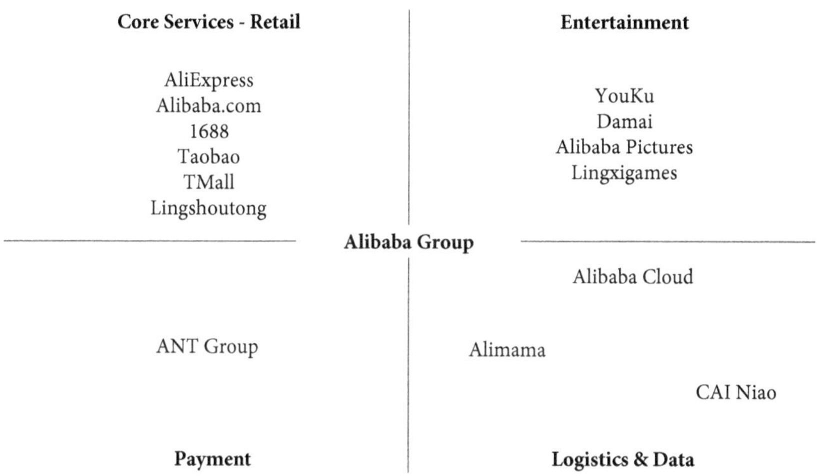

Figure 2.6 Alibaba's Ecosystem

Another significant home-grown ecosystem is the Tencent ecosystem. Tencent earned the first barrels with the instant messaging platform QQ in 1998 but has

[156] For a concise identification of the issues, see M Jacobides and I Lianos, 'Ecosystems and Competition Law in Theory and Practice', Centre for Law, Economics and Society Research Paper Series (January 2021).

[157] F Zhu and Q Liu, 'Competing with Complementors: An Empirical Look at Amazon.com' (2018) 39 Strategic Management Journal 2618.

[158] See, in particular, with reference to EU merger control, chapter VI.

[159] See the website of Alibaba Group, <https://www.alibabagroup.com/about-alibaba#history-and-milestone> (accessed 21 September 2023).

gradually grown into a giant ecosystem 'with core focuses on gaming, social media and networking (i.e. WeChat), FinTech (i.e. WeChat Pay), cloud computing and digital content'.[160]

Chinese scholars and judicial authorities have also noted the anticompetitive concerns in the platform ecosystems. For example, in the case of *Tencent v Kobay Network Technology and Haiyi Network Technology Co Ltd*, the court held that Tencent's platform ecosystem, typified by its WeChat service, was in line with the concept of a business ecosystem as 'an economic community constructed by organizations and individuals that interact with each other'.[161] It belongs to the innovative business model of platforms in digital markets, and legal protection is expected to be provided for the consequent legitimate commercial interests and competitive advantages. Thus, the court recognized the existence of platform ecosystems and held that competition law makes sense in terms of protecting good competition among platform ecosystems. Some scholars have also shifted attention to the status and application of platform ecosystems in antitrust law.[162] It is believed that the platform ecosystem operates at four levels: the collection of multiple commodities and markets, the correlation and crossover between multiple commodities, the effective internalization of multiple levels of complementarity, and the centralized resource allocation mechanism. At the same time, in the internal coordination of the ecosystem with the above four levels, the efficient operation of the ecosystem as a whole is realized through three mechanisms: data utilization, algorithm operation, and the formulation and implementation of platform rules. There is a large number of practical scenarios utilizing digital platform ecosystems worldwide. As for the competitive assessment, it is recommended to incorporate the perspective of digital platform ecosystems into each step of the multi-level and multi-type analyses of anticompetitive behaviours, focusing on examining new types of anticompetitive behaviours and exploring a middle path that meets the characteristics of the ecosystem's operation in terms of ex-ante review and ex-post regulation.[163]

However, on the whole, scholars and regulators in China pay inadequate attention to platform ecosystems, and a systematic framework has not been established. A combination of factors has led to such a phenomenon: first and foremost,

[160] Investor Insights Asia, 'Tencent Holdings (Part 1): Introducing Tencent' (25 April 2022 <https://www.investorinsights.asia/post/tencent-holdings-part-1-introducing-tencent> (accessed 21 September 2023).

[161] Hangzhou Intermediate People's Court, *Shenzhen Tencent Computer System Co, Ltd, Tencent Technology (Shenzhen) Co, Ltd v Hangzhou Kebei Network Technology Co, Ltd, Hangzhou Haiyi Network Technology Co, Ltd*, [2019] (杭州科贝网络科技有限公司、杭州海逸网络科技有限公司不正当竞争纠纷案, (2019)浙01民终9556号) (26 August 2020).

[162] X Liu, '数字平台生态系统的反垄断法定位与规制 [Anti-Monopoly Law in Ecosystem of Digital Platform: Its Positioning and Regulation]' (2022) 1 思想战线 [Thinking] 138, 138–148.

[163] *Ibid.*

considering the continuous innovation of technologies such as big data, AI, and blockchain, the platform ecosystem is still at a fledgling stage and has not yet reached a mature and stable state. Although the digital economy is prone to oligopolistic market structures, technological innovations and consumer preferences have made the market position and competitive landscape of platforms unstable. The formation of platform ecosystems requires a long and challenging process since they have substantial competitive relationships with each other. On the other hand, in China, regulators, judicial officials, and academics may be concerned about platform ecosystems, but they do not have sufficient insights about the application of competition law. Although the concept of platform ecosystems as a whole is mentioned in several case studies, it is not yet clear how to recognize and regulate potential anticompetitive conduct.

IV.2 Choice Architecture and the Power of Defaults

Digital ecosystems' structure, in that they offer an integrated consumer experience within an environment of interconnected products and services, accentuates consumer default biases.[164] For example, let's consider the Google ecosystem, with the offering of a suite of services, such as Search, Android, Gmail, Maps, and Docs, or the Apple ecosystem, combining various Apple devices with the iOS. Both ecosystems offer bespoke experiences to users, thereby preventing them from diverting away from their ecosystem experience.

Such consumer biases can be exploited further through pre-installations and defaults. For example, the CMA market study on mobile ecosystems found that Apple devices (iPhones and iPads) have Apple's Safari web browser pre-installed, whereas Android smartphones usually have Google's Chrome browser pre-installed. Safari and Chrome together account for 90 per cent of mobile devices in the United Kingdom, despite the fact that consumers may download other browsers.[165] In principle, such pre-installation may distort consumer choice and reduce competitive constraints on the incumbents.

[164] See generally, RH Thaler, *Misbehaving: The Making of Behavioral Economics* (WW Norton, 2015); See also A Fletcher, 'The Role of Behavioural Economics in Competition Policy' (2023) in *Cambridge Handbook on the Theoretical Foundations of Antitrust and Competition Law* (CUP, forthcoming) <https://papers.ssrn.com/sol3/papers.cfm?abstract_id=4389681>; CMA, 'Online Choice Architecture—How Digital Design Can Harm Competition and Consumers' (Discussion paper, April 2022) <https://assets.publishing.service.gov.uk/government/uploads/system/uploads/attachment_data/file/1066524/Online_choice_architecture_discussion_paper.pdf> (both accessed 18 August 2023).

[165] CMA, 'Mobile Ecosystems' (Market Study Final Report, 10 June 2022), para 2.27 <https://assets.publishing.service.gov.uk/government/uploads/system/uploads/attachment_data/file/1138104/Mobile_Ecosystems_Final_Report_amended_2.pdf> (accessed 7 June 2024).

In addition, the collection of user data through a wide range of services allows ecosystem orchestrators to offer personalized services, which, on the one hand, enhances users' experience, but, on the other, ensures that users remain locked in within the ecosystem. Consumer choices can also be influenced by the ranking and presentation of certain options.[166] For example, according to a CMA study on mobile devices, the top three links generate more than 70 per cent of the total clicks.[167]

V. Implications for Market Definition and the Assessment of Market Power

V.1 Market Definition

Market definition helps competition authorities to identify the boundaries of competition between firms, in order to assess the competitive constraints they face, both from a product and a geographic dimension.[168] According to the General Court,

> [t]he concept of the relevant market in fact implies that there can be effective competition between the products or services which form part of it and this presupposes that there is a sufficient degree of interchangeability between all the products or services forming part of the same market in so far as a specific use of such products or services is concerned [. . .] The interchangeability or substitutability is not assessed solely in relation to the objective characteristics of the products and services at issue, but the competitive conditions and the structure of supply and demand on the market must also be taken into consideration.[169]

Under the current framework, this is the necessary first step, before the assessment of market power.[170] In the market definition assessment, the competition

[166] CMA, 'Online Choice Architecture' (n164), paras 3.7, 3.11 and 3.12.

[167] CMA, 'Online Search: Consumer and Firm Behaviour—a Review of the Existing Literature' (2017), 3.

[168] European Commission (EU), 'Notice on the Definition of Relevant Market for the Purposes of Community Competition', [1997] OJ C 237/5, paras 2, 7–8; European Commission (EU), 'Commission Notice on the Definition of the Relevant Market for the Purposes of Union Competition Law' C(2024) 1645 (Brussels, 8 February 2024) (Revised Market Definition Notice) para 6.

[169] Case T-427/08 *CEAHR v Commission*, ECLI:EU:T:2010:517, para 67.

[170] The necessity of the market definition exercise is not without criticism. See L Kaplow, 'Why (Ever) Define Markets?' (2010) 124 Harvard Law Review 438. Interestingly, the UK CMA, in its revised Merger Assessment Guidelines, downplays the role of market definition in the analysis. See CMA, 'Merger Assessment Guidelines', CMA 129 (18 March 2021), paras 9.2–9.5. (para 9.2: 'the CMA anticipates that in future, merger assessments will place more emphasis on the competitive assessment as opposed to static market definition').

authorities assess whether products or services are substitutable for customers with respect to demand- and supply-side substitutability.[171]

The technical, economic, and architectural characteristics in the digital economy leading to the rise of powerful platforms and ecosystems have challenged the approach to market definition, primarily given the multi-sided nature of platforms, the emergence of digital ecosystems, the provision of goods and services at zero price, and the importance of data. In *Google Android*, the General Court (GC) set out the general framework for market definition and then proceeded to apply it in the context of digital markets.[172] The GC stated that

> particularly so in the case of markets which [. . .] fall within the digital economy, where traditional parameters such as the price of products or services or the market share of the undertaking concerned may be less important than in traditional markets, compared to other variables such as innovation, access to data, multi-sidedness, user behaviour or network effects.
>
> Thus, in a digital 'ecosystem', which brings together several categories of supplier, customer and consumer and causes them to interact within a platform, the products or services which form part of the relevant markets that make up that ecosystem may overlap or be connected *to* each other on the basis of their horizontal or vertical complementarity. Taken together, the relevant markets may also have a global dimension in the light of the system that brings its components together and of any competitive constraints within that system or from other systems.
>
> Identifying the conditions of competition relevant to the assessment of the position of economic strength enjoyed by the undertaking concerned may therefore require multi-level or multidirectional examination in order to determine the fact and extent of the various competitive constraints that may be exerted on that undertaking.[173]

In its Communication on competition policy that is fit for new challenges, the Commission announced that it will update its notice on market definition.[174] Such an update is warranted given the changes in light of the digitalization and interconnection in the past twenty years.[175] Amongst the changes identified is the fact that the digital economy's share of global gross domestic product (GDP), as well

[171] For a brief account of market definition in competition law assessment, see European Commission (EU), 'Evaluation of the Commission Notice on the Definition of Relevant Market for the Purposes of Community Competition Law' (n152), 4–8.

[172] Case T-604/18 *Google and Alphabet v Commission* (*Google Android*—GC), ECLI:EU:T:2022:541, paras 104–112.

[173] *Ibid*, paras 115–116.

[174] European Commission (EU), 'Communication—a Competition Policy Fit for New Challenges', COM(2021) 713 final (Brussels, 18 November 2021).

[175] *Ibid*, 7.

as the use of online platforms, has risen exponentially. There is an observed high concentration, with the seven large platforms accounting for 69 per cent of the estimated platform economy's EUR 6 trillion valuation.[176] Furthermore, there has been a rise in offering integrated programmes in ecosystem settings as well as the need to evaluate innovation concerns in the competitive assessment.[177] The revised Market Definition Notice has been published in early 2024 and accounts for this reality.[178]

V.1.1 Multi-Sidedness

The EU Expert Report maintained that, with respect to multi-sided platforms, the crucial element for the market definition analysis is the interdependence of different sides. Such interdependence should shift the focus from the analysis of market definition to the analysis of potential anticompetitive strategies and theories of harm.[179]

With respect to market definition in the context of multi-sided platforms, for which concrete guidance is now provided in the Revised Market Definition Notice,[180] the market can be defined either as a single market encompassing both sides or as separate markets on each side. The Commission's past cases have followed both approaches, suggesting that ultimately, market definition is context specific. For example, in the past, the Commission has defined the market for online advertising services separately from other markets for services to other user categories,[181] whereas in the context of online recruitment, a single market for online recruitment services was defined for both sides of recruiters and job seekers.[182] The factors to be taken into account for the assessment include the type of platform and its respective business model, as well as possibilities for substitution for

[176] European Commission (EU), 'Evaluation of the Commission Notice on the Definition of Relevant Market for the Purposes of Community Competition Law' (n152), 13 with further references to the Expert Group for the Observatory on the Online Platform Economy, 'Work Stream on Measurement & Economic Indicators' (Progress Report) <https://platformobservatory.eu/app/uploads/2020/07/ProgressReport_Workstream_on_Measurement_and_Economic_Indicators_2020.pdf> (accessed 7 June 2024).

[177] European Commission (EU), 'Evaluation of the Commission Notice on the Definition of Relevant Market for the Purposes of Community Competition Law' (n152), 13.

[178] Revised Market Definition Notice (n168).

[179] EU Experts Report (n4), 3–4.

[180] Revised Market Definition Notice (n168), paras 94–98.

[181] European Commission (EU), 'Evaluation of the Commission Notice on the Definition of Relevant Market for the Purposes of Community Competition Law' (n152), 54–55 with references to the following cases concerning ad-funded platforms where a separate market for the provision of online advertising services was defined. See cases *Microsoft/Yahoo Search Business* (Case M.5727); *Microsoft/Skype* (Case M.6281) (n130); *Facebook/WhatsApp* (Case M.7217) Commission Decision, C(2014) 7239 final; *Microsoft/LinkedIn* (Case M.8124) (n129); *Google Search (Shopping)* (Case AT.39740) Commission Decision, C(2017) 4444 final and *Google Android* (Case AT.40099), Commission Decision, C(2018) 4761 final (Brussels, 18 July 2018).

[182] European Commission (EU), 'Evaluation of the Commission Notice on the Definition of Relevant Market for the Purposes of Community Competition Law' (n152), 54–55 with references to *Microsoft/LinkedIn* (Case M.8124) (n129).

different user groups and homing decisions.[183] In case multiple markets are defined, network effects are taken into account in the competitive assessment.

It has been suggested that the type of platform (i.e. the distinction between transaction/matching and non-transaction platforms) impacts the market definition analysis.[184] This corresponds with the EU Commission approach, as reflected in the Revised Market Definition Notice, but consensus is yet to emerge with respect to whether a single or multiple markets should be defined. For example, in the case of payment cards (a transaction platform), the EU Commission has defined two distinct product markets on the issuing and acquiring sides, respectively.[185] Contrary to the EU Commission approach, in the case of transaction platforms, it has been argued that a single market should be defined, whereas for non-transaction platforms, multiple markets can be identified.[186] This is because, in the case of transaction platforms, either the transaction takes place on all sides or it does not take place at all.[187] Such an approach was endorsed by the US Supreme Court in *Ohio v Amex*,[188] yet it has been criticized by commentators.[189] Amex provides a transaction platform that intermediates between merchants and cardholders. What distinguishes its business model from other credit cards is the fact that it provides rewards to cardholders, inducing more spending while charging merchants higher fees. In light of such higher fees, merchants may attempt to steer cardholders away from using Amex, and therefore Amex has anti-steering provisions in its respective contracts. The issue in *Ohio v Amex* was whether such provisions constituted unreasonable restraints of trade in violation of section 1 of the US Sherman Act.

[183] Revised Market Definition Notice (n168), para 95; European Commission (EU), 'Evaluation of the Commission Notice on the Definition of Relevant Market for the Purposes of Community Competition Law' (n152), 54–55 with further references to European Commission (EU), 'Support Study Accompanying the Commission Notice on the Evaluation of the Definition of Relevant Market for the Purposes of Community Competition Law' (Final Report) (2019) (Support Study); European Commission (EU), 'Notice on the Definition of the Relevant Market for the Purposes of Union Competition Law' (Draft) (2022) <https://ec.europa.eu/commission/presscorner/detail/en/ip_22_6528> (accessed 7 June 2024), para 95.

[184] Revised Market Definition Notice (n168), para 95.

[185] *Ibid*, para 95 with reference to case *Mastercard* (Case AT.34579), ss 6.2.3 and 6.2.4.

[186] OECD, 'Market Definition in Multi-Sided Markets—Note by Dr Lapo Filistrucchi', DAF/COMP/WD(2017)27/final (12 January 2018), para 50. See also L Filistrucchi, D Geradin, E Van Damme, and P Affeldt, 'Market Definition in Two-Sided Markets: Theory and Practice' (2014) 10 Journal of Competition Law and Economics 293.

[187] OECD, 'Market Definition in Multi-Sided Markets—Note by Dr Lapo Filistrucchi' (n186), para 55.

[188] *Ohio v American Express*, 585 US 138 S Ct 2274 (2018). For a discussion of this case, see G Manne, 'In Defence of the Supreme Court's "Single Market" Definition in Ohio v American Express' (2019) 7 Journal of Accounting and Economics 104; T Wu, 'The American Express Opinion, the Rule of Reason, and Tech Platforms' (2019) 7 Journal of Accounting and Economics 117.

[189] Wu (n188); See also J Newman, 'Ohio v. American Express: The Good, The Bad, and the Ugly' (Network Law Review, 16 July 2018) <https://www.networklawreview.org/ohio-v-amex> (accessed 7 June 2024); H Hovenkamp, 'Platforms and the Rule of Reason: The American Express Case' (2019) Columbia Business Law Review 35; John B Kirkwood, 'Antitrust and Two-Sided Platforms: The Failure of American Express' (2020) 41 Cardozo Law Review 1805.

According to the US Supreme Court majority opinion, there is a single market for credit card transactions, and the plaintiffs failed to show anticompetitive effects in that market, since they focused only on one side of the market, showing that Amex's anti-steering provisions increased merchant fees.[190] Justice Breyer, in his dissenting opinion, made two very important points. First, one critical point that the majority's argument ignored is that 'proof of actual adverse effects on competition is, a fortiori, proof of market power' and, in such circumstances, there is no need to define the market;[191] and second, he stressed the fact that market definition is about substitutes not complements, raising the question of whether merchants, for example, can react to a price increase by switching to being a cardholder.[192]

V.1.2 Ad-Funded Platforms

Another factor that further complicates market definition in the digital economy is the fact that ad-funded platforms offer their products and services at zero monetary price on the users' side, which does not, however, suggest that there is no market for the respective product.[193] Competition authorities, including the EU Commission, have not shied away from defining a separate market for zero-priced goods and services.[194] In particular, the Commission and EU courts have held that

> [t]he fact that a product or service is provided free of charge does not prevent the offering of such a service from constituting an economic activity for the purposes of the competition rules under the Treaty. This is a factor to be taken into account in assessing dominance.[195]

In *Google Shopping*, the Commission defined two relevant product markets: the market for online general search services and the market for online comparison shopping services.[196] According to the Commission, the provision of online general search services constitutes an economic activity, despite being provided free of

[190] *Ohio v Amex* (n188), 15. On the contrary, in the EU, in *Cartes bancaires*, a market for the issue of payment cards was defined. However, the Court of Justice of the European Union held that potential 'interactions between the two facets of a two-sided system' can be taken into account in the analysis of the legal and economic context of the agreement. See Case C-67/13P *Groupement des cartes bancaires (CB) v Commission*, ECLI:EU:C:2014:2204, paras 76–79.

[191] *Ohio v Amex* (n188), Breyer J dissenting, 14.

[192] *Ibid*, 17.

[193] Revised Market Definition Notice (n168), para 97.

[194] European Commission (EU), 'Evaluation of the Commission Notice on the Definition of Relevant Market for the Purposes of Community Competition Law' (n153), 55 with references to the relevant case law. See cases: *Microsoft/Skype* (Case M.6281) (n130); *Facebook/WhatsApp* (Case M.7217) (n182); *Microsoft/LinkedIn* (Case M.8124) (n129); *Google Search (Shopping)* (Case AT.39740) (n181), and *Google Android* (Case AT.40099) (n181).

[195] *Google AdSense* (n121), para 118 with further references to Case T-201/04 *Microsoft v Commission* (n127), paras 966–970; Case T-79/12 *Cisco Systems, Inc. and Messagenet SpA v Commission*, ECLI:EU:T:2013:635, paras 65–74. *Google AdSense*, (n196), para 225.

[196] Case T-612/17 *Google LLC v Commission (Google Shopping)* ECLI:EU:T:2021:763 (*Google Shopping*—GC), para 42.

charge, since internet users agree to allow the collection of their data by the search engine operator. Users' data is subsequently monetized, particularly through display advertising on the results pages. Two-sided platforms strive to attract users' attention, thereby strengthening demand for the paid side, that is advertisers.[197]

Such business models, though, challenge the potential application of traditional economic tools, such as the small but significant non-transitory increase-in-price (SSNIP) test, when defining markets. The SSNIP test essentially measures customer switching in the event of a small but significant non-transitory increase in price.[198] In practice, it has been rarely used by competition authorities when defining the market in a multi-sided platform context.[199] The SSNIP test cannot be applied on the user side of the platform, and if applied on the advertisers' side, it also needs to account for the impact on the users' side.[200]

In zero-priced markets, the emphasis has to shift to factors other than price, such as quality and innovation.[201] Hence, other metrics such as the small but significant non-transitory decrease in quality (SSNDQ) have been suggested.[202] The Commission applied the SSNDQ test in *Google Android*, albeit without any concrete discussion of quality deterioration.[203] Google contested the application of the test, arguing that, given its imprecise nature, it did not know how the test was applied.[204] The GC sided with the Commission and accepted that the SSNDQ test constituted relevant evidence and did not require the definition of a 'precise quantitative standard of degradation of quality of the target product'.[205] Other factors that may influence the Commission market definition analysis in the case of zero monetary price[206] include product functionalities,[207] intended use,[208] industry views on hypothetical substitution and competitive constraints,[209] switching costs, and barriers such as product interoperability and licensing requirements.[210]

Another interesting proposition with respect to attention (ad-funded) platforms is to explore a market for consumer attention where platforms reselling attention

[197] *Ibid*, para 43.
[198] Commission Notice (n169) para 17; Revised Market Definition Notice (n168), para 29.
[199] Support Study (n183), 59.
[200] *Ibid*, 63.
[201] *Ibid*, 61.
[202] OECD, 'Market Definition in Multi-Sided Markets—Note by Dr Lapo Filistrucchi' (n186), paras 113–114.
[203] *Google Android* (Case AT.40099) (n181), paras 297–305.
[204] *Google Android*—GC (n172), para 172.
[205] *Ibid*, paras 173–181.
[206] Revised Market Definition Notice (n168), para 98.
[207] See *Facebook/WhatsApp* (Case M.7217) (n181), paras 24–33 and 51–61 with respect to consumer communication and social networking cases.
[208] See *Google Search (Shopping)* (Case AT.39740) (n181), paras 163–183 with respect to general search services.
[209] See *Microsoft/LinkedIn* (Case M.8124) (n129), paras 106–110 with respect to professional social networking services.
[210] See *Google Android* (Case AT.40099) (n181) with respect to Android app stores (paras 284–305) and licensable smart mobile OS (para 239).

are seen as competitors.[211] Such a proposition is very important given the amount of time consumers spend online. For example, consumers increasingly spend a very large amount of their time on social media.[212] A proposed metric here is the A(ttentional)-SSNIP test, which can measure consumers' reaction in response to additional advertising. When running the A-SSNIP test, the question is whether consumers will switch to other attention platforms if a five-second advertisement is played before every use of Google Search.[213] Viewing attention platforms as competitors irrespective of their specific function (e.g. search engine) can be seen as a way to remedy the observed 'blind spot' in contemporary competition law analysis.[214]

V.1.3 Data Markets

Since data are obliquitous in the digital economy, the question is how they affect the market definition analysis. For example, in the *Facebook/WhatsApp* merger, the Commission refrained from defining a market for the provision of data or data analytics services, since neither party was active in such markets. Facebook collected and analysed user data for targeted advertising but was not selling such data or providing data analytics services. WhatsApp, at the time, was not collecting any data for advertising purposes.[215] Since such data constituted only an intermediary product, an input for the improvement of advertising services, and was not traded on a self-standing basis, no market for data existed.

Such a narrow approach to the data market definition based on the services provided/products traded has been criticized, considering that powerful platforms' business models often rely on the accumulation and exploitation of vast amounts of data. It has been suggested that acquisitions are often driven by the objective of getting hold of valuable data sets. By defining a separate market for data, potential competition between powerful platforms also competing in a market for data can be taken into account.[216] In this vein, in her dissenting statement in *Google/DoubleClick* in the United States, Commissioner Jones Harbour alluded to the possibility of defining potential data markets in the context of data mergers 'comprising data that may be useful to advertisers and publishers who wish to engage in behavioural targeting'.[217]

[211] D Evans, 'Attention to Rivalry among Online Platforms' (2013) 9 Journal of Competition Law and Economics 313, 348.

[212] See, e.g. on the time spent on social media, BroadbandSearch, 'Average Daily Time Spent on Social Media (Latest 2023 Data)' <https://www.broadbandsearch.net/blog/average-daily-time-on-social-media> (accessed 18 August 2023).

[213] Wu, 'Blind Spot' (n136), 797–798.

[214] *Ibid.*

[215] *Facebook/WhatsApp* (Case M.7217) (n181), paras 70–72.

[216] I Graef, 'Market Definition and Market Power in Data: The Case of Online Platforms' (2015) 38 World Competition 473, 492.

[217] FTC, 'Dissenting Statement of Commissioner Pamela Jones Harbour in the Matter of Google/DoubleClick', FTC File No 071-0170 (20 December 2007) <https://www.ftc.gov/legal-library/browse/cases-proceedings/public-statements/dissenting-statement-commissioner-harbour-matter-google

V.1.4 Ecosystem Competition

In the context of consumer-facing ecosystems, the market definition analysis may encompass both specific markets for products and services from a consumer perspective and (possible) ecosystem markets. It may also need to take into account ecosystem-specific aftermarkets, where ecosystems succeed in adopting lock-in strategies for their users.[218] Consumer-facing ecosystems may take the form of aftermarkets and can be conceptualized around a core product and several secondary products. Depending on the level of openness of a given ecosystem, markets may be defined at the level of the ecosystem or there may be different secondary markets.[219] With respect to digital ecosystems, the market definition may rely on similar principles applicable to aftermarkets, and (depending on the specific context) the competition authorities may define a unitary/system market, multiple markets, or dual markets.[220]

Given the nature of ecosystem competition, with digital ecosystems offering a range of products competing intensively over different value propositions, it has been suggested that competition law analysis should move beyond the traditional substitutability approach to market definition.[221]

V.2 Market Power

Competition authorities and courts have been advised to reconsider their approach to market definition as the necessary first step in every competition law analysis and to steer away from a strict market definition in the light of the existence of evidence of market power.[222] Given the complexities inherent in the market definition exercise in digital platforms markets, discussed above, certain practices in the digital economy may provide direct evidence of harm and the concomitant existence of market power enabling incumbents to inflict such harm.[223] Below we discuss various factors that may aid in the assessment of incumbents' market power.

doubleclick>; also 9 <https://www.ftc.gov/sites/default/files/documents/public_statements/statement-matter-google/doubleclick/071220harbour_0.pdf> (both accessed 7 June 2024).

[218] EU Expert Report (n4), 3–4.

[219] Support Study (n183), 82–84.

[220] Revised Market Definition Notice (n168), paras 99–1043.

[221] OECD, 'Ecosystem Competition—a Note by Daniel A. Crane', DAF/COMP/WD(2020)67 (28 October 2020); D Crane, 'Ecosystem Competition and the Antitrust Laws' (2019) 98 Nebraska Law Review 412.

[222] See, e.g. L Kaplow, 'Market Definition: Impossible and Counterproductive' (2013) 79 Antitrust Law Journal 361; J Farrell and C Shapiro, 'Antitrust Evaluation of Horizontal Mergers: An Economic Alternative to Market Definition' (2010) 10 (1) BE Journal of Theoretical Economics, Article 9.

[223] *Ohio v Amex* (n188), Breyer J dissenting. See also S Salop, D Francis, L Sillman, and M Spero, 'Rebuilding Platform Antitrust: Moving on from Ohio v. American Express' (2022) 84 Antitrust Law Journal 883, 896.

Market shares can be a useful first indication of market power and are often calculated based on sales.[224] However, they present only a limited indicator.[225] In the digital economy, other metrics include the number of active users,[226] the number of visits,[227] the number of downloads[228] and interactions, and the platform's transaction value or volume.[229] In zero-price markets, on the consumer side where 'attention platforms' strive for consumer attention with the aim of monetizing such attention on the advertisers' side, it has been suggested that the time spent on the site can serve as a measure of market power.[230]

Franck and Peitz grouped the potential indicators of market power in platform markets. Such indicators include revenue share, user share, user share relative to the number of users, share of usage volume, mark-up/Lerner index, profits, barriers to entry, and direct evidence.[231] Data, network effects, economies of scale, and switching costs can also serve as an indicator of the existence of market power. This is expressly recognized in the German Competition Act section 18(3a), which provides that

> [i]n particular in the case of multi-sided markets and networks, in assessing the market position of an undertaking account shall also be taken of:
> 1. direct and indirect network effects,
> 2. the parallel use of several services and the switching costs for users,
> 3. the undertaking's economies of scale arising in connection with network effects,
> 4. the undertaking's access to data relevant for competition,
> 5. competitive pressure driven by innovation.

Linkages between related markets are another factor that may be considered in the assessment of market power. For example, in *Google Android*, the Commission defined four relevant markets, namely (i) the worldwide market (excluding China) for the licensing of smart mobile OSs; (ii) the worldwide market (excluding China) for Android app stores; (iii) the various national markets, within the EEA, for the provision of general search services; and (iv) the worldwide market

224 Revised Market Definition Notice (n168), paras 105–106.

225 OECD, 'The Evolving Concept of Market Power in the Digital Economy' (OECD Competition Policy Roundtable background note, 2022), 21.

226 *Facebook/WhatsApp* (Case M.7217) (n181), paras 95–98.

227 *Google Search (Shopping)* (n181), paras 273–284.

228 *Google Android* (Case AT.40099) (n181), paras 591–593.

229 With reference to these metrics, see Revised Market Definition Notice (n168), para 108.

230 Wu, 'Blind Spot' (n136), 794–795.

231 F Ju and M Peitz, 'Market Definition and Market Power in the Platform Economy' (CERRE Report, May 2019), 69–70.

for non-OS-specific mobile web browsers.[232] Google was dominant in the first three.[233] In assessing Google's dominance, the Commission also assessed the interconnectedness of these markets as well as the competitive constraints exerted by the Apple ecosystem, which is characterized by the relationship between iOS and the App Store.[234]

Given the characteristics of digital platforms and ecosystems, commentators have highlighted the need to develop new tools and metrics to evaluate both horizontal and vertical interactions in the digital economy.[235] The OECD has examined such new metrics, including platform power, intermediation power, bottleneck power, and portfolio power, amongst others.[236] Platform power essentially stems from, and is defined in relation to, platforms' role and position, which enables platforms to influence multiple markets or multiple sides of a market.[237] Intermediation power refers to the role of platforms in intermediating between different user groups.[238] With respect to intermediation power, the German Competition Act (section 18(3b)) provides that '[i]n assessing the market position of an undertaking acting as an intermediary on multi-sided markets, account shall be taken in particular of the importance of the intermediary services provided by the undertaking for accessing supply and sales markets'. Bottleneck power is associated with the control of a congestion point that has the potential to lead to inefficiencies.[239] This is what distinguishes this concept from the concept of digital gatekeepers, which, on the contrary, are capable of generating efficiencies.[240] Portfolio power connotes the ability to exercise market power from the combination of a portfolio of products.[241] Interestingly, these metrics appear to be captured by the assessment of market power,[242] yet there are proposals to articulate and measure different types of power, such as panopticon power and power from differential dependency between value co-creators, which both extend the concept of power beyond a single market.[243]

[232] *Google Android* (Case AT.40099) (n181), para 120.
[233] *Ibid*, para 121.
[234] *Ibid*, para 270.
[235] Lianos (n139), 648.
[236] OECD, 'The Evolving Concept of Market Power in the Digital Economy' (n225), 22–23.
[237] *Ibid*, 23.
[238] *Ibid*, 24.
[239] *Ibid*, 25 with further references to P Alexiadis and A de Streel, 'Designing an EU Intervention Standard for Digital Platforms', EUI Working Paper RSCAS 2020/14 (2020), 4.
[240] Alexiadis and de Streel (n239), 4.
[241] OECD, 'The Evolving Concept of Market Power in the Digital Economy' (n225), 25.
[242] *Ibid*, 24–25.
[243] I Lianos and B Carballa-Smichowski, 'A Coat of Many Colours—New Concepts and Metrics of Economic Power in Competition Law and Economics' (2022) 18 Journal of Competition Law and Economy 795.

VI. Platform Business Models and Ecosystems

VI.1 Introduction

Powerful platforms exhibit certain common characteristics, yet their business models differ in their details. In terms of these characteristics, the DMA, a Regulation that seeks to complement competition law enforcement against Big Tech companies in the EU, which is applicable to gatekeepers of core platform services,[244] provides a succinct categorization.[245] Such characteristics comprise economies of scale due to near-zero marginal costs of adding new users, network effects, multi-sidedness, intermediation, the dependence of users, lock-in effects, a lack of multi-homing, and data-driven advantages.

Core platform services under the DMA include (i) online intermediation services, (ii) online search engines, (iii) online social networking services, (iv) video-sharing platform services, (v) number-independent interpersonal communication services, (vi) operating systems, (vii) web browsers, (viii) virtual assistants, (ix) cloud computing services, and (x) advertising intermediation services provided by a provider of any of the precious core platform services.[246] Whereas the common characteristics are present in every powerful platform, it is the provision of these various different services that distinguishes the business models employed.

Caffarra and Scott Morton identify three rough groups of platforms, each with a different business model, and argue that such business models have been ignored in the broad-brush DMA obligations, which need clearer organizing principles around business models.[247] The first group is *ad-funded digital platforms*, such as Google (search engines) and Facebook (social media).[248] In essence, the key to their business model is attracting consumers' attention and thereby harnessing their data, which is consequently monetized through targeted advertising.[249] The second group is *transaction or matchmaking platforms*, which includes marketplaces and exchanges. It is comprised of, for example, Amazon as well as Uber, Airbnb, and DoubleClick. This group corresponds to the category of online

[244] DMA (n46), Article 2(2) on 'core platform services' and Article 2(1) and 3 on 'gatekeepers'. On the DMA, see Chapter 3, section V.2.1.

[245] DMA (n46), Recitals 2 and 13. For a detailed discussion of such characteristics, see also this chapter, section III.3.

[246] DMA (n46), Article 2(2). Eight of these ten core platform services were in the Commission's initial proposal, whereas virtual assistants and web browsers were added later during the negotiations. See European Commission (EU), 'Questions and Answers: Digital Markets Act: Ensuring Fair and Open Digital Markets' (Brussels, 2 May 2023) <https://ec.europa.eu/commission/presscorner/detail/en/qanda_20_2349> (accessed 7 June 2024).

[247] C Caffarra and F Scott Morton, 'The European Commission Digital Markets Act: A Translation' (5 January 2021) <https://voxeu.org/article/european-commission-digital-markets-act-translation> (accessed 7 June 2024). Other propositions include the focus on the ecosystem architecture and its governance. See Jacobides and Lianos (n156), 30.

[248] On ad-funded platforms, see CMA, Digital Platforms Report (n6).

[249] *Ibid*, 42.

intermediation services in DMA terms. The third group includes *OS platforms* (operating systems and app stores), such as iOS, the App Store, Google Android, and the Google Play Store. The last two categories of platforms can be grouped into one category—as *platforms funded by transactions.* Contrary to ad-funded platforms, transaction-based platforms, such as Amazon Marketplace or Apple's App Store, are predominantly funded through the commission charged to retailers or app developers, respectively.[250]

Irrespective of the differences in their business models, what these platforms have in common is the development of their respective ecosystems of complementary products/services around their core product/service. Google, for example, has expanded beyond general search and now has a strong position in browsers (Chrome), operating systems (Android) and video streaming (YouTube). Facebook has expanded from social network services into messaging, devices, gaming, and retail.[251] Below, we discuss the structure and architecture as well as the main players in the digital sectors that form the backbone of the digital economy and have attracted competition authorities' and regulators' attention alike under the two-partite distinction—between transaction-based and ad-funded platforms.

VI.2 Transaction-Based Platforms

VI.2.1 Mobile Ecosystems: Operating Systems, App Stores, and Web Browsers

Mobile devices with an internet connection—smartphones and tablets—have become the gateway to an array of online products, services, and content, including music, TV and video streaming, games, fitness tracking, shopping, and banking. They also allow for the control of smart devices. Given their importance, they have attracted regulatory scrutiny. For example, on 15 June 2021, the CMA launched its market investigation into mobile ecosystems, the scope of which was broader than previous studies by other NCAs.[252] The Final Report was published in June 2022.[253] According to the CMA's statement of scope, 'mobile ecosystems' comprise the following core set of products: mobile devices, mobile operating systems, and

[250] *Ibid*, para 2.3.

[251] *Ibid*, para 56. See also this chapter, section IV.1.

[252] See CMA, 'CMA to Scrutinise Apple and Google Mobile Ecosystems' (Press release, 15 June 2021) <https://www.gov.uk/government/news/cma-to-scrutinise-apple-and-google-mobile-ecosystems> (accessed 7 June 2024). See Austrian Regulatory Authority, 'The Open Internet: OS, Apps and App Stores' (Report—English summary, 2019); Authority for Consumers and Markets (ACM), 'Market Study into Mobile App Stores', Report ACM/18/032693 (2019) (ACM Market Study).

[253] CMA, 'Mobile Ecosystems' (Final Report) (n165). The CMA's subsequent decision to open a market investigation reference into mobile browsers and cloud gaming was annulled by the Competition Appeal Tribunal (CAT), since the CMA failed to comply with the statutory deadline for opening such investigation. See *Apple Inc and Others v Competition and Markets Authority* (Case 1576/6/12/23).

mobile apps.[254] The CMA study looks into Apple's and Google's duopoly in the provision of operating systems (iOS and OS), with the combined share of Android and iOS exceeding 99 per cent worldwide,[255] as well as the provision of app stores (Apple and Play Store) and web browsers (Safari and Chrome).

App stores allow users to find and download apps on their mobile devices, while mobile browsers allow users to access the web. As such, these apps collectively are the two 'major access points' for content and service providers to consumers and at least one of each is pre-installed on every mobile device.[256] App stores are two-sided platforms connecting mobile users and app developers and allowing consumers to find and download apps through a centralized marketplace.[257] They also constitute a secondary or after-market to the primary market of mobile devices and associated operating systems since users can only access and use app stores after the purchase of a mobile device.[258] Apple's proprietary App Store is pre-installed on iOS devices and Google's proprietary app store, Google Play Store, is typically pre-installed on Android devices. The difference between Apple and Google here is that, until the adoption of the DMA, only the latter allowed for the installation of other app stores as well as the downloading of apps through a web browser (sideloading), though the Play Store remains by far the most popular app distribution channel.[259] For Apple-iOS devices, native apps could only be distributed through the App Store. Thus, the App Store was the only method of native app distribution, with 100 per cent of native apps on iOS devices being downloaded through the App Store.[260] Native apps are designed for a specific operating system, and hence developers need to produce two different versions for Android and iOS, respectively.[261] Following the adoption of the DMA in the EU,[262] Apple has

[254] CMA, 'Mobile Ecosystems' (Market Study Statement of Scope, 15 June 2021), para 2.

[255] *Ibid*, para 64 with reference to Statcounter Global Stats, 'Mobile & Tablet Operating System Market Share Worldwide' (March 2020–March 2021) <https://gs.statcounter.com/os-market-share/mobile-tablet/worldwide/#monthly-202003-202103> (accessed 7 June 2024). See also CMA, 'Mobile Ecosystems' (Interim Report) (n3), para 3.66. In *Google Android*, the European Commission excluded China from the global mobile OS market, given that Google's presence in China is limited. See *Google Android* (Case AT.40099) (n181), paras 416 et seq. The CMA remarks that although, in China, Android is very popular, smartphones sold in China cannot have any proprietary Google services pre-installed on Android. See CMA, 'Mobile Ecosystems' (Statement of Scope) (n254).

[256] CMA, 'Mobile Ecosystems' (Final Report) (n165), para 2.8.

[257] CMA, 'Mobile Ecosystems' (Statement of Scope) (n254), para 77. See also CMA, 'Mobile Ecosystems' (Interim Report) (n3), para 4.2.

[258] CMA, 'Mobile Ecosystems' (Statement of Scope) (n254), para 77. See also CMA, 'Mobile Ecosystems' (Interim Report) (n3), para 4.2.

[259] CMA, 'Mobile Ecosystems' (Statement of Scope) (n254), paras 78–79, 91.

[260] CMA, 'Mobile Ecosystems' (Final Report) (n165), para 4.34.

[261] CMA, 'Mobile Ecosystems' (Statement of Scope) (n254), para 71. Apps can be written for mobile devices or desktop environments and are generally thought to provide more focused functionalities in comparison to traditional software programs for desktops. See ACM Market Study (n252) into mobile app stores, 20. Native apps should be distinguished from web apps, which, in principle, should work on all browsers and operating systems because of the common standards of open web. See CMA, Mobile Ecosystems (Interim Report) (n3), para 3.

[262] On the DMA obligations, see Chapter III, section V.2.1.1.

proposed changes to its mobile ecosystem, amongst which is allowing sideloading, in order to comply with the DMA obligations.[263] Such proposals have attracted criticism, and their respective impact remains to be seen.[264]

With respect to web browsers, Google Chrome is pre-installed on Android devices and Apple Safari on Apple devices.[265] Other pre-installed apps include utility-style apps (e.g. calendar, calculators, and notepads), and apps for content streaming (Apple Music, Apple TV+, Google TV, YouTube), navigation (Apple Maps, Google Maps), email (Gmail, Apple Mail), and contactless payment services (Apple Pay, Google Pay).[266] In this case as well, Apple has a tighter grip on its ecosystem, which is bound to change post-DMA adoption,[267] limiting pre-installation to its own apps, whereas Android phones allowed pre-installation of original equipment manufacturers (OEMs) and third-party apps.[268] Safari (over 90 per cent) and Chrome (75 per cent) each have very strong shares of browser usage in their ecosystems, with their market position being even stronger in web engines. There are only three browser engines (WebKit by Apple, Blink by Google, and Gecko by Mozilla). On iOS, all browsers are required to use WebKit, and the majority of browsers on Android use Blink.[269]

The report concluded that the two incumbents faced limited competitive constraints from alternative operating system providers[270] and that they enjoy substantial and entrenched market power, which merits intervention.[271]

With respect to the second theme on the distribution of native apps, the report examined whether—given their ownership over the app stores in each respective ecosystem—Google and Apple have market power over the distribution of native apps and whether alternatives exist (either app stores or web-based alternatives and other devices, such as gaming consoles). The report concluded that there is a lack of competition both within and outside their respective ecosystems and that the incumbents enjoy substantial and entrenched market power in native

[263] Apple, 'Update on Apps Distributed in the European Union' <https://developer.apple.com/support/dma-and-apps-in-the-eu> (accessed 25 January 2024).

[264] A Yen, 'Apple's DMA Compliance Plan Is a Trap and a Slap in the Face for the European Commission' (Proton blog, 5 February 2024) <https://proton.me/blog/apple-dma-compliance-plan-trap> (accessed 5 February 2024). See European Commission (EU), 'Commission Sends Preliminary Findings to Apple and Opens Additional Non-Compliance Investigation against Apple under the Digital Markets Act' (Press release, 24 June 2024) <https://digital-strategy.ec.europa.eu/en/news/commission-sends-preliminary-findings-apple-and-opens-additional-non-compliance-investigation> (accessed 24 June 2024).

[265] CMA, 'Mobile Ecosystems' (Statement of Scope) (n254), para 80.

[266] *Ibid*, para 87.

[267] On the proposed changes, see Apple (n263).

[268] CMA, 'Mobile Ecosystems' (Statement of Scope) (n254), para 88.

[269] CMA, 'Mobile Ecosystems' (Interim Report) (n3), para 47. See also CMA, 'Mobile Ecosystems' (Final Report) (n165), para 2.30. Post DMA, Apple has committed to allowing other browser engines. See Apple (n263).

[270] CMA, Mobile Ecosystems (Interim Report) (n3), paras 35–39; CMA, 'Mobile Ecosystems' (Final Report) (n165), para 3.178.

[271] CMA, 'Mobile Ecosystems' (Final Report) (n165), para 3.179.

app distribution.[272] Apple and Google can block apps from being listed on their respective app stores. In that respect, the Interim Report found that Apple has blocked certain types of services altogether (such as cloud gaming services).[273] In addition, app developers are required to use Apple's and Google's respective payment systems for certain in-app transactions, and charge an average commission of 30 per cent.[274] The report also found that, in some respects, Apple has stricter rules in that it has introduced policies and terms, such as the App Tracking Transparency, which, on the one hand, may be detrimental for ad-funded apps, and on the other, nudge users towards apps that make revenue from users' in-app purchases, for which Apple collects a commission.[275] In addition, Apple does not allow for the pre-installation of third-party native apps on iOS devices contrary to Google, which points to the fact that app developers (such as Facebook, Microsoft, and Spotify) have pre-installation agreements with manufacturers.[276] According to the CMA though, such pre-installation potential remains largely an empty shell and does not present a competitive constraint to the Play Store.[277]

With respect to the third theme on the distribution of mobile browsers and browser engines, the market study examined whether the incumbents have market power, given that they own the two largest browsers and browser engines on mobile devices. It was found that restrictions exist regarding web browser choice on iOS. Such restrictions are exacerbated by pre-installation and default choices, the use of certain web standards, and webpage compatibility, as well as the use of their web browsers to shield other activities (app stores and Google's Search advertising).[278] Google and Apple were, thus, found to have substantial market power in the supply of mobile browsers and engines.[279]

The market study also examined concerns that Apple or Google may be using control over their respective app stores to advantage their own apps and services and thereby entrench their market power within app distribution.[280] Examples here include limiting hardware and software functionalities for app developers, including technology allowing contactless payments. Apple appears to be more restrictive in that regard since it controls every aspect of the Apple ecosystem, including hardware. Other examples include the incumbents' power to control the rules of app distribution through the blocking of apps, app ranking, and pre-installing or setting apps as defaults (where, again, Apple is more in control), as

[272] CMA, 'Mobile Ecosystems' (Interim Report) (n3), paras 40–41; CMA 'Mobile Ecosystems' (Final Report) (n165), paras 4.207–4.211.

[273] CMA, 'Mobile Ecosystems' (Interim Report) (n3), para 42.

[274] *Ibid*, para 4.38. In some instances, they apply a lower commission rate of 15 per cent; *Ibid*, para 4.226.

[275] *Ibid*, para 44.

[276] *Ibid*, paras 4.50–4.51.

[277] *Ibid*, para 4.52.

[278] *Ibid*, paras 46–51.

[279] CMA, 'Mobile Ecosystems' (Final Report) (n165), para 5.146.

[280] CMA, Mobile Interim Report (n253), para 52.

well as concerns about Apple's use of app developers' commercially sensitive information.[281] The market study also looked into three specific set of practices, namely rules about payments for in-app purchases as well as Apple's 'App Tracking Transparency' ('ATT') policy and restrictions on cloud gaming.[282]

Some of these practices have already attracted competition law scrutiny by the EU Commission and NCAs.[283] Following the introduction of the DMA, it remains to be seen how changes introduced by the incumbents in order to comply with the DMA obligations may enable more competition within their respective ecosystems.

In China, the mobile ecosystem is dominated by the Android operating system with China-only Android fork versions without any pre-installed Google services.[284] In *Google Android*, the EU Commission concluded that the relevant markets were the worldwide market (except for China) for the licensing of smart mobile OSs and for Android app stores. The Commission reached this conclusion since competitive conditions in China are different. First, most Google apps, including its most popular apps (Google Search, Google Maps, YouTube, and Google Play Store), are unavailable in China. Second, Chinese OEMs pre-install Android forks on their devices aimed at the Chinese market. An example of such Android forks is Aliyun by Alibaba.[285] The Google Play Store is a dominant player in the Android ecosystem outside of China. But in China, every major smartphone manufacturer (such as Huawei, Xiaomi, Oppo, and Vivo) has its own app store. Chinese scholars have noted competition reviews and cases against the mobile ecosystem in Europe and the United States.[286] However, no similar cases have yet emerged in China.

VI.2.2 Retail Marketplaces

Online marketplaces connect consumers and suppliers of goods and services. Examples that can be listed here include Uber, eBay, and Amazon. Amazon, for example, is the leading retail marketplace; however, it does not necessarily maintain a large share of online commerce in every jurisdiction.[287]

[281] *Ibid*, para 53. The CMA has also looked into such practices from a competition law enforcement perspective and managed to secure commitments. See CMA, 'Proposed Commitments Regarding Changes to Google Play's Rules to Allow Certain App Developers to Use Alternative Billing Systems for In-App Purchases' (19 April 2023) <https://www.gov.uk/government/consultations/proposed-commitments-regarding-changes-to-google-plays-rules-to-allow-certain-app-developers-to-use-alternative-billing-systems-for-in-app-purchases> (accessed 7 June 2024). The CMA accepted commitments regarding Google's 'Privacy Sandbox' browser changes and Google's announcement regarding similar proposed Android Privacy Sandbox changes.

[282] CMA 'Mobile Ecosystems' (Interim Report) (n3), para 55.

[283] On these cases, see Chapter 5, sections II.2 and II.5.

[284] See n255 above.

[285] See *Google Android* (Case AT.40099) (n181), paras 402 et seq.

[286] Y Meng, '反垄断法规制平台剥削性滥用的争议与抉择 [Controversies and Choices in Anti-Monopoly Regulation on Exploitative Abuse of Platforms]' (2022) 2 Peking University Law Journal 327, 327–345.

[287] For example, this is the case in the United Kingdom and the United States, but not in Australia. See ACCC, 'Digital Platform Services Inquiry' (n44), 4. This is also the case in Germany, France, and

Retail platforms, as in the case of Amazon, may adopt a dual role: operating a marketplace connecting independent third-party sellers with consumers as well as acting themselves as sellers on the platform. Such a dual role may raise competition concerns with respect to practices that have to do with the placement/ranking of third-party products and potential self-preferencing concerns as well as the use of non-public sellers' data.[288] Other concerns with respect to powerful retail platforms may concern the available avenues for effective dispute resolution and various unfair terms and conditions for third-party sellers.[289]

In China, the leading retail platforms are Taobao (belonging to the Alibaba Group), JD.com, and Pinduoduo. These retail platforms are the protagonists of some of the most high-profile cases in Chinese competition law, which will be discussed in detail in the respective later chapters.

VI.3 Ad-Funded Platforms

VI.3.1 Search Engines

General search engines, in essence, constitute an internet navigation tool, helping consumers to find information following their respective queries. In very simple terms, search engines rely on data and algorithms. They collect data by crawling the web, accumulating information on available webpages and organizing such data into an index. When a user enters a query, search engines use complex algorithms to instantly return the most relevant results from the index.[290] Google Search is the most powerful search engine. Other English-language search engines include Bing (owned by Microsoft), Yahoo Search (owned by Verizon Media), Ecosia, and DuckDuckGo. Apart from Google and Bing, the other search engines do not have their own at-scale index but rather buy organic links and adverts through syndication agreements.[291]

In *Google Android*, the GC discussed Google's business model, which is premised on searches around its flagship Google Search engine.[292] Google offers a range

Spain. See *Amazon Marketplace/Amazon Buy Box* (Joint cases AT.40462 and AT.40703) Commission Decision, C(2022) 9442, para 95. Amazon also has a very strong position in Italy. See Italian Competition Authority (AGCM), 'A528—Antitrust—Amazon Fined over €1,128 Billion for Abusing Its Dominant Position' (9 December 2021) <https://en.agcm.it/en/media/pressreleases/2021/12/A528> (accessed 7 June 2024). On these cases, see Chapter 5, section II.4.

[288] *Amazon Marketplace/Amazon Buy Box* (Joint cases AT.40462 and AT.403703) (n287).

[289] See, e.g. Bundeskartellamt, 'Bundeskartellamt Obtains Far-Reaching Improvements in the Terms of Business for Sellers on Amazon's Online Marketplaces' (Press release, 17 July 2019) <https://www.bundeskartellamt.de/SharedDocs/Meldung/EN/Pressemitteilungen/2019/17_07_2019_Amazon.html;jsessionid=98F173CFCF40CBB4E3AA149FF088832E.1_cid362> (accessed 7 June 2024). On this case, see Chapter 5, section II.4.2.

[290] CMA, Digital Platforms Report (n6), para 3.6.

[291] *Ibid*, para 3.7.

[292] *Google Android*—GC (n172), paras 55 et seq.

of digital products and services to consumers without a monetary charge, thereby collecting vast troves of data, and makes its revenue from its advertising services. In particular, in 2016, 88.7 per cent of Google's total revenues came from online advertising with Google's website, in particular Google Search's homepage, accounting for 80 per cent.[293]

Naturally, ad-funded platforms, in this case search engines, rely on data to 'fuel' their business model. Data collection and processing is controlled by a handful of platforms. Google Search, in the case of search engines, has raised difficult questions at the intersection of competition law, privacy, and consumer protection law.[294]

VI.3.2 Social Media

Social media platforms allow users to create public or semi-public profiles in order to interact and communicate with other users. They have been described as 'online services that allow users to participate in social networking, communicate with other users, and share and consume content generated by other users (including professional publishers)'.[295] They may also offer instant messaging services. The category of social media is rather diverse and encompasses a range of platforms with diverse features and functionalities, such as Facebook, Instagram, YouTube, Twitter, Snapchat, LinkedIn, Pinterest, and TikTok.[296] All social media platforms allow users to create personal profiles and offer various functionalities such as a personalized feed, connection with friends/contacts, followers/subscribers, photo sharing, video sharing, comments, and instant messaging.[297]

Social networks can be seen as a subcategory of social media, with their users valuing primarily the connection with friends and family. For example, the CMA concluded that while YouTube may act as a substitute for Facebook with respect to some functions, such as watching videos, it cannot substitute for Facebook when it comes to networking.[298] This holds true for other social media platforms (excluding Instagram and WhatsApp, which are owned by Facebook).[299]

The DMA lists online social networking services, as a separate category, amongst its core platform services to which it applies.[300] This should not be taken to mean that the Commission perceives this category in a broader manner to also include social media, since social media platforms fall under other core platform services,

[293] *Ibid*, para 56.
[294] ACCC, 'Digital Platforms Inquiry—Final Report' (n116), 5.
[295] *Ibid*, 41.
[296] Office of Communications (OFCOM), 'Online Nation—2021 Report', 32. See also CMA, Digital Platforms Report (n6), para 3.155.
[297] CMA, Digital Platforms Report (n6), with reference to OFCOM (n296).
[298] CMA, Digital Platforms Report (n6), para 3.188.
[299] *Ibid*, para 3.190.
[300] DMA (n46), Article 2(2)(c).

such as (for example) video-sharing platform services or number-independent interpersonal communications services.[301]

Social media, broadly construed, can also be classified as attention platforms,[302] since they compete to attract consumers' attention, with consumers spending time on the platform, and the platforms collecting and monetizing their data through targeted advertising.[303] Since their business models rely on the vast accumulation and monetization of data, concerns with respect not only to competition law, with the vast accumulation of data being translated to market power, but also with respect to privacy and a host of other public interest concerns (e.g. fake news, impact on democracy) have also emerged.[304]

Social media platforms may also expand from their core market into related ones. A good example here is Facebook Marketplace, which intermediates between users and buyers and sellers of a diverse range of goods.[305]

VI.3.3 AdTech/Digital Advertising

Digital advertising powers ad-funded platforms, such as social media and search engines that provide their services free of charge.[306] Here, the focus is on the intermediation activity in digital advertising and ad revenues. Given the growing importance of online advertising (broadly distinguished into search, display, and classified, which is estimated at a global value of USD 360 billion in 2020 with a growth projection of 20.5 per cent during 2021–2026)[307] and the emergence of a handful of intermediaries controlling this sector, a number of competition authorities and regulators have launched market studies into the sector.[308] In the United Kingdom, it was estimated that in 2019, the digital advertising market accounted for 62 per cent of the total advertising spend (up from 25 per cent in 2010) and amounted to a total worth of £15.7 billion.[309]

[301] *Ibid*, Article 2(2)(d) and (e).

[302] See text to n136 above.

[303] See, amongst others, ACCC, 'Digital Platforms Services Inquiry—Interim Report 6: Report on Social Media Services' (March 2023), 7 <https://www.accc.gov.au/system/files/Digital%20platforms%20services%20inquiry%20-%20Interim%20report%206%20-%20Report%20on%20social%20media%20services_0.pdf> (accessed 7 June 2024).

[304] See Chapter 3, section IV.4.

[305] ACCC, 'Interim Report 6' (n303), 70.

[306] For a recent study on the state of digital advertising in the EU, see European Commission (EU), 'Towards a More Transparent, Balanced and Sustainable Digital Advertising Ecosystem: Study on the Impact of Recent Developments in Digital Advertising on Privacy, Publishers and Advertisers' (Final Report, 2023).

[307] See International Mining and Resources Conference (IMARC), 'Global Online Advertising Market Report and Forecast 2021–2026' <https://www.imarcgroup.com/internet-advertising-market> (accessed 7 June 2024).

[308] For studies conducted by EU NCAs, see text to n313 below. Outside the EU, see, e.g. ACCC, 'Feedback Sought on Potential New Rules for Large Digital Platforms' (28 February 2022) <https://www.accc.gov.au/media-release/feedback-sought-on-potential-new-rules-for-large-digital-platforms> (accessed 7 June 2024).

[309] CMA, Digital Platforms Report (n6), para 2.40 with data from the Digital Adspend Report (2019).

Search advertising consists of adverts, usually as text links, appearing following a search query on a search engine. Advertisers pay for their adverts to appear following the entry of particular keywords by the consumer, and payment is made when the consumer clicks on the advert. In simple terms, search advertising uses a 'pull approach', inducing consumer action following their specific request. Display advertising, on the other hand, employs richer content, such as images or video, and employs a 'push approach', where consumers are targeted directly through a combination of various data emanating from their online activity.[310] The display advertising sector comprises two channels, namely owned and operated platforms and the open display market. The former includes, for example, large social media platforms selling advertising inventory directly to advertisers (e.g. Facebook Ads Manager). The majority of publishers sell their advertising inventory on the open display market through a range of intermediaries running auctions for both publishers and advertisers. In the age of programmatic advertising, ads are served in real time through an automated process using complex algorithms.[311] Finally, classified advertising comprises adverts that are listed directly on a specialized website (e.g. rentals) and paid through listing fees.[312]

The French NCA launched a study into display advertising in 2016 and published its findings in 2018.[313] It remarked that '[w]hile very few stakeholders have entered the online advertising market [identifying Criteo as one of these stakeholders] and been able to capture part of its value, the sector's competitive equilibrium is fragile, since stakeholders are confronted with competition from global stakeholders, present at several levels of the value chain (publishing, intermediation), with Google and Facebook leading the pack'.[314] The German NCA has also launched a market study into the online advertising sector.[315] In the United

[310] On the distinction between the pull and push approach, see S Mialki, 'Know before You Spend: The Best Digital Advertising Channels' (28 May 2020) <https://instapage.com/blog/best-digital-advertising-channels> (accessed 7 June 2024).

[311] For an exposition of the AdTech supply chain, see OECD, ' Digital advertising markets – Background note by the Secretariat' (DAF/COMP/WP2(2020)3).

[312] For the distinction, see generally CMA, Digital Platforms Report (n6), paras 2.44–2.55. See also European Commission (EU), 'Online Advertising: The Impact of Targeted Advertising on Advertisers, Market Access and Consumer Choice' (June 2021), 16–18.

[313] AdC, 'Sector-Specific Investigation into Online Advertising' (6 March 2018) <https://www.autoritedelaconcurrence.fr/en/press-release/6-march-2018-sector-specific-investigation-online-advertising> (accessed 7 June 2024). The French NCA examined online search advertising as early as 2010. See AdC, 'Sector Inquiry/Online Advertising' (14 December 2010) <https://www.autoritedelaconcurrence.fr/en/communiques-de-presse/14-december-2010-sector-inquiry-online-advertising> (accessed 7 June 2024). The AdC has also published (jointly with the German NCA) the Report 'Competition Law and Data' (10 May 2016) <https://www.bundeskartellamt.de/SharedDocs/Publikation/DE/Berichte/Big%20Data%20Papier.html;jsessionid=2F34FB1C56475779337616BA96B21934.2_cid381?nn=3591568> (accessed 7 June 2024).

[314] AdC, 'Sector-Specific Investigation into Online Advertising' (n313). See also AdC, 'On Data Processing in the Online Advertising Sector' (6 March 2018) <https://www.autoritedelaconcurrence.fr/sites/default/files/integral_texts/2019-10/avis18a03_en_.pdf> (accessed 7 June 2024).

[315] Bundeskartellamt, 'Bundeskartellamt Launches Sector Inquiry into Market Conditions in Online Advertising Sector' (1 February 2018) <https://www.bundeskartellamt.de/SharedDocs/Meldung/EN/Pressemitteilungen/2018/01_02_2018_SU_Online_Werbung.html> (accessed 7 June 2024). The

Kingdom, the CMA—following such calls from a number of stakeholders[316]—similarly conducted a market study and published its Final Report in July 2020.[317] In July 2021, the Spanish NCA also published a study on the national online advertising sector.[318]

Such studies confirm that digital advertising revenue is largely concentrated on two platforms, Google (search) and Facebook (social media), yet with some smaller players emerging.[319] The CMA has coined search and social media as 'consumer facing markets', where they receive services for 'free', that is without a direct financial cost. At the same time though, they 'pay' through their attention and data, which is then monetized through digital advertising.[320] Search advertising is the highest ad spend in the United Kingdom (£7.3 billion in 2019), with Google earning more than 90 per cent.[321] By comparison, more than half of display advertising (£5.5 billion in 2019) goes directly to Facebook and ca 60 per cent to Facebook and Google combined.[322] The CMA estimated that Google and Facebook earned around 80 per cent of search and display advertising revenue in the United Kingdom in 2019.[323]

Thus, competition law market studies corroborate Google's and Facebook's market power in search and display advertising, respectively. Practices by both platforms have attracted competition law[324] as well as regulatory scrutiny.[325]

Bundeskartellamt has also published a concise report on this issue. See Bundeskartellamt, 'Online Advertising' (Series of papers on 'Competition and Consumer Protection in the Digital Economy', February 2018) <https://www.bundeskartellamt.de/SharedDocs/Publikation/EN/Schriftenreihe_Digitales_III.pdf?__blob=publicationFile&v=5> (accessed 7 June 2024). On the Sector Inquiry Report and Final Report, see Bundeskartellamt, 'Sector Inquiry into Online Advertising' <https://www.bundeskartellamt.de/EN/Tasks/Sector_inquiries/Sector_inquiry_Online_Werbung/Sector_inquiry_OW_node.html#> (accessed 25 June 2024).

316 CMA, 'Online Platforms and Digital Advertising Market Study Statement of Scope' (3 July 2019) <https://assets.publishing.service.gov.uk/media/5d1b297e40f0b609dba90d7a/Statement_of_Scope.pdf> (accessed 7 June 2024), paras 42–47.

317 CMA, Digital Platforms Report (n6).

318 Spanish Competition Authority (CNMC), 'The CNMC Publishes a Study on the Online Advertising Sector in Spain' (Press release, 26 July 2021) <https://www.cnmc.es/sites/default/files/editor_contenidos/Notas%20de%20prensa/2021/20210726_NP_Estudio_Publicidad_Online_en_GB%20.pdf> (accessed 7 June 2024).

319 M Sweeney, 'The Rise of TikTok: Why Facebook Is Worried about the Booming Social App' (*The Guardian*, 9 April 2022) <https://www.theguardian.com/technology/2022/apr/09/rise-of-tiktok-why-facebook-is-worried-booming-social-app?CMP=Share_iOSApp_Other> (accessed 7 June 2024).

320 CMA, 'Online Platforms and Digital Advertising Market Study—Statement of Scope' (n316), paras 8, 31.

321 CMA, Digital Platforms Report (n6), para 2.61.

322 *Ibid*, para 2.62.

323 *Ibid*, para 2.63. See also ACCC, 'Digital Platforms Inquiry—Final Report' (n116), 58 identifying Google's and Facebook's leading position in search and display advertising, respectively in Australia.

324 On the relevant case law see Chapter 5, sections II.3 and II.5. See, e.g. *AdSense* (Chapter 5, section II.3.1.3); *Google AdTech* (Chapter 5, section II.3.1.4); *Display Advertising/Google*—Italy (Chapter 5, text to n206); *Google Ads* and *AdTech*—France (Chapter 5, text to nn 187, 193); *Google AdTech*—UK (Chapter 5, text to n214); *Facebook Classified Ads*—EU (Chapter 5, text to n261); *Facebook/Criteo* Complaint—France (Chapter 5, text to n278); CMA *Facebook Commitments* (Chapter 5, text to n281)

325 See, e.g. the DMA (n46). On the DMA obligations, see Chapter 3, section V.2.1.1.

In China, the leading players in digital advertising include Alibaba, ByteDance, Tencent, and Baidu. According to statistics, the total revenue from digital advertising was estimated to be USD 121.46 billion in 2021, accounting for 79.8 per cent of the total ad spending in China. Compared with 2020, digital ad spending grew by 19.8 per cent.[326]

Baidu is the leader in the field of search advertising, possessing more than 70 per cent of the market share in China.[327] Search advertising has been the cash cow for Baidu for a long period. Nonetheless, Baidu is facing great pressure in terms of competition not only from incumbents like Microsoft Bing and Sougou, but also from new entrants like Alibaba Quark, ByteDance WuKong, and Tencent WeChat Search.

As for display advertising, it covers traditional banner advertising and video advertising, and new formats like influencer advertising and built-in streaming advertising. Tencent takes the lead in the relatively traditional type of social media advertising, banner advertising, and video advertising. With its social media app WeChat and QQ (including Qzone) installed on almost every Chinese mobile phone, Tencent inevitably controls most of the attention of China's digital markets.

The situation is more complicated when it comes to new areas of advertising of built-in streaming advertising or influencer advertising. For example, e-commerce platforms provide built-in streaming services where shops are able to promote their own products. However, it is unfeasible and pointless to calculate the market revenue of such an advertising method since the streaming service instantly transforms to in-platform sales. The Alibaba Group is widely deemed to be the leading player in this regard, although statistics regarding its market share are not available. Also, influencer or key opinion leader (KOL) advertising is the hit currently, but its market revenue is also difficult to estimate, for content related and unrelated to advertising are difficult to distinguish. ByteDance, with its viral app TikTok, is the leader in this category.

In the domain of social media advertising, which is a form of online digital marketing in which paid banner and video ad campaigns are run on social media platforms to reach the target audiences, the main players are Tencent (56 per cent, including Wechat 25 per cent, Tencent QQ 18 per cent, Qzone 13 per cent), ByteDance (18 per cent), Sina (14 per cent), and Baidu (11 per cent).[328]

Banner advertising is one of the most traditional forms of advertising online, allowing anyone to advertise on websites, apps, or social media by using attractive images, shapes, and sizes of displays. In China, Tencent takes up 40 per cent of the

[326] eMarketer, 'Report of China Ad Spending 2022' (18 May 2022) <https://www.insiderintelligence.com/content/china-ad-spending-2022> (accessed 7 June 2024).

[327] Statista, 'Search Advertising—China' (April 2023) <https://www.statista.com/outlook/dmo/digital-advertising/search-advertising/china> (accessed 7 June 2024).

[328] Statista, 'Social Media Advertising—China' (April 2023), <https://www.statista.com/outlook/dmo/digital-advertising/social-media-advertising/china> (accessed 7 June 2024).

market, in which its star products Wechat, QQ, and Qzone account for 18 per cent, 13 per cent, and 9 per cent, respectively. The hit app TikTok of ByteDance contributed 13 per cent of the revenue, and Baidu and Sina account for 10 per cent and 8 per cent, respectively.[329]

Another advertising model is video advertising, which includes all ad formats within webpage-based videos, app-based video players, social media, and streaming apps on computer screens, smartphones, tablets, and other internet-connected devices. Videos that seamlessly match the form and function of the environment (e.g. news websites, video platforms) in which they appear (so-called native advertising) are also included. The leading players in this field are Tencent (30 per cent, including Wechat 13 per cent, Tencent QQ 10 per cent, Qzone 7 per cent), ByteDance (10 per cent), and Sina (7 per cent).[330]

Since 2021, the Chinese government has strengthened its antitrust regulation on platform companies. On 7 February 2021, the Antitrust Commission of the State Council published its Manual on Antitrust for Platform Economy,[331] but it only offers general guidelines for antitrust law enforcement, and the SAMR assumes the most responsibility. Probably as a response to widespread concern about monopolies in digital markets, the SAMR penalized several digital conglomerates, including the Alibaba Group and Meituan, which were notably fined ¥18.2 billion and ¥3.4 billion, respectively for 'either–or choice' requirement when it comes to abuse of dominance.[332] At the same time, in the field of mergers, the SAMR announced forty-three decisions regarding fines for failure-to-notify violations on 20 November 2021, thirty-nine of which involved companies competing in digital markets.[333] On 10 July 2022, twenty-eight failure-to-notify fines were made, twenty-four of which involved Internet companies.[334] In most of these decisions, household names such as Tencent or Alibaba made appearances.

[329] Statista, 'Banner Advertising—China' (April 2023), <https://www.statista.com/outlook/dmo/digital-advertising/banner-advertising/china> (accessed 7 June 2024).

[330] Statista, 'Video Advertising—China' (April 2023) <https://www.statista.com/outlook/dmo/digital-advertising/video-advertising/china#key-players> (accessed 7 June 2024).

[331] 'The Anti-Monopoly Guidelines on the Platform Economy' (n64).

[332] SAMR, 'Administrative Prohibition Decision [2021] No 28' (n65); SAMR, '国家市场监督管理总局行政处罚决定书（国市监处罚〔2021〕74号） [The SAMR Administrative Prohibition Decision [2021] No 74]' (8 October 2021) <https://www.samr.gov.cn/xw/zj/art/2023/art_31910760066b4f69aa119a20dee250ad.html> (accessed 10 April 2024). For a discussion, see Chapter 8.

[333] SAMR, '市场监管总局依法对43起未依法申报违法实施经营者集中案作出行政处罚决定 [The SAMR Made Administrative Prohibition Decisions on Forty Three Cases of Illegal Practices of Mergers That Were Not Notified According with the Law]' (20 November 2021) <https://www.samr.gov.cn/xw/zj/art/2023/art_58890b3964a947438e050bec99133f7e.html> (accessed 13 April 2024). For a discussion, see Chapter 9.

[334] SAMR, '市场监管总局发布未依法申报违法实施经营者集中案行政处罚决定书 [The SAMR Issued Decisions on Administrative Prohibition in the Case of Unlawful Implementation of Operator Concentration without Declaring in Accordance with the Law]' (10 July 2022) <https://www.samr.gov.cn/jzxts/tzgg/xzcf/art/2023/art_e938cefc24774f2483b7394abc47bfba.html> (accessed 7 June 2024). For a discussion, see Chapter 9.

However, in these decisions, the AdTech industry was not the regulatory emphasis. In the cases of abuse of dominance concerning the Alibaba Group and Meituan, the market concerned was online retailing. And in the merger cases, the key factor was whether an acquisition of a certain business ever took place or not. It is clear that a monopoly of platform companies via data accumulation and network effect raised regulatory concern, yet the AdTech industry has not become the eye of the storm.

VII. Conclusion

This chapter has presented the main technological, economic, and architectural characteristics of digital markets. It has also presented the main challenges posed by such characteristics to the application of competition law enforcement and the main players in the digital economy. The aim of the analysis was to set the scene for the ensuing chapters, in order to better understand and contextualize the cases brought by different competition authorities against powerful platforms as well as the regulatory attempts to constrain their market power.

3

Digital Markets and Competition Law

I. Introduction

The current debates with respect to the state of competition law in digital markets have called for a reconceptualization of its respective aims. Linked to this, there has been an observed resurgence of 'fairness' in competition rhetoric. If 'fairness' is becoming, or ought to become, the benchmark of competition law enforcement, we need to carefully construct its content. This is due to the fact that 'fairness' on its own is rather nebulous and, like 'consumer welfare', can be employed as an Orwellian term.[1] The European Data Protection Supervisor's (EDPS's) opinion on effective enforcement in the digital economy employs fairness as the unifying principle for data protection, consumer protection, and competition law.[2] Indeed, this idea of fairness as a unifying principle has been picked up and fleshed out by different commentators, who see the merit in enriching competition law with data protection analysis and vice versa.[3] However, fairness has different content in these areas of law and should not be used interchangeably. It is, thus, imperative, to decipher the proper role of fairness in competition law enforcement, taking into account the changing dynamics in digital markets.

The problem with potential anticompetitive practices in digital markets is that they—often—fall on the borderline between different areas of law, which may serve overlapping, yet distinctive, goals, such as competition, consumer, and data protection law. Therefore, we need to be very careful in deciphering the proper role of competition law in such a complex (digital) environment, lest there is a lurking risk of employing competition law as a trump card, when other legal regimes fail. And while such use may serve an outcome-focused approach to competition law enforcement and may be desirable from a policy perspective, it jeopardizes consistency and legal certainty in competition law enforcement.

[1] Kirkwood and Lande commented that by equating consumer welfare to total welfare, 'Bork used "consumer welfare" as an Orwellian term of art that has little or nothing to do with the welfare of true consumers'. See J Kirkwood and R Lande, 'The Fundamental Goal of Antitrust: Protecting Consumers Not Increasing Efficiency' (2008) 84 Notre Dame Law Review 191, 199.

[2] EDPS, 'European Data Protection Supervisor's Executive Summary of the Opinion of the European Data Protection Supervisor on Effective Enforcement in a Digital Society Economy', [2016] OJ C 463/08.

[3] See, e.g. I Graef and S van Berlo, 'Towards Smarter Regulation in the Areas of Competition, Data Protection and Consumer Law: Why Greater Power Should Come with Greater Responsibility' (2020) 12 European Journal of Risk Regulation 674; I Graef, D Clifford, and P Valcke, 'Fairness and Enforcement: Bridging Competition, Data Protection, and Consumer Law' (2018) 8 International Data Privacy Law 200.

Competition Law and Policy in Digital Markets. Maria Ioannidou and Bingwan Xiong, Oxford University Press.
 DOI: 10.1093/9780191925955.003.0003

At the same time, it should invite an open debate as to where we stand at the moment with respect to enforcement principles and benchmarks, whether these can accommodate the challenges of digital markets, and whether they should be adjusted and how.

Chapter 3 first outlines the competition law framework in the European Union (EU) and China and its interplay with other areas of law (section II). It then moves on to discuss the aims of competition law (section III). The discussion on the multiplicity of aims embraced by competition law enforcement reveals that, historically, competition law has shifted between different aims. Therefore, the emerging popularity of fairness can and should be linked to the role that competition law has played so far in embracing fairness concerns. Section IV then fleshes out the role of the 'fairness' benchmark in competition law by employing EU competition law as the focal point. The discussion highlights the porous nature of fairness as a benchmark,[4] which can expand to embrace various policy aims, from furthering privacy protection to equality and from promoting environmental sustainability to sustainability in the workplace. Section V discusses the regulatory responses in the EU and China to the identified problems in digital markets that further an expanded understanding of competition law enforcement.

II. Competition Law Framework and the Interplay with Other Areas of Law

II.1 Introduction

Competition law and different forms of regulation address 'market failures',[5] with the latter embracing a wider set of societal goals, yet through different means. Competition law seeks to regulate business conduct by imposing certain broadly worded restrictions, whereas regulation is more prescriptive in its scope and content and imposes public constraints on market conduct.[6] This section first briefly presents the framework for competition law enforcement in the EU and China. It then moves on to highlight the interplay between competition law and other areas of law.

[4] On the 'sponge'-like analogy of competition law, see A Ezrachi, 'Sponge' (2017) 5 Journal of Accounting and Economics 49.

[5] The often-listed sources of market failure include market power, public goods, externalities, asymmetric or imperfect information, factor immobility, and lack of clear property rights, whereas recent research extends these to include behavioural biases. See Organisation for Economic Co-operation and Development (OECD), 'Competition Enforcement and Regulatory Alternatives' (OECD Competition Committee discussion paper, 2021), 6 <http://oe.cd/cera> (accessed 7 June 2024).

[6] *Ibid.* For a detailed discussion of the relationship between competition law and regulation, see N Dunne, *Competition Law and Economic Regulation: Making and Managing Markets* (CUP, 2015).

II.2 Competition Law Enforcement: EU

II.2.1 Legal Framework

In EU competition law, the prohibition of anticompetitive agreements and abuse of dominance are enshrined in Articles 101 and 102 of the Treaty on the Functioning of the European Union (TFEU), respectively. With respect to the assessment of potentially anticompetitive agreements, the bifurcated structure of Article 101 TFEU requires first that a prohibited agreement/restriction of competition is established under Article 101(1) TFEU. The parties to the agreement may then argue that their respective agreement should be exempted because it meets the conditions under Article 101(3) TFEU, namely leading to efficiencies accruing to consumers without eliminating competition disproportionately.

The EU Commission, in order to facilitate competition law enforcement as well as infuse it with more legal certainty, reduce its workload, and help companies to self-assess their agreements, has adopted secondary legislation (i.e. block exemption regulations) in order to exempt certain categories of agreements from the application of EU competition law. Chapter 4 discusses in particular the recent adoption of the revised Horizontal Block Exemption Regulations (HBERs), which exempt certain research and development (R&D)[7] and specialization agreements[8] from EU competition rules, and the accompanying guidelines[9] as well as the Vertical Block Exemption Regulation (VBER) and accompanying guidelines.[10] In particular, with respect to the HBERs and accompanying guidelines, Chapter 4 covers certain changes that have been introduced, which now provide a clearer demarcation threshold for companies considering entering into data-pooling agreements as well as clearer guidance on information exchange agreements.[11] Chapter 4 also covers changes introduced by the VBER and accompanying guidelines with respect to the assessment of certain vertical restraints in the digital

[7] Regulation (EU) 2023/1066 of 1 June 2023 on the application of Article 101(3) of the Treaty on the Functioning of the European Union to certain categories of research and development agreements, [2023] OJ L 143/9.

[8] Regulation (EU) 2023/1067 of 1 June 2023 on the application of Article 101(3) of the Treaty on the Functioning of the European Union to certain categories of specialisation agreements, [2023] OJ L 143/20.

[9] European Commission (EU), 'Guidelines on the Applicability of Article 101 of the Treaty on the Functioning of the European Union to Horizontal Co-operation Agreements', C(2023) 3445 final (Brussels, 1 June 2023) <https://competition-policy.ec.europa.eu/system/files/2023-07/2023_revised_horizontal_guidelines_en.pdf> (accessed 7 June 2024). The previous HBERs, in force since January 2011, expired on 31 December 2022, and the new rules entered into force in July 2023. Stakeholders have highlighted their respective limits and room for improvement to adapt to digitization and datafication (as well as sustainability goals). See European Commission (EU), 'Evaluation of the Horizontal Block Exemption Regulations', SWD(2021) 103 final (Staff working document, Brussels, 6 May 2021).

[10] Regulation (EU) 2022/720 of 10 May 2022 on the application of Article 101(3) of the Treaty on the Functioning of the European Union to categories of vertical agreements and concerted practices, [2022] OJ L 134/4 (Vertical Block Exemption Regulations, VBER); European Commission (EU), 'Guidelines on Vertical Restraints', [2022] OJ C 248/1.

[11] On this discussion, see Chapter 4, sections III and IV.

economy.[12] The VBER covers vertical agreements, that is agreements relating to the supply and distribution of goods and services. If such agreements meet the VBER requirements, then Article 101(1) TFEU is not applicable. The VBER is accompanied by the Guidelines on Vertical Restraints ('VRG'), which explain how to apply the VBER and assess agreements that fall outside the VBER scope under Article 101(1) and Article 101(3) TFEU.[13]

Article 102 TFEU prohibits abuse of dominance and imposes restraints on powerful companies. The Commission has issued guidance on the application of Article 102 TFEU with an effects-based approach to exclusionary abuses,[14] which has caused controversy with respect to its nature and influence on the EU courts' case law.[15] The Commission has now partially amended this document to reflect recent case law.[16] It has also announced the prospective adoption of relevant Guidelines.[17] In particular, amongst other changes, the Commission has amended the concept of 'anticompetitive foreclosure' to encompass situations where

> the conduct of the dominant undertaking adversely impacts an effective competitive structure thus allowing the dominant undertaking to negatively influence, to its own advantage and to the detriment of consumers, the various parameters of competition, such as price, production, innovation, variety or quality of goods or services.[18]

[12] See Chapter 4, section V. Vertical restraints are restrictions of competition contained in a vertical agreement. See VBER (n10), Article 1(1)(b). Vertical agreements are agreements between two or more companies that operate, for the purposes of the agreement, at different levels of the production or distribution chain. Cf. VBER, Article 1(1)(a).

[13] The new VBER and new Vertical Guidelines entered into force on 1 June 2022 following a long consultation process on revising and updating the old rules. Public consultation on the draft revised texts took place between 9 July and 17 September 2021, as well as dedicated additional public consultation on information exchange in dual distribution between 4 and 18 February 2022. See European Commission (EU), 'Explanatory Note on the New VBER and Vertical Guidelines' (2022), 1.

[14] European Commission (EU), 'Guidance on the Commission's Enforcement Priorities in Applying Article 82 of the EC Treaty to Abusive Exclusionary Conduct by Dominant Undertakings' (Communication), [2009] OJ C 45/7 (Enforcement Priorities).

[15] See, e.g. F Castillo de la Torre, 'Is the Effects-Based Approach Too Cumbersome?: Taking Stock of Recent Practice and Case Law on Article 102 TFEU' (2023), 3 <https://papers.ssrn.com/sol3/papers.cfm?abstract_id=4395401&download=yes> (accessed 7 June 2024), set forth in A Claici, A Komninos, and D Waelbroeck, (eds), *The Transformation of EU Competition Law: Next Generation Issues* (Kluwer Law International, 2023). See also R Podszun and T Rohner, 'Making Article 102 TFEU Future-Proof—Learnings from the Past (2023), 4 <https://papers.ssrn.com/sol3/papers.cfm?abstract_id=4428170> (accessed 7 June 2024).

[16] Case C-680/20 *Unilever Italia Mkt Operations Srl v Autorita Garante della Concorrenza e del Mercato*, ECLI:EU:C:2023:33; Case T-604/18 *Google and Alphabet v Commission* (*Google Android*), ECLI:EU:T:2022:541.

[17] European Commission (EU), 'Commission Announces Guidelines on Exclusionary Abuses and Amends Guidance on Enforcement Priorities' (Press release, 27 March 2023) <https://ec.europa.eu/commission/presscorner/detail/en/ip_23_1911> (accessed 6 June 2024).

[18] European Commission (EU), 'Amendments to the Communication from the Commission—Guidance on the Commission's Enforcement Priorities in Applying Article 82 of the EC Treaty to Abusive Exclusionary Conduct by Dominant Undertakings' (Amending Communication), [2023] OJ C 116/01 (Amendments to the Guidance), para 19. See also European Commission (EU), 'A Dynamic

Chapter 5 will address this concept, in particular in light of the respective case law in the digital economy.

Finally, EU merger control,[19] an ex-ante tool, completes the EU competition law enforcement framework and is specifically discussed in Chapter 6.

II.2.2 Institutions and Enforcement

The competence to enforce Articles 101 and 102 TFEU is ascribed to the EU Commission and the national competition authorities (NCAs) in the course of public enforcement. Commission decisions are reviewed by the EU courts, first by the General Court (GC) and then by the Court of Justice (CJEU) at last instance. NCAs can enforce Articles 101 and 102 TFEU alongside national competition law, when a given practice may affect interstate EU trade. Their decisions (depending, of course, on the national procedural rules in place) can be reviewed before national courts. Regulation 1/2003 has introduced a decentralized system for the enforcement of EU competition law, with the EU Commission retaining the central role.[20]

EU competition law is enforced mainly through administrative public enforcement mechanisms, either by the Commission or by NCAs. Public enforcement proceedings may lead to the imposition of administrative fines and/or behavioural or structural remedies.[21] In some cases, public enforcement proceedings end in negotiated settlements, that is 'commitments'.[22] Finally, the Commission also has the power to undertake sector inquiries in order to investigate the conditions of competition in a given sector.[23] Important sector inquiries in the digital economy comprise the e-commerce and Internet of Things (IoT) sector inquiries.[24]

and Workable Effects-Based Approach to Abuse of Dominance' (Competition Policy Brief, Issue 1, March 2023).

[19] Council Regulation (EC) 139/2004 of 20 January 2004 on the control of concentrations between undertakings, [2004] OJ L 24/1 (European Union Merger Regulation [EUMR]).

[20] Council Regulation (EC) 1/2003 of 16 December 2002 on the implementation of the rules on competition laid down in Articles 81 and 82 of the Treaty, [2003] OJ L1/1. See also European Commission (EC), 'Notice on Cooperation within the Network of Competition Authorities', [2004] OJ C 101/43; European Commission (EC), 'Notice on the Handling of Complaints by the Commission under Articles 81 and 82 of the EC Treaty', [2004] OJ C 101/65; European Commission (EC), 'Notice on the Cooperation between the Commission and the Courts of the EU Member States in the Application of Articles 81 and 82 EC', [2004] OJ C 101/54. Regulation 1/2003 is currently under review. See European Commission (EU), 'Antitrust: Commission Seeks Feedback on Performance of EU Antitrust Enforcement Framework' (Press release, 30 June 2022) <https://ec.europa.eu/commission/presscorner/detail/en/IP_22_4194> (accessed 23 August 2023).

[21] Regulation 1/2003 (n20) Articles 7 and 23.

[22] *Ibid*, Article 9.

[23] *Ibid*, Article 9.

[24] European Commission (EU), 'Final Report on the E-Commerce Sector Inquiry', COM(2017) 229 final (Brussels, 10 May 2017); European Commission (EU), 'Final Report—Sector Inquiry into Consumer Internet of Things', COM(2022) 19 final (Brussels, 20 January 2022).

Apart from public enforcement, EU competition law can also be enforced by private parties in litigation before national courts, though private enforcement has a more limited role compared to public enforcement.[25]

II.3 Competition Law Enforcement: China

II.3.1 Legal Framework

The regulation of anticompetitive behaviours, or anti-monopolistic behaviours,[26] in China dates back to 1993 when China enacted its Anti-Unfair Competition Law, which provided very sketchy rules on anti-monopolistic behaviours. The body of contemporary antitrust law in China is, however, centred on its Anti-Monopoly Law (<反垄断法>, the 'AML'), which was first adopted in 2007 by the Standing Committee of China's National People's Congress and materially amended in 2022 ('the new AML') by the same body. Ever since the adoption of the AML, China's State Council and pertinent regulatory agencies have formulated a good number of regulations, be it provisions concerning a certain category of monopolistic behaviours or provisions specifically addressing challenging issues in the digital economy, so as to guide the practical enforcement of the AML.

At the time of strengthening the enforcement of AML against violating digital platforms, Chinese legislature, in the new AML, reiterated its determination to regulate anticompetitive behaviours and enhance legal liabilities.[27] Most importantly, the new AML reflects the trend of strengthening regulations in the field of the digital economy, adding fundamental principles regarding competition in digital markets into its general part and expressly stressing that platform operators are prohibited from engaging in monopolistic behaviours by exploiting digital technologies, capital advantages, and platform rules.

Like antitrust laws in many jurisdictions around the world, Article 3 of the AML covers three types of anticompetitive behaviours: monopoly agreements, abuse of dominance, and mergers that have (or may have) the effect of excluding or restricting competition. The abuse of administrative power by administrative organs and public organizations (namely administrative monopolies) is prohibited under Article 10. The three types of non-administrative monopoly will be discussed in

[25] For a succinct exposition of the EU competition law enforcement system, see M Ioannidou, '"Responsive" Remodelling of Competition Law Enforcement' (2020) 40 Oxford Journal of Legal Studies 846.

[26] Literally speaking, when Chinese legal academics speak of anticompetitive behaviours (反竞争行为), they tend to use the term 'monopolistic behaviours', largely because the basic statute regulating anticompetitive behaviours in China is entitled the Anti-Monopoly Law. Therefore, we will use the two terms 'anticompetitive' and 'monopolistic' interchangeably throughout the chapters concerning the jurisdiction of China.

[27] See the new AML, 'Anti-Monopoly Law of the People's Republic of China (2022 Amendment)', Article 3 <https://www.pkulaw.com/en_law/d3236788421feacfbdfb.html> (accessed 7 June 2024).

Chapter 7, Chapter 8, and Chapter 9, respectively, while administrative monopoly will be covered in Chapter 10.

In line with the classic dichotomy under EU competition law, the AML categorizes anticompetitive agreements into two types: horizontal and vertical agreements. The former are concluded between competing undertakings, while the latter are between upstream and downstream enterprises at different levels of the distribution chain. Specifically, Article 17 AML targets horizontal agreements, whereas Article 18 prohibits certain vertical restraints. It is worth noting that Article 18(3) introduces the 'safe harbour' clause into China's competition law framework, which has become a major highlight of the new AML.

With the booming digital economy, competition among platforms demonstrates oligopolistic tendencies, with one or few market players occupying the majority of the market share, which makes the digital markets heavily prone to anticompetitive behaviours. 'Either–or choices' and big-data discrimination, for instance, have evolved into a real headache in the new era of the digital economy.

On 1 August 2019, the General Office of the State Council promulgated 'Guiding Opinions on Promoting the Regulated and Healthy Development of the Platform Economy' (the 'Guiding Opinion').[28] The Guiding Opinion aims to maintain a market order featuring fair competition and stresses the duty of the State Administration for Market Regulation (SAMR) to ensure fair competition in the platform economy. Whilst regulators have expressly denounced exclusive dealing and other platform conduct that might raise anti-monopoly concerns, it was rare for regulatory agencies to take enforcement actions until the Central Economic Work Conference in 2020. The 2020 Central Economic Work Conference, an important meeting that should not be overlooked, pointed out that one of the priorities for 2021 was to 'strengthen anti-monopoly supervision and prevention of disorderly capital expansion'.[29]

Since then, not only have the regulatory agencies, at various levels, accelerated the pace with which the AML is enforced but also the national legislative body has made efforts to amend the AML so as to better respond to challenging issues in the digital era. According to the AML, the Anti-Monopoly Commission of the State Council (the 'Anti-Monopoly Commission') has the duty to formulate and release anti-monopoly guidelines, which are of a 'soft-law' nature but substantively guide the practical enforcement by regulatory agencies. From 2009 to 2020, the Anti-Monopoly Commission released six general guidelines to promote the enforcement of the AML.[30]

[28] Central People's Government of the People's Republic of China, 'Guiding Opinions on Promoting the Regulated and Healthy Development of the Platform Economy, ' (2019) <http://www.gov.cn/gongbao/content/2019/content_5421543.htm> (accessed 7 June 2024).

[29] China Economic Network 'Main Contents of 2020 Central Economic Work Conference' <http://www.ce.cn/ztpd/xwzt/guonei/2020/ba2018_341986/index.shtml> (accessed 30 October 2022).

[30] These include (i) Guidelines of the Anti-Monopoly Commission of the State Council on the Definition of a Relevant Market (24 May 2009); (ii) Anti-Monopoly Guidelines of the Anti-Monopoly

On 7 February 2021, the Anti-Monopoly Commission released a document specifically guiding the enforcement of anti-monopoly law in the field of the digital economy, namely the Anti-Monopoly Guidelines for Anti-Monopoly in the Field of Platform Economy (the 'Guidelines'). The Guidelines are the first to systematically target anticompetitive behaviours in the digital economy in China.[31] In line with the AML, anticompetitive agreements, abuse of a dominant market position, merger, and abuse of administrative power in digital markets are four important aspects to which the Guidelines aim to respond.

The release of the Guidelines provided a promising starting point for promoting the enforcement of anti-monopoly law in China's digital markets. In addition to stressing both aims of fair competition and innovation, the Guidelines adhere to the issue-orientated approach and respond to challenging issues associated with the application of competition law against digital platforms, like hub-and-spoke agreements, algorithmic discrimination, and either–or-choice-like exclusive dealings. In this vein, the Guidelines enumerate a range of essential factors that should be considered by the regulatory agencies when evaluating suspected anticompetitive behaviours.

2023 has witnessed China's continued efforts in enforcing its antitrust law. On 24 March 2023, the SAMR issued the following four revised AML supporting regulations, namely 'Provisions on Curbing the Abuse of Administrative Power to Exclude or Restrict Competition', 'Provisions on the Prohibition of Anti-Competitive Agreements', 'Provisions on the Prohibition of Abuse of Dominant Market Position', and 'Provisions on the Review of Concentrations of Undertakings', which have all taken effective since 15 April 2023. The four provisions were amended to further implement the new AML and to further consolidate China's competition legal framework.

II.3.2 Institutions and Enforcement

The authority to enforce the AML is granted to the SAMR in the course of public enforcement under Article 13 of the new AML. The SAMR was established during the reformation of China's ministerial system in 2018, while previously, the National Development and Reform Commission, Ministry of Commerce, and

Commission of the State Council on Anti-Monopoly in the Automobile Industry (4 January 2019); (iii) Anti-Monopoly Guidelines of the Anti-Monopoly Commission of the State Council on the Intellectual Property Industry (4 January 2019); (iv) Guidelines of the Anti-Monopoly Commission of the State Council for Application of the Leniency Program to Cases Involving Horizontal Monopoly Agreements (4 January 2019); (v) Guidelines of the Anti-Monopoly Commission of the State Council for Undertaking Commitment in Anti-Monopoly Cases (4 January 2019); (vi) Anti-Monopoly Compliance Guidelines for Business Operators (11 September 2020).

[31] The drafting process of the Guidelines overlapped in time with the amending process of the AML. In other words, the draft of the Guidelines was issued for public opinions on 10 November 2020, and the formal version was issued on 7 February 2021. The new AML was issued for public opinions on 2 January 2020 and came into effect on 1 August 2022.

State Administration for Industry and Commerce were in charge of anti-monopoly law enforcement.[32] The establishment of the SAMR has solved the problem of decentralized anti-monopoly law enforcement in China. On 18 November 2021, the Anti-Monopoly Bureau was formally established as a significant branch of the SAMR, further improving the enforcement mechanism of the anti-monopoly system in China.[33] Table 3.1 succinctly presents the various institutions' involvement in competition law enforcement in China.

Table 3.1 Competition law enforcers in China

Time	Department	Authority
Before March 2018	National Development and Reform Commission (NDRC)	Investigating and dealing with price monopoly behaviours
	Ministry of Commerce	Reviewing the concentration of undertakings
	State Administration for Industry and Commerce (SAIC)	Investigating and dealing with anti-competitive agreements other than price monopoly, abuse of market dominance, abuse of administrative power to exclude and restrict competition.
March 2018—November 2021	State Administration of Market Regulation (SAMR)	Investigating and dealing with anti-competitive agreements, abuse of market dominance, abuse of administrative power to eliminate restrictions on competition, and concentration of undertakings
After November 2021	Anti-Monopoly Bureau of the SAMR	Competition Policy Coordination Division: promoting the implementation of competition policy and organizing the implementation of fair competition review system
		Division I: investigating and dealing with anti-competitive agreements, abuse of market dominance, and abuse of intellectual property rights to exclude and restrict competition
		Division II: reviewing the concentration of undertakings

[32] Xinhuanet.com, 'Explanation of the State Council's Institutional Reform Plan at the First Meeting of the 13th National People's Congress on March 13th, 2018' (14 March 2018) <http://www.xinhuanet.com/politics/2018lh/2018-03/14/c_1122533011.htm> (accessed 30 July 2023).

[33] China Development.com, 'The State Anti-Monopoly Bureau Was Formally Established' (19 November 2021) <http://www.chinadevelopment.com.cn/news/zj/2021/11/1753311.shtml> (accessed 30 July 2023).

Competition law enforcement in China has depicted a preference for soft-law interventions. In the early stages of a competition law investigation, regulators often resort to administrative interviews as well as guiding opinions to prompt undertakings concerned into self-reflection and the correction of suspected anti-competitive behaviours.[34] Administrative penalties such as fines and confiscation of illegal income of undertakings are employed as a solid backup where soft interventions fail to hold water.[35]

In parallel with public enforcement by regulatory agencies, there are also a growing number of civil lawsuits claiming compensatory remedies against anti-competitive behaviours in digital markets. Platform competitors, online merchants, and consumers in Chinese digital markets have begun to proactively seek relief before the courts.[36] Moreover, public-interest litigations through procuratorates are also a new facet to be explored in China.[37]

II.4 Competition Law and Its Interplay with Other Areas of Law

The development of digital markets with the emergence of a handful of players controlling key segments of the economy instigated debates with respect to the interplay between competition law and other horizontal regulations, such as data protection, consumer protection, and sustainability.[38] Repeated calls have been made in favour of an integrative approach to consumer harm in digital markets. For example, the EDPS has called for policy convergence and stressed that refusal of access to personal data and opaque or misleading privacy policies may justify 'a new concept of consumer harm for competition enforcement in digital economy' and that competition law enforcement may aid the promotion of privacy-enhancing services and ameliorate consumer control over their respective data.[39] In this vein, the EDPS also proposed the establishment of a Digital Clearing

[34] See cases mentioned in Chapter 7.

[35] See the new AML (n27), Articles 56–59.

[36] For a comprehensive description of the framework of private enforcement of antitrust law in China's digital markets, see Chapter 8.

[37] See the new AML (n27), Article 60, providing that

> [w]here an undertaking implementing any monopolistic act causes any loss to others, it shall assume the civil liability in accordance with the law. Where an undertaking implementing any monopolistic act damages the public interests, the People's Procuratorate at the level of city divided into districts or above may institute civil public interest litigation at the People's Court in accordance with the law.

[38] Cf. OECD, 'Competition Enforcement' (n5), 9–10.

[39] EDPS, Preliminary Opinion, 'Privacy and Competitiveness in the Age of Big Data: The Interplay between Data Protection, Competition Law and Consumer Protection in the Digital Economy', EDPS/2014/06 (March 2014), 26.

House, bringing together regulators with powers to enforce different rules in the EU digital sector.[40]

However, developing such 'a new concept of consumer harm' is daunting, especially if one takes into account that, in the past, neither the Commission nor the CJEU have developed a clear notion of consumer benefit/detriment.[41] However, in the light of the characteristics of digital markets that indeed underline and call for such an interplay, regulators (including competition authorities) should not shy away from cooperating with their counterparts in enforcing consumer and data protection law and developing theories of harm that fit the competition law toolkit.

Commentators and policymakers have long alluded to the interdependency between competition and consumer law.[42] Competition law enforcement contributes towards a wider consumer choice, while consumer law caters for the availability of the necessary information to consumers for the exercise of such choice.[43] More recently, with the advent of digital markets where consumer data serve as an important input for the delivery of various products and services, the commonalities between data protection and competition law have gained centre stage.[44]

Similarly to the commonality trait of consumer and competition law (namely furthering consumer interests), data protection and competition law enhance individuals' interests from different perspectives: competition law does so from the macroscopic view of preserving competitive markets, whereas data protection law does so from the microscopic perspective of individual transactions preserving the integrity of decision making relying on the necessary consent for data processing.[45]

[40] EDPS, Opinion 8/2016, 'On the Coherent Enforcement of Fundamental Rights in the Age of Big Data' (23 September 2016), 3; European Parliament, 'European Parliament Resolution of 20 February 2017 on Fundamental Rights Implications of Big Data: Privacy, Data Protection, Non-Discrimination, Security and Law Enforcement, Recital R', Report A8-0044 (2017) <https://www.europarl.europa.eu/doceo/document/A-8-2017-0044_EN.html> (accessed 7 June 2024).

[41] M Ioannidou, *Consumer Involvement in Private EU Competition Law Enforcement* (OUP, 2015), with further references to N Reich, 'Competition Law and the Consumer' in L Gormley (ed), *Current and Future Perspectives on EC Competition Law* (Kluwer Law International, 1997), 126, 137; M Hutchings and P Whelan, 'Consumer Interest in Competition Law Cases' (2006) 16 Clinical Psychology Review 182, 186.

[42] OECD, 'The Interface between Competition and Consumer Policies' (Policy Roundtables) DAF/COMP/GF(2008), 10; Office of Fair Trading (OFT), 'Joining Up Competition and Consumer Policy', OFT 1151 (December 2009), para 1.2; For a thorough analysis of the relationship between consumer and competition law, see K Cseres, *Competition Law and Consumer Protection* (Kluwer Law International, 2005) especially chapter 7.

[43] N Averitt and R Lande, 'Using the "Consumer Choice" Approach to Antitrust Law' (2007) 74 Antitrust Law Journal 175; N Averitt and R Lande, 'Consumer Sovereignty: A Unified Theory of Antitrust and Consumer Protection Law' (1997) 65 Antitrust Law Journal 713;. N Averitt, 'Protecting Consumer Choice: Competition and Consumer Protection Together' in J Drexl and others (eds), *More Common Ground for International Competition Law?* (Edward Elgar, 2011), 36. According to Nihoul, this is, indeed, the approach adopted in the EU. See P Nihoul, 'Is Competition Law Part of Consumer Law?' in J Drexl and others (eds), *More Common Ground for International Competition Law?* (Edward Elgar, 2011) 36, 46.

[44] See, e.g. F Costa-Cabral and O Lynskey, 'Family Ties: The Intersection between Data Protection and Competition in EU Law' 54 (2017) Common Market Law Review 11, 15.

[45] *Ibid.*

At the same time, what consumer and data protection law have in common, which further influences the role of consumers as market actors invigorating the competitive process through their choice-making powers, is the consumer image as a rational market actor. However, insights from the behavioural economics literature increasingly challenge this assumption, since different biases affect consumers' decision making.[46] For example, the status quo bias in the case *Google Shopping* is important in construing and understanding the theory of harm.[47] Status quo bias explains why consumers are more likely to retain the status quo and remain with the default option.[48] Thus, favouring its own comparison shopping service and demoting competing shopping services has an impact on effective competition and consumer choice because of the fact that consumers are reluctant to exercise such choice, even though they have access (albeit more restricted due to the demotion) to competing services. Behavioural economics can also explain the 'privacy paradox' in data protection law whereby, despite their expressed concerns about privacy, consumers do not act upon them and are eager to give access to their data in exchange for various services.[49]

Already there have been instances where competition authorities have had a constructive cooperation with data protection authorities, with the CJEU confirming that this is, indeed, the correct approach with respect to data-related abuses.[50] The German NCA, for example, cooperated with the data protection authorities in the Facebook case and stated unequivocally that

> [m]onitoring the data processing activities of dominant companies is therefore an essential task of a competition authority, which cannot be fulfilled by data protection officers. In cases of market dominance a competition authority must take into account data protection principles, in particular in the assessment of whether terms and conditions for the processing of data are appropriate. In this respect there is an interface between competition law and data protection law.

[46] See, e.g. OECD, 'Roundtable on Demand-Side Economics for Consumer Policy: Summary Report', DSTI/CP(2006)3 final (20 April 2006), 11; C Jolls, C Sunstein, and R Thaler, 'A Behavioral Approach to Law and Economics' (1998) 50 Stanford Law Review 1471; T Ulen, 'Information in the Market Economy—Cognitive Errors and Legal Correctives' in S Grundmann, W Kerber, and S Weatherill (eds), *Party Autonomy and the Role of Information in the Internal Market* (De Gruyter 2001), 98.

[47] On this case see Chapter 5, section II.3.

[48] See, e.g. M Stucke, 'Behavioral Economics at the Gate: Antitrust in the Twenty-First Century' (2007) 38 Loyola University of Chicago Law Journal 513, 528.

[49] R Gross and A Acquisti, 'Information Revelation and Privacy in Online Social Networks' (2005) Proceedings of the 2005 ACM Workshop on Privacy in the Electronic Society 71; C Hoffmann, C Lutz, and G Ranzini, 'Privacy Cynicism: A New Approach to the Privacy Paradox' (2016) 10(4) Cyberpsychology: Journal of Psychosocial Research on Cyberspace; S Athey, C Catalini, and C Tucker, 'The Digital Privacy Paradox: Small Money, Small Costs, Small Talk' (2017) National Bureau of Economic Research Working Paper Series; S Kokolakis, 'Privacy Attitudes and Privacy Behaviour: A Review of Current Research on the Privacy Paradox Phenomenon' (2017) 64 Computers and Security 122.

[50] Case C-252/21 *Meta Platforms and Others*, ECLI:EU:C:2023:537.

> The Bundeskartellamt closely cooperated with data protection authorities in this case which explicitly supported the authority's proceeding.[51]

The above brief exposition of the linkages between competition law and consumer, as well as data protection law, vividly highlights the existing need to consider a more integrative approach to competition law enforcement. Such approach can be condoned in light of the multiple aims of competition law enforcement discussed in the ensuing section III.

III. Aims of Competition Law and the Role of Fairness

Even since its adoption, competition law and policy has been undertaking a constant 'soul-searching' exercise.[52] And whereas there have been voices in favour of a unitary goal in competition law enforcement,[53] a historical account suggests that the very nature and wording of competition law provisions allow the embracing of a multitude of aims.[54] At the same time, some of these aims have guided competition law since its inception,[55] while others inform competition law enforcement at different points in time, depending on the changing socioeconomic realities.

As the EU Commission has rightly observed—and as is, in fact, historically reflected in competition law enforcement—'competition policy cannot be pursued in isolation, as an end in itself, without reference to the legal, economic, political and social context'.[56] Such a statement is, indeed, buttressed by the fact that various different competition law enforcement goals have been embraced in different

[51] Bundeskartellamt, 'Background Information on the Bundeskartellamt's Facebook Proceedings' (7 February 2019). On this case, see Chapter 5, section II.5.

[52] The use of this term is inspired by A Ezrachi and M Stucke, 'The Fight over Antitrust's Soul' (2018) 9 Journal of European Competition Law & Practice 1; E Fox, 'The Battle for the Soul of Antitrust' (1987) 75 California Law Review 917; P Akman, 'Searching for the Long-Lost Soul of Article 82 EC' (2009) 29 Oxford Journal of Legal Studies 267.

[53] See, e.g. F Easterbrook, 'The Limits of Antitrust' (1984) 63 Texas Law Review 1; O Odudu, *The Boundaries of EC Competition Law* (OUP, 2006), 159. See also R Blair and D Sokol, 'The Rule of Reason and the Goals of Antitrust: An Economic Approach' (2012) 78 Antitrust Law Journal 471, 472. In contrast, Stucke argues that a single well-defined objective for competition law is unrealistic: M Stucke, 'Reconsidering Antitrust Goals' (2012) 53 Boston College Law Review 551.

[54] For an empirical account confirming this, see K Stylianou and M Iacovides, 'The Goals of EU Competition Law—A Comprehensive Empirical Investigation', KONKURRENSVERKET (28 January 2021), 5 <https://papers.ssrn.com/sol3/papers.cfm?abstract_id=3735795> (accessed 7 June 2024).

[55] A useful analogy is the one proposed by Ezrachi viewing competition law as a Sponge. See Ezrachi, 'Sponge' (n4).

[56] European Commission (EC), 'XXIInd Report on Competition Policy 1992' (Brussels, Luxembourg 1993). See P Marsden, 'Checks and Balances: European Competition Law and the Rule of Law' (2009) 22 Loyola Consumer Law Review 51, 59 quoting Judge Cooke, the Judge Rapporteur in Microsoft, who stated that 'these Article [101 and 102 TFEU] cases are 20 percent fact, 20 percent law and 60 percent policy'.

jurisdictions.[57] EU competition law enforcement, for example, has been shaped by three main aims, namely the promotion of the competitive process, market integration, and the protection of consumer welfare. At the same time, the teleological interpretation of competition law provisions in the light of other EU Treaty provisions has allowed room for various public interest objectives in competition law analysis.[58]

However, even if one accepts the core aims of EU competition law, these still remain sufficiently open-ended to accommodate different considerations. For example, even if consumer welfare has been the lodestar of competition law enforcement, at least in rhetorical terms, the term has been interpreted differently.[59] Under the influence of the Chicago School, consumer welfare was equated to total welfare.[60] Yet, such an approach to consumer welfare is not endorsed by EU competition law, which (even in its wording)[61] embraces a distributive element and rejects the total welfare standard. The Commission, even in its 'First Report on Competition Policy', stated that: 'such a [competition] policy encourages the best possible use of productive resources for the greatest possible benefit of the economy as a whole and for the benefit in particular of the consumer'.[62] Furthermore, the Commission acknowledges that long-term consumer benefits should be accounted for, thereby preserving firms' incentives to innovate.[63]

[57] See, e.g. OECD, 'The Objectives of Competition Law and Policy', CCNM/GF/COMP(2003) (29 January 2003), 3 < https://one.oecd.org/document/CCNM/GF/COMP(2003)3/en/pdf > (accessed 7 June 2024); International Competition Network (ICN), 'Report on the Objectives of Unilateral Conduct Laws, Assessment of Dominance/Substantial Market Power, and State Created Monopolies' (May 2007); ICN, 'Unilateral Conduct Workbook' (April 2012), chapter 1: 'The Objectives and Principles of Unilateral Conduct Laws'.

[58] M Ioannidou, *Consumer Involvement in Private EU Competition Law Enforcement* (n41), 15–25.

[59] On 'consumer welfare', see ICN, 'Competition Enforcement and Consumer Welfare' (2011). On the different perceptions of 'consumer welfare' by economists, lawyers, and courts, see B Orbach, 'The Antitrust Consumer Welfare Paradox' (2010) 7 Journal of Competition Law and Economics 133. On the various nuances of the consumer welfare standard, see OECD, 'The Consumer Welfare Standard—Advantages and Disadvantages Compared to Alternative Standards' (OECD Competition Policy Roundtable background note, 2023) <www.oecd.org/daf/competition/consumer-welfare-standard-advantages-and-disadvantages-to-alternative-standards-2023.pdf> (accessed 7 June 2024). On the role of consumer welfare in EU competition law, see A Komninos, '"Consumer Welfare" and the EU Courts: An Unexpected Refuge for a Persecuted Concept?' in O Andriychuk (ed), *Antitrust and the Bounds of Power—5 Years On* (Hart, 2023), 73.

[60] R Bork, *The Antitrust Paradox* (2nd edn, Maxwell Macmillan International, 1993), 91; D Ginsburg, 'Judge Bork, Consumer Welfare, and Antitrust Law' (2008) 31 Harvard Journal of Law and Public Policy 449.

[61] The exempted agreement under Article 101(3) TFEU should '[allow] consumers a fair share of the resulting benefit'.

[62] European Commission (EC), 'First Report on Competition Policy' (Brussels, Luxembourg, 1972), 12.

[63] European Commission (EC), 'Guidelines on the Application of Article 81(3) of the Treaty', [2004] OJ C 101/08, Guidelines on Article [101(3)] TFEU para 87 ('the fact that pass-on to consumers occurs within a certain time lag does not in itself exclude the application of [Article 101(3)]' though 'the greater the time lag, the greater must be the efficiencies to compensate also for the loss to consumers during the period preceding the pass-on').

The promotion of consumer welfare can be seen as the outcome of the competitive process,[64] embracing not only price effects but also quality, choice, and innovation.[65] 'Consumer well-being'[66] may be perceived as synonymous to a broader understanding of consumer welfare—encompassing various dimensions of quality and redistributive aims.[67] Such an understanding is, in fact, in sync with the notion of consumer welfare under EU competition law and is sufficiently flexible to accommodate adverse effects on consumer interests in digital markets, where products and services are usually distributed without a monetary exchange on one side of the platform.

In the EU, there has been an observed resurgence of fairness in the competition policy discourse.[68] Similarly in the United States, scholars and enforcers associated with what has come to be known as the 'new Brandeis' movement or 'hipster antitrust' have started to challenge the prevailing consumer welfare paradigm.[69] Fairness is not a brand new concept in competition law enforcement. From its inception, US antitrust law incorporated fairness concerns.[70] Similarly, EU competition law casts its net to capture 'unfair purchase or selling prices or other unfair trading conditions' (102(a) TFEU), or discrimination (102(c) TFEU), provided, of course, that all of the conditions of Article 102 TFEU are met, or ensure that

[64] Case C-377/20 *Servizio Elettrico Nazionale SpA, ENEL SpA and Enel Energia SpA v Autorità Garante della Concorrenza e del Mercato*, ECLI:EU:C:2021:998, Opinion of AG Rantos, paras 94–100.

[65] See, e.g. European Commission (EU), 'Guidelines on the Assessment of Horizontal Mergers under the Council Regulation on the Control of Concentrations between Undertakings', [2004] OJ C 31/5, para 8; European Council (EC), 'Guidelines on the Application of Article 81(3) of the Treaty', [2004] OJ C 101/97, paras 21, 24; Enforcement Priorities (n14), paras 5–6, 19; Amendments to the Guidance (n18), para 19. See also Case C-377/20 *Servizio Elettrico Nazionale, ENEL SpA, Enel Energia SpA v Autorità Garante della Concorrenza e del Mercato and Others*, ECLI:EU:C:2022:379, para 48. See also OECD, 'Advantages and Disadvantages of Competition Welfare Standards—Note by Greece', DAF/COMP/WD(2023)21 (Note prepared by I Lianos and C Milliou, 2021), paras 14–17.

[66] See, e.g. Joined Cases T-213/01 and T-214/01 *Österreichische Postsparkasse and Bank für Arbeit und Wirtschaft v Commission* [2006] ECR II-1601, para 115. See also AG Wahl's Opinion in Case C-525/16 *MEO v Autoridade da Concorrência*, ECLI:EU:C:2017:1020, para 64:

> [t]herefore, even where an undertaking is charged higher prices than those applied to other undertakings and, as a result, suffers (or considers that it suffers) discrimination, the conduct in question will be caught by Article 102 TFEU only if it is established that it is likely to restrict competition and diminish the well-being of consumers).

[67] A Ezrachi, 'EU Competition Law Goals and the Digital Economy', Oxford Legal Studies Research Paper No 17/2018 <http://www.ssrn.com/abstract=3191766> (accessed 7 June 2024). Komninos interprets such references to 'consumer well-being' as a mere 'translation glitch' from French to English, which should have been translated as consumer welfare instead. See also Komninos (n59), 78–80.

[68] D Gerard, 'Fairness in EU Competition Policy: Significance and Implications' (2018) 9 Journal of European Competition Law & Practice 211, 211.

[69] L Khan, 'The New Brandeis Movement: America's Antimonopoly Debate' (2018) 9 Journal of European Competition Law & Practice 131. 'Hipster antitrust' was a term coined by Konstantin Medvedovsky. See N Tiku, 'Do Not Mistake Orrin Hatch for #HipsterAntitrust' (Wired, 3 August 2017) <https://www.wired.com/story/orrin-hatch-antitrust-hipster-antitrust> (accessed 7 June 2024). On 'hipster antitrust', see Competition Policy International (CPI) Antitrust Chronicle (Spring 2018); KG Elzinga and M Webber, 'Louis Brandeis and Contemporary Antitrust Enforcement' (2017) 33 Touro Law Review 277.

[70] C Grandy, 'Original Intent and the Sherman Antitrust Act: A Re-Examination of the Consumer-Welfare Hypothesis' (1993) 53 Journal of Economic History 359, 363.

consumers are afforded 'a fair share of the resulting benefit' under Article 101(3) TFEU. Even the TFEU Preamble refers to 'fair competition'. Yet, such references do not necessarily elevate 'fairness' as an objective of competition law, and even if they do, 'fairness' as an abstract concept needs to be defined if it is to be translated into a manageable legal standard.[71] In seeking a workable definition of fairness, the Commission's and EU court's decisional practice may offer some guiding principles. At the same time, the policy discourse and ever-evolving market realities may stretch the limits of fairness beyond its jurisprudential contours.

In China, the AML explicitly pursues multiple goals amongst which fair competition stands out.[72] As is provided in Article 1 of the new AML, '[t]he present Law is enacted for the purpose of preventing and restraining monopolistic practices, protecting fair market competition, encouraging innovation, improving economic efficiency, safeguarding the interests of consumers and the general public, and promoting the sound development of the socialist market economy'. The fundamental role of competition policy (which pursues fairness, innovation, efficiency, and consumer welfare) has been guaranteed by the law.

The goal of encouraging innovation is expressly added into China's competition law framework. In digital markets, according to the SAMR, the AML aims to stimulate innovation. Specifically, an orderly, open, and inclusive environment for development and competition is to be created, thus reducing barriers to market entry and guiding and encouraging undertakings to devote more to technological innovation, quality, and service improvement.[73] The rise of the digital economy, driven by technological innovations and new business models, always brings challenges, keeps reshaping existing legal regimes, and (to some extent) presents an image of 'illegal arising' at an early stage.[74] To strike a delicate balance between the maintenance of market order for fair competition and the additional value brought by disruptive innovation, China's administrative agencies tend to first take soft interventions to tackle suspected anticompetitive acts before strictly enforcing the law against anticompetitive acts. By adopting such a distinct 'dual-track' approach in China,[75] China is paving the way for the rise of an innovative economy with regard to both policy and law enforcement.

[71] N Dunne, 'Fairness and the Challenge of Making Markets Work Better' (2020) Modern Law Review 8.

[72] M Colino, 'The Antitrust F Word: Fairness Considerations in Competition Law', Research Paper No 2018-09 (Chinese University of Hong Kong, Faculty of Law, 2018), 13; M Furse, 'Evidencing the Goals of Competition Law in the People's Republic of China: Inside the Merger Laboratory' (2018) 41 World Competition 129.

[73] Office of the Central Cyberspace Affairs Commission, 'Responsible Comrades of the Anti-Monopoly Bureau of the SAMR Answered Questions on the Guidelines' (8 February 2021) <http://www.cac.gov.cn/2021-02/08/c_1614358492110420.htm> (accessed 30 July 2023).

[74] L Hu, '非法兴起：理解中国互联网演进的一个视角 [Illegal Arising: A Perspective for Understanding China's Internet Evolution]' (2016) 5 Beijing Cultural Review 121, 125.

[75] On the Chinese 'dual-track' approach, see section V.3.3 below.

China also acknowledges the indispensable status of protecting consumer welfare in competition law enforcement.[76] The consumer welfare test can be applied to determine an abuse of market dominance or illegal mergers, or it can be used on its own as a standard in the exemption review of anticompetitive agreements, thus achieving the legislative purpose of anti-monopoly law, which is to safeguard consumers' interests.[77] Apart from traditional issues regarding price changes, problems brought by data and algorithms with respect to privacy and personal information security in Chinese digital markets fall within the remit of protecting consumer interests.

Whether and how competition law can be applied to protect the interests of personal information in China is a matter of great controversy. Some scholars believe that the Personal Information Protection Law has its own limitations and that competition law therefore has a role to play and can fill in its gaps. Specifically, the Personal Information Protection Law has been intended to solve the problems from an individual perspective instead of at the macro level. Hence, remedy for the damage to personal information rights and interests caused by anticompetitive acts in digital markets cannot be effectively guaranteed, which provides a good reason for the antitrust law to intervene, especially considering its legislative purpose and enforcement practices.[78] Meanwhile, Chinese scholars also do not coincide in opinion on whether competition law should be directly or indirectly applied to the protection of personal information.[79] Nonetheless, others contend that due to the limitations in digital market competition such as information asymmetry and cognitive limitations of consumers, establishing an antitrust law violation is not an appropriate way to promote data privacy protection.[80] Although there is no formal case in practice of the direct application of antitrust law to protect personal information,[81] scholars have made it clear that the protection of personal information in China should rely on the combination of consumer protection law and public law.[82] In particular, with the advent of the Internet and the reality of the big data

[76] H Jiao, '反垄断法上的竞争损害与消费者利益标准 [Competitive Harm in Anti-Monopoly Law and Its Relationship with Consumer Interests]' (2022) 2 Nanjing University Law Journal 11.

[77] Y Zhang, '反垄断法中的消费者福利标准：理论确证与法律适用 [The Consumer Welfare Standard in Anti-Monopoly Law: Theoretical Confirmation and Legal Application]' (2013) 31(3) Tribune of Political Science and Law 102.

[78] YE Ming and J Zhang, '反垄断法保护个人信息权益的理据与路径 [The Rationale and Path of Protecting the Interests of Personal Information through Antitrust Law]' (2023) 37(1) 华中科技大学学报 社会科学版 [Journal of Huazhong University of Science and Technology (Social Science Edition)] 87.

[79] W Han, '数字经济中的隐私保护与支配地位滥用 [The Privacy Protection and the Abuse of Dominance in the Digital Economy]' [2020] 1 Journal of University of Chinese Academy of Social Sciences 37. Also see H Jiao, '个人信息的反垄断法保护：从附属保护到独立保护 [Antitrust Law Protection of Personal Information: From Subsidiary to Independent Protection]' [2021] 4 Law Science 108.

[80] J Li, '互联网反垄断能促进数据隐私保护吗 [Can Antitrust Law Improve Data Privacy in the Internet Industry?]' [2021] 5 Journal of Business Economics 92.

[81] Ming and Zhang (n78), 90.

[82] X Ding, '个人信息私法保护的困境与出路 [The Dilemma of Private Law Protection of Personal Information and a Way Out of It]' [2018] 6 法学研究 [Chinese Journal of Law] 205.

era, platforms, data, and algorithms leave space for the protection of personal information from the perspective of public law,[83] which might also spawn an opportunity for the application of competition law in the digital markets.

In conclusion, it appears that competition law is undergoing different evolutionary stages and has historically embraced a wider set of aims. In EU competition law, while fairness has informed competition law and policy, it has yet to be elevated as a self-standing enforcement aim, whereas in China, the AML explicitly protects fair market competition.

IV. Fairness in Competition Law: Changing Benchmarks?

IV.1 Introduction

This section discusses the various shades and understandings of fairness using the perception of fairness under EU competition law as a starting point. The discussion is structured from the narrow to the wider readings of fairness. First, it links fairness with its EU ordoliberal tradition. It then discusses the role of fairness in protecting the interests of less efficient rivals, before examining whether fairness can accommodate various dimensions of quality and, in particular, privacy. Finally, it assesses whether fairness can cast the net wider to address wider societal problems.

IV.2 Fairness: Ordoliberal Tradition

Promoting the competitive process and attaining economic efficiency have been identified as the two core objectives of competition law, although the notion of these aims varies widely across different jurisdictions.[84] The promotion of the competitive process, thereby promoting equality of opportunity to participate in market competition, links back to the ordoliberal tradition of EU competition law.[85] Ordoliberals

[83] X Ding, '个人信息公私法融合保护的多维解读 [A Multidimensional Interpretation of the Integration of Public and Private Laws for the Protection of Personal Information]' [2022] 5 Research on Rule of Law 25.

[84] OECD, 'The Objectives of Competition Law and Policy' (n57), 3, para 20.

[85] H Buxbaum, 'German Legal Culture and the Globalisation of Competition Law: A Historical Perspective on the Expansion of Private Antitrust Enforcement' (2005) 23 Berkley Journal of International Law 101, 106; D Gerber, 'Constitutionalising the Economy: German Neo-Liberalism, Competition Law and the "New" Europe' (1994) 42 American Journal of Comparative Law 25, 64; contra Akman, 'Searching for the Long-Lost Soul of Article 82 EC' (n52); P Akman, 'The Role of Freedom in EU Competition Law' (2013) 34 Legal Studies 183, 213. On the different influences in EU competition law and distinguishing between the political (both ordoliberal and Keynesian) and the judicial arena, see S Ramirez Perez and S van de Scheur, 'The Evolution of the Law on Articles 85 and 86 EEC [Articles 101 and 102 TFEU]—Ordoliberalism and Its Keynesian Challenge' in K Patel

were sceptical of private economic power and sought ways to prevent its potential harmful effects.[86] In so doing, they focused on the competitive structure, the protection of market players' economic freedom, and competition as a process as ends in themselves.

The traces of its ordoliberal tradition are pronounced in early case law applying Article 102 TFEU. Abuse is described as an 'an *objective concept*' linked to a dominant position,

> which is such as to *influence the structure of a market* where, as a result of *the very presence of the undertaking* in question, *the degree of competition is weakened* and which, through recourse to methods different from those which condition normal competition in products or services on the basis of the transactions of commercial operators, has the effect of hindering the maintenance of the degree of competition still existing in the market or the growth of that competition [emphasis added].[87]

Thus, dominant firms have a 'special responsibility' not to impair competition.[88]

The protection of the competitive market structure and '*competition as such*' has left its mark on CJEU case law.[89] The court has clarified that, 'not every exclusionary effect is necessarily detrimental to competition' and '[c]ompetition on the merits may, by definition, lead to the departure from the market or the marginalisation of competitors that are less efficient and so less attractive to consumers from the point of view of, among other things, price, choice, quality or innovation'.[90] Thus, it appears that competition law protects the competitive process with respect to preventing the marginalization of equally efficient rivals. However, efficiency seems to embrace a wider set of factors and is not restricted

and H Schweitze (eds), *The Historical Foundations of EU Competition Law* (OUP, 2013), 19, 21, 37. For a detailed account of the history and development of EU competition law, see D Gerber, *Law and Competition in Twentieth Century Europe: Protecting Prometheus* (OUP, 2001); A Weitbrecht, 'From Freiburg to Chicago and Beyond: The First 50 Years of European Competition Law' (2008) 29 European Competition Law Review 81.

[86] See Gerber, 'Constitutionalising the Economy' (n85), 49–56; Gerber, *Law and Competition in Twentieth Century Europe* (n85), chapter 7; C Ahlborn and C Grave, 'Walter Eucken and Ordoliberalism: An Introduction from a Consumer Welfare Perspective' (2006) 2 Competition Policy International 197 for an overview of the main concepts of ordo-liberalism. See also W Möschel, 'The Proper Scope of Government Viewed from an Ordoliberal Perspective: The Example of Competition Policy' (2001) 157 Journal of Institutional and Theoretical Economics 3, 4.

[87] Case 85/76 *Hoffman-La Roche v Commission*, ECLI:EU:C:1979:36, para 91.

[88] Case 322/81 *Michelin v Commission*, ECLI:EU:C:1983:313, para 57. See also Case T-83/91 *Tetra Pak v Commission*, ECLI:EU:T:1994:246, para 114. See K McMahon, 'A Reformed Approach to Article 82 and the Special Responsibility Not to Distort Competition' in A Ezrachi (ed), *Article 82 EC: Reflections on Its Recent Evolution* (Hart, 2009), chapter 7, 125.

[89] See, e.g. Case C-8/08 *T-Mobile Netherlands*, ECLI:EU:C:2009:343, para [38]; Case C-501/06P *GlaxoSmithKline*, ECLI:EU:C:2009:610, para 63. See also Case C-95/04 *British Airways plc v Comm'n*, 2007 ECR I-2331, Opinion of AG J Kokott, para 68.

[90] Case C-209/10 *Post Danmark I*, ECLI:EU:C:2012:172, para 22. See also Case C-52/09, *TeliaSonera*, ECLI:EU:C:2011:83, para 64.

solely to price and output restrictions; rather, it expands to cover quality and innovation.[91]

IV.3 Fairness as Equality of Opportunities

A discussion that has emerged with respect to the Commission's enforcement activity against Big Tech is whether it departs from the 'more economic approach' pronounced in recent years as the lodestar of competition law enforcement.[92] At its core, the 'more economic approach' promotes an enforcement standard based primarily on efficiency considerations. Anticompetitive foreclosure does not therefore capture any foreclosure of even inefficient competitors but appears to be linked with the exclusion of as-efficient rivals.[93] However, in certain instances, the CJEU is prepared to accept that even less efficient rivals may exert a competitive constraint upon dominant firms. In *Post Danmark II*, the CJEU accepted that in the light of very large market share and the structural advantages conferred on the dominant undertaking, inter alia, by its statutory monopoly, the application of the as-efficient-competitor test was of no relevance 'inasmuch as the structure of the market makes the emergence of an as-efficient competitor practically impossible'.[94] The court further stated that 'in a market [. . .] access to which is protected by high barriers, the presence of a less efficient competitor might contribute to intensifying the competitive pressure on that market and, therefore, to exerting a constraint on the conduct of the dominant undertaking'.[95]

Anticompetitive foreclosure is not judged solely with respect to price effects but also with respect to the impact on other competitive parameters, namely quality, choice, and innovation.[96] Related to this question is whether there exists a duty of vertically integrated dominant firms not to favour their own businesses to their competitors' detriment (self-preferencing) and whether

[91] In this respect, see European Commission (EU), 'Guidelines on the Assessment of Horizontal Mergers' (n65), para 8; European Council (EC), 'Guidelines on the Application of Article 81(3) of the Treaty' (n65), paras 21, 24; Enforcement Priorities (n14), paras 5–6.

[92] See, e.g. European Commission (EU), 'Guidelines on the Assessment of Non-Horizontal Mergers' (18 October 2008) OJ C 265/6 (Non-Horizontal Merger Guidelines); Enforcement Priorities (n14); and European Commission (EU), 'Guidelines on Vertical Restraints' (19 May 2010) OJ C 130/1.

[93] See Case C-280/08P *Deutsche Telekom*, ECLI:EU:C:2010:603, on margin squeeze practices endorsing an 'as-efficient competitor' test; Case C-52/09 *TeliaSonera Sverige* (n90), para 43; Case C-209/10 *Post Danmark A/S* (n90), paras 21–22; C-413/14P *Intel*, ECLI:EU:C:2017:632, para 139 on exclusive dealing and conditional rebates.

[94] Case C-23/14 *Post Danmark* [2015] *A/S*, ECLI:EU:C:2015:651, para 59.

[95] *Ibid*, para 60. See also European Commission (EU), 'Guidance on the Commission's Enforcement Priorities in Applying Article 82 of the EC Treaty to Abusive Exclusionary Conduct by Dominant Undertakings', (n14), para 24.

[96] Amendments to the Guidance (n18), para 19.

there is a duty of equal treatment or non-discrimination and under which conditions.[97]

In *Google Shopping*, the Commission—confirmed by the GC—found that Google was favouring its own comparison shopping service at the expense of its competitors' services and such conduct constituted an abuse under 102 TFEU.[98] The contentious issue here was whether the classification of Google's conduct as favouring allowed the Commission to circumvent the conditions applicable in refusal to deal.[99] *Google Shopping* is discussed in detail in Chapter 5. For the purposes of this chapter, and on the question of whether fairness has emerged as an enforcement objective, it suffices to say that the GC made an explicit reference to the objective of undistorted competition implying that 'competition takes place on a fair basis'.[100] The GC relied on the general principle of equal treatment under EU law, and the fact that an abuse may take the form of an unjustified difference in treatment,[101] and found that the Commission was right in identifying favouring as 'a departure from competition on the merits' as long as it had taken into account the effects and relevant circumstances of favouring, such as the importance of Google traffic.[102]

In *Google Android*, the Commission found that Google had violated Article 102 TFEU through tying, exclusivity payments, and supplementary anti-fragmentation practices with respect to its mobile operating system, Android.[103] With respect to these practices, the Commission followed previous case law, yet the analysis regarding consumer harm and the impact on innovation admittedly appears rather short. Given the short analysis, it can be argued that the Commission abandoned the more economic approach in order to advance fair market outcomes for other market participants.[104] Yet, the Commission analysis, albeit brief, follows previous case law and thus shows that such fairness considerations were present in competition law analysis long before its recent resurrection. Most importantly though, such shade of fairness appears to be more pronounced in the authorities' case selection and prioritization.

[97] On these questions see, amongst others, E Valdivia, 'The Scope of the "Special Responsibility" upon Vertically Integrated Dominant Firms after the Google Shopping Case: Is There a Duty to Treat Rivals Equally and Refrain from Favouring Own Related Business?' (2018) World Competition 43; B Vesterdorf, 'Theories of Self-Preferencing and Duty to Deal—Two Sides of the Same Coin?' 1(1) Competition Law & Policy Debate 4 (2015); R Nazzini, 'Google and the (Ever-Stretching) Boundaries of Article 102 TFEU' (2015) 6(5) Journal of European Competition Law and Practice 301; P Akman, 'A Preliminary Assessment of the European Commission's Google Search Decision' (2017) 3 CPI Antitrust Chronicle 7.

[98] Case T-612/17 *Google LLC v Commission*, ECLI:EU:T:2021:763, para 123.

[99] *Ibid*, para 137.

[100] *Ibid*, para 433.

[101] *Ibid*, para 166.

[102] *Ibid*, paras 174–175.

[103] On this case, see Chapter 5, section II.3.

[104] Dunne, 'Fairness and the Challenge of Making Markets Work Better' (n71), 24.

IV.4 Fairness as Quality: Privacy as a Dimension of Quality

Dimensions of quality and innovation can inform competition law analysis within the more traditional paradigm of 'fairness', that is preserving the competitive process and competition on the merits in a bid to prevent the marginalization of equally efficient rivals, efficiency being influenced by price, choice, quality, and innovation. Thus, the notion of fairness here can embrace different dimensions of quality, with privacy being one such dimension. The question of whether data protection and privacy emerges as a competition law issue invites multiple answers.[105] To unravel and understand the different approaches, we place them on a spectrum, starting with the rather limited role under traditional competition law analysis to the public interest approach, that is fairness in its own right.

IV.4.1 Data Protection and Privacy: A Competition Law Issue?

The CJEU has clearly carved out data protection issues from the scope of competition law, an approach also advocated by certain commentators.[106] In *Asnef-Equifax*, the court stated that 'any possible issues relating to the sensitivity of personal data are not, as such, a matter for competition law, they may be resolved on the basis of the relevant provisions governing data protection'.[107] Similarly, in the context of merger control, while the Commission has examined whether data accumulation/combination may confer a competitive advantage upon incumbent firms to the detriment of competitors,[108] it has cautiously excluded privacy-related concerns from the scope of EU competition law.[109] Whereas the Commission has taken into account the applicable data protection legal framework when examining parties' potential to combine data,[110] it has gone on to assess the impact on competition assuming that such data use is lawful.[111] It would be interesting to also question the possible impact of the unlawful use of such data, which was exactly the issue in the *Facebook Germany* case.[112]

IV.4.2 Privacy as Quality

Competition in offering privacy solutions can be incorporated in the competitive analysis as an aspect of competition on the merits or a more expansive approach

[105] Data protection and privacy, while often taken as synonymous, are two distinct concepts/rights under EU law. See Cabral and Lynskey (n44) 20, with data protection appearing wider and encompassing informational privacy.

[106] See, e.g. M Ohlhausen and A Okuliar, 'Competition, Consumer Protection, and the Right (Approach) to Privacy' (2015) 80 Antitrust Law Journal 121; D Sokol and R Comerford, 'Antitrust and Regulating Big Data' (2016) 23 George Mason Law Review 1129.

[107] Case C-238/05 *Asnef-Equifax*, ECLI:EU:C:2006:734, para 63.

[108] See Chapter 6, section IV.2.2.

[109] See, e.g. *Facebook/WhatsApp* (Case COMP/M.7217) Commission Decision 2014/C 297/04, para 164. See also *Sanofi/Google/DMI JV* (Case M.7813) Commission Decision 2016/C 112/01, para 70.

[110] *Apple/Shazam* (Case M.8788) Commission Decision 2018/C 417/04, paras 224–238.

[111] *Ibid*, para 238.

[112] On this case, see Chapter 5, section II.5.

to consumer welfare, which does not rely solely on price and output parameters but incorporates quality and innovation. As such, competition law can provide a normative benchmark to appreciate and assess potential privacy degradation, which has been identified as an 'internal influence' on competition law enforcement since, in effect, it does not shift the analysis into the public interest terrain.[113]

Viewing privacy as an aspect of quality has been advocated by a number of scholars, with diverse views on the proper role of such privacy consideration in the competition law framework.[114] Given the characteristics of the digital economy, in particular the prevalence of data-driven markets, it appears that competition authorities are more prone to factor in privacy considerations in their respective analytical framework.[115] For example, in EU merger control, the offering of different privacy solutions has been assessed as one parameter of competition. In *Microsoft/LinkedIn*, the Commission identified the risk that the market for professional social services may reach a 'tipping point' in favour of LinkedIn and, should that happen, consumers' detrimental effects, apart from the substantial reduction in consumer choice, would encompass the marginalization of an existing competitor that offers a greater degree of privacy protection, which is an important parameter of competition.[116] Furthermore, in *Google Android*, the GC acknowledged the role of privacy not only as a quality parameter of competition but also as an element of a pluralistic democracy.[117]

IV.4.3 Privacy in Its Own Right

Apart from embedding privacy in the quality assessment, the more complex question is whether privacy can be protected under competition law in its own right. Such an approach can arguably be supported in the EU legal order, given the constitutional recognition of the right to privacy and data protection.[118]

At the current evolutionary stage of competition law, it appears that enforcers are reluctant to invoke competition law against purely privacy related issues. Yet, there are few instances where competition authorities have ventured out into this brave new world.

[113] Cabral and Lynskey (n44) 14.

[114] See, e.g. M Stucke and A Ezrachi, 'When Competition Fails to Optimise Quality: A Look at Search Engines' (2016) 18 Yale Journal of Law and Technology 70; A Grunes and M Stucke, 'No Mistake About It: The Important Role of Antitrust in the Era of Big Data' (2015) 14 Antitrust Source 1; K Bania, 'The Role of Consumer Data in the Enforcement of EU Competition Law' (2018) 14 European Competition Journal 38.

[115] See, e.g. European Commission (EU), 'Commission Notice on the Definition of the Relevant Market for the Purposes of Union Competition Law', C(2024) 1645 (Brussels, 8 February 2024) (Revised Market Definition Notice) para 15..

[116] *Microsoft/LinkedIn* (Case M.8124) Commission Decision 2016/C 388/04, paras 348–350. On this case, see Chapter 6, section III.6.

[117] *Google Android* (n16), para 1028.

[118] See Charter of Fundamental Rights of the European Union, [2012] OJ C 326/391, Articles 7 and 8.

In *Facebook*, the Bundeskartellamt examined (under national competition law) whether Facebook's terms and conditions amounted to the imposition of unfair terms on its users ('exploitative business use') and concluded in February 2019 that the collection and use of data by Facebook from third-party sources (without users' informed consent) violated data protection rules and was abusive under national competition law.[119] In this case, a breach of data protection law was ultimately treated as a breach of competition law. Analytically this can be classified as an exploitative imposition of unfair terms on consumers, ultimately limiting consumer choice and the expected quality (in terms of privacy degradation) of the service provided. Critics of such an approach would conversely argue that privacy is a self-standing concern, not befitting traditional competition law analysis.[120]

IV.5 Fairness as Trust

As noted by Dunne, 'gradually the rhetoric of fairness embraced two further themes: trust and democracy'.[121] The fairness rhetoric embracing the theme of trust can be invoked as a shorthand to accommodate different public-interest considerations in competition law enforcement. For example, EU competition law enforcement may suggest that, at times, public policy considerations (such as the integrity of the legal profession,[122] the proper conduct of sports,[123] or improving employment conditions[124]) are given priority over restrictions of competition, resulting in 'fairer' outcomes and promoting citizens' trust.[125] Nonetheless, it should be highlighted that, more commonly, public-policy justifications have been addressed as a justification (under Article 101(3) TFEU) when evaluating

[119] See Bundeskartellamt, 'Background Information on the Facebook Proceeding' (19 December 2017) <http://www.bundeskartellamt.de/SharedDocs/Publikation/EN/Diskussions_Hintergrundpapiere/2017/Hintergrundpapier_Facebook.pdf?__blob=publicationFile&v=6> (accessed 7 June 2024); Bundeskartellamt, Case B6-22/16; Bundeskartellamt, 'Facebook, Exploitative Business Terms Pursuant to Section 19(1) GWB for Inadequate Data Processing' (15 February 2019) <https://www.bundeskartellamt.de/SharedDocs/Entscheidung/EN/Fallberichte/Missbrauchsaufsicht/2019/B6-22-16.pdf?__blob=publicationFile&v=4> (accessed 7 June 2024). The decision in English is available at <https://www.bundeskartellamt.de/SharedDocs/Entscheidung/EN/Entscheidungen/Missbrauchsaufsicht/2019/B6-22-16.pdf?__blob=publicationFile&v=5> (accessed 7 June 2024).

[120] On this case, see Chapter 5, section II.5.

[121] Dunne, 'Fairness and the Challenge of Making Markets Work Better' (n71), 13.

[122] Case C-209/00 *Wouters* [2002] ECR I-1577.

[123] Case C-519/04P *Meca-Medina* [2006] ECR I-6991.

[124] Case C-67/96 *Albany* [1999] ECR I-5751. See also Case C-413/13 FNV *Kunsten Informatie en Media v Netherlands*, ECLI:EU:C:2014:2411.

[125] In this context, see also the blocking of Penguin/Simon & Schuster merger in the United States in order to protect book authors. See Federal Trade Commission (FTC), 'Justice Department Obtains Permanent Injunction Blocking Penguin Random House's Proposed Acquisition of Simon & Schuster' (31 October 2022) <https://www.justice.gov/opa/pr/justice-department-obtains-permanent-injunction-blocking-penguin-random-house-s-proposed> (accessed 7 June 2024).

the pro-competitive effects of the agreement. Some examples include environmental,[126] employment,[127] and consumer considerations.[128] Despite the fact that these considerations appear to have influenced the analysis to a large extent, the EU Commission has addressed them cautiously in conjunction with the core competition objectives.[129]

Three general points can be drawn from such an approach. First, competition law enforcement is not a monolithic but rather a 'polycentric' enterprise.[130] Thus, where its context permits, it has embraced public interest concerns. Second, it would be wrong to infer from the previous observation a general rule to this direction, and even if we were to draw such a rule, this should be confined in the application of EU competition law, that is it would be context specific. In the strand of 'regulatory competition' cases, the court has transferred and applied free movement justifications to competition law without transferring public policy justifications *in toto* from the area of free movement to that of competition law.[131] Third, it is comforting to acknowledge that competition law enforcement remains sufficiently porous to allow for different societal considerations to permeate the analysis, as was the case in *Albany*. This realization certainly has a role to play in the context of digital markets, given the precarious working conditions for those employed by powerful platforms.[132]

On the second theme, democracy, while not necessarily linked to, or derived from the fairness rhetoric, it has been suggested that competition law's goals include taming market power and thereby preserving the conditions for democracy.[133]

[126] See, e.g. *DSD* (Case COMP/34493) Commission Decision, 2001/837 EC, [2001] OJ L 319/1, paras 143–145; *CECED* (Case IV.F.1/36.718) Commission Decision, 2000/475/EC, [2000] OJ L 187/47, paras 30–37, 48, 51–57; *Exxon-Shell* (Case IV/33.640) Commission Decision, 94/322/EC, [1994] OJ L 144/21, paras 67–68; *Philips-Osram* (Case IV/34.252) Commission Decision, 94/986/EC, [1994] OJ L 378/37, para 25.

[127] *Ford/Volkswagen* (Case IV/33.814) Commission Decision, 93/49/EEC, [1993] OJ L 20/14, para 36, On appeal Case T-17/93 *Matra Hachette v Commission* [1994] ECR-II 595, para 96; *Stichting Baksteen* (Case IV/34.456) Commission Decision 94/296/EC, [1994] OJ L 131/15, paras 27–28; *Synthetic Fibres* (Case IV/30.810) Commission Decision 84/380/EEC, [1984] OJ L 207/17, para 37.

[128] *Asahi/Saint Gobain* (Case IV/33.863) Commission Decision, 94/896/EC, [1994] OJ L 354/87.

[129] G Monti, 'Article 81 EC and Public Policy' (2002) 39 Common Market Law Review 1057, 1078–1079.

[130] I Lianos, 'Polycentric Competition Law' (2018) 71 Current Legal Problems 161; I Lianos, 'Reorienting Competition Law' (2022) 10 Journal of Accounting and Economics 1; OECD, 'Note by Greece' (n65), paras 41–49.

[131] H Schweitzer, 'Competition Law and Public Policy: Reconsidering an Uneasy Relationship: The Example of Art. 81' (2007) 30 EUI Working Papers in Law 3. For the opposite argument inferring a general rule termed as 'European rule of reason', see Monti, 'Article 81 EC and Public Policy' (n129), 1088–1090. See also J Baquero Cruz, *Between Competition and Free Movement, The Economic Constitutional Law of the European Community* (Hart, 2002), 151–153.

[132] For a discussion, see Chapter 4, section II.2.

[133] T Wu, *The Curse of Bigness: Antitrust in the New Gilded Age* (Columbia Global Reports, 2018); G Sitaraman, 'Unchecked Power—How Monopolists Have Flourished and Undermined Democracy?' (The New Republic, 29 November 2018) <https://newrepublic.com/article/152294/unchecked-power> (accessed 7 June 2024).

This debate is more pronounced in a time of sweeping concentration levels not only in tech but across the economy.[134] Empirical evidence has linked market power and market concentration to rising mark-ups.[135] Competition law's potential to tackle the accumulation of economic power has been highlighted since its adoption; in fact, it has influenced and shaped its very adoption.[136]

Another observation with respect to whether competition authorities should devise a more proactive agenda, as well as its respective content, concerns the potential role of competition law in tackling increased concentration in media markets and its impact on democratic processes. In other words, should (and could) competition law be employed as a tool to safeguard democracy? As ambitious as it sounds, such a question can be translated into more familiar competition law terminology. If a platform, for example, indeed controls the social media market, does the platform have a 'special responsibility' not to discriminate between different media outlets? In so doing, competition law enforcement can certainly serve as a tool to materialize fairer or more democratic societal outcomes, and such potential is the more valuable in the digital economy. Yet, it needs to be complemented with tailored regulatory tools, some of which are discussed in section V below.

V. Regulatory Responses

V.1 Introduction

Section IV has illustrated the various conceptions of fairness and discussed the potential of competition law enforcement to embrace such considerations. At the same time, and acknowledging the respective limits of competition law enforcement, regulators have taken active steps to regulate the identified market failures in digital markets. The analysis in this section focuses on the EU and China.[137]

[134] On concentration levels, see, e.g. W Galston and C Hendrickson, 'A Policy at Peace with Itself: Antitrust Remedies for Our Concentrated, Uncompetitive Economy' (Brookings Report, 5 January 2018) <https://www.brookings.edu/research/a-policy-at-peace-with-itself-antitrust-remedies-for-our-concentrated-uncompetitive-economy> (accessed 7 June 2024).

[135] J de Loecker, J Eeckhout, and G Unger, 'The Rise of Market Power and the Macro-Economic Implications' (2020) 135 Quarterly Journal of Economics 561. See J Kwoka, *Mergers, Merger Control, and Remedies* (MIT Press, 2014).

[136] A Ayal, 'The Market for Bigness: Economic Power and Competition Agencies' Duty to Curtail It' (2013) Journal of Accounting and Economics 221, 231.

[137] In the United Kingdom, the Digital Markets, Competition and Consumer Act 2024 (DMCC) has also been adopted, in order to introduce changes in domestic competition legislation (Competition Act 1998 and the Enterprise Act 2002) and improve competition in digital markets (amongst other changes). See UK Parliament, 'Digital Markets, Competition and Consumers Bill' <https://bills.parliament.uk/bills/3453> (accessed 27 May 2024). For regulatory initiatives in the United States, see Congress.gov, 'S. 2992—American Innovation and Choice Online Act (AICOA)' <https://www.congress.gov/bill/117th-congress/senate-bill/2992/text> (accessed 7 June 2024), Congress.gov, 'H.R. 5017—Open App Markets Act' <https://www.congress.gov/bill/117th-congress/house-bill/5017> (accessed

V.2 Regulatory Responses

V.2.1 EU

In the past five years, the EU has been at the forefront of regulating digital markets, emerging as the regulator trailblazer.[138] The main regulatory initiatives, which have introduced a number of acronyms into the legal jargon, include the GDPR,[139] the P2B Regulation,[140] the DMA,[141] the DSA,[142] the AI Act,[143] and in accordance with the European Strategy for Data,[144] the DGA,[145] and the Data Act.[146] The introduction of certain of these regulatory instruments aims at changing Big Tech's incentives, namely from engaging in yearlong antitrust battles to speeding up the ex-ante regulatory process, as is the case in merger control. However, such

7 June 2024), and Congress.gov, 'S.5339—Platform Accountability and Transparency Act' <https://www.congress.gov/bill/117th-congress/senate-bill/5339> (accessed 7 June 2024). For a concise presentation of regulatory developments in other jurisdictions, see United Nations Conference on Trade and Development (UNCTAD), 'Global Competition Law and Policy Approaches to Digital Markets' (2024), 25–35.

[138] For a critical account, see F Erixon, O Guinea, E van der Marel, and E Sisto, 'After the DMA, the DSA and the New AI Regulation: Mapping the Economic Consequences of and Responses to New Digital Regulations in Europe" (European Centre for International Political Economy Occasional Paper 3/2022), 4.

[139] Regulation (EU) 2016/679 of the European Parliament and of the Council of 27 April 2016 on the protection of natural persons with regard to the processing of personal data and on the free movement of such data, and repealing Directive 95/46/EC, [2016] OJ L 119/1 (General Data Protection Regulation, GDPR).

[140] Regulation (EU) 2019/1150 of the European Parliament and of the Council of 20 June 2019 on promoting fairness and transparency for business users of online intermediation services, [2019] OJ L 186/57 (P2B Regulation).

[141] Regulation (EU) 2022/1925 of the European Parliament and of the Council of 14 September 2022 on contestable and fair markets in the digital sector and amending Directives (EU) 2019/1937 and (EU) 2020/1828, [2022] OJ L 265/1 (Digital Markets Act, DMA).

[142] Regulation (EU) 2022/2065 of the European Parliament and of the Council of 19 October 2022 on a single market for digital services and amending Directive 2000/31/EC, [2022] OJ L 277/1 (Digital Services Act, DSA).

[143] Regulation (EU) 2024/1689 of the European Parliament and of the Council of 13 June 2024 laying down harmonised rules on artificial intelligence and amending Regulations (EC) No 300/2008, (EU) No 167/2013, (EU) No 168/2013, (EU) 2018/858, (EU) 2018/1139 and (EU) 2019/2144 and Directives 2014/90/EU, (EU) 2016/797 and (EU) 2020/1828 (Artificial Intelligence Act)

[144] European Commission (EU), 'Communication for the Commission, A European Strategy for Data', COM(2020) 66 final (2020).

[145] Regulation (EU) 2022/868 of the European Parliament and of the Council of 30 May 2022 on European data governance and amending Regulation (EU) 2018/1724, [2022] OJ L 152/1 (Data Governance Act, DGA).

[146] European Parliament (EU), 'Proposal for a Regulation of the European Parliament and of the Council on Harmonised Rules on Fair Access to and Use of Data', COM/2022/68 final (2022) (Data Act). The Data Act entered into force on 11 January 2024. See European Commission (EU), 'European Data Act Enters into Force, Putting in Place New Rules for a Fair and Innovative Data Economy' (Press release, 11 January 2024) <https://digital-strategy.ec.europa.eu/en/news/european-data-act-enters-force-putting-place-new-rules-fair-and-innovative-data-economy> (accessed 28 September 2024); Regulation (EU) 2023/2854 of the European Parliament and of the Council of 13 December 2023 on harmonised rules on fair access to and use of data and amending Regulation (EU) 2017/2394 and Directive (EU) 2020/1828, [2023] OJ L 1/71 (Data Act).

objectives appear to have been met only to some extent, as the EU Commission non-compliance proceedings under the DMA showcase.[147]

The analysis of the complex regulatory framework is beyond the scope of this book. Below, we focus on selected regulations, which were adopted in a bid to control the power of Big Tech and imbue digital markets with more fairness, transparency, and contestability, in particular the DMA and the P2B Regulation. The DMA has a more limited personal scope than the P2B Regulation, since it introduces rules applicable to very large platforms coined as 'gatekeepers'.

V.2.1.1 DMA

In the EU, the EU institutions managed to adopt the DMA very swiftly, in slightly more than a year after it was initially proposed,[148] with the European Parliament Rapporteur, Andreas Schwab, welcoming its adoption by stating that '[t]he time of long antitrust cases is over'.[149] While this remains to be seen, the adoption of the DMA is undoubtedly a welcome development in regulating the conduct of powerful platforms.[150] Whether it will deliver on its promises is a separate issue. The DMA started to apply on 2 May 2023.[151] Potential gatekeepers had to notify the Commission of their CPS by 3 July 2023,[152] with the first designation decisions having been adopted by 6 September 2023.[153] As will be discussed below, the DMA has already generated a flurry of enforcement activity, with no signs of abating.[154]

[147] See text to n183.

[148] European Commission (EU), 'Digital Markets Act: Commission Welcomes Political Agreement on Rules to Ensure Fair and Open Digital Markets' (Press release, 25 March 2022) <https://ec.europa.eu/commission/presscorner/detail/en/IP_22_1978> (accessed 28 September 2024).

[149] S Stolton, 'EU Negotiators Agree New Rules to Rein in Tech Giants' (24 March 2022) <https://www.politico.eu/article/eus-digital-markets-act-adopted> (accessed 7 June 2024).

[150] For example, according to Reuters, the DMA rules on freedom of choice of internet browsers appear to be effective, as Cyprus-based Aloha Browser reported an increase of 250 per cent in EU users as of March 2024, following the enforcement of the DMA. See S Mukherjee and F Yun Chee, 'New Tech Laws Are Working; Small Browsers Gain Market Share' (Reuters, 10 April 2024) <https://www.reuters.com/technology/eus-new-tech-laws-are-working-small-browsers-gain-market-share-2024-04-10> (accessed 7 June 2024).

[151] DMA (n141), Article 54. The Implementing Regulation also entered into force on 2 May 2023; Implementing Regulation (EU) 2023/814 of 14 April 2023 on detailed arrangements for the conduct of certain proceedings by the Commission pursuant to Regulation (EU) 2022/1925 of the European Parliament and of the Council, [2023] OJ L 102/6, Article 12.

[152] European Commission (EU), 'Questions and Answers: Digital Markets Act: Ensuring Fair and Open Digital Markets' (Brussels, 6 September 2023) <https://ec.europa.eu/commission/presscorner/detail/en/qanda_20_2349> (accessed 7 June 2024).

[153] European Commission (EU), 'Commission Designates Six Gatekeepers under the Digital Markets Act' (Press release, 6 September 2023) <https://digital-markets-act.ec.europa.eu/commission-designates-six-gatekeepers-under-digital-markets-act-2023-09-06_en> (accessed 7 June 2024).

[154] For the first year of the DMA's application, see also European Commission (EU), 'Annual Report on Regulation (EU) 2022/1925 of the European Parliament and of the Council on Contestable and Fair Markets in the Digital Sector and Amending Directives (EU) 2019/1937 and (EU) 2020/1828 (Digital Markets Act)', COM(2024) 106 final (Brussels, 6 March 2024). See also A Bacchiega and T

A. Objectives and the 'No Prejudice Clause'

The DMA aims to ensure contestability and fairness in digital markets, whereas it explicitly distinguishes its objectives from the protection of undistorted competition on the market and the actual, likely, or presumed effects of gatekeepers' conduct on competition on a given market.[155] In as much as the DMA's protective scope is different to EU competition law as well as national competition laws, it proclaims that it is without prejudice to their application.[156] Yet, this complementary relationship will need to be better specified,[157] since it risks the invocation of two sets of rules (the ex-ante regulatory DMA and ex-post competition law provisions) against similar conduct. Such application may raise *ne bis in idem* concerns.[158] Arguably though, since the protected legal interest is different (i.e. fairness and contestability under the DMA and the protection of undistorted competition under competition law), this should alleviate any *ne bis in idem* concerns.[159]

The DMA moves away from notions of market power and dominance, which are prevalent in the competition law analysis, and employs additional indicators of economic power such as imbalances in bargaining power,[160] intermediation power,[161] and gateway position.[162] Such indicators, of course, may be indicative of market power, but it also encapsulates potentially different scenarios where

Tombal, 'Agency Insights: The First Steps of the DMA Adventure' (2024) 12 Journal of Accounting and Economics 189.

155 DMA (n141), Recitals 7, 10, 11 Article 1(1) and 1(6).

156 *Ibid*, Article 1(6). The draft DMA Commission proposal mentions explicitly that '[t]he current proposal minimises the detrimental structural effects of unfair practices ex ante, without limiting the ability to intervene ex post under EU and national competition rules' (4). See European Commission (EU), 'Proposal for a Regulation of the European Parliament and of the Council on Contestable and \ fair Markets in the Digital Sector (Digital Markets Act)', COM(2020) 842 final (Brussels, 15 December 2020) (Draft DMA).

157 In this context, see the common position paper published by Germany, France, and the Netherlands on 27 May 2021 calling for a clearer specification of the relation of the DMA to European competition law and a strengthening of Member States' role in the DMA's enforcement, amongst others. See 'Strengthening the Digital Markets Act and Its Enforcement' (27 May 2021) <https://www.bmwi.de/Redaktion/DE/Downloads/M-O/non-paper-friends-of-an-effective-digital-markets-act.pdf?__blob=publicationFile&v=4> (accessed 7 June 2024). See also P Akman, 'Regulating Competition in Digital Platform Markets: A Critical Assessment of the Framework and Approach of the EU Digital Markets Act' (2022) 47 European Law Review 217; N Moreno Belloso and N Petit, 'The EU Digital Markets Act (DMA)—a Competition Hand in a Regulatory Glove' (2023) 48 European Law Review 391.

158 For a discussion, see G Monti, 'The Digital Markets Act—Institutional Design and Suggestions for Improvement', TILEC Discussion Paper DP 2021-004, 14–15 <https://papers.ssrn.com/sol3/papers.cfm?abstract_id=3797730> (accessed 7 June 2024). See also V Robertson, 'The Complementary Nature of the Digital Markets Act and the EU Antitrust Rules' (2024) 12 Journal of Accounting and Economics 325.

159 Case C-117/20 *Bpost SA v Autorité belge de la concurrence*, ECLI:EU:C:2022:202.

160 DMA (n141), Recital 4.

161 *Ibid*, Recital 26.

162 *Ibid*, Recital 33.

competition law provisions may not have been applicable in the absence of a finding of market power and dominance.[163]

B. Personal Scope

In terms of scope, the DMA targets companies that provide 'core platform services' (CPSs)[164] and are designated as gatekeepers following both qualitative and quantitative criteria. The position of a gatekeeper is linked to the accumulation of economic power due to the ability to connect large numbers of business users with end users, allowing them to leverage their advantages (e.g. access to data) and their ability to control 'whole platform ecosystems'. Such characteristics, coupled with the fact that it is extremely difficult for new players to contest the incumbents' position due to high entry barriers and limited access to certain key inputs such as data, raises the likelihood of market failures.[165]

According to Article 3(1) DMA, the qualitative criteria for a gatekeeper's designation include (i) its significant impact on the internal market; (ii) its provision of a CPS, which is an important gateway for business users to reach end users; and (iii) its entrenched and durable position. Such criteria are then further quantified in Article 3(2) DMA. A company shall be deemed to have a significant impact on the internal market when it has an EU annual turnover of more than €7.5 billion in each of the last three financial years, or where it has an average market capitalisation of at least €75 billion in the last financial year and provides the same CPS in at least three Member States.[166] Furthermore, a CPS is deemed to act as an important gateway for reaching end users in the EU, where, in the last financial year, the platform has had at least 45 million monthly active end users and at least 10,000 yearly active business users. An entrenched and durable market position is deemed to exist if the company meets these figures with respect to its CPS active users in each of the last three financial years.

Still, even if an undertaking meets the quantitative criteria, under Article 3(5) DMA, it may attempt to rebut the presumption that the qualitative criteria are met, and thus it should not be designated as gatekeeper. The Commission examined Microsoft's Bing, Edge, and Advertising as well as Apple's iMessage,

[163] *Ibid*, Recital 5.

[164] *Ibid*, Article 2(2). See Chapter 2, section VI.1.

[165] DMA (n141), Recital 3.

[166] The threshold in the Commission proposal was lower (€6.5 billion turnover over three financial year and 65 billion market capitalization) See Draft DMA (n156), Article 3(2). The Parliament, on the other hand, proposed an even higher threshold of €8 billion turnover annually and 80 billion market capitalization. See European Parliament (EU), 'Digital Markets Act: Parliament Ready to Start Negotiations with Council' (Press release, 15 December 2021) <https://www.europarl.europa.eu/news/en/press-room/20211210IPR19211/digital-markets-act-parliament-ready-to-start-negotiations-with-council> (accessed 29 September 2024).

which, despite meeting the quantitative criteria, succeeded in rebutting the presumption.[167] However, arguments can only be put forward with respect to the quantitative criteria for designation, and any economic arguments with respect to market definition or efficiencies will be rejected as not relevant to the designation exercise.[168] The DMA does not allow undertakings to put forward any efficiency justifications, thereby accepting that if a company, by its sheer economic power, meets the designation criteria, market contestability and fairness is in jeopardy.[169]

Pursuant to Article 3(8) DMA, if an undertaking meets the qualitative criteria under Article 3(1) DMA but fails to satisfy each of the quantitative criteria under Article 3(2) DMA, the Commission may still designate it as gatekeeper following a market investigation (Article 17 DMA) by considering the following factors: (i) its size (including turnover and market capitalisation), position, and operations; (ii) the number of business and end users; (iii) any network effects and data-driven advantages; (iv) any scale and scope effects, including with respect to data; (v) potential user lock-in, including switching costs and behavioural biases, reducing the ability to switch or multi-home; (vi) conglomeration or vertical integration; and (vii) any other structural business or service characteristics. Such intervention may be warranted to prevent markets from tipping irreversibly.[170] According to Article 17(4) DMA, when the Commission designates an emerging gatekeeper (i.e. an undertaking that is yet to have an entrenched and durable position, but it is foreseeable that it will acquire such a position in the near future), only certain obligations should apply, which are necessary and proportionate, in order to meet the DMA's objectives, namely Articles 5(3)–(6) and Articles 6(4), (7), (9), (10), and (13).

The Commission has designated the first six gatekeepers—Alphabet, Amazon, Apple, ByteDance (TikTok's parent company), Meta, and Microsoft—for twenty-two CPSs.[171] Apple, Meta, and ByteDance have challenged the respective

[167] European Commission (EU), 'Commission Closes Market Investigations on Microsoft's and Apple's Services under the Digital Markets Act' (Press release, 13 February 2024) <https://digital-markets-act.ec.europa.eu/commission-closes-market-investigations-microsofts-and-apples-services-under-digital-markets-act-2024-02-13_en> (accessed 7 June 2024).

[168] DMA (n141), Recital 23.

[169] On this point, see also *ibid*, Recital 24, which expressly states that 'this Regulation primarily targets large undertakings with considerable economic power rather than medium-sized, small or micro enterprises'.

[170] *Ibid*, Recital 26.

[171] With respect to social networks: TikTok, Facebook, Instagram, and LinkedIn; with respect to intermediation services: Google Maps, Google Play, Google Shopping, Amazon Marketplace, App Store, Meta Marketplace; with respect to advertising: Google, Amazon, Meta; with respect to NIICS: WhatsApp, Messenger; with respect to browsers: Chrome and Safari; with respect to OS: Google Android, iOS, Windows PC OS; with respect to video sharing: YouTube; and with respect to search: Google Search. See European Commission (EU), 'Commission Designates Six Gatekeepers under the Digital Markets Act' (n153).

designation decisions.[172] The Commission has subsequently designated Apple and Bookings as gatekeepers with respect to iPadOS and Booking.com.[173]

C. List of Obligations

The DMA's approach in order to safeguard CPS contestability and fairness is prescriptive in that it provides for a list of conduct obligations applicable to gatekeepers that are necessary to address the risks of harmful effects of their respective practices.[174] Below, we provide a descriptive account of the relevant DMA obligations with links to the respective DMA provisions, as well as related competition law cases, where relevant.[175] Article 5 ('black list') provides for the following directly applicable obligations:

1. unless the user has been presented with the specific choice and provided its GDPR compliant consent, there is a prohibition on:
   a. Processing end users' personal data that use third parties' services (who use gatekeepers' CPS), *for providing online advertising services*;
   b. Combining personal data from the relevant CPS with personal data from any other CPS or any other gatekeeper's services or with personal data from third-party services;
   c. Cross-using personal data from the relevant CPS in other gatekeeper's services and v ice versa;
   d. Signing in end users to other gatekeeper's services of the gatekeeper to combine personal data.[176]

(Article 5(2) DMA—recitals 36–38—limitations on data processing and use— German Facebook *case—provision of online advertising services)*

[172] Cases T-1077/23R *Bytedance v Commission*, ECLI:EU:T:2024:94; Case T-1078/23 *Meta Platforms v Commission*, [2024] OJ C 2024/561; Case T-1079/23 *Apple v Commission*, [2024] OJ C/2024/562; Case T-1080/23 *Apple v Commission*, [2024] OJ C 2024/563. ByteDance also brought an interim measures request, which was dismissed. See Case T-1077/23R *Bytedance v Commission*, ECLI:EU:T:2024:94. Apple can be expected to withdraw its application in Case T-1079/23 following the successful rebuttal for iMessage.

[173] See European Commission (EU), 'Commission Designates Apple's iPadOS under the Digital Markets Act' (Press release, 29 April 2024) <https://ec.europa.eu/commission/presscorner/detail/en/ip_24_2363> (accessed 6 June 2024); European Commission (EU), 'Commission Designates Booking as a Gatekeeper and Opens a Market Investigation into X' (Press release, 13 May 2024) <https://ec.europa.eu/commission/presscorner/detail/en/ip_24_2561> (accessed 7 June 2024).

[174] DMA (n141), Recital 31. For a different approach, see DMCC (n137), which allows more leeway to the UK regulator to tailor the specific obligations imposed on companies with strategic market status. For a discussion, see O Andriychuk, 'Comparing the Incomparable: Analysing UK Digital Markets, Competition and Consumers Bill through the Prism of the DMA' (2023) 3 Concurrences para 17.

[175] On these cases see Chapter 5, section II.

[176] GDPR (n139), Article 4, point 4(11) and Article 7.

2. prohibition on preventing business users from offering their products or services to end users at different prices or conditions from the ones offered over the gatekeeper's online intermediation services through third-party online intermediation services or through their own direct online sales channel

   (Article 5(3) DMA—recital 39—most-favoured-nation clauses (MFNs)—Amazon—Booking—online intermediation services)

3. obligation to allow business users, free of charge, to communicate and promote offers, to end users acquired via its CPS or through other channels, and to conclude contracts with those end users, regardless of whether, for that purpose, they use the CPS of the gatekeeper

   (Article 5(4) DMA—recital 40—EU Apple—encourage multi-homing—online intermediation services)

4. obligation to allow end users to access and use, through its CPS, content, subscriptions, features or other items, by using the software application of a business user

   (Article 5(5) DMA—recital 41)

5. prohibition on preventing or restricting users from raising any issue of the gatekeeper's non-compliance with competent authorities and courts

   (Article 5(6) DMA—recital 42—Amazon Germany commitments)

6. prohibition on requiring users to use, offer, or interoperate with a gatekeeper's identification service, web browser, or payment service (e.g. payment systems for in-app purchases) in the context of services provided by the business users when using core platform services CPS provided by the gatekeeper

   (Article 5(7) DMA—recital 43—Apple in-app purchases)

7. prohibition on requiring users to subscribe to any further CPS listed in the designation decision as a pre-condition in order to be able to use any of that gatekeeper's CPS

   (Article 5(8) DMA—recital 44—Bundling)

8. obligation to provide information on a daily basis free of charge to each advertiser to which the gatekeeper supplies online advertising services regarding
   a. prices,
   b. publisher's remuneration (subject to the publisher's consent), and
   c. metrics upon which the above are calculated

   *(Article 5(9) DMA—recital 45—Transparency in AdTech—*Google AdTech *case)*

9. obligation to provide information on a daily basis, free of charge, to each publisher concerning each advertisement displayed on the publisher's inventory, regarding
   a. publisher's remuneration and the fees paid
   b. the price paid by the advertiser (subject to the advertiser's consent), and
   c. relevant metrics for the calculation of the above

   *(Article 5(10) DMA—recital 45—Transparency in AdTech—*Google AdTech *case).*

Article 6 ('grey list') adds further obligations that are susceptible to being further specified under Article 8 DMA. The Commission may open proceedings in order to assess the gatekeeper's compliance with the relevant obligations, and specify within six months the necessary measures to ensure compliance with such obligations. The gatekeeper may also ask the Commission to open such a procedure in order to determine that its respective measures comply with the obligations.

10. prohibition on using, in competition with business users, non-public generated data or data provided by business users when using the relevant CPS

    (Article 6(2) DMA—recitals 46–48—Amazon EU)

11. obligation to allow end users to easily uninstall any software applications on the gatekeeper's operating system (OS), unless they are essential for the functioning of the OS or the device and cannot be technically offered on a standalone basis by third parties

    (Article 6(3) DMA—recital 49—Android EU)

12. obligation to allow end users to easily change the default settings on the gatekeeper's OS, virtual assistant, and web browser

    (Article 6(3) DMA—recital 49—Android EU)

13. obligation to allow the installation and effective use of third-party software applications or software application stores on its operating system and to allow these to be accessed by means other than the relevant gatekeeper's CPS.

    The gatekeeper may take strictly necessary and proportionate measures to ensure that such applications do not jeopardize the integrity of the gatekeeper's hardware or operating system, provided that such measures are duly justified.

    (Article 6(4) DMA—recital 50—EU Apple—sideloading)

14. obligation not to treat more favourably, in ranking and related indexing and crawling, its own products and services and apply transparent, fair and non-discriminatory conditions to such ranking

    (Article 6(5) DMA—recitals 51 and 52—Google Shopping)

15. obligation not to restrict end users from switching between software applications and services that are accessed using the gatekeeper's CPS

    (Article 6(6) DMA—recital 53—end-user switching)

16. obligation to ensure interoperability for service and hardware providers and business users.

    The gatekeeper may take strictly necessary and proportionate measures to ensure the integrity of the operating system, virtual assistant, and hardware or software features, provided that such measures are duly justified by the gatekeeper.

    (Article 6(7) DMA—recital 57—interoperability)

17. obligation to provide advertisers and publishers with access to the gatekeeper's performance measuring tools and necessary data to undertake their own independent verification of the advertisements inventory

    (Article 6(8) DMA—recital 58—transparency in Ad tech)

18. obligation to provide end users with effective portability of their data, including by providing tools to facilitate such data portability, and by providing continuous and real-time access to such data

    (Article 6(9) DMA—recital 59—data portability end users)

19. obligation to provide business users with effective, high-quality, continuous, and real-time access to, and use of, aggregated and non-aggregated data, including personal data (subject to end users' consent), provided for or generated during the use of the relevant core platform services. CPS

    (Article 6(10) DMA)—recital 60—Access to data—business users)

20. obligation to provide to other online search engines, on their request access, on fair, reasonable and non-discriminatory terms, to ranking, query, and click-and-view data in relation to free and paid searches generated by end users on its online search engines. Any personal data shall be anonymized

    (Article 6(11) DMA—recital 61—online search engines)

21. obligation to provide business users with fair, reasonable, and non-discriminatory general access to its software application stores, online search engines, and online social networking services

    (Article 6(12) DMA—recital 62—FRAND to business users)

22. obligation to have proportionate general conditions for the termination of a core CPS platform service

    (Article 6(13) DMA—recital 63).

Article 7, upon the Parliament's proposal, further introduced the obligation to ensure the interoperability of number-independent interpersonal communications services (NIICS).[177] Following a market investigation under Article 19 DMA, the Commission may add further digital services as CPSs as well as further obligations. Interestingly, the DMA provides that 'in its assessment, the Commission shall take into account any relevant findings of proceedings under Articles 101 and 102 TFEU concerning digital markets as well as any other relevant developments'.[178]

D. Mergers

Article 14 DMA provides that a gatekeeper has to inform the Commission of any intended merger transactions where the parties or the target provide CPS or

[177] I Brown, 'Key Points on DMA Interoperability and Encryption' (1 April 2022) <https://www.ianbrown.tech/2022/04/01/key-points-on-dma-interoperability-and-encryption> (accessed 13 June 2024). NIICS has the same meaning as in Article 2, point (7) of Directive (EU) 2018/1972 (Article 2(9) DMA). See Directive (EU) 2018/1972 of the European Parliament and of the Council of 11 December 2018 establishing the European Electronic Communications Code, OJ L 321 (17 December 2018), 36.

[178] DMA (n141), Article 19(1).

services in the digital sector or enable the collection of data.[179] The Commission shall inform the NCAs about such anticipated transactions and the latter may invoke Article 22 EUMR.[180] Such a provision complements the expansive application of the Article 22 referral system as well as the potential application of Article 102 TFEU by NCAs to merger transactions that fall below the national merger control thresholds.[181]

E. Market Investigations

Under the DMA, the Commission may undertake market investigations in three instances: (i) for the designation of gatekeepers not meeting the DMA quantitative thresholds, and in cases where gatekeepers, despite meeting the thresholds, have attempted to rebut such a presumption (Article 17);[182] (ii) for the imposition of remedies in cases of systematic non-compliance (Article 18); and (iii) for the addition of new services in the list of CPS and new gatekeeper obligations (Article 19).

F. Remedies

In cases of systematic non-compliance, the Commission may impose structural or behavioural remedies (Article 18(1) DMA). It may also prohibit the gatekeeper from entering into merger transactions for a limited period in the digital sector (Article 18(2) DMA). Systematic non-compliance occurs where the gatekeeper has received at least three non-compliance decisions under Article 29 about any of its CPS within eight years (Article 18(3) DMA).

G. Enforcement

The Commission can adopt a decision opening proceedings with respect to issuing a decision on compliance (Article 8), non-compliance (Article 29), and the imposition of fines (Article 30). Compliance has proven a thorny issue, with the Commission first launching proceedings against Apple, Alphabet, and Meta on 25

[179] On 13 July 2023, the European Commission published its second template relating to the gatekeeper's obligation to inform about potential mergers. See European Commission (EU), 'Template Relating to the Obligation to Inform about a Concentration Pursuant to Article 14 of Regulation (EU) 2022/1925 (Digital Markets Act)' (13 July 2023) <https://digital-markets-act.ec.europa.eu/system/files/2023-07/Article%2014%20DMA%20Template%20%28information%20on%20transactions%29%20-%2013-07-2023.pdf>. For the notified transactions, see European Commission, 'List of Acquisitions' <https://digital-markets-act-cases.ec.europa.eu/acquisitions> (both accessed 4 July 2024). At the time of writing Amazon, ByteDance, and Microsoft have notified one transaction each, and Apple has notified three transactions.

[180] DMA (n141), Article 14(5).

[181] See Chapter 6, section III.1.

[182] The Commission has opened market investigations into five rebuttals, namely for Apple's iMessage, Microsoft's Bing, Microsoft Advertising, and Edge, as well as X online social network. It has also launched a qualitative market investigation into Apple's iPadOS that, despite not meeting the quantitative threshold, has been designated as a gatekeeper following the investigation.

March 2024.[183] The Commission investigations concerned Apple's and Alphabet's alleged non-compliance with Article 5(4) DMA with respect to their anti-steering provisions preventing app developers to direct consumers outside their app stores. Apple is also under investigation for a potential breach of Article 6(3) DMA preventing users to easily uninstall software and change defaults and Alphabet with respect to its self-preferencing practices in breach of Article 6(5) DMA, which may favour Google's vertical search services (e.g. Google Shopping or Google Flights) over competing services. Finally, the Commission is investigating Meta for its 'pay-or-consent' model, which may possibly breach Article 5(2) DMA since it does not truly offer users an alternative choice.[184] With respect to these ongoing investigations, the Commission has informed Meta and Apple (with respect to its anti-steering provisions) of its preliminary findings that the companies have breached the DMA.[185] It has also opened a third non-compliance investigation against Apple with respect to its contractual terms potentially breaching Article 6(4) DMA.[186]

The DMA provides the Commission with similar investigative powers to Regulation 1/2003.[187] In particular, the Commission has the power request information (Article 21), take interviews and statements (Article 22), and conduct inspections (Article 23). The Commission may order interim measures (Article 24) as well as accept commitments (Article 25). In cases of non-compliance, the Commission may impose fines of up to 10 per cent of the company's total worldwide turnover in the preceding financial year, which can be doubled (20 per cent) in the case of recidivism, that is when the gatekeeper commits non-compliance with its obligations concerning the same CPS within a period of eight years. It may also impose periodic penalty payments of up to 5 per cent of the total worldwide daily turnover (Article 31).

The Commission has sole enforcement responsibility for the DMA,[188] despite the NCAs' opposition.[189] The Commission is the only competent authority

183 European Commission (EU), 'Commission Opens Non-Compliance Investigations against Alphabet, Apple and Meta under the Digital Markets Act' (Press release, 25 March 2024) <https://digital-markets-act.ec.europa.eu/commission-opens-non-compliance-investigations-against-alphabet-apple-and-meta-under-digital-markets-2024-03-25_en> (accessed 4 July 2024).

184 *Ibid.*

185 European Commission (EU), 'Commission Sends Preliminary Findings to Meta over Its "Pay or Consent" Model for Breach of the Digital Markets Act' (Press release, 1 July 2024) <https://digital-markets-act.ec.europa.eu/commission-sends-preliminary-findings-meta-over-its-pay-or-consent-model-breach-digital-markets-act-2024-07-01_en> (accessed 1 July 2024); European Commission (EU), 'Commission Sends Preliminary Findings to Apple and Opens Additional Non-Compliance Investigation against Apple' (Press release, 24 June 2024) <https://digital-markets-act.ec.europa.eu/commission-sends-preliminary-findings-apple-and-opens-additional-non-compliance-investigation-2024-06-24_en> (accessed 24 June 2024).

186 European Commission (EU), 'Commission Sends Preliminary Findings to Meta (n185); European Commission (EU), 'Commission Sends Preliminary Findings to Apple (n185).

187 Regulation 1/2003 (n20).

188 DMA (n141), Recital 91.

189 European Competition Network, 'Joint Paper of the Heads of the National Competition Authorities of the European Union: How National Competition Agencies Can Strengthen the DMA' (2021), para 19.

for the designation of gatekeepers, issuing compliance decisions, monitoring non-compliance, and imposing sanctions and even behavioural and structural remedies in the case of systemic non-compliance. However, the DMA explicitly provides that the Commission and national authorities cooperate closely and coordinate their enforcement actions to achieve 'a coherent, effective and complementary enforcement of available legal instruments'.[190] The DMA also provides for the cooperation and coordination between the Commission and NCAs through the European Competition Network (ECN).[191] NCAs have to inform the Commission of their intention to launch an investigation against gatekeepers under EU competition law. Such information may be made available to other NCAs.[192] In addition, where an NCA intends to impose obligations on gatekeepers based on national competition laws, it shall, no later than thirty days before its adoption, share the draft measure with the Commission explaining the reasons for the measure. Such information may be communicated to other NCAs as well.[193] NCAs may—on their own initiative—investigate possible non-compliance with gatekeepers' obligations on their territory, if permitted under national law. However, they cannot impose any sanctions under the DMA; they can only inform the Commission, which may, in turn, open its own investigation and relieve the NCA of its competences.[194]

The DMA also provides for cooperation between the Commission and national courts.[195] In a similar manner (as when they apply EU competition law),[196] national courts shall not give a decision that runs counter to a decision adopted by the Commission under the DMA. In addition, they must also avoid issuing a decision that would conflict with a contemplated Commission decision and may assess whether it is necessary to stay their proceedings to that effect.[197]

Given the DMA's scope and potential interplay with other regulatory measures, Article 40 DMA also provides for the establishment of a High Level Group comprising representatives from the following regulators and networks:

(a) Body of the European Regulators for Electronic Communications,
(b) EDPS and European Data Protection Board,
(c) ECN,
(d) Consumer Protection Cooperation Network, and
(e) European Regulatory Group of Audio-Visual Media Regulators.

[190] DMA (n141), Article 37.
[191] *Ibid*, Article 38.
[192] *Ibid*, Article 38(2).
[193] *Ibid*, Article 38(3).
[194] *Ibid*, Article 38(7).
[195] *Ibid*, Article 39.
[196] Regulation 1/2003 (n20), Article 16.
[197] DMA (n141), Article 39(5).

The High Level Group will meet at least once per year at the Commission's request and will provide advice to the Commission with respect to the DMA enforcement and its consistency with a broad range of regulatory instruments.[198]

V.2.1.2 P2B Regulation

The P2B Regulation is applicable to online intermediation services and online search engines, both of which are defined in a technology neutral manner,[199] and aims to promote fairness and transparency for business users.[200] Online intermediation comprises information society services, aiming to facilitate direct transactions between business users and consumers.[201] They include online market places, app stores, and social media.[202] The rationale behind the introduction of the P2B Regulation rests on the acknowledgement of such services' superior bargaining power,[203] whereas the Regulation also stresses the importance of a '*competitive, fair, and transparent online ecosystem*'.[204]

Amongst the transparency obligations for intermediation service providers is to outline the main ranking parameters to business users in order to improve transparency and help them with the presentation of their respective products and services.[205] Such main parameters include 'any general criteria, processes, specific signals incorporated into algorithms or other adjustment or demotion mechanisms used in connection with the ranking'.[206] Online search engines also bear the same obligation with respect to their ranking parameters.[207] However, the obligation to reveal their ranking parameters does not extend as far as revealing their ranking mechanisms, including algorithms.[208]

The P2B Regulation also covers instances where the online intermediation service providers and the online search engines offer goods and services through their own services in competition with business users.[209] In such instances, they bear an

[198] See, e.g. the proposals of the Body of European Regulators for Electronic Communications (BEREC) to ensure the interplay between the European Electronic Communication Code and the DMA with respect to NIICS. See BEREC, 'BEREC Recommends Clarifying the Scope of the Digital Markets Act in Relation to Number-Independent Interpersonal Communication Services (NI-ICS)', BoR (21) 97 (11 June 2021) <https://www.berec.europa.eu/en/document-categories/berec/berec-press-releases/berec-recommends-clarifying-the-scope-of-the-digital-markets-act-in-relation-to-number-independent-interpersonal-communication-services-ni-ics> (accessed 7 June 2024).

[199] P2B Regulation (n140). For a discussion, see C Busch, 'Platform Regulation beyond DSA and DMA: Which Role for the P2B Regulation?' (2024) 12 Journal of Accounting and Economics 201.

[200] P2B Regulation (n140), Article 1(1).

[201] *Ibid*, Recital 10, Article 2(2).

[202] *Ibid*, Recital 11.

[203] *Ibid*, Recital 2.

[204] *Ibid*, Recital 3.

[205] *Ibid*, Recital 24, Article 5.

[206] *Ibid*, Recital 24.

[207] *Ibid*, Recital 26.

[208] *Ibid*, Recital 27. See also European Commission (EU), 'Guidelines on Ranking Transparency Pursuant to Regulation (EU) 2019/1150 of the European Parliament and of the Council', [2020] OJ C 424/1.

[209] P2B Regulation (n140), Article 7.

obligation to act in a transparent manner and offer an appropriate description and considerations for any differentiated treatment.[210] Such differentiated treatment may raise self-preferencing concerns under competition law and is also addressed under the DMA, if service providers qualify as gatekeepers.

With respect to data, the P2B Regulation highlights the importance of data access and use in the online platform economy and provides that online intermediation service providers should give a clear description of their conditions for data access and use.[211] It further provides for an obligation to inform business users of any sharing of their respective data with third parties.[212] Such an obligation does not extend to end users.

Despite the similarity in the objectives between the DMA and the P2B Regulation, the enforcement approach is different.[213] The DMA attributes sole enforcement responsibility to the Commission, whereas the P2B Regulation relies on actions by private parties, with the possibility of involving public authorities depending on the Member State.[214] Under the P2B Regulation, business users may bring an action for damages against providers of online intermediation services in breach of the P2B Regulation. The P2B Regulation also provides for the right (Article 14) of organizations, associations, and public bodies that have a legitimate interest in representing business users to bring proceedings against providers before national courts for remedies, including injunctions.

The P2B Regulation also attempts to facilitate compliance by requiring providers of online intermediation services to provide for an internal complaints handling system (Article 11) and to identify in their terms and conditions two or more mediators with which they are willing to engage to attempt to reach an agreement on the settlement, out of court, of any disputes between the provider and the business user arising in relation to the provision of the online intermediation services concerned (Article 12). It also provides that the Commission shall encourage the drawing up of codes of conduct by providers of online intermediation services and by organizations and associations representing the interests of business users of platforms (Article 17).[215]

[210] *Ibid*, Recitals 30–31.

[211] *Ibid*, Recital 33.

[212] *Ibid*, Recital 34, Article 9.

[213] See also M Ioannidou, 'Unpacking Multi-Level Elements in Digital Markets: Informing Effective Enforcement and Remedial Design in EU Competition Law' in CM Colombo, K Wright, and M Eliantonio (eds), *The Changing Governance of EU Competition Law: A Constitutional Challenge?* (Hart, 2024).

[214] According to the P2B Regulation (n140), Article 15 (Enforcement), '[e]ach Member State shall ensure adequate and effective enforcement of this Regulation'. For example, competition authorities may be given competence to ensure compliance with the rules. See, e.g. Authority for Consumers and Markets (ACM), 'ACM Launches Market Study into the Platform-to-Business Regulation' (22 October 2021) <https://www.acm.nl/en/publications/acm-launches-market-study-platform-business-regulation> (accessed 7 June 2024).

[215] C Caufmann, 'New EU Rules on Business-to-Consumer and Platform-to-Business Relationships' (2019) 26 Maastricht Journal of European and Comparative Law 469.

V.2.2 Member States: The Example of Germany

Apart from regulatory initiatives at EU level, Member States have also been contemplating legislative changes in order to better regulate competition in the digital economy. In this vein, several national competition laws have been amended or are in the process of being amended (in Belgium, Bulgaria, Austria, Romania, Lithuania, Iceland, Germany, and Greece).[216] Naturally, this proliferation of rules at both EU and national level may risk the fragmentation of the EU-legal framework and calls for better coordination mechanisms.[217] In this section, we briefly present the recent amendments in German competition law under its 10th and 11th amendments. The aim is not to present these changes in detail but to thread out some key provisions that will also be discussed in the case law analysis in Chapter 5. Germany has been selected as a key jurisdiction because it not only influences regulatory developments in the EU but has also developed a strong enforcement record against potentially harmful practices by powerful platforms in the digital economy.[218]

The 10th amendment to the German Competition Law (the Act against Restraints of Competition, 10th ARC amendment) took effect on 19 January 2021. The amendment targeted structural competition law problems in a bid to prevent market tipping and leveraging into adjacent markets.[219] Under section 19(a), the German NCA can designate undertakings with 'paramount significance for competition across markets' according to a list of prescribed factors. At the time of writing, the German NCA has already designated Google, Apple, Facebook, Amazon, and Microsoft (GAFAM) as having paramount significance in terms of competition across markets and has a pending investigation against Microsoft.[220] When an undertaking is found to have paramount significance for competition across markets, it should not engage in certain conducts according to section 19a(2). Prohibited conducts include self-preferencing, leveraging (particularly by means of data), envelopment, market tipping, and constraining data

[216] European Commission (EU), 'Summary of the Contributions of the National Competition Authorities to the Impact Assessment of the New Competition Tool' (2020), 11 <www.ec.europa.eu/competition/consultations/2020_new_comp_tool/summary_contributions_NCAs_responses.pdf> (accessed 7 June 2024).

[217] European Commission (EU), 'Impact Assessment Report Accompanying the Proposal for a Digital Markets Act', SWD(2020) 363 final (Staff working document, 2020), 108 ff. For a discussion of this fragmentation risk, see Ioannidou, 'Unpacking Multi-Level Elements in Digital Markets' (n215).

[218] On these cases, see Chapter 5, section III.

[219] T Weck, 'The New Abuse Rules in the German Competition Act—What's in It for the EU?' (*Competition Policy International*, 14 April 2020) <www.competitionpolicyinternational.com/the-new-abuse-rules-in-the-german-competition-act-whats-in-it-for-the-eu> (accessed 7 June 2024); Act against Restraints of Competition in the version published on 26 June 2013: Bundesgesetzblatt I (Federal Law Gazette), 1750, 3245, as last amended by Article 1 of the Act of 18 January 2021 (Federal Law Gazette I, 2) (ARC).

[220] Bundeskartellamt, 'Apple Also Subject to Provisions for Large Digital Companies under Section 19a GWB' (5 April 2023); Bundeskartellamt, 'Examination of Microsoft's Significance for Competition across Markets' (28 March 2023).

portability.[221] Section 19a(2) prohibits such conduct without the need for the competition authority to establish an exclusionary effect. However, the undertaking may put forward an objective justification for its conduct.

Almost two-and-a-half years later, on 4 July 2023, the German Parliament adopted the 11th ARC amendment.[222] Amongst the changes introduced was providing the German NCA with the power to adopt behavioural and structural remedies, including the break-up of an undertaking as an ultima ratio, following a sector inquiry when there is 'substantial and durable disruption to competition'.[223] This process is akin to market investigations in the United Kingdom.[224] Moreover, the 11th amendment lowered the requirements for the disgorgement of financial gains and introduced a contestable assumption for their calculation. Before the adoption of the DMA, the EU Commission was also contemplating the adoption of a New Competition Tool (NCT), introducing a harmonized market investigation framework to tackle structural market problems, though such a proposal was not included in the DMA in the end. In addition to improving disgorgement,[225] the 11th amendment explicitly bestows the power to the German NCA to investigate alleged DMA non-compliance,[226] as well as the power for private parties to claim damages following an infringement of the relevant DMA obligations (Articles 5–7 DMA).[227]

V.3 Regulatory Responses: China

Ever since the Western idea of considering non-price factors (e.g. quality, consumer choice, privacy, and data protection) in anti-monopoly analysis was introduced into China's legal academia,[228] there has been a growing number of legal

[221] According to the President of the Bundeskartellamt, the ARC (n219) is broader than the DMA since it provides only some examples yet leaves space for identifying new anticompetitive conduct. See J Espinoza and E Solomon, 'EU Draft Tech Rules Too "Narrow", Says German Competition Head' (*Financial Times*, 14 July 2021) <www.ft.com/content/6cff1987-9263-4bc6-8d8d-6426ef303325> (accessed 7 June 2024).

[222] N Ina Pauer, 'The 11th Amendment of the German Act against Restraints of Competition: A "New Competition Tool", Facilitated Disgorgement and the DMA's Enforcement' (2023) Journal of European Competition Law & Practice 1. Discussing the proposed amendments, see also F Wagner-von Papp, 'The 11th Amendment to the ARC and Germany's New Competition Tool' (2023) D'Kart Journal, 22–33 <https://www.d-kart.de/en/blog/2023/05/03/the-11th-amendment-to-the-arc-and-germanys-new-competition-tool> (accessed 7 June 2024).

[223] *Ibid*; see section 32f(3) ARC (n222).

[224] On the UK regime, see R Whish, 'New Competition Tool: Legal Comparative Study of Existing Competition Tools Aimed at Addressing Structural Competition Problems with a Particular Focus on the UK's Market Investigation Tool' (Expert Study) (2020) <https://ec.europa.eu/competition/consultations/2020_new_comp_tool/kd0420573enn.pdf> (accessed 2 December 2022).

[225] See section 34 ARC (n219). See also Ina Pauer (n222).

[226] See section 32gARC (n222). See also Ina Pauer (n222). On the Commission–NCA's cooperation under the DMA, see the text to n191 above.

[227] See sections 33, 33b and h ARC (n219). See also Ina Pauer (n222).

[228] W Han and LI Zheng (李正), '反垄断法框架下的数据隐私保护 [Data Privacy Protection under the Framework of Anti-Monopoly Law]' [2017] 中国物价 [China's Prices] 7.

scholars advocating for the importation of such factors in the enforcement of anti-monopoly law in China,[229] although the weight of the aforesaid elements in such an analysis is yet to be determined. In practice, the legislation and regulation have already explored several channels to promote factors far beyond consumer (price) welfare. We herein identify three channels. First, competition laws and regulations have accorded the preservation of innovation with unprecedented weight so as to ensure that consumers can benefit from various dimensions in constantly innovative digital markets. Second, a 'dual-track' procedural approach of enforcement has been well developed by China's regulatory agencies so as to accommodate the disruptive nature of rising digital platforms in a prudent manner. Third, special laws and regulations were introduced to complement competition law enforcement. Below, we briefly outline the role of innovation in competition law enforcement, as well as the 'dual-track' enforcement approach, before discussing data protection legislation, which can be complementary to competition law enforcement in the digital economy.

V.3.1 Towards a More Prominent Role of Innovation

Ever since the Guidelines and the new AML expressly recognized innovation as an essential aim of anti-monopoly law in China, attempts have been made by both theorists and regulatory agencies to clarify the notion of innovation when considering the effects of various types of anti-competitive conduct. Some scholars believe that the core of innovation is new products, new technologies, and new business models, and innovations should be accurately identified from qualitative and quantitative dimensions to alleviate the dilemma in the application of the innovation exemption system.[230] From the perspectives of law and economics, how AML shall promote the innovation of digital platforms is discussed, which includes the introduction of the principle of modesty, the application of different regulatory intensities based on the industry's stage in the life cycle, the adoption of differentiated regulations for leading platforms and small and micro-platforms, and the balancing of social welfare losses through the redistribution of confiscated revenues.[231]

Innovation can be grounds for both exempting anticompetitive conducts from or holding them for legal liabilities. The AML exempts conduct that is conducive to

[229] Y Li, '从价格到质量：数字经济时代反垄断法中消费者福利标准内涵的演变 [From Price to Quality: The Evolution of Standard Connotations of Consumer Welfare in Antitrust Law in the Era of Digital Economy]' [2022] 2 西北民族大学学报 哲学社会科学版 [Journal of Northwest Minzu University (Philosophy and Social Sciences)] 79.

[230] L Wang, '创新目标在《反垄断法》上的定位与实现—兼评《反垄断法（修正草案）》第1条 [Positioning and Realization of Innovation Objectives in the Anti-Monopoly Law—Comment on Article 1 of the Anti-Monopoly Law (Draft Amendment)]' [2022] 1 Journal of China University of Political Science and Law 180.

[231] Z Wu, '反垄断法促进数字平台创新的法经济学分析 [Legal and Economic Analysis of Anti-Monopoly Law Promoting Digital Platform Innovation]' [2023] 37 Contemporary Law Review 44.

innovation and promotes competition more than eliminating or limiting competition. Article 15(1) exempts anticompetitive agreements that increase productivity, distributional efficiency, and innovation efficiency where these gains are shared by consumers.[232] In terms of the exclusion and restriction of competition by the abuse of market dominance, operators are given the defence of 'just cause' under Article 17(1), which is further explained as 'the impact on the business development, future investment and innovation of operators'.[233] Likewise, a merging party may claim an efficiency defence under Articles 27 and 28 for the concentration of undertakings that promotes innovation, considering 'the impact on the impetus of technological innovation, the investment and utilization of technological research and development, and the integration of technological resources'.[234]

Anticompetitive conduct that is destructive to innovation is certainly more of a concern for regulatory agencies in law enforcement in the digital economy.[235] For instance, in the Administrative Sanction Decision for the *Alibaba* case, the SAMR pointed out that the Alibaba Group has impeded innovation and damaged both the competitive order and consumers' interest by requiring its merchants to sell exclusively on its platform ('either–or choice'). By abusing its dominant position, Alibaba 'hinders the free flow of production factors among online retailing platforms, obstructs the matching of supply and demand, and therefore limits the innovative development of the platform economy'.[236] Moreover, it 'impedes the innovation of business model' and consequently 'harms the actual and expected interests of consumers'.[237] Meituan's similar misconduct of imposing 'either–or choice' on vendors has also been regarded by the SAMR as 'impeding the innovative development of the platform economy, weakening the motivation of competitors to reap competitive advantage through the innovation in technology and business model, and reducing consumers' long-term welfare'.[238]

V.3.2 'Dual-Track' Enforcement Approach

Apart from prioritizing the assessment of innovation when considering suspected anticompetitive conduct so as to better preserve the multiple aims of competition law, China's regulatory agencies have, in their procedure, adopted a 'dual-track' approach to enforce the body of anti-monopoly law in China so as to prudently

232 Wang (n230).

233 Provisions on Prohibiting Abuse of Dominant Market Position (2023), Article 22.

234 Provisions on Examination of Concentration of Undertakings (2023), Article 34.

235 Wang (n230).

236 State Administration for Market Regulation (SAMR), '国家市场监督管理总局行政处罚决定书（国市监处〔2021〕28号）[SAMR Administrative Prohibition Decision [2021] No 28]' (10 April 2021) <https://www.samr.gov.cn/xw/zj/art/2023/art_4966dda92ab34c398615f5878c10c8f1.html> (accessed 7 November 2022).

237 *Ibid.*

238 SAMR, '国家市场监督管理总局行政处罚决定书（国市监处罚〔2021〕74号） [SAMR Administrative Prohibition Decision [2021] No 74]' (8 October 2021) <https://www.samr.gov.cn/xw/zj/art/2023/art_31910760066b4f69aa119a20dee250ad.html> (accessed 10 April 2024).

tackle the complexity of the nature of monopolistic behaviours and of the multitude of the aims of competition law in digital markets. The administrative interview has, to some extent, filled in this gap and constituted a dual-track regulatory system, which involves a hard enforcement mechanism plus a soft administrative intervention.

In addition to adopting strict means of law enforcement to deal with anticompetitive practices, incorporating flexible enforcement techniques, such as administrative interviews, might effectively help increase the administrative effectiveness and ease social tensions.[239] Those soft interventions have been frequently employed by both China's central market regulator (the SAMR) and local regulators. Administrative interviews and guidance stand in line with the contemporary regulatory tendency in changing reactive social governance into a preventive one. Administrative interviewing, if properly conducted, serves to guide market participants to correct suspected illegal conduct in an *ex-ante* manner. By explaining and warning potential violators against the repercussions of a potential breach, it may effectively prevent prospective illegal conduct.[240]

As to their legal nature, administrative interviews are, first of all, an administrative act with independent value. In China's law enforcement practice, interviewing suspected violators is not a mandatory pre-procedure before taking formal administrative measures but can be conducted independently without any subsequent legal consequences or reconciliation measures. Second, it is non-compulsory. In this sense, interviewees are left with room to decide whether or not to comply at their discretion. In most cases, however, non-compliance may lead to negative market evaluation, thus leading to the subsequent initiation of a formal investigation. Third, it is a manner of performing lenient administrative guidance. An administrative interview signals the meaning of regulatory leniency because it mainly transmits the regulator's concern about potential violations but does not require the interviewees to fulfil a specific obligation or assume specific legal liability.[241]

Administrative talk is an administrative and supervisory means commonly employed by other jurisdictions,[242] such as the administrative talk for taxation over tea in Canada and the coffee-drinking system in Hong Kong.[243] In China,

[239] Y Li, Z Huang, X Xia, and L Gao, 'Theoretical Analysis and System Improvement of Administrative Interviews in the Field of Internet Information Supervision' (2022) 4 Scientific Journal of Economics and Management Research 393.

[240] Q Meng,' '江苏漫修律师事务所 [Jiang Su Man Xiu Law Firm], 行政约谈法治化研究 [Study on Legalization of Administrative Talk]' (2015) 6 行政法学研究 Xingzheng Faxue Yanjiu [Administrative Law Review] 99, 99–118.

[241] *Ibid.*

[242] YM Lui, 'Tax Audit System Analysis and Revelation of Canada' (2015) 5 Taxation Research 90.

[243] Y Chen and Y Zhou, 'Analysis of the Effectiveness of the Administrative Talk to Environmental Supervision in China' (2016) 4 Open Journal of Business and Management 716.

administrative interviews have become a common method employed by law enforcement agencies,[244] which are supposed to bring about sound regulatory effects.[245] The system of administrative talk for potential monopoly behaviours provides an alternative means of competition law enforcement in the digital economy on a regular basis and may provide new insights for furthering the protection of a free and fair competition environment. Players in the digital marketplaces are required to act ethically while maintaining their capacity for innovation. Although it is equally important to pay attention to the insufficiency of such a soft enforcement mechanism of competition law, and its potential negative impact on legal certainty, regulatory authorities may obtain better opportunities to prevent potential monopolistic behaviours by conducting administrative talks with digital platform operators.

V.3.3 Data Protection under China's Civil Code and PIPL

In addition to preserving innovation and reforming the enforcement procedure, China has also provided legal tools beyond the area of competition law to protect consumers' non-price interests, especially the introduction of a special section on data protection in China's Civil Code[246] and the Personal Information Protection Law (PIPL).[247] In general, Article 1034 of the Civil Code builds up the statutory foundation for personal information protection by stipulating that '[t]he personal information of natural persons is protected by law'.[248] In addition, Article 1035 provides basic principles in processing personal information, namely the principles of lawfulness, justification, and necessity.[249] Article 1038 further establishes the framework of information processors' responsibilities, which fully embodies the respect for the protection of personality and human rights in China's legal system.[250]

[244] *Ibid.*

[245] *Ibid*, 717.

[246] L Wang and B Xiong, 'Personality Rights in China's New Civil Code: A Response to Increasing Awareness of Rights in an Era of Evolving Technology' (2021) 47(6) Modern China 703.

[247] P Cai and L Chen, 'Demystifying Data Law in China: A Unified Regime of Tomorrow' (2022) 12(2) International Data Privacy Law 75.

[248] Civil Code of the People's Republic of China, Article 1034.

[249] *Ibid*, Article 1035.

[250] *Ibid*, Article 1038 provides that

> [a]n information processor shall not disclose or tamper with any personal information collected or stored thereby; and without consent of a natural person, no personal information shall be illegally provided to any other person, excluding the information through which the specific individual cannot be identified after processing and which cannot be restored. An information processor shall take technical measures and other necessary measures to ensure the security of the personal information collected and stored thereby and to prevent information leakage, tampering, and loss; and for any personal information leakage, tampering, or loss that occurs or is likely to occur, remedy measures shall be taken in a timely manner, the natural person shall be notified according to the provisions, and it shall be reported to the competent department.

Following the basic rules prescribed in the Civil Code, Articles 5–9 of the PIPL reconfirm the principles in handling personal information, namely the principles of lawfulness, legitimacy, necessity, and good faith;[251] of limited and minimized collection;[252] of openness and transparency;[253] of quality maintenance;[254] and of responsibility.[255] As for specific rules promoting law enforcement, the 'notice–consent' rule[256] and the rule concerning the means of automated decision making,[257] in particular, carry much weight in the digital markets.

On 16 August 2023, the National Information Security Standardization Technical Committee released the Safety Requirements for Automated Decision-Making of Information Security Technology Based on Personal Information (Draft for Public Opinion, 'Requirements for Automated Decision-Making'), which clearly set out the safety protection requirements of data processing involved in automated decision making by personal information processors, and meanwhile offered guidance on how to fully protect users' rights in the practical application of automated decision making. Article 8 serves as a specific security requirement on algorithms in automated decision making, including general requirements; algorithmic impact assessment; technical principles, logical principles, human intervention requirements, training, and test data requirements; technical documentation requirements; and operational requirements of algorithmic security.[258] The Requirements for Automated Decision-Making is, in its nature, a legal document aiming to enforce the PIPL, especially its Article 24 on automated decision making based on personal information,[259] and not the AML.

In spite of China's adoption of such special laws and regulations to protect privacy and personal information, some Chinese scholars believe that competition

[251] Personal Information Protection Law (PIPL), Article 5.
[252] *Ibid*, Article 6.
[253] *Ibid*, Article 7.
[254] *Ibid*, Article 8.
[255] *Ibid*, Article 8.
[256] *Ibid*, Article 13.
[257] *Ibid*, Article 24.
[258] National Information Security Standardization Technical Committee, 'Safety Requirements for Automated Decision-Making of Information Security Technology Based on Personal Information (Draft for Public Opinion)' (16 August 2023) <https://www.tc260.org.cn/front/bzzqyjDetail.html?id=20230818163540&norm_id=20221102151633&recode_id=52619> (accessed 7 June 2024).
[259] PIPL, Article 24 provides that

> [p]ersonal information processors using personal information for automated decision making shall ensure the transparency of the decision making and the fairness and impartiality of the results, and may not apply unreasonable differential treatment to individuals in terms of transaction prices and other transaction conditions. Information push and commercial marketing to individuals based on automated decision making shall be simultaneously accompanied by options not specific to their personal characteristics or with convenient means for individuals to refuse. Where a decision that may have a significant impact on an individual's rights and interests is made through automated decision making, the individual shall have the right to request clarification from the personal information processor and the right to refuse the processor for making the decision only through automated decision making.

law certainly has a role to play in filling the gap of these special laws and regulations.[260] After all, the PIPL was intended to solve the problems from an individual perspective, rather than to address macroscopic problems arising from the insufficiency of market competition. Hence, considering the harm to privacy and personal information caused by the anticompetitive acts, competition law enforcement can protect such non-price welfare more effectively. Such wider approach to competition law enforcement is also in line with the legislative purpose of China's AML.[261]

Although there is no formal case in which anti-monopoly law has been directly applied to protect privacy and personal information,[262] other non-price factors, such as consumers' freedom of choice, have become a vital consideration during the SAMR's decisions on a good number of cases like the anticompetitive 'either–or choices' requirement made by the Alibaba Group and the administrative limitations on bike-sharing platforms to provide such services in some local cities. In its penalty decision,[263] the SAMR clearly expressed that the availability of free choice for consumers is an important factor in identifying monopolistic behaviours. Such a factor is manifestly important in at least two aspects: first, in determining a dominant market position, the concentration of the relevant market is taken into account, which is based on the number of market operators. That is to say, the decreasing number of market players will undoubtedly circumscribe consumers' freedom of choice, which indirectly exacerbates the negative impact on consumer choice.[264] Second, the infringement on consumers' freedom of choice by the anticompetitive conduct is considered as an independent factor in determining the material harm to market competition. The compulsory 'either–or choices' requirement restricts consumers' right to make free choices. Likewise, in cases where the local regulatory agencies in charge of urban transportation have unjustifiably excluded platforms from providing bike-sharing services, the agencies enforcing anti-monopoly law have even repeatedly stressed that such exclusions apparently reduce consumers' choice of bike-sharing services.

Nevertheless, privacy and personal information protection has not become a key issue in anticompetitive analysis. There is indeed a case in which the largest Chinese academic database, the China National Knowledge Infrastructure (CNKI) was accused of both abusing its market dominance and collecting users' personal information in the absence of necessity and consent. The two illegal conducts were addressed, however, on separate statutory grounds in two different

[260] As to the limits of China's data protection law, see C You, 'Half a Loaf Is Better than None: The New Data Protection Regime for China's Platform Economy' (2022) 45 Computer Law & Security Review 16.

[261] Ming and Zhang (n78).

[262] *Ibid.*

[263] SAMR, '国家市场监督管理总局行政处罚决定书（国市监处〔2021〕28号） [SAMR Administrative Prohibition Decision [2021] No 28]' (n236).

[264] Ming and Zhang (n78).

cases. The CNKI was ordered to stop its illegal acts, and was fined ¥50 million,[265] on the ground of the Cybersecurity Law of the People's Republic of China (PRC), Personal Information Protection Law of the PRC and Administrative Penalties Law of the PRC, rather than competition law. As discussed in Chapter 9, cases may arise before the regulatory agency in which the merger of two digital platforms may result in massive aggregation of personal information. The primary concern of the regulatory agency in such cases would be whether such aggregation would equip the new platform with excessive competitive advantage and reduce the choice of consumers and whether it would be necessary to prohibit personal information aggregation when approving the merger, instead of remedying various infringements to individuals' rights to personal information.

Despite the wide legislative purposes proclaimed by China's competition laws and regulations, China has developed a separate system of law and enforcement institutions for the protection of privacy and personal information, which materially affects the interplay between competition law and other areas of law. The enforcement of competition law can indeed play a role in promoting such an agenda but merely in the context where the detriments to privacy and personal information have anticompetitive effects. The measures tackling such detriments are also limited to the restoration of free competition instead of providing remedies to individual consumers.

VI. Conclusion

The revived debate on the role of competition law enforcement in promoting fairness needs to be disentangled from the underlying political aspirations and tap into the actual potential of competition law to further public interest considerations within the current legal framework. Incidentally, competition law can promote fairness, trust, and democracy; however, one needs to distinguish such welcome by-products from the core function of competition law, namely to preserve competitive market structures. However, competition should not be perceived strictly as focusing on price effects but, rather, should embrace a wider set of factors, such as quality, choice, and innovation. At the same time, competition rules need to be complemented by regulatory instruments in order to address the structural issue of entrenched power in the digital economy. The recent adoption of additional regulatory tools points in that direction.

[265] Office of Central Cyberspace Affairs Commission, 'Administrative Punishment to CNKI' (6 September 2023) <http://www.cac.gov.cn/2023-09/06/c_1695654024248502.htm> (accessed 7 June 2024).

PART B
COMPETITION LAW AND DIGITAL MARKETS IN THE EU

4
Anticompetitive Agreements

I. Introduction

In light of the challenges posed by the digital economy, this chapter explores the impact that the various key attributes of the digital economy (i.e. data and algorithms) and business models (i.e. platformization of the economy) have on the application of Article 101 of the Treaty on the Functioning of the European Union (TFEU) to potential anticompetitive agreements. The focus is on selected contentious issues. In particular, Chapter 4 discusses the following issues. The first is the notion of undertaking in the platform economy. Questions addressed here include whether platforms act as genuine agents of suppliers, whether platform suppliers (e.g. Uber drivers) qualify as independent undertakings, and whether we need to rethink the approach to exemption criteria towards collective bargaining agreements in the gig economy. Second, it discusses algorithm-driven collusive *horizontal agreements*. Here, we examine the potential of algorithms to exacerbate collusion and present the various scenarios of algorithmic collusion as well as the related regulatory responses. Third, we investigate potential pro-competitive horizontal agreements (such as data-pooling agreements). We discuss the application of EU competition law to data-pooling agreements, given their potential to promote innovative products and services, without losing sight of the 'dark side' of possible anticompetitive information exchange. Finally, the chapter discusses challenges with respect to the assessment of vertical agreements in the digital economy.

II. Undertakings in the Digital Economy

II.1 Introduction

In the digital economy, we observe an unprecedented and wide use of platform business models.[1] The role of the major players as an intermediary between suppliers and customers has raised interesting questions with respect to their role as independent undertakings or agents. It has also raised questions with respect to the legal classification of suppliers on some platforms, such as Uber, as self-employed

[1] See Chapter 2, section III.

Competition Law and Policy in Digital Markets. Maria Ioannidou and Bingwan Xiong, Oxford University Press.
 DOI: 10.1093/9780191925955.003.0004

or employees. These questions bear legal significance since if platforms are classified as agents of the suppliers, it follows that any agreement between them cannot be scrutinized under Article 101 TFEU. In this scenario, the platform and the suppliers are perceived to form a single economic entity. Under the single economic entity doctrine, only agreements between independent undertakings fall under Article 101 TFEU.[2] Equally, if suppliers are seen as platform employees, again, Article 101 TFEU will not be applicable since they form a single economic unit with them and do not constitute independent undertakings.[3]

II.2 Platforms as Agents?

An agent is a legal or natural person that acts on behalf of another person, the principal. Agents can negotiate and/or conclude contracts on behalf of the principal. Agents may act in their own name or in the principal's name for the purchase of goods or services by the principal or the sale of goods or services supplied by the principal.[4]

In circumstances where the agent does not act as an independent economic operator and bears no significant financial or commercial risks with respect to the contracts negotiated and/or concluded on behalf of the principal, Article 101 TFEU does not apply.[5] Such risks are distinguished as contract-specific risks, risks with respect to market-specific investments, and risks with respect to other activities in the same product market.[6] However, as the Commission notes, since this is an exception to the application of Article 101 TFEU, it should be interpreted in a narrow manner,[7] and in fact, this is how it has been interpreted with respect to the

[2] Case C-73/95 P *Viho v Commission* [1996] ECR I-5457, para 14. On the single economic entity doctrine, see O Odudu and D Bailey, 'The Single Economic Entity Doctrine in EU Competition Law' (2014) 51 Common Market Law Review 1721.

[3] Joined Cases 40–48, 50, 54–56, 111, 113, and 114/73, *Coöperatieve Vereniging Suiker Unie v Commission*, ECLI:EU:C:1975:174, para 539.

[4] European Commission (EU), 'Guidelines on Vertical Restraints (Communication)', [2022] OJ C 248/1 (Vertical Restraints Guidelines, VRG), para 29. Case C-266/93, *Bundeskartellamt v. Volkswagen AG and VAG Leasing GmbH*, [1995] I-ECR 3477, para 19. Case C-217/05, *Confederación Española de Empresarios de Estaciones de Servicio v. Compañía Española de Petróleos SA*, [2006] ECR I-11987 and Case C-279/06, *CEPSA Estaciones de Servicio SA v. LV Tobar e Hijos SL*, [2008] ECR I-6681. See, for example, I Lianos, "Commercial Agency Agreements, Vertical Restraints, and the Limits of Article 81(1) EC: Between Hierarchies and Networks" (2007) 3 (4) Journal of Competition Law and Economics 625.

[5] VRG (n4), para 30. On the relevant case law Joined Cases 40–48, 50, 54–56, 111, 113 & 114/73, *Suiker Unie v Commission*, [1975] ECR 1663; Case C-266/93 *Bundeskartellamt v Volkswagen AG and VAG Leasing GmbH*, [1995] I-ECR 3477; Case T-56/99 *Marlines v Commission*, [2003] ECR II-5225; Case T-325/01 *Daimler Chrysler v Commission*, [2005] ECR II-3319; Case C-217/05, *Confederación Española de Empresarios de Estaciones de Servicio v Compañía Española de Petróleos SA*, [2006] ECR I-11987 and Case C-279/06 *CEPSA Estaciones de Servicio SA v. LV Tobar e Hijos SL*, [2008] ECR I-6681.

[6] VRG (n4), para 31.

[7] *Ibid*, para 30.

role of platforms. Furthermore, if the agent acts on behalf of a large number of principals, then such an agreement will most likely be caught by Article 101 TFEU.[8]

The Commission seems to have placed emphasis on the latter factor in its revised Guidelines on Vertical Restraints (VRG), where the role of platforms as agents has been clarified and such agreements between platforms and suppliers fall within the scope of Article 101 TFEU. Such clarification is important, since opposing approaches have been expressed in the literature.[9] According to the Commission, platforms generally act as independent economic operators and do not form part of the undertakings for which they provide services, the more so since they act for a very large number of suppliers. Another factor preventing such agreements from being categorized as an agency agreement, thereby falling outside Article 101 TFEU, is the significant power imbalance between the contracting parties, which allows the platform to dictate the conditions for the supply of goods and services on the platform. Finally, platforms typically undertake significant market-specific investments, for example software, advertising, and after-sales services.[10]

II.3 Platform Suppliers as Employees?

The widespread emergence of platforms has challenged labour relations. The related question here is whether platform suppliers are akin to platform employees or whether they qualify as self-employed. This question bears legal significance, since if the former is the case, EU competition law is not applicable. On the contrary, if they are viewed as self-employed, attempts to organize collectively against powerful platforms may be assessed as an anticompetitive agreement. Given the power imbalance between platforms and platform suppliers, it has been suggested that the promotion of collective bargaining between platform suppliers against powerful platforms may counteract the negative effects of such platform power.[11]

The Uber business model can serve as an illustrative case study here. In *Uber Spain*, the Court of Justice of the European Union (CJEU) has held that Uber is a transport service provider and not an information society service provider.[12] An information

[8] *Ibid*, with reference to Case 311/85 ASBL *Vereniging van Vlaamse Reisbureaus contre ASBL Sociale Dienst van de Plaatselijke en Gewestelijke Overheidsdiensten*, EU:C:1987:418, para 20.

[9] P Akman, 'Online Platforms, Agency and Competition Law: Mind the Gap' (2019) 43 Fordham International Law Journal 209.

[10] VRG (n4), para 46.

[11] Brazil, Russia, India, China, and South Africa (BRICS), 'Digital Era Competition: A BRICS View' (BRICS Report, 2019), 384. See also D Melamed and S Salop, 'An Antitrust Exemption for Workers: And Why Worker Bargaining Power Benefits Consumers, Too', Working Paper Series No 579 (2023) < https://papers.ssrn.com/sol3/papers.cfm?abstract_id=433677> (accessed 8 June 2024).

[12] Case C-434/15 *Asociación Profesional Élite Taxi v Uber Systems Spain SL* (*Uber Spain*), ECLI:EU:C:2017:981, para 40. Such an approach was confirmed in *Uber France* by the General Court. See Case C-320/16 *Uber France SAS*, ECLI:EU:C:2018:221, paras 19–21, 24.

society service is 'any service normally provided for remuneration, at a distance, by electronic means and at the individual request of a recipient of services'.[13] The decisive factor for the classification of Uber as a transport service was the fact that the CJEU viewed the intermediation service as an integral part of an overall service whose main component is a transport service, a service which comes under a different legal classification.[14] Based on this finding, for the classification of intermediation platforms providing an overall service, the decisive question now becomes which is the main component of the service, which may lead to arbitrary and inconsistent results.

Contrary to *Uber Spain*, in *Airbnb Ireland*, the CJEU concluded that Airbnb is an information society service, while also providing a number of ancillary services to its core intermediation service.[15] Thus, in *Airbnb Ireland*, contrary to the intervener's arguments, the main component of the overall service provided was not accommodation, thereby leading to the classification of Airbnb as an accommodation service provider.[16] The CJEU distinguished this case from the earlier *Uber Spain*, since, in this case, the link between accommodation and information society services did not justify the classification of Airbnb as an accommodation service and not an information service provider.[17] This is so given Airbnb's compilation of offers through a harmonized format and the provision of search and comparison, which constitutes a service that is not merely ancillary to another service (here, accommodation), which comes under a different legal classification.[18] The CJEU also took into account that Airbnb does not interfere with setting accommodation prices by hosts.[19] Most importantly, though, Airbnb does not exercise the same level of control as Uber does over its drivers.[20]

The UK Supreme Court, in a unanimous ruling, held that Uber drivers should not be treated as self-employed, independent contractors. They should, instead, be treated as workers[21] and are entitled to a number of benefits, including a minimum wage, pensions, and paid holidays.[22] The decisive element here, as in the

[13] Directive (EU) 2015/1535 of the European Parliament and of the Council of 9 September 2015 laying down a procedure for the provision of information in the field of technical regulations and of rules on Information Society services, [2015] OJ L 241/1 (Codification), Article 1(1)(b). See Directive 2000/31, Article 2(a) referring to Directive 98/34/EC (now repealed).

[14] *Uber Spain* (n12), para 40.

[15] Case C-390/18 *Airbnb Ireland*, ECLI:EU:C:2019:1112, paras 49, 69.

[16] *Ibid*, para 51.

[17] *Ibid*, para 52.

[18] *Ibid*, para 54.

[19] *Ibid*, para 56.

[20] *Ibid*, paras 67–68.

[21] For the definition of workers see the Employment Rights Act 1996, section 230(3). The term 'worker' comprises those employed under a contract of employment as well as some self-employed.

[22] *Uber BV and Others (Appellants) v Aslam and Others (Respondents)* [2021] UKSC 5. Contrary to this case, the Supreme Court held that Deliveroo riders do not qualify as workers. See *Independent Workers Union of Great Britain v Central Arbitration Committee and Another* [2023] UKSC 43. The treatment of Uber drivers as employees or independent contractors has led to inconsistent judgments. For example, in cases against Uber in California and Florida, they were considered as workers, whereas in cases in Georgia, Pennsylvania, and Texas, they were considered independent contractors. See J

CJEU case law, is the element of control that Uber exercises over its drivers. Such a legal precedent seems to be in line with the EU approach to the concept of 'worker', which views that '[t]he essential feature of an employment relationship [. . .] is that for a certain period of time a person performs services for and under the direction of another person in return for which he receives remuneration'.[23] In fact, AG Szpunar in *Uber Spain* appeared to treat Uber drivers as false self-employed when stating that

> [w]hile this control is not exercised in the context of a traditional employer–employee relationship, one should not be fooled by appearances. Indirect control such as that exercised by Uber, based on financial incentives and decentralised passenger-led ratings, with a scale effect, makes it possible to manage in a way that is just as—if not more—effective than management based on formal orders given by an employer to his employees and direct control over the carrying out of such orders.[24]

In *Albany*, the CJEU exempted collective labour agreements from the scope of competition law since their respective social policy objectives would be undermined if management and labour were caught by competition law.[25] In *FNV Kunsten*, by relying on *Albany*, the court distinguished between self-employed and 'false self-employed', with the latter being in a comparable situation to employees.[26] The above approach has now been incorporated in the Commission 'Guidelines on the Application of EU Competition Law to Collective Agreements Regarding the Working Conditions of Solo Self-Employed Persons'.[27] The Guidelines clarify, first, that collective agreements by solo self-employed persons whose situation

Nowag, 'When Sharing Platforms Fix Sellers' Prices' (2018) 6 Journal of Accounting and Economics 382, 389. For a comparative study, see C Hiessl, 'Case Law on the Classification of Platform Workers: Cross-European Comparative Analysis and Tentative Conclusions' (2021) 42 Comparative Labour Law & Policy Journal 465.

[23] Case 66/85 *Lawrie-Blum v Land Baden-Wurttemberg* [1986] ECR 2121, para 17. See also Case C-179/90 *Merci Convenzionali Porto di Genova SpA*, ECLI:EU:C:1991:464, para 13; Case C-22/98 *Jean Claude Becu*, ECLI:EU:C:1999:419, para 26. See P Nihoul, 'Do Workers Constitute Undertakings for the Purpose of the Competition Rules?' (2000) 25 European Law Review 408.

[24] Case C-434/15 *Asociacio 'n Profesional Elite Taxi*, EU:C:2017:364, Opinion AG Szpunar, para 52.

[25] Case C-67/96 *Albany* [1999] ECR I-5751, paras 59–60. On this case, see P Camesasca and R van den Bergh, 'Irreconcilable Principles? The Court of Justice Exempts Collective Labour Agreements from the Wrath of Antitrust' (2000) 25 European Law Review 492.

[26] Case C-413/13 *FNV Kunsten Informatie en Media v Netherlands*, ECLI:EU:C:2014:2411, paras 30–32. In *VM Remonts*, the CJEU held that a service provider, even if it presents itself as independent, may act under the direction or control of the undertaking that uses its services. Such notional independence may result in attributing liability to the latter undertaking for the possible anticompetitive conduct of the service provider. See Case C-542/14 *SIA 'VM Remonts'*, ECLI:EU:C:2016:578, para 27.

[27] European Commission (EU), 'Guidelines on the Application of Union Competition Law to Collective Agreements Regarding the Working Conditions of Solo Self-Employed Persons', [2022] OJ C 374/2.

is comparable to that of workers fall outside the scope of Article 101 TFEU; and second, in terms of its enforcement priorities, that the Commission will not intervene in instances of collective agreements of solo self-employed persons that possess unequal bargaining power vis-à-vis their counterparty or parties.[28] The Guidelines carve out three categories of people who are false self-employed whose situation resembles that of workers. First, economically dependent solo self-employed persons comprise persons that earn at least 50 per cent of their income from one counterparty. Given this situation of dependency, they cannot determine their market conduct independently, are more likely to receive instructions, and are integrated with their counterparty, thus forming a single economic entity.[29] The second category comprises the solo self-employed that work 'side by side' with workers. Similar to the first category, they are also likely to receive instructions and do not enjoy independence in delivering the respective service. In addition, they do not undertake commercial risks.[30] The third category consists of those who are solo self-employed that work through digital labour platforms,[31] where the persons that provide their services on the platform (e.g. transportation services) may be in a dependency relationship, especially for reaching customers, and cannot influence their working conditions.[32]

III. Algorithmic Collusion

III.1 Introduction

Online commerce relies, to a large extent, on the use of pricing algorithms.[33] Algorithms allow firms to better optimize their business strategies, including

[28] *Ibid*, para 9.
[29] *Ibid*, paras 23–24.
[30] *Ibid*, para 26.
[31] A digital labour platform is defined as

> any natural or legal person providing a commercial service which meets all of the following requirements: (i) it is provided, at least in part, at a distance through electronic means, such as a website or a mobile application; (ii) it is provided at the request of a recipient of the service; and (iii) it involves, as a necessary and essential component, the organisation of work performed by individuals, irrespective of whether that work is performed online or in a certain location.

See *ibid*, para 2(d).
[32] *Ibid*, para 28.
[33] European Commission (EU), 'Final Report on the E-Commerce Sector Inquiry', SWD(2017) 154 final (2017), para 149 reporting that (already by 2017)

> 53% of the respondent retailers track the online prices of competitors, out of which 67% use automatic software programmes for that purpose. Larger companies have a tendency to tend to track online prices of competitors more than smaller ones. The majority of those retailers that use software to track prices subsequently adjust their own prices to those of their competitors (78%).

improving their pricing and service customization.[34] At the same time, algorithms can be beneficial for consumers by increasing transparency and lowering their search costs. Yet, the widespread use of algorithms also creates potential competition law problems. The risk of algorithmic collusion has been widely discussed by policymakers,[35] competition authorities,[36] and academics alike.[37] While it is theoretically possible to contemplate scenarios where algorithms collude autonomously without any human intervention,[38] and such a risk might be accentuated with the advent of technology, to date it has not materialized, at least in a case pursued by competition authorities.

Notwithstanding the lack of concrete examples of autonomous algorithmic collusion, algorithms present a tool to implement existing collusion between human agents. This section *first* discusses the spectrum of scenarios of collusion involving algorithms, from the more straightforward ones to the still theoretical scenario of algorithmic collusion without human intervention. *Second*, it presents the relevant case law from the EU and selected jurisdictions applying Article 101 TFEU to collusion involving algorithms. Third, it discusses the remaining challenges in the application of Article 101 TFEU, before presenting some proposals for further action in the final section.

III.2 Algorithmic Collusion: Various Scenarios

This section briefly discusses the various scenarios where algorithms can be used as an instrument to monitor, facilitate, or implement collusion. Taking into account human interaction, the scenarios presented range from ones where the algorithms

[34] For the various types of algorithms, see Chapter 2, section II.3.

[35] See, e.g. Organisation for Economic Co-operation and Development (OECD), 'Algorithms and Collusion: Competition Policy in the Digital Age' (2017) <https://www.oecd.org/competition/algorithms-collusion-competition-policy-in-the-digital-age.htm> (accessed 28 August 2023).

[36] See, e.g. Autorité de la Concurrence (AdC) and Bundeskartellamt, 'Algorithms and Competition' (November 2019); Autoridade da Concorrência, 'Digital Ecosystems, Big Data and Algorithms' (Issues paper, July 2019); Competition and Markets Authority (CMA), 'Algorithms: How They Can Reduce Competition and Harm Consumers' (2021); International Competition Network (ICN), 'ICN CWG SG2 Project on "Big Data and Cartels"—the Impact of Digitalization in Cartel Enforcement" (Scoping paper, 28 April 2020).

[37] See, amongst others, A Ezrachi and M Stucke, *Virtual Competition* (Harvard UP, 2016); M Gal, 'Algorithms as Illegal Agreements' (2019) 34 Berkeley Technology Law Journal 67.

[38] Such scenarios are supported by empirical research in a controlled environment. See, e.g. E Calvano, G Calzolari, V Denicolo, and S Pastorello, 'Artificial Intelligence, Algorithmic Pricing and Collusion' (2019) <https://papers.ssrn.com/sol3/papers.cfm?abstract_id=3304991> (accessed 8 June 2024); S Assad, R Clark, D Ershov, and L Xu, 'Algorithmic Pricing and Competition: Empirical Evidence from the German Retail Gasoline Market' Centre for Economic Studies–Institute for Economic Research (CESifo) Working Papers (August 2020); T Klein, 'Autonomous Algorithmic Collusion: Q-Learning under Sequential Pricing' (Tinbergen Institute, November 2021) <https://papers.tinbergen.nl/18056.pdf> (accessed 8 June 2024). See also CMA, 'Pricing Algorithms—Economic Working Paper on the Use of Algorithms to Facilitate Collusion and Personalised Pricing' (2018), paras 6.1 et seq.

merely facilitate pre-existing human interactions to ones where algorithms replace human interaction. In the first two scenarios, algorithms further enhance communication, whereas the last scenario presents an example of tacit collusion facilitated by algorithms.

III.2.1 Existing Human Interaction

In the first category, algorithms may be used to reinforce existing anticompetitive agreements between competitors based on pre-existing direct communications. In such a scenario, which Ezrachi and Stucke label as the 'messenger scenario',[39] algorithms merely facilitate or support existing anticompetitive agreements.[40] In a vertical context, algorithms present a tool for reinforcing fixed or minimum resale price maintenance (RPM), aiding manufacturers to identify possible deviations.[41]

III.2.2 Coordination between Competitors through a Third Party

There are a number of software vendors offering different pricing software programmes that help firms to optimize their pricing policy. Pricing software allows even small firms to resort to dynamic pricing strategies and detect price wars.[42] These programmes come with different degrees of sophistication[43] and offer a hub for various market players to determine their pricing strategy. In this hub-and-spoke scenario,[44] competitors collude through algorithms provided by a third party, and there is no prior direct communication between them. The use of common pricing algorithms allows firms to better predict competitors' market behaviour and reduces strategic uncertainty.

III.2.3 Algorithms Colluding

In this third scenario, different firms use individually different pricing algorithms, which can result in an observed alignment of their behaviour, without any human interaction. Understandably, it is this scenario that raises more challenges for policymakers since they need to decipher whether the observed parallel behaviour can be attributed to some form of coordination or whether it has occurred through self-learning algorithms that have intelligently adapted to each other. Linked to that is whether such algorithmic coordination should be attributed to the undertaking employing such algorithms and under what conditions.

[39] Ezrachi and Stucke, *Virtual Competition* (n37), chapter 5.

[40] AdC and Bundeskartellamt (n36), 27.

[41] See also Autoridade de Concorrencia (n36), 58.

[42] OECD, 'Algorithms and Collusion—Note from Italy', DAF/COMP/WD(2017)18 (2 June 2017), para 5.

[43] Examples of programmes operating on self-learning algorithms include a2i systems (fuel price optimization), Eversight Labs (price optimization for consumer goods companies), and RepricerExpress (price optimization on Amazon). See Klein (n38), 3.

[44] Ezrachi and Stucke, *Virtual Competition* (n37), 250. As an example, see also the RealPage litigation in the United States. See A Ezrachi and M Stucke, 'The Role of Secondary Algorithmic Tacit Collusion in Achieving Market Alignment', Working Paper No CCLP(L)54 (2023), 3–4.

Such a scenario was acknowledged both in the Draft and finally adopted Guidelines on Horizontal Cooperation Agreements, and was distinguished from 'collusion by code'.[45] 'Collusion by code' connotes the situation where competitors deliberately use common behavioural coordination algorithms and falls under the second scenario. This type of collusion is treated as an object restriction. The Revised Horizontal Guidelines (RHG) now clarify that firms employing algorithms cannot escape liability because, arguably, algorithms determined the prices. Algorithms are treated akin to employees or outside consultants under the 'direction or control' of the firm.[46]

Algorithmic collusion under the third scenario (i.e. collusion in the absence of human intervention) feeds into the relevant economic literature on tacit collusion, which has explored many factors affecting the stability of collusion.[47] These factors include the oligopolistic nature of the relevant market, entry barriers, market transparency, and the interaction frequency.[48] As highlighted by competition law scholars, most notably Ezrachi and Stucke, in the future, where the role of human intervention in pricing decisions will be minimized, it is likely that instances of supra-competitive pricing could be attributed to self-learning algorithms interacting with competitors' algorithms and rationally adapting by taking into account different data points.[49]

As the joint study of the French and German competition authorities indicates, to date this scenario has not materialized.[50] This conclusion is also supported by previous research by the OECD, which highlighted that '[i]t is still not clear how machine learning algorithms may actually reach a collusive outcome'.[51] Another potential scenario, which is yet to be tested, is whether algorithms may adopt behaviour similar to explicit rather than tacit collusion. In its submission to the OECD debate, the Commission asked 'whether pricing algorithms could, without

[45] European Commission (EU), 'Public Consultation on the Draft Revised Horizontal Block Exemption Regulations and Horizontal Guidelines' (March 2022) <https://competition-policy.ec.europa.eu/public-consultations/2022-hbers_en> (accessed 29 December 2022) (Draft Guidelines), para 418; European Commission (EU), 'Guidelines on the Applicability of Article 101 of the Treaty on the Functioning of the European Union to Horizontal Co-operation Agreements' (2023) <https://competition-policy.ec.europa.eu/document/fd641c1e-7415-4e60-ac21-7ab3e72045d2_en> (accessed 8 June 2024) (Revised HG, RHG), para 379.

[46] Draft Guidelines (n45); RHG (n45).

[47] M Ivaldi, B Jullien, P Rey, P Seabright, and J Tirole, 'The Economics of Tacit Collusion' (Final Report for DG Competition, March 2003); R Marshall and L Marx, *The Economics of Collusion* (MIT Press, 2012). A final scenario highlighted recently is 'secondary algorithmic tacit collusion', which involves the use of an algorithmic hub-and-spoke arrangement on the primary market coupled with tacit collusion on the secondary market. Even though both the primary and secondary markets are competitive, such a combination may result in anticompetitive effects in the primary market. See Ezrachi and Stucke, 'The Role of Secondary Algorithmic Tacit Collusion in Achieving Market Alignment' (n44), 4.

[48] See Draft Guidelines (n45), para 418.

[49] A Ezrachi and M Stucke, 'Sustainable and Unchallenged Algorithmic Tacit Collusion' (2020) 17 Northwestern Journal of Technology and Intellectual Property 217, 250.

[50] AdC and Bundeskartellamt (n36), 42. See also U Schwalbe, 'Algorithms, Machine Learning, and Collusion' (2019) 14 Journal of Competition Law and Economics 568, 596.

[51] OECD, 'Algorithms and Collusion: Competition Policy in the Digital Age' (n35), 31.

explicit instructions to do so, engage in explicit collusion with each other'.[52] Having said that, there are a number of studies exploring the potential of self-learning algorithms to contribute to collusive outcomes,[53] suggesting that, in controlled environments, this is possible. Yet, this scenario is yet to materialize in real-world settings, with black-box algorithms posing difficult questions for regulators that may be unable to even unpack and decipher the workings of the algorithm itself. The CMA, in its study on pricing algorithms, has pointed to an additional factor, which further complicates the occurrence of collusive outcomes. Arguably, personalized pricing may undermine tacit collusion between algorithms.[54]

III.3 Algorithms Facilitating Existing Collusion: Case Law

Despite the heated debate highlighting potential algorithmic collusion, the case law to date is rather limited. This section discusses European Union (EU) cases as well as selected cases from the United Kingdom and the United States, where the above first and second scenarios have materialized.

III.3.1 Pre-Existing Agreements Implemented through Parties' Algorithms: Case Law Examples

In *Online Posters and Frames: UK*, the CMA concluded that Trod and GB Eye had infringed the Chapter I prohibition (the national equivalent to Article 101 TFEU) because they had agreed not to undercut each other's prices for licensed sport and entertainment posters and frames sold by them on Amazon UK, when there was no other seller offering a lower price.[55] Trod and GB Eye used automated repricing software to implement the arrangement.[56] In fact, the evidence suggested that after trying to implement the arrangement manually, albeit unsuccessfully, it was the use of the repricing software by different third-party providers that gave effect to it.[57]

In this case, the CMA relied on evidence of email correspondence to prove the anticompetitive arrangement.[58] Interestingly, the CMA acknowledged the possible legitimate use of repricing software, yet in this case, it was used as a tool to

[52] OECD, 'Algorithms and Collusion—Note from the European Union' (14 June 2017), para 28.
[53] See n38 above.
[54] CMA, 'Pricing Algorithms' (n38), paras 7.34 et seq.
[55] *CMA, Online Sales of Posters and Frames* (Case 50223) (Decision, 12 August 2016), para 1.3. The CMA imposed a financial penalty on Trod, whereas GBE benefited from full immunity from financial penalties under the CMA's leniency policy. See *ibid*, paras 1.4, 6.6, and 6.7. Following this case, the CMA issued guidance for online sellers. See CMA, 'Price-Fixing: Guidance for Online Sellers' (7 November 2016) <https://www.gov.uk/government/publications/price-fixing-guidance-for-online-sellers/price-fixing-guidance-for-online-sellers> (accessed 28 August 2023).
[56] CMA, *Online Sales of Posters and Frames* (Case 50223) (n55), para 3.46.
[57] *Ibid*, para 3.62, according to an internal email: 'Logistically it is going to be difficult to follow the pricing effectively on a daily basis so I am looking into re-pricing [so]ftware.'
[58] *Ibid*, paras 3.94 et seq.

coordinate prices. The CMA, while acknowledging that online sellers often use repricing software in order to adjust their prices in response to competitors' prices, stated that in this case, such repricing software was used by the parties as the tool to implement their anticompetitive agreement.[59] Such use of repricing software was taken into account by the CMA as one of the factors in assessing the economic and legal context of the agreement and thus classifying it as a restriction by object that was inherently restrictive of competition.[60] In addition, the use of repricing software was taken as an aggravating factor when assessing the seriousness of the infringement for the purposes of calculating the basic amount of the fine, since such use made cheating more difficult.[61]

In *Online Posters and Frames: US*, the US Department of Justice (DoJ) announced a plea-bargaining agreement between David Topkins, a former executive of an online seller of posters and the DoJ. Topkins and other poster-selling firms agreed to fix the prices of certain posters sold online through the Amazon Marketplace.[62] In order to implement the agreement, the co-conspirators adopted specific pricing algorithms in order collect pricing information and coordinate price changes. With respect to this case, the Assistant Attorney General Bill Baer of the DoJ's Antitrust Division emphasized that '[the DoJ] will not tolerate anticompetitive conduct, whether it occurs in a smoke-filled room or over the Internet using complex pricing algorithms'.[63]

In both cases, specific pricing algorithms were used to implement pre-existing price-fixing agreements. As such, there was no difficulty in establishing liability according to 'traditional' competition law concepts. However, the widespread use of algorithmic tools may lend itself to situations of anticompetitive information exchange between competitors through, for example, the apparent unilateral disclosure of information through a commonly used algorithmic tool.[64] Such

[59] *Ibid*, para 5.47.

[60] *Ibid*, para 5.58.

[61] The basic amount of the financial penalty is calculated based on the relevant turnover of the undertaking and the seriousness of the infringement. See *ibid*, paras 6.19, 6.23. For this case, the CMA secured its first director disqualification order against Mr Aston, the managing director of Trod, for five years. See CMA, 'CMA Secures Director Disqualification for Competition Law Breach' (1 December 2016) <https://www.gov.uk/government/news/cma-secures-director-disqualification-for-competition-law-breach> (accessed 24 February 2023). Mr Aston was also sentenced to six months imprisonment in the United States, after he pleaded guilty to collusive price fixing for the sale of posters on Amazon Marketplace in the United States. See Department of Justice (DoJ), 'Former E-Commerce Executive Pleads Guilty to Price Fixing; Sentenced to Six Months' (28 January 2019) <https://www.justice.gov/opa/pr/former-e-commerce-executive-pleads-guilty-price-fixing-sentenced-six-months> (accessed 24 February 2023).

[62] DoJ, 'Former E-Commerce Executive Charged with Price Fixing in the Antitrust Division's First Online Marketplace Prosecution' (6 April 2015) <https://www.justice.gov/opa/pr/former-e-commerce-executive-charged-price-fixing-antitrust-divisions-first-online-marketplace> (accessed 24 February 2023).

[63] *Ibid.* See also S Mehra, 'US v. Topkins: Can Price Fixing Be Based on Algorithms?' (2016) 7 Journal of European Competition Law & Practice 470.

[64] See Draft Guidelines (n45), para 432; RHG (n45), para 396.

disclosures make it easier for firms to predict competitors' future market conduct, even without proof of reciprocal conduct between undertakings.[65] In light of this reality, some jurisdictions have gone a step further and opted for the prohibition of unilateral disclosure of information (e.g. price signalling).[66]

III.3.2 Hub and Spoke, Information Exchange, and Cartel Facilitators

Algorithms may aid companies in sharing information directly or through a third party, such as a software developer.[67] This scenario lends itself to a hub-and-spoke arrangement defined as 'any number of vertical exchanges or agreements between economic actors at one level of the supply chain (the spokes), and a common trading partner on another level of the chain (the hub), leading to an indirect exchange of information and some form of collusion between the spokes'.[68] Different to the cases discussed above, where the implicated parties took part to the anti-competitive arrangement and used repricing algorithms as a tool, here, software developers may be held liable as well. Thus, they should be particularly cautious not to help their clients by providing software that facilitates such anticompetitive agreements.[69]

Depending, of course, on the type of information exchanged,[70] the software developer may be liable as a cartel facilitator. Depending on the context, even when the third party's software facilitates the gathering, processing, and evaluation of public information, an anticompetitive information exchange may be established if such an exchange enables undertakings 'to become aware of that information more simply, rapidly and directly'.[71]

The CNMC, the Spanish national competition authority (NCA), has already issued two decisions fining software developers for their respective involvement in facilitating cartel arrangements. There is also relevant case law in the United Kingdom. In *Real Estate Brokers: Spain*, a case embedding both the first and second scenario,[72] the CNMC fined seven real estate brokers for price fixing and

[65] See, e.g. A Ezrachi and ME Stucke, 'Is Your Digital Assistant Devious?' in D Geradin and I Lianos (eds), *Reconciling Efficiency and Equity* (CUP, 2019), 222; SK Mehra, 'Antitrust and the Robo-Seller: Competition in the Time of Algorithms' (2016) 100 Minnesota Law Review 1323.

[66] See, e.g. Article 1A of the Greek Competition Act (Law 3959/2011 as amended by Law 4886/2022), Government Gazette Issue A 12 (24 January 2022).

[67] RHG (n45), para 401.

[68] OECD, 'Roundtable on Hub-and-Spoke Arrangements—Background Note by the Secretariat', DAF/COMP(2019)14 (2019), para 1.

[69] See to that effect, CMA, 'Amazon Marketplace Online Sellers Fined £160k for Price-Fixing' (7 November 2016) <https://www.gov.uk/government/case-studies/online-sellers-price-fixing-case-study> (accessed 29 December 2022) (Case Study).

[70] For example, the sharing of commercially sensitive information. See RHG (n45), paras 384 et seq.

[71] Case T-587/08 *Fresh Del Monte Produce v Commission*, ECLI:EU:T:2013:129, para 369. See also AdC and Bundeskartellamt (n36), 39.

[72] Spanish Competition Authority (CNMC), 'The CNMC Fines Several Companies EUR 1.25 Million for Imposing Minimum Commissions in the Real Estate Brokerage Market' (Press release, 9 December 2021) <https://www.cnmc.es/sites/default/files/editor_contenidos/Notas%20de%20prensa/2021/20211209_NP_Sancionador_Proptech_eng.pdf> (accessed 8 June 2024).

anticompetitive information exchange as well as the software and data base providers for being cartel facilitators. These brokers operated the so-called multiple listing system (MLS), which allowed them to exclusively share property listings and sales. An MLS member could list a property on the system, allowing others to conclude the transaction and split the commission of the brokerage service between them. The software developers and data base providers in this case were found to have actively contributed to the development and roll-out of the MLS system that allowed for such cartel formation, as well as monitoring and punishing deviations from this anticompetitive arrangement.

In *Tobacco Cartel: Spain*, the CNMC fined three cigarette manufacturers for exchanging sensitive sales data for a period between 2008 and 2017.[73] In addition, the CNMC imposed the largest fine on the distributor that owned a software, which was used by the cigarette manufacturers to compare sales information in real time. The Spanish NCA treated such information exchange as a restriction of competition by effect. The decision is on appeal on the basis that the distributor had legitimate expectations about its respective conduct, and there was no anticompetitive effect.

The Spanish approach in the above cases appears to be reaffirmed in the RHG, where the Commission distinguishes between feeding publicly available information into an algorithmic tool and aggregating sensitive data using a pricing tool, which is provided by one IT company and to which various competitors have access.[74] In addition, the Commission acknowledges the importance of automated real-time information exchange for businesses' ability to compete.[75]

In the *Supply of Gas and Electricity: UK*, the Gas and Electricity Markets Authority (GEMA)[76] imposed a fine on Economy Energy, Economy Energy, E(Gas and Electricity) Ltd (EGEL), and Dyball for an anticompetitive market-sharing/customer-allocation agreement between Economy Energy and EGEL in the supply of gas and electricity to domestic customers in Great Britain. According to the respective agreement, which was supported through information sharing of current customers' details, the two energy suppliers undertook not to actively target each other's customers.[77] Dyball acted as facilitator since it provided the

[73] OECD, 'The Concept of Potential Competition—Note by Spain' (10 June 2021), 8; Competition Policy International (CPI), 'Spain: CNMC Fines Tobacco Companies for 57.7 Million' (15 April 2019) <https://www.competitionpolicyinternational.com/spain-cnmc-fine-to-tobacco-companies-for-57-7-million-euros> (accessed 29 December 2022); CNMC, 'La CNMC sanciona a las principales empresas fabricantes de tabaco y a Logista por una infracción consistente en unintercambio de información estratégica' (Press release, in Spanish) <https://www.cnmc.es/sites/default/files/2951887_14.pdf> (accessed 29 December 2022).

[74] RHG (n45), para 402.

[75] *Ibid*, para 405.

[76] GEMA is the governing body of the independent regulator of energy markets, the Office of Gas and Electricity Markets (Ofgem). GEMA is responsible for enforcement decisions (amongst others).

[77] Ofgem, 'Infringement by Economy Energy, E (Gas and Electricity) and Dyball Associates of Chapter I of the Competition Act 1998 with Respect to an Anti-Competitive Agreement' (26 July 2019), para 1.3 <https://www.ofgem.gov.uk/system/files/docs/2019/07/decision_on_economy_energy_-_e_

common software that facilitated this arrangement by allowing the sharing of customer lists and blocking the acquisition of certain customers and by also sharing itself customer lists and instructions on how to prevent customer switching between the two energy suppliers.[78]

In calculating the financial penalty to be imposed on Dyball as a cartel facilitator, GEMA accepted as a mitigating factor the 'apparently genuine uncertainty of Dyball's directors in its participation in the infringement' and granted a 5 per cent reduction in the fine,[79] especially taking into account the limited number of instances where the EU Commission or a UK competition authority[80] has held an undertaking liable for facilitating anticompetitive conduct between other parties.[81]

According to the CJEU case law, a third party may be held liable for facilitating an anticompetitive agreement.[82] The third party needs to have the intention of contributing through its own conduct to the common objectives of the other participants and, second, it needs to be aware of, or to have reasonably foreseen and been prepared to take the risk for, the actual conduct planned or put into effect by the other undertakings in pursuit of the same objectives.[83]

In *Eturas*, the CJEU, in its preliminary ruling, clarified the awareness condition. Such awareness may be inferred from the specific context of the arrangement. Eturas was providing the E-TURAS online booking system to travel agencies. This booking system was automatically limiting the discount rates that could be applied to clients, reducing discount rates in excess of 3 per cent to 3 per cent.[84] The travel agencies were informed about this change to the E-TURAS booking system. The administrator of the E-TURAS booking system sent a message about limiting discount rates to the travel agencies participating in the system. This message could only be consulted in the 'Notices' section of the information system in question, and the travel agencies did not expressly respond to it.[85] The CJEU emphasized that

gas_and_electricity_-_dyball_associates_infringement_of_chapter_i_ca98_doorstep_sales_redacted_decision_document_26_july_2019.pdf> (accessed 24 February 2023).

[78] *Ibid*, para 1.4. For a chronology of events see para 5.64, para 8.3.

[79] *Ibid*, para 8.46.

[80] In the United Kingdom, apart from the CMA, a number of national regulatory authorities have concurrent competition law powers. On the concurrency regime, see R Whish and D Bailey, *Competition Law* (10th edn, OUP, 2021), Chapter 10, section 8.

[81] Ofgem (n77), para 8.46. See also Case T-180/15 *ICAP v Commission*, ECLI:EU:T:2017:795, paras 291–299, where the GC annulled the Commission's decision due to insufficient reasoning with respect to its methodology in calculating the fine. Upheld on appeal, see Case C-39/18P *Commission v ICAP*, ECLI:EU:C:2019:584.

[82] See also RHG (n45), paras 401 et seq.

[83] Case C-194/14 *P AC-Treuhand v Commission*, ECLI:EU:C:2015:717, para 30 and the case law cited therein. It is not necessary for the third party to be active on the market affected by the agreement. See *ibid*, para 27; *ICAP v Commission* (n81), para 97.

[84] Case C-74/14 *Eturas et al v Lietuvos Respublikos konkurencijos taryba*, ECLI:EU:C:2016:42, para 12.

[85] *Ibid*, para 43.

> if it cannot be established that a travel agency was aware of that message, its participation in a concertation cannot be inferred from the mere existence of a technical restriction implemented in the system at issue in the main proceedings, unless it is established on the basis of other objective and consistent indicia that it tacitly assented to an anticompetitive action.[86]

Thus, in order to be held liable for using software provided by a third party that leads to a collusive outcome, undertakings need to be aware of such a fact and the mere technical restriction does not suffice, unless supported by other indicia. A travel agency could rebut the presumption of having participated in the concerted practice by proving that it publicly distanced itself from that practice or reported it to the administrative authorities, or by adducing other evidence (in this case, for example, evidence of consistently applying higher discounts).[87]

According to *VM Remonts*, a company may be held liable for the conduct of an independent service provider provided that the following conditions regarding intention and knowledge are met. First, the service provider needs to act under the direction or control of the undertaking receiving the service concerned. Alternatively, the undertaking-recipient of the service needs to be aware of the anticompetitive objectives pursued by its competitors and the service provider and have the intention of contributing to them through its own conduct. Finally, liability may be established in instances where the recipient of the service could reasonably have foreseen such anticompetitive acts between its competitors and the service provider and was prepared to accept such a risk.[88]

It follows from the above that where competitors reach a collusive outcome without prior communication through a third party's algorithms, in order to be liable under EU competition law they need to be aware of such a fact or to have reasonably foreseen it. The RHG discuss such instances of indirect information exchange and offer examples, where competitors may use a shared optimization algorithm. Such an algorithm can potentially reach specific business decisions based on the competitors' commercially sensitive information.[89]

In the cases discussed above, the third party acted as a facilitator of an existing anticompetitive agreement. In instances where a platform controls the algorithm, the third party may assume a more active role in facilitating competitors' interaction with their customers, as, for example, in the case of Uber.[90] Uber is a

[86] *Ibid*, para 45.

[87] *Ibid*, paras 46–49. In the end, the Lithuanian Supreme Court acquitted certain travel agencies that had been fined by the Lithuanian NCA due to lack of evidence. See Lithuanian Competition Council, 'Supreme Court Upheld KT Decision on Cartel among Travel Agencies' (Press release, 3 May 2016) <http://kt.gov.lt/en/news/supreme-court-upheld-kt-decision-on-cartel-among-travel-agencies> (accessed 8 June 2024).

[88] *VM Remonts* (n26), paras 29–33. RHG (n45), para 403.

[89] Draft Guidelines (n45), para 436; RHG (n45), paras 401–402.

[90] AdC and Bundeskartellamt (n36), 40.

ride-sharing platform, matching drivers with passengers, and in so doing possibly engages in platform-driven price fixing,[91] since it is the Uber platform[92] and not the drivers that determine the price. In the United States, an action was brought against Uber for illegal price fixing, but this was subsequently abandoned following an appeal court's decision accepting that Uber's terms and conditions include a mandatory arbitration provision.[93] With regard to the possible application of EU competition law against Uber, many interesting questions arise,[94] primarily with respect to whether drivers qualify as undertakings.[95] Provided that Uber drivers are classified as independent contractors, the Uber business model may be seen as assimilating a hub-and-spoke arrangement where Uber, which controls the algorithm and sets the fares, acts as a cartel facilitator between the drivers. AG Szpunar has noted that 'the use by competitors of the same algorithm to calculate the price is not in itself unlawful, but might give rise to hub-and-spoke conspiracy concerns when the power of the platform increases'.[96] Alternatively, the Uber business model may be treated as a series of vertical RPM agreements between Uber and its drivers, though under this scenario, there is no service that drivers buy from Uber and then subsequently sell to their customers.[97]

Even under the above scenario, where Uber's business model infringes Article 101 TFEU, it may still be exempted under Article 101(3) TFEU. Under the provision, Uber may argue that its business model has resulted in efficiencies in the form of an innovative approach to transport that caters to consumers' needs. In fact, the Luxembourgish NCA adopted such an approach in a national case against a taxi booking platform and even took into account the positive impact on the environment, since customers are matched with drivers that are closer to them. They also considered that an agreement did not eliminate all competition in the relevant market since the parties had less than a 30 per cent market share.[98]

[91] *Spencer Meyer v Travis Kalanick*, 15 Civ 9796 (2016); US Dist Lexis 43944. See Nowag (n22).

[92] According to T Kalanick (chief executive officer and co-founder of Uber), '[we] are not setting the price. The market is setting the price. We have algorithms to determine what that market is.' See M Wohlsen, 'Uber Boss Says Surging Prices Rescue People from the Snow' (WIRED, 17 December 2013) <https://www.wired.com/2013/12/uber-surge-pricing> (accessed 8 June 2024).

[93] *Meyer v Uber Technologies Inc*, No 16-2750 (2d Cir, 2017). Cases against Uber or similar ride-sharing platforms were brought in other jurisdictions. See H Bekisz, 'When Does Algorithmic Pricing Result in an Intra-Platform Anticompetitive Agreement or Concerted Practice? The Case of Uber in the Framework of EU Competition Law' (2021) 12 Journal of European Competition Law & Practice 217, 230.

[94] See also M Anderson and M Huffman, 'The Sharing Economy Meets the Sherman Act: Is UBER a Firm, a Cartel or Something in Between?' (2017) Columbia Business Law Review 859.

[95] On this point, see section II.3 above.

[96] *Asociacio ́n Profesional Elite Taxi*, Opinion of AG Szpunar (n24), n23.

[97] Nowag (n22), 395–396; Bekisz (n93), 232.

[98] Conseil de la Concurrence, *Webtaxi Sarl*, Conseil de la Concurrence (Decision No 2018-FO-01) (7 June 2018). See Bekisz (n93), 233.

III.4 Algorithms Colluding and the Limits of Article 101 TFEU

In essence, competition law provisions have proved flexible enough to catch instances where algorithms have reinforced anticompetitive agreements or concerted practices. Yet, Article 101 TFEU falls short of addressing situations of conscious parallelism, where clever algorithms merely adapt in the absence of evidence of communication between the parties. The question then is how to distinguish between coordination and mere intelligent adaptation to market conditions, especially when taking into account that algorithms 'expand the grey area between unlawful explicit collusion and lawful tacit collusion'.[99] And given that 'algorithms may enable firms to replace explicit collusion with tacit co-ordination',[100] policy makers need to reflect on whether the deliberate choice of using repricing algorithms leading to price coordination may qualify as a looser form of concerted practice under 101 TFEU in order to address the existing regulatory gap.[101] Alternatively, parallel information signalling may be treated as unlawful coordination, under an effects approach, namely when it results in consumer harm not being offset by efficiencies.[102]

Yet, such an approach cannot be reconciled with the treatment of concerted practices under EU competition law. Each economic operator must independently choose their market conduct.[103] The CJEU has repeatedly highlighted that

> [w]hile it is correct to say that this requirement of independence does not deprive economic operators of the *right to adapt themselves intelligently to the existing or anticipated conduct of their competitors*, it does, none the less, strictly preclude any direct or indirect contact between such operators by which an undertaking may influence the conduct on the market of its actual or potential competitors or disclose to them its decisions or intentions concerning its own conduct on the market where the object or effect of such contact is to create conditions of competition which do not correspond to the normal conditions of the market in question, regard being had to the nature of the products or services offered, the size and number of the undertakings involved and the volume of that market [emphasis added].[104]

[99] OECD, 'Algorithms and Collusion: Competition Policy in the Digital Age' (n35), 25.
[100] *Ibid*, 25.
[101] See also A Ittoo and N Petit, 'Algorithmic Pricing Agents and Tacit Collusion: A Technological Perspective' (2017) <https://papers.ssrn.com/sol3/papers.cfm?abstract_id=3046405> (accessed 8 June 2024) discussing the technological challenges, which undermine Q-learning algorithms' potential to reach tacit collusion.
[102] S Thomas, 'Harmful Signals, Cartel Prohibition and Oligopoly Theory in the Age of Machine Learning' (2019) 15 Journal of Competition Law and Economics 159.
[103] Case 40/73 *Suiker Unie v Commission ECR*, EU:C:1975:174, para 173; Case C-8/08 *T-Mobile Netherlands and Others*, ECLI:EU:C:2009:343, para 32 and the case law cited.
[104] See, e.g. Case C-286/13P *Dole Food and Dole Fresh Fruit Europe v Commission*, ECLI:EU:C:2015:184, para 120 with further references to *T-Mobile Netherlands* (n103), para 33 and the case law cited therein. See also Case T-180/15 *ICAP v Commission* (n81), para 50.

The increasing use of algorithms facilitates such adaptation to market conditions without, arguably, the existence of any prior contact. However, in order to sanction such conduct under EU competition law, an agreement in the form of a 'concurrence of wills'[105] or concerted practice needs to be established. For a concerted practice to exist, the competition authorities need to adduce evidence of 'three Cs', namely market conduct of the undertakings concerned, prior contact between them, and a causal link between the two.[106] In *Hüls*, the CJEU stated that

> subject to proof to the contrary, which the economic operators concerned must adduce, the *presumption* must be *that the undertakings taking part in the concerted action and remaining active on the market take account of the information exchanged with their competitors* for the purposes of determining their conduct on that market. That is all the more true where the undertakings *concert together on a regular basis over a long period* [emphasis added].[107]

In the algorithmic context, the question that arises is if, in order to rebut this presumption, the undertakings should be allowed to adduce evidence to show that self-learning algorithms independently reached a collusive outcome.

In addition, if algorithms are programmed to strategically adjust to competitors' pricing, this may be assessed, depending on the context, and under certain conditions such as anticompetitive concerted practice involving price signalling. The RHG highlighted the fact that

> an undertaking discloses commercially sensitive information through a public announcement (for example, through a post on a publicly accessible website, a statement at a public event or in a newspaper) does not in itself exclude the possibility that the announcement may constitute a concerted practice within the meaning of Article 101(1). Indeed, public disclosure may in some cases form part of a communication channel between competitors to signal future intentions to behave on the market in a specific way, or to provide a focal point for coordination between competitors and thereby fall within Article 101(1).[108]

In *Liner Shipping*, fourteen container liner shipping companies regularly announced their intended future price increases for their services on their websites, via the press, or in other public ways.[109] The price announcements did not give full information on these new prices to customers but only concerned absolute price

[105] See, e.g. Case T-41/96 *Bayer AG v Commission* [1996] ECR II-381, para 69.
[106] See, e.g. Case C-199/92 *Hüls v Commission*, ECR, ECLI:EU:C:1999:358, para 161.
[107] *Ibid*, para 162.
[108] RHG (n45), para 398.
[109] *Container Shipping* (Case AT.39850) Summary of Commission Decision, C(2016) 4215 final, [2016] OJ C 327/4, para 6.

percentage increases. The Commission expressed concerns that this practice may allow the companies to explore their respective pricing intentions and coordinate their behaviour.[110] This case was resolved with commitments.

In some jurisdictions, we also find legislative attempts against price signalling. For example, in Greece, the amended Competition Act incorporated a prohibition against invitations to collude and price signalling.[111]

Table 4.1 summarizes the three scenarios discussed above, the various issues they posed, and their respective assessment to date.

Table 4.1 Scenarios of algorithmic collusion

Scenario	Communication	Issues	Assessment
Traditional	Direct		Aggravating factor—sustainability of collusion
Hub and spoke	Through a third party supplying the algorithm/software platform	'Concerted practice'; liability of third party	Competitors knowingly use the same algorithm
Algorithmic collusion	None	'Concerted practice'	Prohibition of price signalling

III.5 Regulatory Responses

Having discussed potential scenarios of algorithmic collusion and selected case law examples, this section explores possible solutions to the evidential difficulties posed by potentially employing algorithms to reach a collusive equilibrium. As Commissioner Vestager stressed, 'competition enforcers [...] need to make it very clear that companies can't escape responsibility for collusion by hiding behind a computer program'.[112] Yet, it may indeed be possible for companies to escape liability, since coordinated effects can be evidence of a concerted practice if this is the only plausible explanation.[113]

110 *Ibid*, para 9.

111 Article 1A Greek Competition Act (n66). See also Hellenic Competition Commission (HCC), 'Guidelines on the Implementation of Article 1A L. 3959/2011' <https://www.epant.gr/en/legislation/1aen.html> (accessed 8 June 2024). See also J Harrington, 'Collusion in Plain Sight: Firms' Use of Public Announcements to Restrain Competition' (2022) 84 Antitrust Law Journal 521.

112 M Vestager, 'Algorithms and Competition' (Speech, 16 March 2017) <https://wayback.archive-it.org/12090/20191129221651/https://ec.europa.eu/commission/commissioners/2014-2019/vestager/announcements/bundeskartellamt-18th-conference-competition-berlin-16-march-2017_en> (accessed 20 January 2021).

113 Joined Cases C-89/85, C-104/85, C-114/85, C-116/85, C-117/85, and C-125/85–C-129/85 *Ahlstrom Osakeyhtio and Others v Commission* [1993] ECR I-1575, para 71.

This section focuses on tacit collusion and does not cover instances where algorithms are programmed to collude. If the evidence suggests that algorithms were programmed in such a way so as not only to independently adapt to each other but also to communicate and reach a collusive outcome, then liability is attributed to the firms employing these algorithms. This situation is no different to employees colluding. To address such situations, undertakings need to promote compliance by design and build their algorithms in a way that does not allow them to collude.[114] Cases such as the Spanish cases discussed above highlight the potential liability of software developers and incentivize programmers to be more cautious when designing their algorithms.[115] Finally, in the RHG, it now becomes clear that firms may be liable for collusion through algorithms when algorithms, like employees or outside consultants, act under the 'direction or control' of the firm.[116]

III.5.1 Revise the Approach to Concerted Practice

The first solution has been alluded to in section III.4 and is linked to the existing limits of the notion of concerted practice under EU competition law. Thus, one way to address instances of independent algorithmic collusion would be to rethink the concept of concerted practice and its applicability to instances of algorithmic collusion, provided that certain conditions are met. Currently, EU competition law catches parallel behaviour only if there is an agreement or concertation between competitors. Since pricing algorithms may arguably support individual incentives to charge supra-competitive prices in the absence of an agreement or concerted practice, from a policy perspective, regulators should be asking the question whether the law should cast the net wider to apply to such conduct. Put differently, is the notion of concerted practice in need of reform so that it also extends to instances of tacit collusion?[117]

The CJEU case law on concerted practice is fact-specific and sufficiently flexible to catch different situations. For example, in *Eturas*, the fact that the travel agencies were using the same pricing software and received a notification of capping discount rates may have sufficed to establish a concerted practice.[118] However, in the absence of such a notification, it would not have been possible to establish a concerted practice.

[114] Vestager (n112).

[115] On these cases, see text to n72 above.

[116] RHG (n45), para 379.

[117] Similarly, the Sherman Act does not catch situations where oligopolists may independently achieve price coordination. For an early discussion, see RA Posner, 'Oligopoly and the Antitrust Laws: A Suggested Approach' (1969) 21 Stanford Law Review 1562, 1576–92; DF Turner, 'The Definition of Agreement under the Sherman Act: Conscious Parallelism and Refusals to Deal' (1962) 75 Harvard Law Review 655. Posner later retracted from his argument to extend the applicability of the Sherman Act to such instances. See R Posner, 'Review of Kaplow, Competition Policy and Price Fixing' (2014) 79 Antitrust Law Journal 761, 763. L Kaplow, 'On the Meaning of Horizontal Agreements in Competition Law' (2011) 99 California Law Review 683. Discussing the 'existing crack in the Sherman Act' and the relevant debate, see S Mehra, 'Antitrust and the Robo-Seller' (n65), 1340–1343.

[118] See text to n84 above.

Tacit collusion may possibly be sanctioned if coupled with certain 'plus factors' that facilitate coordination between firms, including the use of algorithms leading to collusive outcomes.[119] Another possibility is to reverse the presumption. When firms rely on repricing software leading to collusive pricing, then it is for the firm to prove that there was no intention to collude. If collusion is unsustainable in the absence of communication,[120] then if collusion is observed for a period of time, this may presumably be attributed to prior communication. Other proposals include the adoption of specific tests that will prohibit certain pricing algorithms per se.[121] Alternatively, such algorithms may be assessed under an effects approach, depending on the respective market structure and impact on consumer welfare.[122] Other solutions include the widening of competition rules to catch situations of conscious parallelism in the absence of communication.[123]

III.5.2 Ex-Ante Tools: Market Investigations and Beyond

With respect to the possibility of purely algorithmic collusion, researchers and competition authorities broadly accept that this is not a significant threat yet.[124] Notwithstanding the importance of the debate and the risk that such algorithmic collusion may materialize in the future, it appears to be too soon to alter the approach to concerted practice. In effect, such discussions bear importance with respect to competition authorities' treatment of such cases, and their outcome will depend on the evidence at hand and the willingness to bring a test case.

In addition to the ex-post application of competition law, ex-ante tools such as market investigations may be employed in order to identify adverse effects on the competitive process that cannot be pinned down to a specific anticompetitive conduct under Article 101 or 102 TFEU.[125] Market investigations present a useful tool

[119] Gal (n37), 110. 'Plus factors' can be defined as 'economic actions and outcomes, above and beyond parallel conduct by oligopolistic firms, that are largely inconsistent with unilateral conduct but largely consistent with explicitly coordinated action'. See W Kovacic, R Marshall, L Marx, and H White, 'Plus Factors and Agreement in Antitrust Law' (2011) 110 Michigan Law Review 393.

[120] Schwalbe (n50), 597 posing such question.

[121] J Harrington, 'Developing Competition Law for Collusion by Autonomous Artificial Agents' (2019) 14 Journal of Competition Law and Economics 331, 357–358.

[122] For such proposals, see Thomas (n102); Gal (n37), 112.

[123] This is possible, for example, in the United States under the Federal Trade Commission (FTC) Act, section 5. See BRICS Report (n11), 649. See also the recent revision of the Greek Competition Act (n66) and the introduction of Article 1A that includes a prohibition on price signalling under certain conditions. See text to n111 above.

[124] AdC and Bundeskartellamt (n36), 77.

[125] Such a tool exists in some jurisdictions, most notably in the United Kingdom. On the UK competition law regime, see R Whish, 'New Competition Tool: Legal Comparative Study of Existing Competition Tools Aimed at Addressing Structural Competition Problems with a Particular Focus on the UK's Market Investigation Tool' (Expert study, 2020) <https://ec.europa.eu/competition/consultations/2020_new_comp_tool/kd0420573enn.pdf> (accessed 2 January 2023). Such a tool also exists under the Greek Competition Act (n66), Article 11.

to understand the workings of algorithms in e-commerce, since algorithms call for more regulatory oversight.[126]

Regulation could also address the opacity of certain algorithms and enhance transparency. The recently adopted Digital Markets Act (DMA) provides for increased transparency, since it specifically provides for the Commission's power to gain access to any relevant data or algorithms, in whatever format.[127] Ex-ante scrutiny of algorithmic systems may help address any related competition concerns as well as the construction of adequate remedies.[128] Another example comes from the Platform-to-Business (P2B) regulation, which calls for algorithmic transparency when ranking results, though such transparency obligations do not extend to the disclosure of algorithms that would enable consumer deception or result in consumer harm through the manipulation of search results.[129] The Digital Services Act (DSA) also contains provisions with respect to the risks associated with recommender algorithmic systems and algorithmic decision making as well as provisions including the transparency of algorithmic systems.[130] Finally, the Artificial Intelligence (AI) Act aims at addressing various risks (from minimal to unacceptable) raised by AI systems.[131]

III.5.3 Principles by Which to Abide

It is also important to establish principles for algorithmic design. Building competition law principles in with regard to algorithmic design corresponds to the principle of data protection by design embedded in the General Data Protection Regulation (GDPR).[132] These principles should include accountability and

[126] CMA, 'Algorithms: How They Can Reduce Competition and Harm Consumers' (n36).

[127] Regulation (EU) 2022/1925 of the European Parliament and of the Council of 14 September 2022 on contestable and fair markets in the digital sector and amending Directives (EU) 2019/1937 and (EU) 2020/1828, [2022] OJ L 265/1 (Digital Markets Act), Articles 21 and 23.

[128] In this vein, see G Petropoulos, 'The EU's Digital Markets Act' (CPI Columns, May 2021).

[129] Regulation (EU) 2019/1150 of the European Parliament and of the Council of 20 June 2019 on promoting fairness and transparency for business users of online intermediation services, [2019] OJ L 186/57, Article 5(6).

[130] Regulation (EU) 2022/2065 of the European Parliament and of the Council of 19 October 2022 on a single market for digital services and amending Directive 2000/31/EC, [2022] OJ L 277/1 (Digital Services Act), Articles 14, 34, 35, 40, 69, and 72. See also the European Centre of Algorithmic Algorithmic Transparency Home page, <https://algorithmic-transparency.ec.europa.eu/index_en> (accessed 8 June 2024).

[131] Regulation (EU) 2024/1689 of the European Parliament and of the Council of 13 June 2024 laying down harmonised rules on artificial intelligence and amending Regulations (EC) No 300/2008, (EU) No 167/2013, (EU) No 168/2013, (EU) 2018/858, (EU) 2018/1139 and (EU) 2019/2144 and Directives 2014/90/EU, (EU) 2016/797 and (EU) 2020/1828 (Artificial Intelligence Act).

[132] See Article 25(1) GDPR, Regulation (EU) 2016/679 of the European Parliament and of the Council of 27 April 2016 on the protection of natural persons with regard to the processing of personal data and on the free movement of such data, and repealing Directive 95/46/EC, [2016] OJ L 119/1 (General Data Protection Regulation [GDPR]). On this idea, see S Vezzoso, 'Competition by Design' (2017) < https://papers.ssrn.com/sol3/papers.cfm?abstract_id=2986440> (accessed 2 January 2023).

transparency.[133] Companies could be asked to preserve an auditable record of their algorithm development and use.[134] Such requirements would also enhance competition authorities' powers to gather information.

IV. Data-Sharing Agreements

Another issue raised by the digital economy is the traditional competition law approach to information-sharing agreements, since datafication and digitalization have raised the importance of data sharing.[135] The importance of data sharing is highlighted and underpins the European Strategy for Data.[136] At the same time, datafication may challenge the division between pro-competitive cooperation and anticompetitive collusion. According to the EU Experts Report,[137] data pooling may be pro- or anticompetitive, depending on the market power of the incumbents, the type of data shared, and the type of data-sharing arrangement.[138] Data pools may allow firms to offer better-quality products/services than on their own data alone. Yet, data-sharing arrangements may enable the exchange of commercially sensitive information.[139] The Report highlights that data-pooling efficiencies

[133] US Association for Computational Mechanics (USACM), 'Statement on Algorithmic Transparency and Accountability' (12 January 2017) <http://www.acm.org/binaries/content/assets/public-policy/2017_usacm_statement_algorithms.pdf> (accessed 14 February 2023).

[134] Digital Competition Expert Panel, 'Unlocking Digital Competition' (report prepared by J Furman, D Coyle, A Fletcher, D McAuley, and P Marsden) (Furman Report, March 2019), 108.

[135] RHG (n45), para 373.

[136] European Commission (EU), 'A European Strategy for Data', COM(2020) 66 final (Brussels, 19 February 2020) (Communication). In particular, the Data Governance Act aims to increase data sharing in the EU. See Regulation (EU) 2022/868 of the European Parliament and of the Council of 30 May 2022 on European data governance and amending Regulation (EU) 2018/1724 (Data Governance Act), recitals 2 and 3. The Data Act complements the Data Governance Act. See European Commission (EU), 'Proposal for a Regulation of the European Parliament and of the Council on Harmonised Rules on Fair Access to and Use of Data', COM(2022) 68 final (Brussels, 23 February 2022). The Data Act was published in the EU Official Journal in December 2023 and entered into force on 11 January 2024. It will be applicable in September 2025. See also G Schneider, 'Data Sharing for Collaborative Research under Art. 101 TFEU: Lessons from the Proposed Regulations for Data Markets' (2021) 17 European Competition Journal 567 proposing an approach ensuring consistency between the application of competition rules and regulatory initiatives <https://eur-lex.europa.eu/legal-content/EN/TXT/PDF/?uri=CELEX:32022R0868>.

[137] European Commission (EU), 'Competition Policy for the Digital Era' (A Report by J Crémer, Y de Montjoye, and H Schweitzer) (EU Experts Report, 2019), 9, 95. See relevant reference in European Commission (EU), 'Evaluation of the Horizontal Block Exemption Regulation', SWD(2021) 103 final (Staff working document, Brussels, 6 May 2021), 29.

[138] See also B Lundqvist, 'Competition and Data Pools' (2018) 7 Journal of European Consumer and Market Law 146. Data pools connote data-sharing arrangements that contain an element of reciprocity, with at least some member firms contributing data. See EU Experts Report (n137), 92. Conversely, denying access to data may be found to infringe Article 101 TFEU. See European Commission (EU), 'Antitrust: Commission Accepts Commitments by Insurance Ireland to Ensure Access to Its Data Sharing Platform' (30 June 2022) (Case AT.40511). Denying access to data may be caught under 102 TFEU. See Chapter 5 below.

[139] European Commission (EU), 'Guidance on Sharing Private Sector Data in the European Data Economy', COM(2018) 125 final (Staff working document, Brussels, 25 April 2018), 7.

are accepted in the credit[140] and insurance industries[141] and calls for more guidance on the conditions under which data pools may be considered pro-competitive, especially with regard to aggregated data. It also suggests that guidance and a block exemption regulation on data sharing and data pooling may become feasible in the future, with more cumulative experience and after a scoping exercise on the types of data pools and their respective effects.[142]

The RHG now provide clearer guidance for companies considering entering into data-pooling agreements and their respective pro-competitive effects. In particular, with respect to information exchange agreements the public consultation has highlighted that the previous Horizontal Cooperation Guidelines on information-exchange agreements provided insufficient guidance and were too restrictive. In light of this, companies could possibly forego cooperation opportunities. In addition, they have suggested that the guidelines should be updated to reflect digitization challenges, and in particular guidance on data pooling/ data sharing.[143] A similar view has been shared by NCAs. In light of the feedback received, and in order to address the challenges posed by digitization, the Commission has now included in the RHG guidance to assist stakeholders in the self-assessment of data-pooling and data-sharing arrangements.[144] In particular, the RHG clarify that, with respect to potential measures that undertakings may put in place to reduce the risk of anticompetitive information exchange, parties to a data pool should, in principle, have access only to their own information and other participants' final and aggregated information. The management of data pools should be assigned to a trustee that must be subject to strict confidentiality conditions with respect to the information that each participant in the data pool may receive. Also, the collection of information is subject to a proportionality requirement, since the only information collected is the information necessary for implementing the data pool's legitimate purpose.[145]

In addition, refusing access to a shared database may lead to foreclosure, and the assessment under Article 101(1) TFEU will take into account the economic conditions of the relevant market; the purpose of the database; the relevant access

[140] See Case C-238/05 *Asnef-Equifax*, ECLI:EU:C:2006:734.

[141] Pools for the common coverage of a specific category of risks in the form of co-insurance or co-reinsurance were block exempted. See Regulation (EU) 267/2010 of 24 March 2010 on the application of Article 101(3) to certain categories of agreements, decisions and concerted practices in the insurance sector, OJ L 83 (30 March 2010), 1, Article 5. This block exemption expired on 31 March 2017.

[142] EU Experts Report (n137), 93, 109.

[143] European Commission (EU), 'Evaluation of the Horizontal Block Exemption Regulation' (n137), 43–44.

[144] European Commission (EU), 'Revision of the Two Block Exemption Regulations for Horizontal Cooperation Agreements and the Horizontal Guidelines' <https://ec.europa.eu/info/law/better-regulation/have-your-say/initiatives/13058-Revision-of-the-EU-competition-rules-on-horizontal-agreements_en> (accessed 8 June 2021) (Inception Impact Assessment).

[145] RHG (n45), para 408.

conditions; the type of information exchanged (e.g. public or confidential, aggregated or detailed, historical, current or future information); and the frequency with which the database is updated, as well as the information's relevance for setting prices. Parties to such a data-sharing agreement should allow for access on the basis of fair, objective, transparent, and non-discriminatory criteria.[146]

V. Vertical Restraints

V.1 Introduction: Reform of the Rules

In EU competition law, the Vertical Block Exemption Regulation (VBER) and VRG provide a roadmap for companies to self-assess as well as a safe harbour for vertical agreements, when the market power of the parties to the agreement is not substantial, that is where all the parties to the agreement have less than a 30 per cent market share in their respective markets.[147] Linked to this market share threshold, the assumption is that the respective agreement is unlikely to have net negative effects on consumer welfare. However, if a vertical agreement contains hard-core restrains,[148] then the benefit of the VBER ceases to apply, and the agreement must be evaluated under Article 101 TFEU. Hard-core restraints, furthermore, are likely to be classified as restrictions of competition by object.[149] Object restrictions are presumed to have anticompetitive effects and once an object restriction is established, then the burden of proof shifts to the companies involved to argue related efficiencies under Article 101(3) TFEU.

Competition enforcers have increasingly been calling for adjusting and sharpening the competition law regime for the age of online distribution, e-commerce, and 'platformization'.[150] Digitization, interconnection, and 'platformization' have resulted in a radical shift in distribution and consumption and led to new types of vertical restraints such as restrictions on online marketplace sales, restrictions on online advertising, and retail parity clauses. Such concerns underpinned the

[146] *Ibid.*

[147] Regulation (EU) 2022/720 of 10 May 2022 on the application of Article 101(3) of the Treaty on the Functioning of the European Union to categories of vertical agreements and concerted practices, [2022] OJ L 134/4 (VBER), Article 3; VRG (n4), para 23.

[148] These are listed exclusively in Article 4 VBER (n147) and include RPM and restrictions on the distributor's ability to sell into specific territory and customers.

[149] European Commission (EU), 'Guidance on Restrictions of Competition "by Object" for the Purpose of Defining Which Agreements May Benefit from the De Minimis Notice Brussels', SWD(2014) 198 final (25 June 2014) (revised version of 3 June 2015), 5.

[150] C Fonteijn, 'Multichannel Distribution and the Impact of "Footloose" Consumers' (2016) 7 Journal of European Competition Law & Practice 241. On the term 'platformization', see J Hederstrom and L Peeperkorn, 'Vertical Restraints in On-Line Sales: Comments on Some Recent Developments' (2016) 7 Journal of European Competition Law & Practice 10, 17.

Commission sector inquiry into e-commerce[151] and have informed the reform of the VBER and VRG. The main findings of the sector inquiry with respect to e-commerce in consumer goods centred around increased price transparency in digital markets and the observed changing competition law dynamics and distribution models.

First, such *price transparency* allows consumers to compare different products online and increases free-riding concerns, when consumers visit bricks-and-mortar shops and then buy the product online.[152] In light of the increased transparency and search-and-comparison options, competition enforcers may be called upon to reassess approaches towards free-riding. For example, *dual pricing* may be seen as a tool to combat *free-riding*.[153] Additionally, such price transparency enables undertakings to track and adjust to each other's prices through the increasing use of pricing software, which may lead to price coordination at a horizontal level. The Commission cautions that the widespread use of such software may raise competition concerns.[154] At a vertical level, such pricing software makes it easier for manufacturers to detect possible deviations from 'recommended' prices, raising concerns about potential anticompetitive *RPM agreements*.[155]

With respect to the *changing competition dynamics in online markets*, manufacturers increasingly compete on parameters of competition other than price. They place increased emphasis on quality, innovation, and brand image.[156] In addition, the emergence of platform marketplaces enables smaller retailers to market their products to a wider audience across the EU. Such *marketplace competition* may raise manufacturers' concerns with respect to the brand image of the product.[157] Such concerns have forced manufacturers to tighten their grip on their distribution networks in a variety of ways.[158] Manufacturers have increasingly started to sell their products to final consumers through online shops, calling for clarification with respect to the treatment of *dual distribution*. In addition, there has been an observed resurgence in the use of selective distribution systems (SDS), since the latter allow manufacturers to better control the distribution of their respective products both from a quality and price perspective.

To sum up, while the ever-increasing rise in online commerce has boosted dual distribution models, enabling manufacturers to directly distribute their products, at the same time, it has created the need for better control over their distribution

[151] European Commission (EU), 'E-Commerce Final Report SWD' (n33), paras 22–23.

[152] European Commission (EU), 'Final Report on the E-Commerce Sector Inquiry', COM(2017) 229 final (Brussels, 10 May 2017), para 11.

[153] *Ibid*, paras 35, 37.

[154] *Ibid*, para 13. Such concerns were discussed in section III above.

[155] European Commission (EU), 'E-Commerce Final Report' (n152), para 13.

[156] *Ibid*, para 12.

[157] *Ibid*, para 14.

[158] *Ibid*, para 15.

networks. In a bid to control free-riding, preserve their brand image, and maintain price competition, we observe the use of new types of vertical restraints such as restrictions on online advertising and marketplace bans.

Following the findings of the e-commerce sector inquiry, the Commission launched a review process of the rules on vertical restraints in October 2018, with the aim of adapting the rules to account for the gaps and lack of clarity in light of the new market realities with the exponential growth of e-commerce and the rise of online platforms.[159] The review also accounted for the Commission's and NCAs' decisional practice as well as the evolution in the case law.[160] It should be noted that the decisional practice on vertical agreements emanates predominantly from the NCAs and there exists a real risk of diverse interpretations of the rules.[161] On 9 July 2021, the Commission launched a consultation on the draft revised VBER and Vertical Guidelines,[162] with the new rules taking effect in June 2022.[163]

The impact assessment and ensuing consultation focused on four areas where the previous rules needed to be adjusted.[164] The first concerned *dual distribution*, namely situations where a supplier sells its goods or services directly as well as through independent distributors, thereby competing with its distributors at retail level. The second area where the Commission consulted on possible changes was *active sales*. Under the old VBER, restrictions on active sales were permitted in certain instances only; for example, restrictions of active sales into an exclusively allocated territory or restrictions of active and passive sales in the case of a selective distribution network. The Commission sought views on the combination of exclusive and selective distribution systems in the same territory or in different territories and the restriction of sales from outside the territory in which a selective distribution system is operated to unauthorized distributors inside that territory—collecting a mixed range of views.[165] The third set of issues concerned *measures*

[159] Regulation (EU) 330/2010 of 20 April 2010 on the Application of Article 101(3) of the Treaty on the Functioning of the European Union to Categories of Vertical Agreements and Concerted Practices, [2010] OJ L 102/1 (Old Vertical Block Exemption Regulations, Old VBER); European Commission (EU), 'Guidelines on Vertical Restraints', [2010] OJ C 130/1 (Old Vertical Restraints Guidelines, Old VRG).

[160] See, e.g. Case C-230/16 *Coty*, ECLI:EU:C:2017:941.

[161] European Commission (EU), 'Commission Publishes Findings of the Evaluation of the Vertical Block Exemption Regulation' (8 September 2020).

[162] European Commission (EU), 'Commission Invites Interested Parties to Provide Comments on Draft Revised Vertical Block Exemption Regulation and Vertical Guidelines' (9 July 2021), according to which NCAs have 'dealt with more than 90% of vertical cases during the last ten years'.

[163] VBER (n147); VRG (n4). The old VBER expired on 31 May 2022. See old VBER (n159), Article 10. For a concise discussion of the changes, see L Peeperkorn and F Wijckmans, 'The New EU Competition Rules for Supply and Distribution Agreements: No Revolution, But an Evolution of the Effects-Based Approach' (2023) 44 European Competition Law Review 127.

[164] European Commission (EU), 'Summary of the Contributions Received in the Context of the Open Public Consultation on the Impact Assessment for the Review of the Vertical Block Exemption Regulation (EU) No 330/2010', Ref Ares(2021)4119477) (24 June 2021).

[165] *Ibid*, 5–9.

restricting online sales, in particular *dual pricing*—a hard-core restraint under the previous rules—whereby a manufacturer charges a higher price to wholesalers for online distribution compared to the prices charged for offline distribution. Finally, the last area covered was *parity obligations*, namely clauses requiring businesses to offer the same or better terms to their contracting parties compared to the terms offered on any other sales channel, or on the company's direct sales channels, which received mixed opinions as to their pro- and anticompetitive effects.

The new rules provide updated guidance to businesses in light of the new market realities with respect to online sales and restrictions on advertising, while contributing to a more harmonized application of the vertical rules across different Member States.[166] In light of the answers received, the VBER readjusted the safe harbours with respect to the above four areas in a bid to eliminate false positives and reduce false negatives.[167] The Commission has tightened the rules with respect to dual distribution and parity clauses in order to remove from the benefit of the VBER those agreements that cannot be listed with sufficient certainty as efficiency enhancing. First, with respect to *dual distribution*, the proposed changes (Article 2(4)–(6) VBER) aim at excluding from the existing safe harbour scenarios dual distribution arrangements that may give rise to horizontal concerns.[168] Second, with respect to *parity clauses*, the VBER removes the benefit of the safe harbour for across-platform retail parity obligations by providers of OIS (Article 5(1)(d)).[169]

Conversely, the Commission has widened the safe harbour to incorporate situations that will likely be efficiency enhancing. With respect to restrictions on active and passive sales, Article 1(l)–(m) provides a definition, whereas changes are introduced to Article 4 allowing more leeway for setting up an exclusive distribution system and enhanced protection from unauthorized distributors within an SDS. For example, the new VBER introduces the possibility of shared exclusivity under Article 4(b)(i), allowing a supplier to appoint up to five exclusive distributors. Under the new rules, a supplier may require its distributors to pass on to their immediate customers restrictions on active sales.[170] 'Active sales' are defined as actively targeting customers and include targeted advertising, whereas 'passive sales' include sales following unsolicited requests from customers. Setting up a website is a form of passive sales, though operating a website with a top-level domain corresponding to particular territories, or offering languages that are commonly used

[166] European Commission (EU), 'Explanatory Note on the New VBER and Vertical Guidelines' (2022); European Commission (EU), 'Approval of the Content of a Draft for a Commission Regulation on the Application of Article 101(3) of the Treaty on the Functioning of the European Union to Categories of Vertical Agreements and Concerted Practices' C(2021) 5026 final (Brussels, 9 July 2021).

[167] European Commission (EU), 'Explanatory Note' (n166).

[168] See section V.2 below. In the draft VBER, Article 2(4) limited the safe harbour to instances where the parties' aggregated market share in the retail market did not exceed 10 per cent. Following the public consultation, such a proposal was dropped.

[169] VRG, (n4) section 6.2.4.

[170] European Commission (EU), 'Explanatory Note' (n166).

in particular territories and are different from the ones commonly used in the territory where the buyer is established, are a form of active sales.[171] Finally, and in light of the establishment of online sales channels, dual pricing or the imposition of different criteria for online and offline sales are no longer listed as hard-core restraints.[172]

This section discusses the most common types of vertical restraints in digital markets, which have generated enforcement activity by NCAs and have been discussed as part of the reform of the VBER. In particular, the analysis covers more generally various means to control online sales (ban on online sales or online marketplaces and/or differentiation between offline and online sales channels) as well as contractual limitations by online retail platforms (exclusivity obligations/ parity clauses—offering the lowest price on the platform). In particular, the following practices will be discussed: dual distribution; retail most-favoured-nation clauses (MFNs); online sales restrictions (such as marketplace bans, advertising restrictions, and brand bidding); RPM; and minimum advertised prices (MAP), as well as dual pricing.

V.2 Dual Distribution

Dual distribution is covered by the VBER.[173] During the Commission consultation, almost two-thirds of all respondents indicated that they, or their suppliers, engaged in dual distribution (76 out of 118).[174] The VBER was amended with respect to dual distribution in order to address concerns that emerged during the public consultation. The amended rules led to both a narrowing as well as a widening of the safe harbour. In particular, given the rise in the use of dual distribution in the digital era, the old rules may have allowed certain vertical agreements with non-negligible horizontal concerns to slip through the net. Such situations refer, first, to certain instances of information exchange between suppliers and distributors and, second, to hybrid platforms. On the contrary, the rules were extended to cover wholesalers and importers.[175]

Dual distribution is not covered by the VBER in two situations. The first concerns information exchange not directly related to the implementation of the vertical agreement or not necessary for the improvement of the production or distribution of the contract goods or services.[176] These conditions will depend on the

[171] Articles 1(1)(l) and (m) VBER (n147) and VRG (n4), paras 211–215.

[172] European Commission (EU), 'Explanatory Note' (n166); Article 4(e) VBER (n147); VRG (n4), paras 208–210.

[173] Article 2(4) VBER (n147). It was also covered by the previous rules. See Article 2(4) old VBER (n159) and old VRG (n159), para 28.

[174] European Commission (EU), 'Summary of the Contributions' (n164).

[175] European Commission (EU), 'Explanatory Note' (n166).

[176] Article 2(5) VBER (n147).

nature of the distribution agreement.[177] In order to aide businesses to self-assess such agreements, the Guidelines provide both a non-exhaustive list with examples of information exchange that will likely be seen as fulfilling these conditions and a list with factual scenarios that will most likely not be exempted.[178]

The Commission dealt with vertical restraints in dual distribution in a selective distribution system in *Guess*.[179] This decision followed the Commission sector inquiry into e-commerce and concerned a series of hard-core vertical restraints aiming at diverting online sales for Guess products to its own website and restricting intra-brand competition between its authorized distributors.[180] Amongst other restrictions, Guess imposed reporting obligations on its wholesalers in order to control cross-supplies.[181] As such, information exchange was used as a tool to monitor existing hard-core restrictions in the distribution network.[182] The Danish Competition and Consumer Authority dealt with information exchange in the context of dual distribution in *Hugo Boss*. The Danish NCA treated such information exchange as an object restriction in the form of horizontal market partitioning. In this case, Hugo Boss shared information about its planned promotional retail campaigns and respective prices with its distributors. The supplier disregarded the internal firewalls preventing the exposure of its own retail activities to its distributors.[183] The French NCA fined Apple and its two wholesalers in France (Ingram Micro and Tech Data) for dividing clients with respect to the distribution of Apple products (excluding iPhones) between 2005 and 2017.[184] In that regard, Apple and its wholesalers were fined for engaging in a hub-and-spoke information exchange.[185]

The second situation where dual distribution is not covered by the VBER concerns the provision of online intermediation services (OIS)—for example, online

[177] VRG (n4), para 98.

[178] *Ibid*, paras 99–101. See also European Commission (EU), 'Expert Report on the Review of the Vertical Block Exemption Regulation Information Exchange in Dual Distribution' (2022).

[179] *Guess* (Case AT.40428) Commission Decision, C(2018) 8455 final.

[180] On this case, see also below text to n224, 238.

[181] *Guess* (n179), para 69.

[182] European Commission (EU), 'Expert Report' (n178), 13.

[183] Danish Competition and Consumer Authority, 'The Danish Competition Council Has Adopted a Decision Finding the Exchange of Information on Prices, Discounts and Quantities in Relation to Future Sales between Retailers of Clothing Items Illegal' (24 June 2020) <https://www.en.kfst.dk/nyheder/kfst/english/decisions/20200624-the-danish-competition-council-has-adopted-a-decision-finding-the-exchange-of-information-on-prices-discounts-and-quantities-in-relation-to-future-sales-between-retailers-of-clothing-items-illegal> (accessed 9 January 2023). On this case, see European Commission (EU), 'Expert Report' (n178), 14.

[184] AdC, 'Decision 20-D-04 of March 16, 2020 Regarding Practices Implemented in the Apple Products Distribution Sector' (15 June 2020) <https://www.autoritedelaconcurrence.fr/en/decision/regarding-practices-implemented-apple-products-distribution-sector> (accessed 9 January 2023); On appeal, the Paris Court of Appeal reduced the €1.2 billion fine by two-thirds. Apple received a record fine of €1.1 billion, which also covered other anticompetitive practices, namely incentivizing its premium resellers not to undercut its prices and abusing resellers' economic dependence. See Cour d'Appel de Paris RG No 20/08582 (6 October 2022) (in French).

[185] On this case, see European Commission (EU), 'Expert Report' (n178), 16.

e-commerce platforms and app stores—when the OIS provider has a hybrid function. This covers situations where the OIS provider is also a competitor on the relevant market for the sale of the intermediated goods or services.[186] The Guidelines clarify that hybrid-platform, dual-distribution agreements are not an enforcement priority for the Commission in the absence of any object restrictions and significant market power of the platform.[187] Conversely, if such platforms are listed as gatekeepers under the DMA, they may attract Commission scrutiny.

V.3 Retail MFNs

The platformization of the economy has caused a renewed interest and concomitant enforcement wave towards retail MFNs.[188] MFNs, also known as parity clauses/agreements or 'best price guarantees', can be distinguished as narrow or wide. Narrow MFNs prevent suppliers from offering better prices on their own websites compared to the ones offered on platforms' websites, while allowing them to offer different prices to different platforms. Wide MFNs prevent suppliers from offering better prices across the board.[189]

With the exponential advent of e-commerce, there have been a large number of related cases, both at the Commission and at Member State level, involving different platforms.[190] Many of these cases have been resolved with commitments, thereby not

[186] Article 2(6) VBER (n147). VRG (n4), para 104. Online intermediation services follow the same definition as in the Directive (EU) 2015/1535 20 (Codification) (n13), 1; Article 1(1)(e) VBER (n147).

[187] VRG (n4), paras 108–109. See also European Commission (EU), 'Explanatory Note on the New VBER and Vertical Guidelines' (2022), 2 <https://competition-policy.ec.europa.eu/system/files/2022-05/explanatory_note_VBER_and_Guidelines_2022.pdf> (accessed 5 January 2022).

[188] References to MFNs in this section are to retail MFNs. A distinction can be made between wholesale and retail MFNs. Wholesale MFN clauses can be to the advantage of the buyer (most-favoured-customer clause—MFCC) or the seller (most-favoured-supplier clause) and have not been an enforcement priority for the Commission. See F Bostoen, 'Most Favoured Nation Clauses: Towards an Assessment Framework under EU Competition Law', CoRe 223 (2017), 224. On MFCC (applying 102 TFEU though), see *E-book MFNs and Related Matters (Amazon)* (Case AT.40153) Commission Decision, C(2017) 2876 final (4 May 2017). On wholesale MFNs, see J Padilla, S Piccolo, and N Watson, 'The Simple Economics of Wholesale Price-Parity Agreements: The Case of the Airline Tickets Distribution Industry' (2020) 17 Journal of Competition Law and Economics 364.

[189] CMA, 'Private Motor Insurance Market Investigation' (Final Report, 24 September 2014), paras 57 et seq. For a discussion, see contributions at OECD, 'Competition and Across Platform Parity Agreements' (2015) <https://www.oecd.org/daf/competition/competition-cross-platform-parity.htm> (accessed 8 June 2024).

[190] See, e.g. *Apple E-Books* (Case COMP/39.847) Commission Decision, C(2012) 9288 (12 December 2012) <https://ec.europa.eu/competition/antitrust/cases/dec_docs/39847/39847_26804_4.pdf> (accessed 8 June 2024) (addressed to four out of five publishers and Apple) and Commission Decision, C(2013) 4750 (25 July 2013) <https://ec.europa.eu/competition/antitrust/cases/dec_docs/39847/39847_27536_4.pdf> (addressed to Penguin). See also *E-book MFNs and Related Matters (Amazon)* (n188), decided under Article 102 TFEU. See also the UK and German investigations into Amazon's parity clauses (2013) also closed with commitments, with Amazon agreeing to abandon such clauses across the EU. See Office of Fair Trading (OFT), 'Amazon Online Retailer: Investigation into Anti-Competitive Practices', CE/9692/12 (1 October 2013) <https://www.gov.uk/cma-cases/amazon-online-retailer-investigation-into-anti-competitive-practices> (accessed 9 June 2024), Bundeskartellamt,

serving to clarify the law to the requisite standard. Here, the purpose is not to discuss the case law in detail but rather to point to the different approaches. The multiple cases looking at MFNs by online travel agents (OTAs) serve as a good case study.

Since 2010, the application of EU competition law to OTAs' MFNs has generated considerable enforcement activities by NCAs, resulting in different decisions and diverse enforcement approaches.[191] NCAs alleged, amongst others, that OTAs (Booking.com and Expedia—and Hotel Reservation Service in Germany), and the InterContinental Hotels Group (IHG) had MFN clauses in their respective agreements which ensured that the prices listed on OTAs could not be undercut by any other outlet.

The Bundeskartellamt has prohibited such practices, first for wide,[192] and then for narrow MFNs,[193] whereas the French,[194] Italian,[195] and Swedish[196] NCAs have opted for commitment decisions.[197] The latter three NCAs coordinated their investigations and accepted identical commitments from Booking.com to change its wide parity clauses into narrow ones across the EU.[198] Booking.com has applied the narrow parity clause since July 2015 and Expedia has done so since August 2015. Following these changes, though, Loi Macron in France introduced

'Amazon Abandons Price Parity Clauses for Good' (26 November 2013) <https://www.bundeskartellamt.de/SharedDocs/Meldung/EN/Pressemitteilungen/2013/26_11_2013_Amazon-Verfahrenseinstellung.html> (accessed 9 June 2024) (*Amazon Marketplace Germany*).

[191] See, e.g. European Commission (EU), 'Report on the Monitoring Exercise Carried Out in the Online Hotel Booking Sector by EU Competition Authorities' (2016) <https://ec.europa.eu/competition/ecn/hotel_monitoring_report_en.pdf> (accessed 9 June 2024).

[192] Bundeskartellamt, *HRS Bestpreisklausel* (Case B.9—66/10) (20 December 2013).

[193] Bundeskartellamt, FCO Decision (23 December 2015) (Case B9-121/13), Decision (23 December 2015). See S Heinz, 'Online Booking Platforms and EU Competition Law in the Wake of the German Bundeskartellamt's Booking.com Infringement Decision' (2016) 7 Journal of European Competition Law and Practice 530.

[194] AdC, 'Decision 15-D-06 Regarding Practices Implemented by Booking.com B.V., Booking.com France SAS and Booking.com Customer Service France SAS in the Online Hotel Booking Sector' (21 April 2015).

[195] See AGCM (Italian Competition Authority), 'Mercato dei servizi turistici—prenotazioni alberghiere on line' (Case I779) (21 April 2015).

[196] Konkurrensverket, Decision 596/2013 (15 April 2015).

[197] See also the UK investigation, also closed with commitments that focused on discounting practices, OFT, 'Hotel Online Booking: Decision to Accept Commitments to Remove Certain Discounting Restrictions for Online Travel Agents', OFT1514 (31 January 2014) <https://webarchive.nationalarchives.gov.uk/ukgwa/20140402153926/http://www.oft.gov.uk/shared_oft/ca-and-cartels/oft1514dec.pdf> (accessed 9 June 2024). The CMA looked at restrictions in the contracts between the hotel chain IHG and OTAs (Booking.com and Expedia) to offer discounts on room prices to consumers. Such restrictions may amount to RPM. See also Irish investigation; Competition and Consumer Protection Commission (CCPC), 'Commission Secures 5-Year Commitments from Booking.com' (6 October 2015) <https://www.ccpc.ie/business/commission-secures-5-year-commitments-booking-com/#:~:text = Tuesday%2C%206th%20October%202015%3A%20The,agent%20platform%2C%20Booking.com> (accessed 29 April 2024).

[198] European Commission (EU), 'The French, Italian and Swedish Competition Authorities Accept the Commitments Offered by Booking.com' <https://webgate.ec.europa.eu/multisite/ecn-brief/en/content/french-italian-and-swedish-competition-authorities-accept-commitments-offered-booking com> (accessed 9 June 2024).

a blanket prohibition on MFNs in the hotel sector,[199] and the Bundeskartellamt in Germany issued a prohibition decision against Booking.com's narrow parity clauses.[200] Booking.com challenged this decision, which was later overturned by the Düsseldorf Higher Regional Court in June 2019, which ruled that such clauses are necessary for the fair exchange of services between platforms and hotels.[201] However, on 18 May 2021, the Federal Court of Justice overturned this judgment.[202] In 2019, an OTA alleged that its competitors, Booking.com and Expedia, were *de facto* still employing wide price-parity clauses. According to the complaint, Booking.com and Expedia demoted hotel operators that offer cheaper rooms on rival websites.[203]

As a rule of thumb, competition authorities agree that wide MFNs are anticompetitive,[204] whereas the approach is more nuanced with respect to narrow MFNs. The Commission acknowledges that the effects of such clauses may be pro- or anticompetitive, depending on the market characteristics.[205] The distinguishing factor is whether the inter-platform competition is sufficiently strong.

Parity clauses were not listed as hard-core restraints under the previous VBER and were exempted if the parties' market shares did not exceed 30 per cent.[206] With respect to retail parity clauses imposed by platforms, the VBER no longer provides a safe harbour under Article 5(1)(d). This presents a strict approach, since such a restriction still allows for the offering of better terms on other sales channels and presents a reaction to the so-called platformization of the economy and the widespread use of platforms for the supply of a range of goods and services. Across-platform parity clauses are now listed under excluded restrictions and must be assessed individually. Factors to be taken into account in this assessment include (i) the market position of the OIS provider and its competitors, (ii) the share of

[199] Loi Macron was passed on 9 July 2015, following intense lobbying by the European Trade Association of Hotels. See A Ezrachi, 'The Competitive Effects of Parity Clauses on Online Commerce' (2015) 11 European Competition Journal 488, 518. Similarly in Austria, in November 2016, all OTA parity clauses were prohibited by an amendment to the law on unfair competition. See European Commission (EU), 'Report on the Monitoring Exercise Carried Out in the Online Hotel Booking Sector' (n191), 5. Italy has also introduced legislation prohibiting both wide and narrow retail MFNs between OTAs and hotels. See S Long, 'Retail MFNs and Online Platforms under EU Competition Law: A Practical Primer' (CPI Antitrust Chronicle, September 2019) <https://euclid-law.eu/wp-content/uploads/2021/09/Retail-MFNs-and-Online-Platforms-under-EU-Competition-Law-A-practical-primer.pdf> (accessed 9 June 2024).

[200] Bundeskartellamt, FCO Decision (n193). See Heinz (n193).

[201] Judgment, Decision VI-Kart 2/16 (4 June 2019).

[202] Judgment, KVR 54/20 (18 May 2021).

[203] CMA, 'Algorithms: How They Can Reduce Competition and Harm Consumers' (n36), para 2.82. See also M Hunold, R Kesler, and U Laitenberger, 'Hotel Rankings of Online Travel Agents, Channel Pricing and Consumer Protection', ZEW—Centre for European Economic Research, Discussion Paper No 18-059 (2018) <https://papers.ssrn.com/sol3/papers.cfm?abstract_id = 3447828> (accessed 9 June 2024).

[204] CMA, 'Case 50505—Price Comparison Website: Use of Most Favoured Nation Clauses by BGL' (19 November 2020).

[205] EU Experts Report (n137), 5, 55.

[206] European Commission (EU), 'E-Commerce Final Report SWD' (n33), para 621.

buyers covered by the obligations, (iii) the possibility of multi-homing, (iv) barriers to entry in the online intermediation market, and (v) the significance of the direct sales channels and the possibility of delisting.[207] In addition, the DMA imposes a regulatory obligation on gatekeepers not to use either narrow or wide retail MFNs.[208]

On the contrary, narrow parity obligations preventing buyers of the OIS from offering better terms on their own sales channels are still covered by the block exemption, provided that both parties are below the 30 per cent market share threshold, though caution should be exercised in relation to the use of such clauses in concentrated platform markets.[209]

In terms of the assessment of MFN clauses under Article 101 TFEU, the following questions are relevant. First, is there an agreement between the platforms and suppliers or are the platforms genuine agents of the supplier? Second, is this a horizontal or vertical agreement? Does it have as its object or effect the restriction of competition? Is it ancillary to a pro-competitive aim? Can it be exempted under Article 101(3) TFEU?

First, if platforms are listed as genuine agents, the commercial risks remain with the supplier, and therefore there is no agreement under EU competition law. Under this scenario, MFN clauses may be assessed under Article 102 TFEU. Yet platforms, even if they do not take title to the goods and services supplied on the platform (much like genuine agents) and appear to operate on an agency model, where the supplier sets the price and the platform retains a commission fee, do invest significant amounts in promotions and marketing.[210] The last argument was accepted by the Bundeskartellamt in the *HRS* case.[211] In addition, even if they qualify as agents, restrictions on the principal are not covered and, thus, may be assessed under Article 101 TFEU.[212] While this is a contentious issue, the NCAs' decisional practice appears to suggest that suppliers and platforms' arrangements do not qualify as genuine agency agreements. This is also supported by the approach to agency agreements in the VRG.[213]

With respect to whether they qualify as horizontal or vertical agreements, the enforcement record suggests that they qualify as vertical agreements, except for instances where they may contribute towards horizontal collusion[214] or where the platform is active at the suppliers' level as well.[215] MFNs could be seen as a form

207 VRG (n4), para 361.

208 Article 5(3) DMA (n127).

209 European Commission (EU), 'Explanatory Note' (n166). See VRG (n4), paras 253–255.

210 P Akman, 'A Competition Law Assessment of Platform Most-Favored-Customer Clauses' (2016) 1294) Journal of Competition Law and Economics 781, 804–814.

211 Bundeskartellamt, *HRS Bestpreisklausel* (n192), paras 148–149.

212 VRG (n4), paras 18–21.

213 See section II.2 above.

214 *Apple E-Books* (n190).

215 *Amazon Marketplace Germany* (n190).

of RPM, since they are associated with similar theories of harm.[216] For some authors, they constitute 'RPM at its worst',[217] since they have a horizontal element with suppliers offering identical prices across platforms. In terms of effects, competition authorities have discussed softening retail competition between platforms by disincentivizing competition on commission rates charged to suppliers, deterring market entry, and potentially facilitating collusion between suppliers.[218] However, narrow MFNs do not give rise to many concerns associated with wide MFNs.[219] This is confirmed by the approach taken in the new VBER, which lists across-platform MFNs as an excluded restriction, thereby narrowing the scope of the safe harbour.[220]

When it comes to possible exemptions under Article 101(3) TFEU, MFNs could possibly be exempted to prevent free-riding. Platforms lower search costs for consumers, who can first browse on the platform and then visit the supplier's website to buy the product. This is exactly the type of scenario that narrow MFNs intend to prevent in order to protect the platform's investment.

V.4 Online Sales Restrictions: Marketplace Bans, Restrictions on Advertising, and Brand Bidding

The exponential growth of online sales channels has created friction between the treatment of offline and online sales and the extent to which certain restrictions on online sales are permissible. Some of these cases challenge the approach to selective distribution and the ability of suppliers to impose limits on selling online, whereas others may already be covered by the VBER and VRG. The supplier may require the distributor to meet certain quality standards for selling online, or have at least one physical shop in order to join the selective distribution network, or impose certain restrictions on selling on platforms.[221] The question here is whether certain restraints, previously listed as hard core, should have continued to be treated as such or whether suppliers should have been allowed more leeway

[216] OECD, 'Hearing on Across Platform Parity Agreements' (Note by United Kingdom) (27–28 October 2015), para 21.

[217] A Fletcher and M Hviid, 'Broad Retail Price MFN Clauses: Are They RPM "at Its Worst"?' (2016) 81 Antitrust Law Journal 65.

[218] OECD, 'Note by United Kingdom' (n216), 6. On the 'horizontal' effects and 'vertical' effects of MFN clauses, see Fletcher and Hviid (n217).

[219] Ezrachi (n199).

[220] Recently, the Amsterdam District Court has sent a preliminary reference request to the CJEU requiring clarifications (i) on whether wide and narrow retail price MFNs may constitute ancillary restrictions under Article 101(1) TFEU and (ii) on the relevant market definition. See David van Wamel, 'In Search of Clarity: Amsterdam Court Refers Preliminary Questions on Parity Clauses to CJEU' (Kluwer Competition Law Blog, 20 April 2023) <https://competitionlawblog.kluwercompetitionlaw.com/2023/04/20/in-search-of-clarity-amsterdam-court-refers-preliminary-questions-on-parity-clauses-to-cjeu> (accessed 9 June 2024).

[221] Old VRG (n159), para 54; VRG (n4), para 208.

to protect their selective distribution system and the related distributor's incentives. For example, suppliers may strive to maintain online prices at the same level as bricks-and-mortar prices. Should that be listed as anticompetitive RPM?

A complete ban on online sales is considered a hard-core restraint, since, in the VBER lingo,[222] it constitutes a restriction of the territory into which, or of the customers to whom, a distributor may sell the respective goods/services or a restriction of sales to end users by members of a selective distribution system.[223] The new rules now explicitly blacklist clauses that prevent the effective use of the Internet (Article 4(e)). In *Guess*, for example, the Commission held that a contractual term providing that authorized retailers had to obtain explicit written authorization from Guess before selling online without specifying any quality criteria for such authorization constituted a restriction of competition by object. Such a term restricted intra-brand competition and facilitated market partitioning.[224]

However, other restrictions on online sales may fall within the scope of the VBER as they may aim to prevent (though not to ban) retailers from selling online. First, such restrictions may concern the distributor's ability to sell on *online marketplaces*. In *Coty*,[225] the CJEU was asked (in a preliminary reference proceeding) whether, in selective distribution, a contractual ban on selling high-end perfumes through online marketplaces constituted an infringement of Article 101(1) TFEU or a hard-core restriction under Article 4 (old) VBER. By referring to its e-commerce sector inquiry, according to which in online distribution, despite the increasing importance of third-party platforms, over 90 per cent of the distributors surveyed indicated that the main online distribution channel is the distributor's own website,[226] the CJEU concluded that 'a prohibition, [...] imposed on its authorised distributors, on using, in a discernible manner, third-party platforms for the internet sale of luxury goods does not go beyond what is necessary in order to preserve the luxury image of those goods'.[227] This is because the restriction concerns only one specific online channel and other channels remain available.[228] The German NCA was, to some extent, stricter in its treatment of online marketplace bans. In *Adidas*, it closed its investigation after the company stopped implementing a ban on online marketplace sales in its selective distribution network.[229] In *ASICS*, it appeared to suggest that an online marketplace ban constituted a hard-core restraint without addressing the question specifically, since two

222 Article 4(b) and (c) VBER (n147).

223 Hedelstroem and Peeperkorn (n150) 18; Case C-439/09 *Pierre Fabre*, ECLI:EU:C:2011:649; OFT, 'Roma-Branded Mobility Scooters: Prohibitions on Online Sales and Online Price Advertising', CE/9578-12 (5 August 2013).

224 *Guess* (n179), paras 53, 131.

225 *Coty* (n160).

226 *Ibid*, para 54.

227 *Ibid*, para 55.

228 *Ibid*, paras 64–69.

229 Bundeskartellamt, 'Adidas Abandons Ban on Sales via Online Market Places' (Press release, 2 July 2014).

other hard-core restraints had already been ascertained.[230] The new rules provide guidance on the assessment of an online marketplace ban, in line with the CJEU approach.[231]

A second category of online sales restrictions that may benefit from the VBER, depending on their respective scope, concerns *restrictions on online advertising*.[232] For example, a ban on the use of all PCWs amounts to preventing the buyer from using an entire online advertising channel and is listed as a hard-core restriction under Article 4(e) VBER.[233] The German NCA dealt with this issue in *ASICS* and held that prohibiting the use of PCWs in the context of a selective distribution system is a hard-core restriction under Article 4(c) VBER.[234] Arguably, such an approach cannot be reconciled with *Coty*, since a prohibition on the use of PCWs cannot be equated with an in toto ban on online sales.[235]

Another important issue in the context of selective distribution systems is whether, and under what terms, authorized distributors may engage in advertising the respective products online.[236] Keyword advertising has been identified as 'the new frontier of the IP–antitrust interface'.[237] In *Guess*, the Commission imposed a fine on the company for a number of vertical restraints in its selective distribution system in a bid to divert traffic to its own website. Amongst other restrictions, Guess prohibited its authorized distributors from using its brand names and trademarks in online search advertising, in particular in Google Ad Words.[238] The Commission held that such restrictions did not serve the legitimate objective of protecting Guess's brand image.[239] The online search advertising restriction was treated as an object restriction since it reduced authorized retailers' ability to advertise and ultimately to sell the contract products to customers and limited intrabrand competition.[240] A similar approach towards brand bidding was adopted by

[230] The Bundeskartellamt acknowledged that there were conflicting court judgments with respect to the treatment of online marketplace bans in Germany. See Bundeskartellamt, 'Unlawful Restrictions of Online Sales of ASICS Running Shoes' (Case B2-98/11, 13) (13 January 2016). Here, the issues concerned restrictions on brand bidding and the use of price comparison websites (PCWs). See below, text to n243.

[231] VRG (n4), paras 332–334.

[232] *Ibid*, paras 203, 204, 206, 210.

[233] *Ibid*, paras 203, 347.

[234] Bundeskartellamt, 'Unlawful Restrictions of Online Sales of ASICS Running Shoes' (13 January 2016) (n230). See Bundeskartellamt, 'Unlawful Restrictions of Online Sales of ASICS Running Shoes' (26 August 2015) (confirmed on appeal). See German Federal Court of Justice, Case KVR 41/17 (12 December 2017).

[235] In this regard, see T Kuhn and M Rust, 'Between Coty, Guess and the New V-BER—Where Do We Stand on E-Commerce Restrictions?' (2019) 40(8) European Competition Law Review 376, 378.

[236] European Commission (EU), 'E-Commerce Final Report SWD' (n33), para 632.

[237] G Colangelo, 'Competing through Keyword Advertising' (2020) 16 Journal of Competition Law and Economics 306, 346.

[238] *Guess* (n179), paras 40–52.

[239] *Ibid*, para 119.

[240] *Ibid*, para 125.

the German NCA in *ASICS*[241] and *ADIDAS*.[242] In *ASICS*, the Bundeskartellamt held that the restriction on the use of brand names as a key word in paid search engine advertising for the placement of advertisements on third-party websites and backlinks for search engine optimization, as well as the restriction on using price comparison engines to promote sales, constituted hard-core restraints under Article 4(c) (old) VBER since it restricted authorized distributors from reaching customers outside their geographic area via the Internet.[243] These restraints could not be justified because of free-rider considerations protecting the investments in customer services by authorized distributors selling primarily offline. The Dutch NCA has also listed brand bidding as a hard-core restriction.[244] Arguably, such harsh treatment of brand-bidding restrictions is not corroborated by strong empirical and economic evidence at present. To the contrary, since economic theory is inconclusive, and they may lead to both pro and anticompetitive effects such as recovering fixed advertising costs, they need to be subjected to an effects analysis.[245]

The new rules clarify that a prohibition on the use of an entire online advertising channel (such as search engines or price comparison services) and indirect prohibitions on using an entire online advertising channel (like the obligation not to use the supplier's trademarks or brand names to bid in order to be referenced in search engines or providing price-related information to PCWs) constitute hard-core restrictions.[246]

V.5 RPM and MAP

The widespread use of software programmes and price-comparison tools, as well as the ever-increasing use of the Internet as a distribution channel, improve transparency in online markets and facilitate price monitoring, thereby increasing the risk of anticompetitive RPM agreements.[247] Such concerns are corroborated by the NCAs' enforcement activity relating to online RPM.[248] The Commission has also

[241] Bundeskartellamt, 'Unlawful Restrictions of Online Sales of ASICS Running Shoes' (13 January 2016) (n230).

[242] Bundeskartellamt, 'Adidas Abandons Ban on Sales via Online Market Places' (n229), 10.

[243] Bundeskartellamt, 'Unlawful Restrictions of Online Sales of ASICS Running Shoes' (13 January 2016) (n230).

[244] ACM, 'Guidelines Regarding Arrangements between Suppliers and Buyers' (2019), 7. (2019).

[245] E Deutscher, 'Brand Bidding Restraints Revisited: What Is the Appropriate Economic and Legal Framework for the Antitrust Analysis of Vertical Online Search Advertising Restraints?' (2021) 44(4) World Competition 373, 375–376. See also Colangelo (n237), 347–348.

[246] VRG (n4), para 206.

[247] See, e.g. OECD, 'Roundtable on Hub-and-Spoke Arrangements' (n68), 2.

[248] See, e.g. CMA, 'Online Resale Price Maintenance in the Light Fittings Sector' (Case 50343) (3 May 2017); CMA, 'Online Resale Price Maintenance in the Bathroom Fittings Sector' (Case CE/9857-14) (10 May 2016); CMA, 'Online Resale Price Maintenance in the Commercial Refrigeration Sector (Case CE/9856-14) (24 May 2016); CMA, 'Online Resale Price Maintenance in the Digital Piano and Digital Keyboard Sector' (Case 50565-2) (1 August 2019).

imposed fines on four manufacturers of consumer electronics in relation to online RPM, where these manufacturers were using price-monitoring algorithms to implement their anticompetitive agreement.[249] In all these cases, the manufacturers used monitoring algorithms to implement the anticompetitive RPM.

The new rules clarify that requiring the distributor not to advertise prices below the level set by the supplier through the imposition of MAPs amounts to an indirect form of RPM and therefore to a hard-core restriction.[250] MAPs are listed as an indirect form of RPM, even though, in principle, they allow the distributor to sell at a lower than the advertised price; nonetheless, they act as a disincentive for the setting of lower prices since they limit the ability to inform customers about potential discounts.[251] MAPs may, nonetheless, be exempted under Article 101(3) TFEU if the supplier can demonstrate that a distributor regularly resells its product below the wholesale price, as such a practice may negatively affect the product's brand image and subsequently reduce the demand for the respective product as well as reducing the supplier's incentive to make investments in quality and brand image.[252]

Similar restrictions have also been assessed by NCAs. The CMA, in *Pride*, held that Pride, a mobility scooter manufacturer, had asked its distributors not to deviate from its recommended retail prices in online advertising.[253] The CMA, by applying national competition law (since the practices did not affect interstate trade), concluded that the restrictions on online advertising constituted a hard-core/object restriction, since it restricted the territories and customers where the distributors could sell the products.[254]

V.6 Dual Pricing

Dual pricing refers to the situation where the supplier charges higher prices for selling online compared to offline sales, and under the old VBER and VRG framework, it constituted a hard-core restriction.[255] During the Commission

[249] *Asus* (Case AT.40465) Commission Decision, C(2018) 4773 final (2018); *Denon & Marantz* (Case AT.40469) Commission Decision, C(2018) 4774 final (2018); *Philips* (Case AT.4018) Commission Decision, C(2018) 4797 final (2018); *Pioneer* (Case AT.40182) Commission Decision, C(2018) 4790 final (2018).

[250] VRG (n4), para 187. See also the CMA issuing an open letter to suppliers and resellers stating (amongst other things) that minimum advertising practices online can equate to RPM. See CMA, 'Restricting Resale Prices: An Open Letter to Suppliers and Resellers' (20 June 2017).

[251] VRG (n4), para 189.

[252] *Ibid*, para 197.

[253] OFT, 'Mobility Scooters Supplied by Pride Mobility Products Limited: Prohibition on Online Advertising of Prices below Pride's RRP', Decision (27 March 2014) (Pride). See also OFT, 'Roma-Branded Mobility Scooters' (n223); CMA, 'Online Resale Price Maintenance in the Commercial Refrigeration Sector' (n248).

[254] Old VBER (n159), Article 4(b).

[255] *Ibid*, Article 4(b)–(c) and Old VRG (n159), para 52(d).

consultation, the majority of respondents (71 out of all 118 respondents) pointed to concrete benefits from dual pricing, with some respondents stating that the rationale for treating dual pricing as a hard-core restriction based on the concern that this can deter distributors from selling online is outdated.[256]

Under the new rules, dual pricing may benefit from the VBER.[257] The rationale for no longer treating dual pricing as a hard-core restraint is that it potentially incentivizes an appropriate level of investments. However, when the price difference between offline and online channels makes selling on the latter unprofitable or where it limits the quantity of products sold online, it may still qualify as a hard-core restraint since it may be seen as limiting the effective use of the Internet (Article 4(e) VBER). On the contrary, dual pricing is exempted when the price difference between online and offline is related to investment costs incurred by the buyer for each distribution channel.[258]

VI. Conclusion

The digital economy has brought a range of benefits for businesses and consumers alike, yet it has raised new challenges for competition law enforcement. First, the various platform business models have challenged the assessment of the notion of undertaking both in respect to the principal–agent relationship and whether platforms act as agents of suppliers and in respect to the classification of suppliers as employees or self-employed entities. Second, the rise and widespread use of algorithmic tools have tested the limits of competition law tools in addressing various forms of algorithmic collusion. Third, the prevalence of data in the digital economy has allowed new types of information exchange, some of which—such as data pools—may be considered overall pro-competitive in the light of their particular characteristics. Finally, with the fourth industrial revolution forever leaving its imprint on the internet landscape and e-commerce, new modes of online distribution have emerged, presenting novel challenges for competition law enforcement. For example, dual distribution—where suppliers directly distribute their products to end users—has become more widespread. Equally, comparison shopping services, as well as marketplaces have multiplied, and with them the need for suppliers to impose tighter controls over their distribution networks through the use of various clauses (such as MFNs, RPM, or MAP) that may be deemed anticompetitive.

The potential and concomitant challenges of digitalization and platformization have also been taken into account in the revision of the rules applicable to

[256] European Commission (EU), 'Summary of the Contributions Received in the Context of the Open Public Consultation on the Impact Assessment for the Review of the Vertical Block Exemption Regulation' (EU) 330/2010 (2010), 9.

[257] VRG (n4), para 209.

[258] *Ibid.*

horizontal as well as vertical agreements. They have also informed Commission policy and priority setting. Against this background, this chapter has addressed the most pertinent issues with respect to the application of Article 101 TFEU in the digital economy, eventually addressing the broader question of whether EU competition law has been successful in addressing such challenges. The analysis in this chapter points to an overall positive assessment of the current tools.

5
Abuse of Dominance

I. Introduction

Market concentration in the digital economy, with a handful of companies controlling key products and services, has triggered debates with respect to the appropriate role of competition law enforcement.[1] Critics attribute the momentous increase of Google, Apple, Facebook, Amazon, and Microsoft's (GAFAM's) market valuation to their ability to 'beat the antitrust rap'.[2] In the European Union (EU), since *Google Shopping* was launched in 2010,[3] we have seen a flurry of enforcement action against Big Tech both at EU and Member-State level.[4] It is still too early to assess the impact of such actions, yet with the recent adoption of additional regulatory tools,[5] consensus seems to be emerging that competition law tools alone cannot address the adverse effects of the incumbent's entrenched power.

At the time of writing, the Commission and selected national competition authorities (NCAs) have completed cases against Big Tech companies, and there is also a number of ongoing investigations. Section II below embarks on a discussion of the respective case law. Such discussion sets the scene for the ensuing discussion in section III, which presents the alleged problems and categorizes the various theories of harm as well as questioning whether, and how, the latter can be reconciled with recently adopted regulatory tools, primarily the Digital Markets Act (DMA).

[1] See Chapter 2 on the challenges with respect to the application of competition law in the digital economy and Chapter 3 with respect to the aims of competition law enforcement.

[2] A Orlowski, 'Free Market Champions or a Cosy Cartel?' (*The Telegraph*, 5 April 2021), referring to Scott Clelan, saying that 'It's a $4 trillion question—how did Google, Facebook, Microsoft and Apple go from a $1 trillion valuation to a $5 trillion valuation today?' For Cleland, the answer is 'They beat the antitrust rap.'

[3] European Commission (EU), 'Commission Probes Allegations of Antitrust Violations by Google' (Press release, 30 November 2010).

[4] The focus of this chapter is EU competition law enforcement, and it does not discuss the various enforcement actions against Big Tech in other jurisdictions, including the United States, Russia, Turkey, India, South Korea, Japan, and Brazil, amongst others.

[5] See, e.g. Regulation (EU) 2022/1925 of the European Parliament and of the Council of 14 September 2022 on contestable and fair markets in the digital sector and amending Directives (EU) 2019/1937 and (EU) 2020/1828, [2022] OJ L265/1 (Digital Markets Act, DMA). For other regulatory initiatives, see Chapter 3, section V.2.1.

Competition Law and Policy in Digital Markets. Maria Ioannidou and Bingwan Xiong, Oxford University Press.
 DOI: 10.1093/9780191925955.003.0005

II. The Case Law

II.1 Introduction

This section presents the cases against Big Tech before the Commission and selected NCAs. The ensuing discussion focuses on cases at EU level, while also offering selective examples from enforcement efforts at Member-State level. Table 5.1 presents the cases against Google, Apple, Facebook, and Amazon (GAFA) discussed in this chapter, with ongoing cases (at the time of writing) being underlined for ease of reference.

II.2 A Primer: Microsoft

Any discussion of competition law enforcement against GAFA is incomplete without a reference to the *Microsoft (Media Player)* case, the first—and perhaps most influential—case the Commission has brought in digital markets.[6] In this case, the Commission, later confirmed by the EU General Court, found that Microsoft infringed Article 102 of the Treaty on the Functioning of the European Union (TFEU) by committing two counts of abuse: first, by refusing to supply its competitors with interoperability information in order to develop and distribute competing products on the work group server operating systems market;[7] and second, by tying its Media Player to the Windows client PC operating system (OS).[8] The Commission imposed a fine and a set of remedies, requiring Microsoft to supply interoperability information on reasonable and non-discriminatory terms as well as to offer a version of the Windows client PC OS without incorporating the Windows Media Player, at the same time retaining the right to offer them as a bundle.[9]

With respect to *refusal to supply*, despite Microsoft's submissions to the contrary, the General Court (GC) accepted that the Commission analysis was consistent with the case law on refusal to license intellectual property rights.[10] In particular,

[6] *Microsoft* (Case COMP/C-3/37.792) Commission Decision, C(2004)900 final; Case T-201/04 *Microsoft Corp v Commission*, ECLI:EU:T:2007:289. See also *Microsoft (Tying)* (Case COMP/39.530) Commission Decision, C(2013) 1210. In this second *Microsoft (Tying)* case, the Commission imposed a fine on Microsoft for a breach of its 2009 commitments decision. In this case, the alleged abusive tying concerned the tying of Microsoft's Internet Explorer to its dominant Windows client PC operating system (OS). Microsoft offered commitments to address the Commission's concerns and committed to offer Windows users the choice between different web browsers through a choice screen.

[7] *Microsoft (Tying)* (n6), para 36.

[8] *Ibid*, para 43.

[9] *Ibid*, paras 46–49.

[10] On the relevant cases, see Joined Cases C-241/91 P and C-242/91 P *RTE and ITP v Commission*, ECLI:EU:C:1995:98 (*Magill*); Case C-7/97 *Bronner*, ECLI:EU:C:1998:569; case C-418/01 *IMS Health*, ECLI:EU:C:2004:257.

Table 5.1 Cases against GAFAM in the EU

	EU	Germany	France	Italy	Netherlands	United Kingdom
Google	*Google Shopping* (fine, 27 June 2017); Case T-612/17; Case C-48/22P	*Determining 'paramount significance of competition across markets'* (25 May 2021) (section 19a German Competition Act) (PSCAM, 5 January 2022)	*Google Ads* (online search advertising) (fine, 20 December 2019)	*Android auto interoperability/Enel X app* (fine, 13 May 2021)		*Privacy Sandbox* (commitments, June 2021)
	Google Android (fine, 18 July 2018); Case T-604/18; Case C-738/22P (not yet decided)	*Data processing terms* (25 May 2021) (section 19a(2) no 4a German Competition Act) (SO, 23 December 2022)(commitments decision, 5 October 2023)	*Google News Showcase* (interim measures, April 2020) (fine for non-compliance, July 2021) (commitments, June 2022)	*Display advertising/ use of data* (opened in 28 October 2020); case closed following the opening of Commission AdTech investigation		*AdTech* (opened 25 May 2022)
	Google AdSense (fine, 20 March 2019); Case T-334/19; Case C-826/24P (not yet decided)	*Google News Showcase* (4 June 2021) (section 19a German *Competition Act* (commitments, 21 December 2022)				*Header bidding* (partially closed/ partially combined with AdTech investigation, March 2023)
	Online display advertising (launched 22 June 2021) (SO, 14 June 2023)	*Google Maps* (21 June 2022) (section 19a German Competition Act) (proposal from Google, 20 December 2023)	*Adtech/display advertising/auction processes* (fine, 7 June 2021)			*Google Play* (opened, 10 June 2022)*Case closed (DMCC Act potentially applicable)*

(*continued*)

Table 5.1 Continued

	EU	Germany	France	Italy	Netherlands	United Kingdom
Amazon	*Amazon Marketplace* (commitments, 20 December 2022)	*Amazon's terms* (commitments, 17 July 2019)		*Preferential treatment of FBA sellers* (fine, 9 December 2021)		*Use of data/ Amazon's Buy Box* (commitments, 3 November 2023)
	Amazon Buy Box (commitments, 20 December 2022)	*Determining 'paramount significance of competition across markets'* (18 May 2021) (section 19a German Competition Act) (PSCAM, 5 July 2022) on appeal				
		Influencing the pricing of sellers on Amazon Marketplace through price control mechanisms and algorithms (opened, 15 May 2020) (extended to also cover section 19a GWB, 14 November 2022)				
		Amazon and Apple brand-gating agreements (opened, 3 September 2020)(extended to also cover section 19a GWB, 14 November 2022)				
Facebook	*Classified ads sector/use of data* (fine, 14 November 2024)	*Data collection and use* (prohibition decision, 7 February 2019) on appeal	*Online advertising* (commitments, 16 June 2022)			*Use of ad data* (4 June 2021) (commitments, 3 November 2023)

		Linkage between Oculus VR products and Facebook (10 December 2020) (Meta offered remedies, 23 November 2022—case not closed—continue to monitor—also under section 19a German Competition Act); determining 'paramount significance of competition across markets' (28 January 2021) (section 19a German Competition Act) (PSCAM, 5 May 2022)	*Online ad verification* (interim measures, 4 May 2023)			
Apple App	*Ap store practices*; Case T-269/24 on appeal (not yet decided) fine, 4 March 2024 *Apple Pay* (commitments, 11 July 2024) Objections	Determining 'paramount significance of competition across markets' (21 June 2021) (section 19a German Competition Act) (PSCAM, 2 April 2023)	*Anticompetitive distribution practices/abuse of economic dependence* (fine, 16 March 2020)		*App store practices* (decision, 24 December 2021 + periodic penalty payments)	*App store T&C* (4 March 2021) Case closed (DMCC Act potentially applicable)
		Apple's App Tracking Transparency Framework (opened, 14 June 2022)	*Data use for advertising* (Statement of Objections, 27 July 2023)			

Source: Authors.

the refusal does not, in itself, constitute an abuse. However, it may constitute an abuse in the presence of exceptional circumstances, namely, first, when the refusal relates to a product or service that is indispensable for the exercise of a particular activity on a neighbouring market; second, when the refusal excludes any effective competition on that neighbouring market; and third, when the refusal prevents the emergence of a new product for which (potential) consumer demand exists.[11] Arguably, the GC (citing with the Commission analysis) has expanded exceptional circumstances in that first, the product/service of the respective refusal does not have to be indispensable as long as the refusal does not make it economically viable for competitors;[12] second, the refusal does not have to eliminate all competition but only effective competition;[13] and third, the refusal does not have to prevent the emergence of a new product but, rather, may prevent follow-on innovation, since Article 102(b) TFEU refers to not only the limitation of production but also technical development to the prejudice of consumers.[14]

Interestingly, with respect to the assessment of consumer harm, the GC made a statement with respect to the protective scope of competition and the presumed negative impact of the emergence of a very powerful player on the competitive process. The GC stressed that

> it is settled case-law that Article [102 TFEU] covers not only practices which may prejudice consumers directly but also those which indirectly prejudice them by impairing an effective competitive structure. In this case, Microsoft impaired the effective competitive structure on the work group server operating systems market by acquiring a significant market share on that market.[15]

With respect to *tying*, the GC confirmed the Commission decision. It found that all conditions for the finding of an abusive tying under Article 102 TFEU were present, namely that first, the tying (Windows PC OS) and tied products (Windows Media Player) were two separate products; second, Microsoft was dominant in the tying product market; third, customers could not obtain the tying without the tied product; and fourth, such practice resulted in the foreclosure of competition.[16] With respect to the latter condition, the Commission stated that this was not a classical tying case (which, by its nature, is liable to

[11] Case T-201/04 *Microsoft* (n6), paras 331–332.

[12] *Ibid*, para 457. Following *Microsoft*, indispensability now embraces economic indispensability. See B Vesterdorf, 'Article 82 EC: Where Do We Stand after the Microsoft Judgment?' (2008) 1 Global Arbitration Review 1, 7.

[13] Case T-201/04 *Microsoft* (n6), para 563.

[14] *Ibid*, paras 627, 647, and 665. For a discussion of these expansive aspects of the judgment, see A Andreangeli, 'Case T-201/01 *Microsoft v Commission*, Judgment of the Grand Chamber of the Court of First Instance of 17 September 2007' (2008) 45 Common Market Law Review 863, 879–884.

[15] Case T-201/04 *Microsoft* (n6), para 664.

[16] *Ibid*, paras 842, 852–857, 859–862.

foreclose competition) but rather one where tying creates the risk of foreclosing competition in the media players' market as well as negative spillover effects in the other markets, such as client PC OS,[17] given the impact on content providers and software developers in light of the existence of indirect network effects.[18] Thus, the GC has adjusted its test on abusive tying in cases of more complex technological integration.[19]

A final remark on the remedy to address the abusive tying: overall, it was considered unsuccessful, since there was no demand for the version of Windows without the Media Player, and understandably so. It was priced the same as the bundled version and offered a lower functionality.[20]

Following the seminal *Microsoft* case briefly discussed above, on 23 July 2023, the Commission opened a new investigation into Microsoft's alleged abusive tying practices concerning the alleged tying of its communication app Teams with its Office suite.[21]

II.3 Google

II.3.1 EU Cases

II.3.1.1 Google Shopping

A. Theories of Harm

The Commission initiated *Google Shopping* on 30 November 2010, following a number of complaints and cases referred by NCAs, in particular the German NCA.[22] After a protracted investigation and three failed commitment attempts, the Commission issued its infringement decision on 27 June 2017, upheld now by both the General Court and the Court of Justice.[23]

[17] *Ibid*, paras 842, 857.

[18] *Ibid*, para 983.

[19] For a discussion, see Andreangeli (n14), 887–890.

[20] N Economides and I Lianos, 'A Critical Appraisal of Remedies in the EU Microsoft Cases' (2010) 2 Columbia Business Law Review <https://doi.org/10.7916/cblr.v2010i2.2922> (accessed 7 June 2024); J Padilla and C Kalmus, 'Tying and Competition Law: An Overview of EU and National Case Law' (2012) Concurrences No 43907.

[21] European Commission (EU), 'Antitrust: Commission Opens Investigation into Possible Anticompetitive Practices by Microsoft Regarding Teams' (Press release, 27 July 2023); European Commission (EU), 'Commission Sends Statement of Objections to Microsoft over Possibly Abusive Tying Practices Regarding Teams' (Press release, 25 June 2024).

[22] *Google Search (Shopping)* (Case AT.39740) Commission Decision, C(2017) 4444 final (Brussels, 27 June 2017). See also Case T-612/17 *Google LLC v Commission*, ECLI:EU:T:2021:763, paras 21–22. The Federal Trade Commission (FTC) also launched an investigation into Google in 2011, which was closed in 2013, since Google's prominent display of its own search results was viewed as a product improvement. See FTC, 'Statement of the Federal Trade Commission Regarding Google's Search Practices—In the Matter of Google Inc. FTC File Number 111-0163' (3 January 2013).

[23] *Google Search (Shopping)*—Commission Decision (CD) and General Court (GC) (n22); Case C-48/22 P *Google LLC and Alphabet Inc v European Commission*, ECLI:EU:C:2024:726 (*Google Search (Shopping)*—CJEU).

In *Google Shopping*, the Commission found that the more favourable positioning and display of Google's own comparison shopping service (CSS) compared to its competitors in its general search engines results pages infringed Article 102 TFEU.[24] Increased traffic was essential for CSSs, and Google increased traffic to its CSS and decreased traffic to its competitors. This was the more important since the traffic from Google's general results pages constituted a large part of competing comparison services' traffic and thus could not be effectively replaced by other sources of traffic.[25]

According to the Commission, Google's CSS was prominently displayed on its general results pages in an eye-catching manner in dedicated 'boxes', without it being subject to the adjustment algorithms used for general searches. On the contrary, competing CSSs could appear on its general results pages only as general search results (blue links). The latter tended to be given a low ranking due to the application of those adjustment algorithms.[26] The Commission stressed that it did not object to Google's relevance criteria and the fact that Google promoted specialized comparison shopping results it considered relevant, but rather the problem lay in Google not applying the same positioning and display criteria to its own and to competing CSSs, and it did not make the same promotion effort with respect to its own CSS and competing CSSs.[27]

Commentators have disagreed on whether the Commission's approach constituted a 'novel' abuse in the form of self-preferencing.[28] With respect to the abusive conduct at stake, the EU Courts examined the legal classification of favouring adopted by the Commission under Article 102 TFEU and whether such conduct whereby a dominant undertaking favouring its own service at the expense of its competitors' services could be caught under Article 102 TFEU.[29] Google alleged that the Commission committed an error of law since the Commission, by classifying Google's conduct as favouring, in effect circumvented the conditions applicable in refusal to deal.[30] The GC dismissed this argument. In so doing, it based its

[24] *Google Search (Shopping)*—Commission Decision (CD) (n22), para 2.

[25] *Google Search (Shopping)*—General Court (GC) (n22), para 68.

[26] *Google Search (Shopping)*--GC (n22), para 69; *Google Search (Shopping)*—CD (n22), paras 344, 512.

[27] *Google Search (Shopping)*—GC (n22), para 69; *Google Search (Shopping)*—CD (n22), paras 440, 537.

[28] See, amongst others, B Vesterdorf, 'Theories of Self-Preferencing and Duty to Deal—Two Sides of the Same Coin' (2015) 1 Competition Law & Policy Debate 4; N Petit, 'Theories of Self-Preferencing under Article 102 TFEU: A Reply to Bo Vesterdorf' (2015) <https://orbi.uliege.be/bitstream/2268/192437/1/Theories%20of%20Self-Preferencing%20Under%20Article%20102%20TFEU%20A%20Reply%20to%20Bo%20Vesterdorf.pdf> (accessed 7 June 2024); R Nazzini, 'Google and the (Ever-Stretching) Boundaries of Article 102 TFEU' (2015) 6(5) Journal of European Competition Law & Practice 301, 307–310; P Akman, 'The Theory of Abuse in Google Search: A Positive and Normative Assessment under EU Competition Law' (2017) 2 Journal of Law, Technology and Policy 301.

[29] *Google Search (Shopping)*—GC (n22), para 123. *Google Search (Shopping)*—CJEU (n23), paras 97–99.

[30] *Ibid*, para 137. *Google Search (Shopping)*—CJEU (n23), para 65.

analysis on the principle of equal treatment as a general principle of EU law and clarified that an unjustified difference in treatment may constitute an abuse.[31] It then clarified that the Commission did not rely solely on leveraging in order to find an abuse but also assessed Google's practice of favouring its own CSS and its effects on the basis of the relevant circumstances.[32] According to the Commission decision, Google, through leveraging, relied on its dominance in the market for general search services to favour its own CSS by promoting the positioning and display of its own CSS and of its results on its general results pages in comparison to competing CSSs, whose results (due to their inherent characteristics) were susceptible to being demoted on those pages by adjustment algorithms.[33] The GC noted that the importance of Google's traffic and the fact that, in effect, it was not replaceable was taken into account by the Commission 'as *relevant circumstances*' in order for such practices to fall outside the scope of competition on the merits.[34] It concluded that

> the Commission did not merely identify leveraging but, as required by the case-law, classified Google's accompanying practices in law *on the basis of relevant criteria*. Thus, if *the favouring and its effects*, identified in the light of the specific circumstances of the relevant markets, have been validly demonstrated by the Commission, which will be verified having regard to all of the pleas and arguments, the Commission will have been fully entitled to take the view that that favouring was a departure from competition on the merits.[35]

The GC drew a distinction between the present case and the case law on refusal to deal. By characterizing Google's general search results pages as 'infrastructure', it went on to note that such infrastructure can be distinguished from the respective infrastructures in the refusal to deal case law (e.g. tangible or intangible assets such as press distribution networks or intellectual property rights). In contrast to the latter, which draw their value from their exclusive nature, general search results pages are open.[36] In addition, the GC identified an *abnormality* in Google's conduct in favouring its own search results since such conduct is the opposite of the

[31] *Ibid*, para 155. See C Ahlborn, G Van Gerven, and W Leslie, 'Bronner Revisited: Google Shopping and the Resurrection of Discrimination under Article 102 TFEU' (2022) 13 Journal of European Competition Law & Practice 87, 88 arguing that the GC treats self-preferencing (or in the language of its judgment, 'favouring') as a type of discriminatory leveraging abuse.

[32] *Google Search (Shopping)*—GC (n22), paras 166, 175.

[33] *Ibid*, para 167.

[34] *Ibid*, para 174. For an in-depth examination of the notion of 'competition on the merits', see P Colombo, 'Competition on the Merits' (2024) 61 Common Market Law Review 387, 387–416. Colombo argues that 'competition on the merits', as a principle, is at odds with more recent judgments because what would previously have been deemed anticompetitive may now be a standardized practice employed by both dominant and non-dominant undertakings.

[35] *Google Search (Shopping)*—GC (n22), para 175.

[36] *Ibid*, para 177.

economic model for its search engine success. Thus, it is for Google to justify such difference in treatment under competition law.[37]

Moreover, the GC relied on Regulation (EU) 2015/2120[38] to point to a quasi-regulatory obligation for Google. Regulation 2015/2120 establishes a non-discrimination obligation for internet access providers on the upstream market. The GC seems to take into account this general non-discrimination obligation in analysing Google's conduct on the downstream market, given Google's *ultra-dominant position* and its special responsibility not to impair genuine, undistorted competition in the internal market. The GC noted that the fact that such general obligation for non-discriminatory access to online search results does not exist does not call into question the fact that discriminatory treatment may be considered contrary to Article 102 TFEU.[39]

The GC cited with the Commission to find abusive favouring since Google's practices divert traffic from competing comparison services and are capable of having anticompetitive effects.[40] While the GC acknowledges that 'any practice, whether a pricing practice or not, which has exclusionary effects cannot be regarded, on that basis alone, as being anticompetitive',[41] thereby not equating exclusionary conduct with anticompetitive effects, nonetheless, it appears to lower the bar for establishing an abuse. In this instance, it sufficed to show that favouring occurred *in a particular context*. For examining the latter, the Commission relied on three criteria: the importance of Google's traffic, users' behaviour, and the fact that the diverted traffic cannot be effectively replaced.[42] Thus, the court found that the Commission's analysis is consistent with the case law on abusive leveraging[43]

> in so far as it may be concluded that there is an infringement on the basis, *first, of suspect elements in the light of competition law (in particular an unjustified difference in treatment)* which are absent in the case of a refusal of access and, secondly, of *specific circumstances*, [. . .], relating to the *nature of the infrastructure* from

[37] *Ibid*, para 179.
[38] Regulation (EU) 2015/2120 of the European Parliament and of the Council of 25 November 2015 laying down measures concerning open internet access and amending Directive 2002/22/EC on universal service and users' rights relating to electronic communications networks and services and Regulation (EU) 531/2012 on roaming on public mobile communications networks within the Union, [2015] OJ L 310, 1. 1.
[39] *Google Search (Shopping)*—GC (n22), para 180.
[40] *Ibid*, para 195.
[41] *Ibid*, para 195.
[42] *Ibid*, para 196.
[43] *Ibid*, para 334 and case law cited therein, though it is questionable whether the underlying abuse in such cases was a more general category, such as abusive leveraging. See Case 311/84 *Centre belge d'études de marché—Télémarketing (CBEM) v SA Compagnie luxembourgeoise de télédiffusion (CLT) and Information publicité Benelux (IPB)*, ECLI:EU:C:1985:394, para 27; Case C-333/94 P *Tetra Pak v Commission*, ECLI:EU:C:1996:436, para 25; Case T- 228/97, *Irish Sugar plc v Commission*, EU:T:1999:246, para 166; Case T-201/04 *Microsoft* (n6), para 1344.

> which that difference in treatment arises (in this instance, importance and being not effectively replaceable, in particular).[44]

From the latter, it can be inferred that abusive leveraging can be established if the competition authority adduces 'suspect evidence' (i.e. unjustified difference in treatment) plus points to specific circumstances relevant to the infrastructure at issue, namely its importance and the fact that it cannot be effectively replaced.

Apart from the question on establishing abusive leveraging, Google argued that the Commission, in effect, tacitly treated Google's conduct as refusal to deal, without establishing the Bronner indispensability and elimination of all competition on the downstream market criteria.[45] The GC acknowledged that 'Google's general results page has characteristics akin to those of an essential facility, inasmuch as there is currently no actual or potential substitute available that would enable it to be replaced in an economically viable manner on the market'[46] and that the Commission tacitly examined the indispensability condition by finding that 'the traffic generated by Google's general search pages was not 'effectively replaceable' and that other sources of traffic were not "economically viable"'.[47] However, the court distinguished the Bronner refusal to supply from Google's conduct in the present case by stating that

> [a] 'refusal' to supply that warrants the application of the conditions set out in [. . .] Bronner [. . .] implies (i) that it is express, that is to say, that there is a *'request' or in any event a wish to be granted access and a consequential 'refusal'*, and (ii) that *the trigger of the exclusionary effect—the impugned conduct—lies principally in the refusal as such*, and *not in an extrinsic practice such as, in particular, another form of leveraging abuse.*[48]

It follows that the GC accepted the Commission's approach to abusive leveraging capable of having exclusionary effects as the specific form of abuse in *Google Shopping*. The GC approach was confirmed by the CJEU, which rejected the appellants' argument that the General Court applied an incorrect legal test by failing to apply the Bronner criteria, since Google does not refuse access to competing CSSs to its general search results. Instead, it makes such access subject to discriminatory conditions.[49] Furthermore, the CJEU held

[44] *Google Search (Shopping)*—GC (n22), para 197.
[45] *Ibid*, paras 199–206. This was one of the most contentious points in this case. Discussing the indispensability condition, see, e.g. P Ibanez Colomo, 'Indispensability and Abuse of Dominance: From Commercial Solvents to Slovak Telekom and Google Shopping' (2019) 10(9) Journal of European Competition Law & Practice 532; N Dunne, 'Dispensing with Indispensability' (2020) 16(1) Journal of Competition Law and Economics 74.
[46] *Google Search (Shopping)*—GC (n22), para 224.
[47] *Ibid*, para 227.
[48] *Ibid*, para 232.
[49] *Google Search (Shopping)*—CJEU (n23), paras 79, 111–115.

that the GC was correct in its analysis, concluding that Google's conduct departed from competition on the merits. In a statement of principle the Court clarified that

> In order to find, in a given case, that conduct must be categorised as 'abuse of a dominant position' [. . .], it is necessary, *as a rule*, to demonstrate, through the *use of methods other than those which are part of competition on the merits* between undertakings, that that *conduct has the actual or potential effect of restricting that competition by excluding equally efficient competing undertakings* from the market or markets concerned, or by hindering their growth on those markets [. . .].That demonstration [. . .] must however be made in the light of all the relevant factual circumstances, irrespective of whether they concern the conduct itself, the market(s) in question or the functioning of competition on that or those market(s). That demonstration must, moreover, be aimed at establishing, [. . .] that that *conduct, at the very least, is capable of producing exclusionary effects*. In addition, conduct may be categorised as 'abuse of a dominant position' not only where it has the actual or potential effect of restricting competition on the merits by excluding equally efficient competing undertakings from the market or markets concerned, but also where it has been proven to have the *actual or potential effect—or even the object—of impeding potentially competing undertakings at an earlier stage*, through the placing of obstacles to entry or the use of other blocking measures or other means different from those which govern competition on the merits, from even entering that or those market(s)[50] [emphasis added].

So, is this a 'novel' abuse?[51] The Commission, now supported by the GC and the CJEU,[52] argued that its analysis concerning abusive leveraging as an independent form of abuse follows established principles. The above succinct presentation of the decision suggests that the Commission did not come up with self-preferencing as a new form of abuse, at least not vocally. It rather treated Google's conduct as abusive leveraging, though in so doing, it took into account certain elements that are fact specific, namely the unjustified difference in treatment and the specific circumstances, in particular the nature of the infrastructure. Yet, some commentators disagree and rather make the point that the Commission should have been more vocal about its 'progressive policy making',[53] which can be seen not only as permissible but also as desirable.

[50] *Google Search (Shopping)*—CJEU (n23), paras 165–167, 172–174.

[51] On earlier scholarship arguing that Google's conduct does not fit existing categories, see n28 above.

[52] *Google Search (Shopping)*—CJEU (n23).

[53] N Dunne, 'Fairness and the Challenge of Making Markets Work Better' (2020) 84 Modern Law Review 1, 23.

B. Remedies

The Commission imposed a €2.4 billion fine and an equal treatment remedy. It ordered Google to bring its abusive conduct to an end within ninety days and refrain from similar conduct having the same object or effect. The Commission clarified that there are different ways in which Google could comply with that order, yet the company should respect the principle of non-discrimination between Google's CSS and competing CSSs.[54]

The Commission avoided a prescriptive remedy; yet, the adopted equal treatment remedy proved to be difficult to implement. The Commission's approach can be justified under the EU approach to competition law remedies, since the perpetrator is entitled to decide how to comply when there are different options available.[55] In fact, this was also the approach followed in *Microsoft*, since the Commission did not specify how it expected Microsoft to comply.[56]

According to the Commission decision,[57] implementation measures needed to ensure that Google did not treat its competitors 'less favourably' than its own CSS within its general results pages and that any such measure should subject Google's CSS to the 'same [. . .] processes and methods' for positioning and display as those used for its competitors.[58] Following the decision, from 27 September 2017, through an auction mechanism, rival CSS and *Google Shopping* could bid for their ads to be displayed in the shopping unit at the top of the general search results pages.[59] Despite Google's claims about the effectiveness of its devised remedy,[60] competing CSSs view such a remedy as unsatisfactory to restore competition.[61]

A further interesting point with respect to the applicable remedy in *Google Shopping* is its respective interplay with the underlying theory of harm. The

[54] *Google Search (Shopping)*—GC (n22), para 72; *Google Search (Shopping)*—CD (n22), Articles 3 and 4.

[55] Case T-24/90 *Automec*, ECLI:EU:T:1992:97.

[56] Case T-201/04 *Microsoft* (n6).

[57] *Google Search (Shopping)*—CD (n22), paras 699–700.

[58] *Google Search (Shopping)*—GC (n22), para 221.

[59] B Vesterdorf and K Fountoukakos, 'An Appraisal of the Remedy in the Commission's Google Search (Shopping) Decision and a Guide to Its Interpretation in Light of an Analytical Reading of the Case Law' (2018) 9 Journal of European Competition Law & Practice 3.

[60] O Heckmann, 'Changes to Google Shopping in Europe' (Google Ads and Commerce Blog, 27 September 2017) <https://www.blog.google/products/ads/changes-to-google-shopping-in-europe> (accessed 12 January 2023).

[61] 'Letter to Commissioner Vestager by 41 Rival CSS' (28 November 2019), <https://www.hausfeld.com/uploads/documents/final_version_joint_letter_of_css_to_ms_vestager_on_google_shopping-non-compliance_26.11.2019.pdf> (accessed 12 January 2023). See also T Hoeppner, 'Google's (Non-) Compliance with the EU Shopping Decision—a Study Based upon Empirical Data of 25 Comparison Shopping Services' (2020) <https://www.hausfeld.com/uploads/documents/googles_(non)_compliance_with_google_search_(shopping).pdf> (accessed 12 January 2023). On the remedy in *Google Search (Shopping)* (n22), see T Graf and H Mostyn, 'Do We Need to Regulate Equal Treatment? The Google Shopping Case and the Implications of Its Equal Treatment Principle for New Legislative Initiatives' (2020) 11 Journal of European Competition Law & Practice 561 (in favour of the remedy); P Marsden, 'Google Shopping for the Empress's New Clothes—When a Remedy Isn't a Remedy (and How to Fix It)' (2020) 11 Journal of European Competition Law & Practice 553 (against the remedy).

Commission rejected Google's argument that the *Bronner* criteria should apply, since the latter are irrelevant where, in order to bring an infringement to an end, the remedy does not impose a duty to deal on the dominant undertaking requiring Google to transfer assets or enter into agreements with persons with whom it has not chosen to contract.[62] The court, though, has subsequently clarified that '[t]here can be no automatic link between the criteria for the legal classification of the abuse and the corrective measures enabling it to be remedied',[63] and cited with the Commission in distinguishing between active infringements, as is the case in *Google Shopping* and a simple refusal to supply.[64]

C. Private Enforcement

In its press release on *Google Shopping*, the Commission has also underlined the potential civil liability in damages for Google before Member State courts through damages actions brought by affected parties. Such actions, according to the Commission, have been facilitated by the EU Antitrust Damages Directive.[65] *Google Shopping* has, indeed, sparked follow-on damages actions and strengthened private enforcement cases, already brought prior to the Commission decision.[66]

II.3.1.2 Google Android

A. Theories of Harm

Google Android resulted from a relevant complaint lodged by FairSearch on 25 March 2013.[67] Aptoide (16 June 2014), Yandex (15 April 2015), and Disconnect

[62] *Google Search (Shopping)*—CD (n22), para 651 with references to Case T-65/98 *Van den Bergh Foods*, ECLI:EU:T:2003:281, para 161, upheld on appeal in Case C- 552/03P *Unilever*, ECLI:EU:C:2006:607, paras 113 and 137.

[63] *Google Search (Shopping)*—GC (n22), para 244.

[64] *Ibid*, para 247.

[65] Council Directive (EU) 2014/104/EU of 26 November 2014 on certain rules governing actions for damages under national law for infringements of the competition law provisions of the Member States and of the European Union, [2014] OJ L 349/1. See also European Commission (EU), 'Antitrust: Commission Fines Google €2.42 Billion for Abusing Dominance as Search Engine by Giving Illegal Advantage to Own Comparison Shopping Service' (Press release, 27 June 2017). See J Mouton and L Reed, 'Following the Google Shopping Judgment, Should We Expect a Private Enforcement Action?' (2022) 13 Journal of European Competition Law & Practice 154, pointing to difficulties in building a counterfactual and quantify damages in private enforcement.

[66] See, e.g. A Ram, 'European Shopping Sites Sue Google for Abuse of Position' (*Financial Times*, 12 April 2019); R Browne, 'Price Comparison Site Sues Google for $2.4 Billion over Alleged Antitrust Breach" (CNBC, 7 February 2022) <https://www.cnbc.com/2022/02/07/pricerunner-sues-google-for-2point4-billion-over-alleged-antitrust-breach.html> (accessed 7 June 2024). See also Heureka Group, 'Heureka Is Suing Google for an Abuse of Dominance That Harms Online Shoppers and Merchants Alike' (30 June 2020) <https://www.politico.eu/wp-content/uploads/2020/07/Heureka-press-release.pdf> (accessed 7 June 2024). The last case led to a preliminary reference before the CJEU. See Case C-605/21 *Heureka Group as v Google LLC*.

[67] *Google Android* (Case AT.40099) Commission Decision, C(2018) 4761 final. The Department of Justice (DoJ) has also brought a case against Google for similar practices. See DoJ, 'Justice Department Sues Monopolist Google for Violating Antitrust Laws' (Press release, 20 October 2020) <https://www.justice.gov/opa/pr/justice-department-sues-monopolist-google-violating-antitrust-laws> (accessed 7 June 2024). The trial started in September 2023. See M Stoller, 'The First Big Antitrust Trial of the

(1 June 2015) also filed complaints against Google.[68] In *Google Android*, the Commission concluded that Google abused Article 102 TFEU by engaging in four separate abusive practices constituting a single and continuous infringement: first, two separate tying abuses, namely (i) tying the Google Search app with the Play Store app; and (ii) tying Google Chrome with the Play Store and the Google Search app. Restrictions in Google mobile application distribution agreements (MADAs) required manufacturers of mobile devices to pre-install the Google Search and Chrome browser apps in order to obtain license for the Play Store. The second abuse was making the licensing of the Play Store and the Google Search app conditional on anti-fragmentation obligations in the anti-fragmentation agreements (AFAs) obliging manufacturers not to sell devices running Android versions ('Android forks') not approved by Google (non-compatible Android forks). The abuse here concerns only the restriction applied to smart mobile devices on which Google's apps are not pre-installed. The third abuse was committed, under the revenue-sharing agreements (RSAs), by granting revenue share exclusivity payments to original equipment manufacturers (OEMs) and mobile network operators (MNOs) under the condition that they would not pre-install any competing general search service on any device within an agreed portfolio.[69]

The Commission concluded that Google's conduct was part of an 'overall "carrot-and-stick" strategy' towards OEMs and MNOs in order to shield and reinforce Google's dominant position in the market for general search services and thereby increase its revenues in search advertising. This strategy ensures that Google acquires valuable traffic users' data.[70] Overall, it protects the Android ecosystem and restricts competition in the respective markets, namely the market for the licensable smart mobile OSs, Android app stores, general search services, and mobile web browsers.

The Commission decision has been largely upheld by the GC.[71] Google has challenged the Commission's findings that the MADAs, AFAs, and RSAs were abusive.[72]

Century Is About to Start' (BIG, 6 August 2023) <https://www.thebignewsletter.com/p/the-first-big-antitrust-trial-of> (accessed 7 June 2024).

[68] The number of complaints in this case has risen. See *Google Android*—Commission Decision (CD) (n67), para 21, reference being made to seventeen complainants and third parties.

[69] *Ibid*, Article 1(1) and (2).

[70] *Ibid*, para 739.

[71] Case T-604/18 *Google and Alphabet v Commission (Google Android)*, ECLI:EU:T:2022:541 (*Google Android*—General Court (GC).

[72] The other pleas concerned, first, the assessment of market definition and dominance with respect to the market for the licensing of operating systems (OSs), the market for Android app stores, and each national market for general search services in the European Economic Area (EEA). On market definition, see Chapter 2, section V.1. The fifth plea concerned an alleged infringement of Google's rights of defence, and lastly, the sixth plea alleged errors in imposing and calculating the fine.

With respect to the MADA pre-installation conditions, Google argued that the Commission failed to show anticompetitive foreclosure, since there were ample opportunities for competitors and users. First, the Commission failed to establish that the pre-installation conditions created a status quo bias. Second, the Commission ignored the fact that manufacturers were still free to pre-install rival search services and browsers and set them as defaults. The MADA conditions only required that, on devices where OEMs wanted to pre-install the Google Mobile Services (GMS) suite,[73] the home screen had to also display icons for the Play Store, an app folder, and Google Search. Third, the Commission also ignored the fact that there were alternative means for competitors to reach users. Fourth, it did not show that usage shares for Google's search and browser services were attributable to the MADA conditions. Finally, the Commission failed to take into account the full economic and legal context. According to Google, the MADA conditions did not foreclose rivals. On the contrary, they created new opportunities for them.[74]

Google Android is the first case since Microsoft that examines tying practices in technology markets. The latter case concerned technological tying, whereas *Google Android* concerns contractual tying. The conditions for establishing abusive tying are the following: first, the tying and tied products need to be two separate products; second, the need to establish a dominant position in the tying product market; third, the fact that there is no choice for customers or end users to obtain the tying product without the tied product; fourth, the fact that the tying is capable of restricting competition; and fifth, the fact that such practice is not objectively justified.[75]

With respect to the fourth limb of the test, the Commission, with regards to *the tying of the Google Search app with the Play Store*, concluded that Google's conduct was capable of restricting competition based on two premises; *first*, it afforded Google a significant competitive advantage, which cannot be offset by competing general search services providers, and *second*, it enables Google to maintain and strengthen its dominant position, increases entry barriers, decreases innovation, and 'tends to harm, directly or indirectly consumers'.[76] Thus, the Commission adopted a two-step test to assess the restriction of competition. The first focused on establishing Google's competitive advantage and the second showing exclusionary effects leading to consumer harm.[77]

Google's competitive advantage was premised on the following reasons, which were relied upon by the Commission: the significant increase in the number of

[73] Google Mobile Services (GMS) is the bundle of Google apps and services that Google licenses together. See *Google Android*—CD (n67), para 133.

[74] *Google Android*—General Court (GC) (n71), paras 317–319.

[75] *Google Android*—CD (n67), para 741 with references to Case T-201/04 *Microsoft* (n6), paras 859, 862, 864, 867, 869, and 1144–1167.

[76] *Google Android*—CD (n67), para 773.

[77] In this vein, see *Google Android*—GC (n71), paras 305–306.

general searches via smart mobile devices; the nature of pre-installation as an important distribution channel; the fact that it was impossible to uninstall the Google Search app on GMS devices; the fact that competitors cannot offset Google's competitive advantage (through downloads);[78] and the evolution of market shares.[79] The Commission analysis with respect to the second premise on exclusionary effects is rather brief and takes into account the fact that Google's conduct 'makes it harder' for competitors to gain search queries and the respective revenues and data to improve their services, increases barriers to entry in the markets for the provision of search services, and reduces competitors' incentives to innovate.[80] In particular, with respect to consumer harm, the Commission states that 'as a result of Google's interference with the normal competitive process, may see less choice of general search services available'.[81] Similar analysis was followed with respect to the tying of Google Chrome with the Play Store and the Google Search app.[82]

The GC upheld the Commission analysis. In a statement of principle with respect to exclusionary effects, the GC repeated that

> not every exclusionary effect is necessarily detrimental to competition. Competition on the merits may, by definition, lead to the departure from the market or the marginalisation of competitors that are less efficient and so less attractive to consumers from the point of view of, among other things, price, choice, quality or innovation.[83]

It highlighted further that

> [e]xclusionary effects characterise situations in which effective access of actual or potential competitors to markets or to their components is hampered or eliminated as a result of the conduct of the dominant undertaking, thus allowing that undertaking negatively to influence, to its own advantage and to the detriment of consumers, the various parameters of competition, such as price, production, innovation, variety or quality of goods or services.[84]

Thus, exclusionary effects embrace not only situations where competitors' access is eliminated but also where such access is hampered. The GC then clarified that the Commission not only examined the capacity of such conduct to restrict

[78] Despite Google's arguments that the low number of downloads can only be plausibly explained by users' preference to the Google Search app. See *Google Android*—CD (n67), para 811.
[79] *Ibid*, para 775.
[80] *Ibid*, paras 858–866.
[81] *Ibid*, para 863.
[82] *Ibid*, paras 877–992.
[83] *Google Android*—GC (n71), para 278, with reference to C-413/14 P *Intel v Commission*, ECLI:EU:C:2017:632, para 134.
[84] *Google Android*—GC (n71), para 281.

competition but also went further to consider factors which establish that the exclusionary effects are real.[85] In *Google Android*, users had the ability but not the incentive to download rival search engines or browser apps.[86] In addition, the court clarified that with respect to the practices at issue having been implemented for a number of years,

> the difference between 'restriction of competition' and 'capacity to restrict competition' has no bearing on the requisite proof in cases where, as in this instance, the Commission has characterised the restriction of competition on the basis of the effects which the implementation of the practices at issue have had over a significant period of time, effects which may be observed and which enable the Commission to determine the nature and scope of the ensuing anticompetitive foreclosure, and the Court to review those findings.[87]

Google argued that such practices were objectively justified as a monetization strategy for Google's investment in Android and non-revenue-generating apps. The Commission rejected such arguments since Google failed to demonstrate that such practices were necessary to monetize its investment and offer the better user experience claimed. Google also failed to prove that such practices were necessary to avoid charging OEMs a fee for the Play Store.[88]

With respect to Google's practice making the licensing of the Play Store and the Google Search app conditional on the anti-fragmentation obligations in the AFAs, the Commission equally relied on the *Microsoft* test. In particular, the imposition of a supplementary obligation may be caught by Article 102 TFEU provided that the following conditions are met; first, the unrelated nature of the supplementary obligation to the subject of the contract; second, the dominant position in the market in which it offers the product or service; third, no choice with respect to the supplementary obligation; and fourth, capability of the supplementary obligation to restrict competition.[89] The Commission found that Google's conduct was capable of restricting competition with respect to Android forks.[90] The consumer harm consisted in the reduction of choice of smart mobile OSs and general search services. An example of such reduction in consumer choice came from Fire OS, a forked version of Android developed by Amazon, which is generally considered as a high-quality fork of Android but was nonetheless prevented from finding distribution channels by the anti-fragmentation

[85] *Ibid*, para 291.
[86] *Ibid*, para 292.
[87] *Ibid*, para 299.
[88] *Google Android*—CD (n67), paras 993–1008.
[89] *Ibid*, para 1011, with reference to Case T-201/04 *Microsoft* (n6), paras 859, 862, 864, 867, 869, and 1144–1167.
[90] *Google Android*—CD (n67), para 1036.

obligations.[91] According to Google, such conduct was necessary to preserve the Android ecosystem.[92]

The GC annulled the Commission decision with respect to the portfolio-based RSAs. Making portfolio-based revenue share payments conditional on the obligation not to pre-install any competing general search engine was treated as exclusivity payments, which were presumed to be abusive under Article 102 TFEU.[93] In this case, the Commission went on to examine the presumption that Google's portfolio-based revenue share payments were capable of restricting competition.[94] The Commission found that Google's conduct reduced OEMs' and MNOs' incentives to pre-install competing general search services, made access to the national markets for general search services more difficult, and deterred innovation.[95] The Commission claims that such payments reduced the incentives for competing general search service providers to innovate since it affected their incentives to 'invest in developing innovative features, such as innovation in algorithm and user experience design'.[96] It also stated that if such practice did not deter Google's incentive to innovate coinciding with a period of improvement in Google's general search services, Google has not proved the same for competing search engines. Further, absent such RSAs, Google's search engine may have improved even further.[97] This is a largely conspicuous statement, since it is not for the incumbent to prove a 'negative' (namely that its conduct has *not* affected innovation incentive), but rather, the competition authority needs to prove that such conduct had, indeed, had such impact. This part of the judgment is just an assertion, which appears rather unsubstantiated.

Before addressing Google's challenge on this part of the decision, the GC laid out the principles, as developed in the case law,[98] for assessing exclusivity payments. In a nutshell, exclusivity payments are presumed to be capable of restricting competition. However, if the incumbent undertaking puts forward a claim that

[91] *Ibid*, para 1142.
[92] *Ibid*, para 1155.
[93] *Ibid*, para 1188, with further references to Case 85/76 *Hoffmann-La Roche*, ECLI:EU:C:1979:36, para 89; Case C-23/14 *Post Danmark A/S v Konkurrencerådet*, ECLI:EU:C:2015:651, para 27. See also previous two cases, where the GC annulled Commission decisions on exclusivity payments: Case T-286/09 *Intel RENV*, ECLI:EU:T:2022:19 and Case T-235/18 *Qualcomm*, ECLI:EU:T:2022:358. See also Case C-240/22 P *Commission v Intel* (on appeal) (nyd) and Opinion of AG Medina in Case C-240/22 P *Commission v Intel*, ECLI:EU:C:2024:65, arguing that the appeal should be dismissed. See also C-680/20 *Unilever*, ECLI:EU:C:2023:33, para 62, where the CJEU held that when assessing exclusivity clauses, a competition authority should establish, in view of all the relevant circumstances and, where applicable, the economic analyses adduced by the dominant undertaking with respect to the inability of its conduct to exclude as efficient competitors, their respective capability to restrict competition. There is no obligation to run an 'as efficient competitor' test, but in the event that such test is submitted by the dominant undertaking, the competition authority must evaluate it.
[94] *Google Android*—CD (n67), para 1206.
[95] *Ibid.*
[96] *Ibid*, para 1315.
[97] *Ibid*, paras 1321–1322.
[98] *Intel* (n83), paras 137–140.

its respective conduct is not capable of restricting competition, as will most certainly always be the case, the burden of proof shifts, and the Commission needs to analyse 'the various circumstances' that demonstrate the restriction of competition and the alleged exclusionary effects.[99] The relevant circumstances include the dominant position; the market coverage of the challenged conduct; the conditions and arrangements for the pricing practices in question, their duration, and the amounts involved; and the possible existence of an exclusionary strategy against competitors that is at least as efficient as the dominant undertaking.[100] The 'as-efficient-competitor test' ('the AEC test') can be useful in assessing 'the intrinsic capacity of a practice to foreclose competitors which are at least as efficient as the dominant undertaking'.[101] The GC then clarified that the AEC test concerns competitors that are hypothetically equally efficient in terms not only of price[102] but also of choice, quality, or innovation.[103] It specifically stated that

> [t]he AEC test thus constitutes a possible framework for analysing exclusionary effects in relation to a given case and the exclusionary effects alleged. However, it is *only one of several factors* that may be applied in order to establish, *by means of qualitative or quantitative evidence*, whether anticompetitive foreclosure exists for the purposes of Article 102 TFEU [emphasis added].[104]

However, the GC went on to state that if an AEC test is done, it must be done right, and the Commission has the necessary investigative powers to obtain the necessary data.[105] As a point of principle, and before addressing Google's arguments, the GC stated that the Commission analysis, in order to establish that the portfolio-based RSAs were anticompetitive in nature, depends in particular on two sets of considerations: the examination of their respective coverage and the AEC test results.[106]

Google claimed, first, that, contrary to the Commission's assessment, the portfolio-based RSAs did not amount to exclusivity payments. Second, the Commission failed to explain how such practice with limited coverage restricted competition. Third, the Commission failed to prove their respective anticompetitive nature.[107] While rejecting the first two parts of Google's plea, the GC upheld the third part, noting that the coverage of the contested practice is not significant, since it was calculated less than 5 per cent compared to a coverage between 39

[99] *Google Android*—GC (n71), para 639, with reference to *Intel* (n83), paras 137–138.
[100] *Google Android*—GC (n71), para 640, with reference to *Intel* (n83), paras 139–140.
[101] *Google Android*—GC (n71), para 641.
[102] Case C-52/09 *TeliaSonera Sverige*, ECLI:EU:C:2011:83, paras 40–44.
[103] *Google Android*—GC (n71), with reference to Case C-209/10 *Post Danmark*, ECLI:EU:C:2012:172, para 22.
[104] *Google Android*—GC (n71), para 643.
[105] *Ibid*, para 644.
[106] *Ibid*, para 646.
[107] *Ibid*, para 648.

and 85 per cent found to be significant in earlier case law.[108] Importantly though, the GC mentioned as *obiter* that the outcome may have been different had the Commission argued that

> the segment covered by that practice or even just the OEMs and MNOs concerned in this case were of such *strategic importance* that the foreclosure effect attributable to that practice was capable of excluding Google's rival general search services from the relevant markets. Those rival services would then have been deprived of sufficient opportunities to compete on the merits by entering those markets or expanding in them, at a time when, for Google as well as for its competitors, such as Microsoft, it was important to tackle the challenges of the shift from general searches on PCs to general searches on mobile devices.[109]

The GC also accepted Google's arguments with respect to the correctness and validity of the AEC test[110] and annulled this part of the Commission's decision.[111]

With respect to AFAs, the GC upheld the Commission's analysis about their respective potential to restrict competition. The Commission assessed AFAs as a *Microsoft* tying-like abuse.[112] With respect to the restriction of competition, it took into account the following factors: the fact that non-compatible Android forks posed a credible competitive threat, contrary to Android compatible forks; the fact that AFAs hindered the development of non-compatible Android forks; the fact that Google's proprietary application programming interfaces (APIs) were not available to non-compatible Android fork developers, thereby discouraging them from developing apps that run on such OSs; and the fact that Google's maintaining and strengthening its dominance in general search deters innovation and tends to harm—directly or indirectly—consumers.[113] Google argued that non-compatible forks that do not comply with standards set by Google jeopardize the Android ecosystem as a whole, and therefore, AFAs are indispensable for its protection.[114] The GC, interestingly, started its analysis by discussing, first, Google's anticompetitive objective as evidenced by internal documents[115] before examining the respective anticompetitive effects. The latter analysis arguably afforded a large leeway to the Commission since the GC expected Google to establish that non-compatible Android forks 'could not in any event have constituted a competitive threat to it'.[116] In addition, the GC did not accept Google's argument that the failure of

[108] *Ibid*, paras 683–685, 693.
[109] *Ibid*, para 696.
[110] *Ibid*, paras 752, 774, 788, 797, 798, 799.
[111] *Ibid*, paras 800–802.
[112] *Ibid*, para 815. On the conditions, see above text to n75.
[113] *Ibid*, para 816.
[114] *Ibid*, paras 817–818.
[115] *Ibid*, paras 837–841.
[116] *Ibid*, para 847.

non-compatible Android forks (primarily Amazon's Fire OS and Alibaba's Aliyun OS) was attributed to other reasons, such as (for example) hardware failures; the Commission has adduced enough evidence to prove that AFAs and Google's active monitoring of such obligations led to the failure of non-compatible forks.[117] Furthermore, Google challenged the Commission's conclusion that its conduct deterred innovation. The GC held, though, that the Commission did not have to define more precisely which functionalities could have been introduced absent the practice in question.[118]

B. Remedies

The Commission imposed a €4.342 billion fine,[119] ordered Google to end the infringement, to notify the measures it intends to adopt in order to comply with the decision, and to provide periodic compliance reports every six months for a five-year period.[120] Google engaged in ongoing discussions with the Commission and has progressively introduced changes in its mobile ecosystem.

In order to comply with the Commission decision, Google announced the following measures: first, updates to the compatibility agreements with mobile device manufacturers. Android partners that want to distribute Google apps can also build non-compatible, or forked, smartphones and tablets for the European Economic Area (EEA).[121] Second, Google introduced new licensing options, from 29 October 2018, for smartphones and tablets in the EEA. The device manufacturers can now license the Google mobile application suite without the Google Search app or the Chrome browser. This change would have come at price, since Google planned to introduce a new paid licensing agreement for smartphones and tablets in the EEA—given that, according to the company, they will no longer be able to fund the evolution and free distribution of Android through the pre-installation of Google Search and Chrome and bundling with the other Google apps. Google will also have separate licences for the Google Search app and Chrome.[122]

Another change introduced concerned the introduction of choice screens with the option to download search apps and browsers.[123] When they were first introduced, these choice screens—one for search apps and one for browsers—were displayed when a user opened Google Play after receiving an upcoming update.

[117] *Ibid*, paras 850–851.

[118] *Ibid*, para 862.

[119] Reduced to €4.125 billion by the GC.

[120] *Google Android*—CD (n67), Articles 2–4.

[121] H Lockheimer, 'Complying with the EC's Android Decision' (16 October 2018) <https://www.blog.google/around-the-globe/google-europe/complying-ecs-android-decision> (accessed 7 June 2024).

[122] *Ibid*.

[123] P Gennai, 'Presenting Search App and Browser Options to Android Users in Europe' (18 April 2019) <https://www.blog.google/around-the-globe/google-europe/presenting-search-app-and-browser-options-android-users-europe> (accessed 7 June 2024).

The two choice screens each contained a total of five apps, including any already installed, with those apps not already installed included according to their popularity and displayed in a random order.[124]

Following the option to download other search apps and browsers in Google Play, Google further introduced a new way for Android users to select a default search engine to power a search box on their home screen and in Chrome (if installed). Search providers had to apply in order to participate in this choice screen, which appeared when setting up a new Android smartphone or tablet in Europe.[125] Following additional feedback from the Commission, from September 2021, Google opted for making participation in the choice screen free for eligible search providers (instead of going through a sealed bid auction)[126] and increased the number of search providers shown on the screen from the previous four to a maximum of twelve.[127] Evidence suggests that the vast majority of users choose Google Search as their default search engine.[128]

II.3.1.3 Google AdSense

A. Theories of Harm

The Commission started investigating this case in January 2010, following an exchange of information (under Regulation 1/2003, Article 12) with the German NCA that received a complaint by Ciao GmbH and the reallocation of the respective complaint to the Commission.[129] The Commission initiated proceedings against Google (under Regulation 773/2004, Article 2(1)) on 30 November 2010.

Three separate infringements of Article 102 TFEU were found, together constituting a single and continuous infringement, namely that Google concluded agreements with certain publishers requiring them, first, to cover all or most of their search advertising requirements through Google search ads (site exclusivity clause); second, to reserve the most prominent space on their search results pages for a minimum number of Google search ads (placement clause); and third, to

[124] *Ibid.*

[125] P Gennai, 'An Update on Android for Search Providers in Europe' (2 August 2019) <https://www.blog.google/around-the-globe/google-europe/update-android-search-providers-europe> (accessed 7 June 2024).

[126] T Ricker, 'Google Will Charge Search Providers to Be the Android Default in Europe' (The Verge, 2 August 2019) <https://www.theverge.com/2019/8/2/20751353/google-auction-android-search-choice-screen> (accessed 7 June 2024).

[127] O Bethell, 'Changes to the Android Choice Screen in Europe' (8 June 2021) <https://blog.google/around-the-globe/google-europe/changes-android-choice-screen-europe>. See Google Android, 'About the Choice Screen' (updated 12 June 2023) <https://www.android.com/choicescreen> (both accessed 7 June 2024). See also Competition and Markets Authority (CMA), 'Mobile Ecosystems' (Market Study Interim Report, 14 December 2021), para 5.16.

[128] Bethell, 'Changes to the Android Choice Screen' (n127).

[129] *Google Search (AdSense)* (Case AT.40411) Commission Decision, C(2019) 2173.

make changes in the display of competing search ads following Google's approval (authorizing equivalent ads clause).[130]

AdSense is Google's online advertising intermediation platform, in operation since 2003, which brings Google search ads on publishers' websites.[131] Amongst the services provided,[132] AdSense for Search (AFS) delivers Google search ads in response to users' search queries typed in the search box on the publishers' websites.[133] Google had three types of AFS agreements: (i) those that were individually negotiated, paper-based, Google services agreements (GSAs) with large publishers (direct partners); (ii) standard form, non-negotiable, online agreements with smaller publishers (online contracts); and (iii) paper-based, simplified agreements (simplified contracts).[134] Whereas GSAs are the minority, nonetheless they generate the majority of Google's AFS revenue.[135] The old template GSAs (prior to March 2009)[136] included an exclusivity clause (clause 6.1),[137] whereby publishers agreed to obtain search advertising services exclusively from Google, as well as an English clause (clause 6.2) according to which existing customers had to inform Google about contacts with competing services and to allow Google the right of first refusal to match any more competitive offer.[138] Until 15 June 2016, Google progressively transitioned all its EMEA direct partners to the new template GSA.[139] In the latter, the English clause was removed and the exclusivity clause was replaced with the 'Premium Placement and Minimum Google Ads Clause' (clause 7.2b) according to which direct partners cannot display competing ads above, or directly adjacent to, Google's search ads and must request a minimum number of Google search ads in a single block on desktop devices (three) and on mobile devices (at least one).[140] Furthermore, Google appeared to have tight control over the implementation of the GSAs; there was a regular exchange with direct partners, and the latter had to seek Google's approval prior to implementing any changes on the display of competing search ads (authorizing equivalent ads clause).[141] Following the launch of the Commission investigation, Google has informed the Commission that it intends to remove these clauses from the GSAs.[142]

[130] *Ibid*, para 4. The decision was overturned on appeal. See Case T-334/19 *Google and Alphabet v Commission (Google AdSense for Search)*, ECLI:EU:T:2024:634.

[131] *Google Search (AdSense)*—(n129), para 21.

[132] Other services include AdSense for Content (AFC), AdSense for Domains, AdSense for Mobile Applications (AdMob) and AdSense for Shopping (AFSh). See *Google Search (AdSense)*—Commission Decision (CD) (n129), para 21.

[133] *Ibid*, para 22.

[134] *Ibid*, para 76.

[135] *Ibid*, para 79.

[136] *Ibid*, para 81.

[137] *Ibid*, paras 82–85.

[138] *Ibid*, para 86.

[139] *Ibid*, para 89.

[140] *Ibid*, paras 91, 93.

[141] *Ibid*, paras 96–98.

[142] *Ibid*, paras 99–106.

The Commission concluded that these clauses constituted an abuse of Google's dominant position in the online search advertising intermediation market between 2006 and 2016, since

> competition was already weak in the EEA wide market for online search advertising intermediation because of Google's dominant position. Notwithstanding such weak competition, Google entered into agreements with Direct Partners that maintained and strengthened Google's dominant position on that market by stifling any realistic chance of entry and expansion by competing providers of online search advertising intermediation services.[143]

The exclusivity clause constituted an exclusive supply obligation and, according to established case law, amounted to an abuse.[144] According to the Commission, the fact that (i) its customers had to source all or most of their search ads requirements from Google and (ii) Google failed to argue that such clauses were objectively justified or produced countervailing efficiencies suffice for the application of Article 102 TFEU.[145] Such an approach to exclusivity clauses suggests that these clauses amount to a type of 'by-object' abuse, and the Commission does not have to prove their respective capability to restrict competition. Following Google's submissions, the Commission has further clarified that *Intel* does not challenge this conclusion since *Intel* has clarified the *Hoffmann-La Roche* case law only with respect to exclusivity rebates and not to exclusivity obligations in general.[146] The Commission, despite the fact that (according to its analysis of the respective case law) it was not required to prove that these clauses were capable of restricting competition, nonetheless proceeded to an analysis of all the relevant circumstances in that respect.[147]

In assessing the potential restriction of competition, the Commission assessed the potential foreclosure of competing providers, the potential impact on innovation, and the potential consumer harm.[148] However, the assessment with respect to adverse impact on innovation and consumers was rather superficial and hypothetical.[149] Google has attempted to put forward an objective justification for such clauses based on improving users' experience and the quality of search

[143] *Ibid*, para 333.

[144] *Ibid*, para 338, with reference to Case C-86/76 *Hoffmann-La Roche v Commission*, para 89; Case C-62/86 *AKZO v Commission*, para 149; Case T-65/89 *BPB Industries plc and British Gypsum Ltd v Commission*, para 68; Case T-128/98 *Aéeroports de Paris v Commission*, para 170; Case T-66/01 *Imperial Chemical Industries v Commission*, ECLI:EU:T:2010:255, para 315; Case T-155/06 *Tomra v Commission*, ECLI:EU:T:2010:370, paras 208–209.

[145] *Google Search (AdSense)*—CD (n129), paras 341–342.

[146] *Ibid*, para 344.

[147] *Ibid*, para 345, with reference to *Intel* (n83), para 139; Case C-525/16 *Meo-Serviços de Comunicações e Multimédia*, ECLI:EU:C:2018:270, paras 28, 31, and 362.

[148] *Google Search (AdSense)*—CD (n129), paras 362 et seq.

[149] *Ibid*, paras 403–406 with respect to innovation and paras 416–421 with respect to consumer harm.

ads, amongst other considerations. Yet, the Commission rejected those arguments since Google failed to prove how the exclusion of competing providers affected quality and why such ends could not have been served with less restrictive means such as brand guidelines or content policies.[150]

With respect to the premium placement and minimum Google ads clause, to which Google has itself referred as 'relaxed exclusivity',[151] the Commission has similarly concluded that it amounted to an abuse, yet with respect to this clause, the Commission had to run a 'capability' (of affecting competition) assessment.[152] Similarly to the assessment with respect to the exclusivity clause, the Commission's assessment on the potential restriction of competition assessed similar factors (impact on competitors, innovation, and consumer harm) and remained rather superficial with respect to the potential impact on innovation and consumers.[153] When assessing the clause's capability to restrict competition, the Commission took into account Google's dominance and the coverage and duration of the respective agreements.[154] The Commission followed a similar assessment with respect to the authorizing equivalent ads clause.[155]

However, the General Court while upholding most of the Commission's findings, it has annulled the decision in its entirety since, according to the General Court, the Commission failed to assess the duration of the contested clauses, as well as their respective market coverage in 2016. The General Court held that the Commission had not demonstrated that these clauses were capable of having foreclosure effects, did not take into account all relevant circumstances in assessing their duration, and failed to demonstrate that the contested clauses deterred innovation, strengthened Google's dominant position in online search advertising, and resulted in possible consumer harm.[156]

B. Sanctions/Remedies

The Commission imposed a fine and a cease-and-desist order. The fine amounted to €1.49 billion on Google for a single and continuous infringement consisting of three separate infringements corresponding to the three clauses discussed above.[157]

II.3.1.4 Google AdTech

After fining Google three times in *Shopping*, *Android*, and *AdSense*, the Commission has launched a new investigation against Google, this time in its online display

[150] *Ibid*, paras 451–452.

[151] *Ibid*, para 467.

[152] *Ibid*, para 461.

[153] *Ibid*, paras 494 et seq. With respect to innovation, see paras 529–532 and with respect to consumer harm, see paras 538–540.

[154] *Ibid*, para 496.

[155] *Ibid*, paras 565 et seq.

[156] See Case T-334/19 *Google and Alphabet v Commission (Google AdSense for Search)*, ECLI:EU:T:2024:634. On appeal, see Case C-826/24P.

[157] *Google Search (AdSense)*— CD (n129), Articles 1–3.

advertising business.[158] In *AdSense*, the Commission has looked into Google's online search advertising business and the respective contracts with large publishers. Online search advertising constituted a different product market and was distinguished from non-search online advertising based on the following factors, amongst others: the way an ad appears on the screen, its appearance or format, its targeted nature, its ability to convert existing demand into purchases vis-à-vis the creation of brand awareness and new demand, the click-through rate (CTR), and conversion rates.[159]

This investigation looks into Google AdTech business. In simple terms, AdTech intermediates between advertisers and publishers for the selling of ad inventory on publishers' websites in real time.[160] Such a process is complex, involving many different players and layers, yet it has been observed that Google has emerged as the main player in many layers of the AdTech value chain, which (given the observed opacity of the process and the relatively low payments to publishers) may raise competition law concerns.[161] The AdTech value chain comprises three main tools:

1) Publisher ad servers for publishers that are used to manage advertising space on websites and apps ('DoubleClick For Publishers', or 'DFP');
2) Ad buying tools for advertisers that are used to manage their ad campaigns ('Google Ads' and 'DV 360'); and
3) Real time ad exchanges ('AdX').[162]

The Commission will assess whether Google favours its own display advertising technology services in the AdTech supply chain to the detriment of competitors,

[158] European Commission (EU), 'Commission Opens Investigation into Possible Anticompetitive Conduct by Google in the Online Advertising Technology Sector' (22 June 2021) <https://ec.europa.eu/commission/presscorner/detail/en/ip_21_3143>. For similar actions in the United States, see DoJ, 'Justice Department Sues Google for Monopolizing Digital Advertising Technologies' (24 January 2023) <https://www.justice.gov/opa/pr/justice-department-sues-google-monopolizing-digital-advertising-technologies>. For a similar probe in the United States brought by a coalition of US states led by Texas, see Court Listener, 'In Re: Google Digital Advertising Antitrust Litigation' (14 January 2022) <https://www.courtlistener.com/docket/60149069/152/in-re-google-digital-advertising-antitrust-litigation>. See also European Publishers Council (EPC), 'European Publishers Council Files EU Complaint against Google for Anti-Competitive Ad Tech Practices' (11 February 2022) <https://www.epceurope.eu/post/european-publishers-council-files-eu-complaint-against-google-for-anti-competitive-ad-tech-practices>. For a timeline on the latter lawsuit, see American Economic Liberties Project, 'Timeline on Internet Advertising Monopoly Lawsuit' <https://www.economicliberties.us/texas-v-google> (all accessed 7 June 2024).

[159] *Google Search (AdSense)*—CD (n129), paras 135–154. See also Chapter 2, section VI.3.3.

[160] For a discussion of the different players of the AdTech value chain, see D Geradin and D Katsifis, 'An EU Competition Law Analysis of Online Display Advertising in the Programmatic Age' (2019) 15 European Competition Journal 55, 63. For an account of the evolution of AdTech, see M Sweeney, 'The Colourful History of Advertising Technology in Just 63 Slides' (2015) <https://clearcode.cc/blog/the-colorful-history-of-advertising-technology-in-just-63-slides> (accessed 7 June 2024). For a good explanation of AdTech, see I Simpson, 'What Exactly Is AdTech?' (2016) <https://clearcode.cc/blog/what-is-adtech> (accessed 7 June 2024).

[161] Geradin and Katsifis, 'An EU Competition Law Analysis' (n160), 63. See CMA, 'Online Platforms and Digital Advertising' (Market Study—Final Report) (Digital Platforms Report, 1 July 2020), para 68.

[162] European Commission (EU), 'Commission Sends Statement of Objections to Google over Abusive Practices in Online Advertising Technology' (Press release, 14 June 2023) <https://ec.europa.eu/commission/presscorner/detail/en/ip_23_3207> (accessed 7 June 2024).

advertisers, and online publishers. According to the Statement of Objections, since at least 2014, Google has been committing an abuse by first favouring AdX, Google's ad exchange in the auction run by DFP, Google's publisher ad server. Such favouring occurred because AdX was informed in advance of the best competing bid it that had to beat in order to win the auction. Google also favoured AdX because its ad buying tools (e.g. Google Ads) mainly placed bids on AdX and avoided competing ad exchanges. Such concerns were raised by market participants ahead of Google/DoubleClick, but at the time were dismissed in light of credible alternatives to which customers (publishers/advertisers/ad networks) could switch and the fact that network effects were not deemed to be strong enough to induce tipping.[163] The French NCA has also examined practices with respect to Google favouring its AdX platform (i.e. issues with respect to ad selling tools and ad exchanges), examining the competitive harm on the publishers' side.[164]

Interestingly, the Commission had already proclaimed in the Statement of Objections that a behavioural remedy will not suffice. Given Google's presence on all sides of the AdTech value chain, which inherently creates a conflict of interest, a structural remedy of partial divestment is needed to address the identified competition concerns.[165] Google may have explored options to settle this case with the Commission;[166] yet, the Commission issued its Statement of Objections, pressing ahead with the case.[167] After all, the three previous probes against Google suggest that the regulator will not accept commitment in the end.

II.3.1.5 Google–Facebook 'Jedi Blue' Agreement

On 11 March 2022, the Commission announced its investigation into the Google–Facebook agreement, code-named 'Jedi Blue', concerning online display advertising.[168] As described above,[169] Google provides advertising technology intermediation services through real-time auctioning of online display advertising space, including through its 'Open Bidding programme'. Meta participates in such auctions through its 'Meta Audience Network' using Google's and competitors' advertising technology services. The 'Jedi Blue' agreement concerns a

[163] *Google/DoubleClick* (Case M.4731) Commission Decision (11 March 2008), para 310. For a discussion of this case, see Chapter 6, section III.

[164] See section II.3.2.2 below.

[165] European Commission (EU), 'Commission Sends Statement of Objections to Google over Abusive Practices' (n162).

[166] F Yun Chee, 'Google Offers to Settle EU Antitrust Probe into Digital Advertising—Source' (Reuters, 23 September 2021) <https://www.reuters.com/technology/exclusive-google-seeking-settle-eu-antitrust-probe-into-adtech-source-2021-09-23> (accessed 14 June 2024).

[167] European Commission (EU), 'Commission Sends Statement of Objections to Google over Abusive Practices' (n162).

[168] European Commission (EU), 'Antitrust: Commission Opens Investigation into Possible Anticompetitive Conduct by Google and Meta, in Online Display Advertising' (Press release, 11 March 2022) <https://ec.europa.eu/commission/presscorner/detail/en/ip_22_1703> (accessed 7 June 2024).

[169] See text to n160.

2018 agreement between Google and Meta on the participation of Meta Audience Network in Google's Open Bidding programme. The Commission concerns relate to possible exclusion of rival AdTech services competing with Google's Open Bidding programme to the detriment of publishers, and ultimately consumers.[170] On 19 December 2022, the Commission decided to close this case.[171]

II.3.2 Member State Enforcement

II.3.2.1 Germany

A. Section 19(a) German Competition Act

On 19 January 2021, the new, updated German competition rules came into force.[172] Addressing problems related to ecosystems, section 19(a) aims to prevent powerful platforms from entrenching their position in other markets. Under this provision, the Bundeskartellamt can designate undertakings with 'paramount significance for competition across markets' and provides for a list of factors for declaring such a position. If an undertaking is found to have 'paramount significance for competition across markets', then section 19(a)(2) provides an indicative list of prohibited conducts, which include self-preferencing, leveraging (particularly by means of data), envelopment, market tipping, and constraining data portability.[173]

On 25 May 2021, the Bundeskartellamt initiated two proceedings against Google: the first to determine whether the company is of paramount significance for competition across markets and the second, based on this general classification, to review Google's data-processing terms.[174] On 5 January 2022, the Bundeskartellamt announced that it concluded on Google's special status under the new rules. The company has decided not to appeal the decision.[175]

[170] See European Commission (EU), 'Antitrust: Commission Opens Investigation into Possible Anticompetitive Conduct by Google and Meta' (n 168).

[171] See Commission Decision in *Google–Meta (Open Bidding)* (Case AT.40774)—closing proceedings <https://ec.europa.eu/competition/antitrust/cases1/202302/AT_40774_8845087_898_3.pdf> (accessed 7 June 2024).

[172] Act against Restraints of Competition in the version published on 26 June 2013 (Bundesgesetzblatt (Federal Law Gazette) I, 2013, 1750, 3245), as amended by Article 1 of the Act of 18 January 2021 (Federal Law Gazette I, 2). For a discussion on the amendments in German competition law, see Chapter 3, section V.2.2.

[173] According to the President of the Bundeskartellamt, the German Competition Act is broader than the (then draft) DMA, since it provides only some examples, yet leaves space for identifying new anticompetitive conduct. See J Espinoza and E Solomon, 'EU Draft Tech Rules Too "Narrow", Says German Competition Head' (*Financial Times*, 14 July 2021) <http://www.ft.com/content/6cff198792634bc68d8d6426ef303325> (accessed 7 June 2024).

[174] Bundeskartellamt, 'Proceeding against Google Based on New Rules for Large Digital Players (Section 19a GWB)—Bundeskartellamt Examines Google's Significance for Competition across Markets and Its Data Processing Terms' (Press release, 25 May 2021) <https://www.bundeskartellamt.de/SharedDocs/Meldung/EN/Pressemitteilungen/2021/25_05_2021_Google_19a.html?nn=3591568> (accessed 7 June 2024).

[175] Bundeskartellamt, 'Alphabet/Google Subject to New Abuse Control Applicable to Large Digital Companies—Bundeskartellamt Determines "Paramount Significance across Markets"' (5

B. Data-Processing Practices

This probe was opened in May 2021. On 23 December 2022, Google received the Statement of Objections. Given Google's access to a vast amount of user data across its range of different services, the company enjoys a strategic advantage and should allow users a sufficient choice with respect to the processing of their respective data.[176] Google accesses users' data through its own services, namely through Google Search, YouTube, Google Play, Google Maps, and Google Assistant, as well as through its background services via third-party websites and apps, through, for example, the Google Play services. Based on the Bundeskartellamt's preliminary assessment, users are not given enough choice with respect to this far-reaching collection and processing of their data.[177] This case was ultimately resolved with commitments.[178] Google undertook to allow its users to provide free, informed, specific, and unambiguous consent in order for their data to be processed across services.[179]

An interesting point here is the interplay between the Bundeskartellamt investigation and the application of the DMA, which contains specific obligations for gatekeepers when processing personal data.[180] The Bundeskartellamt has clarified that its own investigation is based on the newly acquired powers under German law with respect to companies of paramount significance for competition across markets and, in some respects, exceeds the DMA requirements, whereas the NCA maintains close contact with the Commission on this matter.[181] The commitments offered cover data processing across services that do not qualify as CPSs under the DMA (such as, for example, Google Shopping, Google Play, Google Maps, Google Search, YouTube, Google Android, Google Chrome, and Google's online advertising services).[182] On 6 October 2023, the Bundeskartellamt rendered its decision

January 2022) <https://www.bundeskartellamt.de/SharedDocs/Meldung/EN/Pressemitteilungen/2022/05_01_2022_Google_19a.html> (accessed 7 June 2024). See Case B7-61/21 *Bundeskartellamt Determines Google's Paramount Significance for Competition across Markets*, Commission Decision (30 December 2021).

176 Bundeskartellamt, 'Statement of Objections Issued against Google's Data Processing Terms' (11 January 2023) <https://www.bundeskartellamt.de/SharedDocs/Meldung/EN/Pressemitteilungen/2023/11_01_2023_Google_Data_Processing_Terms.html> (accessed 7 June 2024).

177 *Ibid.*

178 Bundeskartellamt, 'Bundeskartellamt Gives Users of Google Services Better Control over Their Data' (Press release, 5 October 2023) <https://www.bundeskartellamt.de/SharedDocs/Entscheidung/EN/Pressemitteilungen/2023/05_10_2023_Google_Data.html?nn=3591568> (accessed 7 June 2024).

179 *Ibid.* See Decision B7-70/21 <https://www.bundeskartellamt.de/SharedDocs/Entscheidung/EN/Entscheidungen/Missbrauchsaufsicht/2023/B7-70-21.pdf?__blob=publicationFile&v=2> (accessed 7 June 2024).

180 See, e.g. DMA (n5), Article 5(2). On the DMA obligations, see Chapter 3, section V.2.1.1.

181 Bundeskartellamt, 'Statement of Objections Issued against Google's Data Processing Terms' (n173). See Decision B7-70/21 (n179), paras 27, 36, 38.

182 Bundeskartellamt, 'Bundeskartellamt Gives Users of Google Services Better Control over Their Data' (n178). See Decision B7-70/21 (n179), para 40.

in the case to give Google users better control over their data, accepting Google's commitments to put itself under an obligation to grant new choice options or clarify its data-processing terms. Google qualified this as providing its users with options to exercise free and informed consent on how their data is acquired and processed by the company.

C. Google News Showcase

On 4 June 2021, the Bundeskartellamt announced, following a complaint by Corint Media, the opening of further proceedings against Google, this time with respect to Google News Showcase and its announced integration into Google's general search function. This case was opened following the new section 19(a) of the German Competition Act. The German NCA has examined such practice, mainly under its newly adopted legal framework in digital markets, as a possible self-preferencing practice or as an impediment to the services offered by competitors as well as potential unreasonable contractual conditions imposed by Google to publishers by, in particular, making it disproportionately difficult for them to enforce the ancillary copyright for press publishers following the transposition of the Copyright Directive in Germany. It also examined the conditions of access to Google News Showcase.[183]

On 21 December 2022, the Bundeskartellamt announced that it would close the case after Google offered a series of adjustments to its Google news service to the benefit of the publishers. Google committed not to integrate Google News Showcase into Google search results, while it has also introduced changes to facilitate publishers to assert their general ancillary copyright and committed that, in the future, more publishers will be able to participate in Google News Showcase.[184]

D. Google Maps

On 21 June 2022, the Bundeskartellamt announced that it had initiated proceedings against Google with respect to its Google Maps service and possible anticompetitive restrictions to the detriment of competing map service providers.

This proceeding is based on the authority's new and stricter abuse powers. According to the President's statement, the authority has information suggesting that Google restricts the combination of third-party map services with its own, when (for example) embedding Google Maps location data or Google Street View or the search function into maps not provided by Google. The authority will

[183] Bundeskartellamt, 'Bundeskartellamt Examines Google News Showcase' (4 June 2021) <https://www.bundeskartellamt.de/SharedDocs/Meldung/EN/Pressemitteilungen/2021/04_06_2021_Google_Showcase.html> (accessed 7 June 2024).

[184] Bundeskartellamt, 'Improvements for Publishers Using Google News Showcase' (21 December 2022) <https://www.bundeskartellamt.de/SharedDocs/Meldung/EN/Pressemitteilungen/2022/21_12_2022_Google_News_Showcase.html;jsessionid=DB330BF2E344FECF04D06E2216C14EB8.2_cid371> (accessed 7 June 2024). Case V-43/20 *Antitrust Law Examination of 'Google News Showcase'*.

examine whether such practices allow Google to expand its power regarding certain map services. Additionally, the authority will examine the respective licensing terms and conditions when using Google's map services in vehicles.[185] In response, Google proposed to offer the services of the bundle separately to car manufacturers and software developers (i.e. Google Maps OEM Software Development Kit, Google Play Store, and Cloud Custom Assistant).[186]

II.3.2.2 France

A. Google Ads (Formerly AdWords)

Following a complaint in 2015 by Gibmedia, a company publishing weather information sites, company data, and telephone information, some of which are paid services, on 20 December 2019, the French NCA imposed a fine on Google for abusing its dominant position in online search advertising. According to the decision, the rules for the operation of its Google Ads advertising platform were not transparent, difficult to understand, and applied unfairly. In addition to the fine, the French NCA asked Google to clarify the respective rules as well as the procedure for suspending the respective accounts.[187]

With respect to Google's operating rules for Google Ads, the company had already received two interim orders to clarify its rules and apply them in a non-discriminatory manner following respective complaints.[188]

B. Google News Showcase

In April 2020, the French NCA ordered interim measures against Google following complaints by press publishers and the news agency Agence France Presse.[189]

[185] Bundeskartellamt, 'Proceeding against Google for Possible Anti-Competitive Restrictions of Map Services (Google Maps Platform)' (21 June 2022) <https://www.bundeskartellamt.de/SharedDocs/Meldung/EN/Pressemitteilungen/2022/21_06_2022_Google_Maps.html?nn=3591568> (accessed 7 June 2024).

[186] Bundeskartellamt, 'Google Automotive Services Proceeding—Market Test Regarding Commitments Proposed by Google' (20 December 2023) <https://www.bundeskartellamt.de/SharedDocs/Meldung/EN/Pressemitteilungen/2023/20_12_2023_Google_Automotive.html> (accessed 7 June 2024).

[187] AdC (Autorité de la Concurrence), 'The Autorité de la Concurrence Hands Down a €150M Fine for Abuse of a Dominant Position' (20 December 2019) <https://www.autoritedelaconcurrence.fr/en/communiques-de-presse/autorite-de-la-concurrence-hands-down-eu150m-fine-abuse-dominant-position> (accessed 7 June 2024).

[188] AdC, 'The Autorité de la Concurrence Has Ordered Interim Measures against Google' (31 January 2019) <https://www.autoritedelaconcurrence.fr/en/communiques-de-presse/31-january-2019-online-advertising-directory-enquiry-services-0>; AdC, '30 June 2010: Online Advertising Market' (30 June 2010) <https://www.autoritedelaconcurrence.fr/en/communiques-de-presse/30-june-2010-online-advertising-market> (both accessed 7 June 2024).

[189] AdC, 'Related Rights: The Autorité Has Granted Requests for Urgent Interim Measures Presented by Press Publishers and the News Agency AFP (Agence France Presse)' (9 April 2020) <https://www.autoritedelaconcurrence.fr/en/press-release/related-rights-autorite-has-granted-requests-urgent-interim-measures-presented-press>. Decision 20-MC-01 of 9 April 2020 on requests for interim measures by the Syndicat des éditeurs de la presse magazine, the Alliance de la presse d'information générale and others and Agence France-Presse (in English) <https://www.autoritedelaconcurrence.fr/sites/default/files/integral_texts/2020-06/20-mc-01_en.pdf>. (both accessed 7 June 2024).

According to the authority, following the implementation of the Copyright Directive,[190] Google's practices may amount to an exploitative abuse of a dominant position, in particular the imposition of unfair terms with serious and immediate harm to the press sector. Therefore, Google was asked to engage in good-faith negotiations with press publishers and news agencies with respect to the remuneration for the reuse of their content within three months.

The French NCA subsequently fined Google for non-compliance with the respective decision.[191] On 21 June 2020, the French NCA accepted commitments offered by Google. The commitments were revised four times and will be applicable for five years, with the potential to be renewed for another five years.[192]

C. AdTech

On 8 June 2021, the French NCA imposed a €220 million fine and rendered binding for a three year period the commitments offered by Google for alleged abusive conduct in the AdTech industry. The investigation into this case started in June 2019 following complaints by News Corp Inc, Le Figaro group, and the Rossel La Voix group.[193] The Autorité found that Google granted preferential treatment to its proprietary technologies—namely the DFP ad server and the platform for the programmatic sale of DoubleClick AdExchange advertising space (AdX) under the Google Ad Manager, both with regard to the operation of the DFP ad server, which enables publishers to sell advertising space, and its Supply Side Platform AdX sales platform, which organizes the auction process that allows publishers to sell their 'impressions' or advertising inventories to advertisers to the detriment of competitors and publishers.

[190] Directive (EU) 2019/790 of the European Parliament and of the Council of 17 April 2019 on copyright and related rights in the Digital Single Market and amending Directives 96/9/EC and 2001/29/EC, [2019] OJ L 130/92 (Copyright Directive). France was the first Member State to implement the Copyright Directive, which creates a new neighbouring right for publishers. On this case, see D Katsifis, 'The Autorité de la Concurrence Orders Interim Measures against Google in Neighbouring Rights Case' (4 May 2020) <https://theplatformlaw.blog/2020/05/04/the-autorite-de-la-concurrence-orders-interim-measures-against-google-in-neighbouring-rights-case> (accessed 7 June 2024).

[191] AdC, 'Remuneration of Related Rights for Press Publishers and Agencies: The Autorité Fines Google Up to 500 Million Euros for Non-Compliance with Several Injunctions' (13 July 2021) <https://www.autoritedelaconcurrence.fr/en/article/remuneration-related-rights-press-publishers-and-agencies-autorite-fines-google-500-million>. See D Katsifis, 'The Autorité de la Concurrence Fines Google €500 Million for Not Complying with Interim Measures in Neighboring Rights Case' (13 July 2021) <https://theplatformlaw.blog/2021/07/13/the-autorite-de-la-concurrence-fines-google-e-500-million-for-not-complying-with-interim-measures-in-neighboring-rights-case> (both accessed 7 June 2024).

[192] AdC, 'Related Rights: The Autorité Accepts Google's Commitments' (21 June 2022) <https://www.autoritedelaconcurrence.fr/en/press-release/related-rights-autorite-accepts-googles-commitments> (accessed 7 June 2024).

[193] AdC, 'The Autorité de la Concurrence Hands Out a €220 Million Fine to Google for Favouring Its Own Services in the Online Advertising Sector' (7 June 2021) <https://www.autoritedelaconcurrence.fr/en/decision/regarding-practices-implemented-online-advertising-sector>. On this case, see D Katsifis, 'Google Fined €220 Million by French Autorité de la Concurrence for Breaching Competition Law in Ad Tech; Offers Commitments' (8 June 2021) <https://theplatformlaw.blog/2021/06/08/google-fined-e-220-million-by-french-autorite-de-la-concurrence-for-breaching-competition-law-in-ad-tech-offers-commitments> (both accessed 7 June 2024).

The French NCA found that Google had engaged in two distinct 'favouring' practices with respect to its DFP ad server favouring its AdX SSP and, conversely, its AdX SSP favouring its DFP ad server.[194] First, the DFP ad server favoured the AdX bidding platform, in particular because it indicated to AdX the price offered by competing SSP platforms. This information enabled AdX to optimize its bidding process by altering the commission received on impressions sold based on intensity of competition. Second, third-party ad servers faced technical and contractual limitations when using the AdX platform.[195]

Google has applied for a settlement procedure and offered several commitments to address the identified concerns. The commitments aim to improve interoperability between the DFP ad server and competing SSPs and change existing configurations in order to allow publishers that use third-party ad servers to access AdX demand in real time.

The French NCA was the first competition authority to sanction Google's practices on its AdTech business and secure concessions. One point to note is how the French precedent will affect ongoing cases, which look at the same practices in the EU and beyond.[196] Granted, local advertisers and publishers may be affected in a different way, though the practices employed are largely the same.

D. Other Enforcement Actions

In addition to enforcement actions by the French NCA, the Paris Commercial Court, following proceedings lasting more than three years, has imposed a €2 million fine on Google with respect to its app store practices and has given the company three months to modify seven clauses in its distribution contract with a €10,000 daily penalty. This action was brought by the French State, in particular the Directorate General for Competition, Consumer Affairs and Fraud Prevention following Bruno Le Maire's decision.[197]

This decision covers Google's distribution contracts from May 2015 to July 2016. The problematic clauses, amongst others, concern the requirement for app developers to set app prices within a price range defined by Google and to allow Google to collect a 30 per cent commission on each sale.[198]

Other claims brought before French courts concern damages caused by Google abusing its dominant position in the online search advertising market. Mapping

[194] Decision 21-D-11 of 7 June 2021 regarding practices implemented in the online advertising sector (English version), 3 <https://www.autoritedelaconcurrence.fr/sites/default/files/attachments/2021-07/21-d-11_ven.pdf> (accessed 7 June 2024).

[195] *Ibid.*

[196] See text to n158 above.

[197] Similar action was brought against Apple. See text to n298.

[198] C Woitier, 'France: Google condamné à une amende de 2 millions d'euros pour son magasin d'applications' (*Le Figaro*, 29 March 2022) <https://www.lefigaro.fr/secteur/high-tech/france-google-condamne-a-une-amende-de-2-millions-d-euros-pour-son-magasin-d-applications-20220329> (accessed 7 June 2024).

service Navx claimed that Google's cancelling its online advertisement account amounted to an abuse and caused it €23 million in damages. The court dismissed the abuse claim but ordered Google to pay €70,000 for not giving enough notice to Navx before the blocking of its account.[199]

II.3.2.3 Italy

A. *Enel v Google*

The Italian NCA (AGCM) has imposed a ca €100 million fine on Google for refusing Enel X Italia interoperability with Android Auto and thereby unfairly limiting consumer choice with respect to the use of the Enel X Italia app when driving and recharging an electric vehicle. In so doing, Google was found to favour its own Google Maps app.[200] Enel X Italia developed the JuicePass app, which allows consumers to manage all the charging services of an electric vehicle, including finding charging stations, access schedule, costs, and reserving a connector. According to the AGCM, Google did not allow Enel X Italia to develop a compatible version of its JuicePass app for Android Auto. Android Auto is a specific Android feature allowing apps to be used while driving by connecting the mobile phone on the car display.

Google's exclusion of the JuicePass app from Android Auto lasted at least two years. If such conduct continued, the AGCM predicted that it could permanently threaten Enel X Italia's building of a solid user base. And such impact on the growing of its user base would come at a time when there is an observed significant growth in sales of electric vehicles with negative effects on consumer choice, the popularity of electric vehicles, and the use of clean energy, as well as technological progress.[201]

Apart from the fine, the Italian NCA has actively identified the measures that Google needed to adopt as part of its cease-and-desist order, namely the making available to Enel X Italia, as well as to other app developers, of the necessary programming tools to ensure apps' interoperability with Android Auto. The authority monitored such obligations through the appointment of an independent expert.[202]

This decision has been criticized for departing from the EU case law on essential facilities and refusal to supply[203] with respect to the condition of indispensability and elimination of all competition in an adjacent market.[204] Yet, the theory

[199] Navx's case number is 2010/070465. See AR Rego, 'Google Didn't Abuse Dominance in Ending Navx Ad Deal, Says French Court' (MLex, 27 December 2012).

[200] AGCM (Italian Competition Authority), 'A529—ICA: Google Fined over 100 Million for Abuse of Dominant Position' (13 May 2021) <https://en.agcm.it/en/media/press-releases/2021/5/A529> (accessed 7 June 2024). The decision is currently under appeal. See Case C-233/23 *Alphabet (Android Auto)* pending.

[201] AGCM, 'A529—ICA: Google Fined over 100 Million for Abuse of Dominant Position'.

[202] *Ibid.*

[203] See n10.

[204] P Ibanez Colomo, 'The Italian Competition Authority in Enel v Google: Will Bronner and Magill Survive Common Carrier Antitrust?' (27 May 2021) <https://chillingcompetition.com/?s = ENEL+ ITALIA> (accessed 7 June 2024).

of harm followed by AGCM is similar to the 'favouring' theory of harm, followed by the EU Commission in *Google Shopping*.[205]

B. Display Advertising/AdTech

On 28 October 2020, the AGCM opened an investigation against Google for alleged infringements in the Italian market for display advertising.[206] The focus of the investigation is on the discriminatory use of users' data collected through its various applications to the detriment of competitors and consumers. According to the press release, Google may have engaged in 'an internal/external discriminatory conduct' as it refuses competitors access to Google ID decryption keys and excludes third-party tracking pixels, while at the same time employing tracking elements that allow its own advertising intermediation services to achieve a targeting capability, which some equally efficient competitors are not able to replicate.

It appears that this investigation has been the result of a relevant complaint by a local ad lobby group, the Interacting Advertising Bureau (IAB) Italy, according to which the investigation would have been concluded by November 2021.[207] The scope of the investigation appeared to partly overlap with the Commission investigation, so the Italian NCA decided to close its investigation under Regulation 1/2003, Article 11(6) following the opening of the Commission investigation.[208]

II.3.2.4 United Kingdom

A. Google Privacy Sandbox

Privacy Sandbox was announced as an industry-wide initiative to develop new technologies to improve privacy across the web and apps on Android by limiting tracking and providing safer alternatives while keeping an open and accessible web.[209] Despite the laudable objectives of this initiative, concerns were raised over

[205] On *Google Search (Shopping)*, see text to n27. AG Medina has opined that, in this case, it is not necessary to examine the Bronner criteria of indispensability and elimination of all the competition in the neighbouring market. See Opinion of Advocate General Medina in Case C-233/23 *Alphabet Inc, Google LLC, Google Italy Srl v Autorità Garante della Concorrenza e del Mercato*, ECLI:EU:C:2024:694, paras 45–46.

[206] AGCM, 'A542—ICA: Investigation Opened against Google for an Alleged Abuse of Dominant Position in the Italian Market for Display Advertising' (28 October 2020) <https://en.agcm.it/en/media/press-releases/2020/10/A542> (accessed 7 June 2024).

[207] N Lomas, 'Google's Display Advertising Business Is under Antitrust Probe in Italy' (28 October 2020) <https://techcrunch.com/2020/10/28/googles-display-advertising-business-is-under-antitrust-probe-in-italy> (accessed 7 June 2024).

[208] Cleary Antitrust Watch, 'The ICA Closes Investigation into Google's Conduct in the Digital Advertising Sector Following the Opening of Proceedings by the European Commission' (Cleary Gottlieb, 12 October 2021) <https://www.clearyantitrustwatch.com/2021/10/the-ica-closes-investigation-into-googles-conduct-in-the-digital-advertising-sector-following-the-opening-of-proceedings-by-the-european-commission/#_ftnref2> (accessed 7 June 2024).

[209] The Privacy Sandbox, 'Protecting Your Privacy Online' <https://www.privacysandbox.com> (accessed 7 June 2024).

its potential to concentrate online advertising revenue on Google, to the detriment of publishers and consumers.

On 8 January 2021, the CMA announced that it had opened an investigation into Google's plan to remove third parties' cookies from its Chrome browser.[210] In June 2021, the CMA announced its intention to accept commitments.[211] Following two rounds of public consultation and close engagement with market participants and the Information Commissioner, the CMA has accepted commitments, which will apply globally.[212] Commitments include first, the regulatory oversight and involvement of the CMA and the Information Commissioner's Office (ICO) in the development and testing of the proposals. Second, Google undertook to follow a more transparent process, which involves engagement with third parties and the publication of test results. The CMA may ask Google to address issues raised by the CMA or third parties. Third, commitments provide for a standstill obligation, namely that third-party cookies will not be removed until the CMA's competition concerns have been addressed. Fourth, commitments were undertaken to ensure that, when third-party cookies are eventually removed, Google will not acquire an advantage over competitors; and finally, commitments were made with respect to preventing Google from engaging in self-preferencing regarding its own AdTech services. With respect to monitoring such commitments, Google is obliged to submit quarterly compliance reports to the CMA.[213]

B. AdTech

Following the EU,[214] Italian, and French investigations,[215] on 25 May 2022, the CMA launched another investigation into Google's AdTech stack.[216] Given Google's strong position on every layer of the AdTech value chain, the CMA will

[210] CMA, 'CMA to Investigate Google's "Privacy Sandbox" Browser Changes' (8 January 2021) <https://www.gov.uk/government/news/cma-to-investigate-google-s-privacy-sandbox-browser-changes> (accessed 7 June 2024).

[211] CMA, 'Notice of Intention to Accept Commitments Offered by Google in Relation to Its Privacy Sandbox Proposals' (Case No 50972) (11 June 2021) <https://assets.publishing.service.gov.uk/government/uploads/system/uploads/attachment_data/file/992975/Notice_of_intention_to_accept_binding_commitments_offered_by_Google_publication.pdf>. See D Katsifis, 'CMA Publishes Commitments Offered by Google with Respect to Its Privacy Sandbox Proposals, Seeks Comments' (14 June 2021) <https://theplatformlaw.blog/2021/06/14/cma-publishes-commitments-offered-by-google-with-respect-to-its-privacy-sandbox-proposals-seeks-comments> (both accessed 7 June 2024).

[212] CMA, 'CMA to Keep "Close Eye" on Google as It Secures Final Privacy Sandbox Commitments' (Press release, 11 February 2022) <https://www.gov.uk/government/news/cma-to-keep-close-eye-on-google-as-it-secures-final-privacy-sandbox-commitments> (accessed 7 June 2024); CMA, 'Decision to Accept Commitments Offered by Google in Relation to Its Privacy Sandbox Proposals' (Case No 50972).

[213] CMA, 'Decision to Accept Commitments Offered by Google' (n212). See also O Bethell, 'Our Commitments for the Privacy Sandbox' (11 June 2022) <https://blog.google/around-the-globe/google-europe/our-commitments-privacy-sandbox> (accessed 7 June 2024).

[214] See text to n158.

[215] See text to n206 on the Italian investigation and text to n192 on the French investigation.

[216] CMA, 'Investigation into Suspected Anti-Competitive Conduct by Google in Ad Tech' (25 May 2022) <https://www.gov.uk/cma-cases/investigation-into-suspected-anti-competitive-conduct-by-google-in-ad-tech> (accessed 7 June 2024).

examine whether Google limited its ad exchange interoperability with third-party publisher ad servers and/or engaged in contractual tying of those services. It will also examine whether Google favoured its own ad exchange.

C. 'Jedi Blue' Agreement/Header Biding Services

In a similar probe to the EU Commission,[217] on 11 March 2022, the CMA announced that it had launched an investigation into the Google and Meta agreement,[218] examining whether it restricted or prevented the growth of header bidding services. Header bidding services allow publishers to offer their online advertising space to multiple advertisers simultaneously, thereby rendering auctions more competitive. The focus of the CMA investigation was on whether the companies restricted or prevented the uptake of header bidding services and whether Google also affected the ability of other firms to compete with its products in this area, but it also looked into 'header bidding services more widely to see if the firm abused a dominant position and gained an unfair advantage over competitors trying to provide a similar service'.[219] The CMA has subsequently decided to close this case on the Google and Meta anticompetitive agreement and combine the remaining investigation on the alleged abuse with respect to header bidding services with the AdTech investigation.[220]

D. Google Play Store

On 10 June 2022, the CMA, following its mobile ecosystem market study, opened an investigation with respect to Google's in-app purchase (IAP) system. Google has offered commitments on 19 April 2023, allowing the use of alternative payment options by app developers.[221] The CMA has now announced that it has closed this case and the parallel Apple AppStore, with the intention to address any concerns under the new digital markets and competition regime.[222]

E. Private Litigation: Collective Actions

Apart from competition authorities' investigations, Google faces an opt-out collective action before the Competition Appeals Tribunal (CAT) over its Play Store

[217] See text to n168.

[218] CMA, 'CMA Investigates Google and Meta over Ad Tech Concerns' (Press release, 11 March 2022) <https://www.gov.uk/government/news/cma-investigates-google-and-meta-over-ad-tech-concerns> (accessed 7 June 2024).

[219] *Ibid.*

[220] CMA, 'Investigation into Suspected Anti-Competitive Agreement between Google and Meta and Behaviour by Google in Relation to Header Bidding' (Press release, 11 March 2023) <https://www.gov.uk/cma-cases/investigation-into-suspected-anti-competitive-agreement-between-google-and-meta-and-behaviour-by-google-in-relation-to-header-bidding> (accessed 7 June 2024).

[221] CMA, 'App Developers on Google Play Store Offered Payment Choices Following CMA Probe' (Press release, 19 April 2023) <https://www.gov.uk/government/news/app-developers-on-google-play-store-offered-payment-choices-following-cma-probe> (accessed 7 June 2024).

[222] CMA, 'CMA Looks to New Digital Markets Competition Regime to Resolve App Store Concerns' (Press release, 21 August 2024).

charges.[223] According to the notice from the CAT, the claim alleges that Google's commission fee on revenue from digital app purchases breaches competition rules and has resulted in overcharging, which must be compensated. Further, the claim alleges that Google's operational set-up through the app store has shut out competition.

Google also faces a GBP 13.6 billion collective action by UK publishers with respect to its online advertising businesses.[224] A similar action was brought in the Netherlands representing EU publishers.[225] Finally, another hybrid-class action (partly following the Commission decision)[226] was filed before the CAT with respect to Google's practices concerning the Android OS.[227]

II.4 Amazon

II.4.1 EU Cases

On 10 November 2020, the Commission sent a Statement of Objections to Amazon[228] and opened a second investigation with respect to different practices by the retail giant.[229] On 20 December 2022, the Commission accepted commitments for both cases.[230]

[223] Case 1408/7/7/21 *Elizabeth Helen Coll v Alphabet Inc and Others*. For information on this case, see <https://www.catribunal.org.uk/cases/14087721-elizabeth-helen-coll> (accessed 7 June 2024). On a related case, see Case 1378/5/7/20 *Epic Games, Inc and Others v Alphabet Inc, Google LLC and Others*. For information on this case, see <https://www.catribunal.org.uk/cases/13785720-epic-games-inc-and-others> (accessed 4 July 2024).

[224] Reuters, 'Google Faces Claim from UK Publishers over Online Advertising' (30 November 2022) <https://www.reuters.com/technology/google-faces-claim-uk-publishers-over-online-advertising-2022-11-30> (accessed 7 June 2024). See Case 1572/7/7/22; 1582/7/7/23 *Ad Tech Collective Action LLP v Alphabet Inc & Others*. For information on this case, see <https://www.catribunal.org.uk/cases/15727722-15827723-ad-tech-collective-action-llp> (accessed 4 July 2024).

[225] N Lomas, 'Google's Adtech Practices Targeted in UK, EU Antitrust Damages Suits' (13 September 2022) <https://techcrunch.com/2022/09/13/google-adtech-antitrust-damages-lawsuits-uk-netherlands> (accessed 7 June 2024).

[226] See section II.3.1.2 above on *Google Android*.

[227] Case 1606/7/7/23 *Nikki Stopford v (1) Alphabet Inc; (2) Google LLC; (3) Google Ireland Limited; and (4) Google UK Limited*. For information on this case, see <https://www.catribunal.org.uk/cases/16067723-nikki-stopford> (accessed 7 June 2024).

[228] The first investigation was opened on 17 July 2019. See European Commission (EU), 'Commission Opens Investigation into Possible Anti-Competitive Conduct of Amazon' (17 July 2019) <https://ec.europa.eu/commission/presscorner/detail/en/IP_19_4291> (accessed 7 June 2024). See *Amazon Marketplace* (Case AT.40462).

[229] European Commission (EU), 'Commission Sends Statement of Objections to Amazon for the Use of Non-Public Independent Seller Data and Opens Second Investigation into Its E-Commerce Business Practices' (10 November 2020) <https://ec.europa.eu/commission/presscorner/detail/en/ip_20_2077> (accessed 7 June 2024). The second case is *Amazon Buy Box* (Case AT.40703).

[230] European Commission (EU), 'Antitrust: Commission Accepts Commitments by Amazon Barring It from Using Marketplace Seller Data, and Ensuring Equal Access to Buy Box and Prime' (20 December 2022) <https://ec.europa.eu/commission/presscorner/detail/en/ip_22_7777> (accessed 7 June 2024). See *Amazon Marketplace* (Case AT.40462) and *Amazon Buy Box* (Case AT.40703). In September 2023, the FTC and seventeen state attorney generals have brought a complaint against

The first case, *Amazon Marketplace*, concerned alleged abusive practices because Amazon systematically relied on non-public business data of independent sellers who marketed their products on the Amazon Marketplace to benefit its own retail business. The second case concerned possible preferential treatment of its own retail offers and those of Marketplace sellers who make use of the Amazon's logistics and delivery services (Fulfilment by Amazon—FBA). As also encapsulated in the Commissioners' statement on this case, in this and a similar string of cases, the authority is concerned about the dual role of platforms with market power, in this case Amazon's dual role as marketplace and retailer.[231]

With respect to the first practice on the use of non-public sellers' data, it constituted an abuse as it allowed Amazon to leverage its dominant position in marketplace services in France and Germany, which constituted the biggest markets for Amazon in the EU. With respect to the preferential treatment of sellers using FBA, the Commission examined the Amazon's criteria for selecting the winner of the 'Buy Box'. The 'Buy Box' features on the top right section on a product page, where Amazon's customers directly add items in their shopping carts. Amazon sellers fiercely compete to 'win the Buy Box' for a certain product. When a seller wins the 'Buy Box' placement, customers can click the button to directly add the respective product to their carts. The investigation also assessed the criteria for enabling sellers to market their products to Prime users, under its Prime loyalty programme. The Commission investigated whether the criteria for featuring in the 'Buy Box' and selling to Prime users led to preferential treatment of Amazon's retail business or of FBA sellers and preliminarily concluded that Amazon unduly favoured its own retail business and FBA sellers in France, Germany, and Spain.[232]

Interestingly in this case, with respect to the second investigation, the Commission has carved out Italy since the authority has launched an investigation 'on partially similar concerns'.[233] Amazon has challenged this decision since, according to the company, there is an overlap in the scope of the two investigations, yet its action was dismissed.[234] According to the CJEU, since the Commission proceedings had a different territorial scope, the protection against parallel proceedings under Regulation 1/2003, Article 11(6) did not apply.[235]

Amazon's commitments cover the EEA, with the exception of Italy, and will cover a seven-year period for Prime and the Buy Box offer and a five-year period

Amazon alleging illegal monopolization. See FTC, 'FTC Sues Amazon for Illegally Maintaining Monopoly Power' (Press release, 26 September 2023) <https://www.ftc.gov/news-events/news/press-releases/2023/09/ftc-sues-amazon-illegally-maintaining-monopoly-power> (accessed 7 June 2024).

[231] European Commission (EU), 'Commission Sends Statement of Objections to Amazon' (n229).
[232] *Ibid.*
[233] *Ibid.*
[234] Case T-19/21 *Amazon v Commission*, ECLI:EU:T:2021:730. See also Case C-815/21 *Amazon v Commission*, ECLI:EU:C:2023:308.
[235] Case T-19/21 *Amazon v Commission* (n234), para 34.

for the rest of the commitments offered. Amazon committed not to use third parties' data (data-silo commitment) and identify the offers featured in the Buy Box in a non-discriminatory manner. The commitments also include improving the presentation of the second competing Buy Box offer and including a review mechanism if such presentation does not attract adequate consumer attention. Amazon also undertook to inform sellers about the commitments, in order to enable early switching to independent carriers. The company has, in addition, committed to arrange, in accordance with data protection rules, for independent carriers to directly contact their Amazon customers so that they can offer equivalent delivery services to those of Amazon.[236]

II.4.2 Member State Enforcement

II.4.2.1 Germany

A. Amazon's Terms

The Bundeskartellamt managed to secure commitments from Amazon to introduce changes into its business services agreements worldwide, following a brief investigation into its retail business.[237] Commitments concerned amendments to liability provisions, provisions on the termination and blocking of accounts, provisions on the court of jurisdiction, provisions on returns and reimbursement, and provisions on product information, rights of use, product reviews and sellers rating, as well as confidentiality and transparency.

Liability provisions, which excluded practically Amazon's liability, were brought in conformity with European standards for business-to-business (B2B) relations. With respect to the *termination* as well as *blocking of sellers' accounts*, Amazon committed to give thirty days' notice prior to termination of a seller's account and provide information for the blocking of an account. Amazon also changed its *jurisdiction* clause allowing, under certain conditions, the dispute to be brought before domestic courts, thus changing Luxembourg as the only court of jurisdiction. Further, on returns and reimbursement, if sellers consider such decision unjustified, they can object to it and seek compensation from Amazon. With respect to *product information and the rights of use*, Amazon committed to stop the parity requirement, allowing sellers to use material of higher quality or more specific

[236] European Commission (EU), 'Antitrust: Commission Accepts Commitments by Amazon Barring It from Using Marketplace Seller Data' (n230). See *Amazon Commitments to the European Commission* (Cases AT.40462 and AT.40703) <https://ec.europa.eu/competition/antitrust/cases1/202252/AT_40462_8825091_8265_4.pdf> (accessed 7 June 2024).

[237] Bundeskartellamt, 'Bundeskartellamt Obtains Far-Reaching Improvements in the Terms of Business for Sellers on Amazon's Online Marketplaces' (Press release, 17 July 2019) <https://www.bundeskartellamt.de/SharedDocs/Meldung/EN/Pressemitteilungen/2019/17_07_2019_Amazon.html;jsessionid=98F173CFCF40CBB4E3AA149FF088832E.1_cid36>. On this case, see Case Summary (B2-88/18) <https://www.bundeskartellamt.de/SharedDocs/Entscheidung/EN/Fallberichte/Missbrauchsaufsicht/2019/B2-88-18.pdf?__blob=publicationFile&v=5> (both accessed 7 June 2024). See also similar probe by the Austrian National Competition Authority. See Federal Competition Authority, 'BWB Informs: Amazon Modifies Its Terms and Conditions' (Press release, 17 July 2019) <https://www.bwb.gv.at/en/news/news_2019/detail/bwb_informs_amazon_modifies_its_terms_and_conditions-1> (accessed 7 June 2024).

product information and descriptions/images on other websites. Also, with respect to product reviews and sellers' rating, now Amazon's own 'Vine' rating programme, which previously was only available to suppliers of Amazon Retail, will be gradually made available to those marketplace sellers that own a brand name registered with Amazon.[238]

During the proceedings, the Bundeskartellamt maintained close contacts with the Commission and had *also exchanged information on these proceedings with other competition authorities*,[239] in particular the Austrian and Luxembourgish NCAs, since they were also investigating Amazon practices at the time.[240] The Austrian NCA closed its proceedings on the same day, referring to the close cooperation with its German counterpart.[241] In this case, the German NCA managed to secure commitments that applied globally, which shows that NCAs may rise as quasi-global regulatory authorities.

B. Paramount Significance of Competition across Markets

On 18 May 2021, the Bundeskartellamt has opened proceedings against Amazon based on its newly acquired competences to pronounce on a platform's position of paramount significance for competition across markets and the subsequent possibility of taking pre-emptive actions against potential anticompetitive practices.[242] This investigation adds to the list of cases the Bundeskartellamt has opened against Amazon under the abuse control provisions in place, prior to this latest amendment, which are briefly covered below. In July 2022, Amazon was designated as a platform of paramount significance and subjected to stricter national competition rules.[243] Amazon appealed the decision.[244]

[238] Bundeskartellamt, 'Bundeskartellamt Obtains Far-Reaching Improvements in the Terms of Business for Sellers on Amazon's Online Marketplaces' (n237).

[239] *Ibid.*

[240] *Ibid.*

[241] Federal Competition Authority (n237). See also S Heinz, 'Bundeskartellamt Ends Abuse Probe after Amazon Agrees to Changing Business Terms for Dealers' (Kluwer Competition Law Blog, 30 July 2019) <http://competitionlawblog.kluwercompetitionlaw.com/2019/07/30/bundeskartellamt-ends-abuse-probe-after-amazon-agrees-to-changing-business-terms-for-dealers> (accessed 7 June 2024).

[242] Bundeskartellamt, 'Proceedings against Amazon Based on New Rules for Large Digital Companies (Section 19a GWB)' (18 May 2021) <https://www.bundeskartellamt.de/SharedDocs/Meldung/EN/Pressemitteilungen/2021/18_05_2021_Amazon_19a.html;jsessionid=FBE5A2DD3572BB985109D7D1C5D9699A.2_cid362?nn=3591568> (accessed 7 June 2024).

[243] Bundeskartellamt, 'Amazon Now Subject to Stricter Regulations—Bundeskartellamt Determines Its Paramount Significance for Competition across Markets (Section 19a GWB)' (6 July 2022) <https://www.bundeskartellamt.de/SharedDocs/Meldung/EN/Pressemitteilungen/2022/06_07_2022_Amazon.html> (accessed 7 June 2024). Case B2-55/21 *Amazon.com, Inc* is of paramount significance for competition across markets. Amazon has appealed the decision. See Case KVB 56/22 *Amazon vs Bundeskartellamt.*

[244] Bundeskartellamt, 'Extension of Ongoing Proceedings against Amazon to Also Include an Examination Pursuant to Section 19a of the German Competition Act (GWB)' (14 November 2022) <https://www.bundeskartellamt.de/SharedDocs/Meldung/EN/Pressemitteilungen/2022/14_11_2022_Amazon_19a.html?nn=3599398> (accessed 7 June 2024). See Case KVB 56/22 *Amazon vs Bundeskartellamt.*

C. Amazon–Apple Brand-Gating Agreements

This investigation, launched on 3 September 2020,[245] looks into agreements between Amazon and brand manufacturers, including Apple, and the extent to which these may exclude third-party sellers from selling brand products on Amazon Marketplace.[246] The Italian NCA has also launched an investigation into Amazon and Apple's brand-gating agreements.[247]

The Bundeskartellamt has now widened the scope of this investigation to also include potential infringements of newly adopted provision, section 19(a) of the German Competition Act.[248] According to the President of the Bundeskartellamt, Andreas Mundt,

> We are examining in both proceedings whether and how Amazon impedes the business opportunities of sellers that are active on the Amazon marketplace and compete with Amazon's own retail business. Amazon operates the most important marketplace in e-commerce and thus has a key position in that area, which allows the company to set far-reaching rules for competition on its platform. Our new competencies, which are precisely intended to restrict such power to set rules, allow us to intervene more efficiently against Amazon's anti-competitive practices.[249]

D. Algorithmic Pricing/Price Control

According to the authority's press release,[250] there is also an investigation against Amazon, which started on 15 May 2020 and looks into whether Amazon

[245] Bundeskartellamt, 'Das Bundeskartellamt—Schutz des Wettbewerbs in der Digitalwirtschaft' (Stand 1/2022).

[246] L Hornkohl, 'Brand Gating: German Competition Authority Once Again Launches an Investigation into Amazon (and Apple)' (Kluwer Competition Law Blog, 6 November 2020) <http://competitionlawblog.kluwercompetitionlaw.com/2020/11/06/brand-gating-german-competition-authority-once-again-launches-an-investigation-into-amazon-and-apple> (accessed 7 June 2024).

[247] The Italian NCA has concluded that Amazon and Apple infringed Article 101 TFEU by entering into brand-gating agreements restricting sellers' ability to market Apple products and (Apple-owned) Beats products on Amazon.it. This case was annulled for procedural errors. See AGCM, 'I842—Italian Competition Authority: The Fines Applied against Amazon and Apple for Anticompetitive Agreements Have Been Redetermined' (17 December 2021) <https://en.agcm.it/en/media/press-releases/2021/12/I842>; N Lomas, 'Beats: Italian Antitrust Fine for Apple and Amazon Cancelled on Appeal' (3 October 2022) <https://techcrunch.com/2022/10/03/italy-antitrust-amazon-apple-beats-fine-cancelled>. The Spanish NCA has also opened a case on this issue. See CNMC (Spanish Competition Authority), 'The CNMC Initiates Disciplinary Proceedings against Apple and Amazon for Possible Restrictive Competition Practices' (1 July 2021) <https://www.cnmc.es/sites/default/files/3723098_0.pdf. However, the Spanish High Court suspended the €194 million fine imposed on Apple and Amazon, pending appeal of the decision of the CNMC. See Reuters, 'Spain's High Court Suspends $209 Million Fines on Apple, Amazon Amid Appeal' (8 February 2024) <https://www.reuters.com/technology/spains-high-court-suspends-209-mln-fines-apple-amazon-amid-appeal-2024-02-08> (all accessed 7 June 2024).

[248] Bundeskartellamt, 'Extension of Ongoing Proceedings against Amazon' (n244).

[249] *Ibid.*

[250] Bundeskartellamt, 'Proceedings against Amazon Based on New Rules for Large Digital Companies' (n242).

may be influencing the pricing of sellers on Amazon Marketplace through price-control mechanisms and algorithms. This section of this investigation has also been extended to cover section 19(a) of the German Competition Act.[251]

II.4.2.2 Italy

A. Preferential Treatment to Third-Party Sellers

While the Commission's investigation was ongoing, and before the Commission accepted commitments in this case, on 9 December 2021, the Italian NCA imposed a fine over €1,128 billion and behavioural commitments on Amazon for abusing its dominant position since it was giving preferential treatment to those third-party sellers that use Amazon's own logistics and delivery services (FBA), the so-called 'affiliated sellers'.[252] These sellers receive the Prime badge and enjoy a number of benefits, including participation in special sales events like Black Friday, free shipping to Prime clients, and better chances to adjudicate the Buy Box. The Amazon Prime strategy (i.e. the way products are promoted, sold, and delivered) is unique to Amazon Marketplace, shaping value creation and amounting to an ecosystem, which is distinct to other e-commerce platforms.[253]

II.4.2.3 United Kingdom

Apart from its ongoing investigation under its consumer law powers against Google and Amazon over fake reviews,[254] the CMA launched an investigation against Amazon for similar practices and concerns as the EU probe.[255] This case, as the EU probe, was resolved with commitments.[256]

In addition to the public enforcement cases, two collective actions were launched before the CAT with respect to Amazon's 'Buy Box' practices on behalf

[251] Bundeskartellamt, 'Extension of Ongoing Proceedings against Amazon' (n244).

[252] AGCM, 'A528—Italian Competition Authority: Amazon Fined over €1,128 Billion for Abusing Its Dominant Position' (9 December 2021) <https://en.agcm.it/en/media/press-releases/2021/12/A528>. Moreover, the AGCM recently fined Amazon €10 million over unfair commercial practices, denoting a certain trend for antitrust enforcement against tech giants. See AGCM, 'PS12585—Italian Competition Authority: A Sanction of EUR 10 Million to Amazon for Unfair Commercial Practice' (24 April 2024) <https://en.agcm.it/en/media/press-releases/2024/4/PS12585> (both accessed 7 June 2024).

[253] M Jacobides, C Cennamo, and A Gawer, 'Towards a Theory of Ecosystems' (2018) 39 Strategic Management Journal 2255.

[254] CMA, 'CMA to Investigate Amazon and Google over Fake Reviews' (Press release, 25 June 2021) <https://www.gov.uk/government/news/cma-to-investigate-amazon-and-google-over-fake-reviews> (accessed 7 June 2024).

[255] CMA, 'CMA Investigates Amazon over Suspected Anti-Competitive Practices' (6 July 2022) <https://www.gov.uk/government/news/cma-investigates-amazon-over-suspected-anti-competitive-practices> (accessed 7 June 2024).

[256] CMA, 'Decision to Accept Binding Commitments under the Competition Act 1998 from Amazon in Relation to Conduct on Its UK Online Marketplace' (Case No 51184) (3 November 2023).

of consumers,[257] with the CAT favouring one of the two claims to proceed to trial.[258] More recently, another collective action was filed on behalf of UK retailers regarding Amazon's Buy Box.[259] Finally, Amazon is facing a collective action claiming more than £2.7bn in damages for various abusive practices to the detriment of third-party sellers in the United Kingdom.[260]

II.5 Facebook

II.5.1 EU Cases

On 4 June 2021, the Commission opened a formal investigation into Facebook's alleged abusive conduct in its use of advertising data gathered in particular from advertisers so that it can compete with them in markets where Facebook is present, such as classified ads through Facebook Marketplace, another 'dual-role' platform case with potential adverse effects on neighbouring markets—here, online classified ads. The investigation will also look into alleged tying of Facebook online classified ads service 'Facebook Marketplace' to its social network.[261]

On 19 December 2022, Facebook (Meta) received the Statement of Objections on the Commission's preliminary assessment.[262] According to its preliminary assessment, first Meta engaged in abusive tying, thereby foreclosing competitors, since such tying bestows Facebook Marketplace a substantial distribution advantage that cannot be matched by competing online classified ads services. Second, Meta has engaged in the imposition of unfair trading conditions on competitors advertising their services on Facebook or Instagram. In particular, such unfair trading conditions concern the authorization of the use of competitors' ads-related data for the benefit of Facebook Marketplace. The Commission deems Meta's terms and conditions unjustified, disproportionate, and not necessary for providing

[257] Case 1568/7/7/22 *Julie Hunter v Amazon.com, Inc and Others*. For information on this case, see <https://www.catribunal.org.uk/cases/15687722-julie-hunter>; Case 1595/7/7/23 *Robert Hammond v Amazon.com, Inc and Others*. For information on this case, see <https://www.catribunal.org.uk/cases/15957723-robert-hammond> (both accessed 7 June 2024).

[258] Hammond's case was preferred. See [2024] CAT 8.

[259] Bira (British Independent Retailers Association), 'Bira Leads £1 Billion Damages Claim against Amazon by UK Retailers in Landmark Collective Action' (6 June 2024) <https://www.bira.co.uk/news/bira-leads-1-billion-damages-claim-against-amazon-by-uk-retailers-in-landmark-collective-action> (accessed 28 June 2024).

[260] Geradin Partners, 'Amazon Faces £2.7bn Legal Claim for Its Anticompetitive Conduct to the Detriment of Hundreds of Thousands of Independent UK Sellers' <https://media.licdn.com/dms/document/media/D4E1FAQEEaZRUf6kdnA/feedshare-document-pdf-analyzed/0/1719474482835?e=1720656000&v= beta&t=kHnr_IUVyMNyEoNjIu3sMoVUqKSHawZn28XJVu792IY> (accessed 28 June 2024).

[261] European Commission (EU), 'Commission Opens Investigation into Possible Anticompetitive Conduct of Facebook' (4 June 2021) <https://ec.europa.eu/commission/presscorner/detail/en/IP_21_2848> (accessed 7 June 2024). See *Facebook Marketplace* (Case AT.40684).

[262] European Commission (EU), 'Antitrust: Commission Sends Statement of Objections to Meta over Abusive Practices Benefiting Facebook Marketplace' (19 December 2022) <https://ec.europa.eu/commission/presscorner/detail/en/ip_22_7728> (accessed 7 June 2024).

online display advertising services on Facebook and Instagram. The Commission has eventually found an infringement and imposed a fine of €797.72 million on Meta.[263]

II.5.2 Member State Enforcement

II.5.2.1 Germany

A. Paramount Significance of Competition across Markets

On 8 January 2021, only nine days after its tenth competition law amendment came into force, Facebook became the first company to be examined by the Bundeskartellamt under its new competition law powers,[264] and in May 2022, Facebook was given such status, which subjects Meta to stricter rules on abuse of dominance. The company decided not to appeal the decision.[265]

B. Tying Arrangement between Oculus and Facebook

On 10 December 2020, the German NCA launched an investigation against Facebook to examine the relationship between Oculus virtual reality products and the social network and Facebook platform. It appears that the use of the latest Oculus (Quest 2 and Quest Pro) virtual-reality (VR) glasses requires that the user also has a Facebook account. Given Facebook's dominance in social networks in Germany and its growing share in the VR market, such conduct may amount to abusive tying.

The Bundeskartellamt observes that Facebook has started to integrate its VR activities into its social network Facebook.com. The Oculus platform, which was separate from Facebook.com, will be now offered as an additional function on Facebook's social network, under the name 'Facebook Reality Labs'.[266]

In order to address these concerns, Meta has offered to allow the use of Quest 2 and Pro VR glasses without a Facebook account. Users are now given the option to set up the headset through a separate Meta account. The German NCA has welcomed this change but has not terminated its proceedings. The authority pledged

[263] European Commission (EU), 'Commission Fines Meta €797.72 Million over Abusive Practices Benefitting Facebook Marketplace' (Press release, 14 November 2024).

[264] Bundeskartellamt, 'First Proceeding Based on New Rules for Digital Companies—Bundeskartellamt Also Assesses New Section 19a GWB in Its Facebook/Oculus Case' (28 January 2020) <https://www.bundeskartellamt.de/SharedDocs/Meldung/EN/Pressemitteilungen/2021/28_01_2021_Facebook_Oculus.html;jsessionid=FBE5A2DD3572BB985109D7D1C5D9699A.2_cid362?nn=3591568> (accessed 7 June 2024).

[265] Bundeskartellamt, 'New Rules Apply to Meta (Formerly Facebook)—Bundeskartellamt Determines Its "Paramount Significance for Competition across Markets' (4 May 2022) <https://www.bundeskartellamt.de/SharedDocs/Meldung/EN/Pressemitteilungen/2022/04_05_2022_Facebook_19a.html> (accessed 7 June 2024). See Case B6-27/21 *Meta's Paramount Significance for Competition across Markets*.

[266] See Bundeskartellamt, 'Bundeskartellamt Examines Linkage between Oculus and the Facebook Network' (Press release, 10 December 2020) <https://www.bundeskartellamt.de/SharedDocs/Meldung/EN/Pressemitteilungen/2020/10_12_2020_Facebook_Oculus.html> (accessed 7 June 2024).

to keep monitoring the design of users' options as well as data processing and combination issues along the constellation of Meta services also under investigation in the light of section 19(a) of the German Competition Act.[267]

C. Combination of Data from Different Sources: Facebook Exploitative Abuse

In this much-discussed case,[268] initiated in 2016, the Bundeskartellamt examined whether Facebook's terms and conditions, by asking users to accept the 'whole Facebook package' or not to use the platform at all, amounted to the imposition of unfair terms on its users ('exploitative business use'). The Bundeskartellamt concluded, in February 2019, that the collection and use of data by Facebook from third-party sources violates data protection rules and constitutes an abuse under German competition law. The remedy was akin to data divestiture ordering Facebook to stop combining users' data collected on WhatsApp and Instagram. The company was given a year to change its data-collection business model. Following the NCA decision, Facebook has fiercely challenged the decision.[269]

The decision was subsequently suspended in August 2019 by the Higher Regional Court in Düsseldorf, which accepted Facebook's interim measures application.[270] This decision was then overturned by the Federal Court of Justice in June 2020. The Higher Regional Court in Düsseldorf, in order to decide the substance of this case, sent a preliminary reference request to the CJEU to clarify whether Facebook is abusing its dominant position because of the collection and use of user data in violation of the General Data Protection Regulation (GDPR).[271]

The CJEU has now authoritatively answered the complex question of whether a national competition authority, when examining an alleged abuse under

[267] Bundeskartellamt, 'Meta (Facebook) Responds to the Bundeskartellamt's Concerns—VR Headsets Can Now Be Used without a Facebook Account' (23 November 2022) <https://www.bundeskartellamt.de/SharedDocs/Meldung/EN/Pressemitteilungen/2022/23_11_2022_Facebook_VR_Brillen.html> (accessed 7 June 2024).

[268] See, e.g. M Buiten, 'Exploitative Abuses in Digital Markets: Between Competition Law and Data Protection Law' (2021) 9 Journal of Antitrust Enforcement 270; M Botta and K Wiedemann, 'Exploitative Conducts in Digital Markets: Time for a Discussion after the Facebook Decision' (2020) Journal of European Competition Law & Practice 465; G Colangelo and M Maggiolino, 'Data Accumulation and the Privacy–Antitrust Interface: Insights from the Facebook Case' (2018) 8 International Data Privacy Law 224; G Schneider, 'Testing Art. 102 TFEU in the Digital Marketplace: Insights from the Bundeskartellamt's Investigation against Facebook' (2018) 9 Journal of European Competition Law & Practice 213. A Witt, 'Meta v Bundeskartellamt—Data-Based Conduct between Antitrust Law and Regulation' (2024) 12 Journal of Accounting and Economics 345.

[269] For a brief account, see Bundeskartellamt, 'First Proceeding Based on New Rules for Digital Companies' (n264).

[270] Oberlandesgericht Düsseldorf, Case VI-Kart 1/19 (V), *Facebook* (26 August 2019).

[271] Higher Regional Court Düsseldorf, 'Facebook gegen Bundeskartellamt: Ergebnisse des Verhandlungstermins' (24 March 2021 Pressemitteilung No 9/2021) <https://www.olg-duesseldorf.nrw.de/behoerde/presse/Presse_aktuell/20210324_PM_Facebook2/index.php>. For a very informative account of the hearing and the developments in this case, see R Podszun, 'Facebook: Next Step Europe' (D'Kart, 25 March 2021) <https://www.d-kart.de/en/blog/2021/03/25/facebook-next-stop-europe> (both accessed 2 April 2021).

Article 102 TFEU, can rule that the incumbent's terms with respect to personal data processing are not consistent with the GDPR and whether such a finding is also possible when such terms are being simultaneously investigated by the lead supervisory data protection authority under the GDPR.[272] According to the CJEU,

> the compliance or non-compliance [. . .] with the provisions of the GDPR may, depending on the circumstances, be a vital clue among the relevant circumstances of the case in order to establish whether that conduct entails resorting to methods governing normal competition and to assess the consequences of a certain practice in the market or for consumers.[273]

In view of the different objectives of competition and data protection rules, the fact that a competition authority finds a GDPR infringement when assessing an abuse under Article 102 TFEU does not mean that it replaces the assessment of the competent data protection authority,[274] though in light of the principle of sincere cooperation (Article 4(3) Treaty on European Union (TEU)), it needs to cooperate with the competent data protection authorities to ensure the consistent application of the relevant data protection legislation[275] and cannot depart from the latter's decision, if one exists, but only draw conclusions for the application of competition law.[276]

II.5.2.2 France

A. Unfair Terms/Online Advertising Services

Following a complaint from the online advertising company Criteo for unfair terms in accessing Facebook's advertising services, the French NCA accepted commitments addressing the alleged abuse.[277] Facebook unfairly withdrew Criteo's membership in the Facebook Marketing Partners (FMP) programme and restricted Criteo's access to an API, allowing it to use its own bidding and product recommendation technologies.

The French NCA's preliminary assessment considered that such practices were likely, first, to distort competition between online advertising service providers. Second, given Meta's vertical integration, they may lead to foreclosure effects and

[272] Case C-252/21 *Meta Platforms and Others*, ECLI:EU:C:2023:537, para 36.
[273] *Ibid*, para 47.
[274] *Ibid*, para 49.
[275] *Ibid*, para 52.
[276] *Ibid*, paras 56, 62–63.
[277] AdC, 'In the Context of an Investigation Opened before the Autorité in the Online Advertising Sector, Facebook Proposes Commitments' (3 June 2021) <https://www.autoritedelaconcurrence.fr/en/press-release/context-investigation-opened-autorite-online-advertising-sector-facebook-proposes> (accessed 7 June 2024).

weaken the exerted competitive pressure, since Criteo's retargeting technology competes with that of Meta.[278]

B. Online Ad Verification

Following a complaint by Adloox in October 2022 with respect to the conditions for access to Meta's 'viewability' and 'brand safety' partnerships in the online ad verification sector, the French NCA has ordered interim measures against Meta. It ordered Meta to publicize new objective, transparent, non-discriminatory, and proportionate criteria and admit the complainant to these partnerships if it meets these new criteria.[279]

II.5.2.3 United Kingdom

A. Use of Data/Classified Ads/Online Dating

In a similar manner to the announced investigation into the Jedi Blue agreement,[280] the CMA and the Commission have simultaneously opened investigations against Facebook about similar anticompetitive conducts. On 4 June 2021, the CMA announced its investigation into Facebook's online classified ads and online dating business. In particular, the CMA assessed whether Facebook has gained an unfair advantage through its practices on gathering and use of certain data.[281] The CMA accepted Meta's proposed commitments in this case. Meta offered commitments with respect to limiting the use of competitors' advertising data. By putting in place new technical systems and dedicated staff training, it undertook not to use such data for its own online classified ad service, Facebook Marketplace.[282]

B. Private Enforcement/Collective Action before the CAT

As will be discussed in section III.A below, the large data accumulation by digital platforms with market power without 'express' user consent or adequate remuneration has been discussed in the literature as a form of exploitative abuse, either as excessive data extraction akin to excessive pricing or the imposition of

[278] AdC, 'Meta Makes Commitments to the Autorité de la Concurrence' (16 June 2022) <https://www.autoritedelaconcurrence.fr/en/communiques-de-presse/meta-makes-commitments-autorite-de-la-concurrence> (accessed 7 June 2024).

[279] AdC, 'Online Ad Verification: The Autorité de la Concurrence Issues Interim Measures against Meta' (4 May 2023) <https://www.autoritedelaconcurrence.fr/en/article/online-ad-verification-autorite-de-la-concurrence-issues-interim-measures-against-meta> (accessed 7 June 2024).

[280] See text to nn168 and 217.

[281] CMA, 'CMA Investigates Facebook's Use of Ad Data' (4 June 2021) <https://www.gov.uk/government/news/cma-investigates-facebook-s-use-of-ad-data> (accessed 7 June 2024).

[282] CMA, 'Meta Offers to Limit Use of Other Businesses' Ad Data to Address CMA Concerns' (26 May 2023) <https://www.gov.uk/government/news/meta-offers-to-limit-use-of-other-businesses-ad-data-to-address-cma-concerns> (accessed 7 June 2024); CMA, 'Decision to Accept Binding Commitments Offered by Meta on Its Use of Data Obtained through Digital Display Advertising' (Case AT.51013) (3 November 2023).

unfair contract terms. To date, such an approach has been endorsed only by the Bundeskartellamt, based on German competition law.[283]

An opt-out collective action is currently pending before the CAT against Meta, alleging that Facebook abused its dominant position through the imposition of unfair terms/prices. The action claims damages on behalf of ca 44 million consumers (UK Facebook users between October 2015 and December 2019 living in the United Kingdom) for a minimum of £2.3 billion plus interest.[284] After initially staying the collective proceedings order (CPO) application asking the claimant to address inadequacies in the pleading of the alleged abuses as well as improve the methodology for quantifying loss, the CAT has now allowed the case to proceed to trial.[285]

II.6 Apple

II.6.1 EU Cases

On 16 June 2020, the Commission opened investigations into AppStore rules[286] as well as practices regarding Apple Pay.[287] On 30 April 2021, the Commission sent Apple a Statement of Objections with respect to App Store rules for musing streaming apps,[288] and then sent a second Statement of Objections replacing the first one and limiting the scope of the investigation on 28 February 2023. On 2 May 2022, Apple received a Statement of Objections with respect to its Apple Pay Practices.[289]

Apple products enjoy strong brand loyalty with consumers, with Apple having formed a closed ecosystem. Until the adoption of the DMA, the App Store was the only gateway for consumers to download apps in Apple smart mobile devices, and app developers could only reach iOS users via the App

[283] See text to n268 above.

[284] Case 1433/7/7/22 *Dr Liza Lovdahl Gormsen v Meta Platforms Inc and Others*. For information on the progress of the case, see <https://www.catribunal.org.uk/cases/14337722-dr-liza-lovdahl-gormsen> (accessed 7 June 2024).

[285] [2023] CAT 10, 20 February 2023; [2024] CAT 11, 15 February 2024.

[286] European Commission (EU), 'Commission Opens Investigations into Apple's App Store Rules' (16 June 2020) <https://ec.europa.eu/commission/presscorner/detail/en/ip_20_1073> (accessed 7 June 2024). See *Apple—App Store Practices—Music Streaming* (Case AT.40437) and *Apple—App Store Practices—E-books/Audiobooks* (Case AT.40652).

[287] European Commission (EU), 'Commission Opens Investigation into Apple Practices Regarding Apple Pay' (16 June 2020) <https://ec.europa.eu/commission/presscorner/detail/en/ip_20_1075> (accessed 7 June 2024). See *Apple—Mobile Payments—Apple Pay* (Case AT.40452).

[288] European Commission (EU), 'Commission Sends Statement of Objections to Apple on App Store Rules for Music Streaming Providers' (30 April 2021) <https://ec.europa.eu/commission/presscorner/detail/en/ip_21_2061> (accessed 7 June 2024).

[289] European Commission (EU), 'Commission Sends Statement of Objections to Apple over Practices Regarding Apple Pay' (2 May 2022) <https://ec.europa.eu/commission/presscorner/detail/en/ip_22_2764> (accessed 7 June 2024).

Store.[290] In the *AppStore Rules* case, the Commission expressed concerns with respect to the following two mandatory rules in Apple's agreements with music-streaming app developers: first, the use of Apple's proprietary IAP system. Apple charged a 30 per cent commission fee to app developers on every subscription purchased through the IAP, and such fee was passed on to end users by raising prices. Second, the Commission took issues with the so-called 'anti-steering provisions'. Such provisions prevented app developers from informing users of possible alternative purchasing possibilities outside of apps, which are usually cheaper. Such practices, according to the first Statement of Objections, have distorted competition in the market for music streaming services by raising the rival music-streaming app developers' costs and raising consumer prices.[291] In the second Statement of Objections, the Commission, in a rather rare move, limited the scope of its investigation and expressed concerns only with respect to the second practice, concerning the anti-steering provisions. The Commission finally concluded that such anti-steering provisions amounted to an exploitative abuse of imposing unfair trading conditions contrary to Article 102(a) TFEU, resulting in higher prices for consumers and a degradation in users' experience.[292] It imposed a fine of ca €1.8 billion and asked Apple to remove, and not readopt, the anti-steering provisions.[293] Interestingly, the basic amount of the fine was ca €34 million, but the Commission additionally added a lump sum of €1.8 billion to achieve sufficient deterrence.

With regards to its Apple Pay practices, according to the Commission's preliminary assessment, Apple restricted competition in the mobile wallets market on iOS by limiting access to rival mobile wallet app developers to a key technology used for contactless payments with mobile devices in stores ('near-field communication'—NFC—or 'tap and go'). In so doing, it benefited its own mobile payment service, Apple Pay.[294] Interestingly, in this case as well, in the Statement of

[290] For a critical account of Apple's App Store practices, see D Geradin and D Katsifis, 'The Antitrust Case against the Apple App Store (Revisited)', TILEC Discussion Paper No DP2020-035 (2020) <https://papers.ssrn.com/sol3/papers.cfm?abstract_id=3744192>. For the opposite view, see S Voelcker and D Baker, 'Why There Is No Antitrust Case against Apple's App Store: A Response to Geradin & Katsifis', TILEC Discussion Paper No DP2020-035 (2020) <https://papers.ssrn.com/sol3/papers.cfm?abstract_id=3660896> (both accessed 7 June 2024).

[291] European Commission (EU), 'Commission Opens Investigations into Apple's App Store Rules' (n286).

[292] *Apple—App Store Practices (Music Streaming)* (Case AT.40437) Commission Decision (4 March 2024), paras 521–555.

[293] *Ibid*, paras 869–1027. Apple has appealed the decision. See Case T-269/24 *Apple and Apple Distribution International v Commission*. For a discussion of this case, including the Commission approach to this novel type of exploitative abuse where unfair terms are imposed on musing streaming service providers whereas end users suffer harm, see G Monti, 'Exploitative Abuse—Takeaways from the Apple App Store Practices Decision' (2024) <https://papers.ssrn.com/sol3/papers.cfm?abstract_id = 4853304> (accessed 9 October 2024).

[294] European Commission (EU), 'Commission Opens Investigation into Apple Practices Regarding Apple Pay' (16 June 2020) (n287).

Objections, the Commission limited the scope of its investigation, since it no longer pursued issues with measures concerning the integration of Apple Pay on merchant apps. The Commission has ultimately accepted the commitments offered by Apple to make its technology available to rivals. Such commitments followed the Commission's probe and were given at a time when Apple would have to change its practices to comply with the DMA's interoperability obligations.[295]

II.6.2 Member State Enforcement

II.6.2.1 Germany

A. Paramount Significance of Competition across Markets

On 21 June 2021, the Bundeskartellamt initiated proceedings against Apple in its fourth investigation based on its new rules.[296] The German NCA decided that Apple should be afforded such status on 3 April 2023.[297]

B. Apple's App Tracking Transparency Framework

On 19 June 2022, the Bundeskartellamt initiated proceedings against Apple with respect to Apple's tracking rules and the App Tracking Transparency (ATT) Framework, raising concerns about self-preferencing practices.[298]

The ATT Framework was launched with the updates in iOS 14.5 in April 2021 and applies to third-party apps but not to Apple. According to the ATT, users need to opt in to tracking and give their consent to the use and combination of their data via a pop-up when third-party apps are launched for the first time, in addition to the already existing pop-up requesting such consent from users.[299] The ATT was

[295] *Mobile Payments Proposal of Commitments to the European Commission* (Case AT.40452) (19 January 2024) <https://ec.europa.eu/competition/antitrust/cases1/202403/AT_40452_9866037_9192_4.pdf>; final Commission Decision of 11 July 2024 relating to proceedings under Article 102 of the Treaty on the Functioning of the European Union and Article 54 of the Agreement on the European Economic Area—Case AT.40452—Apple—Mobile Payments, C(2024) 4761 (Brussels, 11 July 2024). See also F Yun Chee, 'Exclusive: Apple Offers to Let Rivals Access Tap-and-Go Tech in EU Antitrust Case' (Reuters, 12 December 2023) <https://www.reuters.com/technology/apple-offers-settle-eu-antitrust-charges-apple-pay-sources-say-2023-12-12> (both accessed 7 June 2024). This was also seen in Europe, even following the Commission's decision. See F Yun Chee, 'EU Regulators Assess Apple's Plan for Complying with Music Streaming Order' (Reuters, 8 April 2024) <https://www.reuters.com/technology/eu-regulators-assess-apples-plan-complying-with-music-streaming-order-2024-04-08> (accessed 27 May 2024).

[296] Bundeskartellamt, 'Proceeding against Apple Based on New Rules for Large Digital Companies (Section 19a(1) GWB)—Bundeskartellamt Examines Apple's Significance for Competition across Markets' (21 June 2021) <https://www.bundeskartellamt.de/SharedDocs/Meldung/EN/Pressemitteilungen/2021/21_06_2021_Apple.html?nn=3591568> (accessed 7 June 2024).

[297] Bundeskartellamt, 'Apple Also Subject to Provisions for Large Digital Companies under Section 19a GWB' (5 April 2023) <https://www.bundeskartellamt.de/SharedDocs/Meldung/EN/Pressemitteilungen/2023/05_04_2023_Abscluss_Apple.html> (accessed 7 June 2024).

[298] Bundeskartellamt, 'Bundeskartellamt Reviews Apple's Tracking Rules for Third-Party Apps' (14 June 2022) <https://www.bundeskartellamt.de/SharedDocs/Meldung/EN/Pressemitteilungen/2022/14_06_2022_Apple.html?nn=3591568> (accessed 7 June 2024).

[299] *Ibid.*

launched by Apple as a privacy-enhancing feature. Research suggests that it has resulted in a rise in paid apps over free apps.[300]

Interestingly in the press release, the Bundeskartellamt indicated that this action was taken under the new rules (section 19(a)(2) sentence 1 of the German Competition Act) and Article 102 TFEU, even though Apple was not designated at the time as a platform of paramount importance across markets under the new rules.[301]

II.6.2.2 France

A. Anticompetitive Distribution Practices/Abuse of Economic Dependence

The French NCA has imposed a €1.1 billion fine on Apple for anticompetitive practices within its distribution network with respect to Apple products (excluding iPhones) and abuse of a situation of economic dependence regarding its 'premium' independent distributors.[302]

B. Use of Data for Advertising

The French NCA has sent a Statement of Objections to Apple alleging that the company has implemented discriminatory, non-objective, and non-transparent conditions with respect to the processing of user data for advertising purposes.[303]

C. Other Enforcement Actions

Similar to the action brough against Google before the Paris Commercial Court,[304] Apple has also been fined (ca €1 million) with respect to its App store practices. The decision focused on some terms, which were considered unfair, such as the fact that Apple can reject apps. The court has been criticized for rejecting claims on the abusive nature of Apple's IAP system and the 30 per cent commission rule.[305]

[300] R Kesler, 'The Impact of Apple's App Tracking Transparency on App Monetization' (2022) <https://papers.ssrn.com/sol3/papers.cfm?abstract_id=4090786> (accessed 7 June 2024).

[301] Bundeskartellamt, 'Proceeding against Apple Based on New Rules for Large Digital Companies (Section 19a(1) GWB)' (n290).

[302] AdC, 'Fines Handed Down to Apple, Tech Data and Ingram Micro' (16 March 2020) <https://www.autoritedelaconcurrence.fr/en/article/fines-handed-down-apple-tech-data-and-ingram-micro> (accessed 7 June 2024).

[303] AdC, 'Advertising on iOS Mobile Applications: The General Rapporteur Confirms Having Notified the Apple Group of an Objection' (27 July 2023) <https://www.autoritedelaconcurrence.fr/en/press-release/advertising-ios-mobile-applications-general-rapporteur-confirms-having-notified-apple> (accessed 7 June 2024).

[304] See n196 above.

[305] Foss Patents, 'Paris Commercial Court Declined to Find Fault in Apple's 30% App Tax, Referred to EU Commission Enforcement of Antitrust Law and DMA: French Government Should Appeal Certain Parts' (20 December 2022) <http://www.fosspatents.com/2022/12/paris-commercial-court-declined-to-find.html> (accessed 7 June 2024).

II.6.2.3 The Netherlands

A. App Store

The Association for Consumers and Markets (ACM), as part of its probe against Apple, examined Apple's conditions for using the App Store by app providers that do not compete with Apple's apps, in particular apps related to online dating in the Netherlands.[306] The Dutch NCA (ACM) announced that its investigation could proceed in parallel with the EU probe, with the two authorities maintaining regular discussions.[307] It had ordered the company to adjust the unreasonable App Store conditions applicable to dating-app providers within two months or else pay a periodic penalty of €5 million per week up to a maximum of €50 million.[308] Following the Dutch order, Apple will now allow different methods of payment in Dutch dating apps and not enforce only Apple's payment method or else be excluded from the App Store. According to the ACM, the fact that its investigation focused on the impact of Apple's practices on non-competing apps is what distinguished its own probe from the ongoing Commission investigation.[309]

The ACM also launched an investigation into payment apps' access to NFC technology[310] but decided to close its investigation, despite confirming previously identified anticompetitive concerns. This was because the ACM conducted its investigation under the Interchange Fee Regulation (IFR), which was not suitable to address competition concerns in that case. The ACM called for an amendment to the European rules for payments services (Second Payment Services Directive—PSD2) and for the introduction of the DMA.[311]

[306] ACM, 'ACM Can Continue Its Investigation into the Apple App Store' (22 June 2021) <https://www.acm.nl/en/publications/acm-can-continue-its-investigation-apple-app-store>; ACM, 'ACM Launches Investigation into Abuse of Dominance by Apple in Its App Store' (11 April 2019) <https://www.acm.nl/en/publications/acm-launches-investigation-abuse-dominance-apple-its-app-store> (both accessed 7 June 2024). Initially, the investigation had a wider scope, which was later narrowed down to include a paid dating app. On this case, see F Bostoen, 'The ACM's Apple Decision: To Boldly Go Where No Enforcer Has Gone Before' (2022) 10 Journal of Accounting and Economics 583.

[307] ACM, 'ACM Can Continue Its Investigation into the Apple App Store' (n306).

[308] ACM, 'ACM Obliges Apple to Adjust Unreasonable Conditions for Its App Store' (24 December 2021) <https://www.acm.nl/en/publications/acm-obliges-apple-adjust-unreasonable-conditions-its-app-store>; ACM, 'Apple Changes Unfair Conditions, Allows Alternative Payments Methods in Dating Apps' (11 June 2022) <https://www.acm.nl/en/publications/acm-apple-changes-unfair-conditions-allows-alternative-payments-methods-dating-apps> (both accessed 7 June 2024). Apple had not complied with the order straight away. Periodic penalty payments applied from January 2022 and had reached the maximum of 50 million: ACM, 'Apple Changes Unfair Conditions' (11 June 2022).

[309] AdC, 'Fines Handed Down to Apple, Tech Data and Ingram Micro' (n302).

[310] ACM, 'ACM Launches an Investigation into Users' Freedom of Choice Regarding Payment Apps on Smartphones' (4 December 2020) <https://www.acm.nl/en/publications/acm-launches-investigation-users-freedom-choice-regarding-payment-apps-smartphones> (accessed 7 June 2024).

[311] ACM, 'Closure of the Investigation into Payment Apps confirms Need for New Rules' (2 July 2021) <https://www.acm.nl/en/publications/closure-investigation-payment-apps-confirms-need-new-rules> (accessed 7 June 2024).

B. Private Enforcement
The Consumer Competition Claims Foundation has launched a collective action against Apple in relation to its app store practices and the 30 per cent fee charged to app developers for every sale in the App Store. Such fee has allegedly been passed on to consumers, resulting in price increases with a total harm—according to the claimant—amounting to nearly €5 billion.[312]

II.6.2.4 United Kingdom
A. App Store Terms and Conditions
The CMA has launched an investigation into Apple's conduct with respect to the distribution of apps on iOS and iPadOS devices in the United Kingdom. In particular, the CMA was examining the terms about app developers' access to the App Store.[313] The CMA has now announced that it has closed this case, and the parallel *Google Play Store* case, and will examine such practices under the new digital markets and competition regime.[314]

B. Private Enforcement
A collective action is pending before the CAT with a proposed class of approximately 19.6 million consumers.[315] Additionally, another collective action has been brought on behalf of app developers.[316] At the time of writing, the CAT had allowed the former to progress to trial while the latter was at the certification stage.

III. Understanding the Competition Law Theories of Harm: An Exercise in Legal Funambulism

III.1 Introduction

After having discussed the relevant case law against Big Tech companies in the EU, at selected Member State and the UK level, this section threads out some

[312] C Koc, 'Apple Faces Multibillion-Euro Dutch Class Action over App Sales' (29 March 2022) <https://www.bloomberg.com/news/articles/2022-03-29/apple-faces-multibillion-euro-dutch-class-action-over-app-sales> (accessed 7 June 2024).
[313] CMA, 'Investigation into Apple App Store' (updated 21 August 2024) <https://www.gov.uk/cma-cases/investigation-into-apple-appstore> (accessed 7 June 2024).
[314] CMA, 'CMA Looks to New Digital Markets Competition Regime to Resolve App Store Concerns' (Press release, 21 August 2024).
[315] Case No 1403/7/7/21 *Dr Rachael Kent v Apple Inc and Apple Distribution International Ltd.* On this case, see <https://www.catribunal.org.uk/cases/14037721-dr-rachael-kent> (accessed 7 June 2024).
[316] Case No 1601/7/7/23 *Dr Sean Ennis v Apple Inc and Others.* On this case, see <https://www.catribunal.org.uk/cases/16017723-dr-sean-ennis> (accessed 7 June 2024).

enforcement themes by focusing on problematic practices investigated by competition authorities. The aim of the analysis is to categorize the investigated practices, question whether there are emerging trends with respect to specific types of abuse and whether competition authorities expand the limits of current categories, and point to the complementarities between the role of competition law in investigating such abuses and ad hoc regulation in order to address market failures in digital markets.

Interestingly, if one looks at the history of competition law enforcement in technology markets, the incumbents—as perhaps expected—have accused the Commission of expanding the limits of its competence and applying novel theories of harm. For example, this assertion was made in *Microsoft*, where Microsoft criticized the Commission for applying 'a new and highly speculative theory'.[317] Yet, as discussed in Chapter 2, with the emerging new regulations aiming at infusing digital markets with transparency, fairness, and contestability, the pendulum appears to have swung in favour of intervention. Whether competition law is the right tool is a different question, but it has definitely paved the way for the adoption of the DMA, considering the close resemblance of the obligations contained therein with competition law cases.[318]

This section first discusses cases that may result in direct exploitation of consumers and then moves on to analyse various themes with respect to exclusionary abuses. The aim is to distil certain emerging categories of abuses from the existing case law against Big Tech companies. Some of these abuses (e.g. self-preferencing) have also been discussed in various policy reports and have also found their way in newly adopted or contemplated regulatory instruments. In the EU, to the extent that gatekeepers now have to comply with DMA obligations, competition law enforcement with respect to some types of abuse may prove to be redundant.

III.2 Exploitative Abuses

In digital markets, there is an observed resurgence of the competition law's role to discipline powerful platforms for alleged exploitative abuses.

With respect to exploitative abuses, attempting a categorization of existing case law, the first category concerns the *imposition of unfair contractual terms*.[319] The *Facebook* case in Germany may be read in this light.[320] Article 5(2) DMA

317 Case T-201/04 *Microsoft* v *Commission* (n6), para 989. Contra the Commission, *ibid*, paras 1004, 1032, 1033.

318 On this point, see Table 5.2 below. See also N Petit, *Big Tech and the Digital Economy: The Moligopoly Scenario* (OUP, 2020), developing the theory of 'moligopoly' to argue that regulation is better suited to address various non-economic harms such as privacy degradation.

319 See Article 102(a) TFEU.

320 On this case, see text to n267.

prohibiting gatekeepers from combining personal data from the relevant CPS with personal data from any other CPS or any other gatekeeper's services or with personal data from third-party services, subject to users' consent, partially addresses the concerns raised in this case.

In the above detailed exposition of the relevant cases against Big Tech, we find other examples, where the imposition of opaque, unfair, discriminatory, or unreasonable terms has been assessed as an abuse of a dominant position. This was the case, for example, in *Google News* (Germany),[321] *Google AdWords* (France),[322] *Google News* (France),[323] *Amazon Marketplace—Commitments* (Germany),[324] *Facebook Online Advertising Services* (France),[325] *Facebook Online Ad Verification* (France),[326] *Apple Online Dating Apps* (the Netherlands)[327] and *Apple App Store* (United Kingdom).[328] Anti-steering practices were discussed in *Apple App Store* in the EU as an exploitative abuse of imposing unfair trading conditions under Article 102(a).[329] The DMA has introduced tailored obligations for gatekeepers that address such practices (Articles 5(4), 5(5), and 6 (4)).

Preferential and or discriminatory treatment of third parties on the platform can be listed as the second category of exploitative abuse cases in digital markets, comprising the following cases: *Amazon Marketplace* (EU), *Amazon Marketplace* (Italy), and *Amazon Marketplace* (United Kingdom).[330]

Apart from exploitative abuses addressed in the case law, commentators have also discussed potential exploitative practices, given the concentrated nature of digital markets and the prevalence of data-driven business models. In light of these, consumers often have no alternatives and therefore may end up being exploited. Such exploitation may take the form of imposition of unfair terms *in the form of misleading privacy policies*, for example.[331] In addition, where digital platforms have substantial market power, consumers may be directly forced to give away their personal information for lack of other options—on a take-it-or-leave-it basis.[332]

[321] See text to n184 above.
[322] See text to n187 above.
[323] See text to n189 above.
[324] See text to n237 above.
[325] See text to n277 above.
[326] See text to n279 above.
[327] See text to n301 above.
[328] See text to n308 above.
[329] See text to n284. With respect to *Apple App Store (UK)*, see text to n308 above.
[330] On these cases, see text to nn228, 252, and 254 above.
[331] See the speech by G Buttarelli, 'Competition Rebooted: Enforcement and Personal Data in Digital Markets' (Keynote speech at Joint European Railway Agency–European Data Protection Seminar, 24 September 2015) <https://edps.europa.eu/sites/default/files/publication/15-09-24_era_gb_en.pdf> (accessed 7 June 2024).
[332] EDPS, Preliminary Opinion, 'Privacy and Competitiveness in the Age of Big Data: The Interplay between Data Protection, Competition Law and Consumer Protection in the Digital Economy', EDPS/2014/06 (26 March 2014), para 79. For a discussion, see M Ioannidou, '"Digital Agoraphobia": Exploitative Abuses in Digital Markets' in I Kokkoris and C Lemus (eds), *Research Handbook on the Law and Economics of Competition Enforcement* (Edward Elgar, 2022), 369. Cf German *Facebook* case (n265).

In other situations, consumers may be forced to reveal too much personal information, which may amount to excessive data extraction.[333] Collectively, these two situations amount to a market failure, since digital markets fail to accommodate consumers' privacy preferences.[334] Excessive data accumulation can be potentially evaluated under the test established by the court about excessive pricing,[335] though this has not been judicially tested yet. In *United Brands*, a price was deemed excessive when 'it has no reasonable relation to the economic value of the product supplied'.[336] The court applied a two-step test to determine such excessiveness; first, it determined the profit margin and examined 'whether the difference between the costs actually incurred and the price actually charged is excessive' and then looked at 'whether a price has been imposed [. . .] is either unfair in itself or when compared to competing products'.[337] The *United Brands* excessive pricing test can be translated to 'excessive data extraction' situations, that is when there is no reasonable relation between the collected data and the service provided. There needs to be an 'excessive difference' between the data collected (which is the 'price' charged in this case) and the platform's cost for the provision of their respective service. This is the first step of the amended *United Brands* test. In the second step, we assess whether such data collection is, in itself, unfair or in comparison to data collected by competing providers. Understandably, the application of the test in practice raises multiple concerns. First, it is difficult to ascertain the platforms' cost as well as the price for the data collected.[338] Second, unavoidably, the assessment of the 'unfairness' of such data collection is to some extent arbitrary, the more so in instances where users tend to overestimate the service received and underestimate the value of data collected.[339] Also, with respect to the comparison, we need to assess which are the competing products.

[333] K Bania, 'The Role of Consumer Data in Competition Enforcement' (2018) 14 European Competition Journal 38, 63–70; M Botta and K Wiedemann, 'EU Competition Law Enforcement vis-à-vis Exploitative Conducts in the Data Economy Exploring the Terra Incognita', Max Planck Institute for Innovation and Competition Research Paper No 18-08 (2018), 44–45 <https://papers.ssrn.com/sol3/papers.cfm?abstract_id=3184119> (accessed 7 June 2024).

[334] On such market failure, see Botta and Wiedemann, 'EU Competition Law Enforcement' (n333), 27–28. See also N Economides and I Lianos, 'Restrictions on Privacy and Exploitation in the Digital Economy: A Market Failure Perspective' (2020) <https://papers.ssrn.com/sol3/papers.cfm?abstract_id=3686785> (accessed 7 June 2024).

[335] Bania (n333), 65; Botta and Wiedemann, 'EU Competition Law Enforcement' (n333); Economides and Lianos, 'Restrictions on Privacy and Exploitation in the Digital Economy' (n334); V Robertson, 'Excessive Data Collection: Privacy Considerations and Abuse of Dominance in the Era of Big Data' (2020) 57 Common Market Law Review 161.

[336] Case 27/76 *United Brands Company and United Brands Continentaal BV v Commission of the European Communities* [1978] European Competition Review 207, para 250.

[337] *Ibid*, paras 251–252. See also, more recently, Case C-177/16, *Autortiesību un komunicēšanās konsultāciju aģentūra v Latvijas Autoru apvienība v Konkurences padome*, ECLI:EU:C:2017:689.

[338] On this challenge, see Robertson (n335), 173–174.

[339] N Newman, 'The Costs of Lost Privacy: Consumer Harm and Rising Economic Inequality in the Age of Google' (2014) 40 William Mitchell Law Review 849, 857 et seq. See also D Ariely, *Predictably Irrational: The Hidden Forces That Shape Our Decision* (Harper Collins, 2008), chapter 3.

Apart from the difficulties in assessing the economic value, calculating the hypothetical competitive 'price' is also fraught with difficulties. This is the more so given the concentrated nature of digital markets, where the powerful incumbent may be charging supra-competitive 'prices' already. Such difficulties may be countenanced through the use of comparator-based models. In *AKKA/LAA* (Latvian Collecting Societies), the court stated that apart from the *United Brands* test, 'there are other methods by which it can be determined whether a price may be excessive' and 'according to the case-law of the court, a method based on a comparison of prices applied in the Member State concerned with those applied in other Member States must be considered valid', thereby accepting a comparator-based approach.[340] Thus, we may compare between the data requested by the dominant platform compared to other platforms,[341] or the data requested by the same platform for other services, where the incumbent is not dominant.

Another potentially problematic practice is the offering of personalized prices or different contractual terms in general by dominant platforms to consumers or third parties, as this may amount to consumer exploitation.[342] This has yet to be discussed in the relevant case law.

III.3 Exclusionary Abuses

As the above discussion on current enforcement activity against Big Tech has showcased, the majority of cases concern exclusionary abuses.[343] In this section, we attempt a categorization of the various theories of harm, accepting the caveat that a neat categorization is not possible, since cases may deal with various theories of harm.

The first category concerns *self-preferencing or favouring* practices.[344] It would not be an exaggeration to state that *self-preferencing or favouring* has emerged as the most popular theory of harm in cases against powerful platforms in the digital

[340] *Autortiesību un komunicēšanās konsultāciju aģentūra* (n337), paras 37–38.

[341] Botta and Wiedemann, 'EU Competition Law Enforcement' (n333), 45.

[342] OECD (Organisation for Economic Co-operation and Development', 'Personalised Pricing in the Digital Era', DAF/COMP(2018)13 (20 November 2018); OECD, 'Price Discrimination', DAF/COMP(2016)15 (13 October 2016); See also I Graef, 'Consumer Sovereignty and Competition Law: From Personalization to Diversity' (2021) 58 Common Market Law Review 471, arguing that personalized pricing and behavioural manipulation should be treated as an abuse of dominance.

[343] Akman contends that the majority of all competition decisions from the Commission are based on exclusionary rather than exploitative abuse. See P Akman, 'A Critical Enquiry into "Abuse" in EU Competition Law' (2024) 44 Oxford Journal of Legal Studies 405 <https://papers.ssrn.com/sol3/papers.cfm?abstract_id = 4720991> (accessed 7 June 2024).

[344] Bougette, Gautier ,and Marty argue that self-preferencing is an umbrella term embracing different practices, from leveraging to second-line injury, and therefore, depending on the practice, a different economic analysis is warranted. See P Bougette, A Gautier, and F Marty, 'Business Models and Incentives: For an Effects-Based Approach of Self-Preferencing?' (2022) 13 Journal of Economic Competition Law & Practice 136.

economy. Self-preferencing has also been addressed in various competition policy reports on competition law enforcement in the digital economy. For example, the EU Experts Report states that

> Article 102 TFEU does not impose a general prohibition on self-preferencing by dominant firms. In other words, self-preferencing is not abusive per se, but subject to an effects test. However, we believe that self-preferencing by vertically integrated dominant digital platform can be abusive not only under the preconditions set out by the 'essential facility' doctrine but also wherever it is likely to result in a leveraging of market power and is not justified by a pro-competitive rationale. In a market with particularly high barriers to entry and where the platform serves as an intermediation infrastructure of particular relevance, we propose that, to the extent that the platform performs a regulatory function, it should bear the burden of proving that self-preferencing has no long-run exclusionary effects on product markets. Abusive practices of self-preferencing by digital platforms might pose specific challenges for remedies. Where self-preferencing has significantly benefitted a platform's subsidiary by improving its market position vis-à-vis competitors, remedies might need to include a restorative element.[345]

Powerful platforms are often vertically integrated and have ventured from their core services to adjacent markets, forming whole ecosystems of products and services, thereby emerging as quasi-regulators of their respective ecosystems.[346] The flagship case in EU competition law concerning favouring practices by a dominant platform is *Google Shopping*.[347] The analysis examined, first, the element of favouring the dominant platform's own services through leveraging and the concomitant demotion of competitors. This amounted to an unjustified difference in treatment. Second, the analysis examined the respective effects of such a practice on the basis of the relevant circumstances that ousted such practices outside the scope of competition on the merits. Self-preferencing/favouring was treated as a separate form of leveraging abuse and was distinguished from refusal to deal with cases where the competition authority has to prove that access is indispensable and the refusal of such access eliminates all competition on the downstream market. Concerns were raised with respect to this approach constituting a novel type of abuse, lowering the threshold for competition

[345] European Commission (EU), 'Competition Policy for the Digital Era' (A Report by J Crémer, Y de Montjoye, and H Schweitzer) (EU Experts Report, 2019), 7. See also DN Cicilline, 'Investigation of Competition in Digital Markets—Majority Staff Report and Recommendations—Subcommittee on Antitrust, Commercial, and Administrative Law of the Committee on the Judiciary of the House of Representatives' (US Congress Cicilline Report, 2020) <https://www.govinfo.gov/content/pkg/CPRT-117HPRT47832/pdf/CPRT-117HPRT47832.pdf> (accessed 7 June 2024), 322.

[346] See Chapter 2, section IV.

[347] See text to n22 above.

authorities.[348] Such practices concerning self-preferencing in ranking fall now under the scope of the DMA. Article 6(5) now contains an obligation for gatekeepers not to treat more favourably, in ranking and related indexing and crawling, their own products and services and apply transparent, fair, and non-discriminatory conditions to such ranking.[349]

Cases against Big Tech concerning self-preferencing practices, where dominant platforms were treating their own services or products more favourably include *Google AdTech* (EU),[350] *Google News* (Germany),[351] *Google AdTech* (France),[352] *Google Android Auto* (Italy),[353] *Google AdTech* (United Kingdom),[354] *Google Play* (United Kingdom),[355] *Amazon Marketplace* (EU),[356] *Amazon Marketplace* (United Kingdom),[357] *Facebook Marketplace* (EU),[358] and *Facebook Classified Ads/Online Dating* (United Kingdom).[359]

Other instances where the investigated practices can also be classified under favouring include cases where dominant platforms reserve to themselves and do not share valuable information with third parties. Such is the case, for example, in the Google AdTech cases in the EU and United Kingdom.[360] As with other types of self-preferencing practices involving preferential ranking, the DMA also caters, to some extent, for this type of practice by requiring gatekeepers to provide certain information to publishers and advertisers (Articles 5(9) and 5(10)) as well as to provide them with access to gatekeepers' performance-measuring tools and the necessary data to undertake their own independent verification of the advertisements inventory (Article 6(8)).

The second broad category of abusive exclusionary practices concerns data-related abuses. Here, we can first enlist practices involving preferential collection and processing of users' data, allegedly due to privacy concerns. Cases here include *Google Data Processing* (Germany),[361] *Google Privacy Sandbox* (United Kingdom),[362]

[348] On the *Google Search (Shopping)* discussion, see text to n28 above. For a succinct note on whether self-preferencing can be assessed as a refusal to deal, margin squeeze, or tying abuse see OECD, 'Abuse of Dominance in Digital Markets' (2020) <https://webarchive.oecd.org/20211031/566602abuseofdominanceindigitalmarkets2020.pdf> (accessed 7 June 2024), 29 *et seq*. According to the OECD, self-preferencing is a novel type of abuse: OECD, 'Abuse of Dominance in Digital Markets', 36, 54.

[349] For a detailed discussion, see T Hoeppner, *Self-Preferencing in Online Search under Article 6(5) DMA* (Nomos, 2024). See also German Competition Act, section 19(a)(2).

[350] See text to n159 above.

[351] See text to n184 above.

[352] See text to n193 above.

[353] See text to n200 above.

[354] See text to n216 above.

[355] See text to n221 above.

[356] See text to n228 above.

[357] See text to n255 above.

[358] See text to n260 above.

[359] See text to n279 above.

[360] On these cases, see text to n159 and text to n216 above.

[361] See text to n177 above.

[362] See text to n209 above.

Facebook Marketplace (EU),[363] *Facebook Classified Ads/Online Dating* (United Kingdom),[364] and *Apple ATT*.[365] The DMA has now imposed additional regulatory obligations on gatekeepers, preventing them from processing, combining, and cross-using users' personal data without users' consent (Article 5 (2) DMA). Second, another category of exclusionary data-related abuse concerns the preferential use of business users' data. *Facebook Marketplace* in the EU and United Kingdom are examples of cases where this was the investigated theory of harm.[366] Such practices are also covered in the DMA, which restricts gatekeepers' ability to use non-public business users' data in competition with them (Article 6(2)).[367]

The third category concerns more 'traditional' theories of harm, such as tying practices or exclusive dealing, which were examined in the following cases: *Google Android* (EU),[368] *Google AdTech* (United Kingdom),[369] *Google AdSense* (EU),[370] *Facebook Marketplace* (EU),[371] and *Facebook VR Market* (Germany).[372] Such practices often concern the terms under which powerful platforms grant access to their respective products and services, with such terms possibly giving default position to the platform's offerings. The DMA has now complemented competition law enforcement with additional regulatory obligations for gatekeepers to enable end users to easily uninstall any software applications and change default settings on a gatekeeper's OS, virtual assistant, and web browser (Articles 6(3) and 6(4)).

A fourth category concerns cases that deal with restrictions on interoperability as an exclusionary abuse of dominance. Here, we can enlist *Google Maps* (Germany),[373] *Google AdTech* (France),[374] *Google Android Auto* (Italy),[375] *Google AdTech* (United Kingdom),[376] and *Apple Pay* (EU).[377] In the DMA, we now find positive obligations on gatekeepers to ensure interoperability for service and hardware providers and business users (Article 6(7)).

The final category concerns anti-steering practices that were discussed in *Apple App Store* in the EU and United Kingdom.[378] The DMA has introduced tailored obligations for gatekeepers that address such practices (Articles 5(4), 5(5), and 6 (4)).

Tables 5.2–5.5 succinctly summarize the above discussion.

[363] See text to n261 above.
[364] See text to n298 above.
[365] See text to n293 above.
[366] On these cases, see text to nn259 and 279 above.
[367] See also the UK Digital Markets, Competition and Consumer Bill, section 20(3)(b).
[368] See text to n68 above.
[369] See text to n216 above.
[370] See text to n130 above.
[371] See text to n261 above.
[372] See text to n264 above.
[373] See text to n186 above.
[374] See text to n193 above.
[375] See text to n200 above.
[376] See text to n216 above.
[377] See text to n287 above.
[378] On these cases, see text to nn286 and 308 above.

Theories of harm and regulatory obligations: Google

Theories of harm	Antitrust cases	DMA provisions
Favouring/self-preferencing	*Shopping* (EU) *AdTech* (EU) *News* (Germany) *AdTech* (France) *Android Auto* (Italy) *AdTech* (United Kingdom) *Google Play* (United Kingdom)	
Favouring/self-preferencing in ranking	*Shopping* (EU)	6(5) Obligation to not treat more favourably, in ranking and related indexing and crawling, its own products and services and shall apply transparent, fair and non-discriminatory conditions to such ranking
Favouring/opacity of information	*AdTech* (EU) *AdTech* (United Kingdom)	5(9)–(10) Obligation to provide information to publishers and advertisers 6(8) Obligation to provide advertisers and publishers with access to gatekeeper's performance measuring tools and necessary data to undertake their own independent verification of the advertisements inventory
Tying	*Android* (EU) *AdTech* (United Kingdom)	6(3) Obligation to allow end users to easily uninstall any software applications on the gatekeeper's OS, unless they are essential for the functioning of the OS or the device and cannot be technically offered on a standalone basis by third parties 6(4) Obligation to allow end users to easily change default settings on gatekeeper's OS, virtual assistant, and web browser
Exclusivity	*AdSense* (EU)	
Terms and conditions (opaque, unfair, discriminatory, unreasonable)	*News* (Germany) *AdWords* (France) *News* (France)	
Preferential use of data/privacy/data processing	*Data Processing* (Germany) *Privacy Sandbox* (United Kingdom)	5(2) Combining personal data from the relevant CPS with personal data from any other CPS or any other gatekeeper's services or with personal data from third-party services
Restrictions of interoperability	*Maps* (Germany) *AdTech* (France) *Android Auto* (Italy) *AdTech* (United Kingdom)	6(7) Obligation to ensure interoperability for service and hardware providers and business users

Source: Authors.

Table 5.3 Theories of harm and regulatory obligations: Amazon

Theories of harm	Antitrust cases	DMA
Preferential use of data	*Marketplace* (EU) *Marketplace* (United Kingdom)	6(2) Prohibition on using, in competition with business users, non-public generated or provided by business users when using the relevant CPS
Preferential treatment of own services	*Marketplace* (EU) *Marketplace* (United Kingdom)	6(5) Obligation not treat more favourably, in ranking and related indexing and crawling, its own products and services and shall apply transparent, fair and non-discriminatory conditions to such ranking
Preferential/discriminatory treatment of third parties on the platform	*Marketplace* (EU) *Marketplace* (Italy) *Marketplace* (United Kingdom)	
Terms and conditions (opaque, unfair, discriminatory, unreasonable)	*Marketplace* (Germany)	5(6) Prohibition on preventing or restricting users from raising any issue of gatekeeper's non-compliance with competent authorities and courts

Source: Authors.

Table 5.4 Theories of harm and regulatory obligations: Meta

Theories of harm	Antitrust cases	DMA
Preferential use of data	*Marketplace* (EU) *Classified Ads/Online Dating* (United Kingdom)	5(2) processing end users' personal data that use third parties' services (who use gatekeepers' CPS), for providing online advertising services, subject to consent
Preferential treatment of own services	*Marketplace* (EU) *Classified Ads/Online Dating* (United Kingdom)	6(5) Obligation not treat more favourably, in ranking and related indexing and crawling, its own products and services and shall apply transparent, fair and non-discriminatory conditions to such ranking
Tying	*Marketplace* (EU) *VR Market* (Germany)	
Terms and conditions (opaque, unfair, discriminatory, unreasonable)—privacy interplay	*Social Network* (Germany)	5(2) prohibition on combining personal data from the relevant CPS with personal data from any other CPS or any other gatekeeper's services or with personal data from third-party services, subject to users' consent
Terms and conditions (opaque, unfair, discriminatory, unreasonable)	*Online Advertising Services* (France) *Online Ad Verification* (France)	

Source: Authors.

Table 5.5 Theories of harm and regulatory obligations: Apple

Theories of harm	Antitrust cases	DMA
Anti-steering/unfair trading conditions	*App Store* (EU) *App Store* (United Kingdom)	5(4) Obligation to allow business users, free of charge, to communicate and promote offers, to end users acquired via its core platform service or through other channels, and to conclude contracts with those end users, regardless of whether, for that purpose, they use the core platform services of the gatekeeper
		5(5) Obligation to allow end users to access and use, through its core platform services, content, subscriptions, features or other items, by using the software application of a business user
		6(4) Obligation to allow the installation and effective use of third-party software applications or software application stores on its OS and allow these to be accessed by means other than the relevant gatekeeper's core platform services
Restricting interoperability/ favouring	*Apple Pay* (EU)	6(7) Obligation to ensure interoperability for service and hardware providers and business users
Use of data/favouring	*ATT* (Germany)	
Unfair terms	*Online Dating Apps* (Netherlands)	
Unfair terms/IAP	*App Store* (United Kingdom)	5(7) Prohibition on requiring users to use, offer, or interoperate with a gatekeeper's identification service, web browser or payment service (e.g. payment systems for in-app purchases) in the context of services provided by the business users when using core platform services provided by the gatekeeper

Source: Authors.

IV. Conclusion

Chapter 5 has discussed the rich case law on abuse of dominance against Big Tech companies in the digital economy. After presenting the relevant cases at EU, Member State, and UK level, it attempted a categorization of the investigated practices. Such an exercise served to highlight the rather expansive approach to the application of Article 102 TFEU, which appears, though, to have reached its limits in preserving competition in digital markets. Thus, it has been complemented with targeted regulatory rules, which present, to a certain extent, an overlap with the investigated practices under Article 102 TFEU.

6
Mergers and Acquisitions

I. Introduction

The exponential growth of Google, Apple, Facebook, Amazon, and Microsoft (GAFAM) and cultivation of their respective ecosystems did not attract timely competition and regulatory scrutiny, allowing Big Tech to grow their market power. Regulators have noted that

> Many of us are now familiar with the statistic that—between 2008 and 2018 of the 400 acquisitions made globally by the 5 largest digital firms—none has been blocked by competition authorities. But it remains a powerful one. It is very hard to look at those numbers, to look at the state of the relevant markets today, and conclude with hindsight that the balance has been struck correctly.[1]

It appears that lately the tide has turned.[2] Yet, at the core of Big Tech's power and exponential growth is the strategic acquisition of competitors and start-up companies that arguably did not attract the requisite scrutiny. Such serial acquisitions may have also impacted the behaviour of start-ups, with many of them aiming for a potential lucrative acquisition rather than at scaling up as a potential competitive force.[3]

Indeed, over the years, Big Tech companies have completed a large number of acquisitions, with only a few of them having been scrutinized by competition authorities. Even in the low number of instances where competition authorities have reviewed such transactions, the outcome has resulted in a clearance decision. Such a lack of control can be attributed both to procedural as well as substantive factors, which will be later discussed in this chapter with respect to specific transactions. Procedural factors refer to the fact that some merger control systems, including European merger control, rely on a turnover threshold for the notification and subsequent review of transactions.[4] Given that, in Big Tech acquisitions, the target

[1] A Coscelli, 'Ahead of the Curve' (Bannerman Competition lecture, 9 February 2021) <https://www.gov.uk/government/speeches/andrea-coscelli-ahead-of-the-curve-bannerman-competition-lecture> (accessed 28 February 2023).

[2] See Chapter 3, section V.2 for regulatory initiatives and Chapter 5 for a detailed discussion of completed and ongoing competition law cases.

[3] J Laitenberger, 'EU Competition Law in Innovation and Digital Markets: Fairness and the Consumer Welfare Perspective" (Speech, 10 October 2017) <https://ec.europa.eu/competition/speeches/text/sp2017_15_en.pdf> (accessed 17 February 2023).

[4] Council Regulation (EC) 139/2004 of 20 January 2004 on the control of concentrations between undertakings, [2004] OJ L 24/1 (European Union Merger Regulation [EUMR]), Article 1(2). This is the

Competition Law and Policy in Digital Markets. Maria Ioannidou and Bingwan Xiong, Oxford University Press.
 DOI: 10.1093/9780191925955.003.0006

is often a nascent competitor or a start-up company with no significant revenue, it may be the case that such transactions slip through the net.

With respect to substantive factors, as the subsequent discussion will show, it may be the case that competition authorities need to be more cautious when constructing relevant competition theories of harm. Yet, one has to admit that predicting outcomes constitutes an inherent difficulty in merger control, and even more so in fast-moving, dynamic markets. For example, when Google acquired Android back in 2006 for what appears today as a low sum, it was not possible to predict the exponential growth of mobile ecosystems. The world was a very different place. Interesting anecdotes from GAFAM's early years suggest that, at their inception, they too were candidates for potential acquisition by bigger rivals. In Google's early years, Microsoft was perceived as a competitive threat, given the fear that it could build a search function in its next operating system (OS).[5] Facebook has also turned down offers for potential acquisition. It has been rumoured that Viacom offered $750 million for Facebook in January 2006, with Zuckerberg asking for $2 billion, and later that year, Yahoo offered $1 billion for it.[6] We can only imagine how the world would have developed if Google and Facebook had been acquired in their early years.

Chapter 6 first briefly describes the business moves of Big Tech and the acquisition of start-ups over the years (section II). Section III covers the cases of digital mergers reviewed by the EU Commission and selected digital mergers reviewed by the UK competition authorities. Section IV then succinctly discusses the characteristics of digital mergers and related theories of harm. Finally, section V discusses the need to amend the regulatory framework.

II. GAFAM's Acquisitions: A Historical Account

According to a study on the period between 2008 and 2018, Google acquired 168 companies, Facebook 71 companies, and Amazon 60 companies, with the

primary notification threshold. Article 1(3) EUMR provides for a secondary notification threshold. For a discussion of the European Union (EU) system see section III.1 below.

[5] A Fisher, *Valley of Genius: The Uncensored History of Silicon Valley (as Told by the Hackers, Founders, and Freaks Who Made it Boom* (Twelve, 2018).

[6] S Hansell, 'Yahoo Woos a Social Networking Site' (*New York Times*, 22 September 2006) <https://www.nytimes.com/2006/09/22/technology/22facebook.html> (accessed 15 February 2023). Between 2004 and 2007, there were rumours that the following companies had made acquisition offers: Friendster, Google, *The Washington Post*, Viacom, MySpace, News Corp, Viacom, NBC, Viacom Three, Yahoo, AOL, Yahoo Again, Google Again, and Microsoft. See M Hoefflinger, *Becoming Facebook: The 10 Challenges That Defined the Company That Is Disrupting the World* (AMACOM, 2017), chapter 3.

targets being newly found companies of less than 4 years old in the majority of cases.[7] Other studies showcase slightly different numbers,[8] yet what they all have in common is an indication of a very large number of acquisitions by Big Tech companies over the years, fleshing out that Big Tech companies are 'the products of hundreds of mergers'.[9] Big Tech acquisitions, despite signs and calls for stricter scrutiny of the respective deals, show no signs of abating.[10] Empirical literature studying the effects of digital mergers has begun to emerge. For example, Gautier and Lamesch examined GAFAM's acquisitions for the period 2015–2017 and concluded that these acquisitions occurred in their core segments and were followed by product shutdowns in order to integrate the target's assets into their own ecosystem.[11] Koski, Kässi, and Braesemann, by studying Big Tech acquisitions between 2002 and 2018, empirically supported the proposition that such acquisitions create a 'kill zone effect', which decreases entry as well venture capital funding. On the contrary, Ivaldi, Petit, and Ünekbaş focused on transactions reviewed by the Commission in information and communication technology (ICT) industries and showed that no transaction led to the discontinuation of the target's products or reduced competition, thus instructing a more cautious approach to the killer acquisitions theory.[12] Affeld and Kessler have empirically examined acquisitions in the mobile applications market and concluded that half of these apps have been discontinued. The apps that have not been discontinued have become free of monetary charge, while their privacy settings have requested more sensitive permissions since the acquisition.[13]

Below, we present an empirical account of Big Tech's main acquisitions.

[7] E Argentesi et al, 'Merger Policy in Digital Markets: An Ex Post Assessment' (2020) 17 Journal of Competition Law and Economics 95.

[8] M Glick and C Ruetschlin, 'Big Tech Acquisitions and the Potential Competition Doctrine: The Case of Facebook', Institute of New Economic Thinking Working Paper 104s (2019).

[9] T Wu and S Thompson, 'The Roots of Big Tech Run Disturbingly Deep' (New York Times, 7 June 2019).

[10] A Sherman and L Feiner, 'Amazon, Microsoft and Alphabet Went on a Buying Spree in 2021 Despite D.C.'s Vow to Take on Big Tech' (CNBC, 22 January 2022) <https://www.cnbc.com/2022/01/22/amazon-microsoft-alphabet-set-more-deals-in-2021-than-last-10-years.html> (accessed 14 June 2024). According to Dealogic, Alphabet concluded twenty-two deals, Microsoft fifty-six deals, and Amazon twenty-nine deals in 2021.

[11] A Gautier and J Lamesch, 'Mergers in the Digital Economy', Centre for Economic Studies—Institute for Economic Research (CESifo) Working Paper No 8056 (2020).

[12] H Koski, O Kassi, and F Braesemann, 'Killers on the Road of Emerging Start-Ups—Implications for Market Entry and Venture Capital Financing', Research Institute of the Finnish Economy (ETLA) Working Paper 81 (2020). Contra, see M Ivaldi, N Petit, and S Ünekbaş, 'Killer Acquisitions: Evidence from European Merger Cases' (2024) Antitrust Law Journal TSE Working Paper No 13-1420 <https://papers.ssrn.com/sol3/papers.cfm?abstract_id=4407333> (accessed 27 September 2024).

[13] P Affeldt and R Kesler, 'Big Tech Acquisitions—Towards Empirical Evidence' (2021) 12 Journal of European Competition Law & Practice 471.

II.1 Google

Research suggests that Google has been the most active of the GAFAM in terms of merger and acquisition (M&A) activity. Google has acquired a number of companies over the years to boost its mobile ecosystem as well as its machine learning and data science activities, with Deep Mind in 2014 being the most notable acquisition in this field.[14]

Between 2004 and 2014, Google acquired 145 companies, spending more than USD 23 billion.[15] By 2022, this number had risen to 240 acquisitions.[16] Some of the most important transactions, both in terms of value and significance for the development of Google's ecosystem include the acquisition of

- Android Inc—USD 50 million (2006)[17]
- YouTube—USD 1.19 billion (2006)
- DoubleClick—USD 3.2 billion (2008)
- AdMob—USD 681 million (2009)
- Admeld—USD 400 million (2011)
- ITA Software—USD 676 million (2011)
- Motorola—USD 12.4 billion (2011) (sold to Lenovo three years later for USD 2.9 billion)[18]
- Waze—USD 969 million (2013)
- Nest Labs—USD 2.6 billion (2014)[19]
- Fitbit—USD 2.1 billion (2019)
- Looker—USD 2.6 billion (2019)[20]
- Mandiant—USD 5.4 (2022) billion.[21]

Ever since the 2008 acquisition of DoubleClick, Google has, through a series of subsequent acquisitions, emerged as the main player in the AdTech value chain. In 2010, Google acquired AdMob, the leading mobile ad network, and Invite, the

[14] Argentesi et al (n7).

[15] ACCC (Australian Competition and Consumer Commission), 'Digital Platforms Inquiry—Final Report' (June 2019) >, 72–73 <https://www.accc.gov.au/system/files/Digital%20platforms%20inquiry%20-%20final%20report.pdf(accessed 7 June 2024), with further references to J Lipton, 'Google's Best and Worst Acquisitions' (CNBC, 19 August 2014) <https://www.cnbc.com/2014/08/19/googles-best-and-worst-acquisitions.html> (accessed 14 February 2023).

[16] Tracxn, 'Acquisitions by Google' (25 July 2022) <https://tracxn.com/d/acquisitions/acquisitionsbyGoogle> (accessed 7 September 2023).

[17] J Callaham, 'Google Made Its Best Acquisition Nearly 17 Years Ago: Can You Guess What It Was?' (13 May 2022) <https://www.androidauthority.com/google-android-acquisition-884194> (accessed 14 February 2023).

[18] *Ibid.*

[19] ACCC, 'Digital Platforms Inquiry—Final Report' (n15), 73.

[20] G Cuofano, 'Google Acquisitions' (11 February 2023) <https://fourweekmba.com/google-acquisitions> (accessed 7 September 2023).

[21] *Ibid.*

leading demand-side platform (DSP). In 2011, it acquired, AdMeld—the leading supply-side platform (SSP)—which then integrated to AdX.[22] Of the above transactions, only *Google/DoubleClick*, *Google/Motorola Mobility*, and *Google/Fitbit* were reviewed by the Commission. The first two were cleared unconditionally, with the latter being approved subject to remedies.

II.2 Amazon

Amazon has acquired a number of retail operators such as Buy VIP in 2010 and LoveFilm and the Book Depository in 2011. Since 2015, Amazon has acquired a number of companies that are active in the remote storage and file transfer cluster, arguably in a bid to strengthen and expand its own Amazon Web Services.[23] Other acquisitions include Whole Foods Market, a supermarket chain, acquired in 2017 for USD 13.7 billion, and Zappos, an online shoe retailer, acquired in 2009 for USD 1.2 billion.[24] In 2022, Amazon acquired MGM Studios for USD 8.5 billion.[25] As of July 2023, Amazon had acquired ninety-seven companies, having spent USD 44.5 billion.[26]

II.3 Facebook

Facebook was particularly active in the acquisition of companies active in setting up communication apps/tools, with acquisitions including the messaging app Beluga (2011), and later Facebook Messenger, Instagram (2012), and WhatsApp (2014).[27] Facebook has also acquired virtual-reality (VR) companies such as Oculus (2014), Surreal Vision (2015), and Two Big Ears.[28]

[22] D Geradin and D Katsifis, 'An EU Competition Law Analysis of Online Display Advertising in the Programmatic Age' (2019) 15 European Competition Journal 55, 70; See also Autorité de la Concurrence (AdC), Opinion No 18-A-03 (6 March 2018) on data processing in the online advertising sector, para 105.

[23] Argentesi et al (n7).

[24] *Ibid.*

[25] A Malik, 'Amazon Completes $8.5 Billion Acquisition of MGM' (17 March 2022) <https://techcrunch.com/2022/03/17/amazon-completes-its-8-5-billion-acquisition-of-mgm> (accessed 9 June 2024).

[26] Tracxn, 'Acquisitions by Amazon' (20 July 2023) <https://tracxn.com/d/acquisitions/acquisitionsbyAmazon> (accessed 7 September 2023).

[27] The US Federal Trade Commission (FTC) has brought an action against Facebook alleging that Facebook engaged in a systematic anticompetitive strategy to maintain its monopoly in social networks, including through the acquisition of Instagram and WhatsApp. FTC's action seeks (amongst other things) the divestiture of Instagram and WhatsApp. See *FTC v Facebook* (File No 191 0134) (9 December 2020) <https://www.ftc.gov/legal-library/browse/cases-proceedings/191-0134-facebook-inc-ftc-v> (accessed 9 June 2024).

[28] Argentesi et al (n7). For an account of Facebook's acquisitions, see Glick and Ruetschlin (n8), Appendix.

Between 2006 and 2018, Facebook spent more than USD 23 billion acquiring sixty-six companies. This number had risen to ninety-four companies as of 2022,[29] and ninety-six by July 2023.[30] The most important transactions include

- Instagram—USD 715 million (2012)
- Occulus - USD 19 billion (2014)
- WhatsApp—USD 19 billion (2014).

The concept of killer acquisitions, whereby the aim is to 'kill' the target and benefit from its technological innovation, increased in prominence after Facebook's acquisition of WhatsApp and Instagram. Chairman of the US FTC Lina Khan noted that Facebook's illegal conduct through such purchases took place at a key moment of technological transformation, namely the transition from desktop to mobile Internet.[31]

II.4 Apple

Apple has made 107 acquisitions, spending over USD 28.51 billion.[32] Notable transactions include the acquisition of *Beats* for USD 3 billion (2014) and *Shazam* for USD 400 million (2017).

II.5 Microsoft

Microsoft has acquired 202 companies, spending over USD 180.63 billion.[33] Amongst the most important transactions are the acquisition of

- Skype—USD 8.5 billion (2011)
- Nokia—USD 7.2 billion (2014)
- LinkedIn—USD 26.2 billion (2016)
- Github—USD 7.5 billion (2018)
- Nuance Communications—USD 19.7 billion (2021)
- Activision Blizzard—USD 69 billion (2022).

[29] ACCC, 'Digital Platforms Inquiry—Final Report' (n15), 80. See also S Bose, 'Facebook Acquisitions—The Complete List (2022)!' (TechWyse Blog, 17 February 2022) <https://www.techwyse.com/blog/general-category/facebook-acquisitions-infographic> (accessed 9 June 2024).

[30] Tracxn, 'Acquisitions by Facebook' (20 July 2023) <https://tracxn.com/d/acquisitions/acquisitionsbyFacebook> (accessed 7 September 2023).

[31] M Swift, 'Khan Not Ready to Ease Off Throttle at US FTC as She Marks First Year at Helm' (MLex comment, 9 June 2022).

[32] Tracxn, 'Acquisitions by Apple' (20 July 2022) <https://tracxn.com/d/acquisitions/acquisitionsbyApple> (accessed 7 September 2023).

[33] Tracxn, 'Acquisitions by Microsoft' (25 July 2022) <https://tracxn.com/d/acquisitions/acquisitionsbyMicrosoft> (accessed 7 September 2023).

III. Killer Acquisitions: Case Law

III.1 Introduction: The European Union Merger Regulation and Case Allocation

The European Union Merger Regulation (EUMR) is a 'one-stop-shop' mandatory notification system, with mergers meeting certain turnover thresholds having to be notified to the European Commission.[34] The primary thresholds under Article 1(2) EUMR capture transactions where the aggregate worldwide turnover of the merging parties is more than €5 billion combined and the European Union-wide turnover of at least two parties in the transaction is for each €250 million in the European Union (EU). The secondary threshold under Article 1(3) EUMR, which may apply if the transaction does not meet the primary threshold, applies to transactions where the combined worldwide turnover of the parties is €2.5 billion; the EU-wide turnover of at least two of the parties is, for each, more than €100 million in the EU; in each of at least three Member States, the combined aggregate turnover of all the parties is more than €100 million; and in the same three Member States, at least two of the parties to the transaction each achieve €25 million. If these thresholds are met, the transaction needs to be notified to the Commission, unless each of the parties achieves two-thirds of its revenue in one and the same Member State.

Concentrations that do not meet the above thresholds can still be reviewed by the Commission under the EUMR referral mechanisms.[35] According to Article 4(5) EUMR, when a transaction needs to be filed in more than three Member States, the merging parties can file a reasoned submission to the Commission and request that the Commission reviews this transaction. If no Member State that has jurisdiction to review this transaction objects to the Commission asserting jurisdiction, then the transaction is deemed to have an EU dimension.

Apart from the merging parties, Member States can also request that the Commission reviews a transaction. According to Article 22, one or more Member States may request that the Commission examines a transaction that does not have a Union dimension if it affects trade between Member States and threatens to significantly affect competition in the territory of the requesting State. The Commission may also invite Member States to make such a request.[36] Contrary to Article 4(5), where the referral takes place on the request of the merging parties, the Commission may accept the request, even if there is a partial referral by

[34] Articles 4(1), 21(1), and 21(2) EUMR (n4).
[35] European Commission (EU), 'Commission Notice on Case Referral in Respect of Concentrations', [2005] OJ C 56/2.
[36] Article 22(5) EUMR (n4).

some Member States, whereas others choose to apply their own rules on merger control. Such a double application of merger control rules constitutes an exception to the principle of 'one-stop-shop' merger control.[37] Furthermore, the wording of Article 22 does not provide that the referred transaction needs to meet national merger control rules. However, the Commission has, in the past, discouraged national authorities from referring deals that did not fall under their nation merger control rules.[38] The Commission attempted to revise this approach claiming that in light of the particular characteristics of mergers in the digital and pharma sectors, where the target has the potential to develop into an important competitive force in the future (e.g. due to data advantages, innovative products, or intellectual property rights) without at present generating significant turnover, it will accept referrals from Member States even in instances where the national merger control thresholds are not met.[39] In light of such a 'reconceptualization' of the Article 22 referral mechanism, the Commission did not consider it necessary to change the EU merger control notification thresholds from a turnover to a value of the transaction basis.[40] On the contrary, Austria and Germany have changed their respective merger controls to introduce a transaction value-based threshold.[41] *Illumina/Grail* was the first case where the Commission applied this new approach to Article 22 referrals, following a referral request from France, which was joined by Belgium, Greece, Iceland, the Netherlands, and Norway and ultimately prohibited the transaction.[42] However, the CJEU has now authoritatively ruled that such expansive interpretation of Article 22 EURM to capture transactions that are not caught by

[37] See, e.g. *Procter & Gamble/Sara Lee Air Care* (Case M.5828) Commission Decision,(C(2010) 2243. See also *Meta (Formerly Facebook)/Kustomer* (Case M.10262) Commission Decision, C(2022) 409. See R Whish and D Bailey, *EU Competition Law* (OUP, 2021), 895. See also European Commission (EU), European Competition Authorities, 'Principles on the Application, by National Competition Authorities within the ECA, of Articles 4(5) and 22 of the EC Merger Regulation' (2005) <https://ec.europa.eu/competition/ecn/eca_referral_principles_en.pdf> (accessed 23 February 2023), para 18.

[38] M Vestager, 'The Future of EU Merger Control' (Speech, International Bar Association 24th Annual Competition Conference, 11 September 2020); European Commission (EU), 'Guidance on the Application of the Referral Mechanism Set Out in Article 22 of the Merger Regulation to Certain Categories of Cases', C(2021) 1959 final) (26 March 2021) (Article 22 Guidance), para 8.

[39] Article 22 Guidance (n38), paras 9, 11. For a discussion on the 'repurposing' of Article 22 EUMR (n4), see A Tzanaki, 'Dynamism and Politics in EU Merger Control: Appreciating the Gain and the Gap' (2023) <https://papers.ssrn.com/sol3/papers.cfm_abstract_id=4574948> (accessed 6 July 2024).

[40] European Commission (EU), 'Evaluation of Procedural and Jurisdictional Aspect of EU Merger Control', SWD(2021) 66 final (26 March 2021), paras 266–270. Article 22 Guidance (n38), para 10.

[41] Bundeskartellamt, 'Merger Control' <https://www.bundeskartellamt.de/EN/Mergercontrol/mergercontrol_node.html> (accessed 24 February 2023); BWB (Bundeswettbewerbsbehörde), Austrian Federal Competition Authority, 'Merger Control' <https://www.bwb.gv.at/en/merger_control> (accessed 9 June 2024); See joined Guidance issued by the German and Austrian NCAs (National Competition Authorities), 'Guidance on Transaction Value Thresholds for Mandatory Pre-Merger Notification (Section 35(1a) GWB and Section 9(4) KartG)' (January 2022).

[42] *Illumina-Grail* (Case M.10188). See European Commission (EU), 'Commission Prohibits Acquisition of GRAIL by Illumina' (Press release, 6 September 2022). The Commission's approach to the Article 22 EUMR (n4) referral mechanism was upheld by the General Court. See Case T-227/21, *Illumina Grail v Commission*, ECLI:EU:T:2022:447.

other EU or national merger control rules is not allowed.[43] The Commission has also accepted two more referral requests of this kind, in *Qualcomm/Autotalks*[44] and *EEX/Nasdaq Power*,[45] yet both transactions have subsequently been abandoned. Finally, following *Towercast*, transactions below the EU and national merger control thresholds may be reviewed by NCAs under Article 102 of the Treaty on the Functioning of the European Union (TFEU) on abuse of dominance. NCAs have to establish that the acquirer is dominant in the relevant market and that the acquisition will result in a substantial impediment to effective competition.[46]

As succinctly shown in section II above, Big Tech has been very active in acquiring a number of nascent companies. Interestingly, very few of those cases were reviewed by the Commission; and even in those cases that were reviewed, most of them did not have an EU dimension under Article 1 EUMR. For example, in *Google/DoubleClick*, the transaction was reviewed by the Commission at the request of the notifying party under Article 4(5) EUMR, since the transaction was capable of being reviewed under the national competition laws of at least three Member States (Germany, Greece, Portugal, Spain, and the United Kingdom).[47] This was also the case in *Facebook/WhatsApp*, where the Commission reviewed the transaction at the request of the merging parties under Article 4(5) EUMR.[48] In *Apple/Shazam*, the Commission ascertained jurisdiction following a referral request pursuant to Article 22(1) by the Austrian NCA, which had jurisdiction to review the deal under its national merger control. The Austrian NCA was joined by France, Iceland, Italy, Norway, Spain, and Sweden.[49] Similarly, in *Facebook/Kustomer*, the Commission ascertained jurisdiction following an Article 22 EUMR request by Austria, where the deal had to be notified. Austria was joined by Belgium, Bulgaria, France, Iceland, Ireland, Italy, the Netherlands, Portugal, and

[43] Advocate General (AG) Emiliou Opinion concluded that the General Court judgment should be set aside. See Opinion of AG Emiliou in Joined Cases C-611/22 P and C-625/22 P, ECLI:EU:C:2024:264. The CJEU sited with the AG Opinion. See Joined Cases C-611/22 P and C-625/22 P, ECLI:EU:C:2024:677.

[44] European Commission (EU), 'Mergers: Commission to Assess the Proposed Acquisition of Autotalks by Qualcomm' (Daily News, 18 August 2023) <https://ec.europa.eu/commission/presscorner/detail/en/mex_23_4201> (accessed 9 June 2024). His deal has been abandoned. See, for example, Autotalks, 'Qualcomm ends bid to buy Israel's Autotalks after antitrust probe' (22 March 2024) <https://auto-talks.com/qualcomm-ends-bid-to-buy-israels-autotalks-after-antitrust-probe/>.

[45] European Commission (EU), 'Mergers: Commission to Assess the Proposed Acquisition of Nasdaq Power by EEX' (Daily News, 21 August 2023) <https://ec.europa.eu/commission/presscorner/detail/en/mex_23_4221> (accessed 9 June 2024). This deal has also been abandoned. See, for example, 'Nasdaq announces termination of previously announced agreement with EEX' (26 June 2024) <nasdaq-announces-termination-previously-announced-agreement-eex>

[46] Case C-449/21 *Towercast*, Judgment of 16 March 2023, ECLI:EU:C:2023:207. The Belgian NCA has already applied *Towercast*, in *Proximus/EDPnet*. See Decision No ABC-2023-RPR-17 (21 June 2023) (in French) <https://www.belgiancompetition.be/sites/default/files/content/download/files/ABC-2023-RPR-17%20PUB.pdf> (accessed 9 June 2024).

[47] *Google/DoubleClick* (Case M.4731) Commission Decision, C(2008) 927, para 7.

[48] *Facebook/WhatsApp* (Case M.7217) Commission Decision, C(2014) 7239, paras 9–12.

[49] *Apple/Shazam* (Case M.8788) Commission Decision, C(2018) 5748 (6 September 2018), para 8.

Romania.[50] *Facebook/Kustomer* tested the 'one-stop-shop' principle upon which the EUMR is premised, since Germany also reviewed the deal, ultimately reaching a clearance decision.[51]

All of the Big Tech acquisitions reviewed by the Commission were cleared, with only *Microsoft/LinkedIn*, *Google/Fitbit*, and *Meta/Kustomer* being cleared with commitments. This section discusses the GAFAM acquisitions reviewed by the Commission, while acknowledging that there is also a growing review of digital mergers by NCAs.[52] With respect to national merger control, this chapter discusses certain digital mergers reviewed by the Competition and Markets Authority (CMA). The United Kingdom has been chosen amongst other EU jurisdictions for three reasons. First, because of its share-of-supply test as a jurisdictional threshold in UK merger control,[53] it was able to review transactions that slipped through the EUMR net when the United Kingdom was part of the Union. Second, the CMA has risen as one of the most influential authorities in merger control globally. Third, it will be interesting to see whether the United Kingdom adopts a divergent merger control approach post-Brexit.

III.2 Google's Acquisitions

The Commission has reviewed and cleared four acquisitions by Google, three of them unconditionally. *Google/Fitbit* was cleared with commitments. Below, a brief account of these transactions is provided, whereas *Google/DoubleClick* and *Google/Fitbit* are discussed in more detail; the former given its importance for Google, which has emerged as the most powerful player in the AdTech value chain, and the latter because of the complex issues it raises with respect to data accumulation and the development of Google's ecosystem.

III.2.1 *Google/DoubleClick*

Google notified its proposed acquisition of DoubleClick in 2007. DoubleClick's activity focused mainly on ad-serving technology for website publishers, advertisers, and advertising agencies. At the time, it was also launching an intermediation

[50] *Meta (Formerly Facebook)/Kustomer*—Commission Decision (CD) (n37), para 6.

[51] Bundeskartellamt, 'Bundeskartellamt Clears Acquisition of Kustomer by Meta (Formerly Facebook) (B6-21/22)' (28 June 2022) <https://www.bundeskartellamt.de/SharedDocs/Entscheidung/EN/Fallberichte/Fusionskontrolle/2022/B6-21-22.pdf?__blob = publicationFile&v = 3> (accessed 24 February 2023). The Higher Regional Court of Düsseldorf concluded that the Bundeskartellamt had wrongly asked Meta to notify the deal under the transaction value notification threshold, since Kustomer did not have a substantial operation in Germany. See judgment of 23 November 2022—Kart 11/21 (V).

[52] Discussing selected national merger cases in digital markets, see European Commission (EU), 'Merger Review in Digital and Technology Markets: Insights from National Case Law' (Final Report, prepared by V Robertson, 2022).

[53] Enterprise Act 2002, section 23.

(ad-exchange) platform.[54] The relevant markets included the provision of online advertising space, online advertising intermediation, and the provision of online display ad-serving technology.[55] Google was identified as the leading provider of online advertising, in particular search ad space in the European Economic Area (EEA), as a publisher on its own search engine webpage.[56] It also acted as an intermediary with its ad network (AdSense). DoubleClick was the leading provider of ad-serving technology to third parties, whereas Google only provided ad-serving technology as an ancillary service to its offer of online ad space (and not on a standalone basis). Therefore, they were not deemed to be direct competitors.[57]

III.2.1.1 Potential Competition

The Commission assessed Google's intention to develop a new ad-serving product for advertiser-side display ad serving, management, and reporting. Google Ad Manager for Advertisers (GFA) was in the early stages of development, as was Google's publisher-side ad-serving solution, Google for Publishers (GFP).[58] Several third parties argued that the transaction would eliminate potential competition, since DoubleClick was planning to provide ad intermediation services.[59] The Commission dismissed such arguments, due to the low likelihood of DoubleClick emerging as an effective competitive force in the ad intermediation market and the fact that there would be a sufficient number of competitors post-merger.[60] The Commission also assessed whether DoubleClick's data accumulation by its ad-serving business would allow it to rise as an effective player in the ad intermediation market. It concluded that it did not give it a strong advantage in that regard since any network effects in the ad intermediation market would be derived from those that could arise in the ad-serving market through the cross-use of data created through the use of DoubleClick for Advertisers (DFA) or DoubleClick for Publishers (DFP). However, this was considered unlikely, given the importance that publishers and advertisers place on confidentiality.[61]

III.2.1.2 Non-Horizontal Theories of Harm

With respect to non-horizontal theories of harm, the Commission investigated the following: (i) potential foreclosure based on DoubleClick's market position in

[54] *Google/DoubleClick* (n46), para 5.
[55] *Ibid*, paras 44–81.
[56] *Ibid*, para 95.
[57] *Ibid*, para 192.
[58] *Ibid*, para 215.
[59] *Ibid*, paras 221–222.
[60] See, e.g. European Commission (EU), 'Guidelines on the Assessment of Horizontal Mergers under the Council Regulation on the Control of Concentrations between Undertakings', [2004] OJ C 31/5 (EU HMG), para 60. See *Google/DoubleClick* (n46), paras 224–278.
[61] *Google/DoubleClick* (n46), paras 275–276.

ad serving, (ii) potential foreclosure based on Google's market position in search advertising and online ad intermediation services, and (iii) potential foreclosure based on the combination of DoubleClick's and Google's databases on customer-provided data through their online behaviour.[62]

With respect to the first theory of harm (i.e. anticompetitive foreclosure due to DoubleClick's position in ad serving), the Commission assessed (i) the ability to foreclose, (ii) the incentives to foreclose, and (iii) the overall impact on effective competition.[63] With respect to the ability to foreclose, the Commission concluded that DoubleClick could not exercise significant market power,[64] the data on actual switching indicated that the switching costs were manageable,[65] the combination of customers' databases would not provide a competitive advantage,[66] and the network effects were not sufficiently strong to induce tipping.[67] It also concluded that the merged entity was unlikely to have incentives to foreclose intermediation competitors.[68] Finally, according to the Commission, even if the merged entity had the ability and incentive to foreclose, it would be unlikely for rivals to be marginalized and customers harmed in the long run.[69]

With respect to the second theory of harm (i.e. potential foreclosure due to Google's strong position in search advertising and ad intermediation services through bundling Google's search ad and/or ad intermediation services with DoubleClick's ad serving), the Commission equally held that Google may have the ability to foreclose its rivals, but it would most likely not have such an incentive and, in any event, even if adopted, such a strategy would not have a significant detrimental effect on competition since a number of financially strong, vertically integrated rivals would not be foreclosed.[70]

Finally, with respect to the third theory of harm about combining CPI data, the Commission concluded that even if the parties' data collections were available as input for DoubleClick, it would be unlikely that its competitiveness would be enhanced in such a way that would confer on the merged entity a competitive advantage that could not be matched by its competitors, since the combination of data about searches with data about users' web surfing behaviour was already available to a number of Google's competitors.[71]

[62] *Ibid*, para 288.
[63] EU HMG (n59), para 94. See *Google/DoubleClick* (n46), para 293.
[64] *Google/DoubleClick* (n46), para 296.
[65] *Ibid*, para 297.
[66] *Ibid*, para 298.
[67] *Ibid*, para 310.
[68] *Ibid*, para 325.
[69] *Ibid*, para 326.
[70] *Ibid*, para 332.
[71] *Ibid*, paras 364–365.

III.2.1.3 Privacy and Consolidation in the AdTech Supply Chain

Privacy concerns were also raised with respect to this deal by consumer organizations and privacy groups.[72] The Commission, though, did not address such concerns and reiterated in the decision that its conclusion to clear this transaction was based on a competition law assessment, and as such, it was without prejudice to data protection and the privacy regulatory framework.[73]

III.2.1.4 Comment

Although it is, indeed, difficult to foresee the future, the Commission nonetheless identified possible concerns with this merger, as the above analysis showcases, but was quick to dismiss them. Arguably, in its assessment, the Commission failed to take into account the complementarities between the merging parties' products, as well as the economies of scope, and to properly assess the impact on competition in the long run.[74] The US FTC also closed its investigation with a 4–1 majority.[75]

Following the acquisition of DoubleClick as well as other acquisitions in the AdTech sector that were not scrutinized by the Commission,[76] Google has risen as the number one player in the AdTech supply chain, attracting both competition law and regulatory scrutiny, as the discussion in Chapter 5 has revealed.

III.2.2 Google/Motorola Mobility

In 2011, Google acquired Motorola Mobility, a smartphones and tablets manufacturer. The Commission looked into *two vertical relationships*: first, the Android OS as a key input into smartphones, and second the standard essential patents (SEPs) (owned by Motorola) as key inputs for smartphones. The Commission also examined the *conglomerate relationship* between smartphones and related intellectual property (IP) rights with the online services offered by Google.[77] With respect to the Android OS, the Commission concluded that Google would not have the incentive to favour Motorola's access to Android over other original equipment manufacturers (OEMs) post-transaction, given that this would jeopardize Google's main revenue source, online advertising.[78] With respect to SEPs,

[72] See, e.g. P Meller, 'E.U. Group Says Google–DoubleClick Deal Will Harm Privacy' (20 December 2007); L Rosencrance, 'Privacy Groups Say Google–DoubleClick Merger Will Hurt Consumers' (20 December 2007) <https://www.computerworld.com/article/2538252/privacy-groups-say-google-doubleclick-merger-will-hurt-consumers.html> (accessed 9 June 2024).

[73] *Google/DoubleClick* (n46), para 368.

[74] J Van den Boom and P Samranchit, 'Digital Ecosystem Mergers in Big Tech—a Theory of Long-Run Harm with Applications' (2022) 13(5) Journal of European Competition Law & Practice 365, 368.

[75] *Google/DoubleClick*, FTC File No 071-0170, Statement of Federal Trade Commission and Dissenting Statement of Commissioner Pamela Jones Harbour.

[76] See, e.g. AdMob.Google, 'We've Officially Acquired AdMob!" (Official blog, 27 May 2010) <https://googleblog.blogspot.com/2010/05/weve-officially-acquired-admob.html> (accessed 24 February 2024).

[77] *Google/Motorola Mobility* (Case COMP/M.6381) Commission Decision, C(2012) 1068 (13 February 2012), para 63.

[78] *Ibid*, paras 86–94.

the Commission concluded that the transaction would not affect the market situation.[79] The Commission equally dismissed conglomerate concerns and cleared the transaction unconditionally.

The Ministry of Commerce of the People's Republic of China (MOFCOM) cleared this transaction with conditions, with Google undertaking that its Android platform would remain open and free, the treatment of OEMs would be non-discriminatory, and that it would accede to Motorola's fair, reasonable, and non-discriminatory (FRAND) commitments.[80]

III.2.3 Google/Sanofi/Digital Marketing Institute Joint Venture (DMI JV)

In August 2015, Google formed a joint venture with Sanofi—a pharmaceutical manufacturer. The JV would offer services for diabetes treatment and management, including data collection, processing, and analysis.[81] The Commission reviewed various horizontal and conglomerate concerns and ultimately cleared the transaction.

III.2.4 Google/Fitbit

The *Google/Fitbit* deal was announced in November 2019.[82] Fitbit is a leading technology company in activity trackers and smartwatches, possessing one of the world's largest health-data databases.[83] The acquisition was cleared by the EU Commission in December 2020 after Google offered a remedies package.[84] The company committed not to use Fitbit's data for advertising. It also committed to allowing users to share its data with competitors. Following the Commission decision, Google completed the transaction, even though it was still under investigation, at the time, by the ACCC and the US Department of Justice (DoJ). Interestingly, the ACCC rejected similar remedies. The UK CMA has also hinted that such behavioural remedies would not have been acceptable in the United Kingdom due to difficulties with monitoring and implementation.[85]

[79] *Ibid*, paras 105–160.

[80] J Hua Su, 'China's Ministry of Commerce Conditionally Clears the Google/Motorola Mobility Deal' (Kluwer Competition Law Blog, 19 May 2012) <https://competitionlawblog.kluwercompetitionlaw.com/2012/05/19/china-conditionally-clears-google-motorola-mobility> (accessed 9 June 2024).

[81] *Sanofi/Google/DMI JV* (Case M.7813) Commission Decision, C(2016) 1223 (23 February 2016), para 5.

[82] Business Wire, 'Fitbit to Be Acquired by Google' (1 November 2019) <https://www.businesswire.com/news/home/20191101005318/en/Fitbit-to-Be-Acquired-by-Google> (accessed 28 February 2023).

[83] *Ibid.*

[84] *Google/Fitbit* (Case M.96960) Commission Decision, C(2020) 9105.(XX) (17 December 2020).

[85] ACCC, 'ACCC Rejects Google Behavioural Undertakings for Fitbit Acquisition' (Press release, 22 December 2020) <https://www.accc.gov.au/media-release/accc-rejects-google-behavioural-undertakings-for-fitbit-acquisition> (accessed 28 February 2023). See Coscelli (n1).

III.2.4.1 Relevant Markets

Given Google's ecosystem of complementary services, multiple markets were examined in this transaction, namely the markets for (i) wrist-worn wearable devices (without further division between smartwatches and fitness trackers);[86] (ii) licensable smart mobile OSs and the market for wrist-worn wearable devices OSs (Wear OS);[87] (iii) Android app stores and r Wear OS and Fitbit devices app stores;[88] (iv) general search services;[89] (v) search advertising and display advertising;[90] (vi) the provision of online advertising intermediation services subdivided in the supply of (a) search ad network services, (b) display ads SSP services for publishers, (c) display ads DSP services for advertisers, (d) display ad network services, (e) display ads publisher ad-server services, (f) display ads advertiser ad-server services, and (g) the supply of analytics services;[91] (vii) health and fitness apps;[92] (viii) r the retail provision of mobile payment services;[93] (ix) navigation apps;[94] (x) virtual assistants;[95] (xi) digital music distribution services;[96] (xii) digital translation services;[97] (xiii) the provision of cloud infrastructure and data analytics in digital health care;[98] (xiv) patient monitoring;[99] (xv) the provision of data for medical research and real-world evidence;[100] and (xvi) corporate wellness programmes.[101]

III.2.4.2 Horizontal Effects: Data Power

Proceeding with the competitive assessment, after having discussed the parties' market shares in the above markets, the Commission identified the affected markets.[102] The only horizontally affected market in the traditional sense (i.e. where the parties had more than a 20 per cent combined market share) was the mobile payment services market.[103] However, *potential horizontal effects* of this transaction were examined by the Commission with respect to the impact of the acquisition of Fitbit's data on search services, online advertising, and digital health care.[104]

86 *Google/Fitbit* (n83), para 79.
87 *Ibid*, para 100.
88 *Ibid*, para 125.
89 *Ibid*, para 142.
90 *Ibid*, para 155.
91 *Ibid*, para 168.
92 *Ibid*, para 186.
93 *Ibid*, para 201.
94 *Ibid*, para 217.
95 *Ibid*, para 231.
96 *Ibid*, para 248.
97 *Ibid*, para 260.
98 *Ibid*, para 274.
99 *Ibid*, para 285.
100 *Ibid*, para 296.
101 *Ibid*, para 309.
102 For a graphic exposition, see *ibid*, table 26.
103 The concerns here were dismissed, given the number of competitors and Fitbit's low market share. See *ibid*, paras 386–387.
104 *Ibid*, para 385.

With respect to online advertising services, the potential combination of these data sets, despite the existing regulatory restrictions, would give an important data advantage, rendering the entry or expansion of rivals very difficult, if not impossible.[105] Such concerns were corroborated by the vast majority of respondents in the market investigation, who expressed concerns that, by virtue of the increase in Google's data power, competitors would not be able to offer the same level of personalization and appeal to advertisers, which would lead to a price increase and choice reduction.[106] Thus, the transaction would strengthen Google's dominant position in online search advertising and possibly in online display advertising and the supply of AdTech services.[107]

With respect to digital health-care services and data-related concerns, the Commission noted that there were alternative data providers and concluded that the combination of the Fitbit and Google databases would not create a significant impediment to effective competition since the parties were neither actual nor potential competitors. Neither party was actively marketing users' health data, the transaction was unlikely to impact the development of the digital health-care services market, and Fitbit's users' health data were not Google's driver for this acquisition.[108] Furthermore, there was a large number of players in this market,[109] and many new initiatives, with Amazon's Halo being given as an example.[110]

III.2.4.3 Potential Competition

It should be noted that the Commission, in a rather cursory analysis, dismissed the impact of the transaction on potential competition arising from Google's potential entry into the market for the supply of smartwatches.[111] This was despite the fact that Alphabet's subsidiary, Verily, had already developed the Verily Study Watch and was collecting various data health information.[112]

III.2.4.4 Vertical Effects: Input Foreclosure from Access to Fitbit Data

With respect to vertically affected markets, the Commission examined potential vertical effects with respect to potential input foreclosure from access to Fitbit data to the detriment of digital health-care service providers. The Commission also examined input foreclosure to the detriment of wrist-worn wearable suppliers

[105] *Ibid*, paras 402, 411–412.
[106] *Ibid*, para 450.
[107] *Ibid*, para 468.
[108] *Ibid*, paras 483–488.
[109] *Ibid*, paras 490–494.
[110] *Ibid*, para 495. Anticompetitive horizontal effects arising from the combination of Fitbit's and Google's data sets with respect to general search were also dismissed. See *ibid*, paras 469–474.
[111] *Ibid*, paras 392–398.
[112] *Ibid*, n260. At the time of writing, it was still not commercially available. See <https://verily.com/solutions/study-watch> (accessed 2 March 2023).

from access to Wear OS,[113] Google apps and services,[114] Google Play,[115] and Google Search,[116] as well as input foreclosure to the would not have the ability to foreclose since the largest smartwatch suppliers detriment of app developers from access to Fitbit app stores.[117]

As far as foreclosing access to Fitbit's data to the detriment of digital health care service providers was concerned, the Commission concluded that Google would have both the incentive and ability to restrict access to Fitbit's Web application programming interface (API), and such restriction would negatively affect app developers and websites, including nascent innovative companies.[118]

III.2.4.5 Conglomerate Effects: Leveraging Market Power from Android OS to Wearables

Furthermore, the Commission examined potential conglomerate effects arising from the potential leveraging of Google's market power in Android OS to the supply of wrist-worn wearable devices.[119] Such a practice was examined as a form of technical tying, with Google tying the use of Fitbit smartwatches with the Android OS through improved performance compared to competing products.[120] The Commission concluded that Google had both the incentive and ability to engage in such a strategy and that such technical tying through the degrading interoperability of rivals with the Android OS would have a significant effect on competition.

III.2.4.6 Access to Commercially Sensitive Information

Finally, potential non-horizontal effects with respect to Google getting access to commercially sensitive information from third-party apps through Fitbit were also examined;[121] however, the Commission dismissed such concerns, since—amongst other reasons—this would not materially increase Google's information about its competitors, and such data are not unique.[122]

[113] Such concerns were dismissed, given that Google operate their own proprietary OS. Also, it would not have the incentive, given that its business model relies on the widest possible distribution of Wear OS. See *Google/Fitbit* (n83), paras 544, 558, 560.

[114] Such concerns were dismissed, since Google apps are only available on smartwatches running on Wear OS (and recently on Apple and Fitbit watches). See *ibid*, paras 578, 598.

[115] Here, the Commission concluded that any foreclosure strategy would not significantly affect competition, as such a strategy could possibly affect only non-integrated wearable OEMs and only if they could not enter into agreements with Android smartphone OEMs to appear in their app stores. Garmin was identified as the largest competitor that could potentially be affected. See *ibid*, paras 647–648.

[116] Such concerns were dismissed. See *ibid*, para 678.

[117] Such concerns were also dismissed. See *ibid*, para 709.

[118] *Ibid*, paras 529–531.

[119] *Ibid*, para 390.

[120] *Ibid*, para 718.

[121] *Ibid*, para 391.

[122] *Ibid*, paras 838, 839, 845.

III.2.4.7 Remedies

In order to address the Commission's concerns with respect to the potential combination of data and their respective impact on online advertising, potential foreclosure of rivals through restricting access to Fitbit's data, and degrading interoperability with Android OS, Google offered a package of three commitments. The first was the 'Ads Commitment', according to which the company would not use data related to health-and-fitness activity location and measured body data for advertising purposes and would keep these data separate. The second was the 'Web API Access Commitment', according to which third parties would have access without charge, following user consent, to a series of measured body data. Finally, the third was the 'Android APIs Commitment', according to which the parties would keep licensing for free public APIs, which allow interoperability between rival wearable devices and the Android OS on smartphones and offer at least the functionalities of the APIs existing at the date of this decision.[123]

III.2.4.8 Comment

The Commission's decision has been criticized for failing to adopt a broader ecosystem approach as per the Commission Report on Digital Markets and for not examining the potential of this transaction to replicate the duopoly on mobile OSs in the area of wrist-worn, wearable devices as well as Google's potential to dominate digital health care due to its vast data accumulation.[124] In addition, other significant risks identified concerned 'platform envelopment', the extension of monopoly power, and possible consumer exploitation in health care and health insurance, which also raises important privacy concerns.[125]

III.3 Amazon's Acquisitions

The Commission has only reviewed *Amazon/MGM* and *Amazon/iRobot.*

III.3.1 *Amazon/MGM*

The *Amazon/MGM* deal was notified to the Commission on 8 February 2022, since the transaction met the primary thresholds under Article 1(2) EUMR[126] and

[123] *Ibid*, para 896.

[124] J Modrall, 'Google/Fitbit—The EU Commission Misses a Step' (17 June 2021) <https://competitionlawblog.kluwercompetitionlaw.com/2021/06/17/google-fitbit-the-eu-commission-misses-a-step> (accessed 3 March 2023).

[125] G Spagnolo et al, 'Google/Fitbit Will Monetise Health Data and Harm Consumers' (30 September 2020) <https://cepr.org/voxeu/columns/googlefitbit-will-monetise-health-data-and-harm-consumers> (accessed 6 March 2023).

[126] *Amazon/MGM* (Case M.10349) Commission Decision, C(2022) 78/05, paras 1, 5.

was cleared unconditionally following a Phase I investigation. Amazon's ecosystem comprises a wide range of products and services, including retail and technology services, consumer electronics, and the production and supply of audio-visual (AV) content through Prime Video. MGM is an entertainment company producing and distributing AV content.[127]

Relevant markets in this transaction included (i) the production and supply of AV content,[128] (ii) the wholesale supply of TV channels,[129] (iii) the retail supply of AV services,[130] and (iv) production and licensing of distribution rights for theatrical release.[131] These markets are defined along national lines or linguistically homogeneous areas.[132]

With respect to horizontally affected markets, both parties are active in the production and licensing of distribution for theatrical release, yet their combined market share does not exceed 10–20 per cent in any EEA country. There are also competitors with higher market shares.[133]

With respect to vertically affected markets, the Commission examined potential rival subscription-based video-on-demand (SVOD) platforms' foreclosure from accessing MGM's AV content, but dismissed such concerns given the highly competitive nature of the market for AV content supply and the plethora of available content,[134] customers' multi-homing,[135] and the existence of strong competitors.[136] In terms of vertical effects, the Commission also looked into potential foreclosure of AV content producers, but such concerns were also dismissed given that the market for AV content supply is highly competitive and Amazon would need a variety of content, which cannot be covered by MGM's library alone.[137] The Commission also examined and dismissed possible foreclosure of cinemas from access to MGM's content in general and with respect to the Bond franchise in particular.[138]

Potential anticompetitive conglomerate effects of this transaction were also examined by the Commission, but such concerns were dismissed.[139] Such effects concerned potential leveraging of Amazon's strengthened position in the market for the AV content retail supply into the marketplace services market.

[127] *Ibid*, paras 2–3.
[128] *Ibid*, para 36.
[129] *Ibid*, para 54.
[130] *Ibid*, para 74.
[131] *Ibid*, para 88.
[132] *Ibid*, paras 40, 58, 78, 93.
[133] *Ibid*, para 144.
[134] *Ibid*, para 200.
[135] *Ibid*, para 206.
[136] *Ibid*, para 208.
[137] *Ibid*, para 232.
[138] *Ibid*, paras 264, 275.
[139] *Ibid*, para 312.

III.3.2 Amazon/iRobot

This transaction was notified to the Commission on 1 June 2023. iRobot is a producer of robot vacuum cleaners (RVCs). Amazon offers an online marketplace for third-party retailers and also itself acts as a retailer of various products (including RVCs).

Amazon/iRobot has raised concerns with respect to Amazon's ability to restrict competition in the RVC market and strengthen its position in the market for the provision of online marketplace services by obtaining access to iRobot's user data. The transaction had been referred to an in-depth Phase II investigation,[140] and according to the Statement of Objections, the Commission was concerned that Amazon may engage in self-preferencing practices as—post transaction—it could have both the ability and incentive to foreclose competing RVC producers by restricting and/or degrading access on Amazon, including delisting and reducing visibility on Amazon Marketplace.[141] The deal was ultimately abandoned in the light of intense regulatory scrutiny by the EU Commission and the US FTC.[142]

Interestingly, this case has already been cleared by the UK CMA following a Phase I review.[143] Such an approach is in contrast with the CMA's arguably stricter approach to digital mergers following the blocking of *Meta/Giphy*[144] and *Microsoft/Activision*[145] and the updated Merger Guidelines[146] that contemplate ecosystem-based theories of harm.[147]

[140] *Amazon/iRobot* (Case M.10920) Commission Decision, C(2023) 202/12. See European Commission (EU), 'Mergers: Commission Opens In-Depth Investigation into the Proposed Acquisition of iRobot by Amazon' (Press release, 6 July 2023) <https://ec.europa.eu/commission/presscorner/detail/en/ip_23_3702> (accessed 9 June 2024).

[141] European Commission (EU), 'Commission Sends Amazon Statement of Objections over Proposed Acquisition of iRobot' (Press release, 27 November 2023) <https://ec.europa.eu/commission/presscorner/detail/en/IP_23_5990> (accessed 9 June 2024).

[142] European Commission (EU), 'Statement by Executive Vice-President Vestager on Announcement by Amazon and iRobot to Abandon Their Transaction' (Press release, 29 January 2024) <https://ec.europa.eu/commission/presscorner/detail/en/statement_24_521https://ec.europa.eu/commission/presscorner/detail/en/statement_24_521>. See FTC, 'Statement Regarding the Termination of Amazon's Proposed Acquisition of iRobot' (Press release, 31 January 2024) <https://www.ftc.gov/news-events/news/press-releases/2024/01/statement-regarding-termination-amazons-proposed-acquisition-irobot>; Amazon, 'Amazon and iRobot Agree to Terminate Pending Acquisition' (Press release, 29 January 2024) <https://press.aboutamazon.com/2024/1/amazon-and-irobot-agree-to-terminate-pending-acquisition> (all accessed 9 June 2024).

[143] CMA, 'Amazon's Purchase of Roomba Maker Cleared by CMA' (16 June 2023) <https://www.gov.uk/government/news/amazon-s-purchase-of-roomba-maker-cleared-by-cma> (accessed 9 June 2024)

[144] See text to n338 below.

[145] See text to n306 below.

[146] CMA, 'Merger Assessment Guidelines', CMA 129 (18 March 2021) (CMA MAG), paras 7.14, 7.19, 7.30, 7.34.

[147] T Smith, 'Amazon/iRobot: Does Amazon Have an Incentive to Preference Its Own Products?' (13 July 2023) <https://theplatformlaw.blog/2023/07/13/amazon-irobot-cma> (accessed 9 June 2024).

III.4 Facebook's Acquisitions

The Commission has reviewed only two Facebook (Meta) transactions to date. The first (*Facebook/WhatsApp*) was cleared unconditionally, whereas the second (*Meta/Kustomer*) was cleared following a Phase II investigation with commitments. Neither case met the EUMR turnover thresholds, but nonetheless, they were referred to the Commission either by the merging parties (*Facebook/WhatsApp*) or by NCAs (*Meta/Kustomer*).

III.4.1 Facebook/WhatsApp

Facebook acquired WhatsApp in 2014. Both companies seek to attract consumer attention. This transaction fell below the EUMR thresholds, but nonetheless, the Commission asserted jurisdiction at the request of the merging parties under Article 4(5) EUMR.[148] With respect to this transaction, the Commission examined whether, post-merger, the merged entity could use WhatsApp users' data to improve targeted advertising.[149] Such behaviour would have strengthened Facebook's position in the online advertising market.

III.4.1.1 Theories of Harm: Online Advertising

The two theories of harm examined in this respect were whether Facebook could strengthen its respective position in online advertising by (i) introducing advertising on WhatsApp and/or (ii) employing WhatsApp as a potential source of user data in order to improve Facebook's targeted advertising outside WhatsApp.[150] The Commission concluded that these were unlikely to materialize since, post-transaction, there would remain a number of providers of online advertising space.[151]

III.4.1.2 Data Concentration: Privacy

The data aspects examined concerned only potential data concentration to the extent that such concentration may strengthen Facebook's position in the online advertising market. Any privacy issues relevant to this transaction were deemed to fall outside of the scope of competition law.[152]

In this transaction, the Commission, while acknowledging the growing importance that consumers place on privacy,[153] did not examine the potential impact on

[148] *Facebook/WhatsApp* (n47), paras 9–12.
[149] *Ibid*, section 5.3.2.
[150] *Ibid*, para 167.
[151] *Ibid*, paras 177, 188.
[152] *Ibid*, para 164. See FTC action against Facebook alleging that the acquisitions of Instagram (2021) and WhatsApp Facebook were part of a systematic strategy to eliminate possible threats to its social network monopoly. See n27 above.
[153] *Facebook/WhatsApp* (n47), para 87 ('the importance of [privacy and security] varies from user to user but which are becoming increasingly valued, as shown by the introduction of consumer communications apps specifically addressing privacy and security issues').

the offering of privacy solutions and whether, post-transaction, Facebook could change WhatsApp's privacy terms and conditions to the detriment of consumers, thereby also removing an important competitive constraint on its own privacy conditions.[154]

III.4.1.3 Role of Network Effects

With respect to the role of network effects in this transaction the Commission noted that

> [t]he existence of network effects as such does not a priori indicate a competition problem in the market affected by a merger. Such effects may however raise competition concerns in particular if they allow the merged entity to foreclose competitors and make more difficult for competing providers to expand their customer base. Network effects have to be assessed on a case-by-case basis.[155]

In this case, the Commission concluded that their respective role in preventing entry or expansion was mitigated by the following factors: the contestable nature of the market for consumer communications apps, consumers' multi-homing, and the lack of lock-in effects (despite the fact that some third parties highlighted the merged entities' ability to limit data portability).[156] However, as stated in the decision, for the sake of completeness, the Commission examined whether the transaction would strengthen the network effects but concluded that this was unlikely to happen, since it would require a certain degree of inter-platform integration, which was unlikely to happen.[157] The Commission accepted the parties' arguments that such integration between Facebook and WhatsApp would pose substantial technical difficulties, despite third parties' claims to the contrary.[158]

And if merger control inherently involves a prediction about the future evolution of market conduct and structure, in *Facebook/WhatsApp*, the Commission did not perform well in this exercise. According to its decision, '[a]ny forced transfer of WhatsApp users onto the Facebook social network (for example, by compelling WhatsApp users to register on Facebook) may alienate users and cause their outflow to competing consumer communications apps'.[159]

[154] F Costa-Cabral and O Lynskey, 'Family Ties: The Intersection between Data Protection and Competition in EU Law' 54 (2017) Common Market Law Review 11, 26. See also E Deutscher, 'How to Measure Privacy-Related Consumer Harm in Merger Analysis' (PhD thesis, European University Institute, 2018), 7–9.

[155] *Facebook/WhatsApp* (n47), para 130.

[156] *Ibid*, paras 131–135.

[157] *Ibid*, paras 136–139.

[158] *Ibid*, paras 138–139.

[159] *Ibid*, para 160.

III.4.1.4 Fallen Promises

In 2016, just two years after the transaction, Facebook began to integrate WhatsApp users' data into Facebook. The Commission imposed a fine of €110 million on Facebook for providing misleading information.[160] Apart from the Commission's action under the merger control rules, this change in its data policies resulted in a flurry of enforcement actions, primarily by data and consumer protection authorities.[161]

III.4.2 Meta/Kustomer

This transaction did not meet the EUMR turnover thresholds. The Austrian NCA, which had jurisdiction to review this deal, referred it to the Commission with the support of other Member States (Belgium, Bulgaria, France, Iceland, Ireland, Italy, the Netherlands, Portugal, and Romania), with the exception of Germany.[162] The Commission cleared this transaction with commitments following an in-depth Phase II investigation.

Kustomer offers software designed to help companies' customer services to interact with consumers and address consumer queries with respect, for example, to a late delivery. Such software, in technical jargon, is termed software-as-a-service (SaaS) customer relation management (CRM) software. Such CRM software integrates with many B2C communication channels (including Messenger, Instagram, and WhatsApp[163]) through an API.[164] These communication channels provide an important input for CRM software manufacturers, which allows businesses to communicate with consumers.

III.4.2.1 Non-Horizontal Concerns: Input Foreclosure

The Commission assessed potential anticompetitive effects flowing from this transaction as a result of a potential input foreclosure strategy of Kustomer's rivals. Post-transaction, Meta might restrict or degrade the API access to its B2C messaging channels on the market for the supply of CRM software (and the narrower market for the supply of customer service and support CRM software).[165]

With respect to vertical foreclosure, the Commission concluded that there was even a strong probability[166] that Meta had both the ability and the incentive to

[160] European Commission (EU), 'Mergers: Commission Fines Facebook €110 Million for Providing Misleading Information about WhatsApp Takeover' (Press release, 18 May 2017) <https://europa.eu/rapid/press-release_IP-17-1369_en.htm> (accessed 9 June 2024).

[161] On these actions, see I Graef, D Clifford, and P Valcke, 'Fairness and Enforcement: Bridging Competition, Data Protection, and Consumer Law' (2018) 8 International Data Privacy Law 200, 201–202; N Zingales, 'Between a Rock and Two Hard Places: WhatsApp at the Crossroad of Competition, Data Protection and Consumer Law' (2017) 33 Computer Law & Security Review 553.

[162] *Meta/Kustomer* (n37), para 6.

[163] *Ibid*, para 3.

[164] *Ibid*, paras 46–48.

[165] *Ibid*, para 167.

[166] On this high standard of proof, see Case C-376/20 P *Commission v CK Telecoms UK Investments*, ECLI:EU:C:2023:561, para 87. The CJEU held that the General Court (GC) had committed an error in

foreclose competing CRM software suppliers by restricting or degrading API access to its B2C messaging services, with such a strategy likely to result in significant anticompetitive effects.[167] This was because Meta would have the ability to foreclose, since its B2C messaging channels (Messenger, WhatsApp, and Instagram) are an important input for the downstream market;[168] Meta holds market power in the upstream B2C messaging services market;[169] and Meta has the ability to restrict or degrade access to its APIs,[170] as well as the ability to target specific CRM software providers, with the latter not being able to work around such a strategy.[171] It would also have the incentive to foreclose since, first, the benefits from such a strategy would be 'numerous, diverse and significant',[172] flowing from increased SaaS revenues,[173] from data accumulation used in targeted online display advertising,[174] and from luring business customers to Meta's ecosystem of products (e.g. Facebook Marketplace and Shops).[175] Second, Meta would also have the ability to limit losses from such foreclosure, with switching having been estimated as sufficiently significant to limit such losses.[176] Such a foreclosure strategy, the Commission concluded, would have significant effects on competition; in this regard, the Commission noted, amongst other factors, the importance of innovation in the CRM software services market, with many start-ups developing new products.[177]

III.4.2.2 Horizontal Effect: Data Accumulation

The Commission also assessed the impact of Meta's data accumulation on the market for online display advertising as a potential horizontal effect.[178]

With respect to horizontal effects, in a similar vein as in *Google/Fitbit*, even though there were no horizontally affected markets in the traditional sense, the Commission examined potential data effects from this transaction.[179] Although the Commission accepted that Meta would accumulate additional data, which could improve its online display advertising services, it noted that such data

law requiring the Commission to meet a 'strong probability' standard for proving a significant impediment to effective competition. See *Commission v CK Telecoms*, para 88. See Case T-399/16, *CK Telecoms UK Investments Ltd v European Commission*, ECLI:EU:T:2020:217, para 118.

[167] *Meta/Kustomer* (n37), para 241.
[168] *Ibid*, paras 243–256.
[169] *Ibid*, paras 257–272.
[170] *Ibid*, paras 273–293.
[171] *Ibid*, paras 294-302.
[172] *Ibid*, para 317.
[173] *Ibid*, paras 318–322.
[174] *Ibid*, paras 323–362.
[175] *Ibid*, paras 376–382.
[176] *Ibid*, paras 383–429.
[177] *Ibid*, paras 444–484.
[178] *Ibid*, para 169.
[179] *Ibid*, para 515.

accumulation would not be likely to significantly impede effective competition in online display advertising. This was due to the fact that first, such data accumulation would not significantly increase entry barriers and, second, because competitors may still access Kustomer's business customers data, or access similar data sets through alternative means, for example partnerships with other CRM software suppliers.[180]

III.4.2.3 Conglomerate Effects

Finally, the Commission assessed conglomerate effects with respect to Meta's potential leveraging of its market power from the online display advertising to the supply of CRM software.[181] Such concerns were dismissed because Meta would lack the ability to foreclose, since the market investigation showed that online display advertising and CRM software are usually purchased separately.[182]

III.4.2.4 Remedies

In order to address vertical foreclosure effects, Meta offered access to its APIs commitments, which, following the market testing phase, were extended from the five years originally offered to ten years.[183]

III.5 Apple's Acquisitions

The Commission has reviewed and cleared two of Apple's acquisitions to date, the first (*Apple/Beats*) following a Phase I investigation and the second (*Apple/Shazam*) following a Phase II investigation.

III.5.1 Apple/Beats

Apple announced its plan to acquire Beats Electronics, a headphones and audio speakers manufacturer, and Beats Music, a music-streaming application provider, in May 2017. The transaction met the secondary thresholds under the EUMR and was ultimately cleared by the Commission following a Phase I review.[184]

III.5.1.1 Horizontal Effects

The Commission concluded that the transaction was not likely to raise concerns in the headphones market in the light of the parties' market shares being lower than

180 *Ibid*, paras 571, 585, 586.
181 *Ibid*, para 171.
182 *Ibid*, paras 610, 614.
183 *Ibid*, paras 661–683.
184 *Apple/Beats* (Case M.7290) Commission Decision, C(2014) 5448.

20 per cent,[185] the fact that the parties were not close competitors,[186] the fact that there was sufficient competition among global competitors,[187] and the fact that there were low entry barriers, with ten competitors having entered the market in the past five years.[188]

Similarly, the Commission's horizontal concerns in the music-streaming market were equally dispelled, since Beats was not active in the EEA and was not considered an important constraining force as a potential competitor, since existing established players (Spotify and Deezer) already exerted a significant competitive constraint on Apple.[189]

III.5.1.2 Vertical Effects

The Commission dismissed vertical effects with respect to Apple's ability and incentive to use its bargaining power derived from the strong presence of iTunes to convince record labels not to provide content to rival music-streaming services.[190] Similarly, its vertical concerns with respect to reducing interoperability between iOS and competing music-streaming apps of competitors were dismissed.[191]

III.5.2 Apple/Shazam

This deal was announced in December 2017 and was the first transaction where the Commission engaged in an in-depth review of the impact of data accumulation on competition. The Commission acquired jurisdiction to review the transaction following an Article 22 EUMR referral request by Austria (later joined by France, Iceland, Italy, Norway, Spain, and Sweden).[192]

In *Apple/Shazam*, the Commission referred the transaction for a Phase II in-depth investigation since it appeared that it would significantly impede effective competition due to the following non-horizontal, non-coordinated effects: first, possible foreclosure of competitors providing automatic content recognition (ACR) software solutions, including music recognition apps after pre-installing Shazam on iOS, or integrating Shazam with iOS, or degrading the interoperability of ACR solutions provided by Shazam's competitors on iOS; and second, possible foreclosure of competitors of digital music-streaming apps due to Apple's access to commercially sensitive information about its rivals post-transaction.[193]

[185] *Ibid*, para 23.
[186] *Ibid*, para 28.
[187] *Ibid*, para 29.
[188] *Ibid*, para 30.
[189] *Ibid*, para 36.
[190] *Ibid*, paras 41–42.
[191] *Ibid*, paras 44–45.
[192] *Apple/Shazam* (n48), paras 7–9.
[193] *Ibid*, para 11. A similar approach was taken in *Google/Fitbit* (n83) and *Meta/Kustomer* (n37). See, e.g. *Meta/Kustomer* (n37) para 519.

III.5.2.1 Non-Horizontal Effects: Competitors' Foreclosure Due to Access to Commercially Sensitive Information

With respect to the second theory of harm, the Commission, while acknowledging the regulatory constraints based on data protection and privacy as well as contractual constraints that may limit Apple's ability to use such data in the future, nonetheless went on to assess the impact on competition, provided that such use was lawful.[194] This is a rather interesting qualification, since it raises the question as to what would happen if the use of such data was in breach of the regulatory framework. The Commission concluded that even if the merged entity had the ability and incentives to place competing providers of digital music-streaming apps at a competitive disadvantage by using the customer information, such practices (e.g. targeted advertising) were unlikely to negatively impact effective competition.[195] The Commission, in a somewhat alarming statement for privacy sceptics, acknowledged that Apple's ability to target subscribers of competing music-streaming services following the transaction would not increase materially since there existed several other providers (such as Facebook, Google, and Twitter), which would allow for similar targeting to Apple of such 'music enthusiasts', even in the absence of the transaction. Equally, Apple Music rivals may rely on these third parties.[196]

III.5.2.2 Non-Horizontal Effects: Remaining Concerns Regarding Competitors' Foreclosure

With respect to potential foreclosure of competitors of digital music-streaming apps, the Commission also examined the following set of practices, despite the fact that—according to the Commission—Shazam's high market shares did not translate into a high degree of market power. The first was the leveraging of the merged entity's market position from the market of music-recognition apps to the market for digital music-streaming apps. These practices included denying or degrading access of competitors to Shazam's referral mechanism. The second was restricting competitors' access to the Shazam app as an advertising tool and confining its use only to Apple Music. The third was integrating Shazam's music-recognition functionalities within the Apple Music apps while denying similar levels of integration to competitors. Finally, the fourth was denying competitors' access to Shazam user data as an important input to improve existing, or offer additional functionalities, on digital music-streaming apps.[197] Following its assessment, the Commission concluded that even if the merged entity was likely to have both the ability and incentive to engage in such practices, these practices were unlikely to have a negative impact on competition in the market for music-streaming apps.[198]

[194] *Apple/Shazam* (n49), para 238.
[195] *Ibid*, para 246.
[196] *Ibid*, para 248.
[197] *Ibid*, paras 272–274.
[198] *Ibid*, section 8.4.2.2.

Finally, and similarly to the previous analysis with respect to foreclosure concerns of competing providers of music-streaming apps, with respect to potential foreclosure of competing providers of ACR software solutions, including music-recognition apps, the Commission concluded that even if the merged entity were to engage in such practices, these would not have a negative impact on competition.[199]

III.6 Microsoft's Acquisitions

Compared to the other Big Tech companies, the Commission has reviewed a comparatively large number of Microsoft's acquisitions. These transactions are presented below, while emphasis is given to those that raised issues from a competition law perspective. *Microsoft/Github, Microsoft/Zenimax*, and *Microsoft/Nuance* were referred to the Commission at the request of the parties under Article 4(5) EUMR, while the remaining transactions met the EUMR thresholds, either primary or secondary.

III.6.1 Microsoft/Yahoo

In July 2009, Microsoft's acquisition of Yahoo's internet search and online search advertising businesses was announced. The transaction fell under the secondary EUMR thresholds.[200]

In this decision, the Commission, while acknowledging the distinct characteristics of online search advertising as a targeting devise compared to online display advertising as a brand-building awareness mechanism, left the market definition open since, under any definition, no competitive concerns were raised.[201]

In examining the market characteristics of online advertising, the Commission assessed the two-sidedness of search engines,[202] the importance of innovation,[203] and the existence of entry barriers.[204] In terms of market shares, the Commission noted that on the user side, Google was the leader, with Microsoft and Yahoo having small market shares, and thus the transaction did not give rise to affected markets based on the volume of either search queries or paid search queries. However, given that, in this market, the emphasis is on quality and innovation competition and the existence of high entry barriers, the Commission looked into possible effects of this transaction.[205]

199 *Ibid*, section 8.4.3.
200 *Microsoft/Yahoo! Search Business* (Case COMP/M.5727) Commission Decision, C(2010) 1077, paras 27–28.
201 *Ibid*, paras 74–75.
202 *Ibid*, paras 100–108.
203 *Ibid*, paras 109–110.
204 *Ibid*, para 111.
205 *Ibid*, paras 118–119.

This transaction was cleared in Phase I, given the low market shares of the merged entity coupled with Google's entrenched market position in the relevant markets. In fact, the Commission acknowledged that the transaction was procompetitive, since it would allow the parties to compete more effectively with Google.[206]

III.6.2 Microsoft/Skype

This deal was announced in May 2011. The Commission asserted jurisdiction under the EUMR secondary thresholds.[207] It defined two separate relevant product markets for consumer and enterprise communication services.[208] Further segmentation according to functionalities (IM and voice and video calls), according to whether they were provided on different platforms (PCs, tablets, smartphones) and according to OSs (Mac, Android, Windows, Linux) as well as customer size for enterprise communications was left open, since even under a narrower market definition, the transaction did not raise concerns for competition.[209]

III.6.2.1 Consumer Communication Services

The Commission noted that consumer communication services were a nascent and growing sector,[210] there had been a shift from desktop to other devices, such as smartphones and tablets,[211] and they were mostly provided for free.[212] Given that these are free services, market shares based on the volume of unique users are more representative, yet given the dynamic nature of this sector, they offer only a limited account of potential competitive strength.[213] Furthermore, in the consumer communication services market, competition is driven by innovation and quality,[214] and entry barriers are low since consumers can easily download such services,[215] network effects are not strong, and consumers multi-home.[216] The existence of low entry barriers is corroborated by the rapid expansion of new entrants.[217]

III.6.2.2 Horizontal Effects

The Commission assessed potential horizontal effects in the consumer communications market, since both Microsoft, through the Windows Live Messenger (WLM), and Skype offer consumer communication services primarily on

206 *Ibid*, paras 252–256.
207 *Microsoft/Skype* (Case COMP/M.6281) Commission Decision, C(2011) 7279, paras 5–6.
208 *Ibid*, para 17.
209 *Ibid*, paras 29, 37, 42–43, 51, 55, 57, 62, 63.
210 *Ibid*, paras 70–72.
211 *Ibid*, paras 73–74.
212 *Ibid*, para 75.
213 *Ibid*, paras 78–80.
214 *Ibid*, paras 81–84.
215 *Ibid*, para 87.
216 *Ibid*, paras 91–92.
217 *Ibid*, para 93.

Windows-based desktops.[218] Whereas in instant messaging (IM) and voice calls, the increment was lower than 5 per cent and the transaction did not raise concerns,[219] with respect to video calls, it would lead to the creation of the number one player.[220] However, in light of the factors discussed above (namely, the fact that the markets shares are not indicative, the importance of innovation, and the rapid growth of new entrants, and consumers' multi-homing,[221] as well as the competitive constraints from many current market players, primarily Google and Facebook),[222] the transaction did not raise anticompetitive concerns.

III.6.2.3 Conglomerate Effects

The Commission also examined potential conglomerate effects arising from Microsoft leveraging its market power through, for example, degrading Skype's interoperability with competing OSs or conversely degrading competing communication services' interoperability with Windows OS.[223] Microsoft could also potentially tie Windows with Skype, or Skype with Office, or commercially bundle Skype with Windows.[224] However, the Commission found that even though Microsoft would have the ability to engage in such practices, it would lack the incentives.[225]

III.6.2.4 Enterprise Communications Services

In the enterprise communications market, Lync (offered by Microsoft), even though it had a market share of 10–20 per cent, was perceived by market participants as an important player. Lync had also entered the market a year prior to the transaction and gained rapid expansion.[226] However, Skype was not considered a market player in this market, notwithstanding the fact that the Commission noted that it had recently revised its strategy towards small and medium-sized enterprises (SMEs) and enterprise communications.[227] In the market for SMEs communication services, Skype and Microsoft were not considered close competitors.[228] In addition, there were numerous players in the market for enterprise communications.[229] As with the consumer communication services market, similar conglomerate effects were examined but ultimately dismissed.[230]

[218] *Ibid*, para 96.
[219] *Ibid*, paras 110–119.
[220] *Ibid*, para 120.
[221] *Ibid*, paras 121–123, 130.
[222] *Ibid*, para 124.
[223] *Ibid*, paras 135–136.
[224] *Ibid*, paras 137–138.
[225] *Ibid*, paras 143–158.
[226] *Ibid*, para 191.
[227] *Ibid*, paras 192, 196.
[228] *Ibid*, para 197.
[229] *Ibid*, para 200.
[230] *Ibid*, paras 203–222.

The transaction was ultimately cleared in Phase I, and the decision was confirmed by the GC.[231] However, the Commission appears to have disregarded concerns about economies of scope and the integration of the acquiring technologies into Microsoft's existing offers. Microsoft had integrated Skype with Lync to develop Skype for Business, which was then developed to Microsoft Teams.[232]

III.6.3 Microsoft/General Electric (GE) JV

Microsoft and GE announced the creation of a joint intelligence platform for medical data analysis offering health professional advanced analytical tools in December 2011. This JV was cleared by the Commission under the simplified procedure.[233]

III.6.4 Microsoft/Nokia

This deal was announced in September 2013. This transaction gave rise to *horizontal overlaps* between the parties' activities in the development, manufacturing, and sale of smartphones and tablets. Yet, the combined market share was below 15 per cent, and thereby it did not raise any serious concerns for competition.[234]

In addition, the Commission examined *non-horizontal (vertical) effects* with regard to Microsoft's ability and incentive to foreclose competing OEMs by restricting the access to its mobile OS, its Skype and Office apps, and the interoperability between Microsoft's mail server software and competing devices,[235] but ultimately dismissed them.[236]

Finally, the Commission also examined concerns with respect to Nokia's conduct post-transaction about its portfolio of SEPs and non-SEPs relevant for smart mobile devices, and dismissed them. Since this transaction concerned Nokia's Devices & Services Business, and these concerns were relevant for the business retained by Nokia,[237] the Commission ascertained that they fell outside the scope of the EUMR.[238] However, even if they had fallen within EUMR's scope, they would not have raised competitive concerns.[239]

It should be noted that despite this deal being cleared by the Commission in Phase I, MOFCOM—the Chinese Competition Authority at the time—cleared it with conditions.[240]

[231] Case T-79/12 *Cisco Systems Inc v Commission*, ECLI:EU:T:2013:635.
[232] Van den Boom and Samranchit (n73), 368.
[233] *Microsoft/GE/JV* (Case COMP/M.6474) Commission Decision, C(2012) 1017.
[234] *Microsoft/Nokia* (Case COMP/M.7047) Commission Decision, C(2013) 8873, paras 88–91.
[235] *Ibid*, para 92.
[236] *Ibid*, paras 95–184.
[237] *Ibid*, para 222.
[238] *Ibid*, para 224.
[239] *Ibid*, para 238.
[240] N Lomas, 'Microsoft's $7.2BN Deal to Buy Nokia's Devices Business Gets the Nod in China' (8 April 2014) <https://techcrunch.com/2014/04/08/nokia-soft-china-approval> (accessed 9 March 2023).

III.6.5 Microsoft/LinkedIn

This deal was announced in June 2016 and was notified to the Commission in October 2016.[241] The relevant markets were the market for PC OSs (where Microsoft is active with Windows OS),[242] the market for PC productivity software (Microsoft Office),[243] the market for CRM software (Microsoft Dynamics),[244] the market for sales intelligence solutions (LinkedIn Sales Navigator),[245] the market for enterprise communication services (Microsoft Skype for Business),[246] the market for professional social network (PSN) services (LinkedIn),[247] the market for online recruitment services,[248] and the market for online advertising where both parties are active, leaving open the possibility for further segmentation between search and non-search advertising, or advertising on social networking (SN) websites or by device platform, since under any market definition, the transaction did not raise concerns.[249]

III.6.5.1 Horizontal Effects: Data Combination

With respect to horizontal effects, the Commission noted that both parties were active in the online non-search advertising, yet they had a relatively small market share of 5–10 per cent in any EEA Member State, and the market was fragmented, with Facebook and Google being the market leaders.[250] Equally, the Commission dismissed horizontal concerns related to the combination of parties' data post-merger. The Commission reached this conclusion by taking into account 'as a preliminary remark' the fact that such data combination could be implemented to the extent allowed by the applicable data protection rules and noted that the General Data Protection Regulation (GDPR) may limit Microsoft's ability to collect and process users' data since it strengthens existing rights and empowers individuals by giving them more control over their personal data.[251]

The transaction, however, provided that such combination complied with the data protection framework, could still have raised horizontal concerns by first increasing the parties' market power in a hypothetical market for data and/or by increasing entry barriers for actual or potential competitors. Second, even if such combination was not intended or technically feasible, merging parties may have been competing on the basis of data pre-merger, with such competition being eliminated post-merger.[252] The Commission concluded that the transaction did

241 *Microsoft/LinkedIn* (Case COMP/M.8124) Commission Decision, C(2016) 8404, para 1.
242 *Ibid*, paras 9, 15.
243 *Ibid*, paras 20, 25.
244 *Ibid*, paras 31, 50.
245 *Ibid*, paras 58
246 *Ibid*, paras 75,
247 *Ibid*, para 117.
248 *Ibid*, paras 128, 147.
249 *Ibid*, paras 152–161.
250 *Ibid*, para 171.
251 *Ibid*, paras 177–178.
252 *Ibid*, para 179.

not give rise to serious doubts with respect to the above identified concerns for three reasons. First, the parties (with limited exceptions) did not make their data available to third parties. Second, post-merger there would still be a large amount of data available for advertising purposes. And third, the parties were small players in this sector, and there was limited competition between them.[253]

III.6.5.2 Non-Horizontal Effects: Conglomerate Effects—Foreclosure of Competing CRM Software Providers

In terms of non-horizontal effects, the Commission examined first the potential conglomerate effects from any future foreclosure of competing CRM software providers. According to the Commission, the CRM software solutions market was fragmented, and the main players were Salesforce, SAP, Oracle, Microsoft, and Adobe.[254] Microsoft was the fourth player, with a low market share of 0–5 per cent.[255] Sales intelligence solutions were viewed complementarily to CRM software solutions.[256] This market was fragmented as well, with LinkedIn's worldwide market share being below 20–30 per cent and below 10–20 per cent in the EEA.[257] Based on the above, the Commission concluded that the merged entity would have neither the ability nor the incentive to engage in leveraging through bundling or tying its sales intelligence solutions to the CRM software solutions, and any such potential conduct would not have adverse effects on competition.[258]

III.6.5.3 Non-Horizontal Effects: Vertical Effects—Input Foreclosure Regarding LinkedIn's Data

Second, the Commission examined vertical effects with respect to any future input foreclosure strategy adopted by Microsoft. In particular, it looked into whether Microsoft could restrict access to LinkedIn's data (as the input) for machine-learning purposes to competing CRM software solution providers,[259] but dismissed such concerns given that (amongst other things) LinkedIn data is not unique, and there are other sources available.[260]

III.6.5.4 Non-Horizontal: Conglomerate Effects—Foreclosure of PSN Service Providers

Third, the Commission examined conglomerate effects with respect to potential foreclosure of competing PSN services providers.[261] In PSN services, LinkedIn

[253] *Ibid*, paras 180–181.
[254] *Ibid*, paras 193–194.
[255] *Ibid*, para 211.
[256] *Ibid*, paras 206, 218.
[257] *Ibid*, para 217.
[258] *Ibid*, paras 220–245.
[259] *Ibid*, para 246.
[260] *Ibid*, para 262.
[261] *Ibid*, para 279.

was the market leader, with very high market shares in the EEA.[262] Similarly, Microsoft was the market leader for the provision of PC OSs[263] and productivity software.[264] Given its very high market shares, the Commission considered that the merged entity could have both the ability and incentive to engage in leverage into the PSN services market.[265] In particular, the practices identified concerned the pre-installation of LinkedIn on Windows PCs and the integration of LinkedIn features into Office and denying similar integration to competitors through denying access to Microsoft's APIs.[266] Such practices raised concerns, as noted by the Commission, especially in the light of the power of defaults resting on an identified users' inertia driven by the 'status quo bias'.[267] The Commission analysis concluded that Microsoft would have both the ability and incentive to engage in such foreclosure practices post-transaction, and the latter would significantly impact competition in the market, granting an unrivalled advantage to LinkedIn.[268] According to the Commission analysis, such practices would lead to market tipping in favour of LinkedIn, especially in the light of networks effects in the PSN services market.[269] Such a negative effect of the network effects in this case was not likely to be mitigated by user multi-homing or potential entry.[270] In a Statement of Principle, the Commission highlighted the fact that networks effects have to be assessed on a case-by-case basis, given that

> [t]he existence of network effects as such does not a priori indicate a competition problem in the market affected by a merger. Such effects may however raise competition concerns in particular if they allow the merged entity to foreclose competitors and make more difficult for competing providers to expand their customer base.[271]

Market tipping would lead to consumer harm in the form of reduced choice as well as the potential marginalization of an existing competitor that offers an enhanced privacy solution.[272]

III.6.5.5 Other Non-Horizontal Concerns

Finally, the Commission assessed and dismissed potential conglomerate effects with respect to the foreclosure of competing online recruitment service

[262] *Ibid*, paras 286.
[263] *Ibid*, paras 288–289.
[264] *Ibid*, paras 291–293.
[265] *Ibid*, para 295.
[266] *Ibid*, para 302.
[267] *Ibid*, para 309.
[268] *Ibid*, para 338.
[269] *Ibid*, paras 339–340.
[270] *Ibid*, para 344.
[271] *Ibid*, para 342.
[272] *Ibid*, paras 349–350.

providers,[273] and of competing enterprise communication service providers,[274] as well as potential vertical effects with respect to foreclosure of competing software productivity providers.[275]

III.6.5.6 Remedies

In the light of the above-identified concerns about potential foreclosure of competing PSN service providers, Microsoft offered remedies early on during Phase I, covering a five-year period, namely the Integration Commitments to address concerns about the possible integration of LinkedIn features into Office and the Pre-Installation Commitments to address concerns about potential pre-installation of LinkedIn on Windows PCs.[276]

III.6.6 Microsoft/Github

Microsoft announced the prospective acquisition of Github, a software development platform, in June 2018. This transaction did not meet the EUMR notification thresholds; nonetheless, the company referred it to the Commission under Article 4(5) EUMR since it fell under national merger control rules in four Member States.[277] The Commission assessed the following concerns: first, horizontal effects related to the supply of DevOps tools; second, conglomerate effects on competing DevOps tools and/or competing infrastructure-as-a-service/platform-as-a-service (IaaS/PaaS) since GitHub had more than 30 per cent of the potential market for source code-hosting services for version control and collaboration; and finally, non-horizontal concerns with respect to potential refusal or degrading access to GitHub's data.[278]

III.6.6.1 Horizontal Effects

Horizontal effects in the potential overall market for DevOps tools were dismissed since there was limited overlap between the parties, while there were many competitors that were active in the market.[279] Equally, the Commission concluded that the transaction would not give rise to anticompetitive horizontal effects in the potential market for source code-hosting services for version control and collaboration since Microsoft's online hosting platform (Visual Studio Teams Services—VSTS) and on-premise solution did not present a credible alternative to GitHub's online source code-hosting platform and on-premise solution, respectively; the parties were not close competitors; sufficient alternative providers would remain

[273] *Ibid*, para 368.
[274] *Ibid*, para 406.
[275] *Ibid*, para 381.
[276] *Ibid*, paras 407–409, 410, 435.
[277] *Microsoft/Github* (Case M.8994) Commission Decision, C(2018) 7020, paras 8–11.
[278] *Ibid*, paras 78–80.
[279] *Ibid*, para 81.

on the market post-merger; switching was fairly easy and was further facilitated by users' multi-homing; network effects were counterbalanced by the possibility of switching; and Microsoft would not have the incentive to block the portability of data to a rival version control service.[280] Finally, the Commission dismissed horizontal concerns in the potential market for code editors and integrated development environments (IDEs) since there was a large number of competitors and GitHub's offering (Atom IDE) is open source, so it would be easy for developers to fork the code and launch a copy in the event that Microsoft stopped supporting Atom.[281]

III.6.6.2 Non-Horizontal Effects

Conglomerate concerns with respect to competing DevOps tools were dismissed as well, since according to the Commission's analysis, Microsoft would have neither the ability nor the incentive to foreclose competing DevOps tools providers by further integrating Microsoft's DevOps tools with GitHub.[282] With respect to conglomerate effects regarding competing IaaS/PaaS, the Commission concluded that Microsoft would not have the ability or incentive to foreclose competition by further integrating Microsoft's Azure with GitHub or by degrading or limiting the interoperability of competing IaaS/PaaS with GitHub.[283] Vertical concerns with respect to Microsoft's refusal or degradation of access to GitHub's data to its downstream competitors of DevOps tools and/or IaaS/PaaS were also dismissed.[284]

III.6.7 Microsoft/Zenimax

This deal was announced in September 2020. The transaction was reviewed by the Commission following the parties' reasoned submission under Article 4(5) EUMR since it was capable of being reviewed in Austria, Cyprus, and Germany.[285] The Commission assessed potential customer foreclosure to Microsoft's console specific digital storefronts (the Microsoft and Xbox Store) for competing publishers of console videogames. Such concerns were dismissed since, despite being technically possible, the merged entity would lack the ability and incentive to engage in such a strategy as there were sufficient economic alternatives for competitors to sell their output in the downstream market.[286] In the light of such alternative distribution channels, such a strategy would not have an effect on competition.[287] Furthermore, the Commission evaluated the potential input foreclosure

[280] *Ibid*, paras 93–106.
[281] *Ibid*, paras 108–109.
[282] *Ibid*, para 114.
[283] *Ibid*, para 125.
[284] *Ibid*, paras 139–140.
[285] *Microsoft/Zenimax* (Case M.10001) Commission Decision, C(2021) 1607, para 7.
[286] *Ibid*, paras 69, 82.
[287] *Ibid*, para 89.

emanating from foreclosing access to ZeniMax digital console video games for competing console video game distributors. Despite ZeniMax's popular game offerings (e.g. 'The Elder Scrolls' and 'Fallout'), the merged entity would not have the ability or incentive to foreclose competing console distributors by refusing to offer ZeniMax games to rival consoles or degrading the terms for offering such games.[288] However, even if they were to implement such a strategy, the latter would not have an effect on competition, since rival consoles could still benefit from the large number of video games available.[289]

III.6.8 Microsoft/Nuance

The deal was announced in April 2021. The transaction was reviewed by the Commission following the parties' reasoned submission under Article 4(5) EUMR since it was capable of being reviewed in Austria, Denmark, and Germany.[290]

The markets affected by this transaction were the following: transcription software, customer engagement solutions, cloud computing services, enterprise communication services, productivity software, and customer relationship management software.[291]

The Commission assessed first horizontal overlaps with regard to transcription software (including its use for accessibility purposes) and customer engagement solutions.[292] It concluded that there were no horizontally affected markets.[293]

Second, it looked into vertical effects stemming from the vertical relationship between Microsoft's cloud computing services (upstream) and Nuance's provision of transcription software for health care (downstream).[294] In particular, the Commission assessed potential input foreclosure by restricting access to Microsoft's cloud services and data analytics to rival health-care transcription software providers. It concluded that Microsoft would not have the ability to engage in such foreclosure given that there were other important providers of cloud computing services, with Amazon being the most powerful followed by Microsoft, Google, Alibaba, and IBM.[295] The Commission further assessed potential customer foreclosure by Microsoft restricting access to Nuance to rival cloud computer service providers. Such concerns were also dismissed due to a lack of ability and incentive to foreclose as well as anticompetitive effects.[296] In addition, the Commission

[288] *Ibid*, paras 102, 115.
[289] *Ibid*, para 125.
[290] *Microsoft/Nuance* (Case M.10290) Commission Decision, C(2021) 9923, para 8.
[291] *Ibid*, para 10.
[292] *Ibid*, para 98.
[293] *Ibid*, para 102 (customer engagement solutions market), para 111 (health-care transcription software market), para 117 (transcription software market outside health care), para 123 (potential market for accessibility software).
[294] *Ibid*, para 99.
[295] *Ibid*, para 132.
[296] *Ibid*, paras 144–147.

looked into potential input foreclosure by restricting access to Nuance's data, but such concerns were dismissed. The Commission first acknowledged that there was no market for medical data, and in any event, even if such a market existed, Nuance did provide its data to any third parties.[297] In a similar vein as in *Apple/Shazam*, the Commission pointed to existing data protection regulatory limitations for the combination of such data.[298] However, even if such combination were allowed, according to the results of the Commission's market investigation, Nuance's database did not constitute an important input for any downstream market.[299]

Finally, the Commission evaluated conglomerate effects with respect to a number of markets: Nuance's transcription software for health care and Microsoft's enterprise communication services, as well as Microsoft's CRM software; and Nuance's transcription software outside health care and Microsoft's productivity software, as well as Microsoft's PC OS.[300] Such concerns were dismissed due to a lack of incentive and ability as well as potential effects on competition in all of the above markets.[301]

III.6.9 Microsoft/Activision

The deal was announced in January 2022. Following its in-depth Phase II investigation, the Commission cleared the transaction with commitments.[302] Activision has developed many popular games, including 'Call of Duty'. Microsoft (amongst others) is a distributor for console games and also offers the Xbox console, together with a wide range of other products and services, including the PC 'Windows' OS.[303]

III.6.9.1 Vertical Effects: Rival Consoles

The Commission concluded that Microsoft would lack the incentive to refuse to distribute Activision's games to Sony via its console Sony PlayStation. To the contrary, since Sony is the leading distributor of console games, Microsoft would have strong incentives to continue distributing Activision's games to Sony. However, even if Microsoft engaged in such refusal, Sony could counteract such an attempt to weaken its position given its strong market position and extensive games catalogue.[304]

III.6.9.2 Vertical Effects: Cloud-Streaming Services

On the contrary, the Commission concluded that the transaction would have a negative impact on the distribution of PC and console games via cloud streaming services, since Microsoft may distribute Activision games exclusively on its own

[297] *Ibid*, para 150.
[298] *Ibid*, paras 155–160.
[299] *Ibid*, para 162.
[300] *Ibid*, para 100.
[301] *Ibid*, in particular, paras 184, 201, 223, 236, 253, 265.
[302] *Microsoft/Activision Blizzard* (Case M.10646) Commission Decision, C(2023) 3199; European Commission (EU), 'Commission Clears Acquisition of Activision Blizzard by Microsoft, Subject to Conditions' (Press release, 15 May 2023).
[303] *Microsoft/Activision Blizzard* (n301).
[304] *Ibid*.

platform (Game Pass Ultimate). Cloud game streaming, despite its current limited use, constitutes an innovative market segment, which, in the future, may transform online gaming. Such exclusive distribution of Activision games on Microsoft's own cloud game-streaming service could further strengthen Windows' position in the PC OS market, in the event that Microsoft hinders or degrades the streaming of Activision's games on PCs using other OSs.[305]

III.6.9.3 Remedies

In order to address the Commission's concerns regarding the distribution of PC and console games via cloud streaming, Microsoft offered a package of ten-year licensing commitments allowing consumers to stream all Activision Blizzard PC and console games via any cloud game streaming services.[306]

On the contrary, the UK CMA blocked the deal based on the same theory of harm, considering the remedies offered inadequate.[307] Following the decision not to grant FTC's preliminary injunction to block the deal in the United States, it seems that the CMA approach is the odd one out.[308] Following this outcome in the United States, in an unexpected move, the CMA issued a statement stating that the authority was prepared to consider Microsoft's proposals to restructure the transaction in order to address its concerns and agreed with the parties to stay litigation in the United Kingdom.[309] On 22 August 2023, the parties notified to the CMA Microsoft's acquisition of Activision, excluding Activision's global cloud streaming rights outside the EEA. All current and future Activision games released in the next fifteen years will be divested to Ubisoft Entertainment SA (Ubisoft). This was treated as a separate merger investigation by the CMA, which ultimately cleared the transaction.[310]

III.7 GAFAM Acquisition Reviewed in the EU

Table 6.1 summarizes the GAFAM transactions reviewed by the Commission.

[305] *Ibid.*

[306] *Ibid.*

[307] CMA, 'Anticipated Acquisition by Microsoft of Activision Blizzard, Inc' (Final Report, 26 April 2023) <https://assets.publishing.service.gov.uk/media/644939aa529eda000c3b0525/Microsoft_Activision_Final_Report_.pdf>. See also CMA, 'Microsoft/Activision Deal Prevented to Protect Innovation and Choice in Cloud Gaming' (Press release, 26 April 2023) <https://www.gov.uk/government/news/microsoft-activision-deal-prevented-to-protect-innovation-and-choice-in-cloud-gaming> (both accessed 9 June 2024).

[308] S Palma and R Waters, 'US Judge Denies FTC Attempt to Block Microsoft's Activision Deal' (*Financial Times*, 11 July 2023). See *FTC v Microsoft*, Case No 23-cv-02880-JSC <https://s3.documentcloud.org/documents/23870711/ftc-v-microsoft-preliminary-injunction-opinion.pdf> (accessed 9 June 2024).

[309] Palma and Waters (n307). See Case 1590/4/12/23 *Microsoft Corporation v Competition and Markets Authority*, [2023] CAT.

[310] CMA, 'Microsoft/Activision Blizzard (Ex-Cloud Streaming Rights) Merger Inquiry' (22 August 2023) <https://www.gov.uk/cma-cases/microsoft-slash-activision-blizzard-ex-cloud-streaming-rights-merger-inquiry> (accessed 9 June 2024).

Table 6.1 GAFAM acquisitions

Company	Phase I clearance	Phase I commitments	Phase II clearance	Phase II (abandoned)	Phase II commitments
Google (Alphabet)	*Google/Motorola Mobility*		*Google/DoubleClick*		*Google/Fitbit*
	Google/Sanofi/JV				
Apple	*Apple/Beats*		*Apple/Shazam*		
Facebook (Meta)	*Facebook/WhatsApp*	*Meta/Kustomer*			
Amazon	*Amazon/MGM*			*Amazon/iRobot*	
Microsoft	*Microsoft/Yahoo*	*Microsoft/LinkedIn*			*Microsoft/Activision*
	Microsoft/Skype				
	Microsoft/GE/JV (Simplified proc)				
	Microsoft/Nokia				
	Microsoft/Github				
	Microsoft/Zenimax				
	Microsoft/Nuance				

III.8 United Kingdom

The UK experience is briefly discussed—since the CMA has risen as one of the leading authorities in examining tech deals. In addition, it will be interesting to see how its approach will develop post-Brexit, especially with respect to deals that have to be reviewed by both the Commission and the CMA. This is even more interesting, given the fact that the CMA has already issued a prohibition decision against Meta on the basis of the impact on dynamic competition and vertical effects,[311] as well as a very controversial decision against Microsoft regarding the acquisition of Activision.[312]

The CMA has also commissioned a merger retrospective study in order to evaluate UK competition authorities' past decisional practice with respect to digital mergers.[313] Amongst the cases reviewed were *Facebook/Instagram* and *Google/Waze*, discussed below. Interestingly, the study, while highlighting the importance of the selected counterfactual and the difficulties in assessing anticompetitive effects with countervailing efficiencies, stressed that the analysis was overly focused on the users' side of the market, overlooking other sides in a multi-sided market setting and disregarding the importance of the respective services' monetization strategy.[314]

Finally, the CMA has updated its Merger Assessment Guidelines to take into account the characteristics of digital mergers, including a new section on the assessment of potential and dynamic competition.[315]

III.8.1 Facebook/Instagram

With respect to this transaction, in a very short decision the Office of Fair Trading (OFT) examined *two unilateral effects theories of harm*, namely actual competition in the supply of photo apps and potential competition in the supply of social network services.[316] With respect to the former, the OFT concluded that there already exist several relatively strong competitors exerting a stronger constraint on Instagram than Facebook's new app. In addition, the responses in the market investigation indicated that photo apps are not attractive to advertisers on a stand-alone basis but as a complement to social networks.[317] However, in order to assess the closeness of competition, the OFT relied on the number of app downloads,

[311] CMA, 'CMA Orders Meta to Sell Giphy' (Press release, 18 October 2022) <https://www.gov.uk/government/news/cma-orders-meta-to-sell-giphy> (accessed 16 May 2024).

[312] See text to n306 above.

[313] Lear, 'Ex-Post Assessment of Merger Control Decisions in Digital Markets' (Final Report, prepared by E Argentesi et al) (Lear Report, 9 May 2019), ii.

[314] *Ibid*, xii.

[315] CMA, 'Merger Assessment Guidelines' (n145), section 5.

[316] OFT, 'Anticipated Acquisition by Facebook Inc of Instagram Inc', ME/5525/12 (14 August 2012), para 14.

[317] *Ibid*, para 21.

and whilst acknowledging that 'this is an imprecise measure of market share', it nonetheless maintained that 'it gives some indication of the availability and popularity of other photo sharing apps'.[318] It has been suggested, though, that merely downloading an app is not an accurate metric for user engagement but, rather, authorities should use other metrics, such as the number of active users over a period of time.[319]

With respect to the latter, the OFT examined the possible loss of potential competition in the supply of online display advertising.[320] The authority acknowledged that it is likely that Facebook was aware of Instagram's growing user base. Instagram was declared Apple's App of the Year in 2011 and its users included high-profile individuals, such as Barack Obama.[321] It concluded that, based on the evidence, Instagram would not compete with Facebook in the short run and that, at the moment, other firms (Google, Yahoo, and Microsoft) compete against Facebook for brand advertising.[322]

The OFT then examined and dismissed *two vertical theories of harm*, namely potential foreclosure of competing social networks by preventing Instagram users from uploading their photos to Facebook and potential foreclosure of other photo apps by limiting users from uploading their photos to Facebook.[323] According to the OFT, even if the merged entity had the technical ability to engage in foreclosure strategies, it would not have the incentive to do so.

What is missing from the OFT's analysis is the assessment of potential competition between Facebook and Instagram in the market for attention.[324] Empirical data post-merger suggest that by increasing Facebook's user base and users' engagement, Instagram's acquisition substantially increased its attractiveness to advertisers.[325] Yet ultimately, and despite the criticism levelled against the OFT's assessment, it is difficult to predict which counterfactual is more likely.[326]

[318] *Ibid*, para 17.

[319] Argentesi et al (n7), 117.

[320] Interestingly, in para 14, the OFT refers to potential competition in the supply of virtual social network services and then moves on to discuss online display advertising. See OFT, 'Anticipated Acquisition by Facebook Inc of Instagram Inc' (n315). This is explicable by the nature of social networks as two-sided markets. See *ibid*, para 7:

> Social networks are two-sided markets. They compete to add users and to attract advertising revenue. Advertisers are willing to pay to purchase advertising space on the social networks' sites and apps based on the number of users that the network has and the information that the networks records on those users (for example, their demographics).

[321] *Ibid*, para 25.

[322] *Ibid*, paras 28–29.

[323] *Ibid*, para 30.

[324] Argentesi et al (n7), 118–119.

[325] *Ibid*, 122–123. See also Lear Report (n312), vi–vii.

[326] Argentesi et al (n7, 126.

III.8.2 Google/Waze

Google (through its wholly owned subsidiary Motorola Mobility Holding) acquired Waze in 2013.[327] Waze provides turn-by-turn, maps-based services[328] on mobile devices, whereas Google Maps is available on the Internet, including mobile devices.[329] Thus, the OFT examined whether the merger would potentially result in the loss of a growing and innovative rival that exerted a constraint on Google, which may grow increasingly strong in the future with the result that innovation incentives would be reduced and consumers would be presented with services of lesser quality.[330] In assessing the unilateral horizontal effects of the transaction, the OFT relied on data for downloads and usage in 2012 for both the iOS and Android platforms provided by the parties.[331] The OFT took into account evidence about the functionality of the parties' applications, quality, and coverage, internal documents, and third-party views and concluded that, at the moment, Waze did not present a strong competitive constraint on Google in the United Kingdom.[332] In terms of potential competition, the OFT noted that Waze had expanded it user base in a short time period, and its growth had been faster than competing applications.[333] The OFT assessed whether its growth could accelerate due to network effects in mapping and community as well as through potential partnerships.[334] It concluded that Waze had not achieved sufficient scale in the United Kingdom to benefit from 'significant and insuperable' network effects, and overall, it had not appeared to emerge as a disruptive competitive force.[335] In addition, Apple Maps represents a strong competitive constraint on Google Maps, and other providers also exert some, although a rather limited, competitive constraint.[336] Based on the above, the OFT cleared the transaction.

However, what is missing from its analysis is the assessment of the possible impact of the transaction on the advertising side of the market.[337] Furthermore, Apple Maps is only available on iOS devices, therefore rendering questionable whether it exerts a strong competitive constraint.[338]

[327] OFT, 'Completed Acquisition by Motorola Mobility Holding (Google, Inc) of/Waze Mobile Limited', ME6167/13.
[328] Turn-by-turn navigation systems are updated based on factors such as traffic and road conditions and provide the user with up-to-date directions for a selected route in the form of spoken and/or visual instructions. See *ibid*.
[329] *Ibid*, paras 2–3.
[330] *Ibid*, paras 26–28.
[331] *Ibid*, para 29.
[332] *Ibid*, paras 31, 39.
[333] *Ibid*, paras 41–42.
[334] *Ibid*, para 44.
[335] *Ibid*, paras 49–52.
[336] *Ibid*, para 74.
[337] Argentesi et al (n7), 128.
[338] *Ibid*, 129.

III.8.3 Facebook/Giphy

Facebook completed Giphy's acquisition on 15 May 2020. The CMA asserted jurisdiction on the basis of the share-of-supply test.[339] Following the CMA's prohibition decision, Facebook was forced to sell Giphy as the only way to address the CMA's concerns, namely the removal of Giphy as a potential competitor in the display advertising market and the reduction of competition between social media platforms.[340]

III.8.3.1 Horizontal Effects: Loss of Dynamic Competition in Display Advertising

Prior to the merger, Giphy had introduced innovative advertising services and was planning to expand these outside the United States, including in the United Kingdom. Such services had the potential to compete with Facebook's display advertising services as well as encourage greater innovation from other market players, such as social media services and advertisers. Facebook had terminated Giphy's advertising services, thereby eliminating an important source of potential and dynamic competition.[341]

II.8.3.2 Vertical Effects: Input Foreclosure by Limiting Access to Giphy's Database for Rival Social Media

The CMA concluded that the transaction would allow Meta to strengthen its already powerful position in social media by limiting competitors' access to Giphy graphics interchange formats (GIFs) and driving more traffic to Meta-owned sites—Facebook, WhatsApp, and Instagram.[342]

The CMA rejected the behavioural remedies offered by Meta and ultimately concluded that only Giphy's divestiture would address its concerns.[343]

339 CMA, 'Completed Acquisition by Facebook, Inc (now Meta Platforms, Inc) of Giphy, Inc' (Final Report, 30 November 2021), para 3.50.

340 CMA, 'CMA Directs Facebook to Sell Giphy' (Press release, 30 November 2021) <https://www.gov.uk/government/news/cma-directs-facebook-to-sell-giphy> (accessed 9 June 2024).

341 CMA, 'Completed Acquisition by Facebook, Inc (now Meta Platforms, Inc) of Giphy, Inc' (n339), section 7. Facebook appealed (Case 1429/4/12/21). The Competition Appeals Tribunal (CAT) rejected all of Meta's substantive grounds of appeal and upheld one procedural ground related to flaws in confidentiality redactions; it quashed the Final Report and remitted the case back to the CMA for reconsideration. See *Meta v CMA*, [2022] CAT 26. The Final Report following the remittal inquiry confirmed the theories of harm investigated in the first report. See CMA, 'Completed Acquisition by Facebook, Inc (now Meta Platforms, Inc) of Giphy, Inc' (Final Report on the case remitted to the CMA by the Competition Appeal Tribunal, 18 October 2022). On 30 June 2023, the CMA approved the purchase of Giphy by Shutterstock. See CMA, 'Facebook, Inc (Now Meta Platforms, Inc)/Giphy, Inc Merger Inquiry' (updated 30 June 2023) <https://www.gov.uk/cma-cases/facebook-inc-giphy-inc-merger-inquiry> (accessed 9 June 2024).

342 CMA, 'Completed Acquisition by Facebook, Inc (now Meta Platforms, Inc) of Giphy Inc' (n338), section 8.

343 *Ibid*, section 11.

IV. Killer Acquisitions: Theories of Harm

IV.1 Introduction: Characteristics of Digital Mergers

Section III has discussed the GAFAM transactions that have been reviewed, and ultimately cleared, by the European Commission. Below, we present the main characteristics of digital mergers that contextualize the assessment of merger transactions in the digital economy. Such transactions take place in dynamic markets, and for years they were viewed under the lens of the 'garage myth' and the potential next 'big thing' that could challenge the existing powerful players. They often concern nascent companies that are taken over for substantial amounts but that are yet to generate the turnover necessary to trigger merger control rules. The substantive analysis of such transactions is itself complicated due to the characteristics of the digital economy discussed in Chapter 2, such as the prevalence of multi-sided platforms, the emergence of digital ecosystems, the existence of network effects, and the role of data in merger assessments.[344] Finally, past experience with the few transactions that have been reviewed points to difficulties in devising remedies as well as the incumbent's tendency to misrepresent their ability to cross-share data between the different services they offer.

The FTC complaint against Facebook, by relying on internal documents, highlights the mechanics behind start-up acquisitions. To quote an email exchange between Mark Zuckerberg and Facebook's Chief Financial Officer David Ebersman, Zuckerberg explains that

> [t]here are network effects around social products and a finite number of different social mechanics to invent. Once someone wins at a specific mechanic, it's difficult for others to supplant them without doing something different. It's possible someone beats Instagram by building something that is better to the point that they get network migration, but this is harder as long as Instagram keeps running as a product. [Integrating Instagram's functions into Facebook] is also a factor but in reality we already know these companies' social dynamics and will integrate them over the next 12–24 months anyway. The integration plan involves building their mechanics into our products rather than directly integrating their products if that makes sense.... [O]ne way of looking at this is that what we're really buying is time. Even if some new competitors spring [. . .] up, buying Instagram, Path, Foursquare, etc now will give us a year or more to integrate their dynamics before anyone can get close to their scale again. Within that time, if we incorporate the social mechanics they were using, those new products won't get much traction since we'll already have their mechanics deployed at scale.[345]

[344] See Chapter 2, sections III.3 and IV.

[345] *FTC v Facebook* (1:20-cv-03590) (9 December 2021) <https://www.ftc.gov/system/files/documents/cases/051_2021.01.21_revised_partially_redacted_complaint.pdf> (accessed 9 June 2024), para 14.

Below, we thread out and briefly discuss the main characteristics of digital mergers.

IV.1.1 Dynamic Markets and the Garage Myth

In digital mergers, the market dynamics may arguably change very quickly, and current incumbents may be easily displaced by innovative start-ups. The often-repeated dictum that 'competition is only a click away' fuels Big Tech arguments that competition authorities should be cautious in reviewing such transactions. For example, in *Google/DoubleClick*, the notifying parties, with reference to the history of Internet search in the 1990s, with Excite being succeeded by AltaVista and then Lycos, submitted that search advertising is a dynamic market, where technological developments easily impact market positions.[346] Yet, the myth of the start-up garage has begun to wane,[347] since the path to success is dependent on a multitude of variables, such as access to finance and talent as well as links with research universities.[348]

In dynamic markets with frequent entries and short innovation cycles, proxies such as market share may not be an indicator of market power.[349] For example, the Commission found that the consumer communications sector exhibits such characteristics and therefore even large market shares may change and do not necessarily allude to market power.[350] On the contrary, Shazam, a company providing music recognition services, was found not to be a start-up company, given that it is in operation for almost twenty years and launched its first smartphone app in 2008.[351]

IV.1.2 Low Turnover–High Value Targets

Despite the Big Tech acquisition spree, very few of these transactions have been reviewed by competition authorities, since they have not met the turnover thresholds for the application of merger control rules. Some of these transactions have been reviewed by NCAs where the applicable domestic merger control rules allowed for alternative thresholds (apart from turnover), such as the 'share-of-supply' test in the United Kingdom.[352] When Facebook acquired Instagram in 2012 for USD 300 million and 22,999,412 shares of Facebook common stock, Instagram had 13 employees and had not generated any turnover since it was established.[353] The UK

[346] *Google/DoubleClick* (n46), para 335 and fn 170.

[347] Microsoft, Google, Amazon, and Apple claim that they started in garages. See World Economic Forum, 'Forget the Start-Up Garage Myth. We Need Golden Triangles and Super Clusters' (3 November 2016) <https://www.weforum.org/agenda/2016/11/the-startup-garage-myth> (accessed 17 February 2023).

[348] Laitenberger (n3).

[349] *Apple/Shazam* (n48), para 162.

[350] *Facebook/WhatsApp* (n47), para 99; *Cisco Systems Inc* (n230), para 69.

[351] *Apple/Shazam* (n48), para 162.

[352] See text to nn52 and 338.

[353] OFT, 'Anticipated Acquisition by Facebook Inc of Instagram Inc' (n315), paras 2–5. Instagram users' base, though, grew rapidly from 1.4 million users in January 2011 to around 24 million users in February 2012. See *ibid*, para 36.

competition authority ascertained jurisdiction based on the share-of-supply test, since both parties were active in the supply of virtual social networking services; Facebook's respective share of supply was over 25 per cent and Instagram's acquisition would have resulted in an increment.[354]

IV.1.3 Challenges in Predicting the Outcome of the Transaction

Network effects in digital markets transform competition dynamics in that competition is for the market rather than in the market. As a result, smaller competitors or potential entrants may exert a competitive threat. Network effects cement dominance and may lead to markets tipping; at the same time, though, they may allow new entrants to scale up quickly and challenge the incumbents.[355]

As stated in the respective Guidelines, '[n]etwork effects occur when the value of a product for a customer increases when the number of other customers also using it increases. Examples include communication devices, specific software programmes, products requiring standardisation, and platforms bringing together buyers and sellers.'[356] The Commission has repeatedly acknowledged that the existence of network effects does not prejudice the outcome of the assessment, but rather it has to be assessed on a case-by-case basis whether they lead to competitors' foreclosure or hampering rivals' ability to expand their customer basis. Network effects may be mitigated in the presence of multi-homing or by potential entry.[357]

For example, in *Microsoft/Skype*, the Commission examined network effects.[358] Respondents indicated that network effects in the consumer communications markets constitute a barrier to expansion, since the larger the number of users a provider of communications has, the easier it is to further grow its user base.[359] However, the Commission accepted that network effects are mitigated by the fact that there is an observed degree of consumer multi-homing between various providers of consumer communications services,[360] as well as low barriers to expansion since new entrants have succeeded in increasing their active users.[361]

In contrast, the assessment in *Microsoft/LinkedIn* concluded that the pre-installation of a LinkedIn application on Windows PCs, the integration of LinkedIn features into Office, and the denial of access to Microsoft APIs were likely to foreclose LinkedIn's competitors and have a negative impact on competition among

354 *Ibid*, para 5.

355 Glick and Ruetschlin (n8), 6.

356 European Commission (EU), 'Guidelines on the Assessment of Non-Horizontal Mergers under the Council Regulation on the Control of Concentrations between Undertakings' (18 October 2008) OJ C 265/6 (Non-Horizontal Mergers Guidelines, NHMG), para 62, n4.

357 *Google/DoubleClick* (n46), paras 342, 344.

358 *Microsoft/Skype* (n206).

359 *Ibid*, para 91.

360 *Ibid*, para 92. On the impact of consumer multi-homing, see (amongst others) S Athey, E Calvano, and J Gans, 'The Impact of Consumer Multi-Homing on Advertising Markets and Media Competition' (2018) 64 Management Science 1574.

361 *Microsoft/Skype* (n206), para 93.

PSN services. Such negative effects would be exacerbated by the presence of network effects in the absence of multi-homing and potential entry with respect to PSN services.[362] The transaction was cleared following commitments addressing these concerns.

Empirical research suggests that the majority of Big Tech acquisitions concern relatively young companies, with most targets being aged four years or younger.[363] Given the fact that the respective companies' future evolution at the time of the acquisition is uncertain, it is more difficult to make future predictions about the merger outcomes and the counterfactual in the absence of the merger.

IV.1.4 Zero-Price Markets/Attention Markets

Apart from the strong presence of network effects, mergers in digital markets often take place in *attention/zero priced markets*. The often-repeated quote that 'if you don't pay for the product, then you are the product' encapsulates the business model of ad-based digital platforms striving to attract consumer attention and thereby consumer data, in order to monetize these data on the advertising side of the multi-sided market. Thus, mergers between companies operating on an ad-funded business model aiming to capture consumer attention increase their respective market power in these advertising markets, irrespective of the substitutability of their offers.[364] In this case, multi-homing, which can be assessed as a mitigating factor of the exacerbation of network effects, increases the market power of the incumbents when it takes place between the merging parties' products.[365]

IV.1.5 Difficulties in Devising Remedies and Following through Promises

For digital mergers, in those instances that have been reviewed by competition authorities, it has been very difficult to devise appropriate remedies. Such remedies need to be forward looking and ideally easy to monitor, not allowing any leeway for the incumbents to circumvent them. In addition, competition authorities need to hold incumbents accountable if they do not follow through with the promises made during the merger review process.

For example, when Facebook acquired WhatsApp, it pledged not to share any data—a promise that has subsequently been broken.[366] Another example comes from *Google/DoubleClick*, where Google promised to keep information collected through Gmail separate from information on data-browsing records; later, it

[362] *Microsoft/LinkedIn* (n240), paras 302, 339–340, 351–352.
[363] Gautier and Lamesch (n11), 14; Lear Report (n312), ii.
[364] For an assessment of potential anticompetitive effects, see A Prat and T Valletti, 'Attention Oligopoly' (2022) 14 American Economic Journal: Microeconomics 530.
[365] Argentesi et al (n7), 107.
[366] See n158.

announced that browsing information 'may be' combined with information collected through Gmail and other Google services.[367]

IV.2 Theories of Harm

Chapter II has discussed in particular the challenges pertaining to the market definition analysis and the assessment of market power in the digital economy.[368] Such a discussion is, of course, relevant for the assessment of digital mergers as well. Starting from the multi-sided nature of platforms and the pervasiveness of digital ecosystems, here we focus on some selected issues that often play an important role in the substantive analysis of digital mergers. Overall, non-price considerations such as innovation, quality, and privacy have a larger role to play in digital mergers. Yet, despite the fact that non-price effects are taken into account and mentioned in the relevant merger guidelines,[369] cases where non-price effects have played a central role as well as the availability of dedicated analytical tools for their assessment are rather limited.[370]

IV.2.1 Conglomerate Concerns: Ecosystem Competition

Mergers in the digital economy take place between companies that control their own digital ecosystems, offering a range of complementary products and services. As such, they raise conglomerate concerns, which traditionally have been less central in merger control, since they are perceived to be less likely to impact on effective competition and may result in efficiencies.[371] Since the Commission's controversial assessment of conglomerate effects in *GE/Honeywell*[372] and *Tetra Laval/Sidel*,[373] the Commission has only rarely

[367] T Valletti, '"An Offer We Can't Refuse": How We Gave Away Our Data and Made Big Tech What It Is Today' (18 January 2021) <https://www.promarket.org/2021/01/18/facebook-whatsapp-terms-of-service-ads-data-privacy/https://www.promarket.org/2021/01/18/facebook-whatsapp-terms-of-service-ads-data-privacy> (accessed 20 February 2023).

[368] See section V.

[369] EU HMG (n59), para 8; CMA MAG (n145), paras 2.4–2.5.

[370] OECD (Organisation for Economic Co-operation and Development), 'Considering Non-Price Effects in Merger Control—Background Note by the Secretariat', DAF/COMP(2018)2 (2018), para 3. For a list of cases in the United Kingdom where non-price effects were the main factor in the analysis, see CMA MAG (n145), n16.

[371] NHMG (n355), paras 11–14. For a detailed discussion, see OECD, 'Roundtable on Conglomerate Effects of Mergers—Background Note', DAF/COMP(2020)2 (24 May 2020).

[372] *General Electric/Honeywell* (Case COMP/M.2220) Commission Decision, [2004] OJ L 48/1, upheld in Case T-210/01 *General Electric Company v Commission*, ECLI:EU:T:2005:456. In this case though, the GC was critical of the Commission's conglomerate effects analysis and upheld the decision on the basis of the horizontal effects assessment.

[373] *Tetra Laval/Sidel* (Case COMP/M.2416) Commission Decision, [2004] OJ L 43/13, annulled by the EU courts. See Case T-5/02 *Tetra Laval v Commission*, ECLI:EU:T:2002:264, upheld in Case C-12/03P *Commission v Tetra Laval*, ECLI:EU:C:2005:87.

examined conglomerate effects.[374] This trend has been reversed with respect to digital mergers reviewed by the Commission, where conglomerate effects have been reviewed in ten cases.[375] The majority of these cases were cleared unconditionally, whereas *Microsoft/LinkedIn*, *Google/Fitbit*, and *Meta/Kustomer* were cleared following commitments to address conglomerate concerns.

It has been proposed that merger control should tighten its assessment when it comes to conglomerate effects of digital mergers. This is because complementarities and economies of scope resulting from conglomerate mergers, even though they may result in short-term efficiencies, are harmful in the long run because they lead to anticompetitive foreclosure. Thus, such long-run anticompetitive effects need to inform the competition authorities' analysis.[376] Given the propensity of digital mergers to raise conglomerate effects concerns, new theories of harm have been proposed. Envelopment, for example, refers to a dominant platform's strategy to enter another platform market through tying or bundling. In this scenario, network effects arising from its user databases and economies of scope arising from the sharing of data and technology will make it difficult for the competing platforms to challenge the incumbent.[377]

Competition authorities have become increasingly concerned about conglomerate effects, even though policy pronouncements appear more often than actual enforcement efforts. For example, in the updated UK CMA Merger Assessment Guidelines, the assessment of conglomerate effects appears prominently, and they are also discussed with respect to digital markets.[378] The CMA acknowledges that conglomerate effects may be more pronounced in nascent and digital markets

> as new customers may be more easily diverted between firms, scaling particularly critical, competitors more easily marginalised, and the future benefits of controlling these markets especially large. However, these anticompetitive effects may not emerge in full until after the market has reached maturity, so in assessing

[374] See, e.g. *Lagardère/Natexis/VUP* (Case COMP/M.2978) Commission Decision, C(2003) 5277; and *Procter & Gamble/Gillette* (Case COMP/M.3732).

[375] *Microsoft/GitHub* (n276), paras 76 et seq; *Microsoft/LinkedIn* (n240), paras 185 et seq; *Microsoft/Skype* (n206), paras 133 et seq; *Microsoft/Nuance* (n289), paras 165 et seq; *Sanofi/Google/DMI JV* (n80), paras 78 et seq; *Google/Motorola Mobility* (n76), paras 161 et seq; *Google/DoubleClick* (n46), paras 289 et seq; *Google/Fitbit* (n83), paras 710–815; *Apple/Shazam* (n48), paras 189 et seq; *Meta/Kustomer* (n37), paras 587 et seq. For an analysis, see A Witt, 'Who's Afraid of Conglomerate Mergers?' (2022) 67 Antitrust Bulletin 208.

[376] Van den Boom and Samranchit (n74), 365.

[377] OECD, 'Executive Summary of the Roundtable on Conglomerate Effects of Mergers', DAF/COMP/M(2020)1 ANN2 final (4 February 2021), 3. See also D Condorelli and J Padilla, 'Harnessing Platform Envelopment in the Digital World' (2020) 16 Journal of Competition Law and Economics 143.

[378] CMA MAG (n146), paras 7.30–7.37. See, e.g. para 7.30 ('[f]or example, it may only offer the products as a bundle, integrate them within a digital ecosystem, or offer customers of the adjacent product a discount if they also purchase its focal product, potentially through increasing the stand-alone price of the adjacent product'), para 7.31.

> these mergers the CMA may focus on their impact on the structure of the market and competition over the longer term. Such an assessment will likely be subject to a degree of uncertainty, but this will not in itself preclude the CMA from concluding that the SLC [substantial-lessening-of-competition] test is met on the basis of all the available evidence.[379]

The emergence of multi-product and multi-actor ecosystems[380] explains the reinvigoration of conglomerate—and, more generally, non-horizontal—concerns in digital mergers. Yet, the analysis of conglomerate concerns is still engrained in a more traditional approach to foreclosure theories of harm tied to specific markets rather than a more holistic ecosystem-based approach. This should not detract from the fact that competition authorities have reluctantly started to evaluate ecosystem-based theories of harm in merger control. For example, the German NCA looked into conglomerate effects with respect to the strengthening of Meta's ecosystem in *Meta/Kustomer*, which was cleared unconditionally.[381] The authority considered that it was likely that the respective ecosystem would be strengthened; however, it did not refer the case for a Phase II investigation, given its inability to prove this to the requisite legal standard. More recently, the Commission has blocked the acquisition of eTraveli, a flight online travel agent (OTA), by Booking, the leading hotel OTA in the EEA, on the basis of an ecosystem-based theory of harm. According to the Commission, the transaction would have allowed Booking to expand its travel services ecosystem, since the acquisition of eTraveli would have substantially increased traffic for Booking.[382]

IV.2.2 Data and Privacy Considerations

The prevalence of data in the digital economy has called for a reconceptualization of competition law enforcement and raised questions with respect to the assessment of various data and privacy concerns in competition law analysis.[383] The tide has now turned, and it seems that academics, policymakers, and competition authorities have reached an agreement with respect to the assessment of privacy as a competition parameter, though different opinions are expressed as to the exact

[379] *Ibid*, para 7.37.

[380] On ecosystems, see Chapter 2, section IV.

[381] European Commission (EU), 'Merger Review in Digital and Technology Markets' (n51), 8, 76. Bundeskartellamt 'Bundeskartellamt Clears Acquisition of Kustomer by Meta (Formerly Facebook)', *Kustomer/Meta (Formerly Facebook)*, B6-21/22B7-119/21 (11 February 2022) <https://www.bundeskartellamt.de/SharedDocs/Meldung/EN/Pressemitteilungen/2022/11_02_2022_Meta_Kustomer.html> (accessed 9 June 2024).

[382] European Commission (EU), 'Mergers: Commission Prohibits Proposed Acquisition of eTraveli by Booking', Case M.10615 (Press release, 25 September 2023).

[383] On data, see Chapter 2, section II.4 and Chapter 3, section IV.3. While data protection and privacy protection concerns may be used interchangeably by the Commission, there are differences between the two. See O Lynskey, *The Foundations of EU Data Protection Law* (OUP, 2015), 10–11.

role of privacy in competition law assessment.[384] The EU Commission, in its revised Notice on Market Definition, explicitly acknowledges that privacy, as an aspect of quality, constitutes a parameter of competition.[385]

In merger control, the transactions reviewed by the Commission to date, while assessing the potential impact of data combination post-merger, have largely dismissed concerns with respect to data accumulation and privacy. For example, in *Google/DoubleClick*, the Commission concluded that even if the parties combined their CPI data, it would be unlikely that the merged entity would be conferred such a competitive advantage since such data were already available to a number of Google's competitors.[386] In *Microsoft/LinkedIn*, the Commission found that the combination of data did not raise competition concerns for online advertising. According to the Commission, any such data combination could only be implemented to the extent allowed by data protection law and the newly adopted—at the time—GDPR could possibly further limit Microsoft's ability to access and process its users' personal data in the future since 'the new rules will strengthen the existing rights and empowering individuals with more control over their personal data (i.e. easier access to personal data; right to data portability; etc.)'.[387] Yet, such an assessment overlooks the fact that an adverse effect on privacy, impacting competition and resulting in consumer harm, can be implemented without necessarily constituting a breach of data protection rules.[388]

Data privacy considerations were largely left out of the Commission analysis. In *Google/DoubleClick*, for example, the Commission expressly mentioned that its decision appraised the transaction exclusively based on the EUMR and was without prejudice to obligations imposed by other data protection and privacy regulations.[389] In other cases, privacy has been considered as an element of quality. In *Microsoft/*

[384] In this vein, see (amongst others), W Kerber, 'Digital Markets, Data, and Privacy: Competition Law, Consumer Law, and Data Protection', ZWB Joint Discussion Paper Series in Economics No 14 (2016); G Colangelo and M Maggiolino, 'Data Protection in Attention Markets: Protecting Privacy through Competition?' (2017) 8 Journal of European Competition Law & Practice 363; SY Esayas, 'Data Privacy in European Merger Control: Critical Analysis of Commission Decisions Regarding Privacy as a Non-Price Competition' (2019) 40 European Competition Law Review 166; MC Wasastjerna, 'The Implications of Big Data and Privacy on Competition Analysis in Merger Control and the Controversial Competition-Data Protection Interface' (2019) 30 European Business Law Review 337; M MacCarthy, 'Privacy as a Parameter of Competition in Merger Reviews' (2020) 72 Federal Communications Law Journal 1. Expressing the opposite 'purist' approach, see M Ohlhausen and A Okuliar, 'Competition, Consumer Protection, and the Right (Approach) to Privacy' (2015) 80 Antitrust Law Journal 121; D Sokol and R Comerford, 'Antitrust and Regulating Big Data' (2016) 23 George Mason Law Review 1129.

[385] European Commission (EU), 'Notice on the Definition of the Relevant Market for the Purposes of Union Competition Law', [2024] OJ C 1645, para 15.

[386] *Google/DoubleClick* (n47), paras 364–365.

[387] *Microsoft/LinkedIn* (n241), paras 176–178.

[388] E Deutscher, 'The Role of Privacy in Merger Control—Limiting Principles, Theories of Harm, and Operationalisation' in M Ioannidou and D Mantzari (eds), *Research Handbook on Competition Law and Data Privacy* (Edward Elgar, forthcoming), 31.

[389] *Google/DoubleClick* (n47), para 368.

LinkedIn, the Commission concluded that potential foreclosure of PSN service providers would have had a negative effect on competition since it may have led to the marginalization of existing or potential competitors offering better privacy protection than LinkedIn, thereby restricting consumer choice.[390] The Commission, based on the market investigation results, acknowledged that privacy constituted an important competition parameter and drove customer choice and stated that such a finding was consistent with the findings in *Facebook/WhatsApp*.[391] However, in *Facebook/WhatsApp*, the Commission clarified that any privacy-related concerns arising from the increased data concentration were to be assessed under EU data protection and not competition rules. Any potential data concentration was analysed only to the extent that it was likely to strengthen Facebook's position in the online advertising market,[392] instead of also looking at the reduction in privacy protection as a concrete privacy harm resulting from the elimination of competition between Facebook, which accumulated large amounts of personal data, and WhatsApp, which offered enhanced privacy protection to its users.[393]

In *Apple/Shazam*, the Commission assessed the combination of the respective parties' data sets. It considered Shazam's Customer Information[394] as commercially sensitive information on Apple Music's rivals in the market for digital music-streaming apps.[395] When assessing its respective ability to put competitors at a competitive disadvantage, the Commission analysis relied on the regulatory data protection constraints placed on the merged entity with respect to the use of such data.[396] Similarly, when assessing whether denying competitors' access to Shazam user data (as an important input to improve existing or offer additional functionalities on the digital music-streaming app) could lead to anticompetitive foreclosure, the Commission concluded that first Shazam user data did not appear to be an important input.[397] Second, Shazam user data were not unique so as to confer a significant 'data advantage', and competitors could access similar databases. In order to arrive at this conclusion and compare such databases, the Commission employed four relevant metrics, namely the variety, velocity, volume, and value of the data. According to the Commission, '[t]hese metrics, the so called "Four Vs", comprise the four key parameters that are increasingly used to assess the commercial and thus competitive relevance of large datasets'.[398] Yet, absent from the

390 *Microsoft/LinkedIn* (n241), paras 350–351.
391 *Ibid*, with references to *Facebook/WhatsApp* (n48), paras 87, 102 and n79.
392 *Facebook/WhatsApp* (n48), para 164.
393 Deutscher, 'The Role of Privacy in Merger Control' (n388).
394 *Apple/Shazam* (n49), para 214.
395 *Ibid*, para 220.
396 *Ibid*, paras 225–235.
397 *Ibid*, para 316.
398 *Ibid*, para 317, with reference to the joint report of the AdC and the Bundeskartellamt, 'Competition Law and Data' (10 May 2016) <https://www.bundeskartellamt.de/SharedDocs/Publikation/DE/Berichte/Big%20Data%20Papier.html;jsessionid=2F34FB1C56475779337616BA96B21934.2_cid381?nn=3591568> (accessed 7 June 2024).

Commission analysis was the potential ability to engage in enhanced user profiling resulting from the combination of the respective data sets.[399]

IV.2.3 Innovation Competition

Section II has briefly outlined the rampant merging activities of Big Tech. Such acquisitions often take place in fast-moving, dynamic markets, raising potential questions with respect to the impact on innovation. For example, evidence suggests that GAFAM have been particularly keen on acquiring artificial intelligence (AI) start-ups,[400] or generally investing in AI companies without necessarily triggering merger control rules.[401]

When reviewing a merger, the EU Commission assesses its impact on competition and, in particular, on various different factors such as price, output, choice, quality, and innovation.[402] With respect to innovation, the EU HMG provide that

> [i]n markets where innovation is an important competitive force, a merger may increase the firms' ability and incentive to bring new innovations to the market and, thereby, the competitive pressure on rivals to innovate in that market. Alternatively, effective competition may be significantly impeded by a merger between two important innovators, for instance between two companies with 'pipeline' products related to a specific product market. Similarly, a firm with a relatively small market share may nevertheless be an important competitive force if it has promising pipeline products.[403]

Even though innovation is an important parameter in digital markets, the Commission is yet to address such a consideration with respect to digital mergers,[404] though this has been examined in the agrochemical sector. In *Dow/Dupont*, the Commission elaborated for the first time on an innovation theory of harm, stating that firms were also competing in 'innovation spaces'.[405] In *Dow/Dupont*,

[399] On such a privacy harm theory of harm, see Deutscher, 'The Role of Privacy in Merger Control' (n388), with further references to relevant cases where such considerations were also overlooked. See *Google/DoubleClick* (n47), *Facebook/WhatsApp* (n48), *Microsoft/LinkedIn* (n241), and *Google/Fitbit* (n84).

[400] Laitenberger (n3).

[401] On the recent debate about AI partnerships and acqui-hires, see, e.g. Bundeskartellamt, 'Cooperation between Microsoft and OpenAI Currently Not Subject to Merger Control' (Press release, 15 November 2023) <https://www.bundeskartellamt.de/SharedDocs/Meldung/EN/Pressemitteilungen/2023/15_11_2023_Microsoft_OpenAI.html>; CMA, 'CMA Seeks Views on AI Partnerships and Other Arrangements' (Press release, 24 April 2024) <https://www.gov.uk/government/news/cma-seeks-views-on-ai-partnerships-and-other-arrangements> (both accessed 2 May 2024) with respect to *Microsoft/Inflection AI*, *Amazon/Anthropic*, and *Microsoft/Mistral AI*.

[402] EU HMG (n60), para 8. See also CMA MAG (n146), paras 2.5, 2.17, 2.18, 5.18.

[403] EU HMG (n60), para 38.

[404] For cases where the Commission assessed the impact on innovation, see European Commission (EU), 'EU Merger Control and Innovation' (Policy brief, April 2016).

[405] *Dow/Dupont* (Case M.7932) Commission Decision, C(2017) 1946 (23 March 2017).

the Commission looked in detail into the merging parties' incentives to innovate post-merger and concluded that the merger would negatively impact on innovation since it would reduce the parties' incentives to develop new pesticides.[406]

Kenneth Arrow famously argued that '[t]he preinvention monopoly power acts as a strong disincentive to further innovation'.[407] Market concentration has a negative impact on innovation.[408] At the other end of the spectrum, Schumpeter maintained that powerful firms have both the ability and greater incentives to innovate.[409] Aghion and colleagues argued that the relationship between competition and innovation can be depicted as an inverted U-curve. Competition triggers innovation incentives only if competition is not intense. On the contrary, intense competition reduces innovation rewards, thereby also impacting innovation incentives.[410] Shapiro has made the proposition that even though they seem irreconcilable, Arrow's and Schumpeter's views are, indeed, compatible and mutually reinforcing and offered a conceptual framework based on the principles of appropriability, contestability, and synergies to assess the impact of competition on innovation.[411]

Overall, the assessment of a merger's impact on innovation will depend on the particular market structure.[412] Various analytical tools have been proposed for assessing a merger's future impact on innovation, including the definition of innovation[413] and technology markets,[414] evaluating whether the merger would lead to a significant impediment to industry innovation,[415] and examining the merger's impact on the merging parties' incentives and ability to innovate.[416] Past merger cases have relied on various types of evidence in order to assess the state of innovation and impact post-merger, including evidence on the importance of innovation activities to the merging parties and consumers, evidence on the firms that

[406] *Ibid.* See M Bourreau and A de Streel, 'Digital Conglomerates and EU Competition Policy' (March 2019) < https://papers.ssrn.com/sol3/papers.cfm?abstract_id=3350512> (accessed 9 June 2024), 28–29.

[407] K Arrow, 'Economic Welfare and the Allocation of Resources to Invention' in *The Rate and Direction of Inventive Activity: Economic and Social Factors* (Princeton UP, 1962), 609, 620.

[408] *Ibid.*

[409] J Schumpeter, *Capitalism, Socialism and Democracy* (Harper & Brothers, 1942).

[410] P Aghion et al, 'Competition and Innovation: An Inverted-U Relationship' (2005) 120 Quarterly Journal of Economics 701; P Aghion et al, 'The Effects of Entry on Incumbent Innovation and Productivity' (2009) 91 Review of Economics and Statistics 20.

[411] C Shapiro, 'Competition and Innovation: Did the Arrow Hit the Bull's Eye?' in J Lerner and S Stern (eds), *The Rate and Direction of Inventive Activity Revisited* (University of Chicago Press, 2011), 361, 363.

[412] OECD, 'Considering Non-Price Effects in Merger Control' (n369), para 9.

[413] R Gilbert and S Sunshine, 'Incorporating Dynamic Efficiencies Concerns in Merger Analysis: The Use of Innovation Markets' (1995) 63 Antitrust Law Journal 569.

[414] M Katz and H Shelanski, 'Mergers and Innovation' (2007) 74 Antitrust Law Journal 1.

[415] N Petit, 'Significant Impediment to Industry Innovation: A Novel Theory of Harm in EU Merger Control?', White Paper 2017-1 (2017) <https://orbi.uliege.be/bitstream/2268/207345/1/SSRN-id2911597.pdf> (accessed 9 June 2024).

[416] Shapiro, 'Competition and Innovation' (n411).

are undertaking or could undertake relevant innovation efforts, and evidence on the nature of the respective firms' innovation rivalry.[417]

With respect to digital mergers, the assessment of their respective impact on innovation is complex. As noted in the EU Experts Report, Big Tech acquisitions of innovative start-ups may involve a different kind of 'kill zone', one that reduces the start-ups' incentives to invest in innovation out of fear that such innovation may end up being copied or acquired.[418] Such a 'kill-zone' effect has led to calls for the articulation of an innovation theory of harm, where competition authorities would assess the post-merger cannibalization effects on the incumbent's incentives to delay or withdraw the target's innovation.[419] Yet, the EU Experts Report recognizes that in digital mergers, the more plausible scenario is that—instead of killing the target's innovation—the latter is integrated in the incumbent's ecosystem, possibly having an efficiency rationale and thus requiring a more complex assessment of the theory of harm.[420] Such a scenario is corroborated by empirical evidence regarding Big Tech acquisitions, where the branded product may be either maintained or incorporated in the incumbent's ecosystem.[421]

IV.2.4 Potential Competition

Another concern with respect to digital mergers has to do with the likelihood of the target growing into an effective competitive thread in the future, even if this is not the case at the time of the merger.

A fact pattern that has been identified with respect to mergers in digital markets is the strategy of incumbents to acquire promising firms that operate in an adjacent market. Examples of such moves include Google's acquisitions of YouTube (2006) and DoubleClick (2007) and Facebook's acquisitions of Instagram (2012) and WhatsApp (2014).[422] However, at the time of the transaction, it may be more complicated to prove with a sufficient degree of certainty that potential competition exists.[423]

[417] OECD, 'Considering Non-Price Effects in Merger Control' (n369), 20.

[418] European Commission (EU), 'Competition Policy for the Digital Era' (A Report by J Crémer, Y de Montjoye, and H Schweitzer) (EU Experts Report, 2019), 117. Developing a model on the 'kill-zone' effect, see S Krishna Kamepalli, R Rajan, and L Zingales, 'Kill Zone', National Bureau of Economic Research Working Paper 27146 (2020) <https://www.nber.org/system/files/working_papers/w27146/w27146.pdf> (accessed 9 June 2024).

[419] Krishna et al (n418), with reference to Bourreau and de Streel (n406), 30.

[420] As such, this has been termed nurturer—rather than killer acquisition. See E Calvano and M Polo, 'Market Power, Competition and Innovation in Digital Markets: A Survey' (2021) 54 Information Economics and Policy 1, 13. A useful distinction here is between disruptive and sustaining innovation, with Big Tech being likely to discontinue disruptive innovations while promoting sustaining innovations that strengthen their value chain. See M Stucke and A Ezrachi, 'Innovation Misunderstood' (2023) <https://papers.ssrn.com/sol3/papers.cfm?abstract_id=4547201> (accessed 9 June 2024), 25.

[421] Gautier and Lamesch (n11).

[422] C Shapiro, 'Antitrust in a Time of Populism' (2018) 61 International Journal of Industrial Organization 714, 740.

[423] EU Expert Report (n418), 112.

Motta and Peitz have developed a framework in order to assess a merger's impact on potential competition.[424] They also point out the difficulties that competition authorities face in proving the impact on potential competition since they have to prove that the target is more likely than not to develop into a competitive threat and substantiate such an assessment with documents that cannot be easily obtained, not least because of the fact that such clear plans, at an early stage of a start-up's acquisition, have not yet been drafted.[425]

V. The Way Forward

V.1 Introduction

In light of the rather laissez-faire approach to digital mergers to date, several proposals have been put forward in order to render merger control more effective. Such proposals concern the amendment of both the procedural and the substantive rules.

V.2 Change of Procedural Rules

The Commission, in the past, has explored the possibility of complementing the current turnover thresholds for merger notification with transaction value thresholds.[426] Even though certain Member States have opted for the introduction of alternative thresholds,[427] the Commission has not seen the need to amend the EU merger control rules.[428] This is in line with the EU Experts Report's recommendations, according to which, in light of the additional administrative burden and impact on legal certainty, it would have been premature to amend the EUMR turnover threshold.[429] After all, under EU competition law, competition authorities may review transactions even though the merger thresholds are not met, even though

[424] M Motta and M Peitz, 'Big Tech Mergers' (2021) 54 Information Economics and Policy 1.

[425] *Ibid*, 14; EU Experts Report (n418), 119.

[426] Other proposals concern the introduction of an economic goodwill test, representing the difference between the target's net tangible assets and the transaction value. See A McLean, 'A Financial Capitalism Perspective on Start-Up Acquisitions: Introducing the Economic Goodwill Test' (2020) 17 Journal of Competition Law & Economics Journal of Competition Law and Economics 141, 162.

[427] See above text to n41 with respect to Austria and Germany. The UK merger control could capture certain digital mergers under the share-of-supply test. See cases above in the text to n311.

[428] On the relevant consultation, see European Commission (EU), 'Consultation on Evaluation of Procedural and Jurisdictional Aspects of EU Merger Control' (2016) <https://competitionpolicy.ec.europa.eu/publicconsultations/2016mergercontrol_en> (accessed 9 June 2024). See European Commission (EU), 'Evaluation of Procedural and Jurisdictional Aspects of EU Merger Control', SWD(2021) 66 final (26 March 2021), paras 266–270 <http://2017_comp_003_evaluation.pdf>.

[429] EU Experts Report (n418), 113–116.

the *Illumina/Grail* CJEU ruling limited such possibility. After the *Illumina/Grail* CJEU ruling, the wide interpretation of the Article 22 EUMR referral mechanism, which allowed a merger to be referred to the Commission even though the national merger control thresholds were not met, is no longer possible.[430] However NCAs still retain the ability to review transactions that do not meet their respective national merger control thresholds under Article 102 TFEU.[431]

V.3 Change of Substantive Rules

The EU Experts Report has proposed changes with respect to the assessment of substantive theories of harm in digital mergers, where incumbents enjoy strong data advantages and network effects. The potential harm of such acquisitions may not be adequately encapsulated in input foreclosure conglomerate theories of harm but rather needs to account for the overall bolstering of the incumbent's ecosystem power.[432] Thus, in order to address 'false negatives', the report proposes that where the target is active in a related market and has the potential to grow into a competitive threat beyond that market, the analysis should follow the logic of a horizontal merger analysis and examine whether the incumbent and the target are active in the same 'technological' or 'users' space'. The competition authorities should inquire into whether the target has the potential to grow into a competitive threat in that technological/users' space or ecosystem, whether its acquisition would increase the market power therein, and whether there are merger specific efficiencies.[433] The Report also proposes a widening of the concept of potential competition.[434] Ultimately, these proposals concern a rethinking and, to some extent, targeted widening of the existing tools but do not extend as far as suggesting a reversal of the burden of proof, although it may be suggested that this is the case.[435]

In a similar vein, the Furman Report in the United Kingdom calls upon the CMA to take a long-run-effects approach to digital mergers and assess the impact

[430] See text to n43 above.

[431] See text to n45 above. Criticism was levelled against these alternative mechanisms because they may be seen as a threat to the EU one-stop shop merger control system and adversely impact legal certainty. See, e.g. J Mulder and W Sauter, 'A New Regime for Below Threshold Mergers in EU Competition Law? The Illumina/Grail and Towercast Judgments' (2023) 11(3) Journal of Antitrust Enforcement 544, with further references.

[432] EU Expert Report (n418), 11.

[433] *Ibid*, 116–117.

[434] *Ibid*, 119.

[435] UK House of Lords Select Committee on AI, 'A New Pro-Competition Regime for Digital Markets', CP 489 (July 2021), paras 189–191 <https://assets.publishing.service.gov.uk/government/uploads/system/uploads/attachment_data/file/1003913/Digital_Competition_Consultation_v2.pdf> (accessed 9 June 2024).

on dynamic competition.[436] Companies with a strategic market status should be required to report their anticipated mergers to the CMA.[437] More importantly, though, the Furman Report proposed an amendment to the substantive test for the evaluation of mergers, from a 'balance-of-probabilities' to a 'balance-of-harm' approach, where the CMA could have taken into account the scale and likelihood of harm to potential competition and innovation.[438] Such an approach would lead to the blocking of transactions when they are expected to cause more harm than good.[439] Other proposals have concerned the lowering of the intervention threshold in Phase II (in essence, using the same standard as in Phase I) from 'a more likely than not' for the SLC to occur to a 'realistic-prospect' test.[440]

Others have considered the reversal of the *burden of proof* from the competition authorities to prove anticompetitive harm to the merging parties to prove that the merger will not harm competition,[441] or the introduction of a rebuttable presumption that the merger will harm competition.[442]

The above proposals, both in the EU and the United Kingdom, have not found their way into the respective legislative proposals. Legislators have not gone as far as proposing changes with respect to the burden or the standard of proof and have merely adopted notification requirements for Big Tech companies.[443] The standard of proof in EU merger control is a 'balance-of-probabilities' test. In order to prohibit a transaction, the Commission, relying on a 'sufficiently cogent and consistent body of evidence', needs to demonstrate 'that it is more likely than not' that the transaction will result in a significant impediment to effective competition.[444]

[436] Digital Competition Expert Panel, 'Unlocking Digital Competition' (Report prepared by J Furman, D Coyle, A Fletcher, D McAuley, and P Marsden) (Furman Report, March 2019), 12.

[437] *Ibid.* This is the only proposal with respect to merger control that found its way into the Digital Markets, Competition and Consumers Act 2024.

[438] Furman Report (n436), 13.

[439] *Ibid*, para 3.88.

[440] UK House of Lords Select Committee on AI, 'A New Pro-Competition Regime for Digital Markets' (n434), paras 189–191. Such proposals were not endorsed by the UK government in the end. HM Government (UK), 'Government Response to the Consultation on a New Pro-Competition Regime for Digital Markets', CP 657 (May 2022), para 113.

[441] United States House of Representatives, 'Majority Staff Report and Recommendations—Subcommittee on Antitrust, Commercial, and Administrative Law of the Committee on the Judiciary' (October 2020) <https://www.govinfo.gov/content/pkg/CPRT-117HPRT47832/pdf/CPRT-117HPRT47832.pdf>, 328; Stigler Committee on Digital Platforms, 'Final Report' (2019) <https://www.sipotra.it/wp-content/uploads/2020/02/Stigler-Committee-on-Digital-Platforms-Final-Report.pdf>; 16-17. H.R.3826—Platform Competition and Opportunity Act of 2021; T Valletti, 'How to Tame the Tech Giants: Reverse the Burden of Proof in Merger Reviews' (Promarket, 28 June 2021) <https://www.promarket.org/2021/06/28/tech-block-merger-review-enforcement-regulators> (all accessed 9 June 2024).

[442] ACCC, 'Digital Platforms Inquiry—Final Report' (n15), 108–109.

[443] In the EU, see Article 14 DMA. See Chapter 3, text to n150. In the United Kingdom, see n437.

[444] Case C-376-20 P *Commission v CK Telecoms UK Investments* (n166), para 87. The CJEU held that the GC had committed an error in law requiring the Commission to meet a 'strong probability' standard for proving a significant impediment to effective competition. See *ibid*, para 88. See Case T-399/16 *CK Telecoms UK Investments Ltd v Commission* (n166), para 118.

Finally, other proposals concern the potential to tame Big Tech market power, partly attributed to serial acquisitions, through the imposition of structural remedies. The latter are presented as more effective than behavioural, rule-making conduct remedies.[445] Yet, others doubt the efficiency of structural remedies and prescribe more caution. Whereas it is true that breaking up a super-dominant digital incumbent will increase competition, at the same time, it will prevent consumers from interacting with others. Thus, consumers may progressively switch to the same network to increase their social interactions, thereby leading to market tipping.[446]

VI. Conclusion

Chapter 6 discussed the challenges involved in assessing digital mergers by powerful Big Tech companies. The analysis gave both an account of Big Tech's merger activity, most of which has remained unreviewed and unchallenged by competition authorities, and an exposition of all of the GAFAM mergers reviewed by the EU Commission. It also discussed selected transactions reviewed by the UK CMA and its predecessor. Furthermore, it threaded out the key characteristics and main theories of harm with respect to digital mergers, as well as the challenges involved in reviewing such deals. In light of such challenges, various proposals have been put forward in order to amend the jurisdictional thresholds and substantive assessment rules. Yet, the pendulum, at this stage, has not struck in the other direction. Despite the mounting criticism regarding the perceived under-enforcement against Big Tech deals, the EU legislature has not introduced any changes in EU merger control apart from the notification requirement in the DMA coupled with a failed expansive interpretation of the EU merger referral system.

[445] J Kwoka and T Valletti, 'Unscrambling the Eggs: Breaking Up Consummated Mergers and Dominant Firms' (2021) 30 Industrial and Corporate 1286. See also the US case, *FTC v Facebook* (pending) <https://www.ftc.gov/legal-library/browse/cases-proceedings/191-0134-facebook-inc-ftc-v> (accessed 9 June 2024). The FTC had not challenged *Facebook/Instagram* and *Facebook/WhatsApp* (n47)—how can they now bring this case?

[446] A de Corniere, 'Should We Break Up Big Tech?' (*The Economist*, 7 November 2019) <https://thetseconomist.wordpress.com/2019/11/07/should-we-break-up-big-tech> (accessed 9 June 2024).

PART C

COMPETITION LAW AND DIGITAL MARKETS IN CHINA

7
Anticompetitive Agreements

I. Introduction

In the digital economy, a significant number of anticompetitive agreements are reached with the facilitation of information technology.[1] In the European Union (EU), for example, there have been investigations both at the EU and Member State levels, resulting in prohibition decisions and fines to combat those anticompetitive practices that are detrimental to competition. In comparison, Chinese competition law enforcement seems to focus on abuse of market dominance and mergers in digital markets. As for anticompetitive agreements, however, formal and stringent administrative measures are rarely taken.

Article 3 of the Anti-Monopoly Law of the People's Republic of China (AML) stipulates three types of anticompetitive behaviours: first, anticompetitive agreements; second, abuse of dominance; and third, mergers that have, or may have, the effect of excluding or restricting competition. Agreements that are detrimental to competition are often used in various traditional industries in China. The Chinese competition authorities have realized the adverse effects they bring about and have thus been accustomed to adopting sanctions and remedies such as fines and restitution to regulate violating behaviours in these industries. In digital markets, there is also a variety of anticompetitive agreements in business practice: some involve price restrictions, some come down to sales volume, and others even step into brand new fields, such as algorithms. Accordingly, there have been laws and regulations as a specific response to potential anticompetitive behaviours in China's huge digital economy, not only involving traditional factors such as sales volume and price but also targeted at new-born technology like algorithms. Typical examples include the amendments made in the new AML tackling digital markets and the rich rules in the Guidelines.[2]

When we probe into the anti-monopoly enforcement mechanism, what is intriguing is that the EU authorities tend to take a firm line on anticompetitive agreements reached by digital platform giants, conducting formal investigations and imposing penalties. China, however, takes a relatively different approach, although the tone of anti-monopoly enforcement against digital platforms has grown firmer

[1] NV Deltsova and OM Storozhenko, 'Anti-Competitive Agreements in the Digital Economy Conditions: Legal Aspects' (2021) 106 European Proceedings of Social and Behavioural Sciences 1458.

[2] See Chapter 2, section II.3; Chapter 3, section V.3.

Competition Law and Policy in Digital Markets. Maria Ioannidou and Bingwan Xiong, Oxford University Press.
 DOI: 10.1093/9780191925955.003.0007

in recent years. For anticompetitive agreements, traditional industries are usually the area where there is a high frequency of violating activities. In the Annual Report of China on Anti-Monopoly Law Enforcement (2021) released by the State Administration for Market Regulation (SAMR), for example, it was pointed out that the competition authorities had carried out thirty investigations against anticompetitive agreements and imposed eleven administrative penalties thereon, with the fines totalling ¥1,673 million (ca €240 million). The cases regarding anticompetitive agreements in 2021 involved one industry association and forty-three enterprises, which were mainly distributed in traditional industries such as medicine, materials construction, gas, and other relevant areas.[3]

Such a lack of enforcement begs the question as to whether the practice of anticompetitive agreements is absent in Chinese digital markets or the law addressing such a practice is inadequate. When looking beyond China's formal enforcement of competition law against anticompetitive agreements, it should be noted that the law in China is definitely not a paper tiger that allows platforms to conclude anticompetitive agreements. There have been a good number of cases, in fact, that have come to the attention of Chinese competition authorities. Some were filed for investigation but eventually dropped before formal investigations were initiated, and others were not even filed at all.

In a nutshell, such low-level enforcement is basically associated with two reasons: first, the current maturity of China's digital markets and the state of competition therein do not provide a solid ground fostering the conclusion of typical anticompetitive agreements, especially in the absence of platforms' market dominance and negotiating powers with absolute advantage. Second, innovation has become an essential element that is heavily considered and evaluated by the Chinese competition authorities in AML enforcement. Especially, Chinese central government has made innovation a paramount focus in its national economic agenda so as to rectify its long-lasting reliance on exports and investment for economic growth. The introduction of the five-year-long 'Internet Plus' initiative in 2015 by the State Council has given digital technologies like big data and cloud computing primary importance for promoting traditional manufacturing and service economies.[4] Thus, the regulatory authorities tend to let the bullets of seemingly violating business models fly for a while before firm evidence of the adverse effects of anticompetitive behaviours arise.

Before a particular suspected anticompetitive violation reaches scale effect, the regulatory authorities in China usually take precautionary measures of prior warning and education, whilst the AML is always viewed as the last resort to rectify

[3] SAMR, '中国反垄断执法年度报告 (2021) [Annex of Annual Report of China on Anti-Monopoly Law Enforcement (2021)]' (8 June 2022) <https://www.samr.gov.cn/xw/zj/art/2023/art_bfac0acc333e4bd0be85adf099272047.html> (accessed 27 September 2022).

[4] A Zhang, 'Agility over Stability: China's Great Reversal in Regulating the Platform Economy' (2022) 63(2) Harvard International Law Journal 457, 471–474.

market failure. Hence, instead of conducting a formal investigation into anticompetitive agreements and imposing direct penalties on such monopolistic behaviours, the Chinese regulators tend to resort to what we call 'soft enforcement' of the law against them in the first instance, for example administrative interviews or administrative talks.[5] Formal investigations and stringent prohibition decisions are likely to follow where such soft interventions fail to rectify suspected violating behaviours. Such a 'dual-track' approach of enforcement of competition law with Chinese characteristics not only applies to the conclusion of anticompetitive agreements but also to other forms of anticompetitive misconducts.

Hence, this chapter presents the law enforcement against anticompetitive agreements in China's digital markets as follows. Section II briefly explains the infeasibility of concluding anticompetitive agreements in China's current digital markets, which includes both internal and external reasons. A key external reason comes from the 'dual-track' approach with Chinese characteristics, which has already been introduced at some length in Chapter 3 and will be illustrated with laws and regulations, academic debates, and cases in sections III and V.

II. Infeasibility of Anticompetitive Agreements in China's Digital Markets

In traditional industries, given the large number of competitors or potential competitors, undertakings aiming to obtain monopolistic benefits often resort to anticompetitive agreements. However, there are few cases of formal law enforcement against anticompetitive agreements in Chinese digital markets, as both horizontal and vertical agreements are difficult either to reach or to identify.

On the one hand, it is difficult to reach a horizontal agreement between platforms. At present, the competition among major platforms is still fierce, and charging commission is only one of the main competition parameters among platforms, while each platform still has its own distinct competitive advantages, such as fees for sales promotion and services like data analysis for marketing and advertising. In the case of online retail platforms, for instance, with the gradual development of digital markets, the overall quantity of existing online retailers has stabilized, and new entrants still have a long way to go before extending their influence. Nonetheless, as several managers from the departments of marketing and legal affairs from giant digital platforms like Alibaba Group and Meituan.com commented, major platforms are still fiercely competing for existing online retailers at this moment.[6]

[5] See Chapter 3, section V.3.

[6] Interview with two managers of the Department of Legal Affairs from Alibaba Group (20 September 2022) and a marketing manager from Meituan.com (10 March 2022).

Therefore, it is unlikely that platform-like undertakings will take out horizontal agreements as a preferential competing strategy, which is subject to Article 17 of the new AML in digital markets. More specifically, for one thing, platforms are unlikely to fix prices or limit sales with their rivals. For another, it is also unrealistic for platforms to segment the market, given the cross-territorial nature of businesses facilitated by digital platforms.[7] Moreover, against the backdrop of cross-border e-commerce, platforms can hardly reach horizontal agreements so as to scarcely limit platform competition, be it at the domestic or international level, since competition takes place simultaneously on both sides.

On the other hand, vertical agreements concluded in the absence of platform power are rare. This is largely because platforms can hardly bring about substantial anticompetitive effects by merely reaching vertical agreements on a narrow scale, that is concluding an 'either–or' choices agreement between the platform and only a few online merchants. However, in order to make such 'either–or' agreements universally binding, the platform inevitably has to call the shots on a wide scale in the relevant market, which involves the issue of a dominant position, thus likely making the problem investigated transform into another form of monopoly: abuse of dominance.[8]

Such an attitude of intervention is widely taken by the regulatory authorities in the face of anticompetitive behaviours in China's digital markets. For example, before the Guidelines came into effect, most-favoured-nation clauses (MFNs) were accepted by small and medium online merchants so as not to lose any opportunity to trade on major retail platforms. However, it becomes almost impractical when it comes to the implementation of such vertical agreements. Once there is one platform that breaks the intra-platform balance by offering special rewards to certain merchants in exchange for more competitive selling prices, the balance facilitated by such agreements is prone to collapse internally. In particular, since the Guidelines clearly regulate MFNs and the regulatory policies for the digital economy industry have become more stringent ever since 2020, such behaviour is much more easily detected. Therefore, digital platforms tend to be cautious about entering into such agreements.[9] All in all, anticompetitive agreements are almost unfeasible in China's current digital markets.

[7] F Xiao and W Wei, '数字经济发展对市场分割的影响研究 [On the Influence of Digital Economy Development on Market Segmentation]' (2013) 15 Journal of Commercial Economics 111, 111–112. See also World Economic Forum, 'Competition Policy in a Globalized, Digitalized Economy Report' (2019), 15.

[8] See Chapter 8, section V.1.

[9] Interview with a manager of the Department of Legal Affairs from Alibaba (September 2022).

III. The Chinese Regulatory Framework of Anticompetitive Agreements

III.1 The New AML on Anticompetitive Agreements in Digital Markets

The amendments to the rules on anticompetitive agreements in the new AML are particularly notable, including, in particular, five aspects: (i) the definition of anticompetitive agreements is prescribed in a separate clause,[10] (ii) the rules on the identification of vertical agreements have been refined,[11] (iii) the long-called-for safe harbour for vertical agreements has been provided,[12] (iv) organizers or substantial facilitators have been targeted in the form of hub-and-spoke conspiracy,[13] and (v) the liability for anticompetitive agreements has been enhanced.[14] Tables 7.1–7.3 refer to the last three material improvements, which were made as a specific response to the prevailing concerns about anticompetitive agreements emerging in China's digital markets.

III.2 The Guidelines on Anticompetitive Agreements in Digital Markets

In order to provide competition authorities with effective guidance for strengthening the enforcement of AML in the field of platform economy, the Anti-Monopoly Commission released the Guidelines soon after the 2020 Central Economic Work Meeting, clarifying the definition of relevant markets, the form of horizontal and vertical agreements, hub-and-spoke agreements, collaborative practices, and other related factors.[15] It provides a clearer determination and standards for the enforcement of anti-monopoly law in digital markets. Below, we provide a concise account of the relevant provisions related to anticompetitive agreements in the Guidelines.

[10] '中华人民共和国反垄断法（2022修正）[Anti-Monopoly Law of the People's Republic of China (2022 Amendment)]' (promulgated by the Standing Committee of the National People's Congress, 24 June 2022, effective 1 August 2022), Article 17 <https://www.pkulaw.com/en_law/d3236788421feacfbdfb.html> (accessed 30 May 2024) (AML).

[11] *Ibid*, Articles 17 and 18.

[12] *Ibid*, Article 18.

[13] *Ibid*, Article 19.

[14] *Ibid*, Article 56.

[15] Anti-Monopoly Commission of the State Council, '国务院反垄断委员会关于平台经济领域的反垄断指南（国反垄发〔2021〕1号）[Anti-Monopoly Guidelines on the Platform Economy]' (7 February 2021), Articles 4–9 <https://www.gov.cn/xinwen/2021-02/07/content_5585758.htm> (accessed 7 November 2022).

Table 7.1 Defence clause of anti-competitive effect and safe harbours clause

AML 2008	AML 2022
Article 14 Business operators are prohibited from reaching any of the following monopoly agreements with their trading parties: 1. Fixing the price of products for resale to a third party; 2. Restricting the minimum price of products for resale to a third party; or 3. Other monopoly agreements as determined by the AML enforcement authority of the State Council.	Article 18 (*newly added provisions*) Business operators are prohibited from reaching any of the following monopoly agreements with their trading parties: 1. Fixing the price of products for resale to a third party; 2. Restricting the minimum price of products for resale to a third party; or 3. Other monopoly agreements as determined by the AML enforcement authority of the State Council. An agreement specified in subparagraph (1) or (2) of the preceding paragraph, which, as the business operator is able to prove, has no effect of precluding or restricting competition, shall not be prohibited. If the business operator is able to prove that its share of the relevant market is lower than the standard established by the AML enforcement authority of the State Council, and satisfies the other conditions specified by the AML enforcement authority of the State Council, the agreement shall not be prohibited [italicized words added].

Source: The translation of AML 2008 is taken from pkulaw.com with minor revisions <https://pkulaw.com/en_law/503218397088141cbdfb.html> accessed 7 July 2024; the translation of AML 2022 is taken from pkulaw.com with minor revisions <https://pkulaw.com/en_law/d3236788421feacfbdfb.html> accessed 7 July 2024.

Table 7.2 Hub-and-spoke agreements

AML 2008	AML 2022
	Article 19 (*newly added provision*) A business operator shall not arrange or provide substantive assistance for other business operators to reach monopoly agreements.

Source: the translation of AML 2008 is taken from pkulaw.com with minor revisions <https://pkulaw.com/en_law/503218397088141cbdfb.html> (accessed 7 July 2024); the translation of AML 2022 is excerpted from pkulaw.com with minor revisions <https://pkulaw.com/en_law/d3236788421feacfbdfb.html> (accessed 7 July 2024).

Table 7.3 Enhanced liabilities for violation

AML 2008	AML 2022
Article 46 Where a business operator enters into and implements a monopoly agreement in violation of this Law, the AML enforcement authority shall order it to cease the violation, confiscate its illegal proceeds, and impose a fine of not less than 1% nor more than 10% of its sales for the previous year. Where the reached monopoly agreement has not been implemented, a fine of less than 500,000 *yuan* may be imposed. Where a business operator that is engaged in a monopoly agreement reports, on its own initiative, the monopoly agreement to the AML enforcement authority and provides material evidence, the authority may, at its discretion, mitigate or exempt the business operator from penalty. Where a trade association arranges for the business operators in the industry to enter into a monopoly agreement in violation of this Law, the AML enforcement authority may impose a fine of less than 500,000 *yuan*; and in the case of a grave violation, the authority in charge of the registration of social organizations may revoke the registration of the trade association.	Article 56 Where a business operator enters into and implements a monopoly agreement in violation of this Law, the AML enforcement authority shall order it to cease the violation, confiscate its illegal proceeds, and impose a fine of not less than 1% nor more than 10% of its sales for the previous year or *if there are no sales for the previous year, a fine of not more than 5 million yuan*; or may impose a fine of not more than *3 million yuan if the monopoly agreement entered into has not been implemented.* If the legal representative, the primary person in charge, or any directly liable person of the business operator is personally liable for entering into the monopoly agreement, he or she may be fined no more than *1 million yuan* [emphases added]. Where a business operator that is engaged in a monopoly agreement reports, on its own initiative, the monopoly agreement to the AML enforcement authority and provides material evidence, the authority may, at its discretion, mitigate or exempt the business operator from penalty. Where a trade association arranges for business operators in the industry to enter into a monopoly agreement in violation of this Law, the AML enforcement authority shall order it to make correction, and may impose on it a fine no more than 3 million *yuan*; and in the case of a grave violation, the authority in charge of the registration of social organizations may revoke the registration of the trade association [emphases added].

Source: the translation of AML 2008 is taken from pkulaw.com with minor revisions <https://pkulaw.com/en_law/50321839708814 1cbdfb.html> (accessed 7 July 2024); the translation of AML 2022 is excerpted from pkulaw.com with minor revisions <https://pkulaw.com/en_law/d3236788421feacfbdfb.html> (accessed 7 July 2024).

III.2.1 Innovation Preservation in Anticompetitive Agreements

Among other non-price aims of competition law, the preservation of innovation at both the supplier level and the distribution level has been accorded significant weight for the analysis of anticompetitive agreements in many jurisdictions. Similar to what the EU has emphasized,[16] the Guidelines not only enumerate the

[16] European Commission (EU), 'Communication from the Commission: Commission Notice, Guidelines on Vertical Restrains', C(2022) 248/01, paras 19, 196.

stimulation of 'innovation' as a general guiding principle for the enforcement of the whole body of anti-monopoly law, as already mentioned in Chapter 3, but also specifically stipulate (at the beginning of Chapter 2 on anticompetitive agreements) that detrimental effects on innovation should be considered when determining whether there is an anticompetition agreement falling under Articles 13(6) and 14(3) of the new AML. Moreover, Article 7 (vertical agreements) makes it clear that 'effects on consumers' legitimate rights and interests, innovation and others' should be taken into account when determining whether the conduct under investigation constitutes other concerted practices under Article 14(3) of the new AML.

III.2.2 Across-Platform Parity Agreements

Across-platform parity agreements (APPAs), or MFN clauses, are typical anticompetitive agreements in digital markets.[17] The Anti-Monopoly Guidelines on the Platform Economy (Draft for Public Opinions) (the 'Draft Guidelines') explicitly mentioned about MFN clauses but merely focused on whether they constituted vertical agreements. Namely, paragraph 2, Article 7 of the Draft stated that '[t]o analyse whether an MFN clause constitutes a vertical monopoly agreement, the operator's business motivation to enter into such clause and its ability to control the market, and the impact of implementing such clause on such factors as market competition, consumer interests and innovation shall be comprehensively considered'. In comparison, the Guidelines, in its paragraph 2, Article 7, eventually replace the expression 'MFN clause' with a more detailed description of suspicious conduct and acknowledge the possibility of constituting the abuse of market dominance. After all, if a dominant digital platform enters into MFN clauses with its merchants, it may not only reduce the merchants' possibilities to explore new operational strategies but also prevent rival platforms from expanding their business by taking advantage of more favourable trade conditions possibly supported by novel business models or technological reforms.[18]

Article 7 (vertical agreements)

Operators in the platform economy and their counterparties may reach vertical agreements on fixing resale prices and minimum resale price limitation, among others, by the following methods:[19]

[17] For the treatment in the EU, see Chapter 4, section V.3.

[18] C Tan, '互联网平台经济下最惠国条款的反垄断法规制 [Antitrust Regulation against MFN Clauses in the Internet Platform Economy]' (2020) 22(2) Journal of Shanghai University of Finance and Economics 138, 138–152.

[19] The translation of the Anti-Monopoly Guidelines on the Platform Economy (n15) is excerpted from pkulaw.com with minor revisions (italicized words were added by the author for illustrative purposes): Anti-Monopoly Commission of the State Council, '国务院反垄断委员会关于平台经济领域的反垄断指南（国反垄发〔2021〕1号）[Anti-Monopoly Guidelines on the Platform Economy]' (7 February 2021) (English translation) <https://pkulaw.com/en_law/dec522cd66c7b43ebdfb.html> (accessed 9 June 2024).

(1) Setting prices automatically by technical means;
(2) Unifying prices by taking advantage of the platform rules;
(3) Limiting prices directly or indirectly by taking advantage of the data and algorithms;
(4) Restricting other trading conditions through technical means, platform rules, data, algorithms and other methods, to eliminate and restrict market competition.

The conduct whereby a platform operator requires an in-platform operator to provide trading terms equal or superior to those on other competing platforms in terms of product prices, quantity and other respects, may constitute an anticompetitive agreement or abuse of dominant market position.

When analysing whether the above conduct constitutes a vertical agreement prohibited by Article 14(3) of the Anti-Monopoly Law, we may comprehensively consider the platform operator's market power, the competitive situation in the relevant market, the degree of hindrance to other operators from entering into the relevant markets, the impact on customers' interests and innovation, and other factors.

III.2.3 Hub-and-Spoke Agreements

Hub-and-spoke agreements present a mixture of horizontal and vertical elements. Articles 13 and 14 AML prohibit horizontal and vertical agreements, respectively. This divide between horizontal and vertical agreements falls short when it comes to the assessment of hub-and-spoke conspiracy. Article 8 of the Guidelines circumvents such a dichotomy under the AML. Instead, it provides a set of factors so as to effectively assess whether a suspected agreement constitutes hub-and-spoke conspiracy.

Article 8 (*hub-and-spoke agreements*) [20]
In-platform operators with competitive relationships may, by virtue of the vertical relationships with platform operators, or through organization and coordination by platform operators, reach a hub-and-spoke agreement that has the effect of a horizontal agreement. When analysing whether such agreements are anticompetitive agreements as prohibited by Articles 13 and 14 of the Anti-Monopoly Law, it may be considered whether in-platform operators with competitive relationships have reached and implemented anti-competitive agreements by technical means, platform rules, data, algorithms and other methods to eliminate and restrict competition in relevant markets.

[20] Italicized words were added by the author for illustration purposes.

III.2.4 Data in Anticompetitive Agreements

The Guidelines take full account of data that could facilitate the reach of anticompetitive agreements. Article 5 stresses the possibility of achieving 'other concerted practices' through data. Article 6 stipulates that horizontal agreements could be concluded via 'making use of data to achieve coordination and consistency'. Article 7, in its first paragraph, clearly articulates the concern that '(business operators) could directly or indirectly fix prices by making use of data' and that '(business operators) could impose other trade conditions by making use of data to eliminate or restrict competition'. Also, as mentioned above with respect to hub-and-spoke agreements, when determining whether such agreements fall under Articles 13 or 14 AML, the competition authority shall consider whether competing merchants trading on the same platform have reached and implemented agreements through data and other means, thus eliminating or restricting competition in the relevant market, in accordance with Article 8 (hub-and-spoke agreement) of the Guidelines.

Article 5 (*form of anti-competitive agreements*) [21]

An anti-competitive agreement in the field of platform economy refers to any agreement, decision or other concerted conduct by business operators to exclude or restrict competition. Agreements or decisions may be in written or oral form. The term 'other concerted conduct' refers to the conduct whereby operators do not explicitly enter into an agreement or decision, but are actually coordinated through data, algorithms, platform rules or other means, except for price following and other parallel conduct conducted by the relevant operators based on their independent expression of intent.

Article 6 (*horizontal agreements*)

Operators in the platform economy with competitive relationships may reach horizontal agreements on price fixing, market segmentation, restriction on production (sales) volume, restriction on new technology (product), and horizontal boycott, among others, by the following methods:

(1) Using the platform to collect and exchange price, sales volume, cost, client or other sensitive information;
(2) Using technical means for communication;
(3) Using data, algorithms, platform rules, etc., to achieve coordination and consistency; and
(4) Using other ways that help achieve collaboration.[22]

[21] Italicized words were added by the author for illustration purposes.
[22] Italicized words were added by the author for illustration purposes.

For the purposes of these Guidelines, the price includes, but is not limited to, product prices as well as commission, handling fees, membership fees, promotion fees and other service fees charged by operators.

III.2.5 Algorithms in Anticompetitive Agreements

The Guidelines also take into account the role of algorithms in reaching anticompetitive agreements. Among various categories of algorithms envisaged by theorists, it is still quite controversial as to whether 'automated' algorithms could take place in real business in digital markets.[23] The Guidelines do not categorize various forms of algorithmic collusion. Instead, they provide, in Articles 5–7 outlined above, an approach of a case-by-case analysis, in combination with considering technical development and the evolution of business models.

IV. Reflections on the Assessment of Anticompetitive Agreements in Digital Markets

Anticompetitive agreements can be reached through multiple means. In digital markets, however, such agreements facilitated by the application of big data and algorithms have recently triggered particular social concerns, both in China[24] and around the world. China's legislation and regulation have made good efforts to address the problems that are detrimental to competition in digital markets. Amongst these efforts, the mechanism of algorithm audit has been proposed as a notable resolution. According to the Guidelines, concerted conduct may also refer to conduct whereby undertakings do not explicitly enter into an agreement or decision but are coordinated through data, algorithms, platform rules, or other means.[25] One of the effective methods to tackle the detriments to competition in digital markets posed by the anticompetitive agreements relying on big data and algorithms is to establish an algorithm audit system both from the internal and external side. Through ensuring the transparency and equity of an algorithm, auditing serves to tackle both anticompetitive agreements and abuse of dominance. The Algorithmic Recommendation

[23] S Li, C Xie, and E Feyler, 'Algorithms & Antitrust: An Overview of EU and National Case Law' (2021) e-Competitions Special Issue Algorithms & Antitrust 3. Also see E Calvano, G Calzolari, V Denicolo, and S Pastorello, 'Artificial Intelligence, Algorithmic Pricing, and Collusion' (2020) 110(10) American Economic Review 3268, 3268–3269; World Economic Forum (n7), 8.

[24] W Han, Y Gao, and A Deng, 'Algorithmic Price Discrimination on Online Platforms and Antitrust Enforcement in China's Digital Economy' (The Antitrust Source, August 2018) <https://www.americanbar.org/content/dam/aba/publications/antitrust/magazine/archived/2018/august/algorithmic-price-discrimination-online-platforms.pdf> (accessed 11 April 2024).

[25] Anti-Monopoly Commission of the State Council (n15), Articles 6–7.

Regulations, however, only cover algorithmic recommendation services, which are widely employed in cases of abuse of market dominance. Chapter 8 will look further into the problems arising from the introduction of big data and algorithms, as well as the corresponding audit mechanism in China's digital markets.

There are still other obstacles to the effective regulation of anticompetitive agreements, however, that are waiting to be overcome. Whilst the current legal system has steered significant attention to aspects of new technology, strengthening law enforcement against anticompetitive behaviours such as 'prohibiting and exempting' resale price maintenance, problems still exist at the level of implementation, such as how to precisely formulate the black-letter law and how to establish implementing mechanism.

IV.1 Highlighting the Rules of the New AML on Anticompetitive Agreements

IV.1.1 Vertical Agreements

IV.1.1.1 Safe Harbours

The new AML introduces a 'safe harbour', under which vertical agreements can be exempted if the market share threshold is met.[26] It sets two prerequisites for its application: first, the market share is lower than the standards set by the SAMR; and second, other conditions stipulated by the SAMR are met. Compared to the 'safe harbour' in the EU, first, one of the most important similarities for its application is the criterion for market share. However, the legislature eventually abandoned the requirement of specifying market share directly due to the diversity and complexity of digital undertakings' business models. Instead, it authorized the anti-monopoly law enforcement agency of the State Council to further clarify the specific market share standards of 'safe harbour' and the meaning of 'other conditions' in the provisions. Second, the new AML states that the 'safe harbour' rule is only applicable to vertical agreements, and it needs further clarification as to whether different conditions are set.

IV.1.1.2 Resale Price Maintenance (RPM) Agreements

The new AML provides that an agreement that limits or fixes resale prices will not be prohibited if the parties can prove that it does not have the effect of restricting or eliminating competition. This rule was actually adopted from the approach taken by the Shanghai High People's Court and Guangdong High People's Court. According to previous decisions delivered by the two courts, RPM agreements are

[26] AML (n10), Article 18.

presumed to be unlawful unless the defendant can establish that the agreement is not anticompetitive under the AML.[27] The new AML recognizes such a rule-of-reason approach by putting the burden of proof on the concerned undertakings to provide that it does not eliminate or restrict competition and by repositioning the definition of anticompetitive agreements.[28]

IV.1.2 Hub-and-Spoke Conspiracy

The concept of 'hub-and-spoke conspiracy' is introduced, for the first time in Chinese law, with a separate clause set up in the Guidelines. However, the Guidelines are vague about its nature and application.[29] The new AML further stipulates that '[b]usiness operators shall not organize other business operators to reach anti-competitive agreements, or provide substantive assistance for other business operators to reach anti-competitive agreements'.[30] At the same time, it clarifies that the legal liability of the organizers and facilitators is the same as that of the operators who conclude and implement an anticompetitive agreement.[31]

IV.1.2.1 Identification of the 'Hub-and-Spoke Conspiracy' in Digital Markets

In the digital economy, the platform has a vertical relationship with the operators on the platform and benefits from more convenient information exchanges. At the same time, considering the fact that platform rules and algorithms are usually consistent with operators on the platform, platforms are more likely to reach collaborative behaviours with the facilitation of platform rules and algorithms. In this regard, the Guidelines have already noted that it is necessary to determine whether platform operators have employed technical tools, platform policies, data, and algorithms to negotiate and implement violating agreements, including collaborative behaviours, when examining anticompetitive agreements in the digital markets.[32]

IV.1.2.2 Potential Factors to Be Considered

At present, there has been no case in China in which the competition authority has enforced the rule against hub-and-spoke conspiracy. Based on the new AML and

[27] Shanghai High People's Court, *Wuhan Hanyang Guangming Trading Co, Ltd v Shanghai Hanmou Tire Sales Co, Ltd*, [2018] (武汉市汉阳光明贸易有限责任公司与上海韩某轮胎销售有限公司纵向垄断协议、滥用市场支配地位纠纷案, (2018)沪民终475号) (30 July 2020). See also Guangdong Higher People's Court, *Dongguan Hengli Guochang Electric Appliance Store v Dongguan Shengshi Xinxing Geli Trading Co, Ltd*, [2016] (东莞市横沥国昌电器商店与东莞市晟世欣兴格力贸易有限公司等纵向垄断协议纠纷案, (2016)粤民终177号) (19 July 2018).

[28] AML (n10), Article 18.

[29] Anti-Monopoly Commission of the State Council (n15), Article 8.

[30] AML (n10), Article 19.

[31] *Ibid*, Article 56.

[32] Anti-Monopoly Commission of the State Council (n15), Articles 6, 8.

the Guidelines, two major factors may become the focus of determining hub-and-spoke conspiracy in future cases in digital markets. First, in-platform vendors need to have reached horizontal agreements, such that they have engaged in collaborative behaviours through unified algorithms and platform rules. Second, the platform must have played an organizational role or provided substantive assistance to the conclusion of such horizontal agreements.[33]

IV.1.3 Enhanced Penalties

Legal accountability has its inherent value, including both sanctioning violations and providing relieves.[34] To ensure an adequate deterrent effect, the new AML materially enhances the cap of penalties against a broad range of targets (especially fines for violations such as jump-dealing and non-implementation of anticompetitive agreements and behaviours organized by trade associations), from ¥500,000 (ca €63,830) to ¥3,000,000 (ca €382,980). Remarkably, the new AML introduces a punitive penalty, in its Article 63, which multiplies fines by between two and five times the original penalty where the violation has particularly serious circumstances, social impacts, or consequences. In addition to sharply raising the level of penalties against platform undertakings, the new AML introduces legal liabilities to a wide range of individuals, including legal representatives and the person in charge or directly responsible, as well as organizers, aiders, and abettors involved in 'hub-and-spoke' conspiracies.

China's previous enforcement of anti-monopoly law suggests that anticompetitive behaviours are mainly conducted by business operators instead of individuals, particularly in cases associated with abuse of dominant position and mergers. Nevertheless, it has been recently stressed among Chinese scholars that individuals may also become the subjects of anticompetitive agreements and shall be held accountable therefor. Certain specialized markets are primarily composed of occupations or professionals with the drive and aptitude to engage in anticompetitive behaviours. Anticompetitive agreements are more likely to take place due to the substantial asymmetry in transaction information.[35] Although professional associations or trade associations in China with professional or vocational participation usually have the status of subjects in litigation and can be classified as 'unincorporated organizations', with the diversification of market participators,

[33] J Hao, '论我国垄断协议类型序列的立法完善 [On the Legislative Improvement of the Sequence of Types of Anti-Competitive Agreements in China]' (2022) 1 Journal of China University of Political Science and Law 211, 211–216. See also BC Weber, 'Hub-and-Spoke Conspiracies: Can Big Data and Pricing Algorithms Form the Rim?' (2023) 26 SMU Science and Technology Law Review 25.

[34] J Shi, '个人反垄断义务和责任的制度完善及其实施 [Implementation and Improvement of Individual Antitrust Obligations and Responsibilities]' (2022) 5 China Journal of Applied Jurisprudence 60.

[35] *Ibid.*

those organizations without independent subject status may still contribute to facilitating illegal behaviours that are detrimental to competition.[36] Therefore, it is indispensable to impose personal liability for anticompetitive behaviours, in terms of civil, administrative, and even criminal contexts.[37]

Some amendments in the new AML were indeed made in the absence of specific rules tackling digital markets. The general principles and rules do not make special distinctions between the traditional industries and digital markets. Nonetheless, the social backdrop against which these amendments were carried out makes it quite clear that the new AML is aimed, at least in part, at providing better statutory grounds for regulatory enforcement in digital markets and putting forward new requirements for the fair competitive behaviour of operators in the era of the digital economy. The Guidelines released before the new AML and other regulatory documents introduced around the amendment of the AML have provided rich materials for the interpretation of these general principles and rules at a time when enforcement activity is still lacking.

IV.2 Highlighting the Rules of the Guidelines on Anticompetitive Agreements

In the field of platform economy, big data and algorithms can facilitate new forms of collusion. The characteristics of anticompetitive agreements have therefore changed greatly compared with traditional ones, which calls for the reformation of antitrust regulation.

First, the Guidelines make it clear that the application of digital technology has only altered how anticompetitive agreements are reached and implemented, not their fundamental nature. The Guidelines point out that in the platform economy, operators may engage in anticompetitive agreements with the facilitation of platforms, technical means, data, and algorithms and other ways promoting synergy. Nonetheless, such monopolistic behaviours are still, in essence, agreements, decisions, or other synergetic acts employed by business operators to exclude or limit market competition. Therefore, the challenge in the implementation of the Guidelines still lies in finding sufficient evidence to prove the intention of platform operators, so as to determine whether there is an anticompetitive agreement.

Second, in light of the wide recognition of the anticompetitive nature of MFN clauses practised by digital platforms in western jurisdictions, the Guidelines also take the stand, though not in a direct manner, that the MFN clauses may constitute one type of vertical agreements. However, this provision is not clearly reflected in

36 *Ibid.*
37 *Ibid.*

the new AML. From the perspective of EU competition law, enforcement relating to the MFN clauses has steadily become a major hot spot, with parallel antitrust actions in the fields of online hotel booking and e-book distribution.[38]

Third, the Guidelines incorporate exclusive agreements into the scope of the regulation of vertical agreements, so as to meet the inherent demands of antitrust law to regulate the wide practice of 'either–or' choice by major platforms.[39] It should be noted that, as with the MFN clauses, in addition to vertical agreements, if the platform operator holds a dominant market position, the 'either–or' behaviour may also constitute an abuse of dominant market position, but the latter is applied under more stringent conditions.

Fourth, hub-and-spoke agreements are included.[40] This is mainly for the reason that in reality, the boundaries between horizontal and vertical agreements are not always clear-cut, as there is crossover or overlap between them. This provision is also reflected in the new AML.

V. Major Cases of Anticompetitive Agreements in China's Digital Markets

Meituan, Alibaba, Tencent, ByteDance, and Baidu are some of the domestic digital goliaths that compete with global ones such as Amazon, Apple, and others in the Chinese market. While the practice of anticompetitive agreements have emerged in multiple business sectors in Chinese digital markets, major platforms, especially in the fields of local life services (e.g. on-demand food delivery), have caught the attention of Chinese competition authorities. Anticompetitive behaviours are mostly associated with price fixing, which poses a notable threat to the maintenance of a free and competitive market. Anticompetitive agreements, as expressly prohibited by Article 16 of the new AML, are typically concluded to fix pricing, split markets, or restrict production.[41] As aforementioned, a dual-track approach of enforcement has been adopted by Chinese competition authorities to deal with anticompetitive agreements in digital markets,[42] which involves a hard enforcement mechanism plus a soft administrative intervention. Distinctive from formal investigation and stringent administrative punishment, soft administrative interviews are more frequently applied in the resolution of anticompetitive agreements in China.

[38] See Chapter 4, section V.3.

[39] Anti-Monopoly Commission of the State Council (n15), Article 7.

[40] *Ibid*, Article 8.

[41] CCCS (Competition and Consumer Commission), 'What Are Anti-Competitive Agreements and Why Are They Bad?' (28 February 2019) <https://www.cccs.gov.sg/anti-competitive-behaviour/anti-competitive-agreements> (accessed 27 September 2022).

[42] See text to n5 above.

V.1 Meituan

Meituan is an online 'local-life' service platform, best known for its on-demand food delivery service. Over time, Meituan has evolved into an all-in-one super app with third-party services in locally found services and products like tourism-related businesses, entertainment, restaurants and more. Meituan charges a commission per transaction, depending on the nature of the business.

Since Meituan does not provide goods itself, it relies heavily on the vendors who have joined the platform to maintain its competitiveness. When vendors entered into Meituan's platform in 2018, they were required to make an 'either–or' choice. In other words, merchants were asked to choose one platform over another. Such an exclusive choice between platforms materially constrained their freedom to manage their business operation, and at the same time disrupted the normal business rhythm in the food-takeaway market. It also undermined consumers' choice of merchants available on rival platforms. Such behaviour is of a sophisticated nature and may constitute both an abuse of market dominance and an anticompetitive agreement. On 20 September 2017, Huaian's Municipal Market Supervision Administration received a report stating that Meituan had been engaging in unfair competition. The Administration then launched an investigation. In 2018, the Wuxi Administration for Industry and Commerce launched an early investigation into Meituan's engagement in anticompetitive conduct with the intention of crowding out rival platforms by locking vendors on its own platform.

In April 2021, the SAMR launched a formal investigation into Meituan's abuse of its dominant market position in the online food and beverage delivery service market in China. The SAMR eventually found that Meituan used to compel vendors to sign exclusive cooperation agreements with it by way of implementing discriminating rates, postponing vendors' store openings, and collecting exclusive partnership deposits. Such behaviours, according to the SAMR, not only unjustifiably undermined the competition among on-demand delivery platforms but also harmed the legitimate interests of the vendors on the platform, ultimately harming the interests of consumers.[43] According to the prohibition decision released by the SAMR on 8 October 2021, (i) Meituan was ordered to cease its illegal conducts, including revamping its operations and filing self-rectification compliance reports to the SAMR for the next three years; and (ii) Meituan was fined 3 per cent of the sales volume in China in 2020, amounting to ¥3,442 million (ca €450 million) in total. What's more, Meituan was required to refund exclusive partnership deposits to vendors on the platform, amounting to ¥1.3 billion (ca €0.17 billion).

[43] SAMR, '国家市场监督管理总局行政处罚决定书（国市监处罚〔2021〕74号） [SAMR Administrative Prohibition Decision [2021] No 74]' (8 October 2021) <https://www.samr.gov.cn/xw/zj/art/2023/art_31910760066b4f69aa119a20dec250ad.html> (accessed 10 April 2024).

Although the investigation and prohibition decision were largely grounded on Meituan's abuse of dominant position in the on-demand delivery market, the SAMR certainly took notice of the anticompetitive agreements involved. When describing the misconduct of the platform, the prohibition decision repeatedly mentioned the agreements signed by the vendors with the platform and the anticompetitive effects thereof. On the same day as the administrative punishment of Meituan, the SAMR issued an administrative instruction letter, advising Meituan on how to conduct self-investigation and rectification in accordance with its written decision.[44] In the instruction letter, the SAMR clearly pointed out that Meituan should not implement anticompetitive agreements to exclude and restrict market competition by way of technical means, platform rules, data, and algorithms.[45]

China's competition authorities tend to tackle Meituan-like anticompetitive behaviours on the ground of abuse of market dominance instead of anticompetitive agreements, largely because of the special structure of the rules on anticompetitive agreements. Specifically, when choosing the statutory grounds on which prohibition decisions can be delivered, competition authorities often have to consider the availability of evidence and the level of difficulty in presenting sound arguments. With regard to the vertical agreements between the platform and its vendors, paragraph 1 of Article 18 in the new AML (Article 14 in the old AML) provides three prohibitive scenarios: (i) fixing the prices of products resold to a third party, (ii) restricting the lowest prices for products resold to a third party, and (iii) other anticompetitive agreements confirmed as such by the authority for enforcement of the AML under the State Council.

While the first two scenarios cover agreements involving pricing, the third one is no more than an open-ended clause that is subject to an *ad hoc* decision and susceptible to questioning of its substantive and procedural justification. Hence, the competition authorities in China are inclined to resort to the rules on the abuse of market dominance so as to avoid such a challenge from the incumbent platform. Nonetheless, there are still cases (although they are quite rare) in which similar open-ended clauses on the abuse of market dominance are applied, with the most typical being the *Tetra Pak* case.[46] The competition authority concerned found that *Tetra Pak* had, in effect, excluded competitors from the liquid-food packaging

[44] SAMR, '国家市场监督管理总局行政指导书（国市监行指〔2021〕2号） [Administrative Guidance [2021] No 2]' (8 October 2021) <https://www.samr.gov.cn/jzxts/tzgg/xzcf/art/2023/art_e10040bb366242629925685accabfab2.html> (accessed 10 April 2024).

[45] SAMR, '国家市场监督管理总局行政处罚决定书（国市监处〔2021〕2号） [SAMR Administrative Prohibition Decision [2021] No 2]' (27 January 2021) <https://www.samr.gov.cn/jzxts/tzgg/xzcf/art/2023/art_783f995cdfe440eabcdf886a5cd8c97f.html> (accessed 10 April 2024).

[46] SAIC (State Administration for Industry and Commerce), '工商总局依法对利乐滥用市场支配地位案作出行政处罚 [SAIC Imposed Administrative Punishment on Tetra Pak for Abusing Its Dominant Market Position in Accordance with Law]' (16 November 2016) <https://www.gov.cn/xinwen/2016-11/16/content_5133237.htm> (accessed 3 October 2023).

market by using loyalty discounts. Due to the ambiguous nature of loyalty discounts, after prudent deliberation,[47] the competition authority concerned eventually decided the case on the ground of the open-ended scenario provided by item 7 of paragraph 1, Article 17 of the old AML.[48]

V.2 Community Group Buying

In September 2016, there was a group of individuals roaming around the main shopping and residential areas of Changsha. On the one hand, they rallied the locals to sign up for the WeChat group purchases for the neighbourhood. On the other, they bargained with the store owners to get the best deal. Platforms providing community group buying services in second-tier cities soon exploded, and such a model gradually matured in 2018 as group-buying websites in China, such as Pinduoduo, have prevailed in the online retail market. Under such business models, residents place online orders on the platforms and pick up their chosen products (e.g. vegetable, meats) offline at pick-up sites. The platforms also provide a delivery service. Customers can therefore enjoy a lower price, which is thought to change their way of shopping and to reduce the costs of sellers by virtue of bulk deliveries. Typically, these websites feature a 'discount of the day', which becomes active if a predetermined number of users commit to purchasing the goods.

However, with strong capital influx into this field, some community group-buying platforms started to subsidize online retailers and were complained about for conducting inappropriate price-dumping by coordinating online retailers. Aside from subsidies, platforms also control the sales volume in several ways. For instance, platforms like Pinduoduo always take a 'limited-time' or 'limited-sales' selling strategy. Such a limitation is, to some extent, comparable to production control, which involves an agreement between competitors to limit the quantity of goods available in the market. By controlling the supply of certain products, big platforms may be able to increase prices and eventually obtain monopolistic profits.[49]

These business practices emerged at a time when China was trying to contain the COVID-19 pandemic. While sales of fresh produce, daily necessities, and other products skyrocketed and the platforms reaped great profits, the expansion of group-buying platforms was widely considered to exert an anticompetitive impact on the industry of on-site retail and to be detrimental to product supply.[50] On 22

[47] X Fu and G Tan, 'Abuse of Market Dominance under China's Anti-Monopoly Law: The Case of Tetra Pak' (2019) 54(2) Review of Industrial Organization 409, 409–434.

[48] Item 7 covers 'other acts of abuse of dominant market positions confirmed as such by the authority for enforcement of the Anti-Monopoly Law under the State Council'.

[49] CCCS (n41).

[50] J Zou, '拼多多上线《48小时保供套餐》，到达集单数量需求即可下单 [Pinduoduo Online "48 Hours Guarantee Package" Orders Can Be Placed When Arriving at the Set Single Number of

December 2020, the SAMR, alongside other central regulatory agencies, held an administrative guidance meeting with six major platforms, including Alibaba and Tencent, in order to preserve the competition order of community group buying, instructing these platforms to strictly abide by the nine requirements proposed,[51] one of which requires that anticompetitive agreements of any kind (such as those concerning fixed prices, production, and sales volume limitation or market division) shall not be reached or implemented in violation of the law.[52]

Nonetheless, these platforms did not strictly comply with these prohibitions after the meeting. Hence, the SAMR initiated further regulatory actions against the low-priced and market-disruptive practices by several community group buying platforms.[53] Intriguingly, the regulatory measures against the platforms that subsidized community group buying were also not mainly grounded on the rules on anticompetitive agreements in the AML but on Article 14 of the Price Law: 'for the purpose of crowding out competitors or monopolizing the market, dumping at prices below cost disrupts the normal order of production and operation and damages other operators' rights and interests'.[54] On this ground, the SAMR imposed

Demand]' (8 April 2022) <https://www.thepaper.cn/newsDetail_forward_17519276> (accessed 13 October 2023). See also S Lu, '疫情《重燃》需求， 盒马再战社区团购 [Epidemic Rekindles Demand, He Ma Fights Again for Community Group Buying]' (31 May 2022) <https://baijiahao.baidu.com/s?id=1734335845096995123&wfr=spider&for=pc> (accessed 13 October 2023).

[51] SAMR, '市场监管总局联合商务部召开规范社区团购秩序行政指导会 [SAMR and MOFCOM Jointly Held an Administrative Guidance Meeting to Regulate the Order of Community Group Buying]' (22 December 2020) <https://www.gov.cn/xinwen/2020-12/22/content_5572312.htm> (accessed 27 September 2022). The nine requirements are: (1) It shall not conduct low-priced dumping, price collusion, price gouging, price fraud, etc. In addition to price reductions in accordance with laws to deal with fresh products, seasonal products, backlogs of products and other products, it shall not dump products at a price below cost for the purpose of crowding out competitors or take the monopoly position. (2) It shall not reach or implement any form of anticompetitive agreement such as fixing prices, limiting the quantity of goods produced or sold, or dividing the market. (3) It shall not carry out acts of abuse of dominance such as predatory pricing, refusal to deal, or tying without justifiable reasons. (4) It shall not unlawfully implement mergers excluding or restricting competition. If the merger reaches the notification standard, it shall notify in advance. (5) It shall not engage in unfair competition such as commercial confusion, false propaganda, commercial defamation, etc., which endangers the market environment of fair competition. It shall not fabricate or disseminate false information or conduct misleading commercial propaganda, damage the business reputation of competitors, the reputation of goods, deceive and mislead consumers. (6) It shall not take advantage of data to harm the legitimate rights and interests of consumers. (7) It shall not use technical means to impair the order of competition and hinder the normal operation of other market players. It shall not make use of service agreements, transaction rules, and technology to impose unreasonable restrictions or conditions on the transactions of operators on the platform, transaction prices and transactions with other operators, or charge unreasonable fees to operators on the platform. (8) It shall not illegally collect or use consumers' personal information, which may bring about security risks. (9) It shall not sell counterfeit or shoddy goods, endangering the safety and security of consumers.

[52] *Ibid.*

[53] B Yin, '《菜蓝子》电商鏖战 [Cailanzi e-Commerce Fierce Battle]' (2021) 6 Shanghai Informatization 34.

[54] Y Si, '依法规范社区团购市场秩序努力营造公平有序的市场环境—市场监管总局对五家社区团购企业不正当价格行为作出行政处罚答记者问 [Standardizing the Market Order of Community Group Purchase in Accordance with Laws and Striving to Create a Fair and Orderly Market Environment—The State Administration for Market Regulation Imposes Administrative

an administrative punishment of RMB 1.5 million (ca €0.20 million) on four community group-buying enterprises on 3 March 2021, namely Orange Optimization (Beijing) Technology Development Co, Ltd, Shanghai Yucan Information Technology Co, Ltd, and Shenzhen Meituan Youxuan Technology Co, Ltd, imposing an administrative penalty of RMB 500,000 (ca €65,100) on Wuhan Seven Delicious Technologies Co, Ltd.[55]

V.3 Sharing Economy

The sharing economy, like bicycle sharing and rechargeable battery sharing, has experienced tremendous growth in China over the past decade. In recent years, the AML's restrictions on 'concerted price increases' may have been broken by the sharing economy, although no formal investigation has been launched.

Bicycle sharing is considered an environmentally friendly way of commuting,[56] providing a solution to the 'last mile' trouble and promoting the development of the sharing economy.[57] The most famous Chinese dockless bike-sharing business—'ofo'—began in September 2015 and rapidly expanded its business scale. In addition to this start-up, at least twenty-five other bike-sharing companies entered the market in 2016.[58] The bike-sharing industry flourished in 2017. Many start-ups, financed by venture capital poured into the market, including leaders like Ofo, Mobike, Bluegogo, and Hellobike.[59] Not only did the number of bike-sharing companies climb to nearly seventy in 2017,[60] but also the quantity of users also increased by 108.1 per cent in the second half of 2017 compared to that in the first half of the same year.[61]

Punishment on Five Community Group Purchase Enterprises for Their Unfair Price Practices]' (2021) 6 China's Food 26.

[55] SAMR, '国家市场监督管理总局行政处罚决定书（国市监处〔2021〕38号） [SAMR Administrative Prohibition Decision [2021] No 38]' (27 May 2021) <https://www.samr.gov.cn/xw/zj/art/2023/art_054aa1dab46d4cb8a760e2f46e290d5b.html> (accessed 10 April 2024).

[56] Ministry of Transport, '关于鼓励和规范互联网租赁自行车发展的指导意见 [Guiding Opinions on Encouraging and Regulating the Development of Internet Bicycle Rental]' (1 August 2017) <http://www.gov.cn/xinwen/2017-08/03/content_5215640.htm> (accessed 27 September 2022).

[57] The 'last mile' trouble refers to the last mile between the public transportation and the destination, for example the walking distance between a subway station and a person's office building.

[58] P Chen, '近30家厂商逐鹿共享单车 冬天过后将洗牌 [Nearly 30 Companies Competing in Bike Sharing, There Would Be a Shuffle after the Winter]; (6 January 2017) <http://www.nbd.com.cn/articles/2017-01-06/1067717.html> (accessed 27 September 2022).

[59] CNNIC (China Internet Network Information Center), '第41次"中国互联网络发展状况统计报告" [41st Statistical Report on Internet Development in China]' (31 January 2018) <http://www.cac.gov.cn/2018-01/31/c_1122347026.htm> (accessed 27 September 2022).

[60] Ministry of Transport, '交通运输部运输服务司司长徐亚华解读《关于鼓励和规范互联网租赁自行车发展的指导意见》 [Interpretation of the Guiding Opinions on Encouraging and Regulating the Development of Internet Bicycle Rental by Yahua Xu, the Director of the Transportation Service Department of the Ministry of Transportation]' (4 August 2017) <http://www.gov.cn/xinwen/2017-08/04/content_5215971.htm> (accessed 27 September 2022).

[61] CNNIC (n59).

However, the market became considerably concentrated in 2017. In the second half of 2017, many medium and small bike-sharing companies exited the market due to a lack of continuous funding by venture capital as competition rose tremendously. Some companies were unable to refund deposits to their customers, which caused serious social issues.[62] At the end of 2017, ofo and Mobike became the two dominant companies in the bike-sharing market.[63] Subsequently, the bike-sharing industry experienced a bust in 2018.[64] For example, the increase rate in the number of users slowed down to 11 per cent in comparison to that of 2017. What's more, as of March 2018, thirty-four of the seventy less competitive bike-sharing companies had gone bankrupt.[65]

Among those companies that survived, Mobike was acquired by Meituan, Bluegogo was acquired by Didi, and Hellobike was invested in by Alibaba.[66] Competition was becoming even more fierce. The bike-sharing industry in China was capital driven in the early stage of its development, when investors were desperately chasing profits. Investors were more inclined to quit funding new projects when the unsustainable market made them realize that such a business model might not generate promising profits. It has been reported that Qingju still cannot compensate for its loss in 2021.[67] To deal with the hardship associated with continuous financing, platform undertakings in this market seemed to unanimously raise the price in the hope of earning profits in the future. Consequently, from 2020 to 2022, shared bicycles increased in price several times, even up to 50 per cent, sparkling public discontent.[68]

The recharge-sharing industry has had a similar development cycle to Didi, going from grandeur to misery. 2017 was the time when shared charges were born. Customers' reliance on mobile devices, together with developments like the emergence of online payment systems and the explosive growth of online social media,

[62] *Ibid.*

[63] *Ibid.*

[64] CCTV Finance, '全国12城市叫停新增投放 共享单车开始骑向海外 [Twelve Cities Stopped the Increase of Shared Bikes, Share Bikes Started to Turn to Overseas Markets]' (21 December 2017) <https://www.nbd.com.cn/articles/2017-12-21/1174097.html> (accessed 27 September 2022).

[65] HE Changtang, '共享单车应该免押 [Shared Bikes Should Be Free from Deposits]' (18 March 2018) <https://baijiahao.baidu.com/s?id=1595249240416216665&wfr=spider&for=pc> (accessed 27 September 2022).

[66] CNNIC, '第42次《中国互联网络发展状况统计报告》 [42nd Statistical Report on Internet Development in China]' (20 August 2018) <https://www.cac.gov.cn/2018-08/20/c_1123296882.htm> (accessed 27 September 2022).

[67] See C Chen et al, '共享充电宝、共享单车齐涨价引争议，共享经济变贵还是变味？[The Simultaneous Price Increase of Shared Power Banks and Bike-Sharing Services Has Sparked Controversy: Is the Sharing Economy Getting More Expensive or Has It Taken on a Different Flavour?]' (20 September 2022) <https://new.qq.com/rain/a/20220920A014NS00> (accessed 27 September 2022).

[68] B Shao, '最高涨价50%！美团骑行卡也全面开涨，共享单车还划算吗？[With the Highest Price Increase of 50%, Meituan Ride Cards Start to Increase in Price. Is Bike Sharing Still a Good Deal?]' (ThePaper.cn, 14 August 2022) <https://www.thepaper.cn/newsDetail_forward_19442011> (accessed 2 May 2024).

contributed significantly to the industry's explosive growth in shared rechargeable batteries. In the initial stage, the companies adopted low price subsidies to expand their market share, but slowly, they entered a phase of sustained losses. Since the second half of 2019, the rechargeable battery-sharing industry has increased its prices several times, with the rent rising from ¥1 (ca €0.14) per hour to ¥2 per hour. According to the 2022 Market Research Report on China's Charger-Sharing Industry, in the first half of 2022, the average daily capital flow of the top companies in the industry dropped by varying degrees compared to the same period last year. Energy Monster, which was once known as the top recharge-sharing undertaking, has been losing nearly ¥100 million (ca €13.84 million) every quarter since it was listed.[69] Surprisingly, rechargeable battery rentals have become priced by the minute, and the daily rental cap is constantly being increased upwards, with the daily maximum even reaching ¥99 (ca €13.7), directly catching up with the price of buying one. With such circumstances comes stringent regulation.[70]

Collaborative acts refer to acts of coordination between operators in the absence of a clear agreement or decision.[71] Price fixing, which occurs when rival businesses agree to fix, control, or maintain the pricing of goods or services, is suspected to be the cause of the concurrent cooperative acts of price increases, covering both direct and indirect forms of fixed pricing.[72]

Due to the fact that current regulations are still catching up with how the sharing economy works, businesses in such a field operate within legal grey areas. The AML, however, seems to have stayed relatively dormant, while this innovative business has been expanding, for the reason that the sharing industry is suspected of violating the AML, but ultimately no formal investigation has been filed. Following the typical dual-track approach, in June 2021, the SAMR held an administrative guidance meeting, requiring eight enterprises engaging in the sharing industry (including Hellobike, Qingju, Meituan, Energy Monster, Little Electric, Caller, Street Electric, and Search Electric) to rectify suspected violating conducts by a deadline, clarify their pricing rules, and strictly adhere to price indication requirements. The eight interviewees were companies operating bike-sharing and

[69] Orient Webcasting, '头豹发布2022年中国共享充电宝行业市场研究报告 [2022 Market Research Report on China's Charger-Sharing Industry Released by Toubao]' (5 August 2022) <http://caijing.chinadaily.com.cn/a/202208/05/WS62ecbd71a3101c3ee7ae280e.html> (accessed 27 September 2022).

[70] P Shui, '垄断就涨价？ 共享充电宝集体涨价， 市场监管总局出手遏制 [Monopolies Lead to Price Increases? The Collective Price Hike of Shared Charging Stations Prompts Regulatory Intervention by the SAMR]' (2 September 2021) <https://www.sohu.com/a/487251053_100082204> (accessed 27 September 2022).

[71] SAMR (State Administration for Market Regulation), '禁止垄断协议规定 [Provisions on Prohibiting Anticompetitive Agreements]' (promulgated by SAMR, 10 March 2023, effective 15 April 2023), Article 5, para 3 <https://www.pkulaw.com/chl/13f8f20ffb8edd3cbdfb.html?keyword=%E7%A6%81%E6%AD%A2%20%E5%8F%8D%E5%9E%84%E6%96%AD%E5%8D%8F%E8%AE%AE&way = listView> (accessed 30 May 2024).

[72] CCCS (n11).

portable charger-sharing businesses. As disclosed at the time, the six portable charger-sharing brands that participated in the rectification had a total of 4.26 million cabinets, accounting for about 80 per cent of the market share. Currently, numerous bike-sharing and charger-sharing companies are on the way to working on implementing appropriate usage-based rates and deposit waivers based on client credit ratings.[73]

Didi, the largest e-hailing service platform in China, is a reflection of both the success of the sharing economy here and the hurdles the enforcement of anti-monopoly law faces. Predatory pricing is considered by scholars to be one of the most common anticompetitive concerns revealed in the operation of Didi.[74] In order to solve this issue, it is anticipated that the core aim of efficiency demonstrated in the AML will be reinforced, which may enable law enforcement agencies to break free from the constraints of conventional antitrust paths and try more adaptable and effective methods to balance corporate conduct and market welfare.[75] Meanwhile, the ongoing innovation of business models and the discipline of digital markets shall also been respected. Protecting innovation plays a vital role in the development of the digital economy.[76]

V.4 MFN Clauses

Similarly, the practice of MFN clauses in China's digital markets in recent years has attracted the attention of regulatory agencies and provides a supplementary perspective to understanding China's enforcement practice against anticompetitive agreements. A seller's commitment to treat a buyer in the same manner as its best, most-preferred client is known as an MFN.[77] Such contractual terms are often drafted for pricing arrangements but may also extend to other aspects of trade, such as payment terms or access to supply.

[73] V Sago, 'Bike Sharing in China—From Bicycle Graveyards to a Regulated Industry' (Georgetown Environmental Law Review, 29 April 2020) <https://www.law.georgetown.edu/environmental-law-review/blog/bike-sharing-in-china-from-bicycle-graveyards-to-a-regulated-industry/#_ftn5> (accessed 27 September 2022).

[74] J Cai, 'The Sharing Economy and China's Antimonopoly Law: From the Didi Case to Regulatory Challenges' (2020) 28(1) Asia Pacific Law Review 159.

[75] *Ibid.*

[76] L Wang, '创新目标在《反垄断法》上的定位与实现—兼评《反垄断法（修正草案）》第1条 [Positioning and Realization of Innovation Objectives in the Anti-Monopoly Law—Comment on Article 1 of the Anti-Monopoly Law]' (2022) 1 Journal of China University of Political Science and Law 173, 173–185.

[77] SW Smith and W Stephen, 'When Most-Favored Is Disfavored: A Counselor's Guide to MFNs' (2013) 27(2) Antitrust 10, 10–14; MFNs in the digital economy are also called 'platform most-favoured-nation' (PMFN) clauses. See H Jiao, '互联网平台最惠国条款的反垄断法适用 [Application of Anti-Monopoly Law of the Most-Favoured-Nation Clauses on the Internet Platform]' (2021) 2 Journal of Business Economics 74.

The competition authorities in Europe and the United States have carried out numerous anti-monopoly investigations into the practice of MFN clauses, especially in online booking, e-book selling, and price comparison websites.[78] For instance, the MFN clauses between hotels and the booking platform Hotel Reservation Service (HRS) was found unlawful by the Bundeskartellamt in Germany. Article 1 of the German Act against Restraints of Competition and Article 101 of the Treaty on the Functioning of the European Union (TFEU), which consider MFN clauses to constitute anticompetitive agreements, served as the statutory ground for the ruling.[79]

In spite of the widespread academic and policy concerns over the growing practice of MFN clauses in China's digital markets,[80] there have been very few formal investigations into such practices by any digital platform yet in China. Or at the very least, no official regulatory decision has been made public in mainland China,[81] while the regulatory agency in the jurisdiction of Hong Kong investigated the MFN conduct by Ctrip, one of the major online booking platforms in China.[82] Nonetheless, the SAMR took express notice of the practice of MFN clauses by Tencent Music Group when issuing the prohibition decision on Tencent Music Group's illegal merger with China Music Corporation. While the decision primarily addressed the exclusive licensing deals in order to restore the competitiveness in the relevant market, it also clearly required Tencent not to enter into exclusive agreements with upstream copyright holders via abandoning exclusive copyright.[83] Chinese legal scholars widely view such an anticompetitive business model with high prepayments as a variant of the MFN clause as well.[84]

Given the size of China's digital economy, it is certainly reasonable to assume that digital platform operators may have concluded MFN clauses with their

[78] P Akman, 'A Competition Law Assessment of Platform Most-Favored-Customer Clauses' (2016) 12(4) Journal of Competition Law and Economics 781.

[79] Bundeskartellamt, *HRS-Hotel Reservation Service*, 9th Decision Division, B9- 66/10 (20 December 2013). On the assessment under EU competition law, see Chapter 3, section V.3.

[80] Tan (n16).

[81] X Yi and G Tian, 'China Responding to Regulatory Challenges of IT Industry Competition: A Quick Guide to the Anti-Monopoly Guidelines for Platform Economy (Draft for Comment)' (Zhong Lun Law Firm, 16 November 2020) <https://www.lexology.com/library/detail.aspx?g=7b929b9aa51e4dc593dd2e0ea6b42d88> (accessed 4 October 2023).

[82] Hong Kong Competition Commission, '关于网上旅行社根据"竞争条例"第60条所作出的承诺 [The Commitments Made by Online Travel Agents under Section 60 of the Competition Ordinance]' (13 May 2020) <https://www.compcomm.hk/tc/enforcement/registers/commitments/commitments_online_travel_agents.html> (accessed 4 October 2023).

[83] SAMR, '国家市场监督管理总局行政处罚决定书（国市监处〔2021〕67号） [SAMR Administrative Prohibition Decision [2021] No 67]' (24 July 2021) <https://www.samr.gov.cn/zt/qhfldzf/art/2021/art_61810ad454524ec2b9cb38c78f3d793c.html> (accessed 7 November 2022).

[84] S Li, '数字音乐独家版权模式解除与反垄断—以对腾讯音乐的反垄断调查为例[Dismantling of the Exclusive Copyright Model for Digital Music and Antitrust—An Example of Antitrust Investigation on Tencent Music Group]' (2022) 4 China Price 69, 70. Also see J Long, '数字音乐版权独家授权的竞争风险及其规制方法 [Competition Risks of Digital Music Copyright Exclusive Authorization and Its Solutions]' (2020) 34(2) Journal of Huazhong University of Science and Technology (Social Science Edition) 83, 86.

merchants. However, the conclusion of MFN clauses may not have become a scalable business practice, largely because, on the one hand, powerful platforms have multiple strategies that could be more effective than MFN clauses to maintain their monopolistic status.[85] On the other hand, the intensive enforcement actions taken by Chinese competition authorities against digital platforms have probably made digital giants highly cautious of such practice, which could be easily detected. Taking Ctrip as an example, it now controls more than 70 per cent of China's online booking business following many rounds of profitable equity acquisitions.[86] Ctrip might probably have adapted its business strategy after learning about the potential risk from the cases of Booking.com and HRS.[87]

Apart from the low level of MFN clause practice in China's digital markets, the availability of statutory ground for MFN clauses may also bring challenges for the regulatory agencies to tackle such a practice. Unlike the structure of MFN clauses in traditional industries, such clauses concluded in digital markets are essentially 'third-party agreements' that limit the price at which the merchants can charge individual consumers leveraging the power of platforms.[88] Based on current law enforcement in China, the significant concealment of 'collusion' between the platforms and merchants makes it difficult to identify such anticompetitive agreements in digital markets. Therefore, as aforementioned, it is not clear whether a platform's behaviour constitutes by nature an anticompetitive agreement or abuse of market dominance.

As illustrated in the previous cases, it is undeniable that, more often than not, regulators tend to adopt gentle measures like administrative guidance, constituting a dual-track mechanism system with a distinct Chinese flavour.[89] And regulators seemly tend to tackle such behaviours, if found to be materially anticompetitive, on the ground of the abuse of market dominance or even other areas of law, such as price law, rather than directly addressing behaviours of an MFN nature.[90] The recent revision of the Guidelines on Anti-Monopoly Compliance for Business Operators ('the Compliance Guidelines' for short) by the Anti-Monopoly and

[85] See J Sun and Y Song, '数字经济背景下最惠国待遇条款的反垄断合理分析 [The Antitrust Rule-of-Reason Analysis of MFN Clauses in the Context of the Digital Economy]' (2018) 12 Electronics Intellectual Property 12, 17.

[86] Ctrip, '供应链及品牌力筑核心壁垒， 国际化布局有望贡献增量 [Supply Chain and Brand Power to Build Core Barriers, International Layout Is Expected to Contribute to the Increase]' (Research Report, 1 October 2023) <https://www.vzkoo.com/read/20231001fc3e5cb1f4b75791873d7f52.html> (accessed 4 October 2023).

[87] According to an interview with a manager of Ctrip.

[88] Jiao (n77).

[89] For example, on 27 October 2020, under the guidance of the Beijing Municipal Bureau of Market Regulation and the Chaoyang District Market Regulation Bureau, the Self-Discipline Convention of Internet Travel Service Industry was officially released, which was jointly initiated and formulated by five Internet travel service enterprises, namely Tongcheng Yilong, Ctrip, Meituan, Mafengwo, and Qunar. See M Xin, '携程参与《互联网旅游服务行业自律公约》制定 用服务和技术为行业赋能 [Ctrip Participated in the Formulation of the "Internet Travel Service Industry Self-Discipline Convention" to Empower the Industry with Services and Technology]' (27 October 2020) <https://baijiahao.baidu.com/s?id=1681674965693421580&wfr=spider&for=pc> (accessed 4 October 2023).

[90] Han, Geo, and Deng (n24).

Anti-Unfair Competition Commission of China's State Council arguably suggests a similar stance. The SAMR released the first version of the Compliance Guidelines in 2020 and released a draft revision of the Compliance Guidelines (Draft for Consultations) on 21 March 2024. A reference case included in the draft revision explicitly directs undertakings to take effective measures to monitor and prevent anticompetitive business practices such as exclusive cooperation, MFN clauses, and vertical agreements.[91] Nonetheless, such a reference case was eventually deleted from the final revision of the Compliance Guidelines.[92]

VI. Conclusion

The recent changes made in Chinese laws and regulations on anticompetitive agreements in digital markets are notable. The amended AML added a 'safe-harbour' clause and a 'hub-and-spoke conspiracy' clause in the chapter on anticompetitive agreements, alongside an enhanced liability for anticompetitive agreement violations, in response to challenges presented by digital markets. The Guidelines also referred to innovation preservation, APPA, 'hub-and-spoke agreements', and data and algorithms, in the chapter on anticompetitive agreements.

Although the issue of anticompetitive agreements has raised great regulatory concern, it is worth noting that formal prohibition decisions were rarely made on the ground of anticompetitive agreements in actual cases, compared with multiple prohibition decisions on abuse of dominance and failure to notify. Especially when compared to its EU counterpart, Chinese competition law enforcement seems to focus more on the abuse of market dominance and mergers in digital markets rather than anticompetitive agreements. Formal and stringent administrative measures are rarely taken to address anticompetitive agreements. Two factors have contributed to this situation. On the one hand, it is still infeasible for platforms to conclude anticompetition agreements in China's digital markets at this stage. Fierce competition across multiple segments on both sides of the market prevents platforms from reaching horizontal agreements, whereas vertical agreements employed by platforms often fall within the scope of abuse of dominance. On the other hand, regulatory bodies in China tend to take the 'dual-track' approach, where formal investigations and informal interventions are combined to tackle suspected conclusions of anticompetitive agreements.

[91] SAMR, '经营者反垄断合规指南（征求意见稿）[Guidelines on Anti-Monopoly Compliance for Business Operators (Draft for Consultations)]', Reference Case No 23 (promulgated by the SAMR, 21 March 2024) <https://www.samr.gov.cn/jzxts/tzgg/zqyj/art/2024/art_3ed68bc139684c7c92487e2e5f12c31e.html> (accessed 1 May 2024).

[92] SAMR, '经营者反垄断合规指南 [Guidelines on Anti-Monopoly Compliance for Business Operators]' (promulgated by the SAMR, 24 April 2024) <https://www.samr.gov.cn/zw/zfxxgk/fdzdgknr/jzzcxds/art/2024/art_2d4b1705febf41c38856dda554e84857.html> (accessed 1 May 2024).

8
Abuse of Dominance

I. Introduction

The years after China's Central Economic Work Conference in 2020 have witnessed a good number of cases in which the competition authorities of China have made high-profile prohibition decisions against the abuse of dominant positions in its digital markets. Among the eleven cases of abuse of market dominance that the State Administration for Market Regulation (SAMR) formally investigated in the year immediately following Communist Party of China's (CPC's) Central Economic Work Conference in December 2020, for example, there were three cases involving digital platforms and eight cases involving traditional industries like the pharmacy, water, and energy sectors.[1] Compared with the number of cases formally investigated in 2020 (eighteen cases in total, one concerning digital platforms) and 2019 (fourteen cases in total, none in digital economy), in 2021, the number materially increased.[2]

According to the official statistics of the SAMR, the total penalties in 2021 imposed by the competition authorities nationwide regarding abuse-of-dominance cases amounted to ¥23.57 billion (ca €3.03 billion), approximately 91.88 per cent of which were imposed on violating digital platforms.[3] Notably, the SAMR first fined the Alibaba Group ¥18.23 billion (ca €2.35 billion), about 4 per cent of Alibaba's 2019 domestic revenues, and then fined Meituan ¥3.44 billion (ca €0.44 billion), about 3 per cent of Meituan's 2020 domestic revenues.[4]

[1] Unfair overpricing and tied sales are prevalent in China's traditional industries. In recent years, China has stepped up its anti-monopoly enforcement in the fields of application programming interfaces (APIs), water supply, power supply, gas supply utilities, etc. See SAMR, '中国反垄断执法年度报告 (2021) [Annex of Annual Report of China on Anti-Monopoly Law Enforcement (2021)]' (8 June 2022) <https://www.samr.gov.cn/xw/zj/art/2023/art_bfac0acc333e4bd0be85adf099272047.html> (accessed 7 November 2022).

[2] G Shao, '2021年反垄断执法数据分析：滥用市场支配地位 [Analysis of Anti-Monopoly Enforcement Data in 2021: Abuse of Dominance]' (14 March 2022) <https://weibo.com/1794930063/LjIqo3OIh> (accessed 7 November 2022). In 2022, a total of thirteen cases of abuse of market dominance were formally investigated by the SAMR, among which one case involved digital platforms (the case of *CNKI*). See SAMR, '中国反垄断执法年度报告 (2022) [Annual Report of China on Anti-Monopoly Law Enforcement (2022)]' (9 June 2023) <https://www.samr.gov.cn/xw/zj/art/2023/art_38056964cf5449daa346237200e24da0.html> (accessed 27 January 2024).

[3] Shao (n2), 30.

[4] *Ibid*, 30. See also X Li and Y Yin, 'China Fines Meituan $533m for Monopolist Practices, Milder Than Alibaba Due to Difference in Rectification Moves' (Global Times, 8 October 2021), 30 <https://www.globaltimes.cn/page/202110/1235798.shtml> (accessed 27 September 2022).

Competition Law and Policy in Digital Markets. Maria Ioannidou and Bingwan Xiong, Oxford University Press.
 DOI: 10.1093/9780191925955.003.0008

On 10 April 2021, the SAMR issued a prohibition decision finding that the Alibaba Group had abused its market dominance by requiring its merchants to sell exclusively on its platform ('either–or choice'). The decision resulted in a penalty of ¥18.23 billion (ca €2.35 billion) being imposed. On 8 October 2021, the SAMR imposed a penalty of ¥3.44 billion (ca €0.44 billion) on Meituan, since Meituan had forced vendors to conclude tied sales agreements. To enforce such agreements, Meituan implemented discriminatory rates and other platform rules against dissenting vendors.[5] Moreover, Shanghai Administration for Market Regulation (Shanghai AMR) imposed a penalty of ¥116.86 million (ca €15.06 million) on Sherpa's, a popular food and beverage delivery platform serving English-speaking consumers, for its similar tied sales misconduct with online food sellers.

In addition to tied sales, another focus of China's recent law enforcement against the abuse of market dominance has been the exploitation of data advantages by dominant digital platforms. A sizable portion of cases accordingly encompass data-related monopolies.[6] As ever-increasing amounts of data are being collected by digital platforms, valuable opportunities for the innovation of business models arise, thanks to the development of new products and services in digital markets. Nevertheless, risks may arise simultaneously by means of big data-enabled price discrimination, barriers for new entrants to obtain market access, and personal information infringements. As illustrated in the case of *CNKI* in section V.1.5 of this chapter, the SAMR has attached growing importance to anticompetitive behaviours, driven by data advantages among platform competitors.

As for the practice of law enforcement by competition authorities in this regard, the 'dual-track' approach with Chinese characteristics, mentioned in Chapter 3, section V.3 and elaborated in Chapter 7, has also been employed to address the abuse of market dominance. Formal law enforcement, however, plays a more vital role in this field. Several high-profile cases of formal enforcement, especially against the business practice of 'either–or choice', have taken place in almost every sector of China's digital markets (e-tailing, food delivery, online booking, housing agency, etc.). Giant platforms like the Alibaba Group, Meituan, and Beike were all suspected of abusing their dominance in relevant markets when conducting 'either–or choice' business strategies. Although soft interventions like administrative interviews with those suspected were carried out by the competition authority, almost all of these cases eventually went to formal investigation and prohibition decisions.

Apart from the law enforcement by competition authorities, civil lawsuits claiming compensatory remedies against such abusive behaviours, which will be

[5] Shao (n2). See also J Yan, 'Anti-Monopoly Regulation of Algorithm Collusion in Big Data Era' (2021) 8 International Conference on Machinery, Mechanics, Materials, and Computer Engineering 124.

[6] SAMR (n2). See also S Zheng, 'JD Wins $140 Million Damages from Alibaba in Antitrust Suit' (Bloomberg News, 29 December 2023) <https://news.bloomberglaw.com/antitrust/jd-wins-1b-yuan-in-damages-in-anti-monopoly-case-against-alibaba> (accessed 25 January 2024).

further elaborated on in this chapter, are taking place subsequent to these prohibition decisions. Platform competitors, in-platform merchants, and consumers that are adversely affected by such anticompetitive behaviours have also proactively sought relief from the courts. For example, on 29 December 2023, in a case related to the prohibition decision against the Alibaba Group, JD.com announced that it had won the lawsuit against the Alibaba Group for its misconduct of 'either–or choice'. Beijing High People's Court, in its judgment, awarded JD.com ¥1 billion (ca €127 million) in damages against its rival, the Alibaba Group.[7] In another case still pending before the court, ByteDance sued Tencent, at the beginning of 2021, for alleged abuse of market dominance for the reason that Tencent, it was claimed, had restricted users' sharing of content from ByteDance's short-video sharing app (Douyin, the Chinese version of TikTok) on its instant communication apps (QQ and WeChat).[8]

The active anti-monopoly law enforcement against the abuse of dominance in digital markets, be it through public enforcement or private litigation, is largely associated with the recent reformulation of China's anti-monopoly laws and regulations, which is pertinent to the challenging issues arising in digital markets. Against such a backdrop, this chapter aims to shed light on how the abuse of dominance in digital markets is addressed by both dimensions of law enforcement and law reformulation in China. We present the regulatory framework for abusive behaviour in this chapter after mapping out the main types of abusive behaviours in digital markets in China, and then reflect on the effectiveness of China's regulatory reform. Major cases concerning abuse of dominance in China's digital markets will further be analysed thereafter.

II. Main Types of Abusive Behaviour in China's Digital Markets

Platform operators in digital markets have been engaging in multiple forms of anticompetitive practices, which disrupt market competition and hinder the welfare of consumers and other stakeholders by way of incurring higher prices and entry barriers.[9] When it comes to the abuse of dominant positions in China's digital markets, anticompetitive behaviours, as mapped out below, mainly include exclusive dealing, deep discounting and predatory pricing, and differentiated treatment. The prevalence of these anticompetitive behaviours has largely catalysed the

[7] F Fan, 'JD wins monopoly lawsuit against Alibaba' (China Daily, 29 December 2023) <https://www.chinadaily.com.cn/a/202312/29/WS658eba2ea3105f21a5079c97.html> (accessed 8 November 2024).

[8] See X Zhou, '北京知识产权法院正式受理抖音诉腾讯垄断纠纷案 [Beijing Intellectual Property Court Formally Accepts ByteDance v. Tencent in Terms of Monopoly Dispute]' (7 February 2021) <http://www.techweb.com.cn/it/20210207/2825270.shtml> (accessed 11 March 2023).

[9] L Rana and N Nagpal, 'Abuse of Dominant Position in Digital Markets' (Bar and Bench, 2 June 2022) <https://www.barandbench.com/view-point/abuse-of-dominant-position-in-digital-markets> (accessed 7 November 2022).

reformulation of the laws and regulations tackling the new forms of abusive behaviours in digital markets. Before moving on to the details of such a reformulation, we sketch out these behaviours and generally comment on the regulatory attitudes thereon, including the emerging mechanism of private enforcement against them.

II.1 Exclusive Dealing

According to Article 22 of the new Anti-Monopoly Law (AML), it is explicitly forbidden for a dominant undertaking to force business partners to conduct their business exclusively with it or its designated subjects in the absence of justifiable reasons.[10] In the most typical form of exclusive dealing in China's digital markets, platform operators require users (typically merchants) on the platform to make 'either–or choice', which means to operate exclusively on one of the competing platforms.

The practice of the 'either–or choice' business strategy by giant platforms has been prevalent in China's digital markets in recent years. By forcing online merchants to make an 'either–or choice' between one platform and its rivals, the platform seeks to exclusively deal with obedient merchants. Such a practice has been widely accused of unfairly exploiting platform advantages, including capital, technology, business scale, etc. The 'either–or choice' may also arise through the exclusion of a specific platform. Some platforms may require platform users to make an 'either–or choice' between themselves and a specific competing platform on the ground of technological incompatibility with such a platform.[11] If merchants breach such a choice, the platform will either directly or indirectly restrict the service quality available to them, or even compel them to withdraw their business presence on rival platforms. Such strategies ultimately bring about lock-in effects, snatching market share from other operators, squeezing out other platforms' business opportunities, and entrenching or enhancing the competitive advantages of digital goliaths.

There has been no unified view on the legal nature of the 'either–or choice' yet. Nonetheless, it is widely agreed that the practice of 'either–or choice' falls under both the domain of anticompetitive agreements and that of abuse of dominance if the undertaking involved enjoys considerable market power.[12] In the practice

[10] DeHeng Law Offices, 'In Brief: Abuse of Dominance in China' (Lexology, 19 March 2020) <https://www.lexology.com/library/detail.aspx?g=7e04484d-f754-4a7e-b698-80d2eb47ce04> (accessed 7 November 2022). Even if the implementer of the 'either–or choice' strategy does not have a dominant market position, and therefore poses a relatively lower impact on market competition than the typical form does, it may also bring about anticompetitive effects. Typically, see the *3Q War* case discussed below.

[11] *Ibid.*

[12] *Ibid.* See Z Xu (ed), '互联网平台《二选一》研讨会观点综述 [Summary of the Views of the Seminar on 'Either–Or Choice' by Platforms]' (25 April 2019) <https://www.imsilkroad.com/news/p/363138.html> (accessed 7 November 2022).

of law enforcement, the Chinese regulatory authorities tend to handle the issue of the 'either–or choice' under the umbrella of the abuse of market dominance, instead of anticompetitive agreements. Legal experts in China also tend to approach the practice of the 'either–or choice' as a type of abusive behaviour.[13] There is the opinion that the 'either–or choice' has the essence of exclusivity, by aiming to exclude competitors by locking in online merchants.[14] There is also the view that the 'either–or choice' refers to excluding competitors by limiting their choices through exclusive deals, refusal to deal, and loyalty discounts.[15]

The business practice of the 'either–or choice' by digital platforms in China did not come into being all of a sudden. It first emerged during the years from 2010 to 2015, when China's digital economy was still in its infancy. Early practices came in forms such as 'price wars' and 'sales promotion wars', aiming to lure platform users and pursuing platform scales. It was alleged to be exclusive dealing for the first time in the high-profile case of *3Q War*, in which the Supreme People's Court (SPC) considered the characteristics of instant communication services when defining the relevant market and assessing platforms' market power.[16] In the second phase, lasting from 2016 to 2018, major digital platforms, especially e-tailing platforms, vigorously invested in shopping festivals (e.g. 'Double 11' and '6.18', two major annual mass-promoting activities in China) and other promotional marketing strategies so as to consolidate their market positions and lock in platform users.[17]

During the third stage, from 2019 onwards, leading digital platforms from a wide range of e-commerce sectors kept escalating the practice of the 'either–or choice'. Such practices eventually evolved into a major problem, plaguing the healthy development of China's digital markets.[18] The E-Commerce Law of China that aims to provide a general regulatory framework for e-commerce came into effect on 1 January 2019. For the first time during China's long march to address the 'either–or choice' practice, it struck a clear tone on the illegality of the 'either–or choice' at the level of national legislation. It stated that e-commerce platform operators shall not make use of their service agreement, transaction rules, and technology

[13] DeHeng Law Offices (n10). See also the opinion of H Jiao, Deputy Director of Institute of Economic Law, China University of Political Science and Law, in Xu (n12).

[14] See the opinion of H Jiao, Deputy Director of Institute of Economic Law, China University of Political Science and Law, in Xu (n12). See the opinion of W Yao, Director of Antitrust Affairs, NetEase Group, in Xu (n12).

[15] See the opinion of W Yao, Director of Antitrust Affairs, NetEase Group, in Xu (n12).

[16] Supreme People's Court, *Beijing Qihoo Technology Co, Ltd v Tencent Technology (Shenzhen) Co, Ltd, Shenzhen Tencent Computer System Co, Ltd*, [2013] (指导案例78号：北京奇虎科技有限公司诉腾讯科技（深圳）有限公司、深圳市腾讯计算机系统有限公司滥用市场支配地位纠纷案，(2013)民三终字第4号) (8 October 2014). See more details of this case in Section V.1.1 '3Q War': *Qihoo v Tencent*.

[17] See more details of this case in Section V.1.1 '3Q War': *Qihoo v Tencent*.

[18] See the case of the 'Either–Or Choice' below. See SAMR, '国家市场监督管理总局行政处罚决定书（国市监处〔2021〕28号）[SAMR Administrative Prohibition Decision [2021] No 28]' (10 April 2021) <https://www.samr.gov.cn/xw/zj/art/2023/art_4966dda92ab34c398615f5878c10c8f1.html> (accessed 7 November 2022).

to impose unreasonable restrictions or unreasonable conditions on transactions taking place within the platform and with other business partners.[19] Later on, the Guidelines and the new AML paid particular attention to anticompetitive behaviours in digital markets and highlighted abuse-of-dominance cases as a priority for anti-monopoly law enforcement.

II.2 Deep Discounting and Predatory Pricing

The second category of abusive conduct in China's digital markets falls into the scope of price abuse, namely deep discounting and predatory pricing. In their early stages of development, some e-tailing platforms (such as Pinduoduo) might have adopted a business model that prioritized market expansion above profitability by subsidizing users in one way or another so as to attract users and expand user pools. A good number of consumers chose to purchase through such platforms due to the incredibly low prices.[20] In the long run, platforms may make significant gains by exploiting their dominant market positions to compensate for their initial losses.

Article 22 of the new AML expressly prohibits a dominant undertaking from selling products or providing services at a price lower than the cost in the absence of justified reasons. According to the Interim Provisions for Prohibiting Abuse of Market Dominance (hereafter referred to as 'the Interim Provisions'), in the determination of whether products or services are sold at a price below cost, key consideration shall be given as to whether the price is lower than the average variable cost, which is a standard that is also adopted by the European Union (EU).[21] The State Administration for Industry and Commerce established such a standard in early cases, such as Tetra Pak's abuse of dominant market position.[22] The 'Provisions of the Supreme People's Court on Several Issues Concerning the Application of Law in Monopoly Civil Disputes (Draft for Public Comments)' released by the SPC of

[19] MOFCOM (Ministry of Commerce, People's Republic of China), '中华人民共和国电子商务法 [E-Commerce Law of the PRC]' (promulgated by the Standing Committee of the National People's Congress, 31 August 2018, effective 1 January 2019), Article 35 <http://mg.mofcom.gov.cn/article/policy/201912/20191202923971.shtml> (accessed 7 November 2022).

[20] N Misra, 'An Analysis on the Increasing Abuse of Dominance in the Digital Market' (Black n' White Journal, 11 September 2021) <https://bnwjournal.com/2021/09/11/an-analysis-on-the-increasing-abuse-of-dominance-in-the-digital-market> (accessed 7 November 2022).

[21] SAMR, '禁止滥用市场支配地位行为暂行规定 [Interim Provisions on Prohibiting Abuse of Dominant Market Position]' (promulgated by the SAMR, 24 March 2022, effective 1 May 2022), Article 15 <https://sjfg.samr.gov.cn/law/pageInfo/main.main?order = 10&iframe = pageInfo/law_search_new.law_details?lawId = 1654ccdf139f45f22da645587e314e6a> (accessed 25 November 2023).

[22] Tetra Pak is a multinational company supplying liquid food-processing and packaging products. See SAIC (State Administration for Industry and Commerce), '国家工商行政管理总局行政处罚决定书（工商竞争案字[2016]1号） [SAIC Administrative Prohibition Decision [2016] No 1]' (9 November 2016) <https://www.samr.gov.cn/zt/qhfldzf/art/2016/art_8ca2ed4b38d842d7b4c363eaac06c103.html> (accessed 7 November 2022).

China in November 2022, also introduces such a standard in its Article 38. The first paragraph in this Article enumerates average variable cost as a key parameter in assessing below-cost price, while the second paragraph asserts that, in the context of the digital economy, multilateral costs associated with those services and their interactions should also be taken into account.[23]

Deep discounting and predatory pricing in digital markets typically take two forms: first, when platforms lack control over the prices of goods or services they provide, they may resort to discounting or predatory pricing by lowering the commissions charged against engaged merchants; and second, when platforms can determine the selling prices, they may adopt discounting or predatory pricing strategies by lowering prices.[24] As a matter of exemption, selling below cost by a dominant undertaking is justifiable only if it is for (i) the disposal of fresh, seasonal, or overstocked items; (ii) paying off debt, changing production routes, or winding up a business; or (iii) promoting new products within a reasonable period of time.[25] To determine whether certain platforms have abused their dominant market position by selling below cost, it is therefore vital to thoroughly identify the impacts on competition in the relevant market.

In practice, as we mentioned in Chapter 7, community group buying conducted by platforms such as Pinduoduo and Meituan would be primarily treated as a type of anticompetitive agreement. Such anticompetitive behaviour is related to deep discounting and predatory pricing since the prices for community group buyers are normally set below the cost either through direct discounting or through providing coupons.[26] Nevertheless, the low selling prices by virtue of community group buying put in place by Pinduoduo were not decided under the framework of anti-monopoly law. Instead, they were decided on the ground of the Price Law, which does not require the competition authority to strictly establish the dominant position of the investigated undertaking in its relevant market. Moreover, the Price Law provides the competition authority with a more discretionary threshold for punishing 'unfair price' than anti-monopoly law's calculation of the average variable cost. Even if the platform is proved to have a dominant position, its upfront input costs, instead of merely the sale price, should also be taken into account. That said, it becomes even more difficult to evaluate whether a platform has

[23] Supreme People's Court of China, '最高人民法院关于审理垄断民事纠纷案件适用法律若干问题的规定（公开征求意见稿）[Provisions of the Supreme People's Court on Several Issues Concerning the Application of Law in Monopoly Civil Disputes (Draft for Public Comments)]' (promulgated by the Supreme People's Court of China, 18 November 2022) <https://www.court.gov.cn/zixun/xiangqing/380101.html> (accessed 2 December 2022).

[24] Y Wang, Z Wang, and X Sun, 'On Determination of Predatory Pricing by Online Sharing Platforms under the AML' (2017) 3 Journal of Cyber Affairs 60, 60–66.

[25] SAMR, 'Interim Provisions on Prohibiting Abuse of Dominant Market Position' (n21), Article 15.

[26] Beijing Fourth Intermediate People's Court, *Tian Shufeng v Beijing Taobao Technology Co., Ltd.*, [2022] (田淑凤与北京淘宝科技有限公司等信息网络买卖合同纠纷案， (2022)京04民终195号) (23 May 2022).

committed below-cost selling when it provides free or below-cost price products and services.[27]

II.3 Differentiated Treatment

II.3.1 Big Data-Enabled Price Discrimination

The issue of big data-enabled price discrimination arises when digital platforms charge different consumers different prices for identical goods and services based on consumers' personal information, which is collected by profiling technology. Such a business practice uses algorithms to build up consumers' profiles with respect to their personal consumption preferences and financial capacity so as to implement differentiated trading conditions for the same goods or services.

Such business conduct essentially involves differentiated pricing for different consumers and may, at some stages, involve raising prices for loyal clients so as to boost profits. Although such conduct has been clearly identified, it is still debatable as to whether it should be legally classified as price discrimination, price fraud, or abuse of algorithmic power. As a complement to the AML, China's E-Commerce Law aims to 'respect and protect the legitimate rights and interests of consumers such as equality',[28] which may serve as a general but indeterminate statutory ground for the regulation of big data-enabled price discrimination.

Anti-monopoly wise, as a handful of digital platforms control the opportunity to collect and process vast amounts of data, they sit in a better position to exploit consumers' personal preferences.[29] Article 22 of the new AML states explicitly that price discrimination by a dominant undertaking, short of justifiable reasons, constitutes an abusive conduct. Nevertheless, it is still a challenge for the SAMR and the court to determine whether certain practices of price differentiation have sound justifications. After all, it is not abnormal for goods or service providers to charge different trading partners different prices. In principle, price difference within a reasonable scope is legally acceptable, even for dominant platforms. When it comes to the constantly evolving digital markets, it becomes more difficult

[27] Interview with a senior lawyer from Linklaters Beijing Office (April 20, 2021)..

[28] Article 18 of the E-Commerce Law stipulates that

> When providing the results of search for products or services for a consumer based on the hobby, consumption habit, or any other traits thereof, the e-commerce business shall provide the consumer with options not targeting his/her identifiable traits and respect and equally protect the lawful rights and interests of consumers.

English version available at MOFCOM, 'E-Commerce Law of the PRC' (English translation) (29 October 2019) <http://mg.mofcom.gov.cn/article/policy/201912/20191202923971.shtml> (accessed 11 October 2024).

[29] M Ioannidou, '"Digital Agoraphobia": An Enforcement Perspective' in I Kokkoris and C Lemus (eds), *Research Handbook on the Law and Economics of Competition Enforcement* (Edward Elgar, 2022), 369. On such practices and the various risks they pose, see M Stucke, 'Should We Be Concerned about Data-opolies?' (2018) 2 Georgetown Law Technology Review 275.

to set a benchmark to determine the degree of price difference for the establishment of discrimination. There have been several high-profile cases concerning price discrimination in China's digital markets, including, for example, Didi's reported charging of different fares for Apple users and Android users for the same journey and similar conduct by Ctrip. Moreover, as commented on at some length below, Meituan's implementation of price discrimination also triggered intensive academic discussions and received attention from regulatory agencies in 2020.

II.3.2 Self-Preferencing

The business strategy of self-preferencing used to be widely adopted, partly because platform operators generally think that other platform operators will implement the same strategy so as to preserve e-tailing profits for their own interests.[30] Relying on its own market power for the implementation of self-preferencing, platforms bid to expand, consolidate, or enhance their market positions. Such anti-competitive behaviour encompasses a wide range of forms and is prone to bring about the effect of excluding or restricting competition.

Google,[31] Amazon,[32] and other platform giants have been penalized severely by the regulatory agencies in the EU for their practices of self-preferencing, amongst others. In China, self-preferencing has also become a topic of heated discussion. Many legal academics think that self-preferencing may strengthen undertakings' dominant positions, which may subsequently harm the competition in the downstream market and eventually pose a threat to the welfare of consumers.[33]

Such a concern was triggered by a business practice that can be exemplified by Tencent. During the COVID-19 pandemic, demand for remote collaboration software in China surged rapidly. Tencent's WeChat and Tencent Conference, Alibaba's Ding Talk, and ByteDance's Feishu were three major competitive products in this field. In 2020, Tencent blocked Ding Talk and Feishu by not allowing links to these two apps to be shared through WeChat, causing inconvenience to the users of these apps.[34] In the same vein, in 2021, Tencent imposed bans on links to Douyin and Xiaohongshu on WeChat, while those to Tencent Apps could operate normally.[35] In April 2021, an individual user filed an anti-monopoly lawsuit

[30] MA Salinger, 2020, 'Self-Preferencing, The Global Antitrust Institute Report on the Digital Economy' (Boston University Questrom School of Business, 2020), 334.

[31] On the various cases against Google see Chapter 5, section II.3.

[32] On the various cases against Amazon see Chapter 5, section II.4.

[33] Xinhua Net, '《竞争法视野下的平台自我优待》学术研讨会召开 [Seminar on "Self-Preferencing of Platforms in the Perspective of Competition Law" Was Successfully Held]' (28 January 2021) <https://baijiahao.baidu.com/s?id=1690123772257090597&wfr=spider&for=pc> (accessed 10 December 2022).

[34] Sohu News, '微信为争夺在线办公市场封杀钉钉 [WeChat Blocked the Ding Talk for the Online Office Market]' (4 March 2020) <https://www.sohu.com/a/377641393_120003738> (accessed 10 December 2022).

[35] WeChat Security Center, '针对第三方违规导流链接的治理公告 [On the Handling of Third-Party Illegal Infusion Links]' (11 December 2020) <https://mp.weixin.qq.com/s/wrzynlw92rRGo528hZItVg> (accessed 11 March 2023).

against Tencent, claiming that he could neither share content on Douyin with his friends through WeChat nor open links to Douyin on WeChat. On the grounds that Tencent had abused its dominant market position and refused to trade, the user filed a lawsuit in Beijing Intellectual Property Court. Subsequently, Tencent filed a jurisdictional objection. The case is currently under trial.[36]

Nevertheless, there has not yet been any conclusive regulatory enforcement or judicial cases addressing the legality of self-preferencing in China. Actually, there are not yet any formal statutory rules on self-preferencing, in spite of the efforts to formulate such rules by China's central competition authority. In September 2021, for example, the Ministry of Industry and Information Technology (MIIT), the central regulatory authority for Internet supervision in China, reportedly required large tech firms (such as the Alibaba Group, Tencent Holdings, and ByteDance) to stop blocking rivals' links in a closed-door meeting.[37] On 29 October 2021, for example, the SAMR issued the 'Guidelines on Implementing the Main Responsibility of Internet Platforms (Draft for Consultations)', Article 2 of which stipulates the principle of 'equal governance' and demands that 'giant platform operators shall comply with the principles of fairness and non-discrimination when providing relevant products or services, equally treat the platform itself (or affiliated enterprises) and operators within the platform, and not implement self-preferential treatment'.[38]

At a later stage, on 27 June 2022, the SAMR released the 'Provisions on Prohibition of Abuse of Market Dominance (Draft for Consultations)' which, in its Article 20, attempted to explicitly prohibit platform operators from implementing self-preferential treatment in two situations: first, by giving priority to the display or ranking of their own goods; and second, by using the non-public data of business operators on the platform to develop their own products or assist in their own decision-making.[39] The formula in Article 20 intensively borrowed from the

[36] On Tencent's filing of jurisdictional objection, see the public news regarding the case (16 April 2021), *Mr Huang v Tencent Technology (Beijing) Co, Ltd*, [2021] (黄某诉腾讯科技（北京）有限公司滥用市场支配地位纠纷案), (2021)京73民初172号) <https://weibo.com/1765373140/Kb9Cqvyyf> (accessed 11 March 2023).

[37] B Goh and S Yan, 'In Fresh Regulatory Move, China Tells Tech Giants to Stop Blocking Rivals' Links' (Reuters, 13 September 2021) <https://financialnewsletter.com/in-fresh-regulatory-move> (accessed 10 December 2022).

[38] SAMR, '互联网平台落实主体责任指南（征求意见稿）[Guidelines on Implementing the Main Responsibility of Internet Platforms (Draft for Consultations)]' (promulgated by the SAMR, 29 October 2021), Article 2 <https://www.samr.gov.cn/hd/zjdc/art/2023/art_c0086d02fcc544ea9506c997b3ac93c1.html> (accessed 10 December 2022).

[39] Exemptions were also provided in the same Article, including first, displaying or ranking based on fair, reasonable, and non-discriminatory platform rules; second, conforming to proper industry practices and trading customs; and third, other reasons that can prove that the conduct is justifiable. See SAMR, '禁止滥用市场支配地位行为规定（征求意见稿）[Provisions on Prohibition of Abuse of Market Dominance (Draft for Consultations)]' (promulgated by the SAMR, 27 June 2022) <https://www.samr.gov.cn/hd/zjdc/art/2023/art_6dcdc0b84d0040daad1613ec2a12cc90.html> (accessed 10 December 2022).

European court decision against Google's practice of self-preferencing and the regulatory decisions against Amazon in several jurisdictions. The 'Provisions on Prohibition of Abuse of Market Dominance' were eventually adopted on 10 March 2023, which, however, do not contain such a formula anymore. This is mainly because, on the one hand, it is highly controversial among Chinese legal academics as to whether the practice of self-preferencing constitutes an independent form of abusive behaviour or is merely one form of existing anticompetitive behaviour such as differentiated treatment. On the other hand, platform operators found it difficult to apprehend the criteria for the definition of self-preferencing and, therefore, complained to the SAMR about the apparent lack of certainty in this formula. It has also been suggested that the open clause on abusive behaviours could serve to contain the conduct of self-preferencing if such conduct were decided to be anticompetitive in nature.[40]

III. Reforming Legal Regimes for Abusive Conduct in Digital Markets

As a country with an enormously large-scale digital economy, China has taken several steps to reformulate its regulatory framework so as to better address the growing concern of the abuse of dominance by digital platforms. The new AML provides the top-level design among many other institutional changes in recent years to strengthen the regulation against abuse of dominance. The enumeration of abusive behaviours in its earlier version, the AML effective as of 1 August 2008 ('the 2008 AML' or 'the AML'), apparently fell short of coverage of many anticompetitive behaviours conducted by digital platforms with the facilitation of big data and digital technology in general. Article 9 of the new AML generally stipulates that 'operators shall not take advantage of data and algorithms, technology, capital advantages and platform rules to engage in anti-competitive behaviours prohibited by this Law', while Article 22 in the chapter on 'Abuse of Market Dominance' serves as a special provision; both respond to the challenges of the digital economy and highlight the nature of abuse of dominance by platforms.

Under the umbrella of these provisions adopted in the new AML, the Guidelines and the Provisions, as complementary rules, enrich the overall regulatory framework of China's anti-monopoly law on abuse of market dominance in the digital markets.

[40] Interview with two law professors who were involved in the drafting process of the Provisions on Prohibition of Abuse of Market Dominance (December 2023).

III.1 The Adherence to the Principle of False Negatives

'Error cost' is an essential factor for the enforcement of antitrust law. Early literature, advanced by Richard Posner[41] and extended by Paul Joskow and Alvin Klevorick,[42] was quickly accepted by a wide range of theorists and policymakers. Modern antitrust analysts often refer to the framework adopted by Frank Easterbrook in a widely cited article in 1984.[43] According to the views on error cost, antitrust rules are evaluated based on whether they minimize the total social costs. The relevant costs include the costs of 'false positives' (finding violations when the conduct did not harm competition and putting it under the AML), the costs of 'false negatives' (not finding violations when the conduct harmed competition), and the transaction costs associated with the use of legal processes.[44]

In antitrust enforcement, the ideal goal would certainly be to precisely identify and regulate all the behaviours that harm competition. But such a goal is, in fact, so difficult to achieve that the two kinds of errors mentioned above may occur anyhow. Economically speaking, antitrust rules benefit society primarily by deterring harmful conduct. Both of the two errors, however, are detrimental to the overall growth of the economy, since the consequences of the decision or legal rule for conduct are not limited to the parties being investigated by competition authorities but can also extend to other parties that might be targeted by competition authorities. False positives and false negatives could discourage other players from acting lawfully; conversely, they could fail to deter negative behaviours from other participants governed by the same rule.[45] By comparison, false positives are more costly than false negatives and more detrimental to the whole market. Scholars assert that the costs of false positives outweigh those of false negatives, citing the alleged persistence of incorrect judicial precedents: '[i]f the court errs by condemning a beneficial practice', Judge Easterbrook wrote, 'the benefits may be lost for good' through the precedential effect of the judicial decision.[46] Therefore, the antitrust law needs to be applied as the last weapon in the face of anti-competitive business practice, and the establishment of monopolistic behaviours needs to be very stringent. If it is materially hard to determine whether a suspected behaviour

[41] I Ehrlich and RA Posner, 'An Economic Analysis of Legal Rulemaking' (1974) 3 Journal of Legal Studies 257; RA Posner, 'An Economic Approach to Legal Procedure and Judicial Administration' (1973) 2 Journal of Legal Studies 399.

[42] PL Joskow and AK Klevorick, 'A Framework for Analyzing Predatory Pricing Policy' (1979) 89 Yale Law Journal 213, 222–225.

[43] FH Easterbrook, 'The Limits of Antitrust' (1984) 63 Texas Law Review 1. See, e.g. DS Evans and AJ Padilla, 'Designing Antitrust Rules for Assessing Unilateral Practices: A Neo- Chicago Approach' (2005) 72 University of Chicago Law Review 73, 74–75 and n8.

[44] JB Baker, 'Taking the Error Out of "Error Cost" Analysis: What's Wrong with Antitrust's Right' (2016) 13 Washington College of Law Research Paper 5.

[45] *Ibid.*

[46] Easterbrook, (n43), 2. Cf. W. Page, 'Microsoft and the Limits of Antitrust' (2010) 6 Journal of Competition Law and Economics 33, 47.

constitutes a monopoly, it is better to adopt the false-negative approach to let it go rather than risk falling into the trap of a false positive.

In respect of abuse of dominance, the new AML, in its Article 22, further stresses that 'an undertaking with a dominant market position shall not use data, algorithms, technologies, platform rules, etc. to engage in the abuse of a dominant market position as prescribed in the preceding paragraph', referring to a full list of digital acts that may be considered as abuse of dominant position.[47] The regulation of monopolistic behaviours in China, however, be it the making of statutory grounds or their enforcement, adheres to the foundational principle of false negatives. At the legislative level, Article 7 of the new AML provides that 'the undertakings that have dominant market positions shall not abuse their dominant positions to eliminate or restrict competition'. It is clear that the new AML requires enforcement agencies or the courts to consider both abusive conduct (form-based approach) and the anticompetitive effect of such conduct (effects-based approach) in determining the abuse of dominance.[48] Such a provision directs the law enforcement agencies to prudently consider the anticompetitive nature of suspected behaviours. All of this explains why the law enforcement agencies in China's digital markets often prioritize soft enforcement, especially interviewing suspected platforms, so as to avoid stepping into the phase of a formal investigation.[49] And the legislative emphasis on the purpose of 'encouraging innovation' in Article 1 of the new AML in part echoes the adherence to such a principle.[50]

In addition to soft interventions, the wide range of potential defence the suspects might resort to is also in line with China's adherence to the principle of false negatives in antitrust law enforcement. Not all conduct that may have restrictive effects on market transactions by the dominant undertaking is *per se* of an abusive legal nature, and the undertaking under investigation could rebut by proving justifiable reasons to demonstrate that the conduct is not anticompetitive in accordance with Article 22 of the new AML.[51] More broadly, in judicial practice, defence might be sought from the following aspects: (i) the market definition is incorrect, (ii) there is no dominant market position of the undertaking,[52] (iii) there is no

[47] NPC Standing Committee, '中华人民共和国反垄断法（2022修正）[Anti-Monopoly Law of the PRC (2022 Amendment)]' (promulgated by the Standing Committee of the National People's Congress, 24 June 2022, effective 1 August 2022), Article 22 <https://www.pkulaw.com/en_law/d3236788421feacfbdfb.html> (accessed 7 November 2022) (new AML).

[48] See DeHeng Law Offices (n10).

[49] New AML (n47), Article 55.

[50] The purpose of 'encouraging innovation' stipulated in Article 1 of the new AML can be explained from two aspects: first, the government, guided by the principle of false negative in antitrust enforcement, tries to respect the commercial practices innovated by giant undertakings; and second, the AML also aims to maintain the freely competitive markets for start-ups to ensure their chances of competition and innovation.

[51] New AML (n47), Article 22.

[52] *Ibid.* Common arguments for not having the dominant market position are (i) the undertaking's single market share is under 50 per cent, (ii) the undertaking has no ability to control the retail market or procurement market for raw materials, (iii) there is no substantial difference between the undertaking and other competitors on financial status and technical capabilities, (iv) the trading partners are

conduct of abuse, or (iv) the alleged conduct can be justified;[53] or such defence against the claimed losses used in ordinary civil actions such as (v) the plaintiff has no standing to file the lawsuit, (vi) there is no damage to the plaintiff by the alleged conduct, and (vii) there is no causation between the conduct and the alleged damage.[54]

Against this backdrop, a common understanding is still lacking on the accurate role that data could play in implementing anticompetitive behaviours in digital markets and whether it is necessary to take a departure from the conventional principle of false negatives, especially to take a proactive strategy in handling abusive behaviours in digital markets. As a cover piece in *The Economist* famously puts it, data has been recognized as 'the most valuable resource' in the digital world.[55] Considering the scarcity and economic value of data,[56] some states, like China, have expressly recognized data as a new type of factor of production.[57] It enables the advancement of complicated algorithmic operations. Article 22 of the new AML clearly adds that operators with a dominant market position are prohibited from using data and algorithms, as well as platform rules, to set unreasonable barriers to other operators to enter into the market, so as to avoid unfair competition in digital markets. As further demonstrated in the cases of *CNKI*, data may play both roles—as a vehicle for the business operation of an enterprise or as an object for trade—and thus abuse of data advantage may easily bring about anticompetitive effects.[58]

not dependent on the undertaking, (v) the data to determine market share is inaccurate, and (vi) there is no barrier for other undertakings to enter into the relevant market.

[53] New AML (n47), Article 22.

[54] For a survey from the practitioners' perspective, see DeHeng Law Offices (n10); Shaoxing Intermediate People's Court, *Hu Hongfang v Shanghai Ctrip Business Co, Ltd*, [2021] (胡红芳诉上海携程商务有限公司侵权责任纠纷案，(2021)浙06民终3129号) (31 December 2021).

[55] S Jossen, 'The World's Most Valuable Resource Is No Longer Oil, But Data' (*The Economist*, 6 May 2017) <http://www.economist.com/leaders/2017/05/06/the-worlds-most-valuable-resource-is-no-longer-oil-but-data> (accessed 7 July 2022).

[56] H Wang, '数据资产理论 [*Data Asset Theory*]' (China Renmin University Press, 2019), 1–5; W Long, '数据新型财产权构建及其体系研究 [On the Construction of New Data Property and Its System Structure]' (2017) 35(4) Tribune of Political Science and Law 63; F Gao, '数据生产理论—数据资源权利配置的基础理论 [The Theory of Data Production: A Fundamental Theory of the Right Allocation of Data Resource]' (2019) 4 Shanghai Jiao Tong University Law Review 5.

[57] Central Committee of the CPC, '中共中央关于坚持和完善中国特色社会主义制度 推进国家治理体系和治理能力现代化若干重大问题的决定 [Decision of the Central Committee of the Communist Party of China on Major Issues Concerning Adherence to and Improvement of the Socialist System with Chinese Characteristics and Advancement of the Modernization of the National Governance System and Capability]' (adopted at the Fourth Plenary Session of the 19th Central Committee of the Communist Party of China, 31 October 2019) <https://www.gov.cn/xinwen/2020/01/01/content_5465721.htm?eqid=915fb773000307bc0000000264644e94> (accessed 1 June 2024), which emphasizes 'improving the mechanism whereby the contribution to factors of production such as labour, capital, land, knowledge, technology, management and data is valued by the market and remuneration is determined by contribution'.

[58] On this case, see text to section V.1.5 below.

Although it is controversial as to whether data accumulation can, by itself, constitute an independent element of abusive behaviour, it is well accepted that data can at least be used as a crucial vehicle to facilitate anticompetitive practices. Recognizing the role of data-driven platforms in restricting market competition, Article 14 of the Guidelines largely adopts the EU doctrine on an essential facility for the assessment of abuse of market dominance. For the analysis of whether a refusal to transact has been unreasonably committed by a dominant platform, it accords special weight to the suspect's control of an essential facility. According to the essential facility doctrine, an 'essential' or 'bottleneck' facility's owner must grant platform users, be it in-platform merchants or consumers, adequate access to that facility, which was not a conventional tool for the regulation of undertakings' market dominance. Debates, however, have arisen as to whether data could, by itself, constitute 'essential facilities'. The draft of the Guidelines specified multiple factors for determining whether a platform and data are necessary facilities, while the final version kept those factors merely for assessing the necessity of a platform. In the context of the digital economy, it is vital to clarify the legal nature of behaviours in collecting, holding, circulating, or utilizing data. Nonetheless, there is still a long way to go to map out such a nature and formulate systematic rules, which will not be possible until sufficient cases and evidence arise during platform undertakings' wide conduct of data processing activities.

III.2 Rules on Abuse of Dominance in Digital Markets

In digital markets, a good number of platform enterprises have presented unprecedentedly strong market power because of their large business scales. And platforms are prone to take advantage of their dominant market position to implement anticompetitive behaviours that exclude or restrict competition. Apart from modifying the general principle of anti-monopoly law, it is also vital to provide guiding rules, in spite of the non-systemic nature, to better contain the challenges of digital technologies like data and algorithms, as well as platform rules. The amendment of the AML, the making of the Guidelines before such an amendment, and the revision of the Interim Provisions after such an amendment have all aimed to clarify the rules, though under the conventional regulatory umbrella, for the practical assessment of digital platforms' market dominance and the abusive behaviours thereof. The new AML states very generally that special attention should be paid to the application of digital technology, while the two supporting documents provide detailed guidance.

III.2.1 The New AML

Tables 8.1 and 8.2 deal with dominance within the new AML.

Table 8.1 AML Abuse-of-dominance provisions

AML 2008	AML 2022
	Article 9 (newly added provision) A business operator shall not engage in any monopolistic conduct prohibited by this Law by utilizing data and algorithm, technology, capital advantage, or platform rules, among others.
Article 17 A business operator with a dominant market position shall not engage in any of the following conducts of abusing the dominant market position: 1. Selling products at unfairly high prices or buying products at unfairly low prices; 2. Selling products at prices below cost without any justifiable causes; 3. Refusing to trade with a trading party without any justifiable causes; 4. Restricting their trading party so that it may conduct deals exclusively with themselves or with the designated business operators without any justifiable causes; 5. Implementing tie-in sales or imposing other unreasonable trading conditions at the time of trading without any justifiable causes ('tie-in sale' refers to an unfair sale practice in which a business operator bundles other undesirable products with a hot-sale product—noted by the translator for clarification); 6. Applying discriminatory treatments on trading prices or other trading conditions to their trading parties with equal standing without any justifiable causes; or 7. Other forms of abusing the dominant market position as determined by the AML enforcement authority under the State Council. The term 'dominant market position' as mentioned in this Law refers to a market position held by business operators that have the ability to control the price or quantity of products or other trading conditions in the relevant market or block or affect the entry of other business operators into the relevant market.	Article 22 (newly added provision) A business operator with a dominant market position shall not engage in any conduct of abusing a dominant market position specified in the preceding paragraph by utilizing data and algorithm, technology, and platform rules, among others.

Source: the translation of AML 2008 is taken from pkulaw.com with minor revisions, <https://pkulaw.com/en_law/503218397088141cbdfb.html> (accessed 7 July 2024); the translation of AML 2022 is excerpted from pkulaw.com with minor revisions, <https://pkulaw.com/en_law/d3236788421feacfbdfb.html> (accessed 7 July 2024).

Table 8.2 AML provisions on the determination of dominance

AML 2008	AML 2022
Article 18 The dominant market position of a business operator shall be determined according to the following factors:	Article 23 The dominant market position of a business operator shall be determined according to the following factors:
1. The market share of the business operator and its competitive status in the relevant market; 2. The ability of the business operator to control the sales market or the raw material supply market; 3. The financial and technological conditions of the business operator; 4. The extent of reliance on the business operator by other business operators in the transactions; 5. The degree of difficulty for other business operators to enter the relevant market; and 6. Other factors relevant to the determination of the dominant market position of the business operator.	1. The market share of the business operator and its competitive status in the relevant market; 2. The ability of the business operator to control the sales market or the raw material supply market; 3. The financial and technological conditions of the business operator; 4. The extent of reliance on the business operator by other business operators in the transactions; 5. The degree of difficulty for other business operators to enter the relevant market; and 6. Other factors relevant to the determination of the dominant market position of the business operator.
Article 19 Under any of the following circumstances, a business operator may be presumed to have a dominant market position:	Article 24 Under any of the following circumstances, a business operator may be presumed to have a dominant market position:
1. The market share of one business operator accounts for 1/2 or more in the relevant market; 2. The joint market share of two business operators accounts for 2/3 or more in the relevant market; or 3. The joint market share of three business operators accounts for 3/4 or more in the relevant market.	1. The market share of one business operator accounts for 1/2 or more in the relevant market; 2. The joint market share of two business operators accounts for 2/3 or more in the relevant market; or 3. The joint market share of three business operators accounts for 3/4 or more in the relevant market.
Under the circumstance prescribed in Item 2 or 3 of the previous paragraph, if any of the business operators has a market share of less than 1/10, that business operator shall not be considered to have a dominant market position.	Under the circumstance prescribed in Item 2 or 3 of the previous paragraph, if any of the business operators has a market share of less than 1/10, that business operator shall not be considered to have a dominant market position.
A business operator that has been presumed to have a dominant market position shall not be considered as having a dominant market position if the operator can provide opposite evidence.	A business operator that has been presumed to have a dominant market position shall not be considered as having a dominant market position if the operator can provide opposite evidence.

Source: the translation of AML 2008 is taken from pkulaw.com with minor revisions, <https://pkulaw.com/en_law/503218397088141cbdfb.html> (accessed 7 July 2024); the translation of AML 2022 is excerpted from pkulaw.com with minor revisions, <https://pkulaw.com/en_law/d32367884 21feacfbdfb.html> (accessed 7 July 2024).

III.2.2 The Guidelines

The Guidelines were adopted before the revision of the AML, when exclusive dealings imposed by platforms on in-platform merchants were quite prevalent. These exclusive dealings, especially the business practice of the 'either–or choice', not only made headlines then but also triggered regulatory investigations and civil lawsuits. The AML prohibits dominant undertakings from restricting or excluding transactions, short of justifiable reasons, with competing market players. Such a prohibition, at a very general level, is certainly applicable to platform undertakings but is short of practical guidance. The Guidelines were formulated against such a backdrop not only in a bid to guide the judgment of platform undertakings' market dominance but also to specify in detail the factors and scenarios for considering whether a suspected anticompetitive behaviour constitutes exclusive dealing. For the first time in the history of Chinese competition law, it became clear that the business practice of 'either–or choices' by digital platforms may unfairly limit market competition and constitute abuse of dominance. The SAMR's high-profile prohibition decision against the Alibaba Group in 2020 for its business practice of an 'either–or choice' provides a good example in this regard.[59] The pertaining rules in the Guidelines were indeed not directly invoked in this decision, or in other prohibition decisions because, on the one hand, they are thought to be, in nature, guidance on how to interpret and apply authoritative statutory law and, on the other hand, the Chinese competition authorities have not yet developed the custom of invoking guiding documents. Nonetheless, there is no doubt among Chinese legal academics and legal practitioners that the Guidelines have played the *de facto* role of statutory grounds and exerted a great impact on the enforcement of the AML against anticompetitive behaviours in China's digital markets.

The Guidelines, in their Article 14, also specify the factors for addressing differentiated treatment, another prevalent anticompetitive phenomenon in recent years, notably conducted by ticket-booking platforms such as Ctrip and e-hailing platforms such as Didi. With the facilitation of big data and algorithms, some platforms charge existing customers higher prices than new customers. The AML generally prohibits undertakings from abusing their dominant market position by treating identical counterparties differently[60] in terms of trading prices and

[59] SAMR, 'Administrative Prohibition Decision [2021] No 28' (n18).

[60] The term 'counterparties' has been widely used in China's AML and relevant regulations, but it has not been clearly defined. Some scholars think that 'counterparties' refer to either operators or consumers and the term needs to be eventually determined in a case-by-case manner. See J Hao, '反垄断法上的交易相对人及其三重角色 [The Counterparty to a Transaction and Its Triple Role in Antitrust Law]' (2020) 7(7) China Price Regulation and Antitrust 13, 13–14. In terms of system interpretation, the new AML and Guideline distinguish between the concept of operator and consumer with separate provisions (see the Guidelines, Article 14–17; the new AML (n47), Article 17), or incorporate both in the same article (see the Guidelines, Articles 15, 16). In the framework-of-purpose interpretation, the goal of 'fairness' and 'protecting the interests of consumers' are two values pursued by China's AML (see the new AML, Article 1). Therefore, in this chapter, if there is no specific reference, the term 'counterparties' refers to either operators or consumers.

other trading conditions. The Guidelines clarify the factors for the consideration of differential treatment, including differential prices or other trading conditions according to the payment capacity, consumption preferences, and usage habits of the targeted consumers. Regarding the determination of whether the targets are 'identical', the Guidelines provide that the differences in their privacy information, trading history, individual preferences, and consumption habits obtained by the platforms do not affect the determination of 'identical'. The specification of these factors provides the very statutory ground for the competition authorities to tackle the practice of differential treatment by dominant platforms, be it differentiated trading prices or other trading conditions.

As a matter of counterbalance, the Guidelines provide a list of justifiable reasons for the practice of restrictive trading rules by dominant digital platforms, such as selling below cost, refusal to deal, limiting trade, tying or attaching unreasonable trading conditions, and differential treatment. Such conduct by the platform operators concerned does not necessarily constitute an abuse of market dominance if they have justifiable reasons, as stipulated in the Guidelines. The reasons listed in the Guidelines mainly consider the possible commercial reasonableness of the undertakings' behaviours in the digital markets in commercial practice, such as conduct 'to attract new users within a reasonable period of time',[61] 'to make promotions within a reasonable period of time',[62] or 'necessary to protect the interests of counterparties and consumers, intellectual property rights, trade secrets or data security',[63] among other justifiable reasons.[64]

III.2.2.1 Definition of Relevant Markets

The Guidelines devote their chapter III to the determination of abuse of market dominance in digital markets. The draft of the Guidelines attempted to skip the step of a market definition in cases in which the conditions do not allow for accurately defining the market or where market definition is extremely difficult, but there is sufficient evidence to suggest that suspected behaviours are long-lasting and have exerted significant damaging effects, which would only be possible with a dominant market position.

However, such an approach was eventually removed from the final version of the Guidelines. which did not fundamentally deviate from the traditional approach with respect to the relevant market definition. Instead, the Guidelines provide special instructions on the definition of the relevant market for the digital economy.

[61] Anti-Monopoly Commission of the State Council, '国务院反垄断委员会关于平台经济领域的反垄断指南（国反垄发〔2021〕1号） [Anti-Monopoly Guidelines on the Platform Economy]' (7 February 2021), Article 13 <https://www.gov.cn/xinwen/2021-02/07/content_5585758.htm> (accessed 7 November 2022) (the Guidelines).

[62] *Ibid.*

[63] *Ibid*, Article 15.

[64] *Ibid*, Article 14.

More specifically, Article 4(1) and 4(2) of the Guidelines still takes substitution analysis as the basic analytical method for the definition of relevant product markets and geographical markets on a case-by-case basis. Nevertheless, as the following provisions of the Guidelines suggest, special weight is accorded to non-price factors for the substitution analysis, especially for the demand substitution analysis, which is also widely encouraged by Chinese competition law in academia.[65]

Article 4

Due to the complicated business types and changeable competition dynamics, the definition of relevant product markets and relevant regional markets in the field of platform economy needs to follow the general principles determined in the AML and the Guidelines of the Anti-Monopoly Commission of the State Council for the Definition of the Relevant Markets, concurrently in consideration of the characteristics of the platform economy and through specific analysis of individual cases.[66]

(1) Relevant product markets

The basic method for the definition of relevant product markets in the field of platform economy is substitution analysis. When defining relevant product markets in individual cases, substitution analysis may be conducted on the basis of the platform functions, business modes, application scenarios, user groups, multilateral markets, offline trading and other factors; and when the competitive constraints caused by supply substitution on operators' conducts is similar to demand substitution, supply substitution analysis may be considered on the basis of market access, technical barriers, network effects, lock-in effects, transfer costs, cross-border competition and other factors. Specifically, relevant product markets may be defined on the basis of the products of the platform side; and multiple relevant product markets may be respectively defined on the basis of multilateral products involved in a platform, and the interrelationship and interaction between relevant product markets shall be considered. When the cross-platform network effects of a platform may cause sufficient competition constraints on platform operators, the relevant product markets may be defined on the basis of the platform as a whole.

(2) Relevant geographic ma rkets

Demand substitution and supply substitution analysis shall also be adopted for defining relevant regional markets in the field of platform economy. When

[65] See C Zhong, '数字经济平台相关市场界定研究 [On the Definition of Relevant Market in Digital Markets]' (2023) 2 Research Rule of Law 45.

[66] The translation of the Anti-Monopoly Guidelines on the Platform Economy is excerpted from pkulaw.com with minor revisions: Anti-Monopoly Commission of the State Council, '国务院反垄断委员会关于平台经济领域的反垄断指南（国反垄发〔2021〕1号） [Anti-Monopoly Guidelines on the Platform Economy]' (English translation) (7 February 2021) <https://pkulaw.com/en_law/dec522cd66c7b43ebdfb.html> (accessed 9 June 2024).

defining relevant geographic markets in individual cases, actual regions of products selected by most users, users' language preference and consumption habits, provisions of relevant laws and regulations, degree of competition constraint in different regions, online and offline integration, and other factors may be comprehensively assessed and considered.

According to the characteristics of the platform, relevant geographic markets are usually defined as the Chinese market or specific regional markets, and may also be defined as global market on the basis of the circumstances of individual cases.

(3) Role of the definition of relevant markets in various cases
The principle of analysis of individual cases shall be insisted on, and the actual needs of different types of monopoly cases for the definition of relevant markets vary from one another.

To investigate cases of monopoly agreements and cases of abuse of dominant market positions, and to conduct a centralized anti-monopoly review of operators, the relevant markets generally need to be defined.

III.2.2.2 Determination of Market Dominance

The Guidelines provide multiple factors for the determination of platforms' market dominance on the basis of the AML in combination with the characteristics of digital markets.

First of all, market share is the only directly quantifiable indicator in determining market dominance. The case of the 'either–or choice' concerning the Alibaba Group vividly showed the indicative role of market share. Under the characteristics of the digital economy, market share can be examined from three perspectives:

(1) A high percentage of market share can represent an undertaking's market power but does not necessarily mean that a dominant position exists. Considerations like the level of competition in digital markets, an undertaking's ability to control the market, and its financial and technical conditions, the degree of dependence of other undertakings, the ease of entry into the relevant market, and other factors based on the characteristics of the digital economy also count.[67]
(2) Multiple market share metrics may also play a role in the analysis. Sales are the main indicator to calculate market share in traditional antitrust cases. Due to the network effect of platforms, however, sales are not the only criterion for judging the market dominance.[68] The Guidelines

[67] Guidelines (n61), Article 11, terms 1 and 2.
[68] J Sun and Z Zhao, '互联网平台经营者市场支配地位界定的系统性重构—以《反垄断法》第 18 条的修订为中心 [Systematic Reconstruction of the Definition of Market Dominance of Internet Platform Operators—Centering on the Revision of Article 18 of the AML]' (2019) 5 Science, Technology and Law 76.

stipulate, in their Article 11(1), that 'to determine the market share of undertakings in the platform economy, the transaction amount, number of transactions, sales, number of active users, clicks, hours of use or other indicators in the relevant market may be considered'.[69] In the *Alibaba* case, the SAMR also held that the indication of a single indicator is limited in terms of digital markets and therefore calculated Alibaba's market share from two aspects: service revenue and transaction volume.[70]

(3) The duration of market share also serves to indicate market power. Due to the multi-sided nature of platform markets, the anticompetitive effects arising on one side may instantly vanish on the other side. Therefore, the market power of a given platform may not arise in a stable manner.[71] Therefore, the Guidelines clarify that the time dimension shall be considered when assessing the power of an undertaking's market share. In the *Alibaba* case, the SAMR also found that the Alibaba Group had a high market share for an extended period, lasting from 2015 to 2019, and firmly established its market dominance.[72]

Furthermore, an undertaking may be found dominant because of its all-round competence. Still taking the *Alibaba* case as an example, the SAMR combined the financial and technical conditions, the dependence of other undertakings, the associated market power, and other elements in the analysis of the determination of market dominance, which is stipulated in the Guidelines as well.[73]

Article 11

Anti-monopoly law enforcement institutions shall, in accordance with the provisions of Articles 18 and 19 AML, determine or presume that operators have dominant market positions. In consideration of the characteristics of the platform economy, the following factors may be specifically considered:

(1) Market shares of operators and status of competition in the relevant markets. To determine the market share of an operator in the field of platform economy, the proportions of trading amount, trading quantity, sales volume, number of active users, click volume, service time or other indicators in the

[69] Guidelines (n61), Article 11, term 1.

[70] SAMR, 'Administrative Prohibition Decision [2021] No 28' (n18).

[71] P Wu, K Dong, and R Long, Beijing Zhonglun Law Firm, '互联网平台企业的市场支配地位认定 [Determination of Market Dominance of Internet Platform Enterprises]' (Beijing Zhonglun Law Firm, 10 May 2021) <https://www.sohu.com/a/465629816_221481> (accessed 7 November 2022).

[72] SAMR, 'Administrative Prohibition Decision [2021] No 28' (n18).

[73] Guidelines (n61), Article 11, terms 3–5.

relevant markets may be considered, and the duration of such market share may be concurrently considered.

To analyse the status of competition in the relevant markets, the development status of the relevant platform markets, the number of existing competitors and their market shares, the characteristics of competition on the platform, the degree of difference on the platform, the scale economy, and the situation of potential competitors, and innovation and technical changes, among others, may be considered.

(2) The operator's market control capacity. The operator's capacity to control the upstream and downstream markets or other affiliated markets, capacity to hinder or affect other operators' entering the relevant markets, relevant platform operation mode, and network effect, and capacity to affect or decide the prices, traffic or other trading conditions, among others, may be considered.

(3) The operator's financial and technical conditions. The operator's investors, asset scale, source of capital, profitability, financing ability, ability for technical innovation and application, intelligent properties owned, and ability to master and handle relevant data, and the extent to which such financial and technical conditions could facilitate the business expansion of the operator or consolidate or maintain its market position, etc., may be considered.

(4) The degree of dependence of other operators on the operator in the transaction. The transaction relation, transaction volume, the time such a transaction lasts between other operators and the operator, and the lock-in effects, user stickiness, and possibility and switching costs of other operators to switch to another platform, may be considered.

(5) The ease of entry of other operators into the relevant market. Market access, the scale effects of the platform, the scale of capital invested, technology barrier, users' multi-homing, user switching costs, the difficulty for data access, the habits of the users, etc., may be considered.

(6) Other factors. Other factors which are based on the characteristics of the platform economy that determine the dominant market position of the operator may be considered.

III.2.2.3 Types of Abuse of Dominance

To better understand the aforementioned general changes in laws and regulations, we further enumerate the detailed guidance provided by the Guidelines on how to approach the main types of abusive behaviours in China's digital markets, some of which have already been briefly mentioned in the introduction pertaining to these behaviours.

A. Unfair Price Conducts

Article 12

Operators in the field of platform economy with dominant market positions may possibly abuse dominant market positions to sell products at unfairly high prices or purchase products at unfairly low prices. To analyse whether an unfair price conduct is constituted, the following factors may be considered:

(1) Whether the price is significantly higher or lower than the price of the same kind of or comparable products of other similar operators under the same or similar market conditions.
(2) Whether the price is significantly higher or lower than the price of the same kind of or comparable products of operators in the field of platform economy operators under the same or similar market conditions.
(3) Whether an operator in the field of platform economy raises sales price or reduces purchasing price beyond the normal range when the cost is basically stable.
(4) Whether the prices of products sold by an operator in the field of platform economy are raised significantly at a rate higher than the cost growth rate, or the prices of products purchased are lowered significantly at a rate lower than the cost reduction rate.

To determine the same or similar market conditions, the type of platform, operation mode, trading links, cost structure, specific trading conditions and other factors may be generally considered.

B. Sales below Costs

Article 13

Operators in the field of platform economy with dominant market positions may possibly abuse their dominant market position to sell products at prices lower than the costs without justified reasons, to eliminate or restrict market competition.

To analyse whether sale below cost is constituted, whether the operator in the field of platform economy is squeezing out other operators that have competitive relationships by means of a price lower than the cost, and whether there is a possibility for the operator to raise the price to seek illicit profits, or damage the fair market competition or consumers' lawful rights and interests after squeezing out other operators from the market shall be mainly considered.

In the calculation of cost, the cost correlation between various relevant markets in the multilateral markets involved on the platform shall be comprehensively considered generally.

Operators in the field of platform economy may have the following justified reasons for sale below cost:

(1) For developing other businesses on the platform within a reasonable period of time.
(2) For advancing the entry of new products into the market within a reasonable period of time.
(3) For attracting new users within a reasonable period of time.
(4) For carrying out sales promotion activities within a reasonable period of time.
(5) Other reasons that can justify the conduct.

C. Refusal to Trade

Article 14

Operators in the field of platform economy with dominant market positions may possibly abuse their dominant market position by refusing to trade with counterparties without justified reasons, to eliminate or restrict market competition. To analyse whether refusal to trade is constituted, the following factors may be considered:

[...]

5. whether an operator which controls necessary facilities in the platform economy sector is refusing to enter into transactions with counterparts on reasonable terms. In the determination of whether a relevant platform constitutes a necessary facility, it is generally necessary to comprehensively consider the platform's data occupancy status, the substitutability of other platforms, the existence of potential available platforms, the feasibility of it developing into a competitive platform, the degree of dependence of transaction counterparts on the platform, the possible impact of opening the platform on the operator of the platform, and other factors.

D. Restricting Trading

Article 15

Operators in the field of platform economy with dominant market positions may possibly abuse their dominant market position by restricting trading with counterparties without justified reasons, to eliminate or restrict market competition. To analyse whether a restriction on trading is constituted, the following factors may be considered:

(1) Requiring in-platform in-platform operators to choose 'one out of two' competitive platforms or other conduct restricting counterparties to exclusively trade with it.
(2) Restricting counterparties to exclusively trade with operators designated or trade through its designated channel and other restricted methods.
(3) Restricting counterparties not to trade with specific operators.

The aforesaid restrictions may be realised by written agreement, on telephone, in oral form, or through any method as agreed with counterparties, and by actually setting restrictions or obstacles through platform rules, data, algorithms, technology and other manners.

To analyse whether a restriction on trading takes place, the following two circumstances may be mainly considered: first, restrictions imposed upon by platform operators through shielding shops, reducing search rights, restriction on traffic, technical obstacles, deduction of deposits, and other punitive measures may generally be determined as having constituted a restriction on trading, as they may cause direct damage to market competition and consumers' interests. Second, restrictions imposed by platform operators through subsidies, discounts, preference, traffic resource support and other incentive methods may have certain positive effect on the interests of in-platform operators and consumers and overall social welfare, but if there is evidence to prove that the obvious effect of elimination and restriction has been caused to market competition, they may also be determined as having constituted a restriction on trading.

Operators in the field of platform economy may restrict trading for the following justified reasons:

(1) For protecting the interests of counterparties and consumers.
(2) For protecting intellectual property rights, trade secrets or data security.
(3) For protecting specific resource investment in trading.
(4) For safeguarding the reasonable operation mode.
(5) Other reasons that can justify the conduct.

E. Tied Sales or Adding Unreasonable Trading Conditions

Article 16

Operators in the field of platform economy with dominant market positions may abuse their dominant market position by conducting tie-in sales or adding unreasonable trading conditions without justified reasons, to eliminate or restrict market competition. To analyse whether a tie-in sale or adding of unreasonable trading conditions is constituted, the following factors may be considered:

(1) Bundling the sale of different products by taking advantage of standard terms, pop-up windows, necessary operation steps and other methods that cannot be selected, changed or rejected by counterparties.
(2) Forcing counterparties to accept other products through a reduction of search right, traffic restriction, technical obstacles, and other punitive measures.

(3) Adding unreasonable restrictions on trading conditions and methods, service provision methods, payment method and means, and after-sales warranty, among others.
(4) Collecting unreasonable fees besides the trading price.
(5) Compulsively collecting unnecessary user information or adding trading conditions, trading procedures or service items irrelevant to the trading subject matter.

Operators in the field of platform economy may implement a tie-in sale for the following justified reasons:
(1) Complying with the appropriate industry practice and trading practice.
(2) Protecting the interests of counterparties and consumers.
(3) Improving the use value or efficiency of products.
(4) Other reasons that can justify the conducts.

F. Differentiated Treatment

Article 17
Operators in the platform economy sector with a dominant market position may abuse their dominant market position by implementing, without justifiable reasons, differentiated treatment for transaction counterparts with the same transaction terms, so as to eliminate or restrict market competition. In the analysis of whether differentiated treatment is constituted, the following factors may be considered:
(1) Implementing, based on big data and algorithms, differentiated transaction prices or other transaction terms according to transaction counterparts' payment ability, consumption preferences, use habits and other aspects;
(2) Implementing differentiated criteria, rules or algorithms; and
(3) Implementing differentiated terms of payment or transaction modes.
The same terms mean that there are no differences that are substantially affecting transactions between transaction counterparts in terms of transaction security, transaction cost, credit status, transaction link, transaction duration and other aspects. Differences in transaction counterparts' privacy information, transaction history, individual preferences, consumption habits and other aspects obtained by the platform during transactions will not affect the determination that the transaction counterparts have the same terms.

III.2.3 The Provisions

In 2019, the Interim Provisions were issued and implemented as one of the supporting regulations to the AML. In 2023, the Provisions were revised in accordance with the amendments to the AML.[74] The Provisions empower provincial administrations to implement the AML against particular abusive conduct in various markets, aiming to create a coordinated anti-monopoly enforcement network.[75] They outline nine factors for the assessment of market dominance in digital markets.[76] Articles 11–17 of the Guidelines are of the same nature as Articles 7–20 of the Provisions, and some even share the same wording. Article 21 specifically prohibits dominant undertakings from making use of data and algorithms, technologies, and platform rules, etc. to engage in anticompetitive behaviours. Other special provisions are listed below.

Article 4

An anti-monopoly law enforcement institution shall treat all operators equally when investigating and handling abuse of dominant market positions.[77]

Article 5

[. . .]

The relevant product market in the sector of platform economy may be defined based on the products on one side of the platform, or based on the multi-lateral products involved in the platform; the platform as a whole may be defined as a relevant product market or several relevant product markets separately, and the mutual relations and influences between the relevant product markets shall be taken into consideration.

[. . .]

[74] SAMR, '禁止滥用市场支配地位行为规定 [Provisions on Prohibiting Abuse of Dominant Market Position]' (promulgated by the SAMR, 10 March 2023, effective 15 April 2023) <https://www.gov.cn/gongbao/content/2023/content_5754539.htm> (accessed 16 April 2023) (the Provisions).

[75] See CPI (Competition Policy International), 'Year of the Rat: Antitrust in China' (2020) 3 Competition Policy International 11.

[76] According to Article 18 AML and Articles 6–10 of the Provisions, factors such as the competition characteristics of relevant industries, their operating mode, the number of users, network effects, lock-in effects, technical characteristics, market innovation, the ability to grasp and process relevant data, and the market power of operators in related markets may be considered in determining the market dominance of online operators. See SAMR, '禁止滥用市场支配地位行为暂行规定 [Interim Provisions on Prohibiting Abuse of Dominant Market Position]' (promulgated by the SAMR, 26 June 2019, effective 1 September 2019) <http://www.gov.cn/gongbao/content/2019/content_5430507.htm> (accessed 7 November 2022).

[77] The translation of the Provisions is excerpted from pkulaw.com with minor revisions: SAMR, '禁止滥用市场支配地位行为规定 [Provisions on Prohibiting Abuse of Dominant Market Position]' (English translation) (promulgated by the SAMR, 10 March 2023, effective 15 April 2023) <https://pkulaw.com/en_law/4a966fd519ae33cabdfb.html> (accessed 7 July 2024).

Article 6
'Dominant market position' means a market position such that an operator can control the prices, volumes or other transaction conditions of goods or services (hereinafter collectively referred to as 'goods') in a relevant market, or can obstruct or affect other operators from entering into the relevant markets.

For the purposes of this article, 'other transaction conditions' means other factors that can have a substantial impact on transactions on the market, other than the price and quantity of goods, including the varieties and quality of goods, terms of payment, mode of delivery, after-sales services, transaction selection, technical constraints, and so on.

For the purposes of this article, the term 'can obstruct or affect other operators from entering into the relevant markets' includes excluding other operators from entering into the relevant markets, delaying other operators' entering into the relevant markets within a reasonable period of time, or making other operators enter into the relevant markets at substantially increased costs, leading to their inability to conduct effective competition with the existing operators, and other circumstances.

Article 12
According to Article 23 AML and the provisions of Articles 7 to 11 of the Provisions, in the determination of whether a platform operator or other new economic formats hold dominant market positions, the competition characteristics, business models, number of users, network effects, locking effects, technical features, market innovation, capacity of mastering and handling relevant data, the operator's market force in associated markets, and other factors may be considered.

Article 21
A business operator with a dominant market position shall not utilize data, algorithms, technologies and rules of the platform, among others, to conduct acts of abusing its dominant market position as stipulated in Articles 14 to 20 of these Provisions.

As mentioned above, the most notable contribution of the Interim Provisions is the refinement of the criteria for defining the relevant market, which provide enforcement agencies with clearer and more predictable standards, particularly in the context of the digital economy.

IV. Towards a Holistic Approach with Alternative Enforcement Tools

Effective governance of abusive behaviours cannot merely rely on a single regulatory tool, not just because the socio-economic impacts of abusive behaviours can be multifold and can hardly be effectively resolved by a single *ex post* prohibition decision. Especially for a jurisdiction like China, in which the formal enforcement of anti-monopoly law against abusive behaviours by competition authorities in the constantly evolving digital markets is at an early stage, it is vital to take a holistic approach with supplemental enforcement tools so as to make continuing efforts to tackle the abuse of market dominance by digital platforms. For example, the SAMR has become increasingly accustomed to issuing administrative advice for rectifications after making prohibition decisions against violating platforms. More notably, besides the enforcement of anti-monopoly law by China's competition authorities, civil lawsuits against abusing platforms brought before the courts by adversely affected platform competitors, in-platform merchants, and individual consumers have also been exerting pressure on undisciplined platforms.

Even within the realm of enforcement of law by governmental authorities, anti-monopoly law can be enforced in an ex-ante manner. In addition to soft interventions like the aforementioned administrative interviews by competition authorities, some regulatory tools (such as algorithm auditing) carried out by various regulatory agencies may play a supplemental regulatory role in preventing the implementation of abusive conduct with the facilitation of new technologies. That said, it would be helpful to further consider the strengths and limits of two major alternative enforcement tools against platforms' abusive behaviours arising in China—private enforcement of anti-monopoly law by way of civil lawsuits and supplemental regulation of these behaviours with algorithm auditing.

IV.1 Private Enforcement of Anti-Monopoly Law at a Crossroad

As specified by the aforementioned prohibition decisions against the Alibaba Group and Sherpa,[78] the abuse of a dominant position by a platform has far-reaching impacts not only on competing platforms but also on other market participants like in-platform merchants and consumers. In-platform merchants, for instance, would be subject to increased commission or unable to enjoy the

[78] For detailed descriptions of the two decisions, see sections V.1.2 and V.1.4 below.

preferential trading conditions offered by the platforms if they did not comply with the 'either–or choice' requirement of the Alibaba Group or Meituan. The abuse of a dominant position breaks the solid triangular structure among platforms, merchants, and consumers. Although the SAMR has noticed the detrimental impact of abusive behaviours on platform competitors, in-platform merchants, and consumers, it does not normally quantify the actual impacts of such abusive behaviours in its prohibition decisions.[79] Nor has the SAMR ordered any violating platforms, be it the Alibaba Group or Meituan, to compensate the suffering parties.

In parallel with public enforcement, private enforcement of anti-monopoly law may serve as a vigorous response to the loss of the triangular balance. In light of the characteristics of digital markets, business-to-customer (B2C) trades entail inherent risks especially for consumers, which, in turn, complicate their choices, triggering their anxiety, inability, apathy, and lack of trust when engaging in various transactions in digital marketplaces.[80] It is assumed that private participation and litigation of public interest-related disputes facilitate the discovery and rectification of anticompetitive behaviours.[81]

China has also acknowledged the significance of litigation in enforcing antitrust laws and the need to remedy any deficiencies and inadequacies in the legal system. Several recent cases in China have demonstrated predominantly private participation during the enforcement of anti-monopoly law, invariably with the objective of compensating the losses of adversely affected parties.[82]

Civil lawsuits for compensatory remedies against powerful platforms by competing platforms, victimized merchants, and consumers have therefore developed into a focal point of anti-monopoly law enforcement in China. In addition to the lawsuits brought before the courts by competing platforms, in-platform merchants such as taxi drivers have been suing e-hailing car platforms like Didi for their suffering due to unfair ride order dispatching facilitated by dominant e-hailing platforms' algorithmic operations. In addition to individual drivers, the interests of taxi companies have also taken a hit. Troubled by the declining market share, in December 2020, the China Taxi Industry Alliance jointly sent a letter to regulatory agencies petitioning for the protection of their interests and an anti-monopoly investigation into e-hailing platforms.[83]

[79] X Fu and G Tan, 'Abuse of Market Dominance under China's Anti-Monopoly Law: The Case of Tetra Pak' (2019) 54 Review of Industrial Organization 432.

[80] Ioannidou (n29), 369.

[81] F Deng, '反垄断民事诉讼机制的当下选择 [Current Options for Anti-Monopoly Civil Litigation Mechanisms]' (2022) 5 China Academic Journal 72.

[82] See the typical case of *CNKI* in V.1.5.

[83] Sohu Technology, '中国出租汽车产业联盟呼吁继续对滴滴优步合并案展开反垄断调查 [China Taxi Industry Alliance Calls for Continued Anti-Monopoly Investigation of Didi and Uber]' (19 December 2020) <https://www.sohu.com/a/439234215_115565> (accessed 16 March 2023).

Civil lawsuits against anticompetitive platforms for compensatory remedies have reached a considerable scale, sparking a discussion about the effectiveness of civil litigation as a potential means of private enforcement of anti-monopoly law. Article 60 of the new AML (Article 50 of the old AML) stipulates that 'if an operator conducts monopolistic behaviours and causes losses to others, it shall bear civil liability according to law'.[84] This Article authorizes the court to address civil disputes between undisciplined platforms and adversely affected parties. Even when monopolistic allegations have not been decided by competition authorities yet, the courts in China may determine whether the defendant has violated anti-monopoly law in their own judgment. In such circumstances, the courts have to follow the constituent elements under the AML so as to decide whether the defendant has abused its dominant market position.[85]

Nonetheless, as stated by the SPC, Chinese courts are still in the early stage of enforcing the AML through civil lawsuits, especially in the digital markets. The courts, therefore, tend to avoid making such a judgment. Instead, they may choose to decide the case from the perspective of other laws and regulations (e.g. the Anti-Unfair Competition Law, E-Commerce Law, and the Law of Consumer Rights and Interests),[86] in a bid to compensate for civil losses.[87] For instance, in 2021, Hongfang Hu, a VIP customer of Ctrip, sued Ctrip for its data-enabled price discrimination, alleging that she was charged twice the market price for a hotel booking. The court eventually held that Ctrip had committed fraud against Hu and should bear the civil liability.[88] In a press release on 17 November 2022, the SPC stated that the courts in China had concluded 916 civil cases on monopoly and 32,075 civil cases on unfair competition from 2013 to June 2022.[89]

Moreover, the costs and indeterminacy of private actions in anti-monopoly cases are relatively high, with challenges including (i) the ambiguity of the issues at stake, (ii) the difficulty of collecting evidence, (iii) lengthy and complicated procedures, (iv) a heavy burden proof on damages suffered, and (v) the inexperienced of the courts in dealing with such cases.[90] For the litigation mechanism of

[84] New AML (n47), Article 60.

[85] Typically, see *Beijing Qihoo Technology Co, Ltd* (n16).

[86] See, e.g. Zhejiang High People's Court, *Shanghai Lazarus Information Technology Co, Ltd v Beijing Sanfast Technology Co, Ltd Jinhua Branch, etc.* [2021] (上海拉扎斯信息科技有限公司、北京三快科技有限公司金华分公司等不正当竞争纠纷案，(2021)浙民终601号) (8 December 2021).

[87] *Hu Hongfang* (n54).

[88] *Ibid.*

[89] CCTV News, '人民法院严厉制裁垄断行为，维护市场公平竞争 [People's Court Severely Sanction Monopolistic Behaviour and Maintain Fair Competition in the Market]' (17 November 2022) <https://news.cctv.com/2022/11/17/ARTIu7JF8aBGtAf9Oa7ZNkNP221117.shtml> (accessed 2 December 2022).

[90] A Jones and B Sufrin, *EU Competition Law: Text, Cases, and Materials* (5th edn, OUP, 2021), 1086–1087.

anti-monopoly specifically, it is also necessary to clarify the functional role of civil litigation as a tool of anti-monopoly enforcement.[91]

On 18 November 2022, for the purpose of improving the fairness and efficiency of the resolution of anti-monopoly civil disputes and to preserve the fair competition order, the SPC issued the 'Provisions of the Supreme People's Court on Several Issues Concerning the Application of Law in Monopoly Civil Disputes (Draft for Public Comments)' (hereinafter referred to as the 'Draft Provisions for Monopoly Civil Disputes'). To ensure consistency with the latest revision of the AML, the Draft Provisions for Monopoly Civil Disputes provided substantive stands concerning the definition of relevant markets and the determination of market dominance, as well as the burden of proof for the parties.[92] Pursuant to this draft, the newly added Articles 17–19 stipulate the methodology and considerations for the definition of relevant markets. In the field of digital markets, the draft especially emphasizes the focus on the types of digital platforms, the multilateral markets, and the cross-platform network effects of the digital economy, incorporating the interrelationships and impacts between the various relevant markets. Article 16 clarifies the burden of proof in the determination of relevant markets: in cases of abuse of dominance, it is the plaintiff who shall define the relevant market and provide evidence or reasons.

Moreover, Articles 30–43 in the Draft Provisions for Monopoly Civil Disputes cover the abuse of market dominance, among which Article 34 specifically stipulates the factors that the People's Court can comprehensively consider when determining the dominant market position in accordance with Article 23 of the new AML.[93] Article 36 adds a new provision concerning the defendant's proof to rebut the presumption of joint market dominance. Under this provision, when the plaintiff provides evidence that the defendant's market share meets the criteria for presumed joint dominance, the burden of proof shifts to the defendant, who

[91] Deng (n81).

[92] Supreme People's Court of China, 'Provisions of the Supreme People's Court on Several Issues Concerning the Application of Law in Monopoly Civil Disputes (Draft for Public Comments)]' (n23).

[93] Article 34 of the Draft Provisions for Monopoly Civil Disputes (*ibid*) stipulates that

> In accordance with Article 23 of the new AML, to determine the dominant market position of the Internet platforms, the People's Court may take into account the following factors:
>
> (a) The business model of the Internet platform and the actual competitive constraints to which its operator is subjected;
> (b) the market share of the Internet platform operator in the relevant market and the duration of such a market share;
> (c) whether there is a significant network effect, scale effect, scope effect, etc. of the Internet platform services;
> (d) the relevant data, algorithms, technologies, etc. in the hands of the Internet platform operators;
> (e) the impact of the Internet platform operator on adjacent markets or in adjacent markets;
> (f) the degree of dependence of the user or the operator of the platform on the Internet platform operator and the ability to check and balance, use habits, simultaneous use of multiple Internet platforms, the cost of switching to other Internet platform operators, etc;

may rebut the finding of joint dominance by proving that substantial competition exists between the two or more operators involved or that the two or more operators involved as a group are effectively competing with one another in the relevant market.[94]

At present, however, the prevailing attitude among Chinese academics is still that private enforcement of competition law is, in principle, supplementary.[95] In circumstances where the private enforcement of public policy may be the sole solution,[96] the courts shall indeed be encouraged to consider the practical capacity of private parties to monitor violating business activities.[97] Nonetheless, to generally accord the courts with independent power to tackle anticompetitive behaviours by way of civil litigation would probably, on the one hand, incentivize unpredictable amounts of compensatory lawsuits, which may exert undue economic burdens on commercial undertakings given the imposition of heavy regulatory penalties; and on the other hand, the separation of institutional powers between the courts and the competition authorities would also be blurred.[98]

A better option for the court, as some courts have already considered, might be temporal suspension of the proceeding of the civil lawsuit in order to wait for and follow the administrative decision on the anticompetitive nature of disputed behaviours. For example, Beijing High People's Court suspended the aforementioned lawsuit between JD.com and the Alibaba Group for years until the SAMR adopted its prohibition decision against the Alibaba Group. The courts' deference to the decisions of competition authorities on the anticompetitive nature of disputed behaviours is indeed a mechanism to make up for the expertise insufficiency

(g) the willingness and ability of other Internet platform operators to enter the relevant market and the scale requirements, technical requirements, legal restrictions and other market entry barriers faced;
(h) innovation and technological changes in the relevant market;
(i) other factors to be considered.

[94] Article 36 of the Draft (*ibid*) newly adds that

> Where the People's Court presumes, in accordance with Article 24(1)(b) and (c) of the new AML, that two or more operators jointly have a dominant market position, the presumption may be rebutted if the operators have evidence that they meet one of the following circumstances: (a) substantial competition exists between the two or more operators; and (b) the two or more operators as a whole are subject to effective competition from other operators in the relevant market.

[95] J Sun and Y Yu, '消费者数据隐私损害的反垄断司法救济及路径拓展 [Antitrust Judicial Remedies and Expanding Paths for Consumer Data Privacy Damages]' (2023) 4 Legal Forum 23.

[96] MA Cohen and PH Rubin, 'Private Enforcement of Public Policy' (1985) 3 Yale Journal on Regulation 167.

[97] B Xiong and Mateja Durovic, 'The Enforcement of Mandatory Rules against Illegal Contracts' (2021) ASIA Pacific Law Review 15.

[98] J Li, '反垄断私人诉讼困境与反垄断执法的管制化发展 [The Antitrust Private Litigation Dilemma and the Regulatory Development of Antitrust Enforcement]' (2011) 33 Chinese Journal of Law 80.

of the courts and ensure the consistency of state authorities, be it the judicial organ or the administrative branch. In comparison to the anti-monopoly law avoiding approach, the deference approach could arguably promote the integrity of the whole body of competition laws and regulations. That said, before formal regulatory procedures begin, the courts may also consider referring the civil proceeding to competent regulatory authorities, especially the competition authority, so as to fill the expertise gap between the court and the competition authorities. Under this circumstance, although the dispute is privately driven to the court for resolution, it can still proceed and benefit from public competition law enforcement.

IV.2 Algorithm Audits as a Supplemental Tool

IV.2.1 The Role of Algorithm Audits in Tackling Abusive Behaviours

The scale of the big data industry in China has expanded rapidly,[99] which has strongly fuelled platforms' technological and business innovations. A notable example is the wide application of algorithms in almost every corner of platform services. The digital businesses of transportation, retailing, online streaming, social media, and travel booking all rely on algorithms to facilitate their daily business operations and decision-making. Ever since 2020, Chinese regulatory agencies have been advocating for the regulation of algorithms. For instance, the 'Implementation Outline for the Construction of a Rule of Law Society (2020–2025)', issued by CPC Central Committee, proposes to regulate new technology applications such as algorithmic recommendations. The 'Guiding Opinions on Strengthening Overall Governance of Internet Information Service Algorithms', issued by nine departments including the CAC in September 2021, further emphasized the need to 'complete algorithm security regulation mechanisms'.

More recently, in March 2022, the CAC launched the QingLang Operation [清朗运动] special action on algorithm regulation by carrying out on-site inspections on Internet enterprises. The Regulations on the Administration of Algorithmic Recommendation of Internet Information Service (Algorithmic Recommendation Regulations), released by four departments including the CAC in March 2022, are another step forward towards establishing a whole body of rules for algorithmic

[99] During the 5th Digital China Summit, the Cyberspace Administration of China (CAC) released the Digital China Development Report (2021), which shows that from 2017 to 2021, China's overall data production grew significantly, accounting for 9.9 per cent of the global share and ranking second in the world. See Office of the Central Cyberspace Affairs Commission, '数字中国发展报告（2021年）[Digital China Development Report (2021)]' (2 August 2022) <https://www.cac.gov.cn/2022-08/02/c_1661066515613920.htm> (accessed 5 April 2024).

governance.[100] Considering algorithms' potential role in certain cases of abuse by digital platforms and China's active legislation and enforcement with respect to algorithms, algorithm regulation might serve as a supplemental tool for ex-ante intervention in platforms' potential abuse of market dominance.

Among the various means of algorithm regulation, algorithm audit is expected to play a significant role in evaluating algorithm values and promoting algorithm innovation. The application of algorithms in a manner restricting or excluding market competition would exacerbate the abuse of platforms' market dominance, and consequently adversely affect consumers' interests. Robust algorithm audits, even if carried out not specifically for market competition, may still make such abusive behaviours susceptible to regulatory detection since the sharing of information on prospect violations among various regulatory agencies can facilitate the competition authority stepping in.

Actually, the Guidelines had already paid attention to abuse of market dominance facilitated by algorithms before China initiated the aforementioned formulation of systemic rules to regulate the application of algorithms. Considering the fact that platform undertakings can use algorithms to implement refusal to supply, restrictive dealing, and price discrimination, Articles 14 and 15 of the Guidelines explicitly state that operators with a dominant market position are prohibited from applying algorithms to set unreasonable barriers that lead to restrictive dealing or refusal to supply. Their Article 17 further stipulates that operators with a dominant market position shall not implement price discrimination based on algorithms or implement differentiated algorithms for identical counterparties.

Nevertheless, the competition authorities normally enforce these rules in an ex-post manner. The misuse of algorithms will not be investigated by the competition authority until adverse impacts have already come into being. Regular audits of algorithms in an ex-ante manner could arguably prevent a good percentage of prospective abusive use of algorithms by dominant platform undertakings.

IV.2.2 The Implementation of Algorithm Audits in a Unitary System

The matters in need of algorithm auditing and algorithm regulation generally go far beyond market competition. Instead, it is important to monitor potential algorithmic misconduct in every aspect of platform business in which algorithms are frequently employed. Before the release of the Algorithmic Recommendation Regulations, the regulation of algorithms, especially by way of auditing, was conducted in a piecemeal manner. Besides the aforementioned provisions in the Guidelines, the provisions of laws and regulations covering algorithm applications merely focused on one aspect of algorithmic misconduct. For instance, the

[100] B Zhou and Y Wang, '新反垄断法落地， 平台监管如何着棋？[How the New AML Tackles Platform Regulation?]' (财经杂志 [*Caijing Magazine*], 18 August 2022) <https://new.qq.com/rain/a/20220818A08J4900> (accessed 30 October 2022).

Personal Information Protection Law (PIPL) stresses the importance of personal information protection, while the purpose of the E-Commerce Law is to protect consumers' interests.[101] Consequently, algorithm audits have been carried out separately through different compliance procedures.[102]

However, the Algorithmic Recommendation Regulations, China's first legal document with 'algorithm' in the name, were formulated in a bid to provide a comprehensive legal regime to regulate algorithmic recommendation services (rather than algorithmic recommendation technology).[103] The CAC, as specified by Article 3 of the Algorithmic Recommendation Regulations, is the principal regulatory authority for the enforcement of the Algorithmic Recommendation Regulations. Other regulatory authorities shall also get involved in the enforcement where the suspected violation is pertinent to their authorities.[104]

IV.2.3 Algorithm Reviews and Algorithms Inspections

In practice, two major types of algorithm audits have been established in China, namely algorithm review and algorithm inspection. Algorithm review is conducted by platforms as internal evaluations, which shall be periodically reported to the regulatory agencies, while algorithm inspection is carried out by external and independent auditors to assist the regulatory agencies to evaluate the compliance of algorithms and improve information transparency for stakeholders concerning platform businesses.

Algorithm review-wise, according to Article 55 PIPL, personal information processors are obligated to implement internal reviews of algorithms. The QingLang Operation special action on algorithm governance required Internet enterprises to clean up the use of algorithms with reference to relevant legal requirements, to rectify problematic uses of algorithms, and to safeguard the lawful rights and interests of Internet users.

[101] Before the establishment of Algorithmic Recommendation Regulations, all provisions related to algorithm governance were segregated into different laws and regulations with different purposes. For instance, the PIPL sets obligations for personal information processors to conduct security assessments of personal information and ensure the ability of personal information subjects to complain against automated decision making. The E-Commerce Law (n19) stipulates that where an e-commerce business operator provides consumers with search results for goods or services based on consumers' preferences or consumption habits, it shall, in parallel, provide consumers with options that are not targeted at their characteristics.

[102] H Zhang, '算法权力的兴起、异化及法律规制 [The Emergence, Alienation and Legal Regulation of Algorithmic Power]' (2019) 4 Legal Business Research 63.

[103] Article 2(1) indicates that 'the application of algorithmic recommendation technology to provide Internet information services' applies to this regulation.

[104] Besides enforcing the Algorithmic Recommendation Regulations through formal procedures by governmental agencies, the Algorithmic Recommendation Regulations also acknowledge private enforcement in a broad sense; namely, platform users are entitled with the rights to choose and to reject services provided with personalized recommendation, to request for interpretation, and to change and to delete user tags. See Central People's Government of the People's Republic of China, '互联网信息服务算法推荐管理规定 [Algorithmic Recommendation Regulations]' (effective 1 March 2022), Article 17 <https://www.gov.cn/zhengce/2022-11/26/content_5728941.htm> (accessed 5 April 2024).

Algorithm inspection-wise, many jurisdictions do not require all algorithms to be externally inspected, considering the institutional costs as well as the inspection costs.[105] For example, Canada set four levels of impact—no impact, moderate impact, high impact, and very high impact—depending on the level of impact of the algorithm on individuals or communities, health and well-being, economic interests, and the ongoing sustainability of an ecosystem.[106] No peer review is required for algorithms with no impact, at least one peer review is required for algorithms with moderate and high impact, and at least two peer reviews are required for algorithms with very high impact.[107]

As for China, following the QingLang Operation special action on algorithm governance, the CAC took the lead in forming a joint inspection group in conjunction with several other regulatory agencies for the regulation of market competition and industrial development to carry out on-site inspections of around 300 Internet enterprises. The inspections focused on checking enterprise algorithm compliance in the field of antitrust, anti-unfair competition, consumer protection, and labour protection.

Nonetheless, questions still remain as to, first, the qualification of the subject that implements algorithm inspections and, second, the sustainability of algorithm inspections. The joint inspection group formed by the CAC mainly consists of randomly chosen experts of law, economics, and technology from regulatory agencies, think tanks, and universities. It is worthy of deliberation as to whether it is necessary to introduce a licensing regime for algorithm inspectors, as well as internal algorithm reviewers, to ensure accurate and fair auditing. As some commentators have suggested, implementing a licensing regime may require auditors to undergo a standard training process to equip them with the necessary expertise for algorithm auditing.[108] However, given the variety of methods and applications in the algorithmic applications, it is not clear yet as to the expertise that shall be required for licensed auditors. One option is to enrich the composition of the expert panel for algorithm audits and ensure that major algorithmic violations, including the use of algorithms for abusive purposes, can be detected effectively.

Moreover, it is necessary to strike a delicate balance between the frequency of algorithm auditing and the costs arising thereof for both regulatory agencies and platform undertakings. Keeping a certain level of algorithm auditing brings about

[105] Y Zhang and B Zhang, '算法规制的路径创新：论我国算法审计制度的构建 [The Path Innovation of Algorithm Law System: On the Construction of China's Algorithm Audit System]' (2022) 10 e-Government 48.

[106] 'Directive on Automated Decision-Making', Appendix B—Impact Assessment Levels.

[107] *Ibid*, Appendix C—Impact Level Requirements.

[108] M Brundage et al, 'Toward Trustworthy AI Development: Mechanisms for Supporting Verifiable Claims' (ResearchGate, 2020), 12 <https://www.researchgate.net/publication/340662790_Toward_Trustworthy_AI_Development_Mechanisms_for_Supporting_Verifiable_Claims> (accessed 10 April 2024).

multiple merits, including the prevention of abuse of market dominance by digital platforms. Nonetheless, algorithm audit, be it internal review or external inspection, may incur a considerable amount of managerial cost and the risk of infringements of the technological secrets of algorithms.

V. Major Cases of Abusive Conduct in China's Digital Markets

V.1 Prohibition Decisions against the Wide Practice of an 'Either–Or Choice'

As introduced at the outset of this chapter, 'either–or choices' used to be a widely employed business strategy in China's digital markets; in essence, they restrict the freedom of in-platform merchants (or traders, in a broad sense) to deal with competing platforms. The prevalence of the 'either–or choice' business practice in China's digital markets far exceeds that in jurisdictions in Europe and the United States. Contributing factors behind this may include inadequate legislation and law enforcement, deeper integration between online and offline businesses, the unique business models in practice, and China's distinct market environment. Such anticompetitive conduct arose in a large number of digital sectors, including online food delivery, online retailing, and even academic literature database service, although some of these conducts were adopted alongside other forms of abusive conducts.

Ever since the SPC decision on an early version of the 'either–or choice' business practice in the case of *3Q War* in 2014, Chinese competition authorities at both central and local levels have decided several high-profile cases involving the business practice of the 'either–or choice' by dominant platform undertakings. Based on these decisions, we further present how the AML has been enforced against such abusive behaviours in China's digital markets. After the court decision on *3Q War*, we then discuss the most high-profile prohibition decision against the Alibaba Group delivered by the SAMR. Then, we present two administrative prohibition decisions on the 'either–or choice' practice in the on-demand food and beverage delivery markets, which were made by the SAMR and Shanghai AMR, respectively. Finally, we introduce the decision on the abusive conduct of China's largest academic literature database operator, part of which was also, by nature, the business practice of an 'either–or choice'.

V.1.1 '3Q War': *Qihoo v Tencent*

As regards anti-monopoly litigation in the digital economy, one of the earliest high-profile cases was the abuse-of-dominance dispute between Beijing Qihoo Technology Co, Ltd ('Qihoo', its subsidiary as appropriate, '360'), Tencent Technology (Shenzhen) Co, Ltd, and Shenzhen Tencent Computer System Co,

Ltd (together, 'Tencent'). This case was listed by the Approval Committee of the SPC as No 78 guiding case in 2017.[109]

Qihoo and Tencent are two large and popular integrated providers of Internet services in China. Each of the two competitors developed its own free apps, anti-virus software (360 Security) and instant messaging software (QQ), in a bid to establish its own user base. Both of them make profit by ad promotion and charges for value-added services. The disputes between 360 and Tencent took place in 2010 when 360 introduced its 360 Security software enabling users to skip ads that QQ could display. On 14 October 2010, Tencent officially announced that it was suing 360 for unfair competition, demanding Qihoo and its affiliates to cease infringement, to make a public apology, and to pay damages. As an accompanying countermeasure, Tencent declared that it would stop running the QQ software on computers that had installed the 360 software. This '3Q War' was intervened by the MIIT and the Internet Association on 5 November 2010, which required both sides to cease the dispute and resume compatibility with each other. On 14 April 2012, Qihoo filed an anti-monopoly lawsuit against Tencent, claiming that Tencent was dominant in the market of instant messaging software and service and had abused its dominant market position because the defendant had expressly prohibited its users from using Qihoo's '360 Security' software, forcing it to delete 360 Security by refusing to provide relevant services for users who had 360 Security installed.

Qihoo also alleged that Tencent had employed technical means to prevent users who had installed 360 browsers from accessing Qzone (a social networking website provided by Tencent). In addition, Tencent had bundled QQ Computer Manager (an antivirus software) with its instant messaging software and required users to install QQ Doctor, an antivirus application like 360 Safeguard, in the name of upgrading QQ Computer Manager, which constituted bundling.[110] Such behaviour made QQ incompatible with all 360 software, as users were forced either to have QQ or to have 360's antivirus software on their computers, the earliest business practice of an 'either–or choice'. The 'either–or choice'" business requirement by Tencent undermined 360's user pool in antivirus software (360 was said to have lost almost 10 per cent of its users within forty-eight hours).[111]

In the end, both the courts of first instance and second instance rejected all of the claims of the plaintiff.[112] Nonetheless, it is worth noting that the SPC held that

> whether the relevant market should be clearly defined depends on the circumstances of each case. [...] If the market position of the operator and the impact of

[109] *Beijing Qihoo Technology Co Ltd* (n16)

[110] *Ibid.*

[111] DeHeng Law Offices (n10).

[112] *Beijing Qihoo Technology Co, Ltd* (n16); Guangdong High People's Court, *Beijing Qihoo Technology Co, Ltd v Tencent Technology (Shenzhen) Co*, Ltd, [2011] (北京奇虎科技有限公司诉腾讯科技（深圳）有限公司、深圳市腾讯计算机系统有限公司滥用市场支配地位纠纷案，(2011)粤高法民三初字第2号) (20 March 2013).

> the anti-competitive behaviours can be assessed through direct evidence of exclusion or obstruction of competition, it is not necessary in every case of abuse of market dominance to explicitly and clearly define the relevant market.[113]

While the SPC acknowledged the possibility of not defining the relevant market 'explicitly and clearly', it seems that the SPC held that such a practice would only be an exception when the said circumstances apply. The SPC defined the relevant market in this case, namely the instant messaging (IM) services market in China primarily based on demand-side substitutability analysis supplemented by supply-side substitutability (which is in line with the then effective and currently effective Guide of the Anti-Monopoly Committee of the State Council for the Definition of the Relevant Market).

With respect to the dominant market position, while the SPC considered the market share of QQ, which had been more than 80 per cent, the SPC held that a high market share did not necessarily mean a dominant market position, especially in the IM service industry, which is characterized by dynamic competition. Hence, the SPC further looked into the competition status of the relevant market; QQ's ability to control the price, quantity, and other transaction conditions; QQ's financial technological conditions;, the degree of difficulty for other undertakings to enter the relevant market; and whether QQ's conduct of making its software incompatible and requiring exclusive dealing *per se* meant that it had a dominant market position. According to the SPC, all of these factors aside from market share pointed to the absence of a dominant market position for QQ.

While it was not necessary to analyse the effect of the conduct, given that the SPC had already concluded that QQ did not have a dominant market position, it still did so to 'verify whether the conclusion on market dominance is correct'[114] given that the 'boundaries of the relevant market are blurred, and it is not very clear whether the defendant has a dominant market position'.[115] The SPC concluded that the incompatibility of the QQ software did not have significant impacts on consumers, that QQ did not have an obvious motive to eliminate and restrict the competition of the IM services market, and that the incompatibility of the QQ software did not significantly restrict the competition of the security software market of which 360 was a part.

The SPC summarized the following as the key takeaways of the judgment. First, in anti-monopoly cases, the definition of the relevant market is, more often than not, an essential step for analysis. Nevertheless, it depends on the particular situation of the case whether the relevant market can be clearly and explicitly defined. It is not required to formally and precisely define the relevant market in every

[113] *Beijing Qihoo Technology Co, Ltd* (n16).
[114] *Ibid.*
[115] *Ibid.*

instance of abuse of market dominance if the operator's position in the market and the impact of the anticompetitive behaviour can be evaluated through direct evidence of exclusion or obstruction of competition. Second, the hypothetical monopoly test (HMT) is a widely recognized method for market definition. In practice, the HMT can be carried out using either the small-but-significant-non-transitory-increase-in-price (SSNIP) or small-but-significant-non-transitory-decrease-in-quality (SSNDQ) method. Third, considering the characteristics of IM services, such as low cost and high coverage, the relevant geographic market must be defined on the basis of a comprehensive assessment, especially examining the regions where users actually choose a certain service, the existence of foreign competitors, and the speed at which foreign competitors enter into the market. Fourth, in the Internet sector, market share is a preliminary but sometimes misleading indicator of market power. When determining the existence of a dominant position, the importance of market shares might be adapted when necessary.[116] Undoubtedly, the SPC's guiding cases, which demonstrate the analysis roadmap, could also exert profound impacts on how administrative antitrust enforcement is carried out in China's digital markets.[117]

In 2021, seven years after the final decision on the '3Q war', the SAMR and Shanghai AMR successively issued prohibition decisions against platform undertakings for engaging in 'either–or choice' practices.[118] On 13 April 2021, the SAMR, alongside the CAC and State Taxation Administration held a joint meeting with thirty-four platform undertakings, urging them to thoroughly examine and rectify any anticompetitive practices. This was a typical soft intervention in the anti-monopoly enforcement procedure in China. Some platform undertakings have issued their commitments, promising not to engage in anticompetitive practices.[119] These decisions did not just provide guidance on 'either–or choice' practices in Chinese digital markets. More importantly, they illustrated the enforcement trend for platforms regarding abuses of dominance, which appears to have changed tremendously since the so-called '3Q war' era in 2014.

[116] *Ibid.*

[117] CPI, 'Year of the Rat' (n75), 36.

[118] SAMR, 'SAMR Administrative Prohibition Decision [2021] No 28' (n18); Shanghai AMR, '上海市市场监督管理局行政处罚决定书（沪市监反垄处〔2020〕06201901001号） [Shanghai AMR Administrative Prohibition Decision [2020] No 06201901001]' (25 December 2020) <https://www.samr.gov.cn/xw/df/art/2023/art_fb84525d385a489db74615d1939883d0.html> (accessed 7 November 2022).

[119] Pengpai News, '中央网信办、市场监管总局, 税务总局联合召开规范线上经济秩序指导会 [SAMR, Cyberspace Administration, and State Taxation Administration Jointly Held an Administrative Guidance Meeting to Regulate Online Economy Order]' (11 November 2020) <https://www.thepaper.cn/newsDetail_forward_9946345> (accessed 7 November 2022). From 14–16 April 2021, the SAMR disclosed the Commitments of Operation in Compliance with Laws of the thirty-four Internet platform enterprises attending the administrative guidance meeting. See SAMR, '互联网平台企业向社会公开《依法合规经营承诺》（第一批）[Internet Platform Enterprises Publicize "Commitment to Operate in Compliance with Law" to Society (First Batch)]' (14 April 2021) <https://mp.weixin.qq.com/s/SlDlWWOcsEt89isAEJKi3Q> (accessed 7 November 2022).

Below, we examine four typical cases to ascertain how the recent enforcement trend in China is evolving. And particular attention is paid to how, during an investigation, the Chinese authorities define the relevant market and how they establish whether a platform undertaking in digital markets has a dominant position.

V.1.2 The Alibaba Group

In 2015, several days before the 'Double Eleven Shopping Carnival', a major e-commerce platform JD.com (JD) reported to the State Administration for Industry and Commerce (SAIC)[120] that its arch-rival Alibaba was disrupting the market order by coercing retailers on Alibaba's B2C e-commerce platform Tmall to make a choice of the product-promoting activities to join either of the two platforms.[121] From 2017 onwards, reports of e-commerce platforms requiring in-platform merchants to stick to one platform went on not only before major mass promotions[122] but also in the everyday environment.[123] Public allegations made both by competing platforms and merchants on platforms were recurring,[124] and such conduct was also reported to be pervasive among other types of digital platforms—especially food delivery platforms.[125]

For years, despite high-profile recriminations among players before the public and repeated claims to have investigated such conduct by the competition

[120] The SAIC was substituted by, and its functions were integrated into the SAMR in 2018.

[121] iMarkets, '京东举报阿里 称其胁迫商家《二选一》扰乱电商市场秩序 [JD.com Reports That Ali Forced Operators to "Choose One from Two Platforms", Disrupting the Order of E-Commerce Market]' (3 November 2015) <http://finance.ifeng.com/a/20151103/14054426_0.shtml> (accessed 23 January 2020).

[122] J Lei, '京东与阿里大战再起！京东锁定后台强行促销， 天猫逼店铺二选一 [War between JD and Ali Again! JD Locked Backend for Forced Promotions, and Tmall Forced Operators to Choose One from Two]' (7 June 2017) <http://www.hxnews.com/news/cjpd/cjxw/201706/07/1232138.shtml>; Ebrun, '二选一再上演：家居家装品牌被迫签保证书 ["Choosing One Out of Two" Again: Furniture Brands Forced to Sign Guarantees]' (11 June 2018) <http://www.ebrun.com/20180611/281442.shtml> (both accessed 23 January 2020).

[123] Southern Metropolis Daily, '京东唯品会炮轰天猫垄断 天猫回应称对方误导公众 [JD and Vipshop Accuse Tmall of Monopoly, and Tmall Responded That They Misled the Public]' (13 July 2017) <http://finance.sina.com.cn/chanjing/gsnews/2017-07-13/doc-ifyiakwa3982343.shtml> (accessed 23 January 2020).

[124] A high-profile example of public allegations by suppliers on platforms is that, before the 'June. 18 promotion', Galanz posted on its official Weibo several announcements alleging that Tmall had restricted its traffic on Tmall after the company's delegation visited and established a strategic relationship with Pinduoduo. See Hubei Yangtze River Business News, '格兰仕怒怼天猫《二选一》 [A Review of the Chinese Air-Conditioning Industry for 2019: Galanz Accused Tmall for "Choice of One Out of Two]' (19 June 2019) <https://baijiahao.baidu.com/s?id=1636734728435224012&wfr=spider&for=pc> (accessed 10 February 2020).

[125] During the period 2016–2019, local subsidiaries or agencies of Meituan in some provinces received local administrative punishments by local Administrations for Market Regulation or Industry of Commerce for breach of Anti-Unfair Competition Law or local anti-unfair competition provisions for forcing providers to quit other platforms. In April 2018, when Didi, the owner of China's biggest ride-sourcing platform, made its debut in the food-delivery market, both Meituan and Eleme were reported to be forcing providers to quit Didi in Wuxi, which led to an inquiry by Wuxi's Bureau of Industry and Commerce with Meituan, Didi, and Eleme. The Bureau requested that relevant platforms should stop 'illegal conducts that constitute unfair competition and monopoly'.

authorities, there had hardly been any formal enforcement against them, be it by regulatory agencies or through private litigation.[126] Nevertheless, on 16 January 2018, JD brought a civil lawsuit before the Higher People's Court of Beijing against the Alibaba Group and Tmall, claiming that Alibaba and its Tmall had abused their dominant market position by coercing in-platform merchants to make an 'either–or choice'. In July 2019, the SPC rejected Alibaba's appeal of an objection to jurisdiction, ruling that the Higher People's Court of Beijing had jurisdiction over the case.[127] In spite of the resolution of the issue of jurisdiction, the hearing court postponed the decision on the case for years, probably because of the absence of stands from the SAMR on whether such conduct constituted an abuse of dominant market position.

In December 2020, the SAMR initiated the formal investigation of the Alibaba Group for its abuse of dominance in China's online retailing platform service market in accordance with the AML. During the investigation, the SAMR conducted on-site inspections, made inquiries and collected pertinent evidence and materials. It also carried out in-depth inquiries on competing platforms and in-platform merchants. A group of experts, including lawyers and economists, were

[126] Some food-delivery platforms received administrative punishments for breach of Anti-Unfair Competition Law or local anti-unfair competition provisions, rather than the AML. See Lishui AMR, '丽水市市场监督管理局行政处罚决定书（丽市监案〔2016〕25号）[Lishui AMR Administrative Prohibition Decision [2016] No 25]' (19 January 2017) <https://lawhtbprolwkinfohtbprolcomhtbprolcn-s.libvpn.zuel.edu.cn/administrative-punishment/detail/MkUwMDE2MTg2NjY%3D?searchId = c84982bf1a71423492a27873eef0ae29&index = 1&q=%E4%B8%BD%E5%B8%82%E7%9B%91%E6%A1%88%E3%80%942016%E3%80%9525%E5%8F%B7&module=&childModule = all> (accessed 30 May 2024); Jinhua AMR, '金华市市场监督管理局行政处罚决定书（金市监罚字〔2017〕22号）[Jinhua AMR Administrative Prohibition Decision [2017] No 22]' (14 November 2017) <https://lawhtbprolwkinfohtbprolcomhtbprolcn-s.libvpn.zuel.edu.cn/administrative-punishment/detail/MkUwMDM5NDM3MTA%3D?searchId = 0d128d4e58934f51a74937ecac613e34&index = 1&q=%E9%87%91%E5%B8%82%E7%9B%91%E7%BD%9A%E5%AD%97%E3%80%942017%E3%80%9522%E5%8F%B7&module=&childModule = all> (accessed 30 May 2024); Wuxi Bureau of Industry and Commerce, '无锡市工商行政管理局行政处罚决定书（锡工商案〔2018〕00097号）[Wuxi Bureau of Industry and Commerce Administrative Prohibition Decision [2018] No 00097]' (1 April 2018) <https://lawhtbprolwkinfohtbprolcomhtbprolcn-s.libvpn.zuel.edu.cn/administrative-punishment/detail/MkUwMDU3MzM0NDI%3D?searchId = 077706718aaa4ca48a2e4d77e57d4c17&index = 1&q=%E9%94%A1%E5%B7%A5%E5%95%86%E6%A1%88%E3%80%942018%E3%80%9500097%E5%8F%B7&module=&childModule = all> (accessed 30 May 2024); Haiyan AMR, '嘉兴市海盐县市场监督管理局行政处罚决定书（盐市监处字〔2018〕160号）[Haiyan AMR Administrative Prohibition Decision [2018] No 160] (6 July 2018) <https://lawhtbprolwkinfohtbprolcomhtbprolcn-s.libvpn.zuel.edu.cn/administrative-punishment/detail/MkUwMTI5MDQ0NzM%3D?searchId = 106929513a574a67b39aa90c636629f4&index = 1&q=%E7%9B%90%E5%B8%82%E7%9B%91%E5%A4%84%E5%AD%97%E3%80%942018%E3%80%95160%E5%8F%B7&module=&childModule = all> (accessed 30 May 2024); Tongjiang AMR, '巴中市通江县市场监督管理局行政处罚决定书（通市监管罚字〔2019〕3037号）[Tongjiang AMR Administrative Prohibition Decision [2019] No 3037]' (20 March 2019) <https://finance.sina.com.cn/chanjing/gsnews/2019-04-15/doc-ihvhiewr6055953.shtml> (accessed 30 May 2024).

[127] Supreme People's Court, *Beijing Jingdong Century Commerce Co, Ltd v Zhejiang Tmall Network Co, Ltd, Zhejiang Tmall Technology Co, Ltd, Alibaba Group Holding Limited*, [2019] (北京京东世纪贸易有限公司、北京京东三百陆拾度电子商务有限公司诉浙江天猫网络有限公司、浙江天猫技术有限公司、阿里巴巴集团控股有限公司滥用市场支配地位案，(2019)最高民辖终130号) (3 July 2019).

also involved in analysing relevant data and verifying evidence and materials.[128] On 6 April 2021, the SAMR sent an administrative guidance letter to the Alibaba Group, prohibiting it from using technical means, platform rules, data, and algorithms to implement anticompetitive agreements and abuse its market dominance to exclude or restrict market competition.[129] Four days later, a prohibition decision was issued.

According to the decision, the Alibaba Group enjoyed a dominant position in the online retailing platform service market in China, and its business practice of an 'either–or choice' had excluded and restricted competition in such a market; hindered the free flow of goods, services, and resources; affected the innovative development of the platform economy; infringed on the legitimate rights and interests of merchants in the platform; and harmed the interests of consumers. In a word, it had abused its dominant market position as prohibited by Article 17(1)(4) of the 2008 AML. In accordance with Articles 47 and 49 of the 2008 AML, the SAMR issued an administrative prohibition decision in 2021, ordering the Alibaba Group to stop its abusive behaviours and imposing a penalty of 4 per cent of its 2019 sales in China of ¥455.712 billion (ca €63.29 billion), amounting to ¥18.23 billion (ca €2.35 billion) in total. At the same time, the Alibaba Group was required to implement comprehensive self-rectification of its abusive behaviours immediately after the decision.

The SAMR made the following analyses in its decision:

(1) The relevant market is defined as the online retailing platform service market in China on the ground of the 2008 AML and the Guidelines and the characteristics of the platform economy. For the product market, the SAMR distinguished the online retailing market service from the offline one and did not accept further segmentation (e.g. B2C v. C2C, display on the platform v. display via live streaming, short videos, etc.) based on a demand-side and supply-side substitution analysis. Demand substitution analysis wise, online retailing market differs from its offline counterpart in terms of: (a) the geographic and service time coverage; (b) the operating costs for platform operators; (c) the ability to support in-platform merchants to match potential consumers; and (d) the efficiency of demand feedback for in-platform merchants. Correspondingly, from the perspective of consumers, the range of products available for selection, the level of shopping convenience provided thereby, and the efficiency of comparing and matching

[128] MLex Staff, 'Alibaba Fined 18.23 Billion Yuan for Abuse of Dominance in China' (English translation) <https://mlexmarketinsight.com/news/insight/alibaba-fined-18-23-billion-yuan-for-abuse-of-dominance-in-china-english-version>.

[129] SAMR, '国家市场监督管理总局行政指导书（国市监行指反垄〔2021〕1号）[Administrative Guiding Decision [2021] No 1]' (6 April 2021) <https://www.samr.gov.cn/xw/zj/art/2023/art_4966dda92ab34c398615f5878c10c8f1.html> (accessed 7 November 2022).

products vary between the two markets. Finally, the following supply-side factors further demonstrate that the two do not have a close substitution relationship: (a) different profit models—online retailing platform services primarily profit by charging transaction commission and marketing fees to in-platform merchants, while the offline ones mainly profit by charging fixed store rents to operators; and (b) the transition from offline retailing commercial services to online retailing platform services presents greater difficulty.

(2) Alibaba Group enjoyed a dominant position in the relevant market in consideration of the following factors: (a) Alibaba Group's market share exceeded 50% in terms of revenue from the platform service and the transaction volumes on the platforms; (b) the relevant market was highly concentrated based on the Herfindahl-Hirschman Index (HHI) and the Four-firm concentration ratio (CR4); (c) Alibaba Group had a strong ability to control the market, especially the ability to control the price of services, the matching of in-platform merchants with consumers, and the general sales channels for in-platform merchants; it had strong financial resources and advanced technical conditions for the operation of platform service; (d) other business operators were highly dependent on Alibaba Group in terms of transactions (with significant network effects and lock-in effects, Alibaba Group's platform being an important channel for displaying their images, and high switching costs for them to move to another platform); (e) entering the relevant market was difficult due to, for example, mass funding for platform building and brand building including for logistics and payment systems and the fact that online retailing platforms must have sufficient users on one side of the platform for valid market entry; (f) and it had significant advantages in related markets such as logistics, payment, and cloud computing.

(3) Alibaba Group had abused its dominant market position. Since 2015, Alibaba Group had prohibited in-platform merchants from opening stores and participating in promotional activities in other competing platforms, and procured the implementation of such a restriction by applying rewards and punishments to such merchants. Such conduct constituted 'restricting transaction counterparties so that they can only make transactions with the said business operator without justifiable reasons' as prohibited by Article 17(1)(4) of the 2008 AML. Such anti-competitive conduct had in effect caused the following harms: (a) it had excluded and restricted competition in the market of online retailing platform services in China and it had excluded and restricted both current fair competition and potential competition between platform operators in the relevant market, (b) it had harmed the interests of in-platform merchants, including the autonomy for business and the opportunity for intra-brand competition, (c) it had impeded the

> optimisation of resource allocation and restricted the innovative development of the platform economy at large, and (d) it had harmed the interests of consumers, especially consumers' right to free choice and right to fair trade, and, in the long run, undermined the overall level of social welfare.[130]

Taking the above effects into account, the SAMR found that the Alibaba Group had abused its dominance in the online retailing market in China, which was in violation of Article 17(1)(4) of the 2008 AML. In accordance with Articles 47 and 49 of the 2008 AML, and taking into account the nature and severity of Alibaba's abusive conduct, as well as the duration of such conduct, the SAMR eventually decided to order the Alibaba Group to cease its illegal conduct and fined it ¥18.23 billion (ca €2.35 billion), equivalent to 4 per cent of its revenue generated within China in 2019.[131]

V.1.3 Meituan

Meituan is an online 'local-life' service platform best-known for its on-demand food delivery service. Over time, Meituan has evolved into an all-in-one super app with third-party services in locally found services and products, such as tourism-related businesses, entertainment, and restaurants. Meituan charges commission per transaction, depending on the nature and amount of such a transaction. From 2018 onwards, Meituan allegedly started requiring in-platform merchants to make an 'either–or choice' when trading. In other words, merchants were asked to make exclusive choices between Meituan and its competing platforms (e.g. Eleme, Meituan's major competitor in the on-demand food delivery service market in China), which materially restricted the business opportunities of merchants and, at the same time, disturbed the normal business online order and delivery of the food and beverage market.

At the level of public law enforcement, the 'either–or choice' requirement imposed by Meituan was widely complained about for its anticompetitive nature and triggered administrative interventions, though mainly under the umbrella of anti-unfair competition law, among local competition authorities as early as 2017. For example, the AMR in Jinhua City, Zhejiang Province, punished Meituan with a total fine of ¥526,000 (ca €67,512) since it had exploited the advantage of its dominant market position to coerce merchants to conclude a 'commitment letter of cooperation' in June 2017.[132] In May 2018, the AMR in Huai'an City, Jiangsu Province also found that Meituan had conducted unfair competition behaviours

[130] SAMR, 'SAMR Administrative Prohibition Decision [2021] No 28' (n18).

[131] MLex Staff (n128).

[132] Sina Finance, '立案！美团被曝《侵害公共利益》， 地方监管诉苦：多次约谈， 权力有限！ [File a Case! Meituan Was Exposed as "Infringing on the Public Interest", Local Supervision Complained: Repeated Interviews, Limited Power!]' (27 April 2021) <https://finance.sina.com.cn/chanjing/gsnews/2021-04-27/doc-ikmyaawc2098745.shtml> (accessed 22 February 2024).

and imposed a fine of ¥70,000 (ca €8,989.4) thereon.[133] In March 2019, the AMR in Tongjiang County in Bazhong City, Sichuan Province, fined Meituan ¥250,000 (ca €32,110) for its conduct of misleading, cheating, and coercing merchants to modify, close, or uninstall network products or services legally provided by other platforms.[134]

In addition to investigations and prohibition decisions against the practice of the 'either–or choice', local competition authorities also carried out a series of administrative interviews with violating platforms. For instance, in June 2019, it was reported that the AMR in Zibo City, Shandong Province, had held an administrative interview with Meituan due to similar business practices.[135] Moreover, in September 2019, Bazhong AMR interviewed sixteen e-commerce platforms, amongst which Meituan, Eleme, and Suning were mentioned by name in the official press release. During the interview, it was made clear that 'either–or choice' practices were strictly forbidden.[136]

At the level of private enforcement, Meituan and Eleme filed several lawsuits against each other in different local jurisdictions in China on the ground of unfair competition law. For instance, in April 2021, Eleme was ordered by Wenzhou Intermediate People's Court to pay compensation of ¥80,000 (ca €10,275.2) to Meituan, as it had coerced in-platform merchants to make an 'either–or choice' and violated China's Anti-Unfair Competition Law.[137] Correspondingly, Eleme sued Meituan for economic compensation and won the battle eventually. In December 2021, Zhejiang High People's Court found that the conduct of coercing merchants to reach exclusive deals had undermined the openness, sharing, fairness, and order of market competition in the sector of digital economy, which had not only harmed the legitimate rights and interests of other platforms and consumers but also impeded the maximization of the overall welfare of the society. Subsequently, the court ruled that Meituan's conduct of restricting and hindering merchants from trading with its competitor Eleme by means of raising commission

[133] *Ibid.*

[134] Hongxing News, '美团被举报强迫外卖商家独家合作， 四川通江代理商遭罚 25 万 [Meituan Reportedly Forced Takeout Merchants to Work Exclusively with It, and Agents in Tongjiang County, Sichuan Province, Were Fined 250,000 Yuan]' (29 March 2019) <https://baijiahao.baidu.com/s?id=1629318393689842444&wfr=spider&for=pc> (accessed 22 February 2024).

[135] NetEase Hao, '美团：《二选一》被约谈已成常态， 非法窃取商业机密成行业公敌 [Meituan: Interviewed for "Choose One or the Other" Has Become the norm, Illegal Theft of Trade Secrets Become the Public Enemy of the Industry] (19 June 2019) <https://www.163.com/dy/article/EI2L2JRQ05314055.html> (accessed 22 February 2024).

[136] Bazhong AMR Official Site, '巴中市市场监督管理局集中约谈16家驻巴重点电商平台 [Bazhong AMR Interviewed Sixteen Important E-Commerce Platforms Operating in Bazhong at Once]' (7 November 2019) <https://samr.cnbz.gov.cn/xwdt/bjdt/14255821.html> (accessed 22 February 2024).

[137] Wenzhou Intermediate People's Court, *Beijing Sanfast Online Technology Co, Ltd v Shanghai Lazarus Information Technology Co, Ltd Wenzhou Branch, etc.*, [2021] (北京三快在线科技有限公司、上海拉扎斯信息科技有限公司及其温州分公司等不正当竞争纠纷案， (2020)浙03民初407号) (7 April 2021).

and setting unreasonable trading conditions constituted unfair competition as prohibited by Article 2 of the Anti-Unfair Competition Law.[138] In another similar case, Meituan was ordered by Jiangsu High People's Court to compensate Eleme for total economic losses of ¥352 million (ca €45 million).[139]

Nonetheless, those fines or compensation were, at most, a slap on the wrist for a platform company of the size of Meituan. In addition, none of these investigations, decisions, or verdicts were made under the AML. Instead, most of the cases were resolved as matters of unfair competition. However, on 26 April 2021, the SAMR initiated an anti-monopoly investigation into Meituan. On 8 October 2021, the SAMR made the prohibition decision against Meituan, ordering restitution of the ¥1.3 billion (ca €0.18 billion) deposit collected for 'either–or choices', and a fine of ¥3.44 billion (ca €0.44 billion).

According to the decision,[140]

(1) The relevant market in this case was defined as China's market of online food and beverage delivery platform services, a multi-sided market that served restaurant operators and consumers. The distinctive feature of this market was the cross-border network effect, which made the demand for online food and beverage delivery platform services from users on each side closely related. The decision distinguished amongst the market of online delivery platforms, offline restaurants, and first-party delivery provided by restaurants themselves.

The market of online food delivery services and the market of offline restaurant services are not in the same relevant market. The analysis of consumer demand substitution was drawn (i) from the fact that they respectively satisfy consumers' needs for dining at home and dining on-site; (ii) from the fact that online food delivery platforms provide services for displaying, recommending, and comparing food products as well as delivery services, which are distinct from offline restaurants; and (iii) the variety of food products offered by the two differs. Correspondingly, from the perspective of operator demand analysis, online food and beverage delivery platforms provide more transaction opportunities and higher operational efficiency. Finally, on the supply side, the transformation of offline dining services into online food delivery platforms entails high costs, including substantial funds,

[138] *Shanghai Lazarus Information Technology Co, Ltd* (n86).

[139] Huai'an Intermediate People's Court, '淮安中院发布2021年度知识产权司法保护十件典型案例 [Huai'an Intermediate People's Court Release of Ten Typical Cases of Judicial Protection of Intellectual Property Rights for the Year 2021]' (25 April 2022) <http://fy.huaian.gov.cn/col/11895_474188/art/16487424/1650871155464Pq7wSVcr.html> (accessed 22 February 2024).

[140] SAMR, '国家市场监督管理总局行政处罚决定书（国市监处罚〔2021〕74号） [SAMR Administrative Prohibition Decision [2021] No 74] (8 October 2021) <https://www.samr.gov.cn/xw/zj/art/2023/art_31910760066b4f69aa119a20dee250ad.html> (accessed 22 February 2024).

infrastructure, and technological support to reach the critical scale of platform economics.

Similarly, restaurant-operated online food delivery services typically complement rather than substitute online food delivery platform services. On the demand side, there is a significant distinction in terms of the variety of dining options available to consumers and the offerings provided by operators. On the supply side, the restaurant-operated online food delivery services differ significantly from online food delivery platform services in terms of user base, service capacity, technological support, and other aspects.

(2) Meituan enjoyed a dominant position in its relevant market of China's online food and beverage delivery platform service. This conclusion was drawn based on the facts that (i) Meituan had a higher-than-50 per cent market share in the relevant market, as evidenced by its share of service revenue and share of food delivery orders; (ii) the relevant market was highly concentrated; (iii) Meituan possessed strong market control capabilities, exerting a strong influence on service prices, the exposure of operators, and the sales channels of operators; (iv) Meituan had financial and technical resources which solidified and enhanced its market power; (v) restaurant merchants relied heavily on Meituan, given that it served as the primary online sales channel for food delivery and made data migration difficult; (vi) potential platform competitors faced great entry barriers, as new entrants needed to invest heavily in constructing platforms and follow-up marketing, but they also faced difficulties in attracting sufficient consumers and in-platform merchants to reach the critical mass; and (vii) Meituan's expansion into various fields had brought more transaction opportunities to online food delivery platforms, further enhancing its market power.

(3) Meituan was found to have abused its dominant market position in such a market. To begin with, it had forced merchants into exclusivity agreements by charging higher commission to those who resisted, and slowing down their approval to be listed on its application. In addition, to ensure the implementation of its 'either–or' policy, Meituan had incorporated the signing of exclusive cooperation agreements into employee assessments and training and monitored and punished exclusive operators who enter into competing platforms. Such conduct was found to have restricted the competition among platforms in the food and beverage delivery service market in China. Such restrictive behaviour had not only harmed the legitimate interests of in-platform merchants and consumers but also impeded the innovation and development of the platform economy.[141] Eventually, Meituan was, first, ordered to cease its illegal acts, to revamp its operations and to refund exclusive partnership deposits to merchants on the platform, amounting to ¥1.3 billion (ca €0.18

[141] *Ibid.*

billion); and second, fined 3 per cent of its sales volume in China in 2020, amounting to ¥3.44 billion (ca €0.44 billion) in total. In addition, Meituan was required to file self-examination compliance reports to the SAMR for the next three years.

V.1.4 Sherpa's

Sherpa's is a China-based online food delivery platform that connects end users with offline food and beverage merchants through the platform company's website and mobile phone application *Sherpa's*, taking orders from users who are accustomed to speaking English. Established as early as 1999, Sherpa's expanded its scope of platform service to cover Shanghai, Beijing, and Suzhou. From January 2017 to October 2019, Sherpa's used its dominant position in the market for online food delivery platforms providing English-language services in Shanghai to impose an 'either–or' requirement on its partner restaurants. In June 2019, Sherpa's was investigated by the AMR of Shanghai Municipality for its suspected abuse of market dominance through restrictive trading practices, since it had concluded agreements that contained an 'exclusive right-of-delivery clause' with all merchants selling food and beverages on its website or platform. In recognition of Sherpa's dominant position in its relevant market and its abusive conduct of such a business practice, on 25 December 2020, the Shanghai AMR imposed a fine of 3 per cent of the sales for the year 2018 on Sherpa's, amounting to ¥116.8 million (ca €16.2 million) in total.

The prohibition decision of the Shanghai AMR, unlike the aforementioned SAMR decisions, contained many steps of technical analyses of the prerequisites for abusive behaviours:

(1) The relevant market is defined as Shanghai's English-language online food and beverage delivery service market. At the outset, Shanghai AMR defined the relevant geographic market to be the city of Shanghai, for online delivery platforms customarily require consumers to choose the city in which the delivery service is provided and forbid consumers from placing orders across cities. In reaching the definition of the relevant service market, Shanghai AMR conducted a demand-side and supply-side substitutability analysis, as well as the hypothetical monopolist (SSNIP) test. In the substitutability analysis, Shanghai AMR distinguished the market of English-language online food and beverage delivery services from the market of offline restaurants, the market of first-party delivery services provided by restaurants, and the market of Chinese-language online food and beverage delivery. Since the platform operates as a two-sided market, the demand substitution of both consumers and restaurants was also analysed.

The Shanghai AMR specifically addressed the problem of language in this part of the analysis, separating English-using platforms like Sherpa's from Chinese-using platforms like Meituan. On the demand side, it was stressed that language was a major factor in consumers' choice of platforms, for evidence revealed that consumers rarely used platforms in both the English and Chinese version. In addition, English-speaking users were found to have consumer behaviours that were distinct from Chinese-speaking users. For example, English-speaking users tended to have a higher level of consumption, prefer Western-style cuisines and often enjoy pairing their meals with alcoholic beverages, with an average order value of over ¥150 (ca €19.20), while Chinese-speaking users were found to tend to make relatively cheaper orders exceeding ¥100 (ca €12.80) and to prefer Chinese-style cuisines, with an average order value ranging between ¥30 and ¥60 (ca €3.84–7.68). Correspondingly, on the supply side, English-using and Chinese-using platforms usually offered considerably distinctive services in respect of website and application design, restaurant selection, and delivery services, as well as pre-sales and after-sales services. Thus, switching from one language to another would lead to a substantial cost, such as the translation of menus and recruitment of English-speaking employees, with the risk of failing to redeem the investment. To support that there was no substitution between English-using and Chinese-using platforms, an HMT of the SSNIP method was adopted. In the SSNIP test, transaction data of both English and Chinese languages' online delivery platforms from January 2015 to June 2017 was collected and a regression between the number of orders and the amount of delivery fee and commissioning fee was conducted. As a result, the English-using online food and beverage delivery service market was deemed independent from its Chinese-using counterpart.

(2) Sherpa's enjoyed a dominant position in its relevant market. This conclusion was reached considering the facts that (i) Sherpa's had a higher-than-50 per cent market share in the relevant market in terms of daily average order volume, the monthly average number of listed partner restaurants, sales revenue, and the number of users during the period 2017–2019; (ii) Sherpa's had financial and technical resources that were significantly better than those of its competing platforms; (iii) restaurant merchants relied heavily on the services of online delivery that were provided by Sherpa's, given the considerable scale of in-platform restaurant merchants and consumer users thereon; and (iv) other platform operators faced great entry barriers, especially due to network effects. Aside from the need to invest capital and overcome the technological challenges regarding providing a delivery service, new platform operators needed to attract sufficient in-platform restaurant merchants and consumer users, both of which were materially difficult due to network effects.

(3) Sherpa's had abused its dominant market position. It had entered into co-operation agreements with 'exclusive provisions of delivery rights' with all its partner restaurants and required partner restaurants that did not comply with such provisions to delist from other competing platforms. As Sherpa's had a dominant position in the relevant market and there were no justifiable reasons for such conduct, such conduct had excluded and restricted competition in the relevant market:
   (a) Sherpa's conduct had materially limited the transaction and crowded out competitors, as evidenced by data from competing platforms. Ever since Sherpa's launched its 'exclusive-delivery-rights' project, the number of orders, online restaurants, and the amount of revenue of the competing platforms had all exhibited a significant decline, while Sherpa's operation had maintained robust growth. The most notable case was its competing platform Mealbay, which did not endure the decline and had to terminate its online delivery service in December 2017.
   (b) Sherpa's conduct in limiting the transaction was detrimental to the interests of the partner restaurants and users of these restaurants. Aside from the obvious consequence of limiting the choice of both the restaurants and consumers, Shanghai AMR also found that the behaviours of Sherpa's had led to a loss of welfare, namely a rise in the commission fee paid by in-platform restaurants and the delivery fee paid by consumers. Evidence shows that from 2016 to the first half of 2017, competition from new entrants (including EKD, Mealbay, and JSS) led to a decrease in the delivery fee and commission fee on Sherpa's, but the launch of an 'exclusive-delivery-right' delivery fee, which was raised by 45.60 per cent, and a commission fee of 9.33 per cent during the period of 2017–2019.
   (c) There was no justifiable reason for Sherpa's to implement the restricted transaction. Sherpa's claimed that it had restricted transactions to protect its intellectual property. According to Sherpa's, the aim of 'exclusive delivery rights' was to prevent restaurants from using its menus, which were translated and edited by Sherpa's, on competing platforms. In reality, Shanghai AMR found that the menus on Sherpa's were actually translated by the restaurants themselves, while Sherpa's only edited and arranged the menus to be displayed on its application and website and prepared additional translations in exceptional circumstances. Other reasons, such as product safety or investment protection, were also found to be inapplicable in this case.

Therefore, Sherpa's had violated Article 47 of the 2008 AML, and the following administrative penalties were imposed: a fine of 3 per cent of its sales of ¥38.9 billion (ca €5.4 billion) for the year 2018, totalling ¥116.8 billion (ca €16.2 billion).

V.1.5 CNKI

China National Knowledge Infrastructure (CNKI) is one of the largest Chinese academic information databases, which reportedly includes over 200 million academic articles, making it an indispensable database for academic writers in China. However, it is also a huge profit-driven company, largely because of its copyright licensing business, with an enormously broad range of copyright holders. The financial report in the first half of 2018 from CNKI's parent company Tsinghua Tongfang showed that its gross profit rate stood at 58.83 per cent, as reported by Science and Technology Daily.[142]

According to the data of the China Government Procurement Network, the total transaction amount of the database services of CNKI for major universities in 2021 was more than ¥60 million (ca €7.7 million), and the average cost of a single-procurement service for each university was nearly ¥700,000 (ca €89,922), with most of the procurement projects only being used for one year. The single-procurement cost of a single university for the plagiarism detection system also ranged from hundreds of thousands to millions yuan (¥).[143] In recent years, several colleges and universities, including Wuhan University of Technology and Peking University, have either once or several times suspended their subscription with CNKI due to its material price increases. From 2012 to 2021, at least six colleges and universities announced that they were suspending the use of CNKI, and the reason in every case was associated with the excessive increase in price by CNKI.[144] In December 2021, Guo Bing, an academic from the Chinese Academy of Sciences, sued CNKI before the Intermediate People's Court of Hangzhou city, Zhejiang Province, claiming that CNKI not only enjoyed a dominant position in the market of knowledge content and services (academic literature information

[142] People's Daily Overseas New Media, 'China's Largest Online Academic Library CNKI Criticized for Monopoly' (20 February 2019) <http://en.people.cn/n3/2019/0220/c90000-9548124.html> (accessed 7 November 2022).

[143] According to an official announcement, for instance, the transaction amount of CNKI procurement is approximately: Tsinghua University—¥1.79 million (ca €0.23 million). See Tsinghua University, '清华大学中国知网数据库（2023年）采购项目成交结果公告 [Tsinghua University CNKI Procurement Project Transaction Result Announcement (2023)]' (23 December 2022) <https://sbgysfw.sysc.tsinghua.edu.cn/tsinghua.war/tsinghua.api/publish/2022/12/23/1853DA88B6B22CB760B2D3D6BD231031/content.pdf> (accessed 1 May 2024). Shandong University—¥1.05 million (ca €0.14 million). See China Government Procurement Network, '山东大学知网研学平台单一来源成交公告 [Shandong University CNKI Single Source Transaction Announcement]' (16 November 2022) <http://www.ccgp.gov.cn/cggg/zygg/cjgg/202211/t20221116_19022783.htm> (accessed 1 May 2024). Changzhou University—¥530 thousand (ca €68.53 thousand). See Changzhou University, '常州大学中国知网（续订）项目成交公告 [Changzhou University CNKI (Renewal) Project Transaction Announcement]' (31 October 2023) <https://zb.cczu.edu.cn/2023/1031/c8598a344317/page.htm> (accessed 1 May 2024). See also, as summarized by public news, Sina News, '知网的《权力》从何而来？天下苦知网久矣 [Where Does the "Power" of CNKI Come From? We've Been Suffering for a Long Time]' (14 May 2022) <http://k.sina.com.cn/article_5617133817_14ecea8f900100wysh.html> (accessed 1 May 2024).

[144] Lizhi News, '中科院也受不了知网的涨价？没那么简单! [Chinese Academy of Sciences Can't Stand CNKI's Price Hike Either? It's Not That Simple!]' (19 April 2022) <https://baijiahao.baidu.com/s?id=1730511153740211879&wfr=spider&for=pc> (accessed 2 May 2024).

services) but had also abused its market dominance by refusing to open the plagiarism detection service[145] to individuals without justifiable reasons.

Although Guo Bing withdrew the lawsuit on 27 June 2022 because CNKI had started to provide plagiarism-checking detection services directly to individual users, such a high-profile case had attracted the attention of the SAMR. On 13 May 2022, the SAMR launched an anti-monopoly investigation into such a mega-database of Chinese academic literature for its abusive practice of exclusionary dealings with copyright holders, on the one hand, and database users, on the other. On 26 December 2022, the SAMR announced its decision to enjoin further monopolistic practices, and to fine CNKI ¥87.6 million (ca €11.25 million) for its abusive behaviour of its dominant market position.[146]

The SAMR first defined the relevant market as the market of online database services for Chinese academic literature. In the decision, the SAMR illustrated the differences amongst online database services for Chinese academic literature, database services for electronic books, online search services for academic literature, and online database services for academic literature of foreign languages. The SAMR performed a substitution analysis on both the demand- and supply-sides to support this proposition.

In the relevant market of online database services for Chinese academic literature, the SAMR recognized its market dominance in consideration of the following factors in line with the AML and the Guidelines: (i) a market share of over 50 per cent (both in terms of the revenue from database services and the number of downloads during the period 2014–2021); (ii) the relevant market was highly concentrated, and CNKI had kept its competitive advantage for a considerable length of time; (iii) CNKI had a strong ability to control the market for database service users; (iv) CNKI had relatively strong financial and technical conditions; (v) the users, especially for academic research purposes, were highly dependent on the database service of CNKI; (vi) the relevant market had high entry barriers; and (vii) CNKI had significant advantages in markets related to literature database services, such as the markets of plagiarism detection services and platform services for manuscript submission and editing.

It is noteworthy that the SAMR recognized that the network effect present in the operation of CNKI as a two-sided platform contributed to its dominant position.

[145] Ever since 2010, the Chinese Ministry of Education has implemented a strict policy of plagiarism-checking in all academic fields, aiming to combat the widespread academic dishonesty. All dissertations for diplomas are subject to such a checking process. See Academic Degrees Committee of the State Council, '关于在学位授予工作中加强学术道德和学术规范建设的意见 [Opinions on Strengthening the Construction of Academic Ethics and Academic Norms in the Work of Conferring Degrees]', Degree [2010] No 9, (9 February 2010) <http://www.moe.gov.cn/jyb_xxgk/xxgk/neirong/fenlei/sxml_gdjy/gdjy_xyzbtxjs/txjs_xgzc/201005/t20100512_87505.html> (accessed 1 May 2024).

[146] SAMR, '国家市场监督管理总局行政处罚决定书（国市监处罚〔2022〕87号） [SAMR Administrative Prohibition Decision [2022] No 87]' (26 December 2022) <https://www.samr.gov.cn/xw/zj/art/2023/art_0f87ad794f7949c4803dd6c9cc4d2d2a.html> (accessed 16 January 2023).

The reliance on CNKI by both copyright holders and database users strengthened each other. On the one hand, the number of times articles were downloaded or cited on CNKI was a vital indicator in assessing the achievements of copyright holders, including editors of academic journals and researchers. On the other hand, database users, mainly researchers from institutions and universities, relied heavily on CNKI for academic study purposes. Thus, database users without a valid subscription to CNKI would lose access to an enormous amount of academic literature, and copyright holders who could not publish on CNKI would suffer from a loss of readers, which would lead to academic non-achievement. Over time, dependence from each side of the market reinforced dependence from the other.

CNKI was found to have abused its dominant market position by concluding exclusionary agreements with copyright holders in the absence of justifiable reasons and charging database users unfairly high prices. Regarding exclusionary agreements, CNKI was found to have signed exclusive cooperation agreements that prohibited partner academic journal publishers and universities from providing academic papers and dissertations to third parties. Since 2014, the number of universities that had entered into exclusive cooperation agreements with CNKI had grown year by year. As of the end of May 2022, 490 universities, accounting for 63.1 per cent of all its partner universities, had entered into such agreements. To ensure the implementation of exclusive partnerships, CNKI had employed a variety of rewards and sanctions strategies. The SAMR also found that CNKI had violated the AML by charging unfairly high prices, restricting transaction exclusions, limiting market competition, infringing users' legitimate rights and interests, and impeding market innovation for the collection and provision of academic literature.

Consequently, the academic literature database was ordered to desist from further abusive practices and was hit with a fine of 5 per cent of its 2021 domestic sales revenue, though the SAMR made no reference to CNKI's illegal income by virtue of abusive conduct, nor was such an amount confiscated. The SAMR also required that effective remedial measures be implemented by CNKI.[147] On the same day on which the SAMR published the administrative prohibition decision, CNKI published a list comprising fifteen remedial measures covering the following aspects: (i) a non-exclusive partnership with copyright holders, (ii) a substantial price reduction for the database service, (iii) a plan to strengthen the protection of the legal rights and interests of authors, (iv) continuing optimization of relevant services (including providing plagiarism detection services to individual users), and (v) a comprehensive improvement in compliance.[148] According to CNKI,

[147] *Ibid.*

[148] CNKI, '知网，知网整改方案 [China National Knowledge Infrastructure's Rectification Programme]' (26 December 2022) <https://mp.weixin.qq.com/s/oc0xlh31PViQTf5X8WmcYg> (accessed 30 October 2022).

these remedial measures were formulated in accordance with the prohibition decision as well as opinions and suggestions from the public.[149]

The abusive conducts of CNKI differ from the aforementioned 'either–or choice' conduct in two ways. First, the practices of CNKI only fall within a broad interpretation of 'either–or choice', primarily through exclusive dealing agreements with copyright holders. In the aforementioned cases of *Meituan*, *Alibaba*, and *Sherpa's*, the problem of 'either–or choices' exhibited obvious characteristics of e-commerce, where direct contracts were reached between merchants and consumers via the technological infrastructure provided by digital platforms, and platforms abused such infrastructure (algorithms and data) to execute exclusive agreements, crowding out present and potential competition. However, no direct contract was concluded between copyright holders and database users on CNKI, and technological measures were seldom used to enforce exclusive agreements, whereas more traditional means, such as price reduction, were applied. Second, not only does the case against CNKI consist of exclusive agreements with copyright holders, but it also involves excessive pricing to database users based on its market dominance. Issues across the two-sided platform were addressed in this decision.

Yet, CNKI's anticompetitive practices still showed common traits with those of Meituan, Alibaba, and Sherpa's. To begin with, all of these agreements fall within the scope of subparagraph 4, paragraph 1, Article 22 AML, namely exclusive dealing agreements. Moreover, all of these conducts were based on a network effect present in a two-sided platform, where reliance from one side of its counterpart reinforces reliance from the other.

V.2 Comments

V.2.1 Definition of the Relevant Market

As aforementioned, the Chinese competition authorities are still cautious about any material departure from the established analytical framework of anti-monopoly law, especially with respect to the definition of the relevant market. Neither at the legislation level nor at the enforcement level has it abandoned this step in abuse-of-market-dominance cases in digital markets.

In *Qihoo v Tencent*, the SPC indeed stated that '[i]f the market position of the operator and the impact of the anti-competitive behaviours can be assessed through direct evidence of exclusion or obstruction of competition, it is not necessary in every case of abuse of market dominance to explicitly and clearly define the relevant market'. It is merely exceptional to skip the step of

[149] *Ibid.*

defining the relevant market 'explicitly and clearly' where the said circumstances apply.

In its draft for comments issued in November 2020, the Guidelines also proposed that while cases regarding abuse of dominance usually require a definition of the relevant market,

> in specific cases where there is sufficient, direct factual evidence that the conduct that can only be implemented by relying on a dominant market position has continued for a considerable period of time and the detrimental effects thereof are obvious, and that the conditions for precisely defining the relevant market are insufficient or very difficult to satisfy, then it is permissible to directly ascertain that the operator in the platform economy sector has engaged in monopolistic practices without defining the relevant market.[150]

Nonetheless, this provision was eventually not adopted in the final version of the Guidelines, which makes it clear that it is generally required to define the relevant market when reviewing suspected abuse of market dominance.

In the four aforementioned prohibition decisions, the establishment of a relevant market was also a prerequisite for the evaluation of suspected abusive behaviours by the platform concerned. This is in line with the general rule that, as provided for in the Guidelines, the relevant market should be defined first in any case involving the abuse of dominance in digital markets. Nonetheless, when it came to the defining process of the relevant market, the competition authorities all considered the characteristics of two-sided markets, though the analytic technicality varied from one decision to another.[151] In particular, the decisions not only considered the barriers for prospective platforms to reach the necessary scales of both merchants users and consumer users for effective competition but also took into account how the exclusive dealings affected consumers' freedom of choice and the commissioning fees for in-platform merchants on both sides. Even if the copyright holders, in the case of CNKI, did not have direct contractual engagements with CNKI's database users, the network effects were still well recognized by the SAMR based on the factual reliance on CNKI from both copyright holders and database users.

[150] Anti-Monopoly Commission of the State Council, 国务院反垄断委员会关于平台经济领域的反垄断指南（征求意见稿）[The Anti-Monopoly Guidelines on the Platform Economy (Draft for Comments)] (10 November 2020), Article 4.

[151] C Liu et al., King & Wood Mallesons, 'Exploring the Trend of Abuse of Dominance Investigation in China' (China Law Insight, 19 April 2021) <https://www.chinalawinsight.com/2021/04/articles/antitrust/exploring-the-trend-of-abuse-of-dominance-investigation-in-china> (accessed 16 March 2023).

V.2.2 Determination of Market Dominance

When it came to the determination of whether an investigated platform enjoyed a dominant market position, both the SPC and the competition authorities adopted a check-list approach in line with the relevant provisions in the AML and the Guidelines, considering the characteristics of the platform. To be specific, six factors, amongst others, were accorded special weight, including (i) the market share; (ii) the level of competition in relevant markets; (iii) the power to control these markets; (iv) the financial resources and technical conditions (as the digital markets, data, and algorithms were given special attention); (v) the degree to which platform users on both sides were dependent on the platforms; and (vi) entry barriers to potential platform competitors.[152]

Regarding market share, several years after the SPC's ruling in *Qihoo v Tencent*, the competition authorities have become accustomed to consider multiple dimensions, for example in terms of revenues from the platform service and the transaction volumes on the platforms in the *Alibaba* case; in terms of revenue from platform services and order values in the *Meituan* case; and in terms of daily average order volume, the monthly average number of listed restaurants, sales revenue, and the number of users in the *Sherpa's* case).

It is also worth noting that the level of maturity of a given platform business has been given special attention when assessing market dominance ever since the SPC ruled on the dispute in *Qihoo v Tencent*.[153] The immature adaptation phase of antivirus and messaging software, prior to the rise of digital platforms, influenced the SPC's rejection of Qihoo's claim against QQ's market dominance. Before 2021, Chinese competition authorities hesitated to investigate major digital platforms due to concerns about platform business maturity. Thereafter, the three-year prevalence of the 'either–or choice' business practice made authorities confident in the maturity of digital platform models in sectors such as online retailing and on-demand food delivery.

V.2.3 Effects of Suspected Conducts and Justifications

After identifying the dominant market position of an investigated platform, the courts and competition authorities continue to evaluate the effects of the suspected conduct. Such effects are generally considered from the perspective of competing platforms, in-platform merchants, consumers, and the digital economy as a whole.

In all the aforementioned cases where the competition authorities conducted formal investigations, the platforms concerned did not seem to be well prepared to defend their conducts. None of the 'justifiable reasons' raised by the investigated platforms in any of the aforementioned cases were accepted by the competition authorities. According to the Provisions and the Guidelines, exclusive dealings can

[152] In all of the three cases discussed above, the six factors were given varying degrees of attention.
[153] Liu et al. (n151).

be justified for multiple reasons, for example, the conduct is necessary for (i) the protection of product safety; (ii) the protection of the trading counterpart's or the consumer's interest; (iii) the protection of intellectual properties, business secrets, or data security; (iv) the protection of a specific investment for the transaction; (v) maintaining a reasonable business model. In two of the four cases discussed above, the arguments of the Alibaba Group and Sherpa's came within the categories of 'specific investment' and 'intellectual properties', respectively, which were, however, denied by the SAMR and Shanghai AMR.

V.2.4 Procedural Issues and Private Enforcement

Some procedural issues are also worth noticing. In none of the above-mentioned public enforcement cases did the SAMR or local AMR confiscate the illegal gains from the platforms' abusive conduct, though Meituan was required to fully refund the exclusive cooperation deposit of ¥1.3 billion (ca €0.18 billion) to the merchants. In this sense, the deterrence of the enforcement might be questioned. On the other hand, in terms of non-pecuniary punishment, for both the *Alibaba* and *Meituan* cases, as part of its order for the platforms to stop their illegal conduct, the SAMR issued an administrative guidance letter that covered a broader range of compliance requirements including, for instance, consumer protection. The SAMR also required these two platforms to report their compliance status regarding rectifications for three years consecutively. Similarly, in the *CNKI* case, CNKI published a list comprising fifteen remedial measures covering wider aspects than simply abuse of its market dominance.[154] These requirements on conduct might have wider effects than mere penalties.

It is also worth further observing how civil lawsuits will evolve. We did not see much progress in the private AML enforcement with respect to the *Alibaba*, *Meituan*, and *CNKI* cases until the end of 2023. For example, updates on JD's lawsuit against Alibaba's abuse of dominant market position (lodged in 2018) had not been available to the public for a long time, and Guo Bing applied to withdraw the lawsuit against CNKI. Even after the Beijing High People's Court decided the compensation lawsuit between JD and the Alibaba Group on 29 December 2023, the judicial decision was kept confidential from the public, which makes it enormously hard, if not impossible, to ascertain meaningful information on the specific stand of the court. In-platform merchants (especially those that decide to conclude their in-platform businesses), as well as some individual consumers of database services, might be more willing to initiate lawsuits against these platforms if the competition authorities have decided on the abusive nature of suspected platform behaviours, and the Draft (as referred to in section III) proposes effective facilitation to follow-on lawsuits.[155]

[154] CNKI (n148).

[155] Supreme People's Court of China, 'Provisions of the Supreme People's Court on Several Issues Concerning the Application of Law in Monopoly Civil Disputes (Draft for Public Comments' (n23).

VI. Conclusion

The abuse of market dominance by digital platforms has become a central issue of China's antitrust enforcement in recent years, challenging the regulatory capabilities of the competition authorities in China. First, exclusive dealing agreements, taking the form of 'either–or choice' practices, were common among dominant platforms like Meituan or Sherpa's. Second, deep discounting or predatory pricing was employed by platforms in aggressive expansion. Third, differentiated treatments, including price discrimination and self-preferencing, were also implemented by some platforms. These anticompetitive behaviours were often performed via data and algorithms, giving such behaviours a distinct digital characteristic. The newly amended AML, complemented by the recently released Guidelines, provided a new framework under which abusive practices facilitated by digital technologies are specifically addressed. Accordingly, Chinese competition authorities have been making efforts to improve their tools to better examine suspected abusive behaviours. In a very recent case, for example, according to the notice published on the web portal of the Chinese Central Government's Procurement Center, Hunan AMR plans to retain a data analysis service provider, in order to analyse the compliance data collected from Didi and examine whether Didi has conduced abusive behaviours.[156] The notice sheds new light on the latest regulatory efforts towards tackling monopolistic practices facilitated by data-like digital technologies.

Under the general legal framework laid down by the new AML, the regulatory practices against abuse of dominance by digital platforms is advancing towards a more holistic approach, combining civil lawsuits with administrative investigations or interventions. On one hand, while there have been controversies regarding the nature of civil litigation against abusive behaviours, it can still proceed and benefit competition law enforcement. Recent years have witnessed a rise in the numbers of anti-monopoly civil litigation, which is expected to serve a more significant role in the coming years. On the other hand, algorithm auditing, among various means of algorithm regulation, is on its way to playing a supplemental but still vital role in ensuring transparency and promoting innovation. Robust algorithm audits, even if not specifically carried out for preserving competition, may still compel abusive practices to become more susceptible to regulatory detection, facilitating the intervention from competition administrations. Driven by both private entities and public authorities, regulation against abuse of dominance in China's digital markets is experiencing a transformation towards a more integrated approach, aiming for a more effective enforcement.

[156] China Government Procurement Network, '湖南省市场监督管理局反垄断局滴滴网约平台数据分析技术服务采购项目竞争性磋商 [Competitive Consultations for the Procurement Project of Data Analysis Technology Services for Didi Ride-Hailing Platform by the Anti-Monopoly Bureau of Hunan AMR]' (7 February 2024) <https://www.ccgp.gov.cn/cggg/dfgg/jzxcs/202402/t20240207_21526794.htm> (accessed 14 April 2024).

9

Mergers

I. Merger Control Review in Digital Markets: An Overview of China's Recent Stance

I.1 Introduction

In recent years, the number of mergers (literally speaking, operator concentration [*jing ying zhe ji Zhong*])[1] in digital markets has shown a trend of rapid growth. The four largest US technology giant companies (namely, Amazon, Apple, Facebook, and Google) have all accomplished a large number of mergers and acquisitions.[2] China's digital companies have also carried out large-scale merger activities in the past few years, with two giant digital companies being particularly prominent, namely the Alibaba Group and Tencent.[3] Enterprises in the digital markets have been devoted to expanding their business territory through a series of mergers and acquisitions so as to highly penetrate relevant fields and build their own business ecosystems.[4] Merger is a common method of enterprise expansion and does not necessarily bring about anticompetitive effects. From an economic point of view, mergers and acquisitions enable enterprises to rapidly expand their production scale, effectively improve their production efficiency, achieve economies of scale, make technological progress, and explore new markets.[5] Capital and large-scale platform enterprises have presented a high tendency to promote mergers and acquisitions. Competitive platforms that share co-investors are even more likely to merge during their operation.

[1] In this chapter, 'merger' and 'concentration' are used interchangeably.

[2] CB Insights, 'Visualizing Tech Giants' Billion-Dollar Acquisitions' (24 February 2021) <https://www.cbinsights.com/research/tech-giants-billion-dollar-acquisitions-infographic> (accessed 6 October 2023). See also the discussion in Chapter 6.

[3] Tracxn, 'Acquisitions by Alibaba Group' (1999) <https://tracxn.com/d/acquisitions/acquisitions-by-alibaba-group/__sCUDmWYmGfRGPYfdwZSsG6Nbn3N1nNfOs6ZdnpQkBBk> (accessed 6 October 2023); Tracxn, 'Acquisitions by Tencent' (1998) <https://tracxn.com/d/acquisitions/acquisitions-by-tencent/__mCEoYeezWVRwXDPYvOxwsZ5teFVZN7E3Yt0sjW38Ewc> (accessed 6 October 2023).

[4] Y Wang, '数字经济背景下我国经营者集中制度的完善 [The Improvement of the Merger Control System in the Digital Markets in China]' (2022) 1 Journal of China University of Political Science and Law 161.

[5] P Alexiadis and Z Bobowiec, 'EU Merger Review of Killer Acquisitions in Digital Markets—Threshold Issues Governing Jurisdictional and Substantive Standards of Review' (2020) 16(2) Indian Journal of Law and Technology 64, 70–71.

Competition Law and Policy in Digital Markets. Maria Ioannidou and Bingwan Xiong, Oxford University Press.
 DOI: 10.1093/9780191925955.003.0009

Nonetheless, the concentration may lead to, or reinforce, a dominant market position, which may still be abused by the combined entity to make considerable profits by cross-selling services or other marketing strategies, eventually preventing other competitors from entering the relevant market. Moreover, the increase in prices resulting from such mergers will be passed on to consumers, who ultimately bear the cost.[6]

Mergers and acquisitions in China's digital markets mainly feature two characteristics. First, the concentration of operators can be both horizontal and vertical, as well as conglomerate mergers.[7] In the early stage of China's digital economy, there were many platforms operating in similar ways. Mergers and acquisitions, then, were mainly horizontal, such as the merger of Youku and Tudou into Youku Tudou in 2012.[8] As the digital markets evolve towards maturity, platform undertakings shift their attention to both vertical and conglomerate mergers, which brings about stronger effects of industrial resources integration and a higher possibility of market dominance. Meituan's acquisition of Dianping in 2015 and Mobike in 2018,[9] as well as the Alibaba Group's investment in Netease Cloud Music in 2019 are typical examples of such a type of merger.[10] Second, the targeted enterprises in merger and acquisitions vary in scale and include both large and small ones. In particular, the fact that many small and medium-sized companies are involved in the deals, with most of them being start-ups in the infancy stage of development, has attracted widespread concern from regulatory agencies. An important question, worthy of notice in a merger review, is whether such an acquisition aims to stifle business innovation and market competition, constituting a 'killer acquisition' targeting small-sized companies.[11]

Moreover, as mentioned in the previous chapters, the wide application of data is playing an increasingly vital role in the era of the digital economy and has prompted corresponding amendments to the whole body of China's anti-monopoly law. Some large platform operators may abuse the advantages of data, technology, and capital to implement monopolistic behaviours. Mergers are an important business practice for those platform operators to leverage their integrated resources such as data and technology. On the one hand, mergers are beneficial

[6] *United States v Microsoft Corp* [2001] DC Cir, [2001] 253 F.3d [34], [58]: '[T]o be condemned as exclusionary, a monopolist's act must have an "anticompetitive effect" That is, it must harm the competitive process and thereby harm consumers.'

[7] A Jones and BE Sufrin, *EU Competition Law: Text, Cases, and Materials* (OUP, 2011), 1064.

[8] China Daily, '优酷、土豆宣布合并 [Youku's Merger with Tudou]' (13 March 2012) <https://www.chinadaily.com.cn/hqzx/2012-03/13/content_14824708.htm> (accessed 13 April 2024).

[9] Y Qing, 'Analysis of Meituan's Acquisition of Dianping' (2022) 4(7) Academic Journal of Business & Management 81, 81–87.

[10] NetEase, 'Alibaba Acquires Import E-Commerce Platform Kaola from NetEase for Approximately US$2 Billion' (5 September 2019) <https://ir.netease.com/news-releases/news-release-details/alibaba-acquires-import-e-commerce-platform-kaola-netease> (accessed 6 October 2023).

[11] M Roberts, 'Killer Acquisitions and the Death of Competition in the Digital Economy' (2022) 24(1) Transactions: The Tennessee Journal of Business Law 65.

for platform operators to gain market power, help them collect data, expand the advantage of data scale, and reduce competitive pressure from competitors with strength.[12] On the other hand, the traditional antitrust review of mergers is largely centred on the market share of merging parties and the impact of mergers on price. Nevertheless, data-driven mergers for start-ups are often not effectively subject to review by regulatory authorities because the start-ups have too limited a turnover, which brings little change in market share, in terms of meeting the filing standards of the AML.

Generally speaking, merger control in Chinese digital markets demonstrates an increasingly strict trend relying on a comprehensive and holistic regulatory framework.[13] This chapter first sheds light on the increasingly tightening regulation towards merger control review in China's digital markets, which is partly due to the clarification of the stance of Chinese competition authorities on the legality variable interest entities (VIEs). In addition, the stance of the Chinese competition authority on high-profile, cross-border mergers is also commented on, signalling China's supportive attitude towards foreign investments to some degree. In section II, we sketch China's most recent regulatory regimes in the new Anti-Monopoly Law (AML) and other regulations, such as the Guidelines that have been formulated to contain the challenging issues arising in merger control review in digital markets, and reflect on the questions that remain to be answered in judicial practice. In the section III, high-profile cases involving Didi, Huya, NVIDIA, and Tencent are provided to elaborate the landscape of the law enforcement against anti-competitive mergers in China's digital markets.

I.2 The Shift of Attitude towards Merger Control

As mentioned in previous chapters, 2020 was a watershed year, when China started to shift its general attitude towards the enforcement of anti-monopoly law, including merger control in the digital economy. Prior to 2020, the competition authorities had been criticized for their failure to take effective action to examine various mergers and acquisitions in the digital economy.[14] However, since 2020, active enforcement of merger control has been initiated. For example, after the release of the Guidelines in early 2021, which provided specific directions for the

[12] *Ibid*, 61.

[13] L Ding, 'Merger Control Laws and Regulations China 2024' (12 April 2023) <https://iclg.com/practice-areas/merger-control-laws-and-regulations/china> (accessed 2 May 2024). Also see SM Werner and S Du, 'China Increases the Threshold for Merger Control Filing' (Bird&Bird, 2 February 2024) <https://www.twobirds.com/en/insights/2024/china/china-increases-the-threshold-for-merger-control-filing> (accessed 2 May 2024).

[14] N Zhang, '滴滴有没有垄断市场？ 合并优步中国反垄断调查为何两年无果 [Does Didi Qualify as Monopoly Power? Why There's no Result for the Merger Control Case of Uber China]' (30 August 2018) <https://www.thepaper.cn/newsDetail_forward_2390607> (accessed 13 April 2024).

enforcement of anti-monopoly law in digital markets, the SAMR announced forty-three decisions imposing fines for failure-to-notify violations on 20 November 2021, with thirty-nine of these cases involving enterprises competing in the digital economy.[15]

The most decisive factor for the attitudinal shift towards such an active enforcement posture came from China's political determination. As mentioned in Chapter 3, the China Central Economic Work Meeting that was convened in December 2020 listed the regulation of monopolistic behaviours in the realm of the platform economy as a particular issue amongst the key problems to be solved in 2021.[16] This marked a departure from the laissez-faire attitude of regulating competition in China's digital markets, which, as a matter of fact, had been the policy before this meeting. This meeting set the tone that leading firms in the digital economy, which had previously enjoyed certain privileges under the unspoken laissez-faire policy, would be subject to strict regulation by the government, especially regarding monopolistic matters.

Another subtle factor, which contributed towards a more proactive merger control, is the clarification of the stance of Chinese competition authorities on the legality of VIEs, as defined by the Financial Accounting Standards Board (FASB). VIE is the legal structure whereby control over a legal entity may be demonstrated through means other than voting rights.[17] VIEs usually take the form of contracts, designed to transfer the proceeds of a domestic operation to entities registered overseas, in order to escape regulatory initiatives and enable companies to go public in countries like the United States. It is no secret that leading digital platforms in China like the Alibaba Group, JD.com, and Tencent have previously employed this controversial instrument for overseas fundraising.[18] Nonetheless, the law and regulatory authorities in China initially did not provide a clear stance as to the legal status of VIEs therein. While the government wanted to preserve foreign investment within the VIE structure, it was also hesitant to give up the powerful regulatory instrument of declaring VIEs fundamentally illegal.

[15] SAMR, '中国反垄断执法年度报告(2021) [Annex of Annual Report of China on Anti-Monopoly Law Enforcement (2021)]' (8 June 2022) <https://www.samr.gov.cn/xw/zj/art/2023/art_bfac0acc333e4bd0be85adf099272047.html> (accessed 13 April 2024).

[16] H Xin, '中央经济工作会议举行 习近平李克强作重要讲话 [The Central Economic Work Meeting was Held, Xi Jinping and Li Keqiang Made Important Remarks]' (18 December 2020) <https://www.gov.cn/xinwen/2020-12/18/content_5571002.htm> (accessed 13 April 2024).

[17] US Consolidation Guide, '4.1 Determining Whether an Entity Is a VIE' (PWC Viewpoint, 31 December 2022) <https://viewpoint.pwc.com/dt/us/en/pwc/accounting_guides/consolidation_and_eq/consolidation_and_eq_US/chapter_4_equity_met_US/41_determining.html#pwc-topic.dita_4a8ec6fd-3279-4ffd-8f72-58907d6ae2fd> (accessed 13 April 2024).

[18] Y Wu, '43张反垄断罚单腾讯和阿里系领走25张，为何罚金仅50万 [25 Out of 43 Antitrust Fines on Tencent and Alibaba Group: Why the Fine Is Only 500,000 Yuan] (20 November 2021) <https://www.thepaper.cn/newsDetail_forward_15476991> (accessed 9 October 2023); Y Guo, 'VIE架构的监管该何去何从—负面清单时代下的再审视 [What Is the Future of VIE Structure Supervision: A Re-Examination in the Era of Negative Lists]' (2023) 25 Journal of Northeastern University (Social Science) 99, 100–101.

According to unofficial yet professional sources,[19] the uncertain legal status of the VIE structure gave rise to a reluctance regarding merger control enforcement. The mere fact of simply accepting and reviewing merger notifications to form a VIE might imply, at least, that the VIE structure would be a legally acceptable means of conducting mergers and acquisitions (M&As) in China.[20] Since the VIE structure was widely employed by tech companies, the anti-monopoly authorities in effect tended not to accept and review such merger notifications. This became an unwritten rule of the industry.[21] For example, although the M&A case of *Didi and Uber* raised anticompetitive concerns, no concrete action was taken by the Ministry of Commerce, which was responsible for merger control review at the time. Gao Feng, the official spokesman of the Ministry of Commerce, publicly stated that the *Didi and Uber* case was 'under investigation',[22] but no further decisions regarding clearance or prohibition of the merger were ever announced.[23]

This situation changed when the Foreign Investment Law of the People's Republic of China (PRC) was adopted in 2019 and came into effect in 2020. Actually, in the draft proposal announced in 2015, control of equity interest by contract or trust was specifically listed as a form of foreign investment,[24] but this specific wording was eventually deleted in the law that was passed. However, by including the somewhat vague terms 'other similar rights and interests of enterprises' and 'other investment prescribed by laws, administrative regulations or specified by the State Council' in the definition of foreign investment in Article 2, the legislator showed its intention to acknowledge the legal status of VIEs.[25] In the subsequent draft proposal of the aforementioned Guidelines, which was announced in

[19] Interview with a legal expert who was involved in the consultation process held by the competition authority in charge of this matter (19 July 2022). Interview records on file with the author.

[20] See the case of *Didi and Uber*, as further discussed subsequently, for more details.

[21] F Chen, 'Variable Interest Entity Structures in China: Are Legal Uncertainties and Risks to Foreign Investors Part of China's Regulatory Policy?' (2021) 29(1) Asia Pacific Law Review 1, 1–24.

[22] Y Pei, 商务部 · 正在对滴滴和优步中国合并案进行调查 [Ministry of Commerce Claims That the Merger Case of Didi and Uber China Is Currently under Investigation]' (27 July 2017) <https://news.sina.cn/2017-07-27/detail-ifyinryq6571111.d.html> (accessed 13 April 2024).

[23] SAMR, '国家市场监管总局：依据反垄断法及有关规定对滴滴收购优步案件进行调查 [SAMR Investigate the Case of Didi's Acquisition of Uber in Accordance with the Anti-Monopoly Law and Relevant Regulations]' (16 November 2018) <https://www.samr.gov.cn/xw/xwfbt/art/2023/art_3d552be3060b4f70b62908081a579310.html> (accessed 13 April 2024).

[24] Economic and Commercial Office of the Consulate General of the PRC in Los Angeles, '中华人民共和国外国投资法（草案征求意见稿）[Foreign Investment Law of the People's Republic of China (Draft Proposal for Public Opinion)]' (7 July 2015) <http://losangeles.MOFCOM.gov.cn/article/ddfg/tzzhch/201507/20150701035860.shtml> (accessed 13 April 2024).

[25] Translated by Professor Kong Qingjiang of China University of Political Science and Law. See China Daily, 《中华人民共和国外商投资法》（双语对照）[Foreign Investment Law of the People's Republic of China: Bilingual Version]' (22 March 2019) <https://language.chinadaily.com.cn/a/201903/22/WS5c94798ca3104842260b205f.html> (accessed 13 April 2024). See also F Liao, '《外商投资法》：背景、创新与展望 [Foreign Investment Law: Background, Innovation and Outlook]' (2020) 3 Journal of Xiamen University (Arts & Social Sciences) 140, 147.

November 2020 by the State Administration for Market Regulation (SAMR), VIEs also explicitly qualified for competition law scrutiny.[26]

Although there are still no official rules expressly declaring the operation of VIEs lawful in China, since 2020, the SAMR has no longer been reluctant to receive and review merger notifications involving VIEs. A series of mergers initiated by VIE entities were reviewed by the SAMR, involving e-commerce giants such as Tencent and the Alibaba Group, alongside other companies dominating entertainment, retail, and other sectors in China's digital markets. For example, Tencent Holdings, registered in the Cayman Islands, was fined for failure to notify in several cases.[27]

The regulatory control of mergers in digital markets was previously largely centred on notification and review procedures. In general, the Chinese competition authorities have recognized the potential of adverse effects brought about by the capital influx into digital markets and have become proactive in reviewing merger cases in digital markets.[28] Ever since 2020, the SAMR has paid more attention to procedural violations than to the violation of substantive anticompetitive standards by merging digital enterprises. According to Article 58 of the new AML, for instance, the merger itself will not be voided simply due to procedural violation, including the failure to notify the competition authorities, if it is not deemed anticompetitive by the competition authority. However, a fine equal to or less than only ¥5 million (ca €0.65 million) will be imposed because of procedural violations. In practice, the SAMR rarely exercises its power to enjoin or restrict mergers that are notified to its office. For example, in 2021, the SAMR unconditionally cleared 813 mergers (including cases from both digital markets and traditional

[26] See SAMR, '市场监管总局关于《关于平台经济领域的反垄断指南（征求意见稿）》公开征求意见的公告 [Guidelines for Anti-Monopoly in the Field of Platform Economy (Draft Proposal for Public Opinion)]' (promulgated by the SAMR, effective 10 November 2020), Article 18, para 2 <https://www.samr.gov.cn/fldes/tzgg/zqyjgg/art/2023/art_80cfa47c2b9d411c80c036244f3d0d70.html> (accessed 13 April 2024):

> [W]here the concentration of undertakings has reached the notification threshold as prescribed by the State Council, the undertakings shall make a notification to the anti-monopoly law enforcement authority under the State Council in advance, otherwise the concentration shall not be implemented. The concentration of undertakings that involves a protocol control structure falls within the scope of anti-monopoly review of concentration of undertakings.

[27] SAMR, '市场监管总局发布腾讯控股有限公司、深圳市红杉煜辰股权投资合伙企业（有限合伙）收购广西叫酒网络科技有限公司股权未依法申报违法实施经营者集中案行政处罚决定书（国市监处罚〔2021〕132号）[SAMR Administrative Prohibition Decision [2021] No 132] (5 January 2022) <https://www.samr.gov.cn/zt/qhfldzf/art/2022/art_522ef4da559848b78868e5fb618a4050.html>; SAMR, '腾讯控股有限公司收购DeepBlue Alpha Inc.股权案行政处罚决定书（国市监处〔2022〕10号）[SAMR Administrative Prohibition Decision [2022] No 10]' (31 March 2022) <https://finance.sina.cn/chanjing/gsxw/2022-07-10/detail-imizmscv0867332.d.html>; SAMR, '腾讯控股有限公司收购奇秦科技（北京）股份有限公司股权案行政处罚决定书（国市监处罚〔2022〕13号）[SAMR Administrative Prohibition Decision [2022] No 13]' (31 March 2022) <https://finance.sina.com.cn/chanjing/gsnews/2022-07-10/doc-imizirav2716388.shtml> (all accessed 13 April 2024).

[28] W Han and Y Gao, 'Digital Economy Driving China's Antitrust Reform' (2023) 19(1) Competition Law International 95, 102.

industries), approved four mergers with behavioural remedies, and prohibited only one merger.[29]

In exceptional circumstances (e.g. in July 2021), the SAMR imposed a fine of ¥500,000 (ca €64,622) on Tencent for its failure to notify its acquisition of China Music Group, as well as requiring the merged entity and its affiliates to take effective actions to restore competition in the relevant market.[30] The sole prohibition decision involving a digital platform to date was the case of *Huya and DouYu*, in which the SAMR prohibited the proposed merger of two live-streaming platforms on the grounds that it would restrict, or even eliminate, competition in the markets of game live streaming and electronic game services.[31]

I.3 China's Attitude towards Cross-Border Mergers

On 18 May 2023, the SAMR approved the merger of Microsoft and Activision Blizzard unconditionally, joining thirty-seven authorities in other jurisdictions that had also cleared this transaction.[32] The merger between Microsoft and Activision Blizzard is a typical case of vertical integration. Microsoft is active in gaming hardware, namely Xbox consoles, whereas Activision Blizzard produces highly popular gaming software like 'Call of Duty'. The M&A between Microsoft and Activision Blizzard, both of which are competitive within their respective fields, naturally raised competition law concerns. The varied regulatory attitudes on the Microsoft and Activision Blizzard merger may provide us with valuable insights into how political factors affect cross-border merger control in different countries.

The European Union (EU) approved this deal conditionally, directing Microsoft and Activision Blizzard to offer free streaming licences to European Economic

[29] G Shao, '2021年反垄断执法数据统计（2023年2月9日更新）[Antitrust Law Enforcement Statistics of 2021]' (9 February 2023) <https://zhuanlan.zhihu.com/p/343860381> (accessed 13 April 2024).

[30] Han and Gao, 'Digital Economy Driving China's Antitrust Reform' (n28), 103.

[31] SAMR, '市场监管总局关于禁止虎牙公司与斗鱼国际控股有限公司合并案反垄断审查决定的公告 [Announcement of the SAMR on the Anti-Monopoly Review Decision to Ban the Merger of Huya and DouYu]' (10 July 2021) <https://www.samr.gov.cn/fldes/tzgg/ftj/art/2023/art_47b307e668484e83a598add8793dcdca.html> (accessed 16 April 2024). For a list of merger cases of enjoinment or conditional approval, see SAMR, '市场监管总局关于禁止虎牙公司与斗鱼国际控股有限公司合并案反垄断审查决定的公告 [Announcement of the SAMR on the Anti-Monopoly Review Decision to Ban the Merger of Huya and DouYu: Index]' (10 July 2021) <https://www.samr.gov.cn/fldes/tzgg/ftj/index.html> (accessed 7 July 2024).

[32] SAMR, '2023年5月15日—5月21日无条件批准经营者集中案件列表 [List of Unconditional Approval of Mergers from 15–21 May] (30 May 2023) <https://www.samr.gov.cn/fldes/ajgs/wtjjz/art/2023/art_933bfb33968d4799a9lc65ac15c9e507.html> (accessed 13 April 2024). See also R Valentine, 'China Approves Microsoft's Acquisition of Activision Blizzard' (IGN, 23 May 2023) <https://www.ign.com/articles/china-approves-microsofts-acquisition-of-activision-blizzard> (accessed 13 April 2024). For the review of this case in the EU and United Kingdom, see Chapter 6, sections III.6.9 and III.7.

Area (EEA)-based gamers.[33] In the official decision published by the Commission, the horizontal, vertical, and conglomerate effects of the merger were assessed. The Commission deemed the anticompetitive effects of the merger insignificant, except when it came to cloud gaming streaming services.[34] A dominant position on cloud gaming and its impact on European consumers were the main concerns of the European Community (EC), which seemed to be satisfied with the commitments made by Microsoft,[35] which included, for a ten-year period, a 'consumer license' and a 'streaming provider license'. The former allows consumers in the EEA 'to stream, via any cloud game streaming services of their choice, all current and future Activision Blizzard PC and console games for which they have a license', while the latter allows any cloud game streaming service provider to provide EEA game players with any Activision Blizzard's PC and console games.[36]

The UK Competition and Markets Authority (CMA) shared similar concerns with the EU and was not entirely satisfied with the remedies proposed by Microsoft.[37] However, due to political pressure from the clearance decision in many other jurisdictions, the CMA has revised its stance. Although the CMA defended its position in Parliament, MPs were not satisfied with its response.[38] The CMA gave its provisional approval in August 2023, as a result of Microsoft's commitment on selling streaming rights of Activision Blizzard games to Ubisoft for fifteen years, and ultimately approved the transaction.[39]

China followed in the footsteps of the majority and approved the deal. However, analysts have also observed certain subtle factors, specific to China's situation, that contributed to this decision. Prior to the merger control case of *Microsoft/Activision Blizzard*, the cooperation between Activision Blizzard and its Chinese counterpart, NetEase, had just broken off, in January 2023. The termination of this

[33] European Commission (EU), 'Mergers: Commission Clears Acquisition of Activision Blizzard by Microsoft, Subject to Conditions' (15 May 2023) <https://competition-cases.ec.europa.eu/cases/M.10646https://competition-cases.ec.europa.eu/cases/M.10646> (accessed 13 April 2024).

[34] The Commission expressed its concern about the effect of the merger on the market of the cloud streaming service. See *Microsoft/Activision Blizzard* (Case M.10646) Commission Decision, C(2023) 3199, paras 571, 747; On the Commission's assessment of the merger's potential effect on other markets, see paras 200, 211, 215, 226, 242, 255, 303, 399, 455, 614 <https://ec.europa.eu/competition/mergers/cases1/202330/M_10646_9311516_7443_3.pdf>.

[35] *Microsoft/Activision Blizzard* (n34).

[36] European Commission (EU), 'Mergers: Commission Clears Acquisition of Activision Blizzard by Microsoft' (n33).

[37] H Ziady, 'UK Blocks Microsoft Takeover of Activision Blizzard' (CNN News, 26 April 2023) <https://edition.cnn.com/2023/04/26/tech/microsoft-activision-blizzard/index.html> (accessed 2 May 2024).

[38] T Phillips, 'UK MPs Grill Regulator over Microsoft Activision Blizzard Deal Block, Day after EU Grants Approval' (EuroGamer, 16 May 2023) <https://www.eurogamer.net/uk-mps-grill-regulator-over-microsoft-activision-blizzard-deal-block-day-after-eu-grants-approval> (accessed 13 April 2024).

[39] V Kennedy, 'Microsoft's Activision Blizzard Bid Provisionally Approved by UK Regulator' (Eurogamer, 22 September 2023) <https://www.eurogamer.net/microsofts-activision-blizzard-bid-provisionally-approved-by-uk-regulator> (accessed 13 April 2024). For the review of this case in the EU and United Kingdom, see Chapter 6, section III.6.9 and III.7.

profitable cooperation was deemed to be a result of stringent regulations in the gaming industry.[40] The green light given to the merger sends a welcoming signal to the business presence of Microsoft and Activision Blizzard in China, and probably also to other foreign investments. Although some analysts have interpreted this decision differently, arguing that, since Activision no longer operates in China currently, there are no competition law effects at all stemming from this merger,[41] Activision Blizzard's re-initiation of its recruitment in China signals its intention to re-enter the market in China after the closure of its deal with Microsoft.[42] Due to the stringent position on the regulation of market competition, alongside the obstacles arising from the COVID-19 pandemic, some foreign investors are likely to be conservative as to their investment plans in China. Nevertheless, China's approval of the M&A between Microsoft and Activision Blizzard has provided a supportive signal to foreign investments, at least in the pertinent field.[43]

II. China's Legal Framework for Merger Control

At the legislative level, this section sheds light on the provisions regarding merger control in the new AML in China, the Guidelines, the Provisions on the Review of Mergers (revised in 2022) (hereafter referred to as 'the Provisions'), and a rare local implementation document, the 'Anti-Monopoly Compliance Guidelines in the Field of the Digital Economy in Jiangxi Province' (hereafter referred to as 'the Guidelines in Jiangxi Province').[44] These laws and regulations not only set the general requirements for merger review but are also focused on digital markets, considering their unique characteristics at both the central and local levels. For high-profile mergers that may generate anticompetitive effects, according to Article 29 of the new AML, 'restrictive conditions' (or remedies)

[40] A Reynolds, 'Blizzard Entertainment and NetEase Suspending Game Services in China' (Blizzard Entertainment, Inc, 17 November 2022) <https://investor.activision.com/node/35721/pdf> (accessed 2 May 2024).

[41] S Zhang, '中国批准微软收购暴雪，魔兽却回不了中国 [China Clears M&A between Microsoft and Activision Blizzard, But Activision Blizzard Can No Longer Return to China]' (31 May 2023) <https://www.thepaper.cn/newsDetail_forward_23294031?commTag = true> (accessed 13 April 2024).

[42] World of Warcraft Intelligence Bureau, '国服稳了！ 官宣正式通过暴雪收购案，动视暴雪重启中国区招聘！ [China Service Secured: Approval of Acquisition for Activision Blizzard Officialized, Activision Blizzard Restarts Its Recruitment in China]' (31 May 2023) <https://new.qq.com/rain/a/20230531A01RAH00> (accessed 13 April 2024).

[43] Y Chen and Y Pan, 'Foreign Investment Crucial for Economic Growth' (*China Daily*, 5 September 2023) <https://www.chinadaily.com.cn/a/202309/05/WS64f660fea310d2dce4bb3d6f.html>; I Kawate, 'Foreign Investment in China Falls to Lowest Level on Record' (Nikkei Asia, 12 August 2023) <https://www.radionikkei.jp/podcast/lr/_230823.html> (both accessed 13 April 2024).

[44] Jiangxi Market Supervision Administration, '江西省数字经济领域反垄断合规指引 [Anti-Monopoly Compliance Guidelines in the Field of the Digital Economy in Jiangxi Province]' (effective 23 November 2023), Article 11 <http://drc.jiangxi.gov.cn/art/2022/11/23/art_68541_4239578.html> (accessed 13 April 2024).

can be imposed by the competition authority to curb potential anticompetitive effects. Such decisions are typically referred to as 'conditional approvals'. Some recent developments concerning merger control are worthy of special attention, especially those in relation to conditional approvals and the 'stop-the-clock' clause.[45]

II.1 The New AML

The formal introduction of the 'stop-the-clock' mechanism and the adaption of the threshold for merger notification are two of the reforms brought by the new AML, aiming to address platform-specific challenges. The two regimes are largely tailored to resolving the difficulty in deciding the applicability of the notification requirement to merging digital platforms, the turnovers of which are generally below the conventional thresholds for notification. In addition, more stringent liabilities for merger control violations run in parallel with the liability regimes against other forms of anticompetitive behaviours, demonstrating the determination of China's competition authority to tackle anticompetitive behaviours in digital markets.

II.1.1 The 'Stop-the-Clock' Mechanism

As a result of drawing lessons from international practices like those in the EU, one of the significant improvements of the new AML is the introduction of a 'stop-the-clock' mechanism for merger reviews. Currently, notifications filed in China have to be pulled and refiled after a review period of 180 days at the maximum; this process can be repeated in complicated cases, especially those approved with conditions. The new AML, however, empowers the enforcement authorities to suspend the merger review period if the operator fails to submit the required documents and information. Newly emerging circumstances and facts also have a significant impact on the review process.[46]

In the past, competition authorities might have struggled to complete a review within the review period for complex cases. The 'stop-the-clock' mechanism undoubtedly increases the flexibility of the time limit for the review (see Table 9.1), and avoids unnecessary procedural operations caused by rigid period requirements.

[45] CPI (Competition Policy International), 'Year of the Rat: Antitrust in China' (2020) 3 Competition Policy International 47.

[46] MOFCOM (Ministry of Commerce, PRC), '中华人民共和国反垄断法（2022修正）[Anti-Monopoly Law of the PRC (2022 Amendment)]' (promulgated by the Standing Committee of the National People's Congress, 24 June 2022, effective 1 August 2022), Article 32 <https://www.pkulaw.com/en_law/d3236788421feacfbdfb.html> (accessed 7 November 2022) (new AML).

Table 9.1 The AML's 'stop-the-clock' mechanism

AML 2008	AML 2022
	Article 32 (newly added provisions) Under any of the following circumstances, the State Council's AML enforcement authority may decide to suspend the time limit for examination of a concentration between business operators, and inform the business operators in writing: (1) The business operators fail to submit documents and materials as required, rendering the examination work impossible. (2) There arises a new situation or fact which has a material impact on the examination of the concentration between business operators, and the examination work cannot proceed without verification thereof. (3) Any restrictive condition attached to the concentration between business operators needs to be further assessed, and the business operators request suspension. The time limit for examination shall resume on the day when the circumstance for suspension of the time limit disappears, and the State Council's AML enforcement authority shall inform the business operators in writing.

Source: the translation of AML 2022 is taken from pkulaw.com with minor revisions, <https://pkulaw.com/en_law/d3236788421feacfbdfb.html> (accessed 14 June 2024).

II.1.2 Adjustment of the Notification Threshold

The aforementioned 'stop-the-clock' mechanism does allow more room for the authorities to investigate and intervene. Nevertheless, this mechanism on its own does not resolve challenging issues of substances, especially the threshold for mandatory notification. Consistent with global trends, the new AML, in its Article 26, for the first time explicitly grants proactive investigation power to competition authorities when it comes to those mergers that fail to meet the notification thresholds but are evidenced to have, or may have, anticompetitive effects.

Such an adjustment to the notification threshold represents an expansion of the enforcement authority's jurisdiction. The proactive investigation will not only focus on the digital economy but also be applicable across the board, which probably aims to address the so-called 'killer acquisitions' of start-ups and other smaller enterprises.[47] Specifically in the field of the digital economy, dominant platforms may conduct mergers and acquisitions when those enterprises are still relatively small in scale. While the acquisition of start-ups has its rationality, since it provides an essential exit strategy for them, the purpose of the concentration may not be to acquire advanced technology or further develop products. Instead, its aim might

[47] *Ibid.*

Table 9.2 The AML's scope of notification

AML 2008	**AML 2022**
Article 21 Where a concentration of business operators meets the threshold for notification set by the State Council, the relevant business operators shall notify to the State Council's AML enforcement authority in advance. In the absence of such a notification, such concentration may not be carried out.	Article 26 (newly added provisions) Where a concentration of business operators does not meet the threshold for notification set by the State Council, but there is evidence that the concentration of business operators has or may have the effect of excluding or limiting competition, the State Council's AML enforcement authority can require the business operators to notify. Where the business operator fails to make a notification in accordance with the two preceding paragraphs, the State Council's AML enforcement authority shall conduct an investigation pursuant to the law.

Source: the translation of AML 2008 is taken from pkulaw.com with minor revisions, <https://pkulaw.com/en_law/503218397088141cbdfb.html> (accessed 7 July 2024); the translation of AML 2022 is excerpted from pkulaw.com with minor revisions, <https://pkulaw.com/en_law/d3236788421feacfbdfb.html> (accessed 7 July 2024).

be to kill potential competitors in the cradle.[48] As Article 26(2) of the new AML expands the scope of notification of the concentration of operators, the phenomenon of 'killer acquisitions' may be alleviated (see Table 9.2).

II.1.3. A Classification and Grading for Review System

The new AML empowers the competition authorities to nip anticompetitive behaviours in the bud and clarifies the conditions under which an anticompetitive behaviour shall be established. In particular, its Article 37 introduces a classification and grading system for the review of concentration, providing handy and accurate coordination systems for competition authorities to identify potential anticompetitive mergers.

The classification review refers to the need for competition authorities to pay attention to the characteristics of the industry in which the concentration takes place and to strengthen the review of the concentration of enterprises in key industrial sectors. The grading review directs competition authorities to accord weights to the business scope and size of concentrating enterprises. The classification review primarily aims to refine the quality of merger review, while the purpose of the grading review is to ensure the efficient allocation of limited human resources for law enforcement. For now, however, it still remains a declarative provision and

[48] Taufen, '数字经济领域经营者集中审查制度的现状与完善 [Present Situation and Perfection of Merger Review System for Operators in Digital Markets]' (5 October 2021) <https://zhuanlan.zhihu.com/p/417320348> (accessed 2 February 2023).

Table 9.3 The AML's classification and grading system

AML 2008	AML 2022
	Article 37 (newly added provisions) The State Council's AML enforcement authority shall improve the hierarchical classification-based examination system for concentrations between business operators, strengthen in accordance with the law the examination of concentrations between business operators in important fields involving the national economy and people's livelihood, among others, and raise the quality and efficiency of examination.

Source: the translation of AML 2022 is excerpted from pkulaw.com with minor revisions, <https://pkulaw.com/en_law/d3236788421feacfbdfb.html> (accessed 7 July 2024).

has not yet been established with detailed rules in any specific legal document. Scholars hold the opinion that obstacles still exist to the implementation of the classification and grading system for reviewing concentrations in China at the legislative and institutional levels (see Table 9.3).[49]

II.1.4 Enhanced Liabilities for Violations

The new AML has dramatically increased the amount of the penalty against illegal concentrations, and the maximum fine imposed on the entities involved has been changed from the single criterion of ¥500,000 to two different standards, depending on whether the suspected concentration has already incurred, or may have the potential to incur, excluding or restricting effects on competition, namely a fine of less than 10 per cent of the previous year's sales; or a fine of less than ¥5 million (see Table 9.4). Although the increased penalty has not yet been applied in law enforcement targeted at anticompetitive mergers, the enforcement of enhanced liability regimes against other forms of anticompetitive behaviours, as illustrated in Chapter 8 for instance, has already shown the high probability of implementing the enhanced liabilities for violating mergers in China's digital markets.

II.2 The Guidelines

Actually, before the revision of the AML in 2022, the Guidelines had already attempted to provide detailed rules on merger reviews in digital markets. This regulatory document not only clarified the legal nature of VIEs and the applicability

[49] H Duan, '我国经营者集中分类分级审查制度的构建—以新《反垄断法》第37条为分析对象 [The Construction of a Classified and Grading Review System for Concentration of Operators in China—An Analysis of Article 37 of the New AML]' (2022) 39(6) Studies in Law and Business 157.

Table 9.4 The AML's enhanced liabilities for violations

AML 2008	AML 2022
Article 48 Where a business operator implements the concentration in violation of this Law, the State Council's AML enforcement authority shall order it to cease the implementation of concentration, to dispose of shares or assets within a specified period, to transfer the business within a specified period, or adopt other necessary measures to restore the market situation before the concentration, and may impose a fine of less than 500,000 *yuan*.	Article 58 Where a business operator implements a concentration in violation of this Law, which has or may have an effect of precluding or restricting competition, the State Council's AML enforcement authority shall order it to cease the implementation of the concentration, to dispose of shares or assets within a specified period, to transfer business within a specified period, and *to take other necessary measures to restore the state before the concentration*, and *impose a fine of not more than 10% of its sales for the previous year*; or in the absence of any effect of precluding or restricting competition, the State Council's AML enforcement authority shall *impose a fine of not more than 5 million yuan* (*emphasis added*).

of the merger review system on VIEs in digital markets but also addressed the discrepancy between platforms' turnover and their actual market powers by empowering the competition authorities to take proactive action against merging enterprises below the conventional turnover threshold. The Guidelines also pay close attention to data accumulation and innovation, two of the most significant themes in digital markets, and take them into account when assessing the anticompetitive effects of suspected concentrations in digital markets.

II.2.1 Clarifying the Legal Nature of the VIE Structure

The legality of the VIE structure is an age-old problem that remains unsolved in the Chinese legal framework, while such a form never ceases to be a trend and constitutes the basis of many business operations. A VIE structure is a kind of 'contractual control' in essence, wherein the actual controlling party does not necessarily own the shares of the operating entity. To be specific, the *de facto* control on business operations and financial consolidation of a company is carried out through a series of agreements. Such a structure is believed to have first been adopted by Sina.com, and later widely accepted in many other digital sectors, particularly in Internet-related businesses. Chinese enterprises often take advantage of such a structure to seek overseas financing.

However, the adverse impact of the wide application of VIE structures in digital markets has been manifested in recent merger cases, especially regarding the legality of pertinent mergers.[50] The concentration of operators in China's digital

[50] See the case of *Didi and Uber* China.

markets has long been outside of the realm of formal jurisdiction in China, with platform giants such as the Alibaba Group, Tencent, JD, and Didi, and almost all well-known Chinese platforms operating under this structure. The legality of the VIE structure used to be clouded in a grey area due to China's previous qualification restrictions on foreign direct investment, and the attitude of the competition authority towards merger cases involving a VIE structure was also ambiguous. Consequently, merging parties often adopted various tactics to keep an otherwise notifiable transaction involving a VIE structure outside of the merger review process.[51]

In response, Article 18 of the Guidelines specifies that concentrations involving the VIE structure are also subject to notification requirements, thereby falling within the scope of the merger control review. Immediately after the release of the Guidelines, the new AML, in its paragraph 3, Article 25, provided additional ground to cover mergers of platform companies involving VIE structures. This paragraph makes it clear that an operator obtaining control over other operators through contracts or its ability to exert decisive influence on other operators falls under the category of the concentration of operators.

Article 18

Where the concentration of business operators has reached the notification threshold as prescribed by the State Council, the operators shall make a notification to the AML enforcement authority under the State Council in advance, otherwise the concentration shall not be implemented.[52] The concentration of operators that involves a protocol control structure falls within the scope of anti-monopoly review of concentration of operators.[53]

II.2.2 Notification Thresholds Involving Turnover Calculation for Platforms

Aside from the legality of the VIE structure, how the turnover should be calculated for the purpose of assessing market power has also sparked debates over its applicability in digital markets. The Guidelines, in this perspective, are penetrative as they not only set out an inclusive calculative method that takes a wide range of digital factors into consideration (e.g. charging methods and

[51] B Wang, 'China Taxi Industry Alliance Calls for Antitrust Probe into Didi–Uber Merger' (PINGWEST, 31 December 2020) <https://en.pingwest.com/a/8195> (accessed 2 February 2023).

[52] The translation of the Anti-Monopoly Guidelines on the Platform Economy is excerpted from pkulaw.com with minor revisions: Anti-Monopoly Commission of the State Council, '国务院反垄断委员会关于平台经济领域的反垄断指南（国反垄发〔2021〕1号）[Anti-Monopoly Guidelines on the Platform Economy]' (English translation) (7 February 2021) <https://pkulaw.com/en_law/dec522cd66c7b43ebdfb.html> (accessed 14 June 2024).

[53] Anti-Monopoly Commission of the State Council, '国务院反垄断委员会关于平台经济领域的反垄断指南（国反垄发〔2021〕1号）[Anti-Monopoly Guidelines on the Platform Economy] (7 February 2021), Article 18 <https://www.gov.cn/xinwen/2021-02/07/content_5585758.htm> (accessed 7 November 2022) (Guidelines).

business models) but also shed light on possible solutions to address the discrepancy between platforms' turnover and their market power. China's traditional turnover standard is hardly applicable in digital markets, since merging platforms that have strong market power often do not meet the turnover criteria for notification.

In spite of the absence of specific rules on the discrepancy between platforms' turnover and their market power in the Guidelines, the inclusive approach adopted in the Guidelines is intertwined with the provision that, in its Article 8, it requires the competition authority to investigate mergers that fail to meet the turnover standard but may bring about anticompetitive effects.

Article 18 Notification thresholds
In the field of platform economy, the turnover of business operators includes the income derived from the sale of goods and provision of services. Based on industry practices, charging methods, business models, the role of the operator of a platform, etc., the calculation of turnover may be different. For the operator of a platform that only provides information matching and collects service fees such as commissions, etc., the turnover may be calculated based on the service fees charged by the platform and other income derived from the platform; if the operator of the platform participates in the market competition on the side of the platform or plays a leading role, the transaction amount involved in the platform may also be calculated.

Where the concentration of business operators has reached the notification threshold as prescribed by the State Council, the operators shall make a notification to the AML enforcement authority under the State Council in advance, otherwise the concentration shall not be implemented. The concentration of operators that involves a protocol control structure falls within the scope of anti-monopoly review of concentration of operators.[54]

II.2.3 Proactive Investigation by Competition Authorities

Duty of the authority unfulfilled is no different from duty unassigned. The Guidelines ensure their own effectiveness not only by setting the above definitive standards and definitions but also by stating the situations where the competition authorities are obliged to launch an investigation. Article 19 of the Guidelines highlights the need for competition authorities to enhance their proactive approach to law enforcement in cases of concentration in the digital markets. This Article clearly stipulates that when a concentration fails to meet the notification threshold but presents facts and evidence showing that it may have the effect of eliminating

[54] *Ibid*, Article 18.

or restricting competition, the competition authorities should take the initiative to conduct an investigation.

Article 19 Proactive investigation by the anti-monopoly law enforcement authority under the State Council

Where the concentration of operators fails to meet the standards for notification in accordance with Article 4 of the Provisions of the State Council on the Thresholds for Notification of Concentration of Operators, but the facts and evidence collected under the prescribed procedures show that the concentration of operators has or is likely to have the effect of eliminating or restricting competition, the anti-monopoly law enforcement authority under the State Council shall conduct investigation in accordance with the law.

Operators may proactively notify concentration of operators failing to meet the notification thresholds to the anti-monopoly law enforcement institution under the State Council.

The anti-monopoly law enforcement authority under the State Council shall pay great attention to concentration of operators in the field of platform economy in which one operator participating in the concentration is a start-up enterprise or an emerging platform, the turnover of an operator participating in the concentration is relatively law as a free or low-price mode is adopted, the relevant markets are relatively highly concentrated, and the number of participating competitors is small, and shall investigate and handle it in accordance with the law where the concentration fails to meet the thresholds for notification but has or is likely to have the effect of eliminating or restricting competition.

II.2.4 Data Advantages and Innovation

The Guidelines also endeavour to spot and tackle anticompetitive effects on innovation specifically associated with the capacity to acquire and control data. In early cases taking place before the digital era, China's competition authorities were already attempting to appraise the concrete harm to innovation, which is deemed essential for market competition.[55] In *Western Digital/Hitachi*,[56] for example, the Ministry of Commerce of the PRC (MOFCOM) assessed the side effects of mergers on product innovation in the hard-drive industry, where innovation was

[55] W Han and Y Gao, 'The Evaluation of Innovation in Merger Control: A Comparison between China and Other Jurisdictions' (2023) 9 China–EU Law Journal 73.

[56] MOFCOM, '商务部公告2012年第9号 关于附加限制性条件批准西部数据收购日立存储经营者集中反垄断审查决定的公告 [Announcement No 9 of 2012 of MOFCOM on the Decision to Approve the Anti-Monopoly Review of Western Data's Acquisition of Hitachi Storage Operators with Additional Restrictive Conditions]' (2 March 2012) < https://www.mofcom.gov.cn/zcfb/blgg/art/2012/art_3b1e088b249f4417a1820b4021de192b.html > (accessed 15 April 2024).

an essential characteristic. In *NXP/Freescale*,[57] MOFCOM also considered the acquisition's adverse effects on scientific research and technological development and innovation in the market of radio frequency power stations.[58]

In the digital era, data alongside the wide application of algorithms becomes another significant factor that has impacts on market innovation. As a vital entry condition to digital markets, data capacity may enable platform undertakings to obtain an excessive market advantage by providing personalized products or services. Then, the goal of undertakings' merger engagements serves as a critical indicator for determining whether market innovation is likely to be stifled, be it to expand market share, to integrate scientific research with technological development, or to obtain data sets in particular.[59] As a response to a data-enabled monopoly, the Guidelines explicitly direct the competition authority, in its assessment of the competition impact of a merger in digital markets, to consider the capacity of the merging parties to acquire, process, and control data resources, although they remain silent on the practical manner in which to implement such a consideration.

Article 20 Factors to be considered

The anti-monopoly law enforcement authority under the State Council shall, in accordance with Article 27 of the AML and Chapter Ⅲ of the Interim Provisions on Review of Concentration of Operators, assess the competition impacts of a concentration of operators in the field of platform economy. The following factors may be specifically considered in light of the characteristics of platform economy:

(1) The market shares of operators in the relevant market. In the calculation of market share, in addition to taking turnover as an indicator, the proportions of trading amount, trading quantity, number of active users, click volume, usage duration or other indicators in the relevant market may also be considered, and the market share within a relatively long period of time may be comprehensively assessed, in light of the reality, to determine its dynamic trends.

(2) The power of operators to control the market. The following factors may be taken into account: whether the operators have exclusive rights to essential and scarce resources and the duration of such exclusive rights, the stickiness

[57] MOFCOM, '商务部公告2015年第64号 关于附加限制性条件批准恩智浦收购飞思卡尔全部股权案经营者集中反垄断审查决定的公告 [Announcement No 64 of 2015 of MOFCOM on the Decision on the Anti-Monopoly Review of the Concentration of Business Operators in the Approval of NXP's Acquisition of All Equity of Freescale with Additional Restrictive Conditions]' (27 November 2015) <http://www.mofcom.gov.cn/article/zcfb/zcdwmy/201511/20151101196189.shtml> (accessed 15 April 2024).

[58] Han and Gao, 'The Evaluation of Innovation in Merger Control' (n55), 80.

[59] *Ibid*, 84.

and multi-homing characteristics of platform users, the operators' ability to acquire and process data, the control over data interfaces, and the operators' ability to penetrate or expand into other markets, the operators' profitability and profit margin levels, the frequency and speed of technological innovation, the life cycle of products, and whether there exists or is likely to be disruptive innovation, etc.

(3) The degree of concentration of the relevant market. The development status of the relevant platform markets, the number of existing competitors and their market shares, among others, may be considered.

(4) The impact of the concentration of operators on market entry. The situation of market entry, the difficulty for operators to obtain necessary resources and facilities such as technologies, intellectual property rights, data, channels and users, the scale of capital investment needed for entering the relevant market, and the conversion costs of users in various respects such as fees, data migration, negotiation, learning and searching may be considered. The possibility, timeliness and adequacy of entry may also be considered.

(5) The impact of concentration of business operators on technological advancements. The impact of competition between existing market competitors on innovation respects such as technology and business models, on operators' motivation and capacity to innovate may be considered. Whether the acquisition of start-ups or emerging platforms may affect innovation may also be considered.

(6) The impact of concentration of operators on consumers. Whether the operators after concentration have the capacity and motivation to impair the interests of consumers by raising product prices, lowering product quality, reducing product variety, impairing consumers' capacity and scope of selection, treating different groups of consumers differently, and inappropriately using consumer data or other methods may be considered.

(7) Other factors affecting market competition to be considered as deemed by the anti-monopoly law enforcement authority of the State Council, including the impact on other operators and the impact on national economic development.

For a concentration of operators involving bilateral or multilateral platforms, the bilateral or multilateral businesses of the platforms and other businesses engaged in by operators may be comprehensively considered. The externalities of direct and indirect networks may be assessed.[60]

[60] Guidelines (n53), Article 20.

II.3 The Provisions

The new AML and the Guidelines have actually sparked a chain of regulatory changes in terms of concentration review. Further provisions with detailed rules have been devised to guide the competition authorities to assess the anticompetitive effects of merging initiatives in digital markets. In particular, in 2023, the Provisions were formally revised so as to meet the ever-changing market development and the new AML. Specifically, the Provisions set out general considerations for merger review. Paragraph 2 of Article 8 reiterates the power of the competition authority to investigate mergers that fail to meet the traditional turnover standard but may bring about material anticompetitive effects.

II.3.1 Legal Basis for Mergers That Have or May Have Anticompetitive Effects

Article 8

Where a merger does not reach the notification threshold, but there is evidence proving that the merger has or may have the effect of excluding or restricting competition, the SAMR may require the business operators concerned to make a notification and notify them in writing of such a requirement.[61] If the merger has not been implemented, the operators concerned shall not implement the merger before they make the notification or obtain the approval after notification; if the concentration has been implemented, the operators concerned shall make a notification within 120 days as of the date of receipt of the written notice, and take necessary measures such as suspending the implementation of the concentration to reduce the adverse effects of the concentration on competition.[62]

II.3.2 Procedure of Merger Review

In addition to providing substantive rules specifically targeting mergers in digital markets, Article 19 of the Provisions sets the standard for cases eligible for a simple procedure, which is a condition that must be met when the SAMR entrusts provincial competition authorities to carry out local merger reviews as aforementioned.

[61] The translation of the Provisions is excerpted from pkulaw.com with minor revisions: SAMR, '经营者集中审查规定 [Provisions on the Review of Concentration of Undertakings]' (English translation) (promulgated by the SAMR, 10 March 2023, effective 15 April 2023) <https://pkulaw.com/en_law/4a966fd519ae33cabdfb.html> (accessed 14 June 2024).

[62] SAMR, '经营者集中审查规定 [Provisions on the Review of Concentration of Undertakings]' (promulgated by the SAMR, 10 March 2023, effective 15 April 2023), Article 8, <https://www.samr.gov.cn/zw/zfxxgk/fdzdgknr/fgs/art/2023/art_4c34a8aa4e62449ab38233bdbba172a7.html> (accessed 15 April 2024).

Article 19
A merger that falls under any of the following circumstances may be notified as a summary case, and the SAMR shall review the merger under the procedures for summary cases:

(1) where, on the same relevant market, the sum of market shares of the business operators participating in the merger is less than 15%; on the upstream and downstream markets, the market share of each operator participating in the merger is less than 25%; or the market share of operators participating in the merger that are not on the same relevant market and do not have an upstream and downstream relationship is less than 25% in each market relating to the transaction;
(2) where an operator participating in the merger establishes a joint venture outside China which does not engage in economic activities in China;
(3) where an operator participating in the merger purchases the equity or assets of an overseas enterprise which does not engage in economic activities in China; or
(4) where a joint venture jointly controlled by two or more business operators is controlled by one or more of the said operators through the merger.[63]

II.3.3 Digital Factors to Be Considered in Merger Review

Just as the new AML and the Guidelines have been remodelled so as to adapt to digital markets, the Provisions accurately capture the unique features of the digital economy. Comparing Article 20 of the Guidelines with the following provisions, it can be seen that merger review in China's digital markets focuses more on factors such as technological innovation, user data attribution issues, data control processing capabilities, and bilateral or multilateral personalized business models.

Article 33
In the evaluation of the control over the market of business operators that participate in a merger, the following factors may be considered: the market share of the operators that participate in the merger in the relevant market, the degree of substitution of products or services, the capability as well as the financial and technical conditions to control the sales market or the raw material procurement market, the capability to master and process data, as well as the market structure of the relevant market, the production capacity of other operators, the purchasing capability of downstream customers and the capability of switching suppliers, the offsetting effect of access of potential competitors, among others.

[63] *Ibid*, Article 19.

In the evaluation of mergers in a relevant market, the following factors may be considered: the number of operators in the relevant market and the market share, among others.[64]

Article 34
In the evaluation of the impact of a merger on market access, the circumstances in which the business operators affect market access through control of production factors, sales and procurement channels, key technologies, key facilities, data, etc., may be considered, and the possibility, timeliness and adequacy of access shall also be considered.

In the evaluation of the impact of a merger on technological advancement, the impact of the merger on the driving force and capacity of technological innovation, investment in and utilisation of technological research and development, and integration of technological resources, among others should be considered.[65]

II.4 The Guidelines in Jiangxi Province

The new AML stands for an attempt at the national level to regulate platform operators and preserve market competition in digital markets. In the meantime, there have been provincial efforts to translate such a national resolution into more detailed rules. On 17 November 2022, for example, Jiangxi Province issued the first anti-monopoly compliance guidelines in the digital economy in China in accordance with the new AML. It is dedicated to promoting the establishment of a sound regulatory system for ensuring fair competition in the digital markets and guiding platform operators to enhance their awareness of anti-monopoly compliance. The main feature of the Guidelines of Jiangxi Province is to further clarify pertinent rules in the new AML and enumerate high-risk concentrations in digital markets, providing more concrete guidelines for local competition authority.

Article 11
The ways to implement the centralisation of business operators include:

(1) Merger of business operators;
(2) The business operator obtains control over other business operators by acquiring equity or assets;

[64] *Ibid*, Article 33.
[65] *Ibid*, Article 34.

(3) The business operator obtains control over other business operators through contracts or can exert decisive influence on other business operators.[66]

Article 12

The concentrated behaviour of high-risk operators with digital economy characteristics mainly includes:

(1) The business operators participating in the centralisation are start-ups or emerging platforms, and the centralised operators in the digital economy are concentrated due to the adoption of free or low-cost models, with low turnover, high concentration of relevant markets, and fewer competitors;

(2) Business operators in Internet platforms, industrial Internet, meta-universe and other fields change their privacy policies and integrate data between platforms without the permission of anti-monopoly law enforcement agencies.[67]

III. Reflections on Merger Control Review in China's Digital Markets

China's regulatory measures taken upon mergers, including the new AML, the Guidelines, the Provisions, and provincial practices, however, do not aim to restrict merger activity in principle. Rather, M&As are largely encouraged since they are generally thought to be beneficial in terms of complementing each party's strengths, increasing efficiency, and ultimately providing consumers with improved products or services.[68] Nonetheless, as giant platforms continue to expand their market power in digital markets through M&As, they may bring about a wide range of adverse impacts on market competition. Concerned about these problems, China's lawmakers have been devoted, in recent years, to the formulation of a sound system to identify and control anticompetitive mergers in its digital markets.[69] Nevertheless, there are still material questions that remain to be addressed when the competition authority enforces the law against anticompetitive concentrations under the new regime. This section first discusses the new formula of the threshold for mandatory notification in Chinese digital markets and then explores the inclusion of non-price factors in the assessment of anticompetitive effects.

66 Jiangxi Market Supervision Administration (n44), Article 11.

67 *Ibid*, Article 12.

68 X Wang, 反垄断法 [*Antimonopoly Law*] (Law Press, 2011), 270–281.

69 X Wang, '中国数字经济领域反垄断监管的理论与实践 [Theory and Practice of Anti-Monopoly Supervision in China's Digital Economy]' (2022) 42(5) Journal of University of Chinese Academy of Social Sciences 38.

III.1 Threshold for Notification: Turnover, Transaction Value, or Market Value Test

The turnover test, which requires mergers involving companies with a certain amount received in sales for a stated period to be notified to the competition authority, is widely accepted as a reasonable criterion for mandatory notification.[70] Following international practices, the State Council has also adopted the turnover test in the Provisions. Specifically, if the undertakings involved in a merger (i) have a combined global turnover exceeding ¥10 billion (ca €1.3 billion) and two of them have a domestic turnover exceeding ¥400 million (ca €52 million) each or (ii) have a combined domestic turnover exceeding ¥2 billion and two of them have a domestic turnover exceeding ¥400 million (ca €52 million) each, the merger is required to be notified to the SAMR. As a rule of thumb, the turnover test is simple enough to offer the authorities *prima facie* evidence on the magnitude of the merger.

However, the turnover test has been criticized for being unadjusted to the digital age. For example, in the famous merger control case of *Facebook/WhatsApp*, although these two companies were undoubtedly influential within their respective fields, the transaction did 'not have a Union dimension' according to the turnover test result alone.[71] In fact, digital enterprises may have a low turnover and strong market power at the same time.[72] To begin with, it is common for online services to be provided free of charge. Furthermore, digital platform companies usually report commissioning fees as revenue, resulting in turnover calculations that are much lower than those of traditional companies. But these two factors just take up a minor position. The most important reason for the adaption of the turnover calculation is the practice of 'killer acquisitions'. Due to the existence of 'destructive creation' in the digital economy, mature companies seek new entrants with promising ideas, which could threaten their market position and buy out such new entrants. Thus, even acquiring small-scale start-ups can significantly inhibit competition.[73]

In light of the aforementioned considerations, Germany and Austria have developed the 'transaction value test', which has also been advocated by Chinese scholars.[74] 'Transaction value' means 'all assets and other monetary benefits that

[70] R Whish and D Bailey, *Competition Law* (OUP, 2012), 842, 921.
[71] European Commission (EU), 'Case No Comp/M.7217—*Facebook/Whatsapp*, Regulation (EC) No 139/2004 Merger Procedure' (10 March 2014), para 9 <https://ec.europa.eu/competition/mergers/cases/decisions/m7217_20141003_20310_3962132_EN.pdf> (accessed 14 April 2024). On this case, see Chapter 6, section III.4.1.
[72] J Cai, 'The Sharing Economy and China's Antimonopoly Law: From the Didi Case to Regulatory Challenges' (2020) 28(1) Asia Pacific Law Review 159, 169–170.
[73] W Wang, '平台扼杀式并购的反垄断法规制 [An Antitrust Analysis of Platform's Killer Acquisitions]' (2020) 34 Peking University Law Journal 84, 86–89.
[74] Cai (n72), 175; W Wang (n73), 98.

the seller receives from the buyer in connection with the merger in question',[75] which can be generally expressed as the price of the acquisition. In merger cases involving platform enterprises, the transaction value test is preferred because it can better reflect the future value of the acquired firm, that is the potential competition damage caused by the merger.[76] Transaction value works as a subsidiary criterion of the turnover.[77]

Similar cases challenging the turnover test have also taken place in China. The merger case between Didi and Uber (China) provided an early example in this regard. The case was notable because, on one hand, the merging parties were economically significant: Uber China was valued at USD 8.2 billion (ca €7.445 billion) and Didi at USD 28 billion (ca €25.42 billion); on the other hand, Didi had a market share of 85.3 per cent in the e-hailing taxi market at the time, and the acquisition of Uber China would clearly have further increased its market power.[78] However, in this case, Didi had gained its market share by providing a huge amount of subsidies to both e-hailing car drivers and riders in its early stage of operation, resulting in significant losses instead of considerable turnover. Neither merging party met the notification threshold.[79] Actually, ever since the implementation of the 2008 AML, there have been a good number of digital merger cases that have not been notified to the competition authority, such as the merger between Meituan and Dianping and the concentration between Ctrip and Qunar, among others involving mega platforms, such as the Alibaba Group and Tencent.[80] This is largely because, as briefly mentioned in previous sections of this chapter, many of the operators involved in these deals are platform enterprises whose turnover does not meet the minimum threshold as provided in the 2008 AML.

In response, the Chinese government used to propose an approach that was different from the transaction value test. In Article 4 of the draft proposal of an

[75] Bundeskartellamt, 'Guidance on Transaction Value Thresholds for Mandatory Pre-Merger Notification (Section 35 (1a) GWB and Section 9 (4) KartG)' (21 January 2022), para 12 <https://www.bundeskartellamt.de/SharedDocs/Publikation/EN/Leitfaden/Leitfaden_Transaktionswertschwelle_2022.html> (accessed 14 April 2024).

[76] W Wang (n73), 98; Y Tao and K Zhang, '数字经济背景下经营者集中审查制度的困境及完善 [The Dilemma and Improvement of the Review System of Concentrations of Undertakings in the Context of Digital Economy]' (2023) 54 Review of Industrial Economics 136, 143.

[77] Bundeskartellamt (n75), para 3.

[78] 21st Century Business Herald, '滴滴出行或将收购Uber中国垄断问题引关注 [Didi May Acquire Uber China Which Raises Monopoly Concerns]' (1 August 2016) <https://news.sohu.com/20160801/n462031324.shtml> (accessed 2 February 2023).

[79] Y Chen, '《滴滴优步合并案》的调查为何这么难 [Why Is It So Difficult to Investigate the Didi–Uber Merger?]' (29 November 2018) <http://m.eeo.com.cn/2018/1129/342209.shtml> (accessed 2 February 2023).

[80] The merger between Meituan and Dianping: see X Yang, '大众点评和美团《相杀到相爱》全过程解密：资本意志助推 [Dianping and Meituan's "Killing Each Other to Falling in Love" Whole Process Decryption: The Will of Capital Boosts]' (8 October 2015) <https://www.thepaper.cn/newsDetail_forward_1382928>; the merger between Ctrip and Qunar: see X Zhang, '携程和去哪儿宣布合并，百度将成携程第一大股东 [Ctrip and Qunar Announce Merger, Baidu Will Become Ctrip's Largest Shareholder]' (26 October 2015) <https://www.thepaper.cn/newsDetail_forward_1389317> (both accessed 14 April 2024).

amended version of the Provisions released on 27 June 2022, the market value of a party of the concentration, or the estimation of this value, is listed as a complement to the parties' turnover when determining whether there is an obligation to notify. If the target has a market value equal to or over ¥800 million (ca €104 million) and, at the same time, its turnover in China equals or exceeds one-third of its global turnover, the concentration qualifies for mandatory notification.[81] In the official explanation accompanying this text, the drafter from the SAMR states that merger actions taken by larger companies may be more detrimental to competition.

> According to the situation reflected in the notification and review of the cases, large firms usually possess stronger market power, and their mergers are more likely to exclude or inhibit competition. Meanwhile, it is also in accordance with the international trend to pay attention to mergers involving large enterprises. By stipulating the notification threshold of mergers involving large firms, and conducting competition analyses according to law, in respect of mergers that may exclude or inhibit competition, the merger control system is able to prevent market structures that may lead to a monopoly ex ante, reduce anticompetitive harm, fortify the accuracy and effectiveness of anti-monopoly governance, and preserve the innovation of market entities.[82]

This statement neither provides thoughts with details on this issue nor explains why the Austrian and German approach relying on transaction value is not preferred. A possible explanation may be that the market value (or its estimation) had already been employed in two prior documents to differentiate amongst platforms of varying sizes. Namely, the 'Guidelines on Categorization and Classification of Internet Platforms (Draft for Public Opinions)' categorized digital platforms according to the services provided on the platforms and classified them according to their market value (or the estimation thereof); and the 'Guidelines on Enforcement of Internet Platform Responsibility (Draft for Public Opinions)' mainly highlighted the responsibility of extra-large platforms, that is platforms with a market value (or the estimation thereof) of more than ¥1000 billion.[83]

Nevertheless, this draft proposal has been pending since its release. In a later version of the Provisions on Merger Review (经营者集中审查规定) that was

[81] SAMR, '市场监管总局关于公开征求《国务院关于经营者集中申报标准的规定（修订草案征求意见稿）》意见的公告 [Provisions on Threshold for Merger Notification (Draft of Amended Version for Public Opinions)]' (27 June 2022) <https://www.samr.gov.cn/fldes/tzgg/zqyjgg/art/2023/art_1c119d88523f42ca8bb8bb436f364ecb.html> (accessed 14 April 2024).

[82] *Ibid.*

[83] SAMR, '《互联网平台分类分级指南（征求意见稿）》《互联网平台落实主体责任指南（征求意见稿）》[Guidelines on Categorization and Classification of Internet Platforms (Draft for Public Opinions), Guidelines on Enforcement of Internet Platform Responsibility (Draft for Public Opinions)]' (29 October 2021) <https://www.samr.gov.cn/hd/zjdc/art/2023/art_c0086d02fcc544ea9506c997b3ac93c1.html> (accessed 14 April 2024). See also D Lu and X Li, '超大型平台并购初创企业的反垄断法规制研究 [Research on the Anti-Monopoly Regulation of Mergers and Acquisitions of Start-Ups by Mega-Platforms]' (2023) 35 Journal of Chongqing University of Posts and Telecommunications (Social Science Edition) 51, 58.

released on 10 March 2023 and came into effect on 15 April 2023, there is no mention of either the market value test or the transaction value test. Arguably, the transaction value standard serves as a better tool to assess the anticompetitive effects of platform concentrations since it pays more attention to the overall value of the transaction itself, including the value of all of the assets involved in the relevant M&A transactions.[84] For example, in the case of *Didi and Uber China*, although Uber China did not have a large turnover in China, Didi was still willing to acquire it at a high price. This case demonstrates that the transaction value standard can accurately reflect the real economic value and potential of the operator of the merged party, thus reasonably bringing the relevant concentrations into the scope of merger control review and effectively preventing possible competitive harm arising from the concentration of data-driven undertakings.

As clarified by the German Federal Cartel Office (Bundeskartellamt), transaction value is different from the market value of the acquired entity in two ways. First, the transaction value 'is often critically influenced by the buyer's subjective assessment of the development of the undertaking to be acquired after it has been integrated in the buyer's undertaking or corporate group'.[85] In contrast, the market value is most probably a 'stand-alone'[86] valuation that disregards the acquirer's private information and agenda. Second, the transaction value only concerns 'the proposed merger project in question',[87] excluding the equity already held by the acquirer, or held by third parties even after the transaction, whereas the market value includes the full value of the target, regardless of how much equity is actually traded in the transaction.

III.2 Non-Price Factors: Data, Start-Ups and Consumer Choices

Apart from the above controversy regarding the technical standards of the turnover test, there are also divergent views on the weight that the merger control review, alongside the review of anticompetitive agreements and abuse of market dominance, shall accord to non-price factors, such as the advantage of data accumulation, the fostering of innovation from start-ups, and the protection of consumer choice. As sketched out in Chapter 3 with respect to Chinese competition law enforcement, the traditional view prefers to confine competition law within a price-centred framework,[88] while others believe that the AML should evolve to

[84] Bundeskartellamt (n75).
[85] *Ibid*, para 12.
[86] *Ibid*, para 12.
[87] *Ibid*, para 13.
[88] D Sokol and R Comerford, 'Antitrust and Regulating Big Data' (2016) 23 George Mason Law Review 1129; MK Ohlhausen and AP Okuliar, 'Competition, Consumer Protection, and the Right [Approach] to Privacy' (2015) 80 Antitrust Law Journal 121.

encompass these non-price factors.[89] The latter perspective, which is gradually gaining popularity, partly stems from the mainstream theory that the ultimate objective of competition law is to promote consumer welfare.[90]

To begin witht, the intersection of privacy and personal information protection law and monopoly law has drawn significant academic attention, but no formal regulatory response has yet been made in China's anti-monopoly law enforcement. The AML makes no explicit reference to personal information protection,[91] and nor do the Guidelines.

The prevention of the abuse of consumers' personal data by platforms, especially dominant ones, indeed constitutes a legitimate concern for legal intervention. It is also persuasive to believe that the seemingly 'zero-price' services provided by digital platforms actually come as a consideration for the exchange of the commercial value of personal information.[92] That is to say, direct consideration of the protection of personal data does not call for a fundamental departure from the traditional antitrust law approach that centres around price-related factors.

Nevertheless, in China, it is not necessarily required to address such an issue within the framework of anti-monopoly law. Instead, as already mentioned in Chapter 3, it is still reasonable and feasible to address it mainly under the framework of the data protection regime, which, after all, does not require significant alterations to the system of anti-monopoly. As an example, the right to data portability, as stipulated in paragraph 3, Article 45 of the PIPL, is one of the approaches to address the competition concerns related to personal data.[93] Also, Article 58 of the Personal Information Protection Law (PIPL) imposes additional protective obligations on platform companies operating important business that have a large number of users or a diverse and complicated service.

According to an interview with an expert in such a field,[94] when it comes to domestic mergers involving platform enterprises, the competition authorities in China may hand over some non-price cases to the Cyberspace Administration of

[89] L O'Callaghan, 'The Intersection between Data Protection and Competition Law: How to Incorporate Data Protection, as a Non-Economic Objective, into EU Competition Analysis' (2018) 21 Trinity College Law Review 109, 111.

[90] I Graef, 'Blurring Boundaries of Consumer Welfare: How to Create Synergies between Competition, Consumer and Data Protection Law in Digital Markets' in M Bakhoum et al (eds) *Personal Data in Competition, Consumer Protection and Intellectual Property Law: Towards a Holistic Approach?* (Springer, 2018), 148–149 <https://link.springer.com/book/10.1007/978-3-662-57646-5>; Whish and Bailey (n70), 19.

[91] Except as an obligation posed on law enforcement authorities in Articles 49 and 66.

[92] H Jiao, '个人信息的反垄断法保护：从附属保护到独立保护 [Anti-Monopoly Protection of Personal Information: From Subsidiary Protection to Independent Protection]' (2021) 4 The Law (法学) 115; B Xiong, J Ge, and C Li, 'Unpacking Data: China's "Bundle of Rights" Approach to the Commercialization of Data' (2023) 13(2) International Data Privacy Law 98.

[93] W Kerber, 'Digital Markets, Data, and Privacy: Competition Law, Consumer Law and Data Protection' (2016) 11 Journal of Intellectual Property Law & Practice 856, 861.

[94] The interview took place at Renmin University of China, Law School (April 17, 2023). Interview records on file with the author.

China in advance before initiating substantive competition reviews, which aids in stripping off issues that could be handled by other regulatory agencies. Despite the coordination of the overlapping personal data problems, the general attitude towards anti-monopoly law in China at this stage is that the problems shall be reviewed in light of the present framework of AML and PIPL, instead of being brought up as a separate problem of the AML.

Second, the problem of killer acquisitions also challenges the current method of merger control review. As aforementioned, mature companies may initiate killer acquisitions to eliminate potential competition pressures from start-ups.[95] This issue is less prevalent in traditional industries, where innovation does not occur at the same pace as within the digital economy. The Anti-Monopoly Commission of the State Council specifically addressed this problem in the Guidelines. In paragraph 3, Article 19, the Commission states that mergers involving start-up platforms should raise significant regulatory concerns. Furthermore, Article 20 of the Guidelines directs the competition authorities to consider the potential impacts of the merger on innovation, requiring prudent consideration of the impact of the acquisitions involved on the competition over technological innovation and business model innovation, especially on the motivation and capacity of market players to pursue innovation. Such impacts associated with the acquisition of start-ups and emerging platforms should be given special attention.[96]

Third, it has been argued that mergers of platform enterprises may eliminate the options available to consumers.[97] Although consumer choice is widely considered a form of consumer welfare protected by competition law,[98] it remains unclear as to how this argument is specifically applied to digital markets. A major concern in this respect is that vertical integration may allow parties to refuse data sharing without justifiable reasons.[99] Hence, when it comes to the review of data-driven operators, the measure taking the traditional notion of market share as the evaluation index of market power probably overlooks the role of data resources.[100] In digital markets, the market share of an enterprise does not necessarily reflect its real market influence. Start-up enterprises, despite their small scale, have accumulated a large amount of high-value user data resources, which materially adds to the weight of their market dominance. This argument also applies to other forms of intangible property, particularly standard essential patents.

[95] W Wang (n73).
[96] Guidelines (n53), Article 20.
[97] L Wang, '数据驱动型并购中竞争损害的新面向及救济理念革新 [New Characteristics of Competition Harm in Data-driven Mergers and Concept Renovation of Antitrust Remedy]' (2021) 23 Journal of Shanghai University of Finance and Economics 138, 143–144.
[98] H Jiao, '反垄断法上的竞争损害与消费者利益标准 [Competitive Harm in Anti-Monopoly Law and Its Relationship with Consumer Interests]' (2020) 2 Nanjing University Law Journal 11, 11–13.
[99] *Ibid*, 143.
[100] Y Wang (n3), 166.

Thus, during the review process, it is essential to assess whether the enterprise controls data-like important essential facilities in the field of the digital economy, taking into consideration factors such as data volume and the overall impact of the merger on the whole digital ecology.[101] In cases where the concentration of digital platforms may result in a massive aggregation of personal information and excessive competitive advantage, the appropriate tool for the competition authority is probably prohibiting personal information aggregation when approving the merging initiative, instead of remedying various infringements to individuals' rights to personal information.

To address this issue, as mentioned in Chapter 8, the new AML, in paragraph 2 of its Article 22, explicitly outlaws the abuse of dominance using data, algorithms and technology, as well as platform rules. Article 14 of the Guidelines re-emphasizes this position by making clear reference to platforms that may be qualified as essential infrastructures.

IV. Major Mergers in China's Digital Markets

The previous parts introduced the most recent legislative progress in China's practice in promoting competition in digital markets, including the new AML, the Guidelines, and the Provisions, which are established with more details and specified standards and which, hence, have prompted provincial efforts. Moreover, the competition authority is not content with merely improving the law. Instead, substantial progress can also be seen in the practice of the intended regulations.

Ever since 2021, the SAMR has actually decided on a large number of merger cases in which platform enterprises have mainly violated their procedural obligation to notify the competition authority before implementing mergers. On 12 March 2021, the SAMR released the 'Administrative Prohibition Decisions on Ten Cases of Illegal Mergers in the Field of Digital Economy', involving the Alibaba Group, Baidu, Didi, and other entities, all of which were considered to have violated Article 21 of the 2008 AML.[102] On 7 July 2021, the SAMR released the 'Administrative Prohibition Decisions on Twenty-Two Cases of Illegal Mergers in the Field of Digital Economy', focusing on mergers conducted by Didi, the Alibaba Group, and Tencent (eight involving Didi, six involving the Alibaba Group, and five involving Tencent), as well as one involving Suning and Meituan.[103] On 29

[101] H Duan and B Shen, '互联网经济领域反垄断中的《必要设施理论》研究 [A Study of the Necessary Facilities Theory in Antitrust in the Digital Economy]' (2020) 4 Chinese Applied Law 49.

[102] SAMR, '市场监管总局依法对互联网领域十起违法实施经营者集中案作出行政处罚决定 [Administrative Prohibition Decisions on Ten Cases of Illegal Mergers in the Field of Digital Economy]' (13 March 2021) <https://www.samr.gov.cn/xw/zj/art/2023/art_1f22ec38ab104caca3b754b5b7b644a6.html> (accessed 2 February 2023).

[103] SAMR, '市场监管总局依法对互联网领域二十二起违法实施经营者集中案作出行政处罚决定 [Administrative Prohibition Decisions on Twenty-Two Cases of Illegal Mergers in the Field of

November 2021, the SAMR released the 'Administrative Prohibition Decisions on Forty-Five Cases of Illegal Mergers in the Field of Digital Economy', which included thirty-six cases in total. The primary targets of the penalties were Tencent and the Alibaba Group, with thirteen cases involving Tencent and eleven involving the Alibaba Group, while the remaining cases involved companies like Meituan, JD, Sina, 58 Tongcheng, and other platform operators.[104]

We will now have a further look at several high-profile cases involving Didi and NVIDIA, as well as Tencent and its subsidiary Huya, in which the platform concentrations were held by China's competition authorities to be materially anticompetitive.

IV.1 Didi

IV.1.1 *Didi/Kuaidi*

Didi Chuxing Technology Co, Ltd (Didi), China's leading domestic e-hailing service provider, took up more than 50 per cent of the domestic market in 2014. It faced intensive competition from a local rival, Kuaidi, and the entry of US-based Uber into the Chinese ride-hailing market. In the face of the increasingly complex and ever-changing landscape of China's ride-hailing market, Didi's next step was to maintain and bolster its leadership in the nascent ride-hailing service market.[105] Didi Kuaidi was the result of a merger that occurred in February 2015 between Tencent-funded mobile taxi-service app Didi, and its rival Kuaidi, which was strongly backed by China's e-commerce giant, the Alibaba Group.

In 2015, Didi and Kuaidi, the two leading players in China's e-hailing industry, merged to form Didi Kuaidi, which was valued at about USD 6 billion (ca €5.45 billion) at that time, in an effort to head off Uber's expansion throughout China. This merger was neither notified to nor reviewed by the competition authority. As announced, the new undertaking would run on a co-chief executive officer (CEO) basis and would keep the original structure of their respective human resources. Didi and Kuaidi would continue to run their businesses in parallel, retain their brands, and remain independent.[106] Meanwhile, Didi Kuaidi actively

Digital Economy]' (7 July 2021) <https://www.samr.gov.cn/xw/mtjj/art/2023/art_7ff4790437fa4d1789b734d95d98168a.html> (accessed 2 February 2023).

[104] SAMR, '市场监管总局依法对43起未依法申报违法实施经营者集中案作出行政处罚决定 [Administrative Prohibition Decisions on Forty-Three Cases of Illegal Mergers in the Field of Digital Economy]' (20 November 2021) <https://www.samr.gov.cn/xw/zj/art/2023/art_58890b3964a947438e050bec99133f7e.html> (accessed 2 February 2023).

[105] CEIBS (China–Europe International Business School), 'Lessons from the Didi Dache and Kuaidi Dache Taxi-App Merger' (14 April 2015) <https://www.ceibs.edu/lessons-didi-dache-and-kuaidi-dache-taxi-app-merger> (accessed 2 February 2023).

[106] Z Liu, 'Kuaidi Marries Didi: End of the Battle or a New Beginning?' (*China Daily*, 16 February 2015) <http://www.chinadaily.com.cn/business/tech/2015-02/16/content_19600016_3.htm> (accessed 2 February 2023).

pursued global growth. For example, it invested in and partnered with Lyft, Uber Technologies Inc's (Uber's) major competitor in the United States. However, the competitive environment of the e-hailing service market was constantly evolving. Didi Kuaidi carefully created a portfolio of strategies to sustainably compete in both the local and global markets.[107]

In 2015, Kuaidi held a 56.5 per cent share of China's taxi-hailing app market, while Didi accounted for 43.3 per cent as of December, according to research consultancy Analysis International.[108] The merged Didi Kuaidi won a considerable chunk of the private car-hailing market, holding an 83 per cent share (versus Uber, in second place, at 16 per cent).[109] Questions lingered about the long-term outcome of Didi Kuaidi versus Uber. Neither undertaking was profitable, partly due to the large subsidies offered to drivers to maintain competitiveness; efforts to phase them out had alienated their driver base.[110] Behind such a commercial strategy loomed the future anticompetitiveness concerns of these platforms.

IV.1.2 *Didi/Uber*

China's giant Didi Kuaidi dominated the business of e-hailing taxis in China, but Uber had been making waves, both in business and legal circles, with its peer-to-peer rides model.[111] In response to this competitive landscape, the ride-hailing giant Didi, along with Uber China, the largest player in China's online car-hailing market, announced a merger in 2016. This merger was one of the most important digital mergers that came under scrutiny by the SAMR, which had assumed the responsibilities of China's MOFCOM in regard to such matters. The merger, valued at USD 35 billion (ca €31.78 billion), created a giant platform in China's ride-hailing market and raised concerns about potential monopolistic practices.

According to the agreement concluded by the two parties, Didi and Uber Global would hold shares in each other and would become minority shareholders of each other. The merger also marked the end of China's ride-hailing competition war, with Didi winning nearly 90 per cent of the market.[112] Intending to safeguard fair competition and consumer interests in China's taxi-hailing market, MOFCOM's antitrust department had already held two meetings with Didi on 7 and 17 August 2016, and had even requested information from them on the Uber deal.[113]

[107] N Su, Y Fang, and Y Yang, 'Main Case Didi Kuaidi' (Harvard Business Publishing Education, 12 April 2016) <https://hbsp.harvard.edu/product/W16197-PDF-ENG?Ntt = Main%20case%20Didi%20Kuaidi> (accessed 15 April 2024).

[108] Liu (n106).

[109] See T Tai, 'Didi Kuaidi & and China's Car-Hailing Market' (Harvard Business School, 4 December 2015) < https://d3.harvard.edu/platform-rctom/submission/didi-kuaidi-chinas-car-hailing-market/ > (accessed 2 February 2023).

[110] E Crouch, 'China's Ride Wars: Uber vs. Didi Kuaidi' (Tech in Asia, 30 October 2015) <https://www.techinasia.com/infographic-didi-kuaidi-uber> (accessed 2 February 2023).

[111] *Ibid.*

[112] B Wang (n51).

[113] CCTV News, '商务部：开展滴滴优步合并案反垄断调查 两次约谈滴滴 [MOFCOM: Anti-Monopoly Investigation into Didi–Uber Merger: Two Interviews with Didi]' (2

According to Reuters, however, Didi said that neither firm had formally notified China's competition authorities for a formal review since Uber's revenues in China did not meet the threshold required for a merger control review.[114] However, the takeover would likely constitute a monopoly as the two might have more than a 90 per cent of the market share in China. Although some experts described the end to the fierce competition in the manner of a 'price war (subsidizing drivers and riders)' as rational business practice, many warned of a monopoly that could result in higher taxi fares immediately after the implementation of the platform concentration.[115] MOFCOM also vowed to comprehensively assess the deal's impact on market competition and industrial development as well as its possible harms to the interests of consumers.[116] However, defining the market was challenging since e-hailing was a new business model on a global scale. In addition, the nature of the platform made it hard to calculate the market share of Didi. Three years after the announcement of the merger, the investigation was still ongoing in accordance with the AML by the SAMR.[117]

Ever since the implementation of the merger between Didi and Uber China, there have been heated debates in China, mainly over merging parties' duty to notify the competition authority and the substantial anticompetitive effects of such a concentration.

The first debate centres on whether the two parties are obliged to take the initiative to notify the competition authority. As provided in Article 3 of the 'Provisions on Threshold for Merger Notification' (2008) ('the 2008 Provisions'), if during the previous fiscal year, the total global turnover of all business operators participating in the concentration exceeded RMB 10 billion (or RMB 40 million in mainland China), and if at least each of the two operators had a turnover exceeding RMB 400 million within mainland China, a notification must be lodged in advance before the concentration is implemented. Before closing the merger, neither Didi nor Uber reported it to, or obtained approval from, the competition authority in China.

As to the merger notification threshold for Didi and Uber China, some commentators hold that turnover should be calculated with net income (profit),

September 2016) <https://news.cctv.com/2016/09/02/ARTIJgQdeT2nSZSNETXi5zq8160902.shtml> (accessed 13 October 2023).

[114] K Grandhi, 'China Launches Anti-Monopoly Investigation into Uber–Didi Deal' (*International Business Times*, 16 February 2009) <https://www.ibtimes.co.uk/china-launches-anti-monopoly-investigation-into-uber-didi-deal-1579350> (accessed 2 February 2023).

[115] Beijing Review, 'Is Didi's Dominance Equal to a Monopoly?' (21 October 2016) <http://www.china.org.cn/opinion/2016-10/21/content_39539886.htm> (accessed 2 May 2024).

[116] CCTV News, 'MOFCOM: Anti-Monopoly Investigation into Didi–Uber Merger' (n113).

[117] CCTV News, '国家市场监管总局：依据反垄断法及有关规定对滴滴收购优步案件进行调查 [SAMR: Ongoing Investigation into Didi–Uber Merger According to the Old AML and Relevant Regulations]' (16 November 2018) <http://news.cctv.com/2018/11/16/ARTIFgxAD8eTn8YU2mY5HJYM181116.shtml> (accessed 13 October 2023).

excluding the costs that such platforms have paid to e-hailing taxi drivers, riders, and other business partners in forms like commissions, coupons. and dividends. Nevertheless, the constantly changing business models of e-hailing platforms make it quite difficult to conduct such a calculation. The amount of such platforms' net income even becomes negative at a certain stage of business development.[118]

In contrast, many others insist on taking gross turnover as the notification threshold, that is calculating all the fares that Didi and Uber collected from taxi riders in the first place.[119] The net income of Didi may, indeed, fail to meet the conventional merger notification threshold. Nevertheless, Didi has gained more than a 90 per cent share in the e-hailing taxi service market and therefore could exert a significant impact on the structure and competition dynamics of China's e-hailing taxi service market.[120] According to these commentators, while the requirements for voluntary notification are unclear, MOFCOM could still initiate a monopoly investigation based on Article 4 of the 2008 Provision under its own judgment. However, this Article has remained a dormant clause ever since it came into effect in 2008.[121]

The second debate focuses on the approach to analysing the anticompetitive effects of such concentration. To address this, it is necessary to first determine the relevant market. The traditional approach relies primarily on demand-side substitution and the hypothetical monopolist test to determine the relevant market.[122] However, the most recent viewpoint proposes a different solution for the analysis of mergers taking place in digital markets, holding that large platform undertakings, primarily engaged in facilitating transactions, should be defined as an independent market. To take this a step further, if a large platform undertaking were defined as a market, it would also be unnecessary to determine the relevant market that was being monopolized.[123] In the case of *Didi–Uber*, if Didi and Uber China were each to constitute a market, their merger would be a merger of two markets. Didi provides comprehensive urban transportation services such as taxi-hailing, carpooling, hitchhiking, and so on to nearly 300 million users in more than 400 cities in China. By contrast, the main business of Uber China lies in carpooling and hitchhiking. Therefore, the merger, in essence, will mainly affect the dedicated car market within the territory of China.

[118] L Jiang, '互联网双边市场经营者集中申报标准之困境 [The Dilemma of Standards for Mergers in Bilateral Internet Markets]' (2017) 19 Journal of Southeast University (Philosophy and Social Science) 21, 22.

[119] Q Gao and H Su, '滴滴合并优步案的反垄断分析 [Anti-Monopoly Analysis on Didi's Merger with Uber]' (2019) 6 Journal of North China Electric Power University (Social Sciences) 78, 79. See also Jiang (n118).

[120] Cai (n72), 170–175.

[121] A Yuan, 'Didi and Uber China's Merger from an AML Perspective' (In House Community, 14 March 2017) <https://www.inhousecommunity.com/article/didi-uber-chinas-merger-anti-monopoly-law-perspective> (accessed 2 February 2023).

[122] See new AML (n46), Article 15.

[123] Yuan (n121).

Meanwhile, the special characteristics of the e-hailing service market need to be considered. MOFCOM did not intervene in the merger case of *Didi–Uber*, probably due to the distinct nature of the e-hailing taxi industry, which involves specific competition dynamics in the digital markets. The core competitiveness of companies involving digital economy lies in their user base. Therefore, in order to enhance their competitiveness, platform operators must reduce the cost of users, improve the profits of merchants, and attract as many sellers and users as possible.[124] In addition to the lower migration costs of users, the unique competition dynamics also affect the judgment of whether the merger and acquisition should be prohibited.[125] After the merger, Didi–Uber will march into many fields such as car rental, special cars, express cars, hitchhiking, and so on. Given its substantial business scale, the chances are that Didi–Uber may strengthen its dominant position and transmit its dominance to other areas, potentially hindering fair competition in a wide range of transportation-related ecosystems.

IV.2 *Huya/DouYu*

HUYA Inc (Huya) and DouYu International Holdings Limited ('DouYu') are two of the largest Tencent-backed game-streaming platforms providing video game live-streaming services in China. While Huya has a 40 per cent market share, DouYu holds 30 per cent. Huya and DouYu first announced a USD 6 billion (ca €5.45 billion) merger deal in October 2020. However, the SAMR blocked the merger initiative following an anti-monopoly investigation, stating that the merger between Huya and DouYu would give Tencent control over the merged entity:

From the perspective of different key indicators such as revenue, number of active users, and resources for streamers, the total share is very substantial, and the elimination and restriction of competition can be foreseen.[126]

This case is the first instance in which the Chinese regulators have prohibited a concentration of operators in its digital markets. Tencent claimed that it would abide by the SAMR's decision, comply with all regulatory requirements, operate in accordance with relevant laws and regulations, and fulfil its social responsibilities.[127] Huya's merger with DouYu was reported to create a live game-streaming behemoth with a dominant market share, a major strategic advantage over its

[124] Cai (n72), 168.

[125] Gao and Su (n119), 82–83.

[126] SAMR, '市场监管总局关于禁止虎牙公司与斗鱼国际控股有限公司合并案反垄断审查决定的公告 [Antitrust Review Decision on Prohibiting the Merger of Huya and DouYu]' (10 July 2021) <https://www.samr.gov.cn/fldys/tzgg/ftj/art/2023/art_a04ceb782566465082e165f0a86f5580.html> (accessed 15 April 2024).

[127] Associated Press, 'Chinese Regulator Halts Huya–DouYu Game-Streaming Merger' (Market Watch, 10 July 2021) <https://www.marketwatch.com/story/chinese-regulator-halts-huya-douyu-game-streaming-merger-01625932174?tesla = y> (accessed 2 February 2023).

peers, leadership in technology, and better access to top streamers. Combined, DouYu and Huya were estimated to dominate the world's second-largest market for live streaming of games, with close to an 80 per cent market share. 'If Huya merges with DouYu, Tencent will solely control the merged entity', said the SAMR.[128]

The SAMR grounded its prohibitive decision on Article 28 AML and Article 35 of the Interim Measures for the Review of Concentration of Undertakings, and explained the decisions as follows:

(a) As for relevant markets: The merger involved two related markets within China, one for online game operation services and the other for live game broadcasting. The SAMR held that Huya and Douyu have horizontal overlap in the game live broadcast, entertainment live broadcast, e-commerce live broadcast and short video markets. Tencent is engaged in online game operation services upstream of game live broadcast. Therefore, the relevant market should be defined as the market of game live broadcast, entertainment live broadcast, e-commerce live broadcast and short videos in China.

(b) As for the competition analysis, according to Article 27 of the AML, the SAMR thoroughly analysed the party's centralisation in the relevant market, its control power, the market concentration, and the impact of the concentration on downstream user enterprises and other relevant operators. The impact of such concentration was believed to have or may have the effect of excluding and restricting competition in the relevant market. More specifically, this concentration would strengthen Tencent's dominant position in the game live broadcast market in China, with the effect of excluding and limiting competition. Furthermore, this concentration would enable Tencent to have a two-way blockade capability in the upstream online game operation service market in China and the downstream domestic game live broadcast market, which may have the effect of excluding and limiting competition. Although Tencent had made a commitment to obtaining conditional approval, the competition authority believed that this commitment did not address the restriction of competition in this case and thus rejected the proposal for conditional approval.[129]

The deal between Huya and DouYu was reported to be terminated on 11 July 2021, amid China's tightening anti-monopoly law enforcement against tech companies. Although the competition authority in China had already enhanced its scrutiny over concentrations of tech undertakings before blocking this deal, such

[128] S Wei, 'Huya, DouYu Abandon Game-Streaming Merger after Regulators Block Deal' (Tech Node, 13 July 2021) <https://technode.com/2021/07/13/huya-douyu-abandon-game-streaming-merger-after-regulators-block-deal> (accessed 2 February 2023).

[129] SAMR, 'Announcement of the SAMR on the Anti-Monopoly Review Decision to Ban the Merger of Huya and DouYu' (n31).

scrutiny was primarily conducted against procedural violations, especially against the failure to notify before closing the deals involved. Since December 2020, the SAMR has acclaimed that forty-four digital platforms have failed to notify to the competition authority, including the Alibaba Group, Tencent, Didi, and other platform enterprises.[130]

The pre-emptive supervision over the deal between Huya and DouYu was said to have raised the curtain of ex-ante regulatory mode, which departs from the ex-post approach in regulating anticompetitive agreements and abuse of market dominance[131] and has enriched the regulatory tools of China's competition authority against violating concentrations. Technical tools like data-facilitated automatic information collection systems are also being employed to complement such enforcement. For example, Zhejiang Province is running an online 'pre-warning and alert system', which enables competition authorities to collect data from other regulatory authorities (e.g. the taxation department) and detect potential anticompetitive dealings in advance.[132] Although the actual functionality of such technical tools remains to be tested, constant technological and institutional improvement on the collection of data concerning financing activities at the early stage of concentration deals may make proactive regulation feasible.

IV.3 *NVIDIA/Mellanox*

An acquisition, announced on 11 March 2019, united the NVIDIA Technology Co, Ltd ('NVIDIA') and Mellanox Technologies, Ltd ('Mellanox'), two of the world's leading companies in high performance and data computing. The consideration of this transaction was USD 6.814 million (ca €6.1867 million). It was reported that this transaction was the second largest transaction in the semiconductor field in the world in 2019, second only to Infineon Technology's acquisition of Cypress Semiconductor Company.[133]

During the review process, the SAMR informed NVIDIA and Mellanox that the proposed concentration was deemed to have, or may have, the effect of eliminating or restricting competition. Several rounds of discussions were held by the SAMR with both the operators and experts on competition. After the evaluation, the

130 Legal Weekly, '虎牙斗鱼合并被否 反垄断监管再迎里程碑式进展 [Anti-Trust Regulation Reaches Another Milestone with the Blocked Merger between Huya and DouYu] (15 July 2021) <http://m.legalweekly.cn/rdcj/2021-07/15/content_8551962.html> (14 October 2023).

131 J Shi, 反垄断法—法典释评与学理探源 [*Anti-Monopoly Law: Interpretation and Theoretical Exploration*] (Renmin University of China Press, 2008), 263.

132 MLex Staff, 'Digital Tools Highlighted in Enforcement Reports of China's Local Market Supervisors' (10 January 2023) <https://mlexmarketinsight.com/news/insight/digital-tools-highlighted-in-enforcement-reports-of-china-s-local-market-supervisors> (accessed 3 April 2023).

133 S Moss, 'Nvidia's $6.9bn Mellanox Acquisition Closes' (Data Center Dynamics, 28 April 2020) <https://www.datacenterdynamics.com/en/news/nvidias-69bn-mellanox-acquisition-closes> (accessed 14 October 2023).

SAMR eventually accepted the additional restrictive conditions commitment submitted by NVIDIA and Mellanox and approved the deal conditionally on 2 April 2020, requiring the two undertakings not to impose mandatory bundling or any other 'unreasonable trading conditions' when selling devices in China.

More specifically, the SAMR, in its Decision,[134] attached the following behavioural relief measures in a bid to prevent the potential impact of this concentration on the global and Chinese graphics-processing-unit (GPU) accelerators, private network interconnection devices, and high-speed Ethernet adapter markets, including (i) not to tie up or discriminate against customers who buy relevant products separately; (ii) to continue to supply the Chinese market under the principles of fairness, reasonableness, and non-discrimination; (iii) to maintain the compatibility of relevant products with third-party products; (iv) to uphold open source commitments; (v) to protect the information of manufacturers of third-party accelerators and network interconnection equipment, and two other confidential remedies.

When assessing the potential impacts of the concentration on market competition, the SAMR reasoned as follows.

IV.3.1 The Relevant Market

After the review, the SAMR held that NVIDIA and Mellanox had a vertical relationship in the market of data centre servers and ordinary Ethernet adapters and were adjacent to the two groups of markets—GPU accelerators and dedicated network interconnection devices and GPU accelerators and high-speed Ethernet adapters. Moreover, the relevant products involved in this case were supplied and procured globally, suppliers competed globally, there were no obvious price differences in the products in different countries, and the proportion of product freight costs in the final price was low. There were no significant cross-border trade barriers, and import and export trade was active. Therefore, the relevant regional markets were defined as within the globe, and the Chinese market was also examined.

IV.3.2 The Competition Analysis

According to Article 27 of the AML, the SAMR thoroughly analysed the operator's centralization in the relevant market from the aspects of its control over the relevant market, the market concentration of the relevant market, and the impact of the concentration on downstream user enterprises and other relevant operators. The SAMR reflected that this concentration would have, or may have, the effect of

[134] SAMR, '市场监管总局关于附加限制性条件批准英伟达公司收购迈络思科技有限公司股权案反垄断审查决定的公告 [Announcement of Anti-Monopoly Review Decisions Regarding Approval of the SAMR on Additional Restrictive Conditions: Nvidia's Acquisition of Equity of Miloth Technology Co, Ltd]' (16 April 2020) <https://www.samr.gov.cn/zt/qhfldzf/art/2020/art_5062ec6932d8429488e4765c83d2d6ea.htmlhttps://www.samr.gov.cn/zt/qhfldzf/art/2020/art_5062ec6932d8429488e4765c83d2d6ea.html> (accessed 17 April 2024).

excluding and limiting competition among global and Chinese GPU accelerators, private network interconnection devices, and high-speed Ethernet adapters.

First, the centralized entity had the ability to eliminate and restrict competitive behaviours in the relevant market. The reasons were (i) the centralized enterprise had strong market power in the GPU accelerator, special network interconnection equipment, and high-speed Ethernet adapter market; (ii) both NVIDIA and Mellanox had strong price control capabilities; (iii) the transaction would enable the centralized entity to provide important GPU accelerator and network interconnection equipment at the same time, further enhancing the control power of both parties in relevant markets; and (iv) the barriers to entry in the relevant markets are high.

Second, after the merger, the entity would have the motivation to exclude and restrict the competition in the relevant market. Accelerator and network interconnection products have great potential for development, and a concentration of operators makes it possible to obtain a broader and brighter development. After the merger, NVIDIA and Mellanox would conduct tying behaviours to increase profits.

Third, the concentration would have, or may have, the effect of excluding and restricting competition in relevant markets. After the concentration, the entity may exclude or restrict market competition through anticompetitive behaviours like tying and refusing to trade. In addition, the centralized entity may exclude or restrict market competition by reducing product interoperability. After the concentration, the entity may use the competitive sensitive information obtained in the process of hardware adaptation to exclude and restrict market competition.

As for NVIDIA's acquisition of Mellanox, in accordance with the AML, the SAMR conducted an in-depth analysis of the impact of this concentration of operators on market competition in terms of the market share of the operators and their control over the market, the market concentration in the relevant market, and the impact of the concentration on downstream user enterprises and other operators concerned, and concluded that the concentration would have, or may have, the effect of excluding or restricting competition in the global and Chinese GPU, dedicated network interconnection equipment, and high-speed Ethernet adapter markets. After the assessment, the SAMR accepted that additional restrictive conditions could reduce the adverse impact of this concentration on competition.[135]

One noteworthy commitment among the conditions for the approval of the concentration by the SAMR was Mellanox's promise to keep the source for point-to-point communications software and aggregate communications software open. During the review process, competitors in China's GPU accelerator market appealed to the SAMR that the concentration between NVIDIA and Mellanox may

[135] *Ibid.*

incur the risk of data concentration because, on the one hand, the integration of a software business into such a hardware business would help NVIDIA to establish a strong cloud computing system and achieve the advantage of data accumulation and, on the other hand, NVIDIA holds a 90 per cent market share in supercomputer accelerators and is likely to take the dominant position therein by 2030.[136] Thus, the enforcement of such a commitment will play a critical role in safeguarding the competition between the merging parties and their competitors in the GPU accelerator market in China.

IV.4 *Tencent/CMC*

Internet giant Tencent offers a range of music services, including an online library of songs and live streaming of performances. It is not alone in the Chinese market, as tech giants such as the Alibaba Group and NetEase have their own platforms. However, Tencent dominates the industry and often serves as the music pipeline for competitors. Ever since 2013, Tencent had been reaching exclusive in-China distribution agreements with several large music producers, including Universal Music Group, Sony Music Entertainment, and Warner Music Group, which accounted for about 70 per cent of global music sales in 2018. Tencent pays the major record labels a fee for the music copyrights and then sublicenses the content copyright to other music-streaming rivals in China, such as music and video platforms operated by the Alibaba Group, NetEase, and ByteDance. Rivals have complained that Tencent paid exorbitant fees for the initial rights and then passed most of the cost on to competitors.

From July 2016 to January 2017, Tencent acquired a majority stake (61.64 per cent) in China Music Corporation (CMC), and restructured CMC and its own online music business into Tencent Music Group (TME), becoming a giant in the music market that controls more than 80 per cent of 'exclusive music library resources'. Such market power and upstream copyright resources enables Tencent to get better terms than its competitors receive or to limit the ability of rivals to enter the market. Tencent's penalty came as the SAMR dusted off an investigation in August 2019 into Tencent's acquisition of CMC that formed TME and its dealings with the world's largest record labels. According to the decision released on 24 July 2021, Tencent was ordered by the competition authority to end such exclusive agreements with music copyright holders.[137]

[136] T Jennewine, 'Why NVIDIA Will Dominate the Data Center by 2030' (The Motley Fool, 10 September 2021), <https://www.fool.com/investing/2021/09/10/why-nvidia-will-dominate-the-data-center-by-2030> (accessed 15 October 2023).

[137] J McDonald, 'China's Tencent Ordered to End Exclusive Music Contracts' (24 July 2021) <https://apnews.com/article/technology-entertainment-business-music-china-bd7e87fdbbce8aad72ae96d8c6c97f07> (accessed 2 February, 2023).

On the grounds of Article 48 and Article 49 AML, the SAMR made the following decisions:[138] first, Tencent and its affiliates were ordered to take the necessary measures to restore the competitive state in the relevant market; second, a maximum fine of RMB 500,000 (ca €67320.12) on Tencent was imposed; third, the concentration of operators had to be notified in accordance with the law; fourth, Tencent was required to comply with the law, by establishing and improving a long-term mechanism for fair participation in market competition. In reaching its decisions, the SAMR took the following stand.

IV.4.1 The Case Constituted an Illegal Concentration of Operators

After the merger in July 2016, Tencent managed to obtain a 61.64 per cent stake in CMC, which fell under the provisions stipulated in Article 20 AML. Tencent's global turnover in 2015 was ¥102.863 billion (ca €13.85 billion), and its turnover in China was ¥96.251 billion (ca €12.96 billion). The global turnover of CMC in 2015 also met the notification standard stipulated in Article 3 of the Provisions on Threshold for Merger Notification. According to Article 21 AML, Tencent was required to notify the merger to the SAMR before completing the registration of equity change on 6 December 2017. Therefore, its failure to notify violated the provisions of Article 21.

IV.4.2 This Case Would Have or May Have the Effect of Excluding or Restricting Competition

According to the provisions of the AML and the Guidelines, considering the characteristics of the digital economy, the relevant market in this case was defined as a horizontal overlap between the two sides of the transaction in China. Moreover, since the authorization of music copyright is limited by the provisions of the copyright laws of various countries and has obvious regional differences, the relevant regional market is therefore defined as within the territory of China. The effects of excluding and limiting competition also existed, which can be mainly summarized as follows. First, after the merger, the entity would have a high market share in the relevant market; second, the main competitors would be reduced in the relevant market; and third, the concentration may further raise the relevant market entry barriers.

In response to the prohibition decision,[139] Tencent formally committed to fully comply with all of the requirements in a timely manner, operating in compliance with laws and regulations, earnestly performing its social responsibilities,

[138] SAMR, '国家市场监督管理总局行政处罚决定书（国市监处〔2021〕67号）[SAMR Administrative Prohibition Decision [2021] No 67]' (24 July 2021) <https://www.samr.gov.cn/zt/qhfldzf/art/2021/art_61810ad454524ec2b9cb38c78f3d793c.html> (accessed 14 April 2024).

[139] S Hu, '腾讯网易回应其关于垄断音乐作品处罚决定：全面接受， 按期整改 [Tencent NetEase Responded to Its Prohibition Decision on Monopoly Music Works: Fully Accept and Rectify on Schedule]' (24 July 2021) <https://www.sohu.com/a/479312888_114941> (accessed 14 April 2024).

and maintaining healthy competition in the market. For the industry, this punitive decision against the failure to notify will certainly incentivize future merging platforms to solicit the attitude of the competition authority on the legality of conceived concentrations and promote a fairer competitive environment for digital business.

In particular, this decision indicates the special attention that the competition authority pays to 'mega mergers' that involve platform undertakings with significant market power in vertical sectors or those with excessively high transaction values. Mega platforms' capacity to leverage their network effects, ecosystem strategies, cross-sector competition, and other advantages may have immense impacts on market competition, especially on market innovation, even if the size of the merged undertaking is small.[140] As mentioned in the opening chapter of this book, non-price factors like innovation and its bearing on the development of the whole national industry have become of vital concern to China's central government. Instead of merely adhering to conventional factors such as market power and the impact on price, the new AML accords special weight to 'innovation' and 'the impact of concentration on the development of national economy' in merger review.[141]

In this case, the SAMR explicitly considered the bearing of the concentration involved on the promotion of industrial innovation. Specifically, Tencent Music's business model of concluding exclusive licensing agreements with music copyrights holders alongside its market power may have exerted adverse impacts on the players in the online music service market in terms of exploring new business models on copyright licensing and music product distribution.[142]

Another anticompetitive issue in this case that overlaps with concentration is therefore the legality of the exclusive licensing between Tencent Music and music copyright holders. As an official from the SAMR commented, China's competition authority pledges to grant 'timely' green lights to merger initiatives concerning digital platforms if there are no anticompetitive effects.[143] The exclusive authorization of digital music copyright involves multiple legal interests and may not necessarily have the effect of excluding or restricting competition. As some commentators have stressed, excessively harsh enforcement on merging initiatives may be equally detrimental to innovation and competition in the digital market since

[140] W Han and Y Gao, 'Challenges and Prospects for Merger Control in China in the Digital Economy' (CPI Antitrust Chronicle, 22 March 2019) <https://www.pymnts.com/cpi-posts/challenges-and-prospects-for-merger-control-in-china-in-the-digital-economy> (accessed 14 April 2024)

[141] R Brandenburger, K Huang, and EX Wang, 'Convergence or Divergence: How Does China Analyse Innovation Concerns in Merger Review?' (2021) 10 Journal of Antitrust Enforcement 63, 65.

[142] SAMR, 'SAMR Administrative Prohibition Decision [2021] No 67' (n138).

[143] MLex Staff, 'Horizontal Merger Guidelines Considered by China's SAMR to Boost Review Regime' (17 January 2023) <https://mlexmarketinsight.com/news/insight/horizontal-merger-guidelines-considered-by-china-s-samr-to-boost-review-regime> (accessed 3 April 2023).

innovation conditioned on sizable undertakings will be prevented.[144] From a practical point of view, the preservation of platform competition should not solely rely on administrative punishment. Instead, diversified regulatory tools such as governmental soft intervention, judicial guidance, and the like should all be taken into account when monitoring and handling anticompetitive concentrations.

To improve corresponding provisions and supporting industrial policies, an approach of prudent macro-supervision should be adopted, especially considering the characteristics of the business models of emerging platforms and the pattern in which business operators and consumers interact. Moreover, a comprehensive regulatory approach should be adopted to achieve a delicate balance between administrative supervision, industrial development, and the overall interests of society.

V. Conclusion

The M&A practices in China's digital market take more flexible formats than in traditional industries. Both horizontal and vertical mergers are common. Killer acquisitions targeted at start-ups, however, may not meet the notification threshold under the old AML; and contractual arrangements (namely, VIE) may achieve desired objectives of a merger without altering the equity structure of any firm. Consequently, mergers potentially detrimental to competition might have gone through without triggering regulatory attention. Eager for aggressive expansion, internet giants in China were proficient in, and used to implementing, unnotified mergers for years, until the competition authorities took a more stringent stance against anticompetitive practices of digital firms.

In response, the new AML and the Guidelines specifically addressed these aforementioned regulatory challenges. The 'stop-the-clock' mechanism gave regulatory bodies a more flexible time frame for complex cases. Adjustments to the notification threshold were made by empowering the competition authorities to require notification as they see fit and by stipulating a more inclusive method evaluating market power. In addition, contractual arrangements like VIEs are now subject to the merger control procedure, according to the Guidelines. Amendments to the merger control system, alongside numerous prohibition decisions on failures to notify, mark a more stringent stance against anticompetitive behaviours in China's digital markets. As for the future, a more comprehensive merger control threshold for digital market is in continued debate. On the one hand, the traditional turnover test has been criticized for being unadjusted to the digital age, unable to cover

[144] J Shi, '加强反垄断监管 促进平台经济在规范中发展 [Strengthen Anti-Monopoly Supervision and Promote the Development of Platform Economy in Regulation]' (10 April 2021) <http://finance.people.com.cn/n1/2021/0410/c1004-32074571.html> (accessed 3 April 2023).

detrimental mergers such as 'killer acquisitions'. Supplemental tests including the 'transaction value test' and 'market value test' have been proposed and discussed by Chinese scholars and authorities. On the other hand, there are also divergent views on the weight that the merger control review shall accord to non-price factors, such as the advantage of data accumulation, the fostering of innovation from start-ups, and the protection of consumer choices. More improvements on the merger control system are already on the way.

10

Administrative Monopoly

I. Introduction

I.1 Background: Decentralized Regulatory Powers in a Unitary Digital Economy

To comprehend why administrative monopoly in digital markets has become a hotspot issue in China, let us first take a brief look at the structure of China's regulatory powers. Although China is politically defined as a unitary nation, its extraordinarily sizable territory and population have made it hardly possible for the central government to implement a totally unified policy throughout its jurisdiction. Instead, in a good number of socio-economic matters, the central government avails local governments the discretion, be it explicitly or implicitly, to translate national legislation and regulations into local versions so as to better keep the law fitting for local conditions.[1] Such a separation of regulatory powers has contributed to a decentralized regulatory style in many respects of social governance. Specifically, the central government controls the appointment of chief local officials and evaluates their performance according to certain criteria, including economic development and regional stability.[2] Hence, a mechanism of competition in both 'bureaucratic and economic markets' is formed, and local officials have high motivation to promote the flourishing of local businesses in economic competition.[3]

The effect of this mechanism is two-fold. On the one hand, it explains China's economic success over the past decades and maintains an experimental environment for public regulations within the unitary political regime of the state. On the other hand, however, it may motivate regional officials to exercise their regulatory power in order to defend local firms against foreign ones. Local governments give full play to the natural advantages of each region respectively, which may lead to a series of invisible market barriers with local protection attributes. In digital markets, taking those businesses that have heavy physical presence, for example

[1] X Zhou,中国国家治理的制度逻辑：一个组织学研究 [*The Institutional Logic of Governance in China: An Organisational Approach*] (SDX Joint Publishing Company, 2017), 14–20.

[2] C Xu, 'The Fundamental Institutions of China's Reforms and Development' (2011) 49 Journal of Economic Literature 1076.

[3] L Zhou, '《官场＋市场》与中国增长故事 ["Bureaucratic and Economic Markets" and China's Growth Story]' (2018) 38(2) Chinese Journal of Sociology 1.

Competition Law and Policy in Digital Markets. Maria Ioannidou and Bingwan Xiong, Oxford University Press.
 DOI: 10.1093/9780191925955.003.0010

(particularly, urban transportation services), local governments may impose excessively high standards for new entrants to obtain access to local markets and reduce the competitive pressure leveraged on incumbent local market players.[4] Similarly, when the business operations in digital markets involve access to scare resources such as data, which are controlled or the control of which is affected by local administration, anticompetitive barriers may also arise for digital platform operators.

In fact, it is not easy to strike a delicate balance between the delegation of regulatory power to local authorities and the central ideology to maintain a unified national market. Ever since the 1980s, China's central government has been making efforts to promote the construction of a unitary market of free business competition. For instance, Article 6 of the 'State Council's Provisional Stipulations on Developing and Preserving Socialism Competition', released in 1980, stresses that competition shall not be inhibited by regional or sectoral barriers.[5]

Nonetheless, the availability of regulatory discretion under China's political system makes the central government uneasy about exerting complete control over every policy adopted by local governments and properly dealing with complicated local situations. Thus, the actual municipal competition landscape depends on the interactions, including conflicts, negotiation, cooperation, and non-cooperation, between local governments and central government.[6]

When it comes to competition law, the recent reformulation of China's central watchdog of market operation (the State Administration for Market Regulation (SAMR), especially the establishment of the Bureau of Anti-Monopoly therein), signals China's determination to bring its anti-monopoly law enforcement into a new stage, as commented on by an official of the Anti-Monopoly Commission of the State Council.[7] Before such reformulation, the regulatory powers for market competition were largely fragmented. In 2008, the State Council of China divided the power of anti-monopoly law enforcement among three central regulatory agencies, namely the National Development and Reform Commission (NDRC), the Ministry of Commerce (MOFCOM) and the State Administration for Industry and Commerce (SAIC). The NDRC was responsible for investigating price violations and price monopolies; the MOFCOM shouldered the responsibility for

[4] For businesses that are facilitated by digital platforms but have weak physical presence in local jurisdictions, say, e-hailing, the immediate and massive introduction of a digital business model could indeed help break local legal barriers to trade nationwide. See L Liu and R Weingast Barry, 'Taobao, Federalism, and the Emergence of Law, Chinese Style' (2018) 111 Minnesota Law Review 1563.

[5] State Council Standing Committee, '国务院关于开展和保护社会主义竞争的暂行规定 [State Council's Provisional Stipulations on Developing and Preserving Socialism Competition]' (17 October 1980) <https://www.beijing.gov.cn/zhengce/zfwj/zfwj/szfwj/201905/t20190523_70377.html> (accessed 9 April 2024).

[6] Zhou, *The Institutional Logic of Governance in China* (n1), 18–19, 29–34, 39–40.

[7] Xinhua, 'China Establishes Anti-Monopoly Bureau to Secure Fair Competition' (*China Daily*, 19 November 2021) <https://www.chinadaily.com.cn/a/202111/19/WS61973a37a310cdd39bc765f5.html> (accessed 8 April 2024).

conducting merger review; and the SAIC was in charge of anti-monopoly law enforcement in relation to anticompetitive agreements, abuse of dominance, and the abuse of administrative power to exclude or restrict competition (except for price monopolies).[8]

The new central agency was established in a bid to consolidate those fragmented powers into a unitary force and enhance the robustness of the enforcement power for market competition throughout the state.[9] Provincial administrations are mainly responsible for enforcement in their respective administrative regions in this regard. The SAMR may also designate provincial regulators to investigate and deal with certain cases. Such a structure mobilizes local law enforcement forces and aims to form a joint anti-monopoly network.[10] Considering the immediate and massive feature of the introduction of digital businesses into a wide range of local jurisdictions, arguably, a consolidated and robust competition authority at the national level would function more effectively in tackling anti-competitive barriers associated with the exercise of administrative powers.

I.2 Legislation and Regulations on Administrative Monopoly in Digital Markets

During China's transition from a planned economy to a market economy, there have been a great number of market-orientated reforms, but administrative controls have still been retained in a wide range of economic sectors such as the aviation, automotive, energy, and medical industries. This control is demonstrated, to some extent, through the adoption of laws and regulations, as well as the implementation of specific administrative acts, which may have the effect of excluding or restricting market competition in the relevant sectors of the economy.[11] So, in pursuit of a unitary national market, China's Anti-Monopoly Law (AML) specifically devotes a chapter to regulating administrative monopolies, in addition to anticompetitive agreements, abuse of market dominance, and mergers with anticompetitive effects.

[8] In accordance with the Reform Programme of the State Council Institutions, which was approved at the first meeting of the Eleventh National People's Congress and Circular of the State Council on the Establishment of Institutions. See State Council, '国务院关于机构设置的通知 [State Council on the Establishment of Institutions]' (21 March 2008) <https://www.gov.cn/zhengce/content/2008-04/26/content_7621.htm> (accessed 9 April 2024).

[9] China Daily, 'Tighter Curbs on Monopoly to Ensure Fair Competition' (*China Daily*, 19 November 2021) <http://www.chinadaily.com.cn/a/202111/19/WS6196de0da310cdd39bc762b0.html> (accessed 2 October 2023).

[10] CPI (Competition Policy International), 'Year of the Rat: Antitrust in China' (2020) 3 Competition Policy International 11.

[11] J Cai and LJ Woon, 'Enforcing China's Anti-Monopoly Law in Regulated Industries: A Study of the Airline Industry' (2021) 9(3) Journal of Antitrust Enforcement 566, 574–584.

In particular, competition policy was formally included in the 2008 AML and further developed in Article 5 of the new AML. Articles 39–44 generally provide for several typical categories of anticompetitive behaviours conducted by administrative agencies or organizations authorized by laws or regulations to administer public affairs. Article 45 enlarges the scope of subjects conducting administrative behaviours so as to cover both governmental agencies and non-governmental organizations that are authorized by laws or regulations to administer public affairs (see Table 10.1).

To enforce the aforementioned rules, the AML and the Guidelines also specified the potential legal consequences of monopolistic administrative conducts. Articles 54 and 55 AML state that competition authorities shall initiate investigations, interview legal representatives or responsible persons of the accountable entity, and request a proposal of improvement measures regarding suspected monopolistic practices. Article 61 provides that internal discipline could be taken against responsible persons (albeit by their own superiors), aside from reports given to superior agencies by competition authorities. Chapter 5 of the Guidelines reiterates the function of competition authorities to investigate and advise. In general, these provisions are more instructive than punitive in nature.

However, for quite a long time, China's legislation on administrative monopoly did not pay attention to the digital economy. The major steps taken upon monopoly in the field of digital economy still target monopolistic behaviours of private platforms, and unregulated administrative monopoly is still at large. Nevertheless, the impact of administrative monopoly in the digital economy has been emerging. In particular, in economic sectors where digital businesses have a heavy physical presence in local jurisdictions and encounter resistance from incumbent offline competitors, or rely on access to scare resources controlled by governmental agencies, these agencies may take advantage of their administrative powers to set legal barriers for platform operators to obtain access to local markets or scare resources or to endorse government-backed organizations to conduct anticompetitive behaviours.[12] Administrative monopolies, of either kind, may occur when platform technologies and business models are applied to regulated industries, as is particularly evident in the sector of urban transportation services.

So far, China's legislative bodies have not perceived administrative monopolies in digital markets as a special hard nut to crack during the legislative process. This is largely because administrative monopolies in China have been unsettled in a good number of major economic sectors, directing the limelight towards legislation at the general level. Predictably, China's legislation and regulation may later be focused on other specific areas, including the digital economy.

[12] EC Ip and KK Hui Fai, 'Judicial Control of Local Protectionism in China: Antitrust Enforcement against Administrative Monopoly on the Supreme People's Court' (2017) 13(3) Journal of Competition Law and Economics 549.

Table 10.1 AML provisions on administrative monopolies in digital markets

AML 2008	AML 2022
	Article 5 (newly added provision) The state shall establish and improve a fair competition review system. In developing provisions involving the economic activities of market participants, administrative organs and organisations authorised by laws or regulations to administer public affairs shall conduct fair competition reviews.
Article 8 Administrative organs and organisations authorised by laws or regulations to administer public affairs shall not abuse their administrative powers to eliminate or restrict competition.	Article 10 Administrative organs and organisations authorised by laws or regulations to administer public affairs shall not abuse their administrative powers to eliminate or restrict competition.
Article 32 Administrative organs and organisations authorised by laws or regulations to administer public affairs shall not abuse their administrative powers to restrict, directly or in disguise, entities or individuals so that they may only deal in, purchase, or use the products supplied by operators designated by such organs and organisations.	Article 39 Administrative organs and organisations authorised by laws or regulations to administer public affairs shall not abuse their administrative powers to restrict, directly or in disguise, entities or individuals so that they may only deal in, purchase, or use the products supplied by operators designated by such organs and organisations.
	Article 40 (newly added provision) Administrative organs and organisations authorised by laws or regulations to administer public affairs shall not abuse their administrative powers by means such as signing cooperation agreements or memorandums with operators to obstruct other operators from entry into the relevant market or unequally treat other operators, eliminating or restricting competition.
Article 36 Administrative organs and organisations authorized by laws or regulations to administer public affairs shall not abuse their administrative powers to compel operators to engage in any monopolistic conduct specified by this Law.	Article 44 Administrative organs and organisations authorized by laws or regulations to administer public affairs shall not abuse their administrative powers to compel, *directly or in disguise,* operators to engage in any monopolistic conduct specified by this Law [emphasis added].
Article 37 Administrative organs shall not abuse their administrative powers to formulate any provisions containing elimination or restriction of competition.	Article 45 Administrative organs and *organisations authorised by laws or regulations to administer public affairs* shall not abuse their administrative powers to formulate any provisions containing elimination or restriction of competition [emphasis added].

Source: the translation of AML 2008 is excerpted from pkulaw.com with revisions, <https://pkulaw.com/en_law/503218397088141cbdfb.html>(accessed 7 July 2024); the translation of AML 2022 is excerpted from pkulaw.com with revisions, <https://pkulaw.com/en_law/d3236788421feacfbdfb.html> (accessed 7 July 2024).

In addition to the aforementioned provisions in the AML, the State Council, in 2016, enacted the 'Opinions of the State Council on Establishing a Fair Competition Examination System in the Building of the Market System' ('the Opinions').[13] Despite the emergence of the digital economy at that time, the Opinions did not bring the issue of administrative monopolies in digital markets to the table. However, the problem of administrative monopolies in digital markets has become increasingly significant since then. In 2021, the SAMR, the NDRC, the Ministry of Finance, MOFCOM, and the Ministry of Justice, alongside several other central regulatory agencies, issued the 'Detailed Rules for the Implementation of the Fair Competition Review System' ('the Detailed Rules').[14] In spite of the comprehensive nature of the Detailed Rules, their Article 13 paragraph 3 explicitly refers to the denial of access to platforms or networks due to the exercise of administrative powers. The backdrop against which the Detailed Rules were formulated also suggests that they serve as a general safeguard for the preservation of market competition against administrative powers in the very sector of China's digital economy.

Detailed Rules for the Implementation of the Fair Competition Review System
Article 13 Market access and exit standards:

(1) No unreasonable or discriminatory access and exit conditions may be set, including but not limited to:
   (a) setting access and exit conditions that are markedly unnecessary or beyond the actual need, which eliminate or restrict a business's participation in market competition;
   (b) setting unequal market access and exit conditions by unreasonable discriminatory treatment of businesses of different ownerships, from different regions or in different forms of organisation, without any basis in laws, administrative regulations, or provisions issued by the State Council;

[13] State Council, '国务院关于在市场体系建设中建立公平竞争审查制度的意见 [Opinions of the State Council on Establishing a Fair Competition Examination System in the Building of the Market System]' (1 June 2016) <https://www.gov.cn/zhengce/content/2016-06/14/content_5082066.htm> (accessed 3 October 2023). English version: State Council, '国务院关于在市场体系建设中建立公平竞争审查制度的意见 [Opinions of the State Council on Establishing a Fair Competition Examination System in the Building of the Market System]' (English translation) (1 June 2016) <https://www.pkulaw.com/en_law/a87136f6ba497fd7bdfb.html> (accessed 14 June 2024).

[14] SAMR, '市场监管总局等五部门关于印发《公平竞争审查制度实施细则》的通知 [Detailed Rules for the Implementation of the Fair Competition Review System]' (29 June 2021) <https://www.gov.cn/zhengce/zhengceku/2021-07/08/content_5623453.htm> (accessed 3 October 2023). English version: SAMR, '市场监管总局等五部门关于印发《公平竞争审查制度实施细则》的通知 [Detailed Rules for the Implementation of the Fair Competition Review System]' (English translation) (29 June 2021) <https://www.pkulaw.com/en_law/00db3f8e67b71091bdfb.html> (accessed 14 June 2024).

(c) setting, whether explicitly or in disguise, obstacles to market access, by recordation, registration, filing, catalog, annual inspection, annual reporting, production under supervision, recognition, certification, accreditation, inspection, testing, determination, designation, allotment, re-inspection, re-examination, replacement of license, or requirement of formation of branch offices, or any other form, without any basis in laws, administrative regulations, or provisions issued by the State Council;

(d) setting, whether explicitly or in disguise, obstacles to market exit, with respect to enterprise deregistration, bankruptcy, listing and transfer, and relocation, among others, without any basis in laws, administrative regulations, or provisions issued by the State Council; and

(e) compelling, whether explicitly or in disguise, enterprises to transfer technology, or setting, whether explicitly or in disguise, obstacles to market exit, by administrative licensing, administrative inspection, administrative penalties, administrative compulsion, or other means.

(2) No concession may be granted to a business without fair competition, including but not limited to:

(a) applying concession to a field of general competition or adding administrative licensing in the name of concession;

(b) failing to specify the term of concession or extending the term of concession without undergoing the statutory procedures;

(c) granting a concession to a particular business directly, instead of doing so in a competitive manner such as bidding or competitive negotiation; and

(d) setting discriminatory conditions to make it impossible for a business to fairly participating in the competition for a concession.

(3) No distribution, purchase, or use shall be limited to the goods or services from a particular business, including but not limited to:

(a) limiting distribution, purchase, or use to the goods or services provided by a particular business, whether explicitly or in disguise, by means such as an express requirement, hint, or refusal, delaying administrative approval, repeated inspections, denying access to a *platform or network*, or granting rewards and subsidies in violation of laws and regulations;

(b) limiting the location, form of ownership or form of organisation of a bidder in bidding or government procurement, or setting other unreasonable conditions to eliminate or restrict businesses' participation in bidding or government procurement activities; and

(c) precluding or restricting potential businesses' supply of goods or services by means such as creating unreasonable project banks, directories, pools of candidates, eligibility pools, or other conditions, without any basis in laws, administrative regulations, or provisions issued by the State Council.

(4) No approval procedures or procedures for prior recordation of an administrative approval nature may be set without any basis in laws, administrative regulations, or provisions issued by the State Council, including but not limited to:

(a) adding any administrative approval items or adding any processes of administrative approval or administrative approval conditions or procedures without any basis in laws, administrative regulations, or provisions issued by the State Council; and

(b) setting any procedures for prior recordation of an administrative approval nature without any basis in laws, administrative regulations, or provisions issued by the State Council.

(5) No approval procedures may be set for industries, fields, and business, among others, outside of a market access negative list, mainly meaning the restriction of market access, whether explicit or in disguise, by means such as prohibiting access or setting limitations on the qualifications of market participants, proportion of shares, scope of business, or business models, without any basis in laws, administrative regulations, or provisions issued by the State Council [emphasis added].[15]

Moreover, the State Council has recently decided to make a special state regulation so as to better implement the institution of fair competition review stipulated in Article 5 of the new AML, on the one hand, and, on the other hand, integrate the fragmented, low-level provisions on fair competition review into a single, high-level state regulation. On 12 May 2024, the SAMR published (in the role of the drafting organ on behalf of the State Council) the draft Regulation on Fair Competition Review for public opinions.[16] Indeed, what the draft regulation includes are still general rules on the prohibition of setting 'unreasonable or discriminatory access or exit conditions or obstacles', and it does not refer to specific matters associated with digital markets. Heightening pertinent provisions to the level of state regulation may, however, by itself improve the authority of these

[15] The translation of the Detailed Rules is excerpted from pkulaw.com with minor revisions: SAMR, 'Detailed Rules for the Implementation of the Fair Competition Review System' (English translation) (n14).

[16] SAMR, '市场监管总局关于《公平竞争审查条例（征求意见稿）》公开征求意见的公告 [Announcement of the State Administration for Market Regulation on Requesting Public Comments on the Regulation on Fair Competition Review (Draft for Public Opinions)]' (12 May 2023) <https://www.samr.gov.cn/hd/zjdc/art/2023/art_647feda81bb249a5981a18c7e5efd4d2.html> (accessed 3 October 2023). English version: SAMR, '市场监管总局关于《公平竞争审查条例（征求意见稿）》公开征求意见的公告 [Announcement of the State Administration for Market Regulation on Requesting Public Comments on the Regulation on Fair Competition Review (Draft for Public Opinions)]' (12 May 2023) <https://www.pkulaw.com/en_law/d713af4239291d827ec31f070b8b2980bdfb.html> (accessed 14 June 2024).

provisions, 'further strengthening the process of fair competition review and curbing local protectionism and administrative monopolies'.[17]

Regulation on Fair Competition Review (Draft for Public Opinions)
Article 12
The policy making authority shall not develop any policy or measure containing any of the following content that restricts market access and exit:
(1) Setting or setting in disguise approval procedures for industries, fields, and business, among others, other than those listed in the negative list of market access.
(2) Illegally establishing or granting a franchise without fair competition.
(3) Restricting or restricting in disguise others' operation, purchase, or use of the goods or services to those provided by specific business entities (hereinafter collectively referred to as the 'goods').
(4) Setting other unreasonable or discriminatory access or exit conditions or obstacles.[18]

At the same time, the NDRC, nicknamed the 'mini State Council',[19] issued the 'Notice Circular on the Establishment of a System for Collecting and Notifying Cases of Violation of the Negative List for Market Access' on 19 November 2021, and also announced the first batch of typical cases of violation of the Negative List for Market Access, including suspected administrative monopolies.[20] In addition to that, the General Office of the State Council issued the 'Opinions on Further Optimizing the Business Environment and Reducing the Institutional Transaction Costs of Market Entities' ('the Opinions on Transaction Costs of Market Entities').[21] It clearly called for 'further eliminating latent thresholds, promoting

[17] SAMR, 'Announcement of the State Administration for Market Regulation on Requesting Public Comments on the Regulation on Fair Competition Review (Draft for Public Opinions)' (n16); SAMR, 'Announcement of the State Administration for Market Regulation on Requesting Public Comments on the Regulation on Fair Competition Review (Draft for Public Opinions)' (English translation) (n16).

[18] The translation of the Regulation on Fair Competition Review (Draft for Public Opinions) is excerpted from pkulaw.com with minor revisions: SAMR, 'Announcement of the State Administration for Market Regulation on Requesting Public Comments on the Regulation on Fair Competition Review (Draft for Public Opinions) (English translation) (n16).

[19] In China, the NDRC is generally referred to as the 'Mini State Council' and is responsible for formulating national development and reform policies in various economic areas and therefore a more powerful central government department than area-specific central authorities.

[20] NDRC, '国家发展改革委关于建立违背市场准入负面清单案例归集和通报制度的通知 [Notice Circular on the Establishment of a System for Collecting and Notifying Cases of Violation of the Negative List for Market Access]' (19 November 2021) <https://www.gov.cn/zhengce/zhengceku/2021-12/16/content_5661450.htm> (accessed 9 April 2024).

[21] General Office of the State Council, '国务院办公厅关于进一步优化营商环境降低市场主体制度性交易成本的意见 [Opinions of the General Office of the State Council on Further Optimizing the Business Environment and Reducing the Institutional Transaction Costs of Market Entities]' (7 September 2022) <https://www.gov.cn/zhengce/content/2022-09/15/content_5709962.htm> (accessed 9 April 2024).

the reduction of access costs for market players', and 'effectively protecting fair competition for market players, and taking special actions to curb the abuse of administrative power to exclude and restrict competition'. The Notice issued by the NDRC, alongside the 'Opinions on Transaction Costs of Market Entities', has led to the release of a series of typical cases of violation of the 'Negative List for Market Access', including a good number of cases regarding an administrative monopoly in sharing-bike markets.[22]

It is also likely that the SAMR will introduce specific regulations under the current legal framework to pointedly address administrative monopolies in digital markets.

In a state like China, where robust governmental regulations and the promotion of market competition are intertwined, the exercise of administrative power has good potential to restrict or eliminate market competition.[23] Therefore, it is vital to apprehend how administrative powers contribute to a market monopoly and are tackled by competition authorities. Against the above backdrop of Chinese laws and regulations on administrative monopolies in digital markets, the remainder of this chapter primarily reflects on how such laws and regulations have been implemented in China's e-hailing market and bike-sharing industry. After providing the socio-economic and technological background for the occurrence of monopolistic administration in these sectors, we introduce and comment on the enforcement measures adopted at different levels to rectify these monopolies.

II. The Case of E-Hailing Regulations

Although there is no specific legislation on administrative monopolies in the digital economy, recently, such monopolies have frequently emerged in practice. In parallel to the campaign to strengthen anti-monopoly enforcement against private platforms, in recent years, China's competition authorities have also accelerated the pace with which anti-monopoly law is enforced against administrative misconduct. The problem of administrative monopoly has been more obvious in the industry of e-hailing taxis, as transportation has always been highly regulated in China. The taxi industry in China was state-owned or collectively owned from 1978 to about 1991 and was subject to stringent approval by the transportation

[22] General Office of the NDRC, '国家发展改革委办公厅关于违背市场准入负面清单典型案例（第四批）的通报 [Circular of the General Office of the National Development and Reform Commission on Typical Cases of Violation of the Negative List for Market Access (Fourth Batch)]' (28 October 2022) <https://www.gov.cn/zhengce/zhengceku/2022-11/10/content_5725955.htm> (accessed 9 April 2024).

[23] Y Huang and Z Deng, '论规制行政垄断的我国〈反垄断法〉特色—兼论行政垄断的政治与经济体制根源 [On the Character of China Anti-Monopoly Law under Controlling Administrative Monopoly]' (2010) 7 Law Science Magazine 50.

authorities. Since 1991, the government has gradually allowed more private investment to enter into this industry, relaxing governmental control thereof.[24]

Before the emergence of e-hailing platforms, the regulatory authorities in charge of transportation were busy with enforcing the legal requirement against unlicensed taxis in response to the petition for sound business environments from licensed taxi drivers.[25] And the illegal nature of unlicensed taxis had availed transportation regulators with solid statutory ground and a high moral standing to detect and punish violating drivers. Nevertheless, the immediate introduction of e-hailing cars into the taxi market quickly changed the landscape of taxi market competition and administrative regulation.

Below, we first look into the social pressures exerted by conventional taxi drivers that drove local governments to adopt anticompetitive regulatory policies for e-hailing taxi service providers. Second, we sketch out the typical regulatory policies that unequally restricted e-hailing taxi service providers' entry into China's taxi service market. Then, we discuss the measures taken at different levels to tackle such administrative monopolies and evaluate their effectiveness.

II.1 Incumbents' Petition for Protectionist Regulation

The emergence of e-hailing cars (and platform business generally) in taxi markets has largely blurred the boundary between legally licensed taxis and illegal ones. E-hailing cars have been increasingly regarded as a welcoming force of competition against incumbent taxi drivers in China's taxi market. On the other hand, the immediate introduction of e-hailing cars into the taxi market has quickly taken over a large share of riding orders from traditional taxi drivers and brought about unprecedented competitive pressure thereon.

In particular, a large group of traditional taxi drivers that invested, in one way or another, a large amount into traditional taxi licences have suffered from drastic depreciation of the market value of licences due to the burgeoning of e-hailing services. The amplified voice of the entrenched incumbents, in forms like petitions, mass protests, and the blocking of roads, has significantly affected local e-hailing regulations, pressurizing local authorities into passing protectionist regulations in their favour.[26] Then, the legal problem of administrative monopoly arose when

[24] Y Sun, '出租车行业政府规制政策变迁轨迹与逻辑—基于间断-均衡理论的解释 [On Changing of the Government Regulations and Policies in Taxi Industry and Its Logic: An Interpretation Based on Intermittent-Equilibrium Theory]' (2021) 34(4) Huxiang Forum 105, 110–113.

[25] State Council, '关于开展打击《黑车》等非法营运专项整治行动的实施方案 [Enforcement Plan to Punish Illegal Operations Including Unlicensed Taxis]' (23 May 2006) <https://www.gov.cn/govweb/gzdt/2006-05/26/content_292364.htm> (accessed 9 April 2024).

[26] L Wang, '共享经济下网约车监管的法律问题研究 [A Study on the Legal Issues of the Regulation of Online Rides in the Sharing Economy]' (2020) 47(2) Seeking Truth 120, 124.

local transportation authorities chose to formulate extraordinarily stringent measures against e-hailing cars.[27]

Actually, the possibility of adopting unfairly stringent measures by local transportation authorities is high in China since the maintenance of social stability is an imperative concern to Chinese governments, at both the central and local levels. In particular, those local governments that have not yet devised effective strategies to deal with the pressures from incumbent taxi drivers are more likely to employ multiple regulatory instruments to inhibit the quick expansion of e-hailing businesses.

II.2 Local Anticompetitive Measures on E-Hailing Taxi Services

The most straightforward way of inhibiting e-hailing cars is to simply impose a quota stipulating the maximum number of vehicles available on platforms.[28] In addition, a good number of cities, including mega cities like Beijing and Shanghai, have imposed a residential requirement requiring e-hailing drivers to have a local *hukou* (permanent local residency).[29] Obtaining a local *hukou* in populated cities is, however, not easy for the majority of e-hailing taxi drivers since most of them are migrant workers coming from other regions, especially economically underdeveloped regions. Thus, the residential requirement constitutes a very high threshold for new entrants to legally access local taxi markets, serving to protect incumbent taxi drivers.

Among many other regulatory measures, the technical requirements for the classes of e-hailing vehicle (e.g. size, fuel efficiency, and purchase price), which are apparently higher than those for traditional taxis, have also put e-hailing taxi service providers in a disadvantageous position in terms of obtaining equal access to these local taxi markets. Some cities require that only limousines are qualified to provide e-hailing car services, and other cities exclude economy vehicles from such services by restricting the vehicle length and wheelbase of e-hailing cars.[30]

[27] Interviews with officials from the Qingdao Bureau of Transportation (29 August 2019, Qingdao).

[28] For example, in 2016, the city of Lanzhou in Gansu Province adopted such a system. See J Liu, '兰州拟限定网约车数量 专家争议政策合理 [Lanzhou Planning to Limit the Number of E-Hailing Cars, Experts Dispute the Rationality of the Policy]' (16 August 2016) <https://china.caixin.com/2016-08-16/100978004.html> (accessed 17 July 2022).

[29] J Yu, '上海出租车非沪籍司机超三成？交委：正研究放宽政策 [The Number of Non-Shanghainese Taxi Drivers May Exceed 30 Per Cent in Shanghai, the Competent Authorities Studying to Moderately Relax Territorial Restrictions]' (China News, 24 June 2019) <https://baijiahao.baidu.com/s?id=1637212786052313659&wfr=spider&for=pc > (accessed 30 October 2024).

[30] Also, the city of Wuhan requires that the price of an e-hailing car should be no less than ¥120k, a standard higher than traditional taxis. As explained by then vice-director of Wuhan Traffic and Transportation Commission, Sun Jiang, 'by stipulating that the price of the vehicle must be over ¥120k, we intend to encourage more high-end vehicles to enter the e-hailing market. See Hubei Daily, '武汉网约车"新政"下周实施 车辆总价要求12万以上 [Wuhan's New Policy on E-Hailing Cars Will Come into Force Next Week, Requiring the Price of the Car Be More than ¥120k]' (15 April 2017) <https://www.hubei.gov.cn/zxjy/rdhy/201704/t20170415_1764294.shtml> (accessed 8 April 2024).

Also, the requirement that the fares collected by e-hailing cars shall exceed certain minimum standards, normally materially higher than those collected by traditional taxi drivers, also serves to heighten the bar for e-hailing taxis to access taxi markets.

At the same time, from an enforcement perspective, local transportation authorities have several tactics of manipulating law enforcement in response to complaints from traditional taxi drivers. One way is to keep silent on the legal status of e-hailing taxis, which was a common practice in the early days of the introduction of this new form of urban transportation service into taxi markets. While regulations on e-hailing platforms were absent, e-hailing taxis could be simply and arbitrarily deemed unlicensed and illegal, and therefore they incurred punishment from transportation regulatory agencies.[31] Also, authorities tasked with enforcing transportation law can either increase the frequency of inspections or acquiesce in the operation of e-hailing businesses through law enforcement.[32]

Actually, before the emergence of e-hailing car services, the condition and service quality of traditional taxis in many cities had long been cause for complaint by passengers. E-hailing car services were immediately welcomed by passengers, largely because of the capability of e-hailing platforms in regard to improving the supply of service providers, the easiness of hailing a car, the relatively lower charges, and the differentiated classes of rider services.[33] The aforementioned regulatory measures imposed on e-hailing taxis by local governments can hardly be justified on the ground of protecting consumer's safety, as transportation authorities have often argued.[34] Instead, they have been widely regarded as an unreasonable limitation for e-hailing taxi service providers to fairly obtain access to taxi markets and compete with incumbent players therein.[35] These regulatory measures, in effect, have not only prevented the whole taxi service market from being innovated with new technologies but also been detrimental to the promotion of passengers' riding choices and transportation welfare.

[31] WC Kirby et al, 'Uber in China: Driving in the Gray Zone' (Harvard Business School Case, January 2016) <https://www.hbs.edu/faculty/Pages/item.aspx?num=50436> (accessed 20 July 2022).

[32] The law enforcement division of the Qingdao Bureau of Transport, for instance, intensified its inspections of e-hailing cars and launched a 100-day random inspection campaign in the downtown area from February to May 2019. See Keke, '青岛市区出租车百日专项整治 网约车也在整治之列 [The 100-Day Special Rectification of Taxis in Qingdao Urban Area, E-Hailing Cars Included]' (15 February 2019) <https://baijiahao.baidu.com/s?id=1625496685514006418&wfr=spider&for=p> (accessed 17 July 2022).

[33] There are certainly shortcomings of e-hailing taxi services, including the abuse of market dominance by major e-hailing platforms, among many other problems. Nonetheless, these shortcomings do not change the overall nature of its great potential in promoting competition in taxi markets and improving the riding convenience of passengers.

[34] For example, Lanzhou required e-hailing taxis to be 1.5 times as expensive as regular taxis, to 'protect consumer rights and interests'. See W Jang, '兰州降低网约车准入门槛 [Lanzhou Lowers Its Thresholds on E-Hailing]' (21 September 2017) <http://it.people.com.cn/n1/2017/0921/c1009-29550869.html> (accessed 9 April 2024).

[35] See J Cai, 'The Sharing Economy and China's Antimonopoly Law: From the Didi Case to Regulatory Challenges' (2020) 28 Asia Pacific Law Review 159, 172–173.

II.3 Attempts to Tackle Anticompetitive Measures

In spite of the contested stands on the orientation to regulate e-hailing taxis between the transportation authority and the competition authority,[36] the latter authority, alongside other central powers, has indeed made attempts, in one way or another, to repeal some of these anticompetitive measures for the development of a unified market in China.[37]

The first type of such attempt is the enforcement of the fair competition review system against local administrative measures that are apparently anticompetitive to e-hailing car service providers. On the ground of the Opinion, one of the regulatory agencies for market competition, then the Anti-Monopoly Bureau in the NDRC, initiated multiple investigations over the years into the regulatory measures for e-hailing in cities like Lanzhou and Quanzhou, which were suspected of violating the Price Law and the AML.[38] Through internal supervisory procedures, the Anti-Monopoly Bureau in the NDRC urged local regulators to repeal the measures that were found to be anticompetitive or in violation of national legislation.

More specifically, Quanzhou city promulgated its local measures on 19 October 2016, namely the 'Detailed Provisions on Management of Operations and Services of E-Hailing Taxis of Quanzhou City',[39] while the city of Lanzhou released its e-hailing regulation on 24 March 2017.[40] A quota restraint on e-hailing taxis was not a common practice owing to its apparent anticompetitive nature and susceptibility

[36] The central transportation authority, the Ministry of Transport, has long shown a conservative stand on the regulation of e-hailing taxis, primarily stressing the necessity of taking various stringent measures for the purpose of maintaining the stability of the whole taxi market and protecting passengers' safety. Nonetheless, many of these measures do not really work to these ends, but bring anti-competitive barriers to new entrants to taxi markets. See B Xiong, '专车拼车管制新探 [Regulating the Peer-to-Peer Transport Service in China: A Perspective from Law and Economics]' [2016] 10(2) Tsinghua University Law Journal 131. Experts Debated the New Regulations Enacted by the Ministry of Transport, and Officials of the Ministry of Transport Responded to the Doubts. See Weiwen, 专家激辩交通部专车新规，交通部官员回应质疑 [Experts debate the Ministry of Transport special car new regulations Ministry of Transport officials respond to questions] (16 October 2015) < https://www.sohu.com/a/35904982_115250 > (accessed 17 July 2022).

[37] J Cai (n35), 177–178.

[38] Guangming Daily, '光明网评论员：落实公平竞争审查，从网约车细则开始 [Implementing Fair Competition Review, Starting with the Concrete Rules on E-Hailing Cars]' (13 November 2017) <https://baijiahao.baidu.com/s?id=1583922156448101294&wfr=spider&for=pc> (accessed 25 August 2022).

[39] Quanzhou Transportation Provisions, '关于印发泉州市网络预约出租汽车经营服务管理实施细则的通知 [Announcement of Issuing the Detailed Provisions on Management of Operations and Services of E-Hailing Taxis of Quanzhou City]' (10 October 2016) <http://jjzd.quanzhou.gov.cn/jtfg/201610/t20161031_408559.htm> (accessed 8 April 2024) (Quanzhou Provisions).

[40] Lanzhou Municipal People's Government, '兰州市人民政府办公厅关于印发兰州市网络预约出租汽车经营服务管理实施细则(试行)的通知 [Announcement of the General Office of the Lanzhou Municipal People's Government on Issuing the Detailed Provisions for the Management of E-Hailing Taxi Operations and Services in Lanzhou (Trial)]' (24 March 2017) <https://www.lawlawing.com/community/380412> (accessed 8 April 2024) (Lanzhou Provisions).

to competition law enforcement.[41] Lanzhou's quota on e-hailing cars, for example, was investigated by the anti-trust division of the NDRC in December 2017.[42] Nonetheless, there was a wide range of other requirements that were regarded as anticompetitive local policies, including the minimum purchase price of the vehicle, the technical specifications of the vehicle, and the residency of the driver.[43] Both cities forbade drivers from signing on to multiple platforms at the same time.[44] The Lanzhou document even required the driver to provide the consumer with phone chargers, tissues, umbrellas, and a wireless connection, which were hardly seen among the regulatory measures for traditional taxis.[45] Quanzhou stated that e-hailing vehicles had to carry positioning devices that supported BeiDou Satellite (BDS) navigation.[46] Quanzhou city also had an unreasonably high insurance threshold (¥1 million for motor vehicle third-party liability insurance, and ¥0.5 million for carrier liability insurance).[47] According to a local taxi driver, these requirements made it almost impossible for existing e-hailing drivers to comply without changing to a new car, which placed a heavy financial burden on them.[48]

Due to the pressure from the NDRC, Quanzhou and Lanzhou revised their provisions on e-hailing regulation before the investigation went through.[49] The requirements regarding the price of the vehicles were lowered, and the residency requirement for drivers was also relaxed.[50] The requirement for BDS positioning devices was abolished and replaced by any positioning device conforming to the national standard.[51] Other unreasonable rules, like the Internet connectivity

[41] Capping the number of e-hailing cars may also exacerbate existing problems of transit inequality, especially for outer borough residents, who suffer from inadequate access to transportation. See KA Laurie, 'Capping Uber in New York City: Ramifications for Rideshares, the Road, and Outer-Borough Residents' (2019) 46 Fordham Urban Law Journal 942, 1002.

[42] Quanzhou City adopted the rule to review e-hailing platforms' offline service capabilities by itself, whereas the Ministry of Transport specified that online service capability should be evaluated and certified by the provincial transport authorities where the platform company is registered. See Quanzhou Municipal People's Government, '泉州发放首张网约车平台经营许可证 [Quanzhou Issued the First Online Car-Hailing Platform Business Licence]' (15 February 2017) <http://www.quanzhou.gov.cn/zfb/xxgk/zfxxgkzl/qzdt/qzyw/201702/t20170215_422995.htm> (accessed 12 October 2022).

[43] R Cai, '泉州、兰州率先重订网约车细则， 下一个是谁？ [Quanzhou and Lanzhou First Amends E-Hailing Provisions, Who's Next?]' (10 November 2017) <https://cj.sina.com.cn/article/detail/5992589948/475742> (accessed 8 April 2024).

[44] Article 25 of Quanzhou Provisions (n39); Article 30 of Lanzhou Provisions (n40).

[45] Article 23 of Lanzhou Provisions, (n40).

[46] Article 12 of Quanzhou Provisions (n39).

[47] *Ibid*, Article 7.

[48] Z Cheng, '泉州调整地方网约车细则 [Quanzhou City Adjusted Detailed Provisions for Online Hailing]' (20 September 2017) <https://jtyst.fujian.gov.cn/zwgk/jtyw/mtsy/201709/t20170928_439039.htm> (accessed 30 October 2024).

[49] *Ibid.*

[50] *Ibid.*

[51] The original Quanzhou Provisions stipulated that the positioning device on the vehicle had to support positioning by BDS, which was repealed in the amended version. See Quanzhou City Transportation Commission, '关于印发调整完善泉州市网络预约出租汽车经营服务管理实施细则的通知 [Announcement of Issuing the Amended Detailed Provisions on Management of Operations and Services of E-Hailing Taxis of Quanzhou City]' (21 September 2017), para 3 <http://www.

requirement and the prohibition on e-hailing car drivers picking up ride orders from multiple platforms, were also deleted.[52] Moreover, Quanzhou also lowered its insurance requirement and allowed more used cars into the market.[53]

The second type of attempt to repeal some of the anticompetitive measures was made by an interior body of China's National People's Congress, which was established recently to record and review the constitutionality of certain central and local regulations, namely the Office for Recording and Reviewing Regulations at the Legislative Affairs Commission of the National People's Congress Standing Committee ('the Office for Recording and Reviewing Regulations'). Since 2019, the Office for Recording and Reviewing Regulations has reviewed the *hukou* requirements for e-hailing drivers in multiple cities and decided that these requirements violate China's labour law and national policies on the promotion of labour mobility and demanded the correction thereof.[54] Although these anticompetitive measures have been repealed, not by the competition authority and not on the ground of the AML, such an attempt, in effect, has broken the unreasonable barriers to fair competition in taxi markets. Hence, in a broader sense, it has served as an enrichment for the channel of competition law enforcement against administrative monopoly in China.

II.4 Assessing the Enforcement against Administrative Monopoly

Despite these attempts to promote competition in China's taxi markets, the effects of this enforcement against administrative monopolies in taxi markets cannot be overblown. After all, the Anti-Monopoly Bureau in the NDRC failed to advance the fair competition investigations into the e-hailing regulatory regimes in many other cities. Likewise, the Office for Recording and Reviewing Regulations did not initiate a thorough review of all local measures on residential requirements, especially those measures that are still in effect in mega cities like Beijing and Shanghai.

It is, first of all, worth noting that the monopolistic situation in China's taxi markets before the introduction of e-hailing taxis took place against quite a special historical background and therefore cannot be easily resolved before mapping out the anticompetitive obstacles formed historically. As aforementioned, the licences for

quanzhou.gov.cn/zfb/xxgk/zfxxgkzl/fgwj/sfggz/201709/t20170921_535530.htm> (accessed 9 April 2024) (Amendment of Quanzhou Provisions).

52 See Amendment of Quanzhou Provisions (n51), para 6.

53 Amendment of Quanzhou Provisions, (n51), paras 4, 5.

54 D Wu, '没有本地户籍开不了出租车？ 属于就业歧视！ 全国人大出手纠正 [Can't Drive a Taxi Without a Local Household Registration? It Is Employment Discrimination! National People's Congress Should Correct]' (20 January 2021) <https://news.southcn.com/node_179d29f1ce/68e99e9c25.shtml> (accessed 17 July 2022).

traditional taxis have gradually become a form of property of their holders,[55] especially taxi drivers, ever since local governments decided to allocate taxi licences through bidding systems or other profit-seeking methods. Even if many taxi licences are held in the name of taxi companies instead of individual taxi drivers, the latter have still become the real licence holders because of companies' various tactics, including long-term subleasing, to transfer these licences to individual drivers.

In cities where taxi licences were legally permitted to be traded, the investments thereon from licence holders became even higher. For many taxi licence holders, their livelihoods were suddenly suffocated by the immediate introduction of massive competitors into taxi markets. Thus, taxi licence holders are dealing with enormously high stakes in exerting pressure on local governments to adopt stronger regulations against the immediate introduction of large numbers of new entrants into taxi markets.

There are, indeed, local governments that have found their own way of compensating adversely affected taxi licence holders so as to mitigate the impacts from e-hailing taxis thereon and diminish the pressure from the incumbents.[56] The local governments in some cities, like Taiyuan and Shenzhen, have sound fiscal conditions and chose to provide monetary or non-monetary subsidies to the adversely affected incumbents. Several other local governments, like Chengdu and Hangzhou, refunded the bidding fees for licences to taxi licence holders.

Nonetheless, the fiscal conditions of many cities do not avail their local governments of the ability to provide sufficient compensation to adversely affected taxi licence holders so as to effectively exchange the opportunity for an environment for adopting lenient regulatory measures on e-hailing taxis and fostering competitive taxi markets. Predictably, the demands from the central competition authority could hardly be materially complied with by these local administrations, and instead, they had to find effective strategies to prevent social instability because of traditional taxi drivers' resistance.

Furthermore, the maintenance of social stability in certain regions, especially in mega cities like Beijing and Shanghai, is of paramount concern for the central government and the whole society in China. For example, although the Office of Regulation Record and Review demanded that cities, including Wuhan and Kunming, remove the residency requirement, similar provisions in the mega cities

[55] For a general argument for the property nature of taxi licences, see KM Wyman, 'Problematic Private Property: The Case of New York Taxicab Medallions' (2013) 30 Yale Journal on Regulation 125, 135–136. See also KM Wyman, 'The New Essentialism in Property' (2017) 9 Journal of Legal Analysis 183.

[56] It is theoretically controversial as to whether it is economically efficient to provide compensation to adversely affected taxi licence holders. See KM Wyman, 'Taxi Regulation in the Age of Uber' (2017) 2(1) New York University Journal of Legislation and Public Policy 1, 84–98; RA Epstein, 'Innovation and Inequality: The Separability Thesis' (2016) 39(1) Harvard Journal of Law and Public Policy 17.

Beijing and Shanghai remain in place.[57] The tension between social stability and market competition in these regions has possibly gone beyond the capacity of the competition authority. Simply pressurizing local transportation officials in these regions to immediately remove regulatory measures that are suspected of being anticompetitive does not actually address the problem.

Similar cases of administrative monopoly have taken place in other markets closely associated with digital platforms over the years as well, where local governments or sectoral regulatory agencies have stood in favour of incumbent market players and excluded the entrance of newly emerging competitive players. For example, the Ministry of Industry and Information Technology once suspended the voice-call services provided by social media apps like Dingding and WeChat in response to resistance from traditional telecommunication operators. The voice-call service provided by these apps significantly diminished the revenue of telecommunication companies.[58] However, such cases of monopoly were far less thorny and easier to handle than the taxi/e-hailing one. The reason is that the introduction of e-hailing has substantially threatened the actual livelihoods of a large number of taxi drivers, causing them to act collectively, which may well raise local stability concerns.

Consequently, the actual landscape of competition in a region is not merely determined by general principles of competition law and economic policies laid down by the central competition authority. It is, instead, determined by the dynamics among concrete concerns, including social stability, prior policies, economic growth, and evaluation from superior authorities.

III. The Case of Bike-Sharing Regulations

III.1 The Emergence of China's Bike-Sharing Industry

The bike-sharing market in China has witnessed another wave of competition law enforcement against administrative monopolies. The history of China's sharing

[57] Article 8 of the 'Detailed Provisions on the Management and Operation of Online Hailed Taxis in Beijing', and Article 9 of 'Several Provisions on the Management and Operation of Online Hailed Taxis in Shanghai' provide that only a person with a permanent local residency can qualify as an e-hailing driver. These articles are still in force on 5 October 2023. The Detailed Provisions and Several Provisions are available at Beijing Municipal Commission of Transport, '北京市网络预约出租汽车经营服务管理实施细则 [Beijing Network Booking Taxi Service Management Implementation Rules]' (16 August 2022) <https://cz.jtw.beijing.gov.cn/ggl/20161221/1482296745211_1.html>; and Shanghai Municipal Transport Commission, '上海市网络预约出租汽车经营服务管理若干规定 [Several Provisions on the Administration of Online Booking Taxi Business Services in Shanghai]' (21 December 2016) <https://jtw.sh.gov.cn/zsk/20210609/0bf46d4e4f514eafb9f0ce2eec3f28e4.html> (both accessed 9 April 2024).

[58] F Wang, '工信部叫停网络通话 影响的可不只是钉钉和微信 [The Ministry of Industry and Information Technology Suspending Voice Calls, Affecting More Than Just Dingding and WeChat]' (25 June 2016) <https://www.jiemian.com/article/713764.html> (accessed 8 April 2024).

economy can be traced back to the mid-2000s, when digital platforms and mobile payment technologies developed rapidly. In 2010, a series of sharing economy platforms emerged in transportation markets, such as car-sharing platforms, laying the foundation for the emergence of the bike-sharing business.

Before the existence of Internet-based shared bikes, Beijing pioneered the introduction of docked public bikes in 2007.[59] These bikes could only be rented and returned at designated docking stations, which somewhat limited the user's flexibility and convenience. Due to the shortage of service quality and commercial promotion for public bikes, as well the high construction cost, the response from both the urban management authorities and consumers was largely lukewarm.

Nonetheless, with the wide introduction of smart phones and digital platforms, the business environment has undergone tremendous changes, leading the sharing economy into a new era. Ever since 2010, companies based on the sharing economy such as Zhihu, Didi Chuxing, Xiaozhu Short-Term Rental, E-Daixi, and 58 Daojia, have emerged one after another, greatly changing the landscape of shared bikes.[60] In 2014, several graduates from Peking University founded Ofo, aiming to solve the problem of the inconvenience of short-distance commuting in urban areas. By May 2015, over 2,000 Ofo shared bikes had been introduced onto Peking University (PKU) campus. These PKU graduates subsequently expanded their service into seven other capital universities and won great popularity from campus users, marking the beginning of the bike-sharing industry in China.

In the early days, sharing bikes were launched in top-tier cities like Beijing, Shanghai, and Guangzhou. Shared bike platforms, taking advantage of smart locks and global positioning system (GPS) technology, achieve dockless parking and allow users to rent and return bikes anytime and anywhere. This provides a perfect answer to the 'last mile problems' during peak commuting hours. China's high population density creates a substantial demand for shared bikes, leading to great potential for the bike-sharing market. The commercial landscape of shared bikes has gradually expanded to other cities, including Chengdu, Hangzhou, Shenzhen, Suzhou, and Nanjing.

To capture a larger market share, sharing-bike platforms employ a considerable workforce to transport and redistribute bikes to key transportation hubs and important commuting intersections. However, such ambitious expansions often lead to excessive deployment and squeeze the limited public space in urban arenas, hence incurring inconvenience to public walking and urban traffic management.

[59] J Wang, '浅谈共享经济发展现状存在的问题及解决措施 [Discussion on the Existing Problems and Solutions of the Development Status of Sharing Economy]' (2020) (21) Inner Mongolia Coal Economy 90.

[60] Y Guo and J Chen, '共享经济的发展历程、分类及商业模式研究 [Research on the Development History, Classification and Business Model of the Sharing Economy]' (2020) 16(9) Science and Technology for Development 1027.

At one time, the number of bike-sharing platforms in Beijing alone reached 16, with over more than 2.35 million bikes on the streets, far exceeding the actual demands of riders.[61] In response, the Beijing Municipal Government carried out administrative interviews with platform enterprises that provided bike-sharing services, requiring these enterprises, on the one hand, to establish parking areas and no-parking zones in a reasonable manner, and, on the other hand, to improve the capacity of user management. User credit management was thus incorporated into the assessment of enterprise service quality, fostering a more equitable market environment.

Nonetheless, with local urban management authorities increasingly intervening in the operation of the bike-sharing business, anticompetitive regulatory measures began to loom large.

III.2 Major Anticompetitive Measures in Bike-Sharing Markets

While big cities like Beijing tended only to guide and regulate the market without imposing anticompetitive measures on bike-sharing platforms, regulatory measures of an anticompetitive nature appeared in some second- and third-tier cities. In extreme cases, anticompetitive measures were imposed to protect the interests of local market players, including state-owned enterprises. In the first type of anticompetitive measure, the Chenggong District of Kunming once prohibited all sharing-bike-platform enterprises except for the Kunming Public Bike Operation and Management Limited Liability Company (a wholly state-owned subsidiary of the Kunming Public Transportation Group) from providing sharing bike services in its district.[62] This policy was adopted against the backdrop of the declining business of public transportation operated by Kunming Group of Public Transportation. Due to adopting such a restrictive policy, the local administration of transportation had to make up for the growing gap between the declining business revenue of the state-owned transportation company and its surplus personnel over the years.[63]

The second type of anticompetitive measure widely employed by local urban management authorities is to cap the number of platform operators that can obtain

[61] B Fang and L Ran, '北京治理共享单车的加减法 [Addition and Subtraction in Beijing's Governance of Shared Bikes]' (13 October 2022) <https://baijiahao.baidu.com/s?id=17465098136852384978&wfr=spider&for=pc> (accessed 9 November 2024).

[62] M Liu, '红星调查：共享单车市场迎来变局， 各地被要求破除垄断 [Red Star Investigation: Bike-Sharing Market Sees Changes as Localities Are Asked to Break Up Monopolies]' (22 November 2022) <https://new.qq.com/rain/a/20221122A0006B00> (accessed 8 April 2024).

[63] Yn House, '云南房网：昆明公交垄断呈贡共享单车业务被叫停， 另一霸王合同也得解除[Kunming Transit Monopoly in Chenggong Bike-Sharing Business Was Called Off, and Another Overbearing Contract Got Rescinded]' (18 November 2022) <https://www.ynhouse.com/news/view-252554.html> (accessed 8 April 2024).

permission to provide bike-sharing services. Local urban management authorities have limited operating permissions in different ways, such as public bidding, competitive negotiations, and the like. For instance, Gaomi Urban Management Bureau selected a single enterprise as the exclusive bike-sharing operator through an open bidding process and entered into a five-year contract with it, which, in essence, was no different from excluding and restricting other qualified bicycle-sharing enterprises with competence and service capability from entering the local market.[64] Similarly, Cangzhou Urban Management Bureau identified one operator as the exclusive bike-sharing operator within a two-year cooperation period by means of competitive negotiation. The Bureau also promised the identified operator an extension of the cooperation contract if the bike-sharing service proved satisfactory, essentially reinforcing the anticompetitive nature of the administrative measures on the bike-sharing business.[65]

The third type of anticompetitive measure is to cap the number of sharing bikes that can be deployed in urban areas, rather than the number of sharing-bike platforms. For example, in December 2020, Cangzhou Urban Management Bureau conducted competitive negotiations and selections in the management of sharing bikes. During this process, the agency claimed that the city could only accommodate around 12,000 sharing bikes due to its scale and population. According to its announcement, which was later refuted by the competition authorities, allowing multiple service providers to offer bike-sharing services in the city may result in resource waste and be burdensome for urban management.[66] The Housing and Urban–Rural Development Bureau of Xuanwei also publicly tendered the operating rights of only 10,000 sharing bikes in its urban area for six years, thereby setting market access conditions and limiting the entry and operation of bike-sharing enterprises.[67]

The fourth type of anticompetitive measure is to first establish franchises and then to allocate sharing-bike operating permissions under the franchises through public auctions. For example, Zhangjiajie in Hunan Province auctioned off a five-year franchise for sharing electric bikes at a price of ¥45 million (ca €5.82 million).[68] This franchise lacked a legal basis and, in effect, imposed restrictions on the entry and operation of other bike-sharing companies.

[64] General Office of the NDRC (n22), Case 8.

[65] Administration for Market Regulation of Hebei Province, '河北省市场监督管理局依法查处沧州市城市管理综合行政执法局滥用行政权力排除、限制竞争行为 [Administration for Market Regulation of Hebei Province Investigated and Dealt with Cangzhou Urban Management Bureau's Abuse of Administrative Power to Exclude and Restrict Competition in Accordance with the Law]' (25 October 2021) <https://www.samr.gov.cn/jzxts/tzgg/qlpc/art/2023/art_867f93a53a0f40a2a44994fa6768f56b.html> (accessed 9 April 2024).

[66] J Wu and Q Xie, '又一地废止与共享单车的"独家合作" 反垄断给城市管理带来新考验 [Another Place Abolished the "Exclusive Cooperation" with Shared Bicycles, and Anti-Monopoly Brought New Challenges to Urban Management]' (11 January 2022) <https://news.qq.com/rain/a/20220111A08OZ800> (accessed 9 November 2024).

[67] General Office of NDRC (n22).

[68] *Ibid*, case 6.

The fifth type of measure suspected of being anticompetitive is to set up market access conditions that are irrelevant to any justifiable consideration for urban management. For example, Longyang District of Baoshan, Yunnan Province, put forward many requirements for bike-sharing enterprises, such as the establishment of a legal person or a branch of a legal person in the local area, and the opening of a specific bank account,[69] which are hardly conducive to the promotion of the quality of bike-sharing services or other concerns about industrial development.

III.3 The Enforcement against Anticompetitive Measures on Bike-Sharing

Since 2018, the Division for the Coordination of Competition Policy of the SAMR has been collecting and publicizing typical cases of abuse of administrative power to restrict and exclude market competition.[70] Since the China Central Economic Work Meeting at the end of 2020, as suggested by the released cases, there has been a significant increase in the number of cases in which competition authorities have enforced the rules on administrative monopolies in the AML against anticompetitive measures on the business of sharing bikes.

In order to provide a comprehensive overview of the different types of restrictive practices, we collected pertinent cases from the 'Typical Cases of Violation of Negative Market Access Lists', as well as 'Cases of Abuse of Administrative Powers to Exclude or Restrict Competition', which were released by the Policy Coordination Division of the SAMR.[71] While some of these cases offer detailed information, specifying the authorities responsible for law enforcement, it is noteworthy that many cases released by the NDRC merely provide a general description of the administrative conduct violating the 'Negative Market Access List' and the measures taken to address such misconduct. It is therefore not clear in these cases whether the law enforcement was carried out by the competition authority, let alone whether the AML was invoked as the statutory ground for such enforcement against violating administrative misconduct. Thus, the inquiry in section III.3 draws heavily on the cases of the SAMR, as well as on cases in the NDRC list that were clearly enforced by competition authorities.

The enforcement in the aforementioned cases bears a striking resemblance in two aspects. First, the authorities in charge of the investigations were mostly provincial Administration for Market Regulation (AMR). Second, Article 32 of the 2008 AML or Articles 39, 40, or 45 of the new AML were invoked as the statutory ground for the decision regarding whether a measure adopted by the local urban

[69] *Ibid*, case 10.

[70] SAMR, '滥用行政权力排除、限制竞争案件 [Cases of Abuse of Administrative Power to Exclude or Restrict Competition]' <https://www.samr.gov.cn/jzxts/tzgg/qlpc/index.html> (accessed 9 April 2024).

[71] There is some overlap between the two case sources.

management bureau was, in nature, an abuse of administrative power to exclude or restrict competition.

In addition to shared statutory grounds, there is much similarity among the rationales for deciding whether the measures under investigation are anticompetitive. First, such a measure is deemed anticompetitive if it deprives consumers of their rights to free choice, which is essential for the assessment in the digital economy.[72] In the bike-sharing industry, indispensable factors such as price, riding experience, availability, unlocking methods, payment methods, the reparation of damaged bikes, and even the appearance of bikes may affect consumers' choices. Second, such a measure may be deemed anticompetitive if it 'excludes and restricts other bike-sharing operators with qualified service capabilities from entering the market in a certain region'.[73] The logic behind that is that if more advanced platforms were not allowed in, there would be insufficient incentives for existing platforms to make improvements, or the shortage of supply would ultimately squeeze the room for consumers' free choice.

Despite these similarities, the cases display substantial differences in the subject matter and forms of law enforcement. Generally speaking, the administrative resolutions can be categorized into two types.

In some cases, it is the AMR that issued an administrative proposal pursuant to Article 51 of the 2008 AML, making specific recommendations for rectification. For example, on 31 May 2022, in accordance with Article 51 of the 2008 AML, the AMR of Shandong Province issued an Administrative Recommendation to the City Government of Gaomi with three requirements. The first was to immediately stop the designation of Weifang Fast Run Company as the only bike-sharing operator enterprise in Gaomi, thereby providing fair competition opportunities for other operators with qualified service capabilities in the market so as to protect consumers' choice. The second was to earnestly implement the fair competition review system, requiring urban management authorities to strictly adhere to fair competition review procedures when formulating local measures involving economic activities, to carefully assess the impact on market competition, and to safeguard a legally sound market environment for fair competition. The third was to require the Gaomi Government to strengthen the supervision and guidance over subsequent policymaking in order to prevent the abuse of administrative power excluding or restricting market competition.[74]

[72] Administration for Market Regulation of Hebei Province (n65). See also SAMR, Division for Coordination of Competition Policy, '2022年制止滥用行政权力排除、限制竞争执法专项行动案件（第一批）[Typical Cases of Violating the Negative List for Market Access (the First Batch)]' (9 June 2022) <https://www.samr.gov.cn/jzxts/tzgg/qlpc/art/2023/art_abcdf27b28e44dab8d1d3ddf24edb6d9.html> (accessed 9 April 2024).

[73] Administration for Market Regulation of Hebei Province (n65). SAMR, Division for Coordination of Policy (n72).

[74] SAMR, Division for Coordination of Competition Policy (n72).

In more cases, the local urban management bureaus rectified their anticompetitive measures on their own during competition authorities' investigations. The bureaus involved usually took active measures to rectify, eliminate negative effects, revoke relevant measures, or make public announcements. As a general practice, the investigated bureaus also submitted rectification reports to the provincial competition authorities, stating their commitment to strictly adhering to the fair competition review system. They tended to make it clear that any future policies and measures concerning market activities would have to go through a fair competition review to prevent the exclusion and restriction of competition. After the local urban authority's rectification measures, the competition authorities usually ended their investigation without any formal decisions.

It is noteworthy that only the earlier cases adopted the method of administrative recommendations. As time went on, the latter way of disposition replaced the former as the predominant solution. One possible reason is the practical impact of the continuous improvement of anti-monopoly legislation and the strengthening of anti-monopoly enforcement after the China Central Economic Work Meeting in 2020. Urban management authorities have become increasingly adept at recognizing mistakes and getting back on track on their own during the investigation process and are no longer in need of suggestions or pressure.

Although local authorities have progressively gained the ability to tackle administrative monopolies, the central government never takes a hands-off approach to such a pressing concern. As evidenced by the fact that the SAMR routinely collects and publicizes such cases, the national competition authority has taken a laudatory stance towards administrative monopoly investigations targeting the bike-sharing industry. Among the cases of abuse of administrative power to exclude or restrict competition published by the SAMR, the portion of cases involving sharing bikes has increased significantly in the last two years. This shows the growing attention paid by the Chinese competition authorities and the strengthening regulatory efforts against administrative monopoly in sharing-bike markets.

Moreover, cases involving sharing bikes even accounted for more than 60 per cent of the typical cases released by the NDRC, in which local administrative measures had violated the negative list for market access (the fourth batch).[75] Predictably, China's competition authorities will continue their efforts to tackle administrative monopolies against free competition in its sharing-bike markets in the foreseeable future.

III.4 Typical Cases

Some typical cases of administrative monopolies in the bike-sharing industry are shown in Table 10.2.

[75] See text at n22.

Table 10.2 Cases on administrative monopolies in the bike-sharing industry

Time and authority	Monopolistic measures	Decisions by competition authorities	Legal grounds	Attitude of the national authority
In August 2021, the Hebei AMR launched an investigation into the administrative monopoly of the Cangzhou Urban Management Bureau.	The Cangzhou Urban Management Bureau authorized a company as the only operator of sharing electric bikes in Cangzhou by means of competitive negotiation.	In accordance with Article 51 of the AML, the Hebei AMR issued an administrative proposal to the Cangzhou Government suggesting that the Cangzhou Government order the Cangzhou Urban Management Bureau to rectify the relevant violations, strengthen the fair competition review process, and restore the order of fair competition in the relevant market.	Articles 32 and 51 AML (2008)	Public cases of SAMR[a]
On 10 March 2022, the Shandong AMR launched an investigation into the administrative monopoly of the Gaomi Urban Management Bureau.	The Gaomi Urban Management Bureau authorized a company as the only operator of sharing power-assisted bikes through a public invitation for bids and signed a five-year contract with the company.	In accordance with Article 51 AML, the Shandong AMR issued an administrative proposal to the Gaomi Government and made the following recommendations: first, the party concerned was ordered to immediately cease designating a single company as the exclusive operator of sharing-bike business in Gaomi to provide fair competition opportunities for other qualified operators in the relevant market and to safeguard consumers' rights of free choice; second, the fair competition review mechanism had to be earnestly implemented, and the parties concerned were required to strictly fulfil the fair competition review procedures when formulating policies and measures relating to the economic activities of market players, carefully assessing the impact on market competition, and safeguarding a fair and competitive market environment in accordance with the law. Third, the government would strengthen the supervision and guidance on the follow-up behaviour of the parties concerned so as to prevent the abuse of administrative power to exclude or restrict market competition.	Articles 32 and 51 AML (2008)	Cases of Special Action to Stop Abuse of Administrative Power to Exclude or Restrict Competition Enforcement 2022 (first batch)[b]

(continued)

Table 10.2 Continued

Time and authority	Monopolistic measures	Decisions by competition authorities	Legal grounds	Attitude of the national authority
On 18 April 2022, the Heilongjiang AMR launched an investigation into the administrative monopoly of the Jiamusi Urban Management Bureau.	The Jiamusi Urban Management Bureau authorised one company as the only operator of sharing bikes through a public invitation for bids. The contract signed with the company stipulated that during the operation period, the Bureau would not introduce other sharing bike service systems into Jiamusi.	During the investigation, the Jiamusi Urban Management Bureau actively rectified the problem, eliminated the adverse impacts, and terminated the exclusive contract. It submitted a rectification report to the Heilongjiang AMR, stating that it would strictly implement the fair competition review, so as to prevent excluding and restricting competition.	Article 40 AML (2022)	Cases of Special Action to Stop Abuse of Administrative Power to Exclude or Restrict Competition Enforcement 2022 (fifth batch)[c]
On 22 August 2022, the Jiangxi AMR launched an investigation into the administrative monopoly of the Ji'an Urban Management Bureau.	The Ji'an Urban Management Bureau authorized one company as the exclusive operator of sharing human-powered and power-assisted bikes through a public invitation for bids.	During the investigation, the Urban Management Bureau actively rectified the problem, submitted a rectification report to the Jiangxi AMR, annulled the relevant contract, and issued a public notice through the official website to fully liberalize the sharing bike market.	Article 39 AML (2022)	Cases of Special Action to Stop Abuse of Administrative Power to Exclude or Restrict Competition Enforcement 2022 (fifth batch)[d]
On 19 September 2022, the Heilongjiang AMR launched an investigation into the administrative monopoly of the Harbin Urban Management Bureau.	The Harbin Urban Management Bureau signed a contract with the winning company in the bidding to provide bike-sharing services in Harbin, which excluded and restricted other companies from participating in the competition in the bike-sharing market in the region.	During the investigation, the Harbin Urban Management Bureau actively rectified the problem, eliminated the adverse impact, and terminated the relevant contract. It submitted a rectification report to the Heilongjiang AMR, stating that it would strictly implement the fair competition review so as to prevent excluding and restricting competition.	Articles 39 and 45 AML (2022)	Public cases of SAMR[e]

On 7 April 2023, the Jiangxi AMR launched an investigation into the administrative monopoly of the Dingnan Urban Management Bureau.	The Dingnan Urban Management Bureau authorized two enterprises through a public invitation for bids to operate sharing electric bikes in Dingnan and signed a contract with them limiting the number of 1,500 bikes to be put into the market and the operation period to 3 years.	During the investigation, the Urban Management Bureau actively rectified the problem, submitted a rectification report to the Jiangxi AMR, terminated the relevant contract, and committed to fully liberalize the sharing electric bike market. It indicated that it would improve the fair competition review mechanism and effectively prevent the exclusion and restriction of market competition.	Article 39 AML (2022)	Public cases of SAMR[f]

[a] Administration for Market Regulation of Hebei Province, '河北省市场监督管理局依法查处沧州市城市管理综合行政执法局滥用行政权力排除、限制竞争行为 [Administration for Market Regulation of Hebei Province Investigated and Dealt with Cangzhou Urban Management Bureau's Abuse of Administrative Power to Exclude and Restrict Competition in Accordance with the Law]' (25 October 2021) <https://www.samr.gov.cn/jzxts/tzgg/qlpc/art/2023/art_867f93a53a0f40a2a44994fa6768f56b.html> (accessed 9 April 2024).

[b] Coordination of Competition Policy of SAMR, 2022 '年制止滥用行政权力排除、限制竞争执法专项行动案件（第一批 [Typical Cases of Violating the Negative List for Market Access (the First Batch)]' (9 June 2022) <https://www.samr.gov.cn/jzxts/tzgg/qlpc/art/2023/art_abcdf27b28e44dab8d1d3ddf24edb6d9.html> (accessed 9 April 2024).

[c] Coordination of Competition Policy of SAMR, 2022 '年制止滥用行政权力排除、限制竞争执法专项行动案件（第五批） [Violating the Negative List for Market Access (the Fifth Batch)]' (11 January 2023) <https://www.samr.gov.cn/jzxts/tzgg/qlpc/art/2023/art_632ec8e460764dc483c12fabcbbe5898.html> (accessed 9 April 2024).

[d] Coordination of Competition Policy of SAMR, '2022年制止滥用行政权力排除、限制竞争执法专项行动案件（第五批） [Violating the Negative List for Market Access (the Fifth Batch)]' (11 January 2023) <https://www.samr.gov.cn/jzxts/tzgg/qlpc/art/2023/art_632ec8e460764dc483c12fabcbbe5898.html> (accessed 9 April 2024).

[e] Administration for Market Regulation of Heilongjiang Province, '黑龙江省市场监督管理局纠正哈尔滨市城市管理局滥用行政权力排除、限制竞争行为 [Administration for Market Regulation of Heilongjiang Province Corrects Harbin Urban Management Bureau's Abuse of Administrative Power to Exclude and Restrict Competition]' (9 May 2023) <https://www.samr.gov.cn/jzxts/tzgg/qlpc/art/2023/art_71eb6f385eec4b498879faf67bf6d28d.html> (accessed 9 April 2024).

[f] Administration for Market Regulation of Jiangxi Province, '江西省市场监管局纠正定南县城市管理局滥用行政权力排除、限制竞争行为 [Administration for Market Regulation of Jiangxi Province Corrects Dingnan Urban Management Bureau's Abuse of Administrative Power to Exclude and Restrict Competition]' (20 June 2023) <https://www.samr.gov.cn/jzxts/tzgg/qlpc/art/2023/art_8afeb16ae95f4dfb8604eba6bf9bae69.html> (accessed 9 April 2024).

IV. The Monopoly of Public Data

As a new essential factor of production and economic resources, data has been widely appraised for its growing economic value. In one of its cover stories, *The Economist* claimed that data has been deemed 'the new oil' and 'the most valuable resource' in the current world.[76] The business model driven by the dual wheels of data and algorithms is prevalent in the ecosystem of many platforms. And huge data collections have availed platforms of a competitive advantage, as well as the opportunity to conduct anticompetitive behaviours. Apart from the abuse of dominance positions involving privately held data, as mentioned in previous chapters,[77] public data has also begun to raise anticompetitiveness concerns in China's digital markets in recent years.

To enrich the applicable scope of anti-monopoly laws against administrative monopoly, this section first explores China's most recent attitude on the debate over the propertization of data resources. Then, we reflect on the anticompetitive barriers to access to public data that are associated with governmental administration of data.

IV.1 Data Propertization and Trading Markets in China

Over the past decade, among many other jurisdictions worldwide, China has primarily placed an emphasis on data governance in two areas: privacy and personal information protection, and data security.[78] However, it was only when national policies explicitly designated data as a factor of production that China began to highlight the significance of exploiting its economic value, while simultaneously addressing privacy and personal information protection and data security.[79]

[76] S Jossen, 'The World's Most Valuable Resource Is No Longer Oil, But Data' (*The Economist*, 6 May 2017) <http://www.economist.com/leaders/2017/05/06/the-worlds-most-valuable-resource-is-no-longer-oil-but-data> (accessed 7 July 2022).

[77] See for instance, Chapter 8, section IV.2.

[78] P Cai and L Chen, 'Demystifying Data Law in China: A Unified Regime of Tomorrow' (2022) 12 International Data Privacy Law 75. See Section III, Chapter 3 and Section IV.2, Chapter 8.

[79] Central People's Government of the People's Republic of China, '中共中央关于坚持和完善中国特色社会主义制度　推进国家治理体系和治理能力现代化若干重大问题的决定 [Decision of the Central Committee of the Communist Party of China on Major Issues Concerning Adherence to and Improvement of the Socialist System with Chinese Characteristics and Advancement of the Modernization of the National Governance System and Capability]' (adopted at the Fourth Plenary Session of the 19th Central Committee of the Communist Party of China, 31 October 2019) <https://www.gov.cn/xinwen/2020-01/01/content_5465721.htm?eqid = 915fb773000307bc0000000264644e94> (accessed 1 June 2024); Central People's Government of the People's Republic of China, '中共中央、国务院关于构建更加完善的要素市场化配置体制机制的意见 [Opinions of the Central Committee of the Communist Party of China and the State Council on the Construction of a More Improved System Mechanism for the Market-Based Allocation of Factors]' (30 March 2020) <https://www.gov.cn/zhengce/2020-04/09/content_5500622.htm> (accessed 1 June 2024).

The 26th meeting of the Chinese Communist Party's (CCP's) Central Committee for Deepening Overall Reform, held on 22 June 2022, deliberated and adopted the 'Opinions on Building the Data Basic Regime to Better Exploit the Value of Data Factors' ('the Basic Regime'), which prescribed the foundational settings for further establishment of a series of data infrastructure systems, especially a modernized property system that aligns with the form and characteristics of data production, with the ultimate goal of stimulating the formation of a well-functioning data market.[80] Actually, the National Data Bureau in China has been drafting a national policy document exclusively delineating the property rights patterns over data, which is going to unfold the framework and contents of China's data property regime in the near future.

Traditionally, the assertion that establishing property rights over data could easily lead to monopolies significantly hindered the introduction of a property regime on data. Instead, a more flexible regulation strategy, including the trade secrets clause or the principles of the Anti-Unfair Competition Law, was advocated to address disputes over multiple stakeholders' claims to access and use data.[81] It is true that data, as a resource with economic value, if it falls under the absolute control of either public or private entities, could indeed lead to the inhibition or exclusion of market innovation and competition associated with the usage of data. Yet, recent legal studies in China have gradually reached a consensus on the introduction of a property rights regime on data and the manner in which to overcome potential monopolistic behaviours regarding data resources.[82]

One the one hand, the mere fact of wide-range data controls by enterprises does not inherently constitute a monopoly, although the advantage of data controls can indeed facilitate holding enterprises to engage in anticompetitive behaviours. On the other hand, the 'false-negative' doctrine in Chinese competition law should still take precedence when determining whether enterprises controlling a massive amount of data have committed a competition law violation. Actually, there have already been cases pending before Chinese courts in which the plaintiffs require the holders of massive amounts of data to perform the duty to supply data. In 2021, for example, Eefung (蚁坊) company filed a complaint at Changsha Intermediate People's Court against Weibo (微梦创科) corporation, a subsidiary of Sina, on

[80] B Xiong, J Ge, and C Li, 'Unpacking Data: China's "Bundle of Rights" Approach to the Commercialization of Data' (2023) 13 International Data Privacy Law 93.

[81] X Mei, '在分享和控制之间数据保护的私法局限和公共秩序构建 [Between Sharing and Control: The Limitations of Private Law and the Building of Public Order in Data Protection]' [2019] 31 Peking University Law Journal 845, 852; X Ding, '数据交易如何破局 [Breaking the Deadlock of Data Trading]' (2022) 2 Oriental Law 144, 151.

[82] X Zhang, '论作为新型财产权的数据财产权 [On Data Property Rights as a New Type of Property Right]' (2023) 4 Social Sciences in China 144; W Liu, '数据产权的法律表达 [Legal Expression of Property Rights in Data]' (2023) 45(3) Chinese Journal of Law 36; B Xiong and J He, '数据确权:理路、方法与经济意义 [Theory, Methodology and Economic Implications of the Delineation of Data Property Rights]' (2023) 45 Chinese Journal of Law 54; L Wang, '数据何以确权 [How Can Data be Right-Sized?]' (2023) 45(4) Chinese Journal of Law 56.

grounds of refusal to supply for Weibo declined to license data accumulated on the Weibo platform to Eefung. The main business of Eefung was the monitoring and analysis of public opinions, which was in direct competition with Yuqing Sina (新浪舆情通, Sina public opinion monitor), another subsidiary of Sina, to whom Weibo data was a key factor in competition. The key issue in this case lies in whether Weibo enjoys a dominant position in the market of public opinion data and, if so, has abused its market dominance.[83]

While the scale of data accumulation and the manner in which data controllers exercise the property rights over data should be taken into special account when assessing the anticompetitive effects of suspected behaviours, straightforwardly rejecting data propertization due to concerns about data-facilitated monopolies is counterproductive. Such rejection fails to adequately apprehend the logic of the data market and therefore overstates the impediment created by property rights-based entitlement to data flow. It fails to fully understand the property rights-based thinking that is implicit in the so-called approach of regulating data behaviours, let alone the overall socio-economic implications of such entitlements.[84]

Granting property rights does not necessarily mean conferring a single ownership of data on a single legal subject. Instead, it needs to follow the general principle of 'standardization of property rights' to construct data project rights modules that are standardized to the extent corresponding to the social proximity of data right holders to the related subjects. The standardization of data property rights can substantially reduce the transaction costs during the interactions between data holders and other subjects and improve data production and the efficiency of data circulation.[85] After all, as recently recognized in China's legal academia, in the absence of a property regime over data, it is hardly possible to protect the interests of data collectors in the scenario of the insolvency of data-processing service providers

[83] It is worth noting that the applicability of the AML in civil litigation involving data licensing is debatable. Some opinions believe that the refusal-to-supply clause (i.e. subpara 3, para 1, Article 22 AML) is applicable, while acknowledging that certain features of denying access of data should be addressed by adjusting the judicial criteria on market definition, market dominance, and abuse of dominance, accordingly. See Beijing High People's Court Civil Tribunal III Research Group, '论数据市场竞争秩序的司法规制路径—保护数据权益与促进数据流通并重 [On the Judicial Regulation Path of Data Market Competition Order—Emphasizing the Protection of Data Rights and the Promotion of Data Circulation at the Same Time]' (2024) 2 Journal of Law Application 122; J Long, '平台拒绝数据许可的反垄断规制—基于反垄断法禁止拒绝交易条款的适用展开 [Anti-Monopoly Regulation of Platforms Refusing to License Data—Based on the Application of Refusal-to-Supply Clause of AML]' (2023) 20 Shanghai Legal Studies 9. Opposing opinions believe that while the refusal to supply in AML and mandatory data licensing share a common policy goal of promoting competition, yet the exclusive control of certain data is not equivalent to market dominance, thus compulsory data sharing should be implemented outside the framework of the AML, as an independent obligation for large platforms. See Q Sun, '论大型平台企业数据交易强制缔约义务 [On Compulsory Contracting Obligations of Large Platform Enterprises in Data Transactions]' (2024) 36 Peking University Law Journal 241. Nevertheless, this debate does fundamentally depart from the 'false-negative' doctrine since, according to the opposing view, the plaintiff still bears the burden of establishing the exclusive control of the data concerned by the defendant.

[84] Xiong and He (n82).

[85] *Ibid.*

and the interests of dealers engaged in exclusive licensing or secured transactions with data as collateral.[86] These transactions are actually not uncommon in China's data markets.

IV.2 Anticompetitive Barriers to Open Access to Public Data

In parallel to the discourse over the propertization of data processed by private firms, the promotion of open access to public data has also occupied the recent policy and academic debates in China, part of which are associated with administrative monopoly in data markets.

Up to now, both Chinese academia and regulators have roughly reached a consensus that, while privacy and personal information protection and data security primarily prevail, extra efforts should also be dedicated to promoting the circulation of data resources so as to better exploit the economic value of data.[87] To combat anti-competitive behaviours in licensing public data, the General Office of the CPC Central Committee and the General Office of the State Council released the *Opinions on Accelerating the Development and Utilization of Public Data Resources* (*Opinions on Public Data*) on September 21, 2024, reiterating the state determination to promote the circulation and utilization of public data. It is noteworthy that the policy document, in its Article 5, expressively prohibits anti-competitive practices of data circulation including abuse of dominance and anti-competitive agreements. [88] One essential issue is how to accelerate the circulation of public data that is directly collected by governmental organs or of a strong public nature. It is therefore vital to delineate the scope of public data that could be accessible to the public.

Opinions on Public Data, in its foreword, defined public data as data "generated in the course of performing statutory duties or providing public services by Party and government organizations, enterprises, and public institutions at all levels." It has also been emphasized in Article 2 that directories of opening up public data shall be compiled and updated, "prioritizing the release of data closely related to people's livelihoods and pressing social demand."[89] It is clear, though, that such expression is undoubtedly subject to interpretation and implementation.

[86] W Cheng, '破产程序中数据权益之保护—以信义义务为视角 [Protection of Data Rights and Interests in Bankruptcy Proceedings: From the Perspective of Fiduciary Duty]' (2022) 4 Law and Economy 115, 123.

[87] Xiong and He (n82), 61.

[88] Xinhua News Agency, '中共中央办公厅 国务院办公厅关于加快公共数据资源开发利用的意见 [General Office of the CPC Central Committee, General Office of the State Council: Opinions on Accelerating the Development and Utilization of Public Data Resources]' (9 October 2024) <https://www.gov.cn/zhengce/202410/content_6978910.htm> (accessed 9 November 2024). (*Opinions on Public Data*)

[89] Ibid.

Technically speaking, public data should be based upon 'public interest' and designated as an extension of the goal of public administration, in order to meet the legislative intent.[90] As a common practice, accessible public data certainly includes that collected by governmental agencies and their subordinates for the purpose of performing legal duties. Additionally, data collected by state-owned enterprises established for the supply of public services (such as water, electricity, and gas supplies) is often considered public.[91] Furthermore, even some data originally collected by private enterprises may, under government coordination, be collectively aggregated and converted into public data. For instance, for the purpose of establishing technological financial infrastructure, the central financial authority established an enterprise, be it state-owned or partly invested by the state, by administrative order, and coordinated the aggregation of data originally collected by private insurance companies.

However, apart from the precarious affirmation that the range of accessible public data could be determined, there still remain various operational loopholes that could potentially enable administrative monopolies to sneak in. For instance, a total of thirty provinces and cities across China had begun to legislate on data by November 2023. At the provincial level, there are nearly 160 policy documents, of which 80 per cent focuses on public data.[92] A rule of 'accessing to local public data through licensing regime' has become a standard model in local administration of data resources. Some local policies even explicitly define a national and local ownership of local public data in order to legitimize their subsequent licensing practices, leading to wide anti-monopoly concerns among legal academia.[93]

Compared with privately owned data, monopolistic concerns concerning government-held public data have received more attention for the following reasons.

First, there is the issue of whether, in the primary market of public data, the government shall directly open public data to a wide range of data users or outsource the right to manage public data to third-party entities. To go a step further, if the latter approach is adopted, as many local data authorities in China do at the moment, there is the issue of whether it is necessary to introduce multiple entities to sustain a certain level of competitiveness. Given the fact that utilizing public

[90] C Zheng and J Tang, '论公共数据的规范含义 [On the Concept of Public Data]' (2021) 6 Fazhi Yanjiu 79.

[91] X Zhang and Q Cao, '公共数据确权授权法律机制研究 [Research on the Legal Mechanism for the Rights to Public Data Ownership and Authorization]' (2023) 3 Journal of Comparative Law 41, 43–44.

[92] L Huang, '时建中：公共数据取之于民，应该用之于民，惠之于民 [Shi Jianzhong: Public Data, Sourced from the People, Should be Used for the People's Benefit and Welfare]' (9 November 2023) <https://mp.weixin.qq.com/s/z5nz-JJxLiGr65vE5YJp2g> (accessed 30 March 2024).

[93] J Shi, '数据基础制度建设的地方立法实践—基于政策文献计量的初步研究 [Local Legislative Practices of Foundational Architecture for Data: A Preliminary Quantitative Research Based on Policy Documents]' (2023) 1 Digital Jurisprudence Review 44, 61, 66, 76–77, 83–84.

data requires substantial technical and financial capacities, third-party entities that meet such prerequisites, rather than the government itself, are likely better suited and thereby justify their participation. Arguably, since public data may involve multiple concerns regarding privacy and personal information protection, trade secrets, and public security, introducing one instead of multiple third-party entities may be more conducive to preserving such values.

However, the anti-competitive concerns of licensing public data to a single entity exclusively are not to be neglected. For example, the Sumscope case decided by Shanghai AMR have prompted reflections over how public data should be licensed, although the data involved in this case was not actually public data. Ningbo Sumscope is a leading financial data service provider, primarily selling real-time bond trading data generated by individual currency brokers, which was licensed exclusively to Sumscope by the brokers. Sumscope was found abuse of dominance for refusing to supply to downstream institutions without justifiable reasons. In this case, Sumscope abused its dominant position not only for obtaining exclusive licensing from upper-stream brokers, but also for participating in the downstream market of trading data of specific bond categories itself.[94] Actually, licensing a certain type of public data exclusively to a single party would be more of a policy concern, in the sense that this party enjoys a dual role both as an agent of public interest, but also as a market participant.

Second, in the secondary market of public data, aside from the questions of whether fees should be charged for the transfer of public data and the amount of such fees, it is even more crucial to clarify the requirements that market participants must meet to access public data. In general, qualification standards should be publicly disclosed in advance, and, for those who meet such standards, data access should remain equal and non-discriminatory. However, in practice, when authorizing third-party entities to manage public data, some local authorities may require such government-backed bodies to selectively provide public data for a designated set of vetted entities. For example, financial data might be available exclusively to large, state-owned commercial banks,[95] which could potentially violate Article 44 AML, as it strictly prohibits market participants from imposing restrictions that hinder competition.

In addition, as mentioned, the government, in its efforts to establish data infrastructure, may collect certain data that was collected by private enterprises and may designate specific entities to utilize such a resource. The aggregation of private data may also raise concerns related to administrative monopolies. Private entities may take advantage of authorized data collected by the government to conduct

[94] G Shao, '初探：公共数据资源开发利用中应当预防的垄断行为 [A Preliminary Exploration: Monopolistic Practices to be Prevented in the Development and Utilization of Public Data Resources]' (1 November 2024) < https://mp.weixin.qq.com/s/tMM8bm_U2H3Lrth0cubkkg> (accessed 9 November 2024).

[95] Interview with manager from Beijing Financial Holdings Group (October 31, 2022).

anticompetitive businesses and operations. For instance, Yuhan (彧菡) Company filed a lawsuit in 2022 against Yuchexing (与车行) Company at Beijing Intellectual Property Court, alleging that the latter abused its dominance in the domestic second-hand car insurance data query service, implementing excessive pricing and discriminatory treatment.[96] This case is also the first anti-monopoly litigation in the realm of public data, for data licensed by Yuchexing were all data collected from China Banking and Insurance Information Technology (CBIT) platform, a state-owned enterprise (SOE) managing banking and insurance data for public interest.[97]

It is noteworthy that different prices charged between members and non-members may not necessarily violate the AML. For example, if insurance companies that provide the data to the designated management platform are treated as members of the platform and are thereby charged lower fees due to their previous contributions, such a discrepancy between the two groups will probably not be deemed anticompetitive according to the AML and, therefore, will not raise the issue of abuse of market dominance.

Furthermore, even if the platform engages in anticompetitive behaviours, it is still necessary to determine the entities actually implementing the monopolistic conduct. If the platform independently carries out exclusionary or anticompetitive conduct, it should be held accountable according to the rules of the AML; if the government mandates certain platforms to engage in monopolistic behaviours, then the government itself, rather than the platform, should be investigated for unlawfully imposing compulsory transactions that could exclude or restrict competition under Article 44 of the new AML.

V. Conclusion

Against the backdrop of a decentralized regulatory power, and competition in both 'bureaucratic and economic markets', regional officials are motivated to exercise their regulatory power in order to defend local firms against foreign ones, hindering effective competition. This fact was observed by the legislature, and was specifically addressed in the 'Abuse of the Administrative Power to Exclude or Restrict Competition' chapter of the AML. The issue remains in the digital era, taking the form of unfair regulations on the e-hailing industry and the shared-bike industry.

[96] Beijing Intellectual Property Court, *Shanghai Yuhan Automotive Technology Co, Ltd v Beijing Yuchexing Information Technology Co, Ltd*, [2022] (上海彧菡汽车科技有限公司诉北京与车行信息技术有限公司滥用市场支配地位纠纷案，(2022)京73民初1330号) (14 April 2023).

[97] Beijing High People's Court Civil Tribunal III Research Group (n83).

Consequently, active measures have been taken to restore competition in such industries. The fair competition review system was set forth by the executive branch to urge local regulators to repeal anticompetitive measures through internal supervisory procedures, whereas the National People's Congress endeavours to preserve competition through the recording and reviewing the constitutionality and legality of local regulations. Investigations are initiated by local AMRs to assess whether a particular policy is anticompetitive, leading to a rather formal recommendation of rectification, or even proactive correction prior to such recommendations. Such a holistic, top-down approach has exhibited its effectiveness in multiple cases and is to be further tested in the future.

Another pressing issue is the circulation of public data. Along with the introduction of a property system for data in the future, how public data, featuring a not-for-profit purpose, shall be licensed or opened to the public in a way in which overall welfare is maximized has attracted continued discussion. Major issues include reasonable prerequisites for market entrance, fair pricing policies, and the viability of third-party management of the data. Since the data property system is still being incubated in China, the debate on these issues is likely to persist in the near future.

PART D

COMPARATIVE ASSESSMENT: NORMATIVE CONCLUSIONS

11
Comparative Conclusions

I. Introduction

In globalized markets, policymakers, enforcers, and market players need to have regard for the objectives and regulatory tools of other jurisdictions. Chapter 11 identifies the more pertinent issues in the European Union (EU) and China and offers comparative conclusions.

The advent of technology has brought sweeping changes in the way we live, displacing existing business models and old consumption habits. Within this new environment, it became evident that the current regulatory tools, including competition law, were in need of a revamp. Such was the reality in both jurisdictions under consideration in this book, namely the EU and China. By covering every area discussed in this book (market definition, anticompetitive agreements, abuse of dominance, merger control, and administrative monopolies) and adopting a comparative approach covering both jurisdictions, this chapter first threads out and succinctly presents the areas where competition law enforcement has proven to be adequate and sufficiently resilient enough to account for such technological challenges ('resilience points'). Second, the chapter discusses changes already introduced in the respective competition law systems ('points of change'), and finally, it identifies areas where challenges remain and that may call for additional reforms in the future ('future challenges'). The discussion first covers EU competition law in the digital era (section II) before moving to its Chinese counterpart (section III). The analysis covers such points with respect to market definition and market power, anticompetitive agreements, abuse of dominance, and mergers, and then offers some reflections. The preceding analysis on resilience points, points of change, and future challenges helps to highlight two normative claims: first, the need for a more holistic integrative approach to competition law enforcement (section IV); and second, the need for a closer regulatory dialogue between the EU and China (section V).

Competition Law and Policy in Digital Markets. Maria Ioannidou and Bingwan Xiong, Oxford University Press.
 DOI: 10.1093/9780191925955.003.0011

II. EU Competition Law Enforcement in Digital Markets: Resilience, Change, and Challenges

II.1 Market Definition and Market Power

The structure of digital markets with the rise of ecosystems offering complementary products and venturing into adjacent markets has challenged the current approach to market definition and the assessment of market power. These issues are discussed first, since they are relevant for the assessment of anticompetitive practices (agreements and abuse of dominance) as well as for merger control.

Issues that call for a reconceptualization of market definition include the multi-sided nature of platform markets, the ad-funded nature of 'free' services, the prevalence of data, and the rise of ecosystem competition.[1] In light of these features, the Commission has undertaken a consultation process in order to update its market definition notice.[2] The adopted changes include an increased focus on elements, other than price, such as innovation and quality and an emphasis on multi-sided markets and digital ecosystems.[3] The 'Revised Market Definition Notice' expressly lists the various parameters of competition, which include price, innovation, and various aspects of quality (including sustainability and the level of privacy protection offered).[4] It also includes chapters about multi-sided platforms and digital ecosystems.[5]

With respect to *market definition* in the context of multi-sided platforms, issues include the existence of one or multiple markets, the impact of indirect network effects on demand substitution, and the offering of products at a zero monetary price on the one side. The 'Revised Market Definition Notice' gives concrete examples from the Commission's decisional practice, where either a single market encompassing both sides or separate markets on each side were defined.[6] Such an analysis would ultimately depend on the specific facts. The

[1] See Chapter 2, section V.1.

[2] European Commission (EU), 'Notice on the Definition of Relevant Market for the Purposes of Community Competition Law', [1997] OJ C 327/5.

[3] European Commission (EU), 'Commission Notice on the Definition of the Relevant Market for the Purposes of Union Competition Law', C(2024) 1645 ('Revised Market Definition Notice'); European Commission (EU), 'Commission Seeks Feedback on Draft Revised Market Definition Notice' (Press release, 8 November 2022) <https://ec.europa.eu/commission/presscorner/detail/en/ip_22_6528> (accessed 7 June 2024).

[4] Revised Market Definition Notice (n 3), para 15. See also European Commission (EU), 'Notice on the Definition of the Relevant Market for the Purposes of Union Competition Law' (Draft) (2022) <https://ec.europa.eu/commission/presscorner/detail/en/ip_22_6528> (accessed 7 June 2024), para 152.

[5] European Commission, 'Notice on the Definition of the Relevant Market (Draft)' (n4), sections 4.4 and 4.5, respectively.

[6] *Ibid*, para 95.

Revised Notice does state, however, that in the presence of important differences in the possibilities of substitution on different sides, then the definition of separate markets may be more appropriate. In order to assess whether important differences exist, factors to take into account include (i) whether the undertakings that offer substitutable products to each user group are different; (ii) the level of product differentiation on each side; (iii) behavioural factors, including potential multi- or single-homing; and (iv) the platform type, that is whether it is a transaction or matching platform.[7] Indirect network effects and zero monetary prices on one side challenge the application of quantitative tools, such as the small-but-significant-non-transitory-increase-in-price (SSNIP) test. The Revised Notice, based on the Commission's decisional practice to date, proposes alternative elements of assessment, such as product functionalities, intended use, and hypothetical substitution, as well as alternative quantitative tools, such as the small-but-significant-non-transitory-decrease-in-quality (SSNDQ) test.[8]

With respect to digital ecosystems, the Notice clarifies that a similar approach may be followed with the definition of aftermarkets, or bundle markets may be followed. Again, this assessment will ultimately rest on the specific facts and be influenced by various factors, including network effects, switching costs, and homing decisions.[9]

The above highlights that there is an evolutionary rather than revolutionary transition to update the market definition exercise. The Commission seeks to update the existing tools and adapt its analysis to reflect the particular characteristics of the digital economy.

Similar adaptation of the existing analytical tools also applies to the assessment of market power.[10] In the digital economy, apart from market shares, metrics that have already been taken into account in the Commission's decisional practice include the number of active users, the number of visits, the number of downloads and interactions, and the platform's transaction value or volume.[11]

Other suggestions about suitable metrics that are yet to inform competition law enforcement include the time spent on each website.[12] Furthermore, various other metrics, such as platform power, intermediation power, bottleneck power, portfolio power, and panopticon power have been proposed by commentators in order

[7] *Ibid.*

[8] *Ibid*, para 98.

[9] *Ibid*, para 103.

[10] See Chapter 2, section V.2.

[11] Revised Market Definition Notice (n3), para 108.

[12] T Wu, 'Blind Spot: The Attention Economy and the Law' (2019) 82 Antitrust Law Journal 771, 794–795.

to better capture the interdependencies in the digital economy.[13] Some of these metrics have also informed recent amendments in national competition laws.[14]

II.2 Anticompetitive Agreements

With respect to the assessment of anticompetitive agreements in the digital economy, the decisional practice to date has shown that the current toolbox and application of Article 101 of the Treaty on the Functioning of the European Union (TFEU) is flexible enough, to some extent at least, to account for the rise of m- and e-commerce, the evolution of business models, and the rapid technological advancements in algorithms, big data, and artificial intelligence (AI). At the same time, the Commission has taken a pragmatic approach and has updated its rules and guidelines with respect to certain practices. Such updates are sometimes premised on existing decisional practice, whereas others represent a more progressive approach or clarify areas where opposing views have been expressed. In that respect, such updates are an amalgam of both clarifications and the envisaged way forward in the application of Article 101 TFEU, rather than a change as such. Yet, here we present them as a change, since they mark important clarifications in the future application of Article 101 TFEU, which were both lacking and much needed. In this section, we first outline the respective areas in Article 101 TFEU assessment, where the enforcement approach has proven resilient and adaptable to technological changes. We then present the recently adopted changes, paving the way for the future application of EU competition law to anticompetitive agreements in the digital economy. Finally, this section briefly outlines the areas where challenges remain.

II.2.1 Resilience

EU competition law enforcement for anticompetitive agreements in the digital economy has proven to be resilient with respect to–algorithmic collusion, when algorithms are used as a tool to reinforce existing human interaction or aide coordination through a third party.[15] The decisional practice to date shows that EU competition law can indeed adapt to such market realities.

[13] I Lianos, 'Competition Law for a Complex Economy' (2019) 50 International Review of Intellectual Property and Competition Law 643; I Lianos and B Carballa-Smichowski, 'A Coat of Many Colours—New Concepts and Metrics of Economic Power in Competition Law and Economics' (2022) 18 Journal of Competition Law and Economy 795.

[14] See, e.g. German Competition Act (section 18(3b)) with respect to intermediation power, Competition Act in the version published on 26 June 2013: Bundesgesetzblatt (Federal Law Gazette) I, 2013, 1750, 3245, as last amended by Article 1 of the Act (25 October 2023), (Federal Law Gazette) I, 294.

[15] See Chapter 4, sections III.1 and III.2.

II.2.2 Change

The Commission has revised its Vertical Block Exemption Regulation and Guidelines to provide legal certainty for the assessment of certain practices.[16] Similarly, the Horizontal Cooperation Guidelines have also been updated to aid stakeholders in their assessment of data-pooling agreements and provide clarifications with respect to the assessment of algorithmic collusion.[17] Finally, the Commission has also issued Guidelines on the Application of EU Competition Law to Collective Agreements Regarding the Working Conditions of Solo Self-Employed People,[18] which are also relevant for the treatment of suppliers in the platform economy.

Areas where the clarifications with respect to current enforcement activity were introduced are the following:

- platforms act as independent undertakings and not as agents;[19]
- platform suppliers are falsely treated self-employed and their situation is akin to workers;[20]
- algorithms colluding autonomously, in the absence of explicit human intervention, can trigger liability for the undertakings employing them;[21]
- according to the RHG, algorithms are deemed to be under the 'direction or control' of the firm and are treated like employees or outside consultants;[22]
- data-pooling agreements can have pro-competitive effects, and this should be reflected in the respective assessment of information exchange agreements, provided certain measures are put in place.[23]

The RHG have provided guidance on data pooling agreements. In particular, the RHG clarify that the parties to a data pool should, in principle, have access only to their own information and other participants' final and aggregated information. The data pools' management should be assigned to a trustee under strict confidentiality conditions. The collection of information should be subject to a

[16] Regulation (EU) 2022/720 of 10 May 2022 on the application of Article 101(3) of the Treaty on the Functioning of the European Union to categories of vertical agreements and concerted practices, [2022] OJ L 134/4 (Vertical Block Exemption Regulations, VBER); European Commission (EU), 'Guidelines on Vertical Restraints, [2022] OJ C 248/1.

[17] European Commission (EU), 'Guidelines on the Applicability of Article 101 of the Treaty on the Functioning of the European Union to Horizontal Co-operation Agreements' (2023) <https://competition-policy.ec.europa.eu/document/fd641c1e-7415-4e60-ac21-7ab3e72045d2_en> (accessed 7 June 2024) (Revised HG, RHG).

[18] European Commission (EU), 'Guidelines on the Application of Union Competition Law to Collective Agreements Regarding the Working Conditions of Solo Self-Employed Persons', [2022] OJ C 374/2.

[19] See Chapter 4, section II.1.

[20] See *ibid*, section II.2.

[21] See *ibid*, section III.2.3.

[22] *Ibid*.

[23] See *ibid*, section IV.

proportionality requirement, with the collected information being necessary for implementing the data pool's legitimate purpose.[24]

- Dual distribution is not covered by the VBER in two situations: first, in the existence of information exchange that is not directly related to the implementation of the vertical agreement or not necessary for the improvement of the production or distribution of the contract goods or services;[25] and second, when the online intermediation service provider has a hybrid function offering goods or services in competition with third parties.[26]
- The VBER lists across-platform parity clauses as excluded restrictions that have to be assessed individually.[27]
- Clauses that prevent the effective use of the Internet are listed as hard-core restrictions.[28] The prohibition of an entire online advertising channel (such as search engines or price comparison services) or indirect prohibitions (such as the obligation not to use the supplier's trademarks or brand names to bid in order to be referenced in search engines) will be treated as hard-core restrictions.[29]
- The imposition of minimum advertised prices (MAPs) is treated as an indirect form of resale price maintenance (RPM) and therefore a hard-core restriction.[30]
- Dual pricing is no longer a hard-core restriction and may benefit from the VBER.[31]

II.2.3 Challenges

With respect to the application of Article 101 TFEU in the digital economy, further challenges to be explored include the treatment of autonomous self-learning algorithms and price signalling.[32]

II.3 Abuse of Dominance

After *Microsoft*,[33] and following a period of feeble enforcement activity against powerful companies in the digital economy, changing market realities and

[24] RHG (n17), para 408.
[25] VBER (n16), Article 2(5). See Chapter 4, section V.2.
[26] VBER (n16), Article 2(6); RHG (n17), para 104.
[27] VBER (n16), Article 5(1)(d). See Chapter 4, section V.3.
[28] VBER (n16), Article 4(e). See Chapter 4, section V.4.
[29] RHG (n17), para 206.
[30] *Ibid*, para 187. See Chapter 4, section V.5.
[31] RHG (n17), para 209. See Chapter 4, section V.6.
[32] See Chapter 4, sections III.3 and III.4.
[33] See Chapter 5, section II.1.

staggering concentration levels have triggered multiple enforcement actions for possible abuse of dominance under Article 102 TFEU at both EU and national Member State level. Such actions have exposed the arguably limited potential of competition law to restrain the anticompetitive activity of Big Tech and restore competitive market conditions. Regulators, cognizant of such a fact, have complemented EU competition law with tailored rules that may infuse more transparency and fairness into digital markets.[34] At the same time, one should not overlook the fact that Article 102 TFEU has proven to be adaptable enough to account for certain practices in digital markets, which may be seen as falling at the intersection between competition and other public interest considerations, such as fairness or privacy. And whereas a lot of ink has been spilled over whether such an approach is permissible (or indeed desirable) under the current EU competition law framework,[35] it is nevertheless true that such enforcement activity does highlight the adaptable nature of EU competition law, albeit it often with a considerable enforcement time lag.

II.3.1 Resilience

Resilience with respect to the application of Article 102 TFEU refers in particular to the existing decisions and ongoing cases against Big Tech companies. A first point to be made here is the observed increased number of exploitative abuse cases against powerful platforms. Such an approach alone represents a shift in the Commission and national competition authorities' (NCAs') case prioritization, which in the past tended to focus more on exclusionary abuses. An example here, where the dominant platform was found liable for the *imposition of unfair contractual terms*,[36] is the *German Facebook* case.[37] Other cases here on the imposition of opaque, unfair, discriminatory, or unreasonable terms include *Google News* (Germany),[38] *Google AdWords* (France),[39] *Google News* (France),[40]*Amazon Marketplace—Commitments* (Germany),[41] *Facebook Online Advertising Services* (France),[42] *Facebook Online Ad Verification* (France),[43] *Apple Online Dating Apps* (the Netherlands),[44] and *Apple App Store* (EU and

[34] See, e.g. Regulation (EU) 2019/1150 of the European Parliament and of the Council of 20 June 2019 on promoting fairness and transparency for business users of online intermediation services, [2019] OJ L 186/57 (P2B Regulation). See also Regulation (EU) 2022/1925 of the European Parliament and of the Council of 14 September 2022 on contestable and fair markets in the digital sector and amending Directives (EU) 2019/1937 and (EU) 2020/1828, [2022] OJ L 265/1 (Digital Markets Act, DMA). Discussing such initiatives, see Chapter 4, section V.2.1.

[35] See the discussion in Chapter 5, section III.

[36] See Article 102(a) TFEU.

[37] On this case, see Chapter 5, text to n268.

[38] See Chapter 5, text to n183.

[39] See Chapter 5, text to n187.

[40] See Chapter 5, text to n189.

[41] See Chapter 5, text to n237.

[42] See Chapter 5, text to n277.

[43] See Chapter 5, text to n279.

[44] See Chapter 5, text to n306.

United Kingdom).[45] *Amazon Marketplace* (EU), *Amazon Marketplace* (Italy) and *Amazon Marketplace* (United Kingdom)[46] concern the preferential and/or discriminatory treatment of third parties on the platform.

With respect to exclusionary abuses, a large number of cases may fall under the category of *self-preferencing or favouring* practices, most notably *Google Shopping*.[47] Other cases include *Google AdTech* (EU),[48] *Google News* (Germany),[49] *Google AdTech* (France),[50] *Google Android Auto* (Italy),[51] *Google AdTech* (United Kingdom),[52] *Google Play* (United Kingdom),[53] *Amazon Marketplace* (EU),[54] *Amazon Marketplace* (United Kingdom),[55] *Facebook Marketplace* (EU),[56] and *Facebook Classified Ads/Online Dating* (United Kingdom).[57] Other cases that can be classified under favouring include instances where dominant platforms reserve valuable information for themselves and do not share it with third parties. Such is the case, for example, in the *Google AdTech* cases in the EU and United Kingdom.[58]

Apart from self-preferencing practices, other cases concern data-related abuses. This category includes practices involving preferential collection and processing of users' data, allegedly due to privacy concerns. Cases here include *Google Data Processing* (Germany),[59] *Google Privacy Sandbox* (United Kingdom),[60] *Facebook Marketplace* (EU),[61] *Facebook Classified Ads/Online Dating* (United Kingdom),[62] and *Apple ATT*.[63] Second, data-related abuses cover the preferential use of business users' data, as was the case in *Facebook Marketplace* in the EU and United Kingdom.[64]

Third, other cases may be associated with more 'traditional' theories of harm, such as tying practices or exclusive dealing. Examples here include *Google Android* (EU),[65] *Google AdTech* (United Kingdom),[66] *Google AdSense* (EU),[67] *Facebook*

45 See Chapter 5, text to nn286, 313.
46 On these cases, see Chapter 5, text to nn228, 252, and 254.
47 See Chapter 5, text to n22.
48 See Chapter 5, text to n158.
49 See Chapter 5, text to n183.
50 See Chapter 5, text to n193.
51 See Chapter 5, text to n200.
52 See Chapter 5, text to n216.
53 See Chapter 5, text to n221.
54 See Chapter 5, text to n228.
55 See Chapter 5, text to n255.
56 See Chapter 5, text to n261.
57 See Chapter 5, text to n280.
58 On these cases, see Chapter 5, text to nn158 and 216.
59 See Chapter 5, text to n176.
60 See Chapter 5, text to n209.
61 See Chapter 5, text to n261.
62 See Chapter 5, text to n281.
63 See Chapter 5, text to n298.
64 On these cases, see Chapter 5, text to nn261 and 281.
65 See Chapter 5, text to n67.
66 See Chapter 5, text to n216.
67 See Chapter 5, text to n129.

Marketplace (EU),[68] and *Facebook VR Market* (Germany).[69] A fourth category includes cases, such as *Google Maps* (Germany),[70] *Google AdTech* (France),[71] *Google Android Auto* (Italy),[72] *Google AdTech* (United Kingdom),[73] and *Apple Pay* (EU),[74] where dominant platforms impose restrictions on interoperability. Finally, other cases concern anti-steering practices, as was the case in *Apple App Store* in the EU and United Kingdom.[75]

II.3.2 Change

Two points can be made with respect to the observed changes in the application of Article 102 TFEU in the digital economy. The first concerns what is perceived as a more progressive approach to alleged abuses in that competition authorities not only pursue more cases on an exploitative abuse theory of harm but also construe exclusionary abuse theories of harm that can be seen as adopting a novel approach, dispensing with a strict effects-based approach. That said, EU competition law has always embraced a wider set of objectives supported by its wording and teleological interpretation.[76] In that sense, the application of Article 102 TFEU against Big Tech does not represent a change but an adjustment of the rules to account for the realities in the digital economy, which is permitted under the current competition law framework and decisional practice. This point is further buttressed by the recent amendments to the Commission Guidance on Article 102 TFEU.[77] The Commission has amended its Guidance to reflect recent case law[78] and has also announced the future adoption of relevant Guidelines[79] Following such changes, the concept of 'anticompetitive foreclosure' encompasses a wide array of situations where a dominant undertaking may adversely affect various competitive parameters, not only focusing on price but also encompassing output, innovation, variety, and quality.[80]

[68] See Chapter 5, text to n261.
[69] See Chapter 5, text to n266.
[70] See Chapter 5, text to n185.
[71] See Chapter 5, text to n193.
[72] See Chapter 5, text to n200.
[73] See Chapter 5, text to n216.
[74] See Chapter 5, text to n287.
[75] On these cases, see Chapter 5, text to nn286 and 313.
[76] See Chapter 3, section IV.
[77] European Commission (EU), 'Guidance on the Commission's Enforcement Priorities in Applying Article 82 of the EC Treaty to Abusive Exclusionary Conduct by Dominant Undertakings', [2009] OJ C 45/7 (Enforcement Priorities). See also Chapter 3, section II.2.1.
[78] See Case C-680/20 *Unilever Italia Mkt Operations Srl v Autorita Garante della Concorrenza e del Mercato*, EU:C:2023:33; Case T-604/18 *Google and Alphabet v Commission* (*Google Android*), EU:T:2022:541.
[79] European Commission (EU), 'Commission Announces Guidelines on Exclusionary Abuses and Amends Guidance on Enforcement Priorities' (Press release, 27 March 2023) <https://ec.europa.eu/commission/presscorner/detail/en/ip_23_1911> (accessed 7 June 2024).
[80] European Commission (EU), 'Amendments to the Communication from the Commission—Guidance on the Commission's Enforcement Priorities in Applying Article 82 of the EC Treaty to Abusive Exclusionary Conduct by Dominant Undertakings', [2023] OJ C 116/01 (Amending Communication), para 19.

A second change concerns the adoption of dedicated regulatory tools complementing competition law enforcement. Here, the DMA complements competition law enforcement, and some of its obligations may even render competition law enforcement obsolete.[81]

II.3.3 Challenges

Challenges going forward include, first, the implementation of the DMA and its effectiveness in infusing digital markets with more contestability and fairness. Second, perceived flaws in competition law enforcement, such as the duration of competition law proceedings and the effectiveness of ensuing remedies, need also be addressed. Third, we also need to account for the better coordination between the various enforcement activities at EU and Member State level under competition law as well as potential coordination between competition law enforcement and future DMA enforcement.[82]

II.4 Mergers

Two points are worth making with respect to EU merger control in the digital economy. First, as was the case in other jurisdictions, very few transactions were reviewed by the EU Commission, given that the EU jurisdictional thresholds were not met. Second, even in the cases reviewed, the Commission has followed a traditional approach to merger assessment and theories of harm, despite concerns being expressed about the impact of certain transactions on the incumbent's ecosystem power and privacy. EU merger control has appeared to be resilient enough in that the existing approach has taken into account public-interest considerations such as privacy, albeit to a limited extent. Such an approach will represent a challenge for the future, namely how to account for the incumbent's acquisitions that strengthen their respective ecosystems. With respect to changes, one can enlist the expansive approach to case referrals under Article 22 of the EU Merger Regulation (EUMR), in order to allow the Commission to review a wider number of transactions.

II.4.1 Resilience

A first point with respect to resilience is the fact that digital mergers often concern digital ecosystems of complementary products and services and thus raise conglomerate concerns. The Commission has traditionally rarely examined conglomerate effects, yet it has often examined such concerns in the digital realm.

[81] See Chapter 5, section III and Tables 5.1–5.5.

[82] See also M Ioannidou, 'Unpacking Multi-Level Elements in Digital Markets: Informing Effective Enforcement and Remedial Design in EU Competition Law' in CM Colombo, K Wright, and M Eliantonio (eds), *The Changing Governance of EU Competition Law: A Constitutional Challenge?* (Hart, 2024).

The majority of digital merger cases were cleared unconditionally, whereas *Microsoft/LinkedIn*, *Google/Fitbit*, and *Meta/Kustomer* were cleared following commitments to address conglomerate concerns.[83]

The EU merger control system has been less resilient in the assessment of data. The Commission to date has assessed the potential impact of data combination post-merger but has largely dismissed concerns with respect to data accumulation and privacy.[84]

II.4.2 Change

The Commission has clarified that, given the fact that mergers in the digital (and pharma) sector may concern a target with the potential to develop in an important competitive force in the future (although they do not have a significant turnover at present), the Commission will be accepting referrals from Member States even in instances where the national merger control thresholds are not met.[85] Such approach has been blocked though by the CJEU following *Illumina/Grail*.[86]

In addition, following *Towercast*, the CJEU has now clarified that transactions below the EU and national merger control thresholds may be reviewed by NCAs under Article 102 TFEU on abuse of dominance.[87]

II.4.3 Challenges

Challenges with respect to EU merger control extend at three levels. First, at the jurisdictional level, it concerns ways to strengthen the Commission's powers to review such transactions. The first challenge is addressed to a very limited extent by Article 14 DMA (since a wider reading of Article 22 EUMR is no longer possible). The latter obliges gatekeepers to inform the Commission of any intended merger transactions where the parties or the target provide core platform service (CPS) or services in the digital sector or enable the collection of data.[88] The Commission shall inform the NCAs about such anticipated transactions and the latter may invoke Article 22 EUMR.[89] The second challenge concerns substantive theories of harm,[90] for example not focusing only on input foreclosure conglomerate theories

[83] See Chapter 6, section IV.2.1.
[84] See *ibid*, section IV.2.2.
[85] European Commission (EU), 'Guidance on the Application of the Referral Mechanism Set Out in Article 22 of the Merger Regulation to Certain Categories of Cases', (C(2021) 1959 final (26 March 2021), paras 9, 11.
[86] See Chapter 6, section III.1.
[87] See Case C-449/21 *Towercast*, ECLI:EU:C:2023:207. See Chapter 6, section III.1.
[88] On 14 July 2023, the European Commission published its second template relating to the gatekeeper's obligation to inform about potential mergers. See European Commission (EU), 'Template Relating to the Obligation to Inform about a Concentration Pursuant to Article 14 of Regulation (EU) 2022/1925' (Digital Markets Act) (updated 13 July 2023) <https://digital-markets-act.ec.europa.eu/system/files/2023-07/Article%2014%20DMA%20Template%20%28information%20on%20transactions%29%20-%2013-07-2023.pdf> (accessed 7 June 2024). See Chapter 3, section V.2.1.1.
[89] DMA (n34), Article 14(5).
[90] See Chapter 6, section IV.

of harm but rather expanding such an approach to evaluate the strengthening of the incumbent's ecosystem power.[91] The third challenge concerns the construction and monitoring of effective remedies. To date, the Commission has accepted behavioural remedies, despite growing concerns about their respective efficacy and the need for structural remedies.[92]

III. Chinese Competition Law Enforcement in Digital Markets: Of Resilience, Change, and Challenges

III.1 Market Definition and Market Power

Article 1, paragraph 4 of the Guidelines makes clear that market definition for the platform economy still follows the approach set forth in the Anti-Monopoly Law (AML) and the 'Guidelines on Market Definition'[93] of 2009. Of course, it is explicitly provided in the Guidelines that characteristics of the platform economy (including market entrance, technological barrier, network effect, and lock-in effects) shall be considered in defining a relevant product market. In multiple cases (for instance, the cases of *CNKI*, *Meituan*, and *Sherpa's*),[94] the authorities made specific reference to issues of technological barriers, network effects, etc. It is noteworthy that a quantitative analysis was also performed by Shanghai AMR in the case of Sherpa's when defining the relevant market.

Likewise, the method by which market dominance is determined in digital markets does not go beyond the general principles laid down by the AML. The Guidelines point out several factors particular to the platform economy, which shall be considered. For example, when defining the market share of a platform, other than traditional indices like turnover or the pecuniary value transacted, other statistics including the number of daily active users/monthly active users (DAU/MAU) or the click-through rate (CTR) can also be used. Also, when evaluating the difficulties encountered by new entrants, factors specific to digital markets, like the scale effect of a platform, technological barriers, user versatility,

[91] European Commission (EU), 'Competition Policy for the Digital Era' (A Report by J Crémer, Y de Montjoye, and H Schweitzer) (2019) (EU Experts Report), 11.

[92] J Kwoka and T Valletti, 'Unscrambling the Eggs: Breaking Up Consummated Mergers and Dominant Firms' (2021) 30 Industrial and Corporate 1286. See also the US case, *FTC v Facebook* (pending) <https://www.ftc.gov/legal-library/browse/cases-proceedings/191-0134-facebook-inc-ftc-v> (accessed 7 June 2024). FTC had not challenged *Facebook/Instagram* and *Facebook/WhatsApp*—how can they now bring this case?

[93] In full, Antimonopoly Commission of the State Council, '国务院反垄断委员会关于印发《关于相关市场界定的指南》的通知 [Antimonopoly Commission of State Council's Guidelines on Definition of Relevant Markets]' (promulgated by the Antimonopoly Committee of the State Council, 6 July 2009).

[94] See Chapter 8, section V.1.

users' cost to switch between platforms, the difficulty to obtain data, and consumer habits shall be assessed.

III.2 Anticompetitive Agreements

III.2.1 Resilience

The general framework of the rules on anticompetitive agreements remains intact, exhibiting strong resilience and significant flexibility. Following the 2022 AML amendment, the definitions, formats, and exemptions of anticompetitive agreements have not been significantly altered.

III.2.2 Change

Amendments were made to the rules on anticompetitive agreements in the new AML, two of which were specifically formulated for practices in the digital market economy:

- The long-called-for safe harbour for vertical agreements has been provided, under which vertical agreements can be exempted if the market share threshold is met. Two prerequisites were set for its application: first, the market share is lower than the standards set by the State Administration for Market Regulation (SAMR); and second, other conditions stipulated by the SAMR are met. In addition, the new AML provides that an agreement that limits or fixes resale prices will not be prohibited if the parties can prove that it does not have the effect of restricting or eliminating competition, putting the burden of proof on the concerned undertakings to provide that it does not eliminate or restrict competition and repositioning the definition of anticompetitive agreements.
- The prohibition of hub-and-spoke conspiracies has been introduced. Organizing other business operators to enter an anticompetitive agreement or providing substantive assistance to other business operators in entering an anticompetitive agreement is prohibited by Article 19 AML.

In order to provide regulatory agencies with effective guidance for strengthening the enforcement of anti-monopoly law in the field of the platform economy, the Anti-Monopoly Commission released the Guidelines soon after the 2020 Central Economic Work Meeting, clarifying the definition of relevant markets, the form of horizontal and vertical agreements, hub-and-spoke agreements, collaborative practices, and other related factors. It provides a clearer determination and standards for the enforcement of the AML in digital markets.

Similar to what was emphasized by the EU, the Guidelines not only enumerate the stimulation of 'innovation' as a general guiding principle for the enforcement of the whole body of anti-monopoly law but also specifically stipulate that the factor of innovation should be considered when determining the legality of a potentially monopolistic agreement.

Paragraph 2, Article 7 of the Guidelines refers to across-platform parity agreements (APPAs), or most-favoured-nation (MFN) clauses with a more detailed description of suspicious conducts and acknowledging the possibility of constituting an abuse of market dominance.

Article 8 of the Guidelines circumvents the possible loophole caused by a dichotomy between horizontal and vertical agreements stipulated by the AML. Instead, it provides a set of factors so as to effectively assess whether a suspected agreement constitutes a hub-and-spoke conspiracy.

The Guidelines take full account of the data and algorithms that could facilitate the reach of anticompetitive agreements.

III.2.3 Challenges

Several obstacles to the effective regulation of anticompetitive agreements, however, are still waiting to be further overcome. The transparency and fairness of algorithms needs to be ensured, highlighting the significance of an algorithm auditing system in the future. Whilst the current legal system has paid significant attention to aspects of new technology, strengthening law enforcement against anticompetitive behaviours like 'prohibiting and exempting' RPM, problems still exist at the level of implementation, such as how to precisely formulate the black-letter law and how to establish implementing mechanisms.

III.3 Abuses of Dominance

III.3.1 Resilience

The antitrust law needs to be applied as the last line in the defence of business practice. The regulation of anticompetitive and monopolistic behaviours in China still adheres to the foundational principle of false negatives. At the legislative level, Article 7 of the new AML provides that 'the undertakings that have dominant market positions shall not abuse their dominant positions to eliminate or restrict competition'. It is clear that the new AML requires enforcement agencies or the courts to consider both abusive conduct (form-based approach) and the anticompetitive effect of such conduct (effects-based approach) in determining an abuse of dominance. Such a provision directs the law enforcement agencies to prudently consider the anticompetitive nature of suspected behaviours.

III.3.2 Change

Aside from the aforementioned changes made to market definition and market dominance, the newly amended AML explicitly prohibits abuse of dominance using 'data, algorithms, technologies and platform rules' (Article 22).

The Guidelines specify in detail the factors and scenarios for considering whether a suspected anticompetitive behaviour constitutes exclusive dealing. For the first time in the history of Chinese competition law, it has become clear that the business practice of 'either–or choices' by digital platforms may unfairly limit market competition and constitute an abuse of dominance. The Guidelines also specify the factors for addressing differentiated treatment, another prevalent anticompetitive phenomenon in recent years. Factors for the consideration of differential treatment include differential prices or other trading conditions according to the payment capacity, consumption preferences, and usage habits of the targeted consumers.

As a matter of counterbalance, the Guidelines provide a list of justifiable reasons for the practice of restrictive trading rules by dominant digital platforms. The reasons listed in the Guidelines mainly involve the possible commercial reasonableness of the undertakings' behaviours in the digital markets in commercial practice, such as conduct 'to attract new users within a reasonable period of time', 'to make promotions within a reasonable period of time', or that is 'necessary to protect the interests of counterparties and consumers, intellectual property rights, trade secrets or data security', among other justifiable reasons.

III.3.3 Challenges

In China, formal enforcement of anti-monopoly law against abusive behaviours by competition authorities is still at an early stage, catching up with the constantly evolving digital markets and the ever-changing business practices thereof. A holistic approach with supplemental enforcement devices is needed so as to make continuing efforts to tackle the abuse of market dominance by digital platforms.

On the one hand, the number of civil litigations against abuse of dominance, amongst other monopolistic practices, has been rising gradually over recent years, pressurizing the courts to explore on procedural rules and substantial tests for on anti-monopoly civil cases. The costs and indeterminacy of private actions in anti-monopoly cases are relatively high, with challenges including (i) the ambiguity of the issues at stake, (ii) the difficulty of collecting evidence, (iii) lengthy and complicated procedures, (iv) a heavy burden of proof on damages suffered, and (v) the inexperienced courts dealing with such an issue. For the litigation mechanism of anti-monopoly specifically, it is also necessary to clarify the functional role of civil litigation as a tool of anti-monopoly enforcement in order to better coordinate court decisions with regulatory investigations.

On the other hand, as emphasized in multiple policy documents, algorithm audit, amongst various means of algorithm regulation, is expected to play a significant role in evaluating algorithm values and promoting algorithm innovation. The system of algorithm auditing is still under development and exploration, presenting several challenges. Most crucially, it is necessary to strike a delicate balance between the frequency of algorithm auditing and the costs arising thereof for both regulatory agencies and platform undertakings.

III.4 Mergers

III.4.1 Resilience

Resilience in respect to merger control in digital era in China includes the general framework of merger control, including the definition of an applicable merger and the exemptions to merger control, which remain basically unchanged and shows its resilience in China's digital markets.

Although alternative tests like the 'transaction value test' and the 'market value test' have been proposed, such tests have not been formally adopted yet to complement the 'turnover' test.

III.4.2 Change

The 2022 AML made specific revisions in the part of merger control in response to challenges presented by digital markets:

- As a result of drawing lessons from international practices like those in the EU, one of the significant improvements of the new AML is the introduction of a 'stop-the-clock' mechanism for merger reviews. The new AML empowers the authorities to suspend the merger review period if the operator fails to submit the required documents and information.
- Consistent with global trends, Article 26 of the new AML, explicitly grants proactive investigation power to anti-monopoly authorities when the mergers do not meet the notification threshold but are evidenced to have, or may have, a monopolistic effect.
- Article 37 of the AML introduces a classification and grading system for the review of concentrations, providing handy and accurate coordination systems for regulatory agencies to identify potential anticompetitive mergers. A classified review requires the regulatory agencies to strengthen their review in key industrial sectors. A graded review directs the regulatory agencies to assign different weights to mergers of businesses of different scopes and sizes accordingly.
- The new AML has dramatically increased the amount of the penalty against illegal concentrations.

The Guidelines were released prior to the 2022 revision of the AML, attempting to provide detailed rules on merger reviews in digital markets.

- They not only clarified the applicability of the merger review system to variable interest entities (VIEs) in digital markets but also addressed the discrepancy between platforms' turnover and their actual market powers by empowering the competition authorities to take proactive action against mergers below the conventional turnover threshold.
- The Guidelines also pay close attention to data accumulation and innovation, two of the most significant themes in digital markets, and take them into account when assessing the anticompetitive effects of suspected concentrations in digital markets.

In addition, the SAMR has also started to take a tougher stance on anti-monopoly enforcement. Ever since 2021, the SAMR has actually decided on a large number of merger cases in which platform enterprises have mainly violated their procedural obligation to notify the competition authority before implementing mergers.

III.4.3 Challenges

Concerned about problems brought about by aggressive expansions of Internet giants, China's lawmakers have been devoted, in recent years, to the formulation of a sound system to identify and control anticompetitive mergers in its digital markets. Nevertheless, there are still material questions that remain to be addressed when the competition authority enforces the law against anticompetitive concentrations under the new regime.

- The turnover test has been criticized for being unadjusted to the digital age. In particular, 'killer acquisitions' may substantially exclude competition without triggering a merger control procedure under the turnover test, since the target acquiree is of low revenue. Cases challenging the turnover test have also taken place in China. Supplementary tests, including the 'transaction value test' and 'market value test' have been proposed by Chinese scholars or authorities, yet no such tests have been adopted.
- There are also divergent views on the weight that the merger control review shall accord to non-price factors, such as the advantage of data accumulation, the fostering of innovation from start-ups, and the protection of consumer choices.

III.5 Administrative Monopoly

Under the regulatory structure in China, administrative monopoly remains a problem in the digital economy. Institutions have been put in place to preserve competition.

The fair competition review system was set forth by the executive branch to urge local regulators to repeal anticompetitive measures through internal supervisory procedures. For example, Quanzhou and Lanzhou have relaxed their requirements on the market entrance of e-hailing taxis under the pressure of such a review. The Guidelines make specific reference to the fair competition review system, emphasizing its anticompetitive role in the platform economy.

The National People's Congress (NPC) endeavours to preserve competition through recording and reviewing the constitutionality and legality of local regulations. For instance, since 2019, the Office for Recording and Reviewing Regulations of the NPC has reviewed the requirement of permanent local residency requirements for e-hailing drivers in multiple cities and decided that these requirements violate China's labour law and national policies on the promotion of labour mobility, and thus demanded the correction thereof.

Investigations are initiated by local administrations for market regulation (AMRs) to assess whether a particular policy is anticompetitive, leading to a rather formal recommendation of rectification, or even proactive correction prior to such recommendations.

A system of sharing or licensing public data without jeopardizing fair competition is under discussion. Issues including market entrance, pricing policy, and third-party management of public data await further resolution.

IV. Comparative Reflections

Based on the markets and ecosystems covered, the main players and the respective problems as well as the resilient points, the recently introduced changes and the future challenges highlighted above, this section allows the drawing of important comparative insights.

First, in both jurisdictions the technological, economic, and architectural characteristics of digital markets discussed in Chapter 2 have prompted regulators to adjust the competition law tools to account for this new reality as well as to adopt additional regulatory instruments. Such efforts mark the end of the era of a rather lax regulatory environment for internet giants.[95] In the EU, for example, the particularities of the digital economy were one of the driving forces behind the revision of the market definition notice, one of the most important policy documents summarizing the Commission and EU courts' practice, since market definition

[95] Arguing that such a change marks the end of a rather lax approach in China, see J Deng, 'The Alibaba Case: An Open Sesame to China's Antitrust Regulation on the Internet Platforms' (2022) 10 Journal of Accounting and Economics 230, 231. On the re-orientation of China's policy against digital platforms, see A Zhang, 'Agility over Stability: China's Great Reversal in Regulating the Platform Economy' (2022) 63 Harvard International Law Journal 457.

constitutes the first step in almost every area of competitive assessment, from anticompetitive agreements to abuse of dominance and merger control.[96] In addition, the wide deployment of algorithms online has been taken into account in the recent revision of the rules on both horizontal and vertical agreements,[97] whereas arguably, the rise of a handful of powerful platforms has prompted the Commission to rethink the once advocated more economic approach to the analysis of abusive practices.[98] Similarly, in China, the AML has been revised in order to address anticompetitive practices facilitated by digital technology. In principle, anticompetitive behaviours implemented with data, algorithms, technology, capital advantages, and platform rules are expressly forbidden by Article 9 AML. Specific provisions including the 'safe-harbour' rule (paragraph 3 of Article 18), the 'hub-and-spoke' conspiracy (Article 19), the 'stop-the-clock' mechanism (Article 32), and a classified and graded merger control system (Article 37), among others, were added to cope with antitrust challenges presented in digital markets. In addition, the Guidelines have also been issued with the aim of achieving a more systematic and effective application of the AML to the platform economy. Equally, both jurisdictions, despite depicting signs of a more expansive and aggressive competition law enforcement approach, have acknowledged the inherent limits of competition law and have complemented such rules with additional and more targeted regulation. The DMA, for example, in the EU, aims to complement competition law enforcement and infuse digital markets with more transparency and fairness.[99] Additional regulatory tools, such as algorithm auditing, and proactive investigations, were also adopted in China. What is more, civil litigation against abusive behaviours for damages has become a new front for the enforcement of antitrust law in recent years and is expected to play an essential role in complementing the enforcement of the AML by competition authorities.

With respect to the treatment of anticompetitive agreements, the 'law in books' appears to be converging in both China and the EU in that they both acknowledge, in recent amendments and with the adoption of guidelines, the challenges posed by the wide deployment of algorithmic tools. Yet, the 'law in action' presents a different picture.[100] In this area, as the discussion in Chapter 7 reveals, the Chinese regulators employ a soft-law approach—which, in this book, is labelled as a dual-track enforcement approach with Chinese characteristics,[101] which explains the lack of enforcement in this area. In the EU, on the other hand, as the discussion in

[96] See Chapter 2, section V.
[97] See Chapter 4, specifically section V.
[98] For the relevant case law, see Chapter 5.
[99] *Ibid.*
[100] For the distinction between the 'law in books' and 'law in action', see the seminal paper by R Pound, 'Law in Books and Law in Action' (1910) 44 American Law Review 12.
[101] See Chapter 7.

Chapter 4 has shown, there is ample case law in this area, both at the EU and even more at the Member State level. Such an approach in China can be attributed to the unique institutional setting. The antitrust regulators in China are very powerful. Their power does not mean, though, that they operate without constraints, since they are indeed constrained by specific bureaucratic rules.[102] However, such power does prompt private parties to settle their cases amicably rather than facing formal procedures, which can lead to hefty fines.

Contrary to anticompetitive agreements, both jurisdictions have been showing a more aggressive enforcement stance against powerful Big Tech companies; the difference here being that the EU has initiated cases against Google, Amazon, Facebook, Apple, and Microsoft (GAFAM), which are all US companies, whereas China has been flexing its muscles against its own digital giants. Most notably, the SAMR has imposed an unprecedented fine against Alibaba of ca €2.4 billion.[103] This is by far the highest fine (and almost three times higher than the second highest one) imposed against a single company in China. High fines against Big Tech companies have also been imposed in the EU. The difference between the two jurisdictions here rests on the length of the investigation as well as the ensuing challenges against the regulators' decision. In the EU, investigations are much more protracted and infringement decisions will most certainly be challenged before the EU courts. Let's take, for example, the *Google Shopping* case. The Commission adopted an infringement decision seven years after the case was launched. The Commission's decision was later challenged before the General Court and, the CJEU, with the latter issuing its decision in 2024, fourteen years after the launch of the investigation. On the contrary, the SAMR adopted the infringement decision against Alibaba in a record time of 108 days, leading Western media coverage to attribute such speed to the purported Chinese government's retaliation against Jack Ma, Alibaba's founder.[104] However, such a take on a case that is in line with the international crackdown against Big Tech arguably presents an 'oversimplification of reality', though the speed of its resolution does, indeed, raise due process issues.[105] Following the adoption of the decision against Alibaba, we observe again the Chinese dual-track enforcement approach in action, since thirty-four tech companies were called to an administrative interview by the SAMR and three other central ministries. The Big Tech firms agreed to remove their exclusionary practices within a month and also released relevant public statements.[106]

[102] A Zhang, *Chinese Antitrust Exceptionalism* (OUP, 2021). For a concise discussion, see The China Project, 'Angela Zhang on Why the West Should Pay More Attention to Chinese Antitrust Law' (24 October 2023) <https://thechinaproject.com/2023/10/24/angela-zhang-on-why-the-west-should-pay-more-attention-to-chinese-antitrust-law> (accessed 7 June 2024).

[103] On this case, see SM Colino, 'The Case against Alibaba in China and Its Wider Policy Repercussions' (2022) 10 Journal of Accounting and Economics 217; Deng (n95).

[104] Colino (n103), 219–220 with references to such press coverage.

[105] *Ibid*, 227.

[106] Zhang, 'Agility over Stability' (n95), 493.

Important commonalities can be observed on the merger front, too. First, both the European and Chinese regulators appear to agree that the merger control rules should be tightened to account for the particularities of the digital economy and the observed high levels of merger activity by Big Tech companies in both jurisdictions. Second, it appears that such an advocated stricter approach is, for the time being, mostly reflected in the application of procedural rules. However, there are signs that it has also permeated substantive assessment, with the Chinese regulators blocking the merger between HUYA and DouYu, and the EU Commission blocking the acquisition of eTraveli by Booking.[107] The Chinese regulators have been proactive and penalized many digital players for gun jumping, though the fines imposed were low.[108] In the EU, the Commission has cast the net wider in the application of Article 22 EUMR, a provision that allows the referral of cases by Member States to the Commission. In so doing, the Commission aspired to capture (amongst others) transactions in the digital sphere that would have otherwise fallen outside the notification thresholds. Yet, the CJEU has put a halt to such expansive approach following *Illumina/Grail*.[109] Third, it appears that both jurisdictions see the value of having the competition authority engage with other regulators when scrutinizing merger cases. However, such consultative processes are closer to the Chinese antitrust DNA in regulatory dialogue that has been triggered by the characteristics of the digital economy, most notably the prevalent role of data. As Zhang points out, China has a unique institutional setting, which is exemplified in its merger control processes with various central ministries with industrial policy agendas being consulted through merger control processes.[110]

V. Normative Reflections

V.1 Towards a More Integrative Approach

The analysis of past competition law enforcement in digital markets in the EU and China has highlighted that the role of competition law as a tool of market monitoring and regulation is 'again' in a transformative state in that it often needs to account for a constellation of different public-interest considerations, beyond competitive market structure and (static) efficiencies. It is 'again' in such a state, since, in the EU, for example, competition law and policy has undergone different evolutionary periods.[111] Arguably, this is just another phase in its development—or even

[107] On the former transaction, see Chapter 9, and on the latter, see Chapter 6, text to n382.
[108] See Chapter 9. See also Deng (n95), 232.
[109] See Chapter 6, section III.1.
[110] Zhang, *Chinese Antitrust Exceptionalism* (n102). For a concise discussion, see the China Project (n102).
[111] On the various phases and aims of EU competition law enforcement, see Chapter 3.

a 'liminal moment'[112]—that accounts for the particular characteristics of digital markets, the role of data, and the meteoric rise of a handful of players.

Chapter 3 discussed the aims of competition law enforcement and has shown that EU competition law has embraced a wider set of aims since its inception.[113] Chinese competition law, modelled upon EU competition law, has explicitly embraced a wider set of aims in its opening provision, Article 1 AML. Given such a background, it should come as no surprise that the current decisional practice is more prone to various public-interest considerations, and rightly so. Below we discuss three examples from EU decisional practice and policy initiatives. First, the cases on abuse of dominance discussed in Chapter 5 were, to some extent, driven by preserving fair market outcomes for other competitors, third-party sellers, and consumers.[114] In fact, such considerations inform, to some extent, the current revision of Article 102 TFEU Guidance,[115] which signals the Commission's departure from the previously advocated more economic approach.[116] Second, given the omnipresence of data in the digital economy, naturally privacy concerns have also permeated competition law analysis. However, whereas privacy concerns have been raised in competition law enforcement, both with respect to abuse of dominance and merger cases, they are taken into account not as a self-standing consideration but only as a parameter of competition, informing competitive assessment. Yet, the mere existence of such considerations has resulted in a more frequent consultation between competition and data protection authorities, which marks another emerging trend in competition law enforcement, that of a more cooperative competition law. Third, the rise of the platform economy challenging traditional labour relationships has also affected competition law enforcement, with the Commission signalling that it is prepared to accept a more lax enforcement of competition law towards platform suppliers.[117] Such public-interest considerations, discussed in these three examples, suggest that competition law assumes a more regulatory role, which in the future may be more difficult to distinguish from the scope of recently adopted regulations to imbue digital markets with more fairness, such as the DMA.[118]

In China, public-interest considerations are potentially more prominent than in the EU, not least because of the proclamation of various objectives in the competition law itself but mainly due to the unique institutional setting and the adopted

[112] Lianos (n13).

[113] See Chapter 3, section III.

[114] For a detailed discussion, see Chapter 5.

[115] Amending Communication (n80).

[116] Discussing this new reality as one example of the emerging new competition law, see P Ibáñez Colomo, *The New EU Competition Law* (Hart, 2023), chapter 2.

[117] European Commission (EU), 'Guidelines on the Application of Union Competition Law to Collective Agreements Regarding the Working Conditions of Solo Self-Employed Persons' (n18). For a discussion see Chapter 4, section II.3.

[118] On the DMA, see Chapter 3, section V.2.1.

'dual-track' enforcement approach, which presents a combination a soft administrative intervention followed, if unsuccessful, by a hard enforcement mechanism.[119] Competition law enforcement has been leveraged by Chinese authorities in a redistributive manner catering for various different interests in the digital economy (consumers, smaller enterprises, and platform suppliers). Meanwhile, Chinese tech firms have quickly adjusted to the regulatory demands.[120] In the *Alibaba* case, the firm committed on its own accord to following the SAMR's administrative guidance to improve the conditions for merchants and reduce their respective fees.[121] Similar redistributive concerns were achieved in other cases that were resolved through a soft-law approach, resulting in companies being vetted to amend their respective business practices. Ten delivery and ride-hailing firms were called in May 2021, by eight central ministries and asked to lower their merchant and driver fees and improve their benefits, safety, and labour conditions.[122] Guidelines by seven central ministries (including the SAMR) followed in July 2021 in order to protect the working conditions and labour rights of platform suppliers as well as set out minimum wage requirements.[123] In a similar vein, and following the opinions for improving the respective labour rights issued by the only legal Chinese labour Union, All-China Federation of Trade Unions, the SAMR, together with seven other regulators, issued relevant guidance. The Guidance aimed to safeguard workers' rights in the gig economy and asked that platforms sign labour contracts when there is a clear labour relationship between them.[124] The application of competition law in order to protect the labour rights of platform suppliers is also a subject of debate that has arisen in the EU and has, to some extent, been addressed through the issuance of relevant Commission guidelines.[125]

The integrative approach to competition law enforcement in China is reflected in the cooperation between different regulators and ministries with different public policy mandates. Such an approach is evident, for example, in the area of merger control and can potentially contribute to facilitating a consensus between

[119] *Ibid*, section V.3.2.
[120] Zhang, 'Ability over Agility' (n95), 498.
[121] *Ibid*.
[122] *Ibid*, 499.
[123] *Ibid*. SAMR, '关于落实网络餐饮平台责任 切实维护外卖送餐员权益的指导意见 [Guidance Opinion on Implementing Internet Catering Platforms' Responsibilities and Strengthening Protection for Delivery Workers' Rights]' (promulgated by the SAMR, 19 July 2021) <https://www.tjxq.gov.cn/zwgk/zfxxgk/zfgbm/scjgj/fdzdgk/zdmsxx/spypjg/202202/W020220210410592915416.pdf> accessed 14 April 2024.
[124] Zhang, 'Agility over Ability' (n95), 502. Ministry of Human Resource and Social Welfare, '关于维护新就业形态劳动者劳动保障权益的指导意见 [Guidance Regarding Safeguarding the Labour Welfare of New Employment Formed Workers]' (promulgated by Ministry of Human Resource and Social Welfare, 16 July 2021) <http://www.gov.cn/zhengce/zhengceku/2021-07/23/content_5626761.htm> (accessed 14 April 2024). See also <https://perma.cc/G4CR-BKYQ> (accessed 7 June 2024).
[125] European Commission (EU), 'Guidelines on the Application of Union Competition Law to Collective Agreements Regarding the Working Conditions of Solo Self-Employed Persons' (n18). See Chapter 4, section II.2.

different stakeholders.[126] Such a cooperative approach between competition authorities and other regulators (such as data protection authorities for example) has started to become the new normal in the EU as well, especially with respect to alleged competition law violations in the digital economy, where data plays a prevalent role.[127] Furthermore, it can be predicted that such cooperation is destined to intensify in the future, given the proliferation of regulatory instruments, such as the DMA, that border competition and data protection law enforcement.[128]

All in all, the characteristics of the digital economy have tested the limits of competition law enforcement and attributed a more regulatory undertone to enforcement. From a normative perspective—responding to the existing needs to tame market power and tackling consolidation—competition authorities should adopt a more integrative approach.[129] It appears that this has been the approach in both the EU and China, albeit through a different approach to enforcement. In the EU, enforcement is overall more formal, whereas in China, a more soft-law approach is often preferred.[130] Such an expansive application of competition law is observed both at the level of establishing an infringement (i.e. when competition law is used as a sword) and in instances where public-interest considerations are employed as justifications for the non-application of competition law (i.e. when competition law is used as a shield).[131] An example of the former (competition as a sword) is the enforcement of Article 102 TFEU against GAFAM, where arguably theories of harm, such as self-preferencing, led to the adoption of a more expansionist approach to the aims of EU competition law embracing fairness and equal treatment considerations.[132] Similarly in China, the application of the AML against Big Tech behemoths, such as Alibaba, are also driven in part by fairness considerations. For instance, the administrative recommendations, issued by the SAMR regarding the *Alibaba* case, specified that the 'right to a fair transaction and free choice' for both merchants and consumers in the platform shall be protected and that Alibaba should 'promote the coordinated development of the platform economy and the real economy'[133] Comments from official media on the *Alibaba* case also made reference to platforms' obligations to ensure fairness and equal treatment and

[126] The China Project (n102).

[127] See, e.g. the German Facebook case in Chapter 5, section II.5.2.1.

[128] See, e.g. DMA (n34), Article 40 on the establishment a high-level group comprising from representatives of different regulators. For a discussion, see Chapter 3, section V.2.1.1, part G.

[129] M Ioannidou, 'The Role of Competition Law Enforcement in Times of Evolving Socio-Economic Governance' in P Valcarcel Fernandez (ed), *Gobernanza económica, regulación y administración de justicia* (Aranzadi Editorial, 2023).

[130] See also K Zheng and F Snyder, 'China and EU's Wisdom in Choosing Competition Soft Law or Hard Law in the Digital Era: A Perfect Match?' (2023) 9 China–EU Law Journal 25.

[131] *Ibid.*

[132] For an analysis of the case law, see Chapter 5.

[133] SAMR, '国家市场监督管理总局行政指导书（国市监行指反垄〔2021〕1号）[SAMR Administrative Guiding Decision [2021] No 1]' (6 April 2021) <https://www.samr.gov.cn/xw/zj/art/2023/art_4966dda92ab34c398615f5878c10c8f1.html> (accessed 14 April 2024).

emphasized consumer protection as an objective of the AML.[134] Scholars' opinions have recognized that anticompetitive practices in the platform economy have deepened the social income gap, hindering the accomplishment of 'common prosperity'. Thus, a more stringent enforcement of the AML is deemed as a path to achieve social fairness.[135] An example of the role of competition law as a shield can be derived from the adopted policy approach in both China and the EU, with respect to the application of competition law to protect labour rights in the gig economy.

V.2 Fostering Regulatory Dialogue

The analysis in this book has shown that the EU and China are struggling with the same problems in the digital economy and, to some extent, have employed their respective competition laws in a similar manner. In both jurisdictions, *a more expansive application of competition law* embracing, beyond the protection of competition and the promotion of consumer welfare, considerations such as fairness of economic outcomes, privacy considerations, and working conditions of platform suppliers, can be observed. Arguably, both the EU and China have adopted an outcome-driven approach to competition law enforcement, where competition law has been employed as a tool to protect other public-interest considerations (such as privacy, for example), which has drawn criticism from some quarters.[136] Understandably, the discussions as to whether such an approach is befitting of the competition law enforcement realm are more pronounced in the EU, given that EU competition law is more mature than its Chinese counterpart, which was only adopted in 2008 and, to some extent, has been enforced under a veil of secrecy.[137]

Both jurisdictions have also *amended or updated* their competition law enforcement approach through the issuance of dedicated guidance and policy documents and have complemented competition law enforcement with *dedicated regulatory instruments*.

Such similarities can provide a springboard for furthering the regulatory dialogue between the two jurisdictions under the auspices of the EU–China

[134] W Zhou, '阿里被罚182亿 互联网平台反垄断破局 [Alibaba Fined for 18.2 bn Yuan, a Breakthrough of Platform Antitrust]' (19 April 2019) <https://www.spp.gov.cn/spp/zdgz/202104/t20210419_516009.shtml> (accessed 10 April 2024).

[135] X Wang, '数字平台反垄断的国际观察与国内思考 [International Observation and Domestic Consideration of Digital Platform Anti-Monopoly]' (2022) 42(5) Journal of University of Chinese Academy of Social Sciences 49, 61–62.

[136] See, amongst others, MK Ohlhausen and AP Okuliar, 'Competition, Consumer Protection, and the Right (Approach) to Privacy' (2015) 80(1) Antitrust Law Journal 121; D Sokol and R Comerford, 'Antitrust and Regulating Big Data' (2016) 23(5) George Mason Law Review 1129.

[137] On these discussions, see Chapter 3.

Competition Policy Dialogue,[138] and should be further explored in the various fora, where officials from both jurisdictions exchange views on their respective enforcement efforts.[139] Chinese competition law has been largely modelled upon EU competition law, with lesser influence from US and Japanese competition law; a 'legal transplant shaped in the mold of Western antitrust laws'.[140] Despite its origins though, Chinese competition law has attracted the criticism that—given the centrality of state control—it is unlikely to develop Western-style antitrust law.[141] To some extent, the 'dual-track enforcement approach' with Chinese characteristics discussed in this book[142] showcases that Chinese competition law has, indeed, made its own path befitting its domestic realities. However, competition law enforcement in the digital economy has indeed proved that Chinese competition law enforcement depicts similarities with its EU counterpart. Importantly, what China can learn from the EU is a more orchestrated enforcement towards Big Tech. Heavy reliance on soft-law enforcement, coupled with a rather piecemeal formal application of competition law against certain players, even though it may be effective, risks jeopardizing legal certainty and the overall system consistency in the long run. Nevertheless, the speed at which the *Alibaba* case was resolved is undoubtedly impressive, irrespective of the alleged underlying political incentives.

The 2022 revision of the AML marks the beginning of a more targeted and formal regulation of anticompetitive practices in the digital market. Rules including 'safe harbour', 'hub-and-spoke conspiracy', and 'stop-the-clock' have been designed specifically for the digital economy, giving the competition authority more effective regulatory instruments in the process of formal investigations and litigation. This trend implies that a more formal enforcement of the AML is probably on its way, following in the footsteps of the EU. However, it could be argued that legal consistency is only one among many policy goals in law enforcement and

[138] European Commission (EU), 'Terms of Reference of the EU–China Competition Policy Dialogue' (2019) <https://competition-policy.ec.europa.eu/system/files/2021-06/China-EU_competition-policy-dialogue_terms-of-reference_en.pdf> (accessed 7 June 2024). See also J Maillo and M Verdeguer, 'The Competition Law Global Governance Dilemma and the EU–China Relationship' (2022) 56 Revista General de Derecho Europeo <https://awards.concurrences.com/IMG/pdf/concurrences_maillo_verdeguer.pdf?105099/d718d0594717aee8c454cd73c04a496d444d980fd4ea4cb411b84cb14b0143f3> (accessed 7 June 2024).

[139] See, e.g. Commission (EU), 'EU–China: Commission and China Hold Second High-Level Digital Dialogue' (Press release, 18 September 2023) <https://ec.europa.eu/commission/presscorner/detail/en/ip_23_4488>. See also European Commission (EU), Competition Cooperation—EU–Asia Partnership, 'Competition Weeks' <https://competitioncooperation.eu/competition-weeks> and European Commission (EU), 'Competition Cooperation'—for example, European Commission (EU), Competition Cooperation, '23rd EU–China Competition Week' (28–31 March 2023) <https://competitioncooperation.eu/23rd-eu-china-competition-week-2-2-2> (all accessed 7 June 2024)

[140] See, e.g. W Zheng, 'Transplanting Antitrust in China: Economic Transition, Market Structure, and State Control' (2010) 32 University of Pennsylvania Journal of International Law 643, 648. See also W Ng, 'Changing Global Dynamics and International Competition Law: Considering China's Potential Impact' (2019) 30 European Journal of International Law 1409, 1417.

[141] Zheng (n140); Ng (n140).

[142] See Chapter 3, sections II.3 and V.3.

that the implications of regulating domestic Big Techs by the SAMR are different from that of regulating US-based ones by the EU after all.[143] Thus, both tough postures and soft measures against leading platforms are still taken strategically, striking a balance amongst various objectives including consumer welfare, the stability of the national economy, and legal consistency. As recently as January 2024, the executive meeting of the State Council deliberated and adopted the 'Guiding Opinions on Promoting High-Quality Development of the Instant Delivery Industry', stressing that the delivery industry had an essential role to play in promoting consumption, ensuring livelihoods, and expanding employment and that a favourable business environment was to be created by the government.[144] While regulation on food safety and traffic safety was also mentioned, beyond doubt, the Guiding Opinions could be construed as an amiable message to take-out delivery giants like Meituan and Eleme regarding all regulatory aspects. The general 'dual-track' approach is likely to be maintained in the foreseeable future, whereas the weight of the respective regulatory measure could be flexibly adjusted to each case and situation.

VI. Conclusion

This chapter has highlighted that the regulators in both China and the EU have, to a large extent, adjusted the competition law tools to account for various challenges in the digital economy and complemented such rules with targeted regulatory instruments. Overall, both jurisdictions depict an interventionist stance, with competition law enforcement embracing wider public-interest considerations while, overall, China adopts more frequently a softer-law approach compared to the EU. The particular characteristics of the digital economy call for a more integrative approach to competition law enforcement and increased regulatory dialogue between the two jurisdictions.

143 Wang (n135), 61–64.

144 Central People's Government of the People's Republic of China, '李强主持召开国务院常务会议 研究全面推进乡村振兴有关举措等 [Li Qiang Presided over the State Council Executive Meeting to Discuss Measures Related to Comprehensively Promoting Rural Revitalization, Etc.]' (22 January 2024) <https://www.gov.cn/yaowen/liebiao/202401/content_6927581.htm> (accessed 11 April 2024).

12
Conclusion

The analysis in this book has discussed competition law enforcement in the digital economy and markets in the European Union (EU) and China. Overall, despite the arguably different models adopted in regulating tech companies—a rights-based model in the EU and a state-driven model in China,[1] our analysis has confirmed important points of convergence with respect to competition law enforcement. First, both jurisdictions showed a marked interest in tackling market power of digital behemoths through the application of competition law. Second, procedurally, they have both repurposed merger control to better fit the challenges of the digital economy, even if substantive analysis may arguably still lag behind. On the contrary, with respect to the treatment of anticompetitive agreements, China has taken a more permissive approach. Even though it has formally modelled its competition law largely on EU competition law and has recently updated its legislation with respect to vertical agreements, enforcement is scarcer in this area.

Another point of convergence is the acknowledgement of the limits of competition law to tame the power of Big Tech and the need to complement the competition law arsenal with additional regulatory tools. In the EU, this is depicted with the introduction of a range of regulations, most prominently with the introduction of the Digital Markets Act (DMA), which has been in force for almost a year at the time of writing and has already attracted its first challenges.[2] China, on the other hand, has amended its legislation and has also adopted soft law to tame platform power.

Further, in stark contrast with the EU, China overall employs often more transactional, negotiated mechanisms to resolve ongoing cases, with businesses in China being more willing to cooperate with antitrust regulators than in other jurisdictions.[3] In addition, the Chinese regulatory landscape permits a more 'idiosyncratic' approach to competition law enforcement, leading to the swifter resolution of cases.[4]

[1] A Bradford, *Digital Empires: The Global Battle to Regulate Technology* (OUP, 2023).

[2] See Chapter 3, section V.2.1.1, part A.

[3] See also A Zhang, *Chinese Antitrust Exceptionalism: How the Rise of China Challenges Global Regulation* (OUP, 2021). For a concise view, see The China Project, 'Angela Zhang on Why the West Should Pay More Attention to Chinese Antitrust Law' (24 October 2023) <https://thechinaproject.com/2023/10/24/angela-zhang-on-why-the-west-should-pay-more-attention-to-chinese-antitrust-law> (accessed 7 June 2024).

[4] A Zhang, 'How Antitrust Facilitates China's Goal to Achieve Technological Self-Sufficiency' (27 June 2022) <https://www.cigionline.org/articles/how-antitrust-facilitates-chinas-goal-to-achieve-technological-self-sufficiency> (accessed 7 June 2024).

Competition Law and Policy in Digital Markets. Maria Ioannidou and Bingwan Xiong, Oxford University Press.
 DOI: 10.1093/9780191925955.003.0012

Decisional practice has highlighted the role and inherent limits of competition law enforcement in tackling various anticompetitive practices in the digital economy. In both jurisdictions, competition law analysis (albeit in different degrees) is infused with public-interest considerations such as fairness and data protection. This is a step in the right direction, given the particularities of digital markets, yet it does present itself as a challenge to legal certainty with respect to the substantive application of competition law in digital markets. Such technological, economic, and architectural particularities were discussed in Chapter 2 in a bid to provide much necessary context against which the ensuing analysis of specific cases should be contextualized and understood. Such particularities have naturally also challenged the role and aims of competition law enforcement, calling for a more inclusive enforcement approach affecting case prioritization as well as outcomes. Chapter 3 has delved into such discussions with respect to the appropriate role of competition law enforcement in the digital economy and its respective aims and has shown that in both the EU and China, competition law is (and has always been) a very powerful tool not only to preserve competitive market structures but also to promote better quality, increased choice, and innovation. Within such a paradigm, fairness in its multiple shades has most definitely a role to play. Yet, competition law, in its quest to achieve the above, needs to be complemented—and has, indeed, been complemented—by additional regulatory tools, thereby raising issues of complementarities and appropriate coordination as well.

Following the analysis in Chapters 2 and 3, the ensuing chapters addressed in detail the decisional practice with respect to anticompetitive agreements, abuse of dominance, and merger control in the EU and China. In China, we have also discussed the problem of administrative monopoly, which has been a rather contentious issues in Chinese legal circles. With respect to competition law enforcement in the EU, Chapter 4 traced the main issues concerning the application of EU competition law to anticompetitive agreements. It assessed first the personal scope of Article 101 of the Treaty on the Functioning of the European Union (TFEU) and how platform business models have impacted the notion of undertaking covering both principal–agent relationships and whether platforms are agents of suppliers and suppliers are platforms' employees or self-employed entities. Chapter 4 further discussed various forms of algorithmic collusion and the assessment of data pools. Finally, it covered various types of vertical restraints that are prevalent in e-commerce and m-commerce, such as most-favoured nations (MFNs), resale price maintenance (RPM), and minimum advertised prices (MAP). Following the discussion on the assessment of anticompetitive agreements in the digital economy, Chapter 5 then delved into a detailed discussion of the multiple cases brought against Big Tech companies, which have rapidly increased in recent years. It covered the relevant cases at EU, selected Member States, and UK level. Such analysis served to highlight an arguably expansive approach to the application of Article

102 TFEU, especially with regards to data collection and processing, as well as control exercised by undertakings within their businesses and the markets concerned. Finally, Chapter 6 focused on merger control and discussed the challenges involved, both procedural and substantive, in assessing digital mergers, namely Big Tech's efforts to achieve network effects, as well as acquiring younger companies which show great potential.

After discussing competition law enforcement in the EU, we moved on to discuss decisional practice in China. Chapter 7 focused on the assessment of anticompetitive agreements and, in stark contrast to the EU, revealed a lack of enforcement. Such low levels of enforcement can arguably be attributed to the rather particular enforcement approach employed by Chinese authorities. Chinese regulators resort to soft enforcement mechanisms such as administrative interviews or administrative talks. Such mechanisms are conducted under the 'big-stick' threat of formal investigations coupled with hefty sanctions. Such a 'dual-track' enforcement approach with Chinese characteristics applies both to anticompetitive agreements, but also—as the subsequent analysis revealed—to other forms of anticompetitive misconducts. Chapter 8 discussed the application of the Anti-Monopoly Law (AML) against powerful platforms. The discussion showed that in recent years, Chinese regulatory authorities at both national and local levels have increasingly investigated suspected abuses in digital markets. Enforcement focused on 'either–or choice' by dominant platforms requiring merchants to operate exclusively on one out of several competing platforms. Further, competition law enforcement against digital giants had become stricter, with Alibaba receiving the highest antitrust fine ever following an antitrust investigation that was completed in record time. Chapter 9 covered the application of Chinese merger control in the digital economy. In line with the international trend, Chinese digital companies have increasingly carried out large-scale merger activities in recent years, which have called for a certain readjustment of the regulatory framework. Concluding the relevant part on the enforcement of competition law in the Chinese digital landscape, Chapter 10 discussed instances of administrative monopoly in the digital economy and the assessment of anticompetitive practices linked to the exercise of administrative powers. Chapter 11 drew together the preceding analysis and argued in favour of an integrative enforcement approach and closer regulatory dialogue between the two jurisdictions, also highlighting areas in which competition law and enforcement could be improved.

Overall, our analysis has highlighted the important role and inherent limits of competition law enforcement in the digital economy in both jurisdictions. With its inherent potential to shape the development of the digital economy, as enforcement intensifies, it will be interesting to assess, in future research, its interplay with newly adopted regulations. Further research should also look into the potential of competition law remedies to infuse more competition into concentrated digital markets as well as the impact of such competition law and regulatory remedies in altering Big Tech business models.[5] Competition law investigations coupled with recently adopted regulations may drive powerful platforms to reconsider established practices. Yet, concerns are voiced with respect to their limited potential, given the lack of contestability in many digital settings, such as mobile ecosystems and online advertising. Such lack of contestability should perhaps shape the approach towards generative artificial intelligence, where arguably (if regulators do not intervene), it will forge a similar path. From a comparative perspective, it will also be interesting to assess the impact of such developments in the digital enforcement landscape in both jurisdictions.

The analysis in this book lends support to the argument that there is, indeed, a new paradigm emerging in EU competition law, with more frequent market shaping and policy driven enforcement, unavoidably coupled with an interaction between competition law and regulation.[6] The analysis also highlights that Chinese competition law, given the domestic socio-economic and political realities, has possessed such attributes from its adoption. Overall, our analysis vividly underlines the ever-changing nature of competition law and its flexibility to adjust to changing market dynamics. In such times of 'legal evolution'—more than ever—different jurisdictions can benefit from policy exchanges in a comparative perspective. The analysis herein is a step in this direction.

[5] M Ioannidou, *Competition Law Remedies in the Digital Economy* (OUP, forthcoming).
[6] P Ibáñez Colomo, *The New EU Competition Law* (OUP, 2023).

Bibliography

I. Books

Andriychuk, O (ed), *Antitrust and the Bounds of Power—25 Years On* (Hart, 2023) <https://www.bloomsbury.com/uk/antitrust-and-the-bounds-of-power--25-years-on-9781509962136/>.

Ariely, D, *Predictably Irrational: The Hidden Forces That Shape Our Decision* (Harper Collins, 2008).

Arrow, K, 'Economic Welfare and the Allocation of Resources to Invention' in *The Rate and Direction of Inventive Activity: Economic and Social Factors* (Princeton UP, 1962), 609.

Averitt, N, 'Protecting Consumer Choice: Competition and Consumer Protection Together' in J Drexl and others (eds), *More Common Ground for International Competition Law?* (Edward Elgar, 2011), 36.

Baquero Cruz, J, *Between Competition and Free Movement, The Economic Constitutional Law of the European Community* (Hart, 2002).

Belleflamme, P and M Peitz, *The Economics of Platforms* (CUP, 2021).

Bennett, A, *The Great Adventure* (Stagedoor, 2014).

Bork, R, *The Antitrust Paradox* (2nd edn, Maxwell Macmillan International, 1993).

Boudreau, K and A Hagiu, 'Platform Rules: Multi-Sided Platforms as Regulators' in A Gawer (ed), *Platforms, Markets, and Innovation* (Edward Elgar, 2009), 163.

Bradford, A, *Digital Empires: The Global Battle to Regulate Technology* (OUP, 2023).

Claici, A, A Komninos, and D Waelbroeck (eds), *The Transformation of EU Competition Law: Next Generation Issues* (Kluwer Law International, 2023).

Colombo, C, K Wright, and M Eliantonio (eds), *The Changing Governance of EU Competition Law: A Constitutional Challenge?* (Hart, 2024)< evolving-governance-of-eu-competition-law-in-a-time-of-disruptions-9781509951796>.

Cormen et al, *Introduction to Algorithms* (2001) <https://dl.ebooksworld.ir/books/Introduction.to.Algorithms.4th.Leiserson.Stein.Rivest.Cormen.MIT.Press.9780262046305.EBooksWorld.ir.pdf>.

Cseres, K, *Competition Law and* Consumer *Protection* (Kluwer Law International, 2005).

Cusumano, MA, A Gawer, and DB Yoffie, *The Business of Platforms: Strategy in the Age of Digital Competition, Innovation, and Power* (HarperBusiness, 2019).

Deutscher, E, 'The Role of Privacy in Merger Control—Limiting Principles, Theories of Harm and Operationalisation' in M Ioannidou and D Mantzari (eds), *Research Handbook on Competition Law and Data Privacy* (Edward Elgar, forthcoming).

Drexl, J et al (eds), *More Common Ground for International Competition Law?* (Edward Elgar, 2011).

Dunne, N, *Competition Law and Economic Regulation: Making and Managing Markets* (CUP, 2015).

Ezrachi, A and M Stucke, *Virtual Competition* (Harvard UP, 2016).

Ezrachi, A and ME Stucke, 'Is Your Digital Assistant Devious?' in D Geradin and I Lianos (eds), *Reconciling Efficiency and Equity* (CUP, 2019), 222.

Fletcher, A, 'The Role of Behavioural Economics in Competition Policy' in *Cambridge Handbook on the Theoretical Foundations of Antitrust and Competition Law* (CUP, forthcoming) <https://papers.ssrn.com/sol3/papers.cfm?abstract_id=4389681> (accessed 18 August 2023).

Fisher, A, *Valley of Genius: The Uncensored History of Silicon Valley (as Told by the Hackers, Founders, and Freaks Who Made It Boom* (Twelve, 2018).

Foroohar, R, *Don't Be Evil: The Case against Big Tech* (Penguin, 2019).

Gerber, D, *Law and Competition in Twentieth Century Europe: Protecting Prometheus* (OUP, 2001).
Gormley, L (ed), *Current and Future Perspectives on EC Competition Law* (Kluwer Law International, 1997).
Graef, I, 'Blurring Boundaries of Consumer Welfare: How to Create Synergies between Competition, Consumer and Data Protection Law in Digital Markets' in M Bakhoum and others (eds), *Personal Data in Competition, Consumer Protection and Intellectual Property Law: Towards a Holistic Approach?* (Springer, 2018), 148.
Grundmann, S, W Kerber, and S Weatherill (eds), *Party Autonomy and the Role of Information in the Internal Market* (De Gruyter, 2001).
Harari, Y, *Homo Deus: A Brief History of Tomorrow* (Penguin, 2015).
Hoefflinger, M, *Becoming Facebook: The 10 Challenges That Defined the Company That Is Disrupting the World* (AMACOM, 2017).
Hoeppner, T, *Selfpreferencing in Online Search under Article 6(5) DMA* (Nomos, 2024).
Ibáñez Colomo, P, *The New EU Competition Law* (OUP, 2023).
Ioannidou, M, *Consumer Involvement in Private EU Competition Law Enforcement* (OUP, 2015).
Ioannidou, M, '"Digital Agoraphobia": Exploitative Abuses in Digital Markets' in I Kokkoris and C Lemus (eds), *Research Handbook on the Law and Economics of Competition Enforcement* (Edward Elgar, 2022), 369.
Ioannidou, M, 'The Role of Competition Law Enforcement in Times of Evolving Socio-Economic Governance' in P Valcarcel Fernandez (ed), *Gobernanza económica, regulación y administración de justicia* (Aranzadi Editorial, 2023).
Ioannidou, M, 'Unpacking Multi-Level Elements in Digital Markets: Informing Effective Enforcement and Remedial Design in EU Competition Law' in CM Colombo, K Wright, and M Eliantonio (eds), *The Changing Governance of EU Competition Law: A Constitutional Challenge?* (Hart, 2024).
Ioannidou, M and D Mantzari (eds), *Research Handbook on Competition Law and Data Privacy* (Edward Elgar, forthcoming).
Jianzhong, SHI, 反垄断法—法典释评与学理探源 [*Antimonopoly Law: Interpretation and Theoretical Exploration*] (Renmin University of China Press, 2008).
Jones, A and B Sufrin, *EU Competition Law: Text, Cases, and Materials* (OUP, 2011).
Jones, A and B Sufrin, *EU Competition Law: Text, Cases, and Materials* (5th edn, OUP, 2021).
Kokkoris, I and C Lemus (eds), *Research Handbook on the Law and Economics of Competition Enforcement* (Edward Elgar, 2022).
Komninos, A, '"Consumer Welfare" and the EU Courts: An Unexpected Refuge for a Persecuted Concept?' in O Andriychuk (ed), *Antitrust and the Bounds of Power—5 Years On* (Hart, 2023), 73.
Kwoka, J, *Mergers, Merger Control, and Remedies* (MIT Press, 2014).
Lerner, J and S Stern, *The Rate and Direction of Inventive Activity Revisited* (University of Chicago Press, 2011).
Lynskey, O, *The Foundations of EU Data Protection Law* (OUP, 2015).
Marshall, R and L Marx, *The Economics of Collusion* (MIT Press, 2012).
Mcmahon, K, 'A Reformed Approach to Article 82 and the Special Responsibility Not to Distort Competition' in A Ezrachi (ed), *Article 82 EC: Reflections on Its Recent Evolution* (Hart, 2009), ch 7.
National Bureau of Economic Research, *The Rate and Direction of Inventive Activity: Economic and Social Factors* (Princeton UP, 1962) https://www.nber.org/books-and-chapters/rate-and-direction-inventive-activity-economic-and-social-factors.
Nihoul, P, 'Is Competition Law Part of Consumer Law?' in J Drexl and others (eds), *More Common Ground for International Competition Law?* (Edward Elgar, 2011), 36.
Odudu, O, *The Boundaries of EC Competition Law* (OUP, 2023).
Pascquale, F, *The Black Box Society* (Harvard UP, 2015).
Patel, K and H Schweitze (eds), *The Historical Foundations of EU Competition Law* (OUP, 2013).
Petit, N, *Big Tech and the Digital Economy: The Moligopoly Scenario* (OUP, 2020).

Ramirez Perez, S and S van de Scheur, 'The Evolution of the Law on Articles 85 and 86 EEC [Articles 101 and 102 TFEU]—Ordoliberalism and Its Keynesian Challenge' in K Patel and H Scgweutze (eds), *The Historical Foundations of EU Competition Law* (OUP, 2013), 19.
Rebala, G, A Ravi, and S Churiwala, *An Introduction to Machine Learning* (Springer, 2019).
Reich, N, 'Competition Law and the Consumer' in L Gormley (ed), *Current and Future Perspectives on EC Competition Law* (Kluwer Law, 1997), 126.
Schumpeter, J, *Capitalism, Socialism and Democracy* (Harper & Brothers, 1942).
Schwab, K, *The Fourth Industrial Revolution* (World Economic Forum, 2016).
Shapiro, C, 'Competition and Innovation: Did the Arrow Hit the Bull's Eye?' in J Lerner and S Stern (eds), *The Rate and Direction of Inventive Activity Revisited* (University of Chicago Press, 2011), 361.
Siebel, T, *Digital Transformation: Survive and Thrive in an Era of Mass Extinction* (Rosetta Books, 2019).
Srnicek, N, *Platform Capitalism* (Polity Press, 2016).
Stucke, M and A Grunnes, *Big Data and Competition Policy* (OUP, 2016).
Thaler, R, *Misbehaving: The Making of Behavioral Economics* (WW Norton, 2015).
Ulen, T, 'Information in the Market Economy—Cognitive Errors and Legal Correctives' in S Grundmann, W Kerber, and S Weatherill (eds), *Party Autonomy and the Role of Information in the Internal Market* (De Gruyter, 2001), 98.
Valcarcel Fernandez, P (ed), *Gobernanza económica, regulación y administración de justicia* (Aranzadi Editorial, 2023).
Wang, H, 数据资产理论 [*Data Asset Theory*] (China Renmin University Press, 2019).
Wang, X, 反垄断法 [*Antimonopoly Law*] (Law Press, 2011).
Whish, R and D Bailey, *Competition Law* (OUP, 2012).
Whish, R and D Bailey, *EU Competition Law* (10th edn, OUP, 2021).
Wu, T, *The Attention Merchants: The Epic Scramble to Get Inside Our Heads* (Knopf, 2016).
Wu, T, *The Attention Merchants: How Our Time and Attention Are Gathered and Sold* (Atlantic Books, 2017).
Wu, T, 'The Curse of Bigness: Antitrust in the New Gilded Age' (2018) Columbia Global Reports.
Zhang, A, *Chinese Antitrust Exceptionalism: How the Rise of China Challenges Global Regulation* (OUP, 2021).
Zhou, X, 中国国家治理的制度逻辑：一个组织学研究 [*The Institutional Logic of Governance in China: An Organisational Approach*] (SDX Joint Publishing Company, 2017).
Zuboff, S, *The Age of Surveillance Capitalism* (Profile Books, 2019).

II. Articles

Adner, R, 'Ecosystem as Structure: An Actionable Construct for Strategy' (2017) 43 Journal of Management 39.
Affeldt, P and R Kesler, 'Big Tech Acquisitions—Towards Empirical Evidence' (2021) 12 Journal of European Competition Law & Practice 471.
Aghion, P et al, 'Competition and Innovation: An Inverted-U Relationship' (2005) 120 Quarterly Journal of Economics 701.
Aghion, P et al, 'The Effects of Entry on Incumbent Innovation and Productivity' (2009) 91 Review of Economics and Statistics 20.
Ahlborn, C and C Grave, 'Walter Eucken and Ordoliberalism: An Introduction from a Consumer Welfare Perspective' (2006) 2 Competition Policy International 197.
Ahlborn, C, G Van Gerven, and W Leslie, 'Bronner Revisited: Google Shopping and the Resurrection of Discrimination under Article 102 TFEU' (2022) 13 Journal of European Competition Law & Practice 87.
Akman, P, 'Searching for the Long-Lost Soul of Article 82 EC' (2009) 29 Oxford Journal of Legal Studies 267.
Akman, P, 'The Role of Freedom in EU Competition Law' (2013) 34 Legal Studies 183.
Akman, P, 'A Competition Law Assessment of Platform Most-Favored-Customer Clauses' (2016) 12(4) Journal of Competition Law and Economics 781.

Akman, P, 'A Preliminary Assessment of the European Commission's Google Search Decision' (2017) 3 CPI Antitrust Chronicle 7.

Akman, P, 'The Theory of Abuse in Google Search: A Positive and Normative Assessment under EU Competition Law' (2017) 2 Journal of Law, Technology and Policy 301.

Akman, P, 'Online Platforms, Agency and Competition Law: Mind the Gap' (2019) 43 Fordham International Law Journal 209.

Akman, P, 'Regulating Competition in Digital Platform Markets: A Critical Assessment of the Framework and Approach of the EU Digital Markets Act' (2022) 47 European Law Review 217.

Akman, P, 'A Critical Enquiry into "Abuse" in EU Competition Law' (2024) 44 Oxford Journal of Legal Studies 405

Alexiadis, P and Z Bobowiec, 'EU Merger Review of Killer Acquisitions in Digital Markets Threshold Issues Governing Jurisdictional and Substantive Standards of Review' (2020) 16(2) Indian Journal of Law and Technology 64.

Alexiadis, P and A de Streel, 'Designing an EU Intervention Standard for Digital Platforms', European University Institute Working Paper RSCAS No 2020/14 (2020).

Anderson, M and M Huffman, 'The Sharing Economy Meets the Sherman Act: Is UBER a Firm, A Cartel or Something in Between?' (2017) Columbia Business Law Review 859.

Andreangeli, A, 'Case T201/01 Microsoft v Commission, Judgment of the Grand Chamber of the Court of First Instance of 17 September 2007' (2008) 45 Common Market Law Review 863.

Andriychuk, O, 'Comparing the Incomparable: Analysing UK Digital Markets, Competition and Consumers Bill through the Prism of the DMA' (2023) 3 Concurrences para 17.

Argentesi, E et al, 'Merger Policy in Digital Markets: An Ex Post Assessment' (2020) 17 Journal of Competition Law and Economics 95.

Armstrong, M, 'Competition in Two-Sided Markets' (2006) 37 Rand Journal of Economics 668.

Athey, S, E Calvano, and J Gans, 'The Impact of Consumer Multi-Homing on Advertising Markets and Media Competition' (2018) 64 Management Science 1574.

Athey, S, C Catalini, and C Tucker, 'The Digital Privacy Paradox: Small Money, Small Costs, Small Talk', National Bureau of Economic Research Working Paper Series (2017).

Averitt, N and R Lande, 'Consumer Sovereignty: A Unified Theory of Antitrust and Consumer Protection Law' (1997) 65 Antitrust Law Journal 713.

Averitt, N and R Lande, 'Using the "Consumer Choice" Approach to Antitrust Law' (2007) 74 Antitrust Law Journal 175.

Ayal, A, 'The Market for Bigness: Economic Power and Competition Agencies' Duty to Curtail It' (2013) 1(2) Journal of Antitrust Enforcement 221.

Bacchiega, A and T Tombal, 'Agency Insights: The First Steps of the DMA Adventure' (2024) 12 Journal of Antitrust Enforcement 189.

Baker, JB, 'Taking the Error Out of "Error Cost" Analysis: What's Wrong with Antitrust's Right' (2016) 13 Washington College of Law Research Paper 5.

Bania, K, 'The Role of Consumer Data in the Enforcement of EU Competition Law' (2018) 14 European Competition Journal 38.

Beijing High People's Court Civil Tribunal III Research Group, '论数据市场竞争秩序的司法规制路径—保护数据权益与促进数据流通并重 [On the Judicial Regulation Path of Data Market Competition Order—Emphasizing the Protection of Data Rights and the Promotion of Data Circulation at the Same Time]' (2024) 2 Journal of Law Application 122.

Bernhardt, L and R Dewenter, 'Collusion by Code or Algorithmic Collusion? When Pricing Algorithms Take Over' (2020) 16 European Competition Journal 312.

Bekisz, H, 'When Does Algorithmic Pricing Result in an Intra-Platform Anticompetitive Agreement or Concerted Practice? The Case of Uber in the Framework of EU Competition Law' (2021) 12 Journal of European Competition Law & Practice 217.

Blair, R and D Sokol, 'The Rule of Reason and the Goals of Antitrust: An Economic Approach' (2012) 78 Antitrust Law Journal 471.

Bostoen, F, 'The ACM's Apple Decision: To Boldly Go Where No Enforcer Has Gone Before' (2022) 10 Journal of Accounting and Economics 583.

Botta, M and K Wiedemann, 'Exploitative Conducts in Digital Markets: Time for a Discussion after the Facebook Decision' (2020) 10(8) Journal of European Competition Law & Practice 465.

Bougette, P, A Gautier, and F Marty, 'Business Models and Incentives: For an Effects-Based Approach of Self-Preferencing?' (2022) 13(2) Journal of European Competition Law & Practice 136.

Bourreau, M and A de Streel, 'Digital Conglomerates and EU Competition Policy' (March 2019) <https://papers.ssrn.com/sol3/papers.cfm?abstract_id=3350512> (accessed 27 September 2024).

Boyd, D and N Ellison, 'Social Network Sites: Definition, History, and Scholarship' (2007) 13(2) Journal of Computer Mediated Communication 210.

Brandenburger, R, K Huang, and EX Wang, 'Convergence or Divergence: How Does China Analyse Innovation Concerns in Merger Review?' (2021) 10 Journal of Antitrust Enforcement 63.

Brin, S and L Page, 'The Anatomy of a Large-Scale Hypertextual Web Search Engine' (1998) 30 Computer Networks 107.

Buiten, M, 'Exploitative Abuses in Digital Markets: Between Competition Law and Data Protection Law' (2021) 9(2) Journal of Antitrust Enforcement 270.

Busch, C, 'Platform Regulation beyond DSA and DMA: Which Role for the P2B Regulation?' (2024) 12 Journal of Accounting and Economics 201.

Buxbaum, H, 'German Legal Culture and the Globalisation of Competition Law: A Historical Perspective on the Expansion of Private Antitrust Enforcement' (2005) 23 Berkley Journal of International Law 101.

Cai, J, 'The Sharing Economy and China's Antimonopoly Law: From the Didi Case to Regulatory Challenges' (2020) 28(1) Asia Pacific Law Review 159.

Cai, J and LJ Woon, 'Enforcing China's Anti-Monopoly Law in Regulated Industries: A Study of the Airline Industry' (2021) 9(3) Journal of Antitrust Enforcement 566.

Cai, P and L Chen, 'Demystifying Data Law in China: A Unified Regime of Tomorrow' (2022) 12(2) International Data Privacy Law 75.

Caillaud, B and B Jullien, 'Chicken & Egg: Competition among Intermediation Service Providers' (2003) 34(2) Rand Journal of Economics 309.

Calvano, E and M Polo, 'Market Power, Competition and Innovation in Digital Markets: A Survey' (2021) 54 Information Economics and Policy 1.

Calvano, E, G Calzolari, V Denicolo, and S Pastorello, 'Artificial Intelligence, Algorithmic Pricing and Collusion' (2019) <https://www.aeaweb.org/articles?id=10.1257/aer.2019062> (accessed 8 June 2024).

Calvano, E, G Calzolari, V Denicolo, and S Pastorello, 'Artificial Intelligence, Algorithmic Pricing, and Collusion' (2020) 110(10) American Economic Review 3268.

Camesasca, P and R van den Bergh, 'Irreconcilable Principles? The Court of Justice Exempts Collective Labour Agreements from the Wrath of Antitrust' (2000) 25 European Law Review 492.

Caufmann, C, 'New EU Rules on Business-to-Consumer and Platform-to-Business Relationships' (2019) 26(4) Maastricht Journal of European and Comparative Law 469.

Chen, F, 'Variable Interest Entity Structures in China: Are Legal Uncertainties and Risks to Foreign Investors Part of China's Regulatory Policy?' (2021) 29(1) Asia Pacific Law Review 1.

Chen, L and Y Han, '责任自治与数字泰勒主义：外卖平台资本的双重管理策略研究 [Self-Governance and Digital Taylorism: A Study on the Due Management Strategy of Takeout Platform Capital]' (2020) 2 清华社会学评论 [Tsinghua Sociological Review] 63.

Chen, Y and Y Zhou, 'Analysis of the Effectiveness of the Administrative Talk to Environmental Supervision in China' (2016) 4 Open Journal of Business and Management 716.

Cheng, X, '大型网络平台违反守门人义务的民事责任 [Civil Liability for Breach of Gatekeeper Obligations by Large Online Platforms]' (2023) 5 法律科学(西北政法大学学报 [Science of Law (Journal of Northwest University of Political Science and Law)] 1.

Cheng, W, '破产程序中数据权益之保护—以信义义务为视角 [Protection of Data Rights and Interests in Bankruptcy Proceedings: From the Perspective of Fiduciary Duty]' (2022) 4 Law and Economy 115.

Cohen, MA and PH Rubin, 'Private Enforcement of Public Policy' (1985) 3 Yale Journal on Regulation 167.

Colangelo, W, 'Competing through Keyword Advertising' (2020) 16 Journal of Competition Law and Economics 306.

Colangelo, G and M Maggiolino, 'Data Protection in Attention Markets: Protecting Privacy through Competition?' (2017) 8 Journal of European Competition Law & Practice 363.

Colangelo, G and M Maggiolino, 'Data Accumulation and the Privacy–Antitrust Interface: Insights from the Facebook Case' (2018) 8 International Data Privacy Law 224.

Colino, M, 'The Antitrust F Word: Fairness Considerations in Competition Law', Research Paper No 2018-09 (Chinese University of Hong Kong, Faculty of Law, 2018).

Colino, SM, 'The Case against Alibaba in China and Its Wider Policy Repercussions' (2022) 10 Journal of Accounting and Economics 217.

Colombo, P, 'Competition on the Merits' (2024) 61 Common Market Law Review 387.

Condorelli, D and J Padilla, 'Data-Driven Envelopment with Privacy-Policy Tying' (Working paper, 2020) <https://papers.ssrn.com/sol3/papers.cfm?abstract_id=3504025> (accessed 18 August 2023).

Condorelli, D and J Padilla, 'Harnessing Platform Envelopment in the Digital World' (2020) 16 Journal of Competition Law and Economics 143.

Costa-Cabral, F and O Lynskey, 'Family Ties: The Intersection between Data Protection and Competition in EU Law' (2017) 54 Common Market Law Review 11.

CPI (Competition Policy International), 'Year of the Rat: Antitrust in China' (2020) 3 Competition Policy International 11.

Crane, D, 'Ecosystem Competition and the Antitrust Laws' (2019) 98 Nebraska Law Review 412.

De Loecker, J, J Eeckhout, and G Unger, 'The Rise of Market Power and the Macro-Economic Implications' (2020) 135 Quarterly Journal of Economics 561.

Deltsova, NV and OM Storozhenko, 'Anticompetitive Agreements in the Digital Economy Conditions: Legal Aspects' (2021) 106 European Proceedings of Social and Behavioural Sciences 1458.

Deng, F, '反垄断民事诉讼机制的当下选择 [Current Options for Antimonopoly Civil Litigation Mechanisms]' (2022) 5 China Academic Journal 72.

Deng, J, 'The Alibaba Case: An Open Sesame to China's Antitrust Regulation on the Internet Platforms' (2022) 10 Journal of Accounting and Economics 230.

Deutscher, E, 'Brand Bidding Restraints Revisited: What Is the Appropriate Economic and Legal Framework for the Antitrust Analysis of Vertical Online Search Advertising Restraints?' (2021) 44(4) World Competition 373.

Ding, X, '个人信息私法保护的困境与出路 [The Dilemma of Private Law Protection of Personal Information and a Way Out of It]' (2018) 6 Chinese Journal of Law 205.

Ding, X, '个人信息公私法融合保护的多维解读 [A Multidimensional Interpretation of the Integration of Public and Private Laws for the Protection of Personal Information]' (2022) 5 Research on Rule of Law 25.

Ding, X, '数据交易如何破局 [Breaking the Deadlock of Data Trading]' (2022) 2 Oriental Law 144.

Duan, H, '我国经营者集中分类分级审查制度的构建—以新《反垄断法》第37条为分析对象 [The Construction of a Classified and Grading Review System for Concentration of Operators in China—An Analysis of Article 37 of the New AML]' (2022) 39(6) Studies in Law and Business 157.

Duan, H and B Shen, '互联网经济领域反垄断中的《必要设施理论》研究 [A Study of the Necessary Facilities Theory in Antitrust in the Digital Economy]' (2020) 4 Chinese Applied Law 49.

Dunne, N, 'Dispensing with Indispensability' (2020) 16(1) Journal of Competition Law and Economics 74.

Dunne, N, 'Fairness and the Challenge of Making Markets Work Better' (2021) 84(2) Modern Law Review 230.
Dunne, N, 'Platforms as Regulators' (2021) 9 Journal of Accounting and Economics 244.
Easterbrook, FH, 'The Limits of Antitrust' (1984) 63 Texas Law Review 1.
Economides, N and I Lianos, 'A Critical Appraisal of Remedies in the EU Microsoft Cases' (2010) 2 Columbia Business Law Review <https://doi.org/10.7916/cblr.v2010i2.2922> (accessed 7 June 2024).
Economides, N and I Lianos, 'Restrictions on Privacy and Exploitation in the Digital Economy: A Market Failure Perspective' (2021) 17(4) Journal of Competition Law and Economics 765.
Ehrlich, I and RA Posner, 'An Economic Analysis of Legal Rulemaking' (1974) 3 Journal of Legal Studies 257.
Eisenmann, T, G Parker, and M Van Alstyne, 'Platform Envelopment' (2011) 32 Strategic Management Journal 1270.
Elzinga, KG and M Webber, 'Louis Brandeis and Contemporary Antitrust Enforcement' (2017) 33 Touro Law Review 277.
Epstein, RA, 'Innovation and Inequality: The Separability Thesis' (2016) 39(1) Harvard Journal of Law and Public Policy 17.
Erixon, F, O Guinea, E van der Marel, and E Sisto, 'After the DMA, the DSA and the New AI Regulation: Mapping the Economic Consequences of and Responses to New Digital Regulations in Europe', European Centre for International Political Economy Occasional Paper 3/2022 (2022).
Esayas, S, 'Data Privacy in European Merger Control: Critical Analysis of Commission Decisions Regarding Privacy as a Non-Price Competition' (2019) 40 European Competition Law Review 166.
Evans, D, 'Attention to Rivalry among Online Platforms' (2013) 9 Journal of Competition Law and Economics 313.
Evans, D and R Schmalensee, 'Markets with Two-Sided Platforms' (2008) 1 Issues in Competition Law and Policy (ABA Section of Antitrust Law) ch 28.
Evans, DS and AJ Padilla, 'Designing Antitrust Rules for Assessing Unilateral Practices: A Neo Chicago Approach' (2005) 72 University of Chicago Law Review 73.
Ezrachi, A, 'EU Competition Law Goals and the Digital Economy' (2018), Oxford Legal Studies Research Paper No 17/2018 <http://www.ssrn.com/abstract=3191766> (accessed 7 June 2024).
Ezrachi, A, 'The Competitive Effects of Parity Clauses on Online Commerce' (2015) 11 European Competition Journal 488.
Ezrachi, A, 'Sponge' (2017) 5 Journal of Accounting and Economics 49.
Ezrachi, A and M Stucke, 'The Fight over Antitrust's Soul' (2018) 9 Journal of European Competition Law & Practice 1.
Ezrachi, A and M Stucke, 'Sustainable and Unchallenged Algorithmic Tacit Collusion' (2020) 17 Northwestern Journal of Technology and Intellectual Property 217.
Ezrachi, A and M Stucke, 'The Role of Secondary Algorithmic Tacit Collusion in Achieving Market Alignment', Working Paper No CCLP(L)54 (2023).
Farrell, J and C Shapiro, 'Antitrust Evaluation of Horizontal Mergers: An Economic Alternative to Market Definition' (2010) 10(1) BE Journal of Theoretical Economics Article 9.
Filistrucchi, L, D Geradin, E Van Damme, and P Affeldt, 'Market Definition in Two-Sided Markets: Theory and Practice' (2014) 10 Journal of Competition Law and Economics 293.
Fletcher, A and M Hviid, 'Broad Retail Price MFN Clauses: Are They RPM "at Its Worst"?' (2016) 81 Antitrust Law Journal 65.
Fonteijn, C, 'Multichannel Distribution and the Impact of "Footloose" Consumers' (2016) 7 Journal of European Competition Law & Practice 241.
Fox, E, 'The Battle for the Soul of Antitrust' (1987) 75 California Law Review 917.
Fu, X and G Tan, 'Abuse of Market Dominance under China's Anti-Monopoly Law: The Case of Tetra Pak' (2019) 54(2) Review of Industrial Organization 409.

Furse, M, 'Evidencing the Goals of Competition Law in the People's Republic of China: Inside the Merger Laboratory' (2018) 41 World Competition 129.

Gal, M, 'Algorithms as Illegal Agreements' (2019) 34(1) Berkeley Technology Law Journal 67.

Gal, M and O Lynskey, 'Synthetic Data: Legal Implications of the Data-Generation Revolution' (2023) 109(3) Iowa Law Review 1087.

Gao, F, '数据生产理论—数据资源权利配置的基础理论 [The Theory of Data Production: A Fundamental Theory of the Right Allocation of Data Resource]' (2019) 4 Shanghai Jiao Tong University Law Review 5.

Gao, Q and H Su, '滴滴合并优步案的反垄断分析 [Antimonopoly Analysis on Didi's Merger with Uber]' (2019) 6 Journal of North China Electric Power University (Social Sciences) 78.

Gautier, A and J Lamesch, 'Mergers in the Digital Economy', Centre for Economic Studies–Institute for Economic Research (CESifo) Working Paper No 8056 (2020).

Geradin, D and D Katsifis, 'An EU Competition Law Analysis of Online Display Advertising in the Programmatic Age' (2019) 15 European Competition Journal 55.

Geradin, D and D Katsifis, 'The Antitrust Case against the Apple App Store (Revisited)', TILEC Discussion Paper No DP2020-035 (2020) <https://papers.ssrn.com/sol3/papers.cfm?abstract_id=3744192> (accessed 27 September 2024).

Gerard, D, 'Fairness in EU Competition Policy: Significance and Implications' (2018) 9 Journal of European Competition Law & Practice 211.

Gerber, D, 'Constitutionalising the Economy: German Neoliberalism, Competition Law and the "New" Europe' (1994) 42 American Journal of Comparative Law 25.

Gilbert, R and S Sunshine, 'Incorporating Dynamic Efficiencies Concerns in Merger Analysis: The Use of Innovation Markets' (1995) 63 Antitrust Law Journal 569.

Ginsburg, D, 'Judge Bork, Consumer Welfare, and Antitrust Law' (2008) 31 Harvard Journal of Law and Public Policy 449.

Glick, M and C Ruetschlin, 'Big Tech Acquisitions and the Potential Competition Doctrine: The Case of Facebook', Institute of New Economic Thinking Working Paper 104s (2019).

Graef, I, 'Market Definition and Market Power in Data: The Case of Online Platforms' (2015) 38 World Competition 473.

Graef, I, 'Consumer Sovereignty and Competition Law: From Personalization to Diversity' (2021) 58 Common Market Law Review 471.

Graef, I and S van Berlo, 'Towards Smarter Regulation in the Areas of Competition, Data Protection and Consumer Law: Why Greater Power Should Come with Greater Responsibility' (2020) 12 European Journal of Risk Regulation 674.

Graef, I, D Clifford, and P Valcke, 'Fairness and Enforcement: Bridging Competition, Data Protection, and Consumer Law' (2018) 8 International Data Privacy Law 200.

Graf, T and H Mostyn, 'Do We Need to Regulate Equal Treatment? The Google Shopping Case and the Implications of Its Equal Treatment Principle for New Legislative Initiatives' (2020) 11 Journal of European Competition Law & Practice 561.

Grandy, C, 'Original Intent and the Sherman Antitrust Act: A Re-Examination of the Consumer-Welfare Hypothesis' (1993) 53 Journal of Economic History 359.

Gross, R and A Acquisti, 'Information Revelation and Privacy in Online Social Networks' (2005) Proceedings of the 2005 ACM Workshop on Privacy in the Electronic Society 71.

Grunes, A and M Stucke, 'No Mistake about It: The Important Role of Antitrust in the Era of Big Data' (2015) 14 Antitrust Source 1.

Guo, Y, 'VIE架构的监管该何去何从—负面清单时代下的再审视 [What Is the Future of VIE Structure Supervision: A Re-Examination in the Era of Negative Lists]' (2023) 25 Journal of Northeastern University (Social Science) 99.

Guo, Y and J Chen, '共享经济的发展历程，分类及商业模式研究 [Research on the Development History, Classification and Business Model of Sharing Economy]' (2020) 16(9) Science and Technology for Development 1027.

Han, W, '数字经济中的隐私保护与支配地位滥用 [The Privacy Protection and the Abuse of Dominance in the Digital Economy]' (2020) 1 Journal of University of Chinese Academy of Social Sciences 37.

Han, W and Y Gao, 'Digital Economy Driving China's Antitrust Reform' (2023) 19(1) Competition Law International 95.
Han, W and Y Gao, 'The Evaluation of Innovation in Merger Control: A Comparison between China and Other Jurisdictions' (2023) 9 China EU Law Journal 73.
Han, W and Z Li, '反垄断法框架下的数据隐私保护 [Data Privacy Protection under the Framework of Antimonopoly Law]' (2017) 7 中国物价 [China's Prices] 34.
Hao, J, '反垄断法上的交易相对人及其三重角色 [The Counterparty to a Transaction and Its Triple Role in Antitrust Law]' (2020) 7 China Price Regulation and Antitrust 13.
Hao, J, '论我国垄断协议类型序列的立法完善 [On the Legislative Improvement of the Sequence of Types of Anticompetitive Agreements in China]' (2022) 1 Journal of China University of Political Science and Law 211.
Harrington, J, 'Developing Competition Law for Collusion by Autonomous Artificial Agents' (2019) 14 Journal of Competition Law and Economics 331.
Harrington, J, 'Collusion in Plain Sight: Firms' Use of Public Announcements to Restrain Competition' (2022) 84 Antitrust Law Journal 521.
Hederstrom, J and L Peeperkorn, 'Vertical Restraints in On-Line Sales: Comments on Some Recent Developments' (2016) 7 Journal of Competition Law & Practice 10.
Heinz, S, 'Online Booking Platforms and EU Competition Law in the Wake of the German Bundeskartellamt's Booking.com Infringement Decision' (2016) 7(8) Journal of European Competition Law & Practice 530.
Hiessl, C, 'Case Law on the Classification of Platform Workers: Cross-European Comparative Analysis and Tentative Conclusions' (2021) 42 Comparative Labour Law & Policy Journal 465.
Hoffmann, C, C Lutz, and G Ranzini, 'Privacy Cynicism: A New Approach to the Privacy Paradox' (2016) 10(4) Cyberpsychology: Journal of Psychosocial Research on Cyberspace.
Hoeppner, T, 'Google's (Non)-Compliance with the EU Shopping Decision—a Study Based upon Empirical Data of 25 Comparison Shopping Services' (2020) <https://www.hausfeld.com/uploads/documents/googles_(non)_compliance_with_google_search_(shopping).pdf> (accessed 12 January 2023).
Hou, H and Y Shi, 'Ecosystem-as-Structure and Ecosystem-as-Coevolution: A Constructive Examination' (2021) 100 Technovation 1.
Hovenkamp, H, 'Platforms and the Rule of Reason: The American Express Case' (2019) Columbia Business Law Review 35.
Hu, L, '非法兴起：理解中国互联网演进的一个视角 [Illegal Arising: A Perspective for Understanding China's Internet Evolution]' (2016) 5 Beijing Cultural Review 121.
Huang, Y and Z Deng, '论规制行政垄断的我国《反垄断法》特色—兼论行政垄断的政治与经济体制根源 [On the Character of China Anti-Monopoly Law under Controlling Administrative Monopoly]' (2010) 7 Law Science Magazine 50.
Hutchings, M and P Whelan, 'Consumer Interest in Competition Law Cases' (2006) 16 Consumer Policy Review 182.
Ibanez Colomo, P, 'Indispensability and Abuse of Dominance: From Commercial Solvents to Slovak Telekom and Google Shopping' (2019) 10(9) Journal of European Competition Law & Practice 532.
Ina Pauer, N, 'The 11th Amendment of the German Act against Restraints of Competition: A "New Competition Tool", Facilitated Disgorgement and the DMA's Enforcement' (2023) 14 Journal of European Competition Law & Practice 354.
Ioannidou, M, '"Responsive" Remodelling of Competition Law Enforcement' (2020) 40 Oxford Journal of Legal Studies 846.
Ip, EC and KK Hiu Fai, 'Judicial Control of Local Protectionism in China: Antitrust Enforcement against Administrative Monopoly on the Supreme People's Court' (2017) 13(3) Journal of Competition Law and Economics 549.
Ittoo, A and N Petit, 'Algorithmic Pricing Agents and Tacit Collusion: A Technological Perspective' (2017) <https://papers.ssrn.com/sol3/papers.cfm?abstract_id=3046405> (accessed 8 June 2024).

Ivaldi, M, B Jullien, P Rey, P Seabright, and J Tirole, 'The Economics of Tacit Collusion', (Final Report for DG Competition, March 2003) *Industrial and Corporate Change*, Volume 30, Issue 5, October 2021, Page 1199.

Ivaldi, M, N Petit, and S Ünekbaş, 'Killer Acquisitions: Evidence from European Merger Cases' (2024) Antitrust Law Journal TSE Working Paper No 13-1420 <https://papers.ssrn.com/sol3/papers.cfm?abstract_id=4407333> (accessed 27 September 2024).

Jacobides, M and I Lianos, 'Ecosystems and Competition Law in Theory and Practice', Centre for Law, Economics and Society Research Paper Series (January 2021).

Jacobides, M, C Cernamo, and A Gawer, 'Distinguishing between Platforms and Ecosystems: Complementarities, Value Creation, and Coordination Mechanisms' (Working paper, 14 October 2020) <https://www.jacobides.com/_files/ugd/0b15b1_7e0678d2815541bb920c77ec41e4d305.pdf> (accessed 18 August 2023).

Jacobides, M, C Cernamo, and A Gawer, 'Towards a Theory of Ecosystems' (2018) 39 Strategic Management Journal 2255.

Jenny, F, 'Changing the Way We Think: Competition, Platforms and Ecosystems' (2021) 9 Journal of Accounting and Economics 1.

Li, J, '互联网反垄断能促进数据隐私保护吗 [Can Antitrust Law Improve Data Privacy in the Internet Industry?]' (2021) 5 商业经济与管理 [Journal of Business Economics] 92.

Jiang, L, '互联网双边市场经营者集中申报标准之困境 [The Dilemma of Standards for Mergers in Bilateral Internet Markets]' (2017) 19 Journal of Southeast University (Philosophy and Social Science) 21.

Jianzhong, SHI, '数据基础制度建设的地方立法实践—基于政策文献计量的初步研究 [Local Legislative Practices of Foundational Architecture for Data: A Preliminary Quantitative Research Based on Policy Documents]' (2023) 1 Digital Jurisprudence Review 44.

Jiao, H, '个人信息的反垄断法保护：从附属保护到独立保护 [Anti-Monopoly Protection of Personal Information: From Subsidiary Protection to Independent Protection]' (2021) 4 Law Science 108.

Jiao, H, '反垄断法上的竞争损害与消费者利益标准 [Competitive Harm in Anti-Monopoly Law and Its Relationship with Consumer Interests]' (2022) 2 Nanjing University Law Journal 1.

Jiao, H, '互联网平台最惠国条款的反垄断法适用 [Application of Antimonopoly Law of the Most Favored Nation Clauses on the Internet Platform]' (2021) 2 Journal of Business Economics 74.

Jolls, C, C Sunstein, and R Thaler, 'A Behavioral Approach to Law and Economics' (1998) 50 Stanford Law Review 1471.

Joskow, PL and AK Klevorick, 'A Framework for Analyzing Predatory Pricing Policy' (1979) 89 YALE Law Journal 213.

Kaplow, L, 'Why (Ever) Define Markets?' (2010) 124 Harvard Law Review 438.

Kaplow, L, 'On the Meaning of Horizontal Agreements in Competition Law' (2011) 99 California Law Review 683.

Kaplow, L, 'Market Definition: Impossible and Counterproductive' (2013) 79 Antitrust Law Journal 361.

Katz, M and H Shelanski, 'Mergers and Innovation' (2007) 74 Antitrust Law Journal 1.

Kerber, W, 'Digital Markets, Data, and Privacy: Competition Law, Consumer Law and Data Protection' (2016) 11 Journal of Intellectual Property Law & Practice 856.

Kesler, R, 'The Impact of Apple's App Tracking Transparency on App Monetization' (2022) <https://papers.ssrn.com/sol3/papers.cfm?abstract_id=4090786> (accessed 27 September 2024).

Khan, L, 'Amazon's Antitrust Paradox' (2017) Yale Law Journal 710.

Khan, L, 'The New Brandeis Movement: America's Antimonopoly Debate' (2018) 9 Journal of European Competition Law & Practice 131.

Kirkwood, J and R Lande, 'The Fundamental Goal of Antitrust: Protecting Consumers Not Increasing Efficiency' (2008) 84 Notre Dame Law Review 191.

Kirkwood, JB, 'Antitrust and Two-Sided Platforms: The Failure of American Express' (2020) 41 Cardozo Law Review 1805.

Klein, T, 'Autonomous Algorithmic Collusion: Q-Learning under Sequential Pricing', Amsterdam Law School Legal Studies Research Paper No 2018-15 (2018).

Klein, T, 'Autonomous Algorithmic Collusion: Q-Learning under Sequential Pricing' (Tinbergen Institute, November 2021) <https://papers.tinbergen.nl/18056.pdf> (accessed 8 June 2024).

Kokolakis, S, 'Privacy Attitudes and Privacy Behaviour: A Review of Current Research on the Privacy Paradox Phenomenon' (2017) 64 Computers and Security 122.

Kovacic, W, R Marshall, L Marx, and H White, 'Plus Factors and Agreement in Antitrust Law' (2011) 110 Michigan Law Review 393.

Kuhn, T and M Rust, 'Between Coty, Guess and the New V-BER—Where Do We Stand on E-Commerce Restrictions?' (2019) 40(8) European Competition Law Review 376.

Laurie, KA, 'Capping Uber in New York City: Ramifications for Rideshares, the Road, and Outer-Borough Residents' (2019) 46 Fordham Urban Law Journal 942.

Lei, W, 'Positioning and Realization of Innovation Objectives in the Anti-Monopoly Law: Comment on Article 1 of the Anti-Monopoly Law (Draft Amendment)' (2022) 1 Journal of China University of Political Science and Law 180.

Li, J, '反垄断私人诉讼困境与反垄断执法的管制化发展 [The Antitrust Private Litigation Dilemma and the Regulatory Development of Antitrust Enforcement]' (2011) 33 Chinese Journal of Law 80.

Li, J, '互联网反垄断能促进数据隐私保护吗 [Can Antitrust Law Improve Data Privacy in the Internet Industry?]' (2021) 5 Journal of Business Economics 92.

Li, S, '数字音乐独家版权模式解除与反垄断—以对腾讯音乐的反垄断调查为例 [Dismantling of the Exclusive Copyright Model for Digital Music and Antitrust: An Example of Antitrust Investigation on Tencent Music Group]' (2022) 4 China Price 69.

Li, S, C Xie, and E Feyler, 'Algorithms & Antitrust: An Overview of EU and National Case Law—Concurrences' (2021) eCompetitions Special Issue Algorithms & Antitrust 3.

Li, Y, '从价格到质量：数字经济时代反垄断法中消费者福利标准内涵的演变 [From Price to Quality: The Evolution of Standard Connotations of Consumer Welfare in Antitrust Law in the Era of Digital Economy]' (2022) 2 Journal of Northwest Minzu University (Philosophy and Social Sciences) 79.

Li, Y, Z Huang, X Xia, and L Gao, 'Theoretical Analysis and System Improvement of Administrative Interviews in the Field of Internet Information Supervision' (2022) 4 Scientific Journal of Economics and Management Research, 393.

Lianos, I, 'Polycentric Competition Law' (2018) 71 Current Legal Problems 161.

Lianos, I, 'Competition Law for a Complex Economy' (2019) 50 International Review of Intellectual Property and Competition Law 643.

Lianos, I, 'Reorienting Competition Law' (2022) 10 Journal of Accounting and Economics 1.

Lianos, I and B Carballa-Smichowski, 'A Coat of Many Colours—New Concepts and Metrics of Economic Power in Competition Law and Economics' (2022) 18 Journal of Competition Law and Economy 795.

Lianos, I, K Hendrik Eller, and T Kleinschmitt, 'Towards a Legal Theory of Digital Ecosystems', University College London, Centre for Law, Economics and Society Research Paper Series No 2 (2024).

Liao, F, '"外商投资法"：背景, 创新与展望 [Foreign Investment Law: Background, Innovation and Outlook]' (2020) 3 Journal of Xiamen University (Arts & Social Sciences) 140.

Hu, L, '非法兴起：理解中国互联网演进的一个视角 [Illegal Arising: A Perspective for Understanding China's Internet Evolution]' (2016) 5 文化纵横 [Beijing Cultural Review] 121.

Liu, L and R Weingast Barry, 'Taobao, Federalism, and the Emergence of Law, Chinese Style' (2018) 111 Minnesota Law Review 1563.

Liu, W, '数据产权的法律表达 [Legal Expression of Property Rights in Data]' (2023) 45(3) Chinese Journal of Law 36.

Liu, X, '数字平台生态系统的反垄断法定位与规制 [Anti-Monopoly Law in Ecosystem of Digital Platform: Its Positioning and Regulation]' (2022) 1 思想战线 [Thinking] 138.

Liu, YM, 'Tax Audit System Analysis and Revelation of Canada' (2015) 5 Taxation Research 90.

Long, J '数字音乐版权独家授权的竞争风险及其规制方法 [Competition Risks of Digital Music Copyright Exclusive Authorization and Its Solutions]' (2020) 34(2) Journal of Huazhong University of Science and Technology (Social Science Edition) 83.

Long, J, '平台拒绝数据许可的反垄断规制—基于反垄断法禁止拒绝交易条款的适用展开 [Anti-Monopoly Regulation of Platforms Refusing to License Data—Based on the Application of Refusal to Supply Clause of AML]' (2023) 20 Shanghai Legal Studies 9.

Long, W, '数据新型财产权构建及其体系研究 [On the Construction of New Data Property and Its System Structure]' (2017) 35(4) Tribune of Political Science and Law 63.

Lu, D and X Li, '超大型平台并购初创企业的反垄断法规制研究 [Research on the Anti-Monopoly Regulation of Mergers and Acquisitions of Start-Ups by Mega-Platforms]' (2023) 35 Journal of Chongqing University of Posts and Telecommunications (Social Science Edition) 51.

Lundqvist, B, 'Competition and Data Pools' (2018) 7 Journal of European Consumer and Market Law 146.

Lycett, M, '"Datafication": Making Sense of (Big) Data in a Complex World' (2013) 22 European Journal of Information Systems 381.

MacCarthy, M, 'Privacy as a Parameter of Competition in Merger Reviews' (2020) 72 Federal Communications Law Journal 1.

Maillo, J and M Verdeguer, 'The Competition Law Global Governance Dilemma and the EU–China Relationship' (2022) 56 Revista General de Derecho Europeo <https://awards.concurrences.com/IMG/pdf/concurrences_maillo_verdeguer.pdf?105099/d718d0594717aee8c454cd73c04a496d444d980fd4ea4cb411b84cb14b0143f3> (accessed 27 September 2024).

Manne, G, 'In Defence of the Supreme Court's "Single Market" Definition in Ohio v American Express' (2019) 7 Journal of Accounting and Economics 104.

Marsden, P, 'Checks and Balances: European Competition Law and the Rule of Law' (2009) 22 Loyola Consumer Law Review 51.

Marsden, P, 'Google Shopping for the Empress's New Clothes—When a Remedy Isn't a Remedy (and How to Fix It)' (2020) 11 Journal of European Competition Law & Practice 553.

McLean, A, 'A Financial Capitalism Perspective on Start-Up Acquisitions: Introducing the Economic Goodwill Test' (2020) 17 Journal of Competition Law and Economics 141.

Mehra, S, 'Antitrust and the Robo-Seller: Competition in the Time of Algorithms' (2016) 100 Minnesota Law Review 1323.

Mehra, S, 'US v. Topkins: Can Price Fixing Be Based on Algorithms?' (2016) 7 Journal of European Competition Law & Practice 470.

Mei, X, '在分享和控制之间数据保护的私法局限和公共秩序构建 [Between Sharing and Control: The Limitations of Private Law and the Building of Public Order in Data Protection]' (2019) 31 Peking University Law Journal 845.

Melamed, D and S Salop, 'An Antitrust Exemption for Workers: And Why Worker Bargaining Power Benefits Consumers, Too', Working Paper Series No 579 (2023) <https://papers.ssrn.com/sol3/papers.cfm?abstract_id = 4336770> (accessed 8 June 2024).

Meng, Q, '江苏漫修律师事务所 [Jiang Su Man Xiu Law Firm], 行政约谈法治化研究 [Study on Legalization of Administrative Talk]' (2015) 6 行政法学研究[Administrative Law Review] 99.

Meng, Y, '反垄断法规制平台剥削性滥用的争议与抉择 [Controversies and Choices in Anti-Monopoly Regulation on Exploitative Abuse of Platforms]' (2022) 2 中外法学 [Peking University Law Journal] 327.

Ye, M and J Zhang, '反垄断法保护个人信息权益的理据与路径 [The Rationale and Path of Protecting the Interests of Personal Information through Antitrust Law]' (2023) 37(1) 华中科技大学学报 社会科学版 [Journal of Huazhong University of Science and Technology (Social Science Edition)] 87.

Monti, G, 'Article 81 EC and Public Policy' (2002) 39 Common Market Law Review 1057, 1078–79.

Monti, G, 'Exploitative Abuse—Takeaways from the Apple App Store Practices Decision' (2024) <https://papers.ssrn.com/sol3/papers.cfm?abstract_id = 4853304> (accessed 9 October 2024).

Moore, J, 'Business Ecosystems and the View from the Firm' (2006) 51 Antitrust Bulletin 31.
Moore, J, 'Predators and Prey: A New Ecology of Competition' (1993) (May/June) Harvard Business Review <https://hbr.org/1993/05/predatorsandpreyanewecologyofcompetition> (accessed 18 August 2023).
Moreno Belloso, N and N Petit, 'The EU Digital Markets Act (DMA)—a Competition Hand in a Regulatory Glove' (2023) 48 European Law Review 391.
Möschel, W, 'The Proper Scope of Government Viewed from an Ordoliberal Perspective: The Example of Competition Policy' (2001) 157 Journal of Institutional and Theoretical Economics 3.
Motta, M and M Peitz, 'Big Tech Mergers' (2021) 54 Information Economics and Policy 1.
Mouton, J and L Reed, 'Following the Google Shopping Judgment, Should We Expect a Private Enforcement Action?' (2022) 13 Journal of European Competition Law & Practice 154.
Mulder, J and W Sauter, 'A New Regime for Below Threshold Mergers in EU Competition Law? The Illumina/Grail and Towercast Judgments' (2023) 11(3) Journal of Antitrust Enforcement 544.
Nazzini, R, 'Google and the (Ever-Stretching) Boundaries of Article 102 TFEU' (2015) 6(5) Journal of European Competition Law & Practice 301.
Newman, N, 'The Costs of Lost Privacy: Consumer Harm and Rising Economic Inequality in the Age of Google' (2014) 40 William Mitchell Law Review 849.
Ng, W, 'Changing Global Dynamics and International Competition Law: Considering China's Potential Impact' (2019) 30 European Journal of International Law 1409.
Nihoul, P, 'Do Workers Constitute Undertakings for the Purpose of the Competition Rules?' (2000) 25 European Law Review 408.
Nowag, J, 'When Sharing Platforms Fix Sellers' Prices' (2018) 6 Journal of Accounting and Economics 382.
O'Callaghan, L, 'The Intersection between Data Protection and Competition Law: How to Incorporate Data Protection, as a Non-Economic Objective, into EU Competition Analysis' (2018) 21 Trinity College Law Review 109.
Odudu, O and D Bailey, 'The Single Economic Entity Doctrine in EU Competition Law' (2014) 51 Common Market Law Review 1721.
Ohlhausen, MK and AP Okuliar, 'Competition, Consumer Protection, and the Right (Approach) to Privacy' (2015) 80(1) Antitrust Law Journal 121.
Orbach, B, 'The Antitrust Consumer Welfare Paradox' (2011) 7 Journal of Competition Law and Economics 133.
Padilla, J and C Kalmus, 'Tying and Competition Law: An Overview of EU and National Case Law' (2012) 43907 Concurrences.
Padilla, J, S Piccolo, and N Watson, 'The Simple Economics of Wholesale Price-Parity Agreements: The Case of the Airline Tickets Distribution Industry' (2020) 17 Journal of Competition Law and Economics 364.
Page, WH, 'Microsoft and the Limits of Antitrust' (2010) 6 Journal of Competition Law and Economics 33.
Parker, G, G Petropoulos, and M Van Alstyne, 'Digital Platforms and Antitrust' (Working paper, 2020) <https://www.bruegel.org/sites/default/files/wp_attachments/WP2020061.pdf> (accessed 18 August 2023).
Peeperkorn, L and F Wijckmans, 'The New Competition Rules for Supply and Distribution Agreements: No Revolution, But an Evolution of the Effects-Based Approach' (2023) 44 European Competition Law Review 127.
Petit, N, 'Theories of Self-Preferencing under Article 102 TFEU: A Reply to Bo Vesterdorf' (2015) <https://orbi.uliege.be/bitstream/2268/192437/1/Theories%20of%20SelfPreferencing%20Under%20Article%20102%20TFEU%20A%20Reply%20to%20Bo%20Vesterdorf.pdf> (accessed 9 June 2024).
Podszun, R and T Rohner, 'Making Article 102 TFEU Future-Proof—Learnings from the Past' (2023) <https://papers.ssrn.com/sol3/papers.cfm?abstract_id=4428170> (accessed 27 September 2024).

Posner, RA, 'Oligopoly and the Antitrust Laws: A Suggested Approach' (1969) 21 Stanford Law Review 1562.

Posner, RA, 'An Economic Approach to Legal Procedure and Judicial Administration' (1973) 2 Journal of Legal Studies 399.

Posner, RA, 'Review of Kaplow, Competition Policy and Price Fixing' (2014) 79 Antitrust Law Journal 761.

Pound, R, 'Law in Books and Law in Action' (1910) 44 American Law Review 12.

Prat, A and T Valletti, 'Attention Oligopoly' (2022) 14 American Economic Journal: Microeconomics 530.

Qing, Y, 'Analysis of Meituan's Acquisition of Dianping' (2022) 4(7) Academic Journal of Business & Management 81.

Roberts, M, 'Killer Acquisitions and the Death of Competition in the Digital Economy' (2022) 24(1) Transactions: Tennessee Journal of Business Law 61.

Robertson, V, 'Excessive Data Collection: Privacy Considerations and Abuse of Dominance in the Era of Big Data' (2020) 57 Common Market Law Review 161.

Robertson, V, 'The Complementary Nature of the Digital Markets Act and the EU Antitrust Rules' (2024) 12 Journal of Accounting and Economics 325.

Rochet, J and J Tirole, 'Platform Competition in Two-Sided Markets' (2003) 1 Journal of the European Economic Association 990.

Rochet, J and J Tirole, 'Two-Sided Markets: A Progress Report' (2006) 3 Rand Journal of Economics 645.

Salop, S, D Francis, L Sillman, and M Spero, 'Rebuilding Platform Antitrust: Moving on from Ohio v. American Express' (2022) 84 Antitrust Law Journal 883.

Schneider, G, 'Testing Art. 102 TFEU in the Digital Marketplace: Insights from the Bundeskartellamt's Investigation against Facebook' (2018) 9 Journal of European Competition Law & Practice 213.

Schneider, G, 'Data Sharing for Collaborative Research under Art. 101 TFEU: Lessons from the Proposed Regulations for Data Markets' (2021) 17 European Competition Journal 567.

Schrepel, T, 'Platforms or Aggregators: Implications for Digital Antitrust Law' (2021) 12(1) Journal of European Competition Law & Practice 1.

Schwalbe, U, 'Algorithms, Machine Learning, and Collusion' (2019) 14 Journal of Competition Law and Economics 568.

Schweitzer, H, 'Competition Law and Public Policy: Reconsidering an Uneasy Relationship: The Example of Art. 81' (2007) 30 EUI Working Papers in Law 3.

Shapiro, C, 'Antitrust in a Time of Populism' (2018) 61 International Journal of Industrial Organization 714.

Shi, J, '个人反垄断义务和责任的制度完善及其实施 [Implementation and Improvement of Individual Antitrust Obligations and Responsibilities]' (2022) 5 China Journal of Applied Jurisprudence 60.

Si, Y, '依法规范社区团购市场秩序努力营造公平有序的市场环境—市场监管总局对五家社区团购企业不正当价格行为作出行政处罚答记者问 [Standardizing the Market Order of Community Group Purchase in Accordance with Laws and Striving to Create a Fair and Orderly Market Environment The State Administration for Market Regulation Imposes Administrative Punishment on Five Community Group Purchase Enterprises for Their Unfair Price Practices]' (2021) 6 China's Food 26.

Smith, SW and W Stephen, 'When Most-Favored Is Disfavored: A Counselor's Guide to MFNs' (2013) 27(2) Antitrust 10.

Sokol, D and R Comerford, 'Antitrust and Regulating Big Data' (2016) 23 George Mason Law Review 1129.

Stucke, M, 'Behavioral Economics at the Gate: Antitrust in the Twenty-First Century' (2007) 38 Loyola University of Chicago Law Journal 513.

Stucke, M, 'Reconsidering Antitrust Goals' (2012) 53 Boston College Law Review 551.

Stucke, M, 'Should We Be Concerned about Data-opolies?' (2018) 2 Georgetown Law Technology Review 275.

Stucke, M and A Ezrachi, 'When Competition Fails to Optimise Quality: A Look at Search Engines' (2016) 18 Yale Journal of Law and Technology 70.
Stucke, M and A Ezrachi, 'Innovation Misunderstood' (2023) 73 American University Law Review <https://papers.ssrn.com/sol3/papers.cfm?abstract_id=4547201> (accessed 27 September 2024).
Stylianou, K and M Iacovides, 'The Goals of EU Competition Law—A Comprehensive Empirical Investigation', KONKURRENSVERKET (28 January 2021) <https://papers.ssrn.com/sol3/papers.cfm?abstract_id=3735795> (accessed 27 September 2024).
Sun, J and Y Song, '数字经济背景下最惠国待遇条款的反垄断合理分析 [The Antitrust Rule-of-Reason Analysis of MFN Clauses in the Context of Digital Economy]' (2018) 12 Electronics Intellectual Property 12.
Sun, J and Y Yu, '消费者数据隐私损害的反垄断司法救济及路径拓展 [Antitrust Judicial Remedies and Expanding Paths for Consumer Data Privacy Damages]' (2023) 4 Legal Forum 23.
Sun, J and Z Zhao, '互联网平台经营者市场支配地位界定的系统性重构—以《反垄断法》第18条的修订为中心 [Systematic Reconstruction of the Definition of Market Dominance of Internet Platform Operators—Centering on the Revision of Article 18 of the AML]' (2019) 5 Science, Technology and Law 76.
Sun, Q, '论大型平台企业数据交易强制缔约义务 [On Compulsory Contracting Obligations of Large Platform Enterprises in Data Transactions]' (2024) 36 Peking University Law Journal 241.
Sun, Y, '出租车行业政府规制政策变迁轨迹与逻辑—基于间断均衡理论的解释 [On Changing of the Government Regulations and Policies in Taxi Industry and Its Logic: An Interpretation Based on Intermittent-Equilibrium Theory]' (2021) 34(4) Huxiang Forum 105.
Tan, C, '互联网平台经济下最惠国条款的反垄断法规制 [Antitrust Regulation against MFN Clauses in the Internet Platform Economy]' (2020) 22(2) Journal of Shanghai University of Finance and Economics 138.
Tao, Y and K Zhang, '数字经济背景下经营者集中审查制度的困境及完善 [The Dilemma and Improvement of the Review System of Concentrations of Undertakings in the Context of Digital Economy]' (2023) 54 Review of Industrial Economics 136.
Thomas, S, 'Harmful Signals, Cartel Prohibition and Oligopoly Theory in the Age of Machine Learning' (2019) 15 Journal of Competition Law and Economics 159.
Turing, A, 'Computing and Machinery Intelligence' (1950) LIX(236) Mind 433.
Turner, DF, 'The Definition of Agreement under the Sherman Act: Conscious Parallelism and Refusals to Deal' (1962) 75 Harvard Law Review 655.
Tzanaki, A, 'Dynamism and Politics in EU Merger Control: Appreciating the Gain and the Gap' (2023) Antitrust Law Journal <https://papers.ssrn.com/sol3/papers.cfm?abstract_id=4574948> (accessed 27 September 2024).
Valdivia, E, 'The Scope of the "Special Responsibility" upon Vertically Integrated Dominant Firms after the Google Shopping Case: Is There a Duty to Treat Rivals Equally and Refrain from Favouring Own Related Business?' (2018) 41 World Competition 43.
Van den Boom, J and P Samranchit, 'Digital Ecosystem Mergers in Big Tech—A Theory of Long-Run Harm with Applications' (2022) 13 (5) Journal of European Competition Law & Practice 365.
Vesterdorf, B, 'Article 82 EC: Where Do We Stand after the Microsoft Judgment?' (2008) 1 Global Arbitration Review 1.
Vesterdorf, B, 'Theories of Self-Preferencing and Duty to Deal—Two Sides of the Same Coin' (2015) 1 Competition Law & Policy Debate 4.
Vesterdorf, B and K Fountoukakos, 'An Appraisal of the Remedy in the Commission's Google Search (Shopping) Decision and a Guide to Its Interpretation in Light of an Analytical Reading of the Case Law' (2018) 9 Journal of European Competition Law & Practice 3.
Vezzoso, S, 'Competition by Design' (2017) <https://papers.ssrn.com/sol3/papers.cfm?abstract_id = 2986440> (accessed 2 January 2023).
Voelcker, S and D Baker, 'Why There Is No Antitrust Case against Apple's App Store: A Response to Geradin & Katsifis', TILEC Discussion Paper No DP20200035 (2020) <https://papers.ssrn.com/sol3/papers.cfm?abstract_id=3660896> (accessed 27 September 2024).

Wachter, S, B Mittelstadt, and L Floridi, 'Why a Right to Explanation of Automated Decision-Making Does Not Exist in the General Data Protection Regulation' (2017) 7(2) International Data Privacy Law 76.

Wagner-von Papp, F, 'The 11th Amendment to the ARC and Germany's New Competition Tool' (2023) D'Kart Journal 22 <https://www.dkart.de/en/blog/2023/05/03/the11thamendmenttothearcandgermanysnewcompetitiontool> (accessed 7 June 2024).

Wang, J, '浅谈共享经济发展现状存在的问题及解决措施 [Discussion on the Existing Problems and Solutions of the Development Status of Sharing Economy]' (2020) 21 Inner Mongolia Coal Economy 90.

Wang, L, '共享经济下网约车监管的法律问题研究 [A Study on the Legal Issues of the Regulation of Online Rides in the Sharing Economy]' (2020) 47(2) Seeking Truth 120.

Wang, L, '数据驱动型并购中竞争损害的新面向及救济理念革新 [New Characteristics of Competition Harm in Data-Driven Mergers and Concept Renovation of Antitrust Remedy]' (2021) 23 Journal of Shanghai University of Finance and Economics 138.

Wang, L, '创新目标在《反垄断法》上的定位与实现—兼评《反垄断法（修正草案）》第1条 [Positioning and Realization of Innovation Objectives in the Anti-Monopoly Law: Comment on Article 1 of the Anti-Monopoly Law (Draft Amendment)]' (2022) 1 Journal of China University of Political Science and Law 173.

Wang, L, '数据何以确权 [How Can Data Be Right-Sized?]' (2023) 45(4) Chinese Journal of Law 56.

Wang, L and B Xiong, 'Personality Rights in China's New Civil Code: A Response to Increasing Awareness of Rights in an Era of Evolving Technology' (2021) 47(6) Modern China 703.

Wang, R, X Chen, and H Chen, 'Research on Agricultural Product Traceability Technology (Economic Value) Based on Information Supervision and Cloud Computing' (2022) Computational Intelligence and Neuroscience.

Wang, X, '数字平台反垄断的国际观察与国内思考 [International Observation and Domestic Consideration of Digital Platform Anti-Monopoly]' (2022) 42(5) Journal of University of Chinese Academy of Social Sciences 49.

Wang, X, '中国数字经济领域反垄断监管的理论与实践 [Theory and Practice of Anti-Monopoly Supervision in China's Digital Economy]' (2022) 42(5) Journal of University of Chinese Academy of Social Sciences 38.

Wang, Y, '数字经济背景下我国经营者集中制度的完善 [The Improvement of the Merger Control System in the Digital Markets in China]' (2022) 1 Journal of China University of Political Science and Law 161.

Wang, Y, Z Wang, and X Sun, 'On Determination of Predatory Pricing by Online Sharing Platforms under the AML' (2017) 3 Journal of Cyber Affairs 60.

Wasastjerna, MC, 'The Implications of Big Data and Privacy on Competition Analysis in Merger Control and the Controversial Competition–Data Protection Interface' (2019) 30 European Business Law Review 337.

Weber, BC, 'Hub-and-Spoke Conspiracies: Can Big Data and Pricing Algorithms Form the Rim?' (2023) 26 SMU Science and Technology Law Review 25.

Wei (韩伟), H, '数字经济中的隐私保护与支配地位滥用 [The Privacy Protection and the Abuse of Dominance in the Digital Economy]' (2020) 1 中国社会科学院研究生院学报 [Journal of University of Chinese Academy of Social Sciences] 37.

Weitbrecht, A, 'From Freiburg to Chicago and Beyond: The First 50 Years of European Competition Law' (2008) 29 European Competition Law Review 81.

Witt, A, 'Who's Afraid of Conglomerate Mergers?' (2022) 67 Antitrust Bulletin 208.

Witt, A, 'Meta v Bundeskartellamt—Databased Conduct between Antitrust Law and Regulation' (2024) 12 Journal of Accounting and Economics 345.

Wu, T, 'Blind Spot: The Attention Economy and the Law' (2019) 82 Antitrust Law Journal 771.

Wu, T, 'The American Express Opinion, the Rule of Reason, and Tech Platforms' (2019) 7 Journal of Accounting and Economics 117.

Wu, Z, '反垄断法促进数字平台创新的法经济学分析 [Legal and Economic Analysis of Anti-Monopoly Law Promoting Digital Platform Innovation]' (2023) 37 Contemporary Law Review 44.

Wyman, KM, 'Problematic Private Property: The Case of New York Taxicab Medallions' (2013) 30 Yale Journal on Regulation 125.

Wyman, KM, 'Taxi Regulation in the Age of Uber' (2017) 2(1) New York University Journal of Legislation and Public Policy 1.

Wyman, KM, 'The New Essentialism in Property' (2017) 9 Journal of Legal Analysis 183.

Xiao, F and W Wei, '数字经济发展对市场分割的影响研究 [On the Influence of Digital Economy Development on Market Segmentation]' (2013) 15 Journal of Commercial Economics 111.

Xiao, H, '算法责任：理论证成, 全景画像与治理范式 [Algorithmic Responsibility: Theoretical Justification, Panoramic Portrait and Governance Paradigm]'(2022) 38(4) 管理世界 [Journal of Management World] 200.

Xiong, B, '专车拼车管制新探 [Regulating the Peer-to-Peer Transport Service in China: A Perspective from Law and Economics]' (2016) 10(2) Tsinghua University Law Journal 131.

Xiong, B and M Durovic, 'The Enforcement of Mandatory Rules against Illegal Contracts' (2021) ASIA Pacific Law Review 15.

Xiong, B and J He, '数据确权:理路, 方法与经济意义 [Theory, Methodology and Economic Implications of the Delineation of Data Property Rights]' (2023) 45 Chinese Journal of Law 54.

Xiong, B, J Ge, and L Chen, 'Unpacking Data: China's "Bundle of Rights" Approach to the Commercialization of Data' (2023) 13(2) International Data Privacy Law 98.

Xu, C, 'The Fundamental Institutions of China's Reforms and Development' (2011) 49 Journal of Economic Literature 1076.

Yan J, 'Anti-Monopoly Regulation of Algorithm Collusion in Big Data Era' (2021) 8 International Conference on Machinery, Mechanics, Materials, and Computer Engineering 124.

Ye, M and J Zhang, '反垄断法保护个人信息权益的理据与路径 [The Rationale and Path of Protecting the Interests of Personal Information through Antitrust Law]' (2023) 37(1) Journal of Huazhong University of Science and Technology (Social Science Edition) 87.

Yin, B, '"菜蓝子"电商鏖战 [Cailanzi Ecommerce Fierce Battle]' (2021) 6 Shanghai Informatization 34.

Zhang, Y, '反垄断法中的消费者福利标准：理论确证与法律适用 [The Consumer Welfare Standard in Antimonopoly Law: Theoretical Confirmation and Legal Application]' (2013) 31 Tribune of Political Science and Law 102.

You, C, 'Half a Loaf Is Better Than None: The New Data Protection Regime for China's Platform Economy' (2022) 45 Computer Law & Security Review.

Zhang, AH, 'Agility over Stability: China's Great Reversal in Regulating the Platform Economy' (2022) 63(2) Harvard International Law Journal 457.

Zhang, L, '算法权力的兴起, 异化及法律规制 [The Emergence, Alienation and Legal Regulation of Algorithmic Power]' (2019) 36(4) Legal Business Research 63.

Zhang, X, '论作为新型财产权的数据财产权 [On Data Property Rights as a New Type of Property Right]' (2023) 4 Social Sciences in China 144.

Zhang, X and Q Cao, '公共数据确权授权法律机制研究 [Research on the Legal Mechanism for the Rights to Public Data Ownership and Authorization]' (2023) 3 Journal of Comparative Law 41.

Zhang, Y, '反垄断法中的消费者福利标准：理论确证与法律适用 [The Consumer Welfare Standard in Anti-Monopoly Law: Theoretical Confirmation and Legal Application]' (2013) 31(3) Tribune of Political Science and Law.

Zhang, Y and B Zhang, '算法规制的路径创新：论我国算法审计制度的构建 [The Path Innovation of Algorithm Law System: On the Construction of China's Algorithm Audit System]' (2022) 10 e-Government 48.

Zheng, C and J Tang, '论公共数据的规范含义 [On the Concept of Public Data]' (2021) 6 Fazhi Yanjiu 79.

Zheng, K and F Snyder, 'China and EU's Wisdom in Choosing Competition Soft Law or Hard Law in the Digital Era: A Perfect Match?' (2023) 9 China–EU Law Journal 25.

Zheng, W, 'Transplanting Antitrust in China: Economic Transition, Market Structure, and State Control' (2010) 32 University of Pennsylvania Journal of International Law 643.

Zhong, C, '数字经济平台相关市场界定研究 [On the Definition of Relevant Market in Digital Markets]' (2023) 2 Research Rule of Law.

Zou, B and Y Wang, '新反垄断法落地, 平台监管如何着棋？ [How the New AML Tackles Platform Regulation?]' (财经杂志 [*Caijing Magazine*], 18 August 2022) <https://new.qq.com/rain/a/20220818A08J4900> (accessed 30 October 2022).
Zhou, H, '《个人信息保护法》守门人条款解析 [Analysis of the "Gatekeeper Clause" of the Personal Information Protection Law]'(2022) 5 法律科学(西北政法大学学报) [Science of Law (Journal of Northwest University of Political Science and Law)] 41.
Zhou, L, '《官场＋市场》》与中国增长故事 ["Bureaucratic & Economic Markets" and China's Growth Story]' (2018) 38(2) Chinese Journal of Sociology 1.
Zhu, F and Q Liu, 'Competing with Complementors: An Empirical Look at Amazon.com' (2018) 39 Strategic Management Journal 2618.
Zingales, N, 'Between a Rock and Two Hard Places: WhatsApp at the Crossroad of Competition, Data Protection and Consumer Law' (2017) 33 Computer Law & Security Review 553.

III. Policy Documents

III.1 European Commission (EU)

European Commission (EU), 'Bilateral Relations with Peoples' Republic of China' <https://competitionpolicy.ec.europa.eu/internationalrelations/bilateralrelations/china_en> (accessed 28 September 2023).
European Commission (EU), 'European Data Strategy' <https://commission.europa.eu/strategyandpolicy/priorities20192024/europefitdigitalage/europeandatastrategy_en> (accessed 18 August 2023).
European Commission (EU), 'List of Acquisitions' <https://digital-markets-act-cases.ec.europa.eu/acquisitions> (accessed 18 August 2023).
European Commission (EU), 'Revision of the Two Block Exemption Regulations for Horizontal Cooperation Agreements and the Horizontal Guidelines' <https://ec.europa.eu/info/law/better-regulation/have-your-say/initiatives/13058-Revision-of-the-EU-competition-rules-on-horizontal-agreements_en> (accessed 8 June 2021) (Inception Impact Assessment).
European Commission (EU), 'The French, Italian and Swedish Competition Authorities Accept the Commitments Offered by Booking.com' <https://webgate.ec.europa.eu/multisite/ecn-brief/en/content/french-italian-and-swedish-competition-authorities-accept-commitments-offered-bookingcom> (accessed 9 June 2024).
European Commission (EU), 'Notice on the Definition of Relevant Market for the Purposes of Community Competition Law', [1997] OJ C 237/5.
European Commission (EU), 'Guidelines on the Assessment of Horizontal Mergers under the Council Regulation on the Control of Concentrations between Undertakings' [2004] OJ C 31/5 (Horizontal Merger Guidelines) <https://eur-lex.europa.eu/LexUriServ/LexUriServ.do?uri=OJ:C:2004:031:0005:0018:en:PDF>.
European Commission (EU), 'Commission Notice on Case Referral in Respect of Concentrations', [2005] OJ C 56/2 <https://eur-lex.europa.eu/legal-content/EN/TXT/PDF/?uri=CELEX:52005XC0305(01)>.
European Commission (EU), 'Guidelines on the Assessment of Non-Horizontal Mergers' (18 October 2008) OJ C 265/6 (Non-Horizontal Merger Guidelines).
European Commission (EU), 'Guidance on the Commission's Enforcement Priorities in Applying Article 82 of the EC Treaty to Abusive Exclusionary Conduct by Dominant Undertakings', [2009] OJ C 45/2.
European Commission (EU), 'Guidance on the Commission's Enforcement Priorities in Applying Article 82 of the EC Treaty to Abusive Exclusionary Conduct by Dominant Undertakings', [2009] OJ C 45/02.
European Commission (EU), 'Guidelines on Vertical Restraints' [2010] OJ C 130/1 (Old Vertical Restraints Guidelines [Old VRG]).
European Commission (EU), 'Summary of the Contributions Received in the Context of the Open Public Consultation on the Impact Assessment for the Review of the Vertical Block Exemption Regulation', (EU) 330/2010 (2010).
European Commission (EU), 'Guidelines on Vertical Restraints' (19 May 2010) OJ C 130/1.

European Commission (EU), 'Commission Probes Allegations of Antitrust Violations by Google' (Press release, 30 November 2010).
European Commission (EU), 'Guidelines on Restrictions of Competition "by Object" for the Purpose of Defining Which Agreements May Benefit from the De Minimis Notice Brussels', SWD(2014) 198 final (25 June 2014) (revised version of 3 June 2015).
European Commission (EU), 'Consultation on Evaluation of Procedural and Jurisdictional Aspects of EU Merger Control' (2016)
European Commission (EU), 'Report on the Monitoring Exercise Carried Out in the Online Hotel Booking Sector by EU Competition Authorities' (2016) <https://ec.europa.eu/competition/ecn/hotel_monitoring_report_en.pdf> (accessed 9 June 2024).
European Commission (EU), 'Synopsis Report on the Public Consultation on the Regulatory Environment for Platforms, Online Intermediaries and the Collaborative Economy' (2016).
European Commission (EU), 'EU Merger Control and Innovation' (Policy brief, April 2016).
European Commission (EU), 'Online Platforms and the Digital Single Market: Opportunities and Challenges for Europe' (Communication, 25 May 2016).
European Commission (EU), 'Final Report on the E-Commerce Sector Inquiry', COM(2017) 229 final (Brussels, 10 May 2017).
European Commission (EU), 'Mergers: Commission Fines Facebook €110 Million for Providing Misleading Information about WhatsApp Takeover' (Press release, 18 May 2017) <https://europa.eu/rapid/pressrelease_IP171369en.htm> (accessed 29 September 2024).
European Commission (EU), 'Antitrust: Commission Fines Google €2.42 Billion for Abusing Dominance as Search Engine by Giving Illegal Advantage to Own Comparison Shopping Service' (Press release, 27 June 2017).
European Commission (EU), 'Stronger Protection, New Opportunities—Commission Guidance on the Direct Application of the General Data Protection Regulation as of May 2018', COM(2018) 43 final (2018).
European Commission (EU), 'Proposal for a Regulation of the European Parliament and of the Council on Promoting Fairness and Transparency for Business Users of Online Intermediation Services', COM(2018) 238 final (Brussels, 24 April 2018).
European Commission (EU), 'Artificial Intelligence for Europe', COM(2018) 237 final (Brussels, 25 April 2018).
European Commission (EU), 'Guidance on Sharing Private Sector Data in the European Data Economy', COM(2018) 125 final (Staff working document, Brussels, 25 April 2018).
European Commission (EU), 'Competition Policy for the Digital Era' (A Report by J Crémer, Y de Montjoye, and H Schweitzer) (EU Experts Report, 2019).
European Commission (EU), 'Support Study Accompanying the Commission Notice on the Evaluation of the Definition of Relevant Market for the Purposes of Community Competition Law' (Final Report, 2019) (Support Study).
European Commission (EU), 'Terms of Reference of the EU–China Competition Policy Dialogue' (2019) <https://competitionpolicy.ec.europa.eu/system/files/202106/ChinaEU_competitionpolicydialogue_termsofreference_en.pdf> (accessed 6 June 2024).
European Commission (EU), 'Digital Single Market: Commission Welcomes European Parliament's Vote on New Rules for Sharing Public Sector Data' (4 April 2019) <http://europa.eu/rapid/pressrelease_STATEMENT191935_en.htm> (accessed 20 August 2022).
European Commission (EU), 'Commission Opens Investigation into Possible Anti-Competitive Conduct of Amazon' (17 July 2019) <https://ec.europa.eu/commission/presscorner/detail/en/IP_19_4291> (accessed 29 September 2024).
European Commission (EU), 'Communication for the Commission: A European Strategy for Data', COM(2020) 66 final (2020).
European Commission (EU), 'Guidelines on Ranking Transparency Pursuant to Regulation (EU) 2019/1150 of the European Parliament and of the Council', [2020] OJ C 424/1.
European Commission (EU), 'Summary of the Contributions of the National Competition Authorities to the Impact Assessment of the New Competition Tool' (2020) <http://www.

ec.europa.eu/competition/consultations/2020_new_comp_tool/summary_contributions_NCAs_responses.pdf> (accessed 7 June 2024).

European Commission (EU), 'Impact Assessment Report Accompanying the Proposal for a Digital Markets Act', SWD(2020) 363 final (Staff working document, 2020).

European Commission (EU), 'A European Strategy for Data', COM(2020) 66 final (Brussels, 19 February 2020) (Communication).

European Commission (EU), 'White Paper on Artificial Intelligence—a European Approach to Excellence and Trust', COM(2020) 66 final (Brussels, 19 February 2020).

European Commission (EU), 'Commission Opens Investigations into Apple's App Store Rules' (16 June 2020) <https://ec.europa.eu/commission/presscorner/detail/en/ip_20_1073> (accessed 29 September 2024).

European Commission (EU), 'Commission Opens Investigation into Apple Practices Regarding Apple Pay' (16 June 2020) <https://ec.europa.eu/commission/presscorner/detail/en/ip_20_1075> (accessed 29 September 2024).

European Commission (EU), 'Commission Publishes Findings of the Evaluation of the Vertical Block Exemption Regulation' (8 September 2020).

European Commission (EU), 'Commission Sends Statement of Objections to Amazon for the Use of Non-Public Independent Seller Data and Opens Second Investigation into Its E-Commerce Business Practices' (10 November 2020) <https://ec.europa.eu/commission/presscorner/detail/en/ip_20_2077> (accessed 29 September 2024).

European Commission (EU), 'Proposal for a Regulation of the European Parliament and of the Council on Contestable and Fair Markets in the Digital Sector (Digital Markets Act)', COM(2020) 842 final (Brussels, 15 December 2020).

European Commission (EU), 'Commission Invites Interested Parties to Provide Comments on Draft Revised Vertical Block Exemption Regulation and Vertical Guidelines' (9 July 2021).

European Commission (EU), 'Evaluation of the Commission Notice on the Definition of Relevant Market for the Purposes of Community Competition Law of 9 December 1997', SWD(2021) 199 final (Staff working document, 12 July 2021).

European Commission (EU), 'Online Advertising: The Impact of Targeted Advertising on Advertisers, Market Access and Consumer Choice (2021).

European Commission (EU), 'Evaluation of Procedural and Jurisdictional Aspect of EU Merger Control', SWD(2021) 66 final (26 March 2021).

European Commission (EU), 'Guidance on the Application of the Referral Mechanism Set Out in Article 22 of the Merger Regulation to Certain Categories of Cases', C(2021) 1959 final (26 March 2021).

European Commission (EU), 'Proposal for a Regulation of the European Parliament and of the Council Laying Down Harmonised Rules in Artificial Intelligence', COM(2021) 206 final (Brussels, 21 April 2021) (AI Act).

European Commission (EU), 'Commission Sends Statement of Objections to Apple on App Store Rules for Music Streaming Providers' (30 April 2021) <https://ec.europa.eu/commission/presscorner/detail/en/ip_21_2061> (accessed 29 September 2024).

European Commission (EU), 'Evaluation of the Horizontal Block Exemption Regulations', SWD(2021) 103 final (Staff working document, Brussels, 6 May 2021).

European Commission (EU), 'Commission Opens Investigation into Possible Anticompetitive Conduct of Facebook' (4 June 2021) <https://ec.europa.eu/commission/presscorner/detail/en/IP_21_2848> (accessed 29 September 2024).

European Commission (EU), 'Summary of the Contributions Received in the Context of the Open Public Consultation on the Impact Assessment for the Review of the Vertical Block Exemption Regulation (EU) No 330/2010', Ref Ares(2021)41194777 (24 June 2021).

European Commission (EU), 'Commission Opens Investigation into Possible Anticompetitive Conduct by Google in the Online Advertising Technology Sector' (22 June 2021) <https://ec.europa.eu/commission/presscorner/detail/en/ip_21_3143> (accessed 7 June 2024).

European Commission (EU), 'Approval of the Content of a Draft for a Commission Regulation on the Application of Article 101(3) of the Treaty on the Functioning of the European Union to Categories of Vertical Agreements and Concerted Practices', C(2021) 5026 final (Brussels, 9 July 2021).

European Commission (EU), 'Communication: A Competition Policy Fit for New Challenges', COM(2021) 713 final (Brussels, 18 November 2021).

European Commission (EU), 'Communication from the Commission: Commission Notice, Guidelines on Vertical Restrains', C(2022) 248/01 (2022).

European Commission (EU), 'Expert Report on the Review of the Vertical Block Exemption Regulation Information Exchange in Dual Distribution' (2022).

European Commission (EU), 'Explanatory Note on the New VBER and Vertical Guidelines' (2022) <https://competition-policy.ec.europa.eu/system/files/2022-05/explanatory_note_VBER_and_Guidelines_2022.pdf> (accessed 5 January 2022).

European Commission (EU), 'Guidelines on the Application of Union Competition Law to Collective Agreements Regarding the Working Conditions of Solo Self-Employed Persons', [2022] OJ C 374/2.

European Commission (EU), 'Guidelines on Vertical Restraints (Communication)' [2022] OJ C 248/1 (Vertical Restraints Guidelines [VRG]).

European Commission (EU), 'Merger Review in Digital and Technology Markets: Insights from National Case Law' (Final Report, prepared by V Robertson, 2022).

European Commission (EU), 'Notice on the Definition of the Relevant Market for the Purposes of Union Competition Law' (Draft) (2022) <https://ec.europa.eu/commission/presscorner/detail/en/ip_22_6528> (accessed 7 June 2024).

European Commission (EU), 'Final Report—Sector Inquiry into Consumer Internet of Things', COM(2022) 19 final (Brussels, 20 January 2022).

European Commission (EU), 'Proposal for a Regulation of the European Parliament and of the Council on Harmonised Rules on Fair Access to and Use of Data, COM(2022) 68 final (Brussels, 23 February 2022).

European Commission (EU), 'Antitrust: Commission Opens Investigation into Possible Anticompetitive Conduct by Google and Meta, in Online Display Advertising' (Press release, 11 March 2022) <https://ec.europa.eu/commission/presscorner/detail/en/ip_22_1703> (accessed 29 September 2024).

European Commission (EU), 'Digital Markets Act: Commission Welcomes Political Agreement on Rules to Ensure Fair and Open Digital Markets' (Press release, 25 March 2022) <https://ec.europa.eu/commission/presscorner/detail/en/IP_22_1978> (accessed 7 June 2024).

European Commission (EU), 'Public Consultation on the Draft Revised Horizontal Block Exemption Regulations and Horizontal Guidelines' (March 2022) <https://competition-policy.ec.europa.eu/public-consultations/2022-hbers_en> (accessed 29 December 2022) (Draft Guidelines).

European Commission (EU), 'Commission Sends Statement of Objections to Apple over Practices Regarding Apple Pay' (2 May 2022) <https://ec.europa.eu/commission/presscorner/detail/en/ip_22_2764> (accessed 29 September 2024).

European Commission (EU), 'Antitrust: Commission Accepts Commitments by Insurance Ireland to Ensure Access to Its Data Sharing Platform' (30 June 2022).

European Commission (EU), 'Antitrust: Commission Seeks Feedback on Performance of EU Antitrust Enforcement Framework' (Press release, 30 June 2022) <https://ec.europa.eu/commission/presscorner/detail/en/IP_22_4194> (accessed 23 August 2023).

European Commission (EU), 'Commission Prohibits Acquisition of GRAIL by Illumina' (Press release, 6 September 2022).

European Commission (EU), 'Commission Seeks Feedback on Draft Revised Market Definition Notice' (Press release, 8 November 2022) <https://ec.europa.eu/commission/presscorner/detail/en/ip_22_6528> (accessed 7 June 2024).

European Commission (EU), 'Antitrust: Commission Sends Statement of Objections to Meta over Abusive Practices Benefiting Facebook Marketplace' (19 December 2022) <https://ec.europa.eu/commission/presscorner/detail/en/ip_22_7728> (accessed 29 September 2024).

European Commission (EU), 'On 19/12/2022, the Commission Decided to Close Antitrust Proceedings in Case AT.40774—Google–Meta (Open Bidding) Agreement, Initiated by the Decision of 11/03/2022' (19 December 2022) <https://ec.europa.eu/competition/antitrust/cases1/202302/AT_40774_8845087_898_3.pdf> (accessed 29 September 2024).

European Commission (EU), 'Antitrust: Commission Accepts Commitments by Amazon Barring It from Using Marketplace Seller Data, and Ensuring Equal Access to Buy Box and Prime' (20 December 2022) <https://ec.europa.eu/commission/presscorner/detail/en/ip_22_7777> (accessed 29 September 2024).

European Commission (EU), 'Amendments to the Communication from the Commission Guidance on the Commission's Enforcement Priorities in Applying Article 82 of the EC Treaty to Abusive Exclusionary Conduct by Dominant Undertakings', [2023] OJ C 116/01 (Amending Communication).

European Commission (EU), 'An EU Initiative on Virtual Worlds: A Head Start Towards the Next Technological Transition' (Call for evidence, 2023).

European Commission (EU), 'Guidelines on the Applicability of Article 101 of the Treaty on the Functioning of the European Union to Horizontal Co-operation Agreements' (2023) <https://competition-policy.ec.europa.eu/document/fd641c1e-7415-4e60-ac21-7ab3e72045d2_en> (accessed 8 June 2024) (revised HG, 'RHG').

European Commission (EU), 'Notice on the Definition of the Relevant Market for the Purposes of Union Competition Law', [2023] OJ C 1645.

European Commission (EU), 'Towards a More Transparent, Balanced and Sustainable Digital Advertising Ecosystem: Study on the Impact of Recent Developments in Digital Advertising on Privacy, Publishers and Advertisers' (Final Report, 2023).

European Commission (EU), 'A Dynamic and Workable Effects-Based Approach to Abuse of Dominance' (Competition policy brief, Issue 1, March 2023).

European Commission (EU), 'Commission Announces Guidelines on Exclusionary Abuses and Amends Guidance on Enforcement Priorities' (Press release, 27 March 2023) <https://ec.europa.eu/commission/presscorner/detail/en/ip_23_1911> (accessed 6 June 2024).

European Commission (EU), 'Speech by President von der Leyen on EU–China Relations to the Mercator Institute for China Studies and the European Policy Centre' (30 March 2023) <https://ec.europa.eu/commission/presscorner/detail/en/speech_23_2063> (accessed 6 June 2024).

European Commission (EU), 'Questions and Answers: Digital Markets Act: Ensuring Fair and Open Digital Markets' (Brussels, 6 September 2023) <https://ec.europa.eu/commission/presscorner/detail/en/qanda_20_2349> (accessed 6 June 2024).

European Commission (EU), 'Commission Clears Acquisition of Activision Blizzard by Microsoft, Subject to Conditions' (Press release, 15 May 2023).

European Commission (EU), 'Guidelines on the Applicability of Article 101 of the Treaty on the Functioning of the European Union to Horizontal Cooperation Agreements', C(2023) 3445 final (Brussels, 1 June 2023) <https://competitionpolicy.ec.europa.eu/system/files/202307/2023_revised_horizontal_guidelines_en.pdf> (accessed 6 June 2024).

European Commission (EU), 'Commission Sends Statement of Objections to Google over Abusive Practices in Online Advertising Technology' (Press release, 14 June 2023) <https://ec.europa.eu/commission/presscorner/detail/en/ip_23_3207> (accessed 6 June 2024).

European Commission (EU), 'Mergers: Commission Opens In-depth Investigation into the Proposed Acquisition of iRobot by Amazon' (Press release, 6 July 2023) <https://ec.europa.eu/commission/presscorner/detail/en/ip_23_3702> (accessed 29 September 2024).

European Commission (EU), 'Commission Fines Illumina and GRAIL for Implementing Their Acquisition without Prior Merger Control Approval', Case M.10483 (12 July 2023) <https://ec.europa.eu/commission/presscorner/detail/en/ip_23_3773> (accessed 29 September 2024).

European Commission (EU), 'Template Relating to the Obligation to Inform about a Concentration Pursuant to Article 14 of Regulation (EU) 2022/1925' (updated 13 July 2023) (Digital Markets Act) <https://digitalmarketsact.ec.europa.eu/system/files/202307/Arti

cle%2014%20DMA%20Template%20%28information%20on%20transactions%29%20%20l3072023.pdf> (accessed 6 June 2024).

European Commission (EU), 'Antitrust: Commission Opens Investigation into Possible Anticompetitive Practices by Microsoft Regarding Teams' (Press release, 27 July 2023).

European Commission (EU), 'Mergers: Commission to Assess the Proposed Acquisition of Autotalks by Qualcomm' (Daily News, 18 August 2023) <https://ec.europa.eu/commission/presscorner/detail/en/mex_23_4201> (accessed 9 June 2024).

European Commission (EU), 'Mergers: Commission to Assess the Proposed Acquisition of Nasdaq Power by EEX' (*Daily News*, 21 August 2023) <https://ec.europa.eu/commission/presscorner/detail/en/mex_23_4221> (accessed 9 June 2024).

European Commission (EU), 'Commission Designates Six Gatekeepers under the Digital Markets Act' (Press release, 6 September 2023) <https://digitalmarketsact.ec.europa.eu/commissiondesignatessixgatekeepersunderdigitalmarketsact20230906_en> (accessed 28 September 2024).

European Commission (EU), 'EU–China: Commission and China Hold Second High-Level Digital Dialogue' (Press release, 18 September 2023) <https://ec.europa.eu/commission/presscorner/detail/en/ip_23_4488> (accessed 6 June 2024).

European Commission (EU), 'Mergers: Commission Prohibits Proposed Acquisition of ETraveli by Booking', Case M.10615 (Press release, 25 September 2023).

European Commission (EU), 'Commission Sends Amazon Statement of Objections over Proposed Acquisition of iRobot' (Press release, 27 November 2023) <https://ec.europa.eu/commission/presscorner/detail/en/IP_23_5990> (accessed 9 June 2024).

European Commission (EU), 'Notice on the Definition of the Relevant Market for the Purpose of Union Competition Law', [2024] OJ C 1645.

European Commission (EU), 'Statement by Executive Vice-President Vestager on Announcement by Amazon and iRobot to Abandon Their Transaction' (Press release, 29 January 2024) <https://ec.europa.eu/commission/presscorner/detail/en/STATEMENT_24_521> (accessed 9 June 2024).

European Commission (EU), 'Annual Report on Regulation (EU) 2022/1925 of the European Parliament and of the Council on Contestable and Fair Markets in the Digital Sector and Amending Directives (EU) 2019/1937 and (EU) 2020/1828 (Digital Markets Act)', COM(2024) 106 final (Brussels, 6 March 2024) (Revised Market Definition Notice).

European Commission (EU), 'Commission Notice on the Definition of the Relevant Market for the Purposes of Union Competition Law', C(2023) 6789 final (Brussels, 2 August 2024).

European Commission (EU), 'Commission Launches Calls for Contributions on Competition in Virtual Worlds and Generative AI' (Press release, 9 January 2024) <https://ec.europa.eu/commission/presscorner/detail/en/ip_24_85> (accessed 24 April 2024).

European Commission (EU), 'European Data Act Enters into Force, Putting in Place New Rules for a Fair and Innovative Data Economy' (Press release, 11 January 2024) <https://digitalstrategy.ec.europa.eu/en/news/europeandataactentersforceputtingplacenewrulesfairandinnovativedataeconomy> (accessed 28 September 2024).

European Commission (EU), 'Commission Notice on the Definition of the Relevant Market for the Purposes of Union Competition Law', C(2024) 1645 (Brussels, 8 February 2024) (Market Definition Notice).

European Commission (EU), 'Commission Closes Market Investigations on Microsoft's and Apple's Services under the Digital Markets Act' (Press release, 13 February 2024) <https://digitalmarketsact.ec.europa.eu/commissionclosesmarketinvestigationsmicrosoftsandapplesservicesunderdigitalmarketsact20240213_en> (accessed 6 June 2024).

European Commission (EU), 'Commission Opens Non-Compliance Investigations against Alphabet, Apple and Meta under the Digital Markets Act' (Press release, 25 March 2024) <https://digitalmarketsact.ec.europa.eu/commissionopensnoncomplianceinvestigationsagainstalphabetappleandmetaunderdigitalmarkets20240325_en> (accessed 4 July 2024).

European Commission (EU), 'Commission Designates Apple's iPadOS under the Digital Markets Act' (Press release, 29 April 2024) <https://ec.europa.eu/commission/presscorner/detail/en/ip_24_2363> (accessed 6 June 2024).

European Commission (EU), 'Commission Designates Booking as a Gatekeeper and Opens a market Investigation into X' (Press release, 13 May 2024) <https://ec.europa.eu/commission/presscorner/detail/en/ip_24_2561> (accessed 7 June 2024).

European Commission (EU), 'Commission Sends Preliminary Findings to Apple and Opens Additional Non-Compliance Investigation against Apple' (Press release, 24 June 2024) <https://digitalmarketsact.ec.europa.eu/commissionsendspreliminaryfindingsappleandopensadditionalnoncomplianceinvestigation20240624_en> (accessed 24 June 2024).

European Commission (EU), 'Commission Sends Statement of Objections to Microsoft over Possibly Abusive Tying Practices Regarding Teams' (Press release, 25 June 2024).

European Commission (EU), 'Commission Sends Preliminary Findings to Meta over Its "Pay or Consent" Model for Breach of the Digital Markets Act' (Press release, 1 July 2024) <https://digitalmarketsact.ec.europa.eu/commissionsendspreliminaryfindingsmetaoveritspayorconsentmodelbreachdigitalmarketsact20240701_en> (accessed 1 July 2024).

European Commission (EU), Competition Cooperation (EU), '21st EU–China Competition Week' (19, 26–28 April 2021) <https://competitioncooperation.eu/21steuchinacompetitionweek2> (accessed 7 June 2024).

European Commission (EU), Competition Cooperation (EU), '23rd EU–China Competition Week' (28–31 March 2022) <https://competitioncooperation.eu/23rdeuchinacompetitionweek222> (accessed 7 June 2024).

European Commission (EU), Competition Cooperation—EU–Asia Partnership, 'Competition Weeks' <https://competitioncooperation.eu/competitionweeks> (accessed 7 June 2024).

European Commission (EU), European Competition Authorities, 'Principles on the Application, by National Competition Authorities within the ECA, of Articles 4(5) and 22 of the EC Merger Regulation (2005) <https://ec.europa.eu/competition/ecn/eca_referral_principles_en.pdf> (accessed 23 February 2023).

III.2 European Commission (EC) and European Economic Commission (EEC)

European Commission (EC), 'First Report on Competition Policy' (Brussels, Luxembourg, 1972).

European Commission (EC), 'XXIInd Report on Competition Policy 1992' (Brussels, Luxembourg, 1993).

European Commission (EC), 'Guidelines on the Application of Article 81(3) of the Treaty' [2004] OJ C 101/08.

European Commission (EC), 'Notice on Cooperation within the Network of Competition Authorities' [2004] OJ C 101/43.

European Commission (EC), 'Notice on the Cooperation between the Commission and the Courts of the EU Member States in the Application of Articles 81 and 82 EC' [2004] OJ C 101/54.

European Commission (EC), 'Notice on the Handling of Complaints by the Commission under Articles 81 and 82 of the EC Treaty' [2004] OJ C 101/65.

III.3 European Data Protection Supervisor

Buttarelli, G, 'Competition Rebooted: Enforcement and Personal Data in Digital Markets' (Keynote speech at Joint European Railway Agency–European Data Protection Supervisor Seminar, 24 September 2015) <https://edps.europa.eu/sites/default/files/publication/150924_era_gb_en.pdf> (accessed 7 June 2024).

EDPS (European Data Protection Supervisor), Preliminary Opinion, 'Privacy and Competitiveness in the Age of Big Data: The Interplay between Data Protection, Competition Law and Consumer Protection in the Digital Economy', EDPS/2014/06 (26 March 2014).

EDPS, 'European Data Protection Supervisor's Executive Summary of the Opinion of the European Data Protection Supervisor on Effective Enforcement in a Digital Society Economy' [2016] OJ C 463/08.

EDPS, Opinion 8/2016, 'On the Coherent Enforcement of Fundamental Rights in the Age of Big Data' (23 September 2016).

III. 4 European Parliament

European Parliament (EU), 'Legislative Train Schedule' <https://www.europarl.europa.eu/legislative-train/theme-a-europe-fit-for-the-digital-age/file-regulation-on-artificial-intelligence> (accessed 8 June 2024).

European Parliament (EU), 'European Parliament Resolution of 20 February 2017 on Fundamental Rights Implications of Big Data: Privacy, Data Protection, Non-Discrimination, Security and Law Enforcement, Recital R', Report A8-0044 (2017).

European Parliament (EU), 'Motion for a European Parliament Resolution on Online Platforms and the Digital Single Market', 2016/2276(INI), Report A8-0204 (2017) <http://www.europarl.europa.eu/sides/getDoc.do?pubRef=//EP//TEXT+REPORT+A820170204+0+DOC+XML+V0//EN> (accessed 18 August 2023).

European Parliament (EU), 'Proposal for a Regulation of the European Parliament and of the Council Laying Down Harmonized Rules on Artificial Intelligence (Artificial Intelligence Act) and Amending Certain Union Legislative Acts', COM/2021/206 final (2021).

European Parliament (EU), 'Digital Markets Act: Parliament Ready to Start Negotiations with Council' (Press release, 15 December 2021) <https://www.europarl.europa.eu/news/en/pressroom/20211210IPR19211/digitalmarketsactparliamentreadytostartnegotiationswithcouncil> (accessed 29 September 2024).

European Parliament (EU), 'Proposal for a Regulation of the European Parliament and of the Council on Harmonised Rules on Fair Access to and Use of Data' (Data Act) COM/2022/68 final (2022).

European Parliament (EU), 'Artificial Intelligence Act: MEPs Adopt Landmark Law' (Press release, 13 March 2024) <https://www.europarl.europa.eu/news/en/press-room/20240308IPR19015/artificial-intelligence-act-meps-adopt-landmark-law> (accessed 24 April 2024).

European Parliament (EU), 'Legislative Resolution of 13 March 2024 on the Proposal for a Regulation of the European Parliament and of the Council on Laying Down Harmonised Rules on Artificial Intelligence (Artificial Intelligence Act) and Amending Certain Union Legislative Acts', COM(2021)0206 (13 March 2024) <https://www.europarl.europa.eu/doceo/document/TA-9-2024-0138_EN.html#title1> (accessed 29 April 2024).

IV. Other International/National Organizations

IV.1 Organisation for Economic Co-operation and Development

OECD (Organisation for Economic Co-operation and Development), 'The Objectives of Competition Law and Policy', CCNM/GF/COMP(2003) (29 January 2003).

OECD, 'Roundtable on Demand-Side Economics for Consumer Policy: Summary Report', DSTI/CP(2006)3 final (20 April 2006).

OECD, 'The Interface between Competition and Consumer Policies' (Policy Roundtables) DAF/COMP/GF(2008) (2008).

OECD, 'The Economic and Social Role of Internet Intermediaries' (April 2010).

OECD, 'Competition and Across Platform Parity Agreements' (2015) <https://www.oecd.org/daf/competition/competition-cross-platform-parity.htm> (accessed 8 June 2024).

OECD, 'Hearing on Across Platform Parity Agreements' (Note by United Kingdom) (27–28 October 2015).

OECD, 'Big Data: Bringing Competition Policy to the Digital Era', DAF/COMP(2016)14 (2016).

OECD, 'Protecting Consumers in Peer Platform Markets: Exploring the Issues' (2016).

OECD, 'Price Discrimination', DAF/COMP(2016)15 (13 October 2016).

OECD, 'Digital Economy Outlook 2017' (2017).

OECD, 'Algorithms and Collusion: Competition Policy in the Digital Age' (2017) <https://www.oecd.org/competition/algorithms-collusion-competition-policy-in-the-digital-age.htm> (accessed 28 August 2023).

OECD, 'Algorithms and Collusion—Note from Italy', DAF/COMP/WD(2017)18 (2 June 2017).

OECD, 'Algorithms and Collusion—Note from the European Union' (14 June 2017).
OECD, 'Algorithms and Collusion—Note from the European Union' (21–23 June 2017).
OECD, 'Considering Non-Price Effects in Merger Control—Background Note by the Secretariat', DAF/COMP/(2018)2 (2018).
OECD, 'Market Definition in Multi-Sided Markets: Note by Dr Lapo Filistrucchi', DAF/COMP/WD(2017)27 final (12 January 2018).
OECD, 'Personalised Pricing in the Digital Era', DAF/COMP(2018)13 (20 November 2018).
OECD, 'Roundtable on Hub-and-Spoke Arrangements—Background Note by the Secretariat', DAF/COMP(2019)14 (2019).
OECD, 'Abuse of Dominance in Digital Markets' (2020) <https://webarchive.oecd.org/20211031/566602abuseofdominanceindigitalmarkets2020.pdf> (accessed 29 September 2024).
OECD, 'Competition in Digital Advertising Markets' (2020) <https://www.oecd.org/en/publications/competition-in-digital-advertising-markets_f2209674-en.html> (accessed 29 September 2024).
OECD, 'Roundtable on Conglomerate Effects of Mergers—Background Note', DAF/COMP/(2020)2 (24 May 2020).
OECD, 'Ecosystem Competition—a Note by Daniel A. Crane', DAF/COMP/WD(2020)67 (28 October 2020).
OECD, 'Digital Competition Policy: Are Ecosystems Different?—Note by Amelia Fletcher', DAF/COMP/WD(2020)96 (9 November 2020).
OECD, 'Taking Ecosystems Competition Seriously in the Digital Economy—Note by Nicolas Petit and David J. Teece' (Hearing on Competition Economics of Digital Ecosystems) DAF/COMP/WD(2020)90 (2 December 2020).
OECD, 'Advantages and Disadvantages of Competition Welfare Standards—Note by Greece', DAF/COMP/WD(2023)21.
OECD, 'Competition Enforcement and Regulatory Alternatives' (OECD Competition Committee discussion paper, 2021) <http://oe.cd/cera> (accessed 29 September 2024).
OECD, 'Executive Summary of the Roundtable on Conglomerate Effects of Mergers', DAF/COMP/M(2020)1 ANN2 final (4 February 2021).
OECD, 'The Concept of Potential Competition—Note by Spain' (10 June 2021).
OECD, 'The Evolving Concept of Market Power in the Digital Economy' (OECD Competition Policy Roundtable background note, 2022).
OECD, 'The Consumer Welfare Standard—Advantages and Disadvantages Compared to Alternative Standards' (OECD Competition Policy Roundtable background note, 2023) <www.oecd.org/daf/competition/consumerwelfarestandardadvantagesanddisadvantagestoalternativestandards2023.pdf> (accessed 29 September 2024).

IV.2 International Competition Network

ICN (International Competition Network), 'Report on the Objectives of Unilateral Conduct Laws, Assessment of Dominance/Substantial Market Power, and State Created Monopolies' (May 2007).
ICN, 'Competition Enforcement and Consumer Welfare' (2011).
ICN, 'Unilateral Conduct Workbook' (April 2012).
ICN, 'ICN CWG SG2 Project on "Big Data and Cartels"—the Impact of Digitalization in Cartel Enforcement' (Scoping paper, 28 April 2020).

IV.3 Securities and Exchange Commission (SEC)

SEC (Securities and Exchange Commission), 'Amazon's Form 8-K' (Commission File No 000-22513) (31 December 2020) <https://d18rn0p25nwr6d.cloudfront.net/CIK0001018724/105ca2e514404fb5815f44f87165ee9a.pdf> (accessed 6 June 2024).
SEC, 'Amazon's Form 10-K' (Commission File No 000-22513) (31 December 2020), <https://d18rn0p25nwr6d.cloudfront.net/CIK0001018724/336d8745ea8240a59acc1a89df23d0f3.pdf> (accessed 6 June 2024).

SEC, 'Facebook's Form 10-K' (Commission File No 001-35551) (31 December 2020), <https://d18rn0p25nwr6d.cloudfront.net/CIK0001326801/4dd7fa7f1a514ed9b9df7f42cc3321eb.pdf> (accessed 6 June 2024).

SEC, 'Apple's Form 10-K' (Commission File No 001-36743) (25 September 2021) <https://d18rn0p25nwr6d.cloudfront.net/CIK0000320193/42ede86f6518450fbc8860211bf39c6d.pdf> (accessed 6 June 2024).

SEC, 'Alphabet Inc's Form 10-K' (Commission File No 001-37580) (28 October 2021) <https://www.sec.gov/Archives/edgar/data/1652044/000165204421000010/goog20201231.htm#id55be7992b374e1a9a2bc48887ddbb3f_16> (accessed 6 June 2024).

IV.4 Monopolkommission (German Monopoly Commission)

Monopolkommission (German Monopolies Commission), 'Competition Policy: Challenges of Digital Markets', Special Report No 68 (2015).

Monopolkommission, 'Algorithms and Collusion' (2018) <https://www.monopolkommission.de/images/HG22/Main_Report_XXII_Algorithms_and_Collusion.pdf> (accessed 14 February 2021).

IV.5 United Nations Conference on Trade and Development

UNCTAD (United Nations Conference on Trade and Development), 'Digital Economy Report' (2019).

UNCTAD, 'Global Competition Law and Policy Approaches to Digital Markets' (2024).

IV.6 Department for Science, Innovation and Technology (UK)

Department for Science, Innovation and Technology (UK), 'A Pro-Innovation Approach to AI Regulation', CP 815 (March 2023).

Department for Science, Innovation and Technology (UK), 'Pro-Innovation Regulation of Technologies Review Digital Technologies' (Report by Sir Patrick Vallance, March 2023).

IV.7 United States House of Representatives

United States House of Representatives, 'Majority Staff Report and Recommendations—Subcommittee on Antitrust, Commercial, and Administrative Law of the Committee on the Judiciary' (October 2020) <https://www.govinfo.gov/content/pkg/CPRT117HPRT47832/pdf/CPRT117HPRT47832.pdf> (accessed 9 June 2024).

IV.8 UK Houses of Parliament

UK House of Lords Select Committee on Artificial Intelligence (AI), 'AI in the UK: Ready, Willing and Able?' (Report of Session 2017–2019, 16 April 2018).

UK House of Lords Select Committee on AI, 'A New Pro-Competition Regime for Digital Markets', CP 489 (July 2021) <https://assets.publishing.service.gov.uk/government/uploads/system/uploads/attachment_data/file/1003913/Digital_Competition_Consultation_v2.pdf> (accessed 9 June 2024).

V. Competition Authorities

V.1 Bundeskartellamt (Germany's Competition Authority)

ACM (Authority for Consumers and Markets), 'Guidelines Regarding Arrangements between Suppliers and Buyers' (2019).

Bundeskartellamt, 'Merger Control' <https://www.bundeskartellamt.de/EN/Tasks/Merger_control/merger_control_node.html> (accessed 24 February 2023).

Bundeskartellamt, 'Amazon Abandons Price Parity Clauses for Good' (26 November 2013) <https://www.bundeskartellamt.de/SharedDocs/Meldung/EN/Pressemitteilungen/2013/26_11_2013_Amazon-Verfahrenseinstellung.html> (accessed 9 June 2024) (*Amazon Marketplace Germany*).

Bundeskartellamt, 'Adidas Abandons Ban on Sales via Online Market Places' (Press release, 2 July 2014).

Bundeskartellamt, 'Unlawful Restrictions of Online Sales of ASICS Running Shoes' (25 August 2015).

Bundeskartellamt, 'Unlawful Restrictions of Online Sales of ASICS Running Shoes' (Case B2-98/11, 13) (13 January 2016).

Bundeskartellamt, 'Background Information on the Facebook Proceeding' (19 December 2017) <http://www.bundeskartellamt.de/SharedDocs/Publikation/EN/Diskussions_Hintergrundpapiere/2017/Hintergrundpapier_Facebook.pdf?__blob=publicationFile&v=6> (accessed 7 June 2024).

Bundeskartellamt, 'Online Advertising' (Series of papers on 'Competition and Consumer Protection in the Digital Economy') (February 2018) <https://www.bundeskartellamt.de/SharedDocs/Publikation/EN/Schriftenreihe_Digitales_III.pdf?__blob=publicationFile&v=5> (accessed 7 June 2024).

Bundeskartellamt, 'Bundeskartellamt Launches Sector Inquiry into Market Conditions in Online Advertising Sector' (1 February 2018) <https://www.bundeskartellamt.de/SharedDocs/Meldung/EN/Pressemitteilungen/2018/01_02_2018_SU_Online_Werbung.html> (accessed 7 June 2024).

Bundeskartellamt, 'Background Information on the Bundeskartellamt's Facebook Proceedings' (7 February 2019) <https://www.bundeskartellamt.de/SharedDocs/Publikation/EN/Pressemitteilungen/2019/07_02_2019_Facebook_FAQs.pdf?__blob=publicationFile&v=6> (accessed 7 June 2024).

Bundeskartellamt, 'Bundeskartellamt Prohibits Facebook from Combining User Data from Different Sources' (Press release, 7 February 2019) <https://www.bundeskartellamt.de/SharedDocs/Meldung/EN/Pressemitteilungen/2019/07_02_2019_Facebook.html> (accessed 7 June 2024).

Bundeskartellamt, 'Facebook, Exploitative Business Terms Pursuant to Section 19(1) GWB for Inadequate Data Processing' (15 February 2019) <https://www.bundeskartellamt.de/SharedDocs/Entscheidung/EN/Fallberichte/Missbrauchsaufsicht/2019/B6-22-16.pdf?__blob=publicationFile&v=4> (accessed 7 June 2024).

Bundeskartellamt, 'Bundeskartellamt Obtains Far-Reaching Improvements in the Terms of Business for Sellers on Amazon's Online Marketplaces' (Press release , 17 July 2019) <https://www.bundeskartellamt.de/SharedDocs/Meldung/EN/Pressemitteilungen/2019/17_07_2019_Amazon.html;jsessionid=98F173CFCF40CBB4E3AA149FF088832E.1_cid36> (accessed 7 June 2024).

Bundeskartellamt, 'First Proceeding Based on New Rules for Digital Companies—Bundeskartellamt Also Assesses New Section 19a GWB in Its Facebook/Oculus Case' (28 January 2020) <https://www.bundeskartellamt.de/SharedDocs/Meldung/EN/Pressemitteilungen/2021/28_01_2021_Facebook_Oculus.html;jsessionid=FBE5A2DD3572BB985109D7D1C5D9699A.2_cid362?nn=3591568> (accessed 7 June 2024).

Bundeskartellamt, 'Bundeskartellamt Examines Linkage between Oculus and the Facebook Network' (Press release, 10 December 2020) <https://www.bundeskartellamt.de/SharedDocs/Meldung/EN/Pressemitteilungen/2020/10_12_2020_Facebook_Oculus.html> (accessed 7 June 2024).

Bundeskartellamt, 'Proceedings against Amazon Based on New Rules for Large Digital Companies (Section 19a GWB)' (18 May 2021) <https://www.bundeskartellamt.de/SharedDocs/Meldung/EN/Pressemitteilungen/2021/18_05_2021_Amazon_19a.html;jsessionid=FBE5A2DD3572BB985109D7D1C5D9699A.2_cid362?nn=3591568> (accessed 7 June 2024).

Bundeskartellamt, 'Proceeding against Google Based on New Rules for Large Digital Players (Section 19a GWB)—Bundeskartellamt Examines Google's Significance for Competition across Markets and Its Data Processing Terms' (Press release, 25 May 2021) <https://www.bundeskartellamt.de/SharedDocs/Meldung/EN/Pressemitteilungen/2021/25_05_2021_Google_19a.html?nn=3591568> (accessed 7 June 2024).

Bundeskartellamt, 'Bundeskartellamt Examines Google News Showcase' (4 June 2021) <https://www.bundeskartellamt.de/SharedDocs/Meldung/EN/Pressemitteilungen/2021/04_06_2021_Google_Showcase.html> (accessed 7 June 2024).

Bundeskartellamt, 'Proceeding against Apple Based on New Rules for Large Digital Companies (Section 19a(1) GWB)—Bundeskartellamt Examines Apple's Significance for Competition across Markets' (21 June 2021) <https://www.bundeskartellamt.de/SharedDocs/Meldung/EN/Pressemitteilungen/2021/21_06_2021_Apple.html?nn=3591568> (accessed 7 June 2024).

Bundeskartellamt, 'Das Bundeskartellamt—Schutz des Wettbewerbs in der Digitalwirtshaft' (Stand 1/ 2022) <https://www.bundeskartellamt.de/SharedDocs/Publikation/DE/Downloads/Liste_Verfahren_Digitalkonzerne.pdf?__blob=publicationFile&v = 6> (accessed 7 June 2024).

Bundeskartellamt, 'Alphabet/Google Subject to New Abuse Control Applicable to Large Digital Companies—Bundeskartellamt Determines "Paramount Significance across Markets"' (5 January 2022) <https://www.bundeskartellamt.de/SharedDocs/Meldung/EN/Pressemitteilungen/2022/05_01_2022_Google_19a.html> (accessed 7 June 2024).

Bundeskartellamt, 'Guidance on Transaction Value Thresholds for Mandatory Premerger Notification (Section 35 (1a) GWB and Section 9 (4) KartG)' (21 January 2022) <https://www.bundeskartellamt.de/SharedDocs/Publikation/EN/Leitfaden/Leitfaden_Transaktionswertschwelle_2022.html> (accessed 14 April 2024).

Bundeskartellamt, 'Bundeskartellamt Clears Acquisition of Kustomer by Meta (Formerly Facebook', *Kustomer/Meta (Formerly Facebook)*, B6-21/22B7-119/21 (11 February 2022) <https://www.bundeskartellamt.de/SharedDocs/Meldung/EN/Pressemitteilungen/2022/11_02_2022_Meta_Kustomer.html> (accessed 9 June 2024).

Bundeskartellamt, 'New Rules Apply to Meta (Formerly Facebook)—Bundeskartellamt Determines Its "Paramount Significance for Competition across Markets"' (4 May 2022) <https://www.bundeskartellamt.de/SharedDocs/Meldung/EN/Pressemitteilungen/2022/04_05_2022_Facebook_19a.html> (accessed 7 June 2024).

Bundeskartellamt, 'Bundeskartellamt Reviews Apple's Tracking Rules for Third-Party Apps' (14 June 2022) <https://www.bundeskartellamt.de/SharedDocs/Meldung/EN/Pressemitteilungen/2022/14_06_2022_Apple.html?nn=3591568> (accessed 7 June 2024).

Bundeskartellamt, 'Proceeding against Google for Possible Anti-Competitive Restrictions of Map Services (Google Maps Platform)' (21 June 2022) <https://www.bundeskartellamt.de/SharedDocs/Meldung/EN/Pressemitteilungen/2022/21_06_2022_Google_Maps.html?nn=3591568> (accessed 7 June 2024).

Bundeskartellamt, 'Bundeskartellamt Clears Acquisition of Kustomer by Meta (Formerly Facebook) (B6-21/22)' (28 June 2022) <https://www.bundeskartellamt.de/SharedDocs/Entscheidung/EN/Fallberichte/Fusionskontrolle/2022/B6-21-22.pdf?__blob=publicationFile&v=3> (accessed 23 February 2023).

Bundeskartellamt, 'Amazon Now Subject to Stricter Regulations: Bundeskartellamt Determines Its Paramount Significance for Competition across Markets (Section 19a GWB)' (6 July 2022) <https://www.bundeskartellamt.de/SharedDocs/Meldung/EN/Pressemitteilungen/2022/06_07_2022_Amazon.html> (accessed 7 June 2024).

Bundeskartellamt, 'Extension of Ongoing Proceedings against Amazon to Also Include an Examination Pursuant to Section 19a of the German Competition Act (GWB)' (14 November 2022) <https://www.bundeskartellamt.de/SharedDocs/Meldung/EN/Pressemitteilungen/2022/14_11_2022_Amazon_19a.html?nn=3599398> (accessed 7 June 2024).

Bundeskartellamt, 'Meta (Facebook) Responds to the Bundeskartellamt's Concerns—VR Headsets Can Now Be Used Without a Facebook Account' (accessed 23 November 2022) <https://www.bundeskartellamt.de/SharedDocs/Meldung/EN/Pressemitteilungen/2022/23_11_2022_Facebook_Oculus.html> (accessed 7 June 2024).

Bundeskartellamt, 'Improvements for Publishers Using Google News Showcase' (21 December 2022) <https://www.bundeskartellamt.de/SharedDocs/Meldung/EN/Pressemitteilungen/

2022/21_12_2022_Google_News_Showcase.html;jsessionid=DB330BF2E344FECF04D06E2216C14EB8.2_cid371> (accessed 7 June 2024).

Bundeskartellamt, 'Statement of Objections Issued against Google's Data Processing Terms' (11 January 2023) <https://www.bundeskartellamt.de/SharedDocs/Meldung/EN/Pressemitteilungen/2023/11_01_2023_Google_Data_Processing_Terms.html> (accessed 7 June 2024).

Bundeskartellamt, 'Examination of Microsoft's Significance for Competition across Markets' (28 March 2023) <https://www.bundeskartellamt.de/SharedDocs/Meldung/EN/Pressemitteilungen/2023/28_03_2023_Microsoft.html?nn=3591568> (accessed 7 June 2024).

Bundeskartellamt, 'Apple Also Subject to Provisions for Large Digital Companies under Section 19a GWB' (5 April 2023) <https://www.bundeskartellamt.de/SharedDocs/Meldung/EN/Pressemitteilungen/2023/05_04_2023_Apple_Abschluss.html;jsessionid=51931A335093425C28795071D578E06C.2_cid387?nn=3591568> (accessed 7 June 2024).

Bundeskartellamt, 'Bundeskartellamt Gives Users of Google Services Better Control over Their Data' (Press release, 5 October 2023) <https://www.bundeskartellamt.de/SharedDocs/Meldung/EN/Pressemitteilungen/2023/05_10_2023_Google_Data.html?nn=3591568> (accessed 7 June 2024).

Bundeskartellamt, 'Cooperation between Microsoft and OpenAI Currently Not Subject to Merger Control' (Press release, 15 November 2023) <https://www.bundeskartellamt.de/SharedDocs/Meldung/EN/Pressemitteilungen/2023/15_11_2023_Microsoft_OpenAI.html> (accessed 2 May 2024).

Bundeskartellamt, 'Google Automotive Services Proceeding—Market Test Regarding Commitments Proposed by Google' (20 December 2023) <https://www.bundeskartellamt.de/SharedDocs/Meldung/EN/Pressemitteilungen/2023/20_12_2023_Google_Automotive.html?nn = 49440> (accessed 7 June 2024).

Bundeskartellamt, 'Sector Inquiry into Online Advertising' <https://www.bundeskartellamt.de/EN/Tasks/Sector_inquiries/Sector_inquiry_Online_Werbung/Sector_inquiry_OW_node.html#> (accessed 25 June 2024).

Bundeskartellamt, 'Verfahren gegen große Digitalkonzerne—auf der basis von § 19a GWB' (July 2024) <https://www.bundeskartellamt.de/SharedDocs/Publikation/DE/Downloads/Liste_Verfahren_Digitalkonzerne.pdf?__blob=publicationFile&v=6> (accessed 7 June 2024).

V.2 Competition & Markets Authority (UK)

CMA (Competition and Markets Authority), *Decision to Accept Commitments Offered by Google in Relation to Its Privacy Sandbox Proposals* (Case No 50972) (11 February 2022).

CMA, 'Private Motor Insurance Market Investigation' (Final Report, 24 September 2014).

CMA, 'Online Resale Price Maintenance in the Bathroom Fittings Sector' (Case CE/9857-14) (10 May 2016).

CMA, 'Online Resale Price Maintenance in the Commercial Refrigeration Sector' (Case CE/9856-14) (24 May 2016).

CMA, *Online Sales of Posters and Frames* (Case No 50972), Decision (12 August 2016).

CMA, 'Amazon Marketplace Online Sellers Fined £160k for Price-Fixing' (7 November 2016) <https://www.gov.uk/government/case-studies/online-sellers-price-fixing-case-study> (accessed 29 December 2022) (Case Study).

CMA, 'Price-Fixing: Guidance for Online Sellers' (7 November 2016) <https://www.gov.uk/government/publications/price-fixing-guidance-for-online-sellers/price-fixing-guidance-for-online-sellers> (accessed 28 August 2023).

CMA, 'CMA Secures Director Disqualification for Competition Law Breach' (1 December 2016) <https://www.gov.uk/government/news/cma-secures-director-disqualification-for-competition-law-breach> (accessed 24 February 2023).

CMA, 'Online Search: Consumer and Firm Behaviour—a Review of the Existing Literature' (2017).

CMA, 'Online Resale Price Maintenance in the Light Fittings Sector' (Case No 50343) (3 May 2017).

CMA, 'Restricting Resale Prices: An Open Letter to Suppliers and Resellers' (20 June 2017).
CMA, 'Pricing Algorithms—Economic Working Paper on the Use of Algorithms to Facilitate Collusion and Personalised Pricing' (2018).
CMA, 'Online Platforms and Digital Advertising Market Study Statement of Scope' (3 July 2019) <https://assets.publishing.service.gov.uk/media/5d1b297e40f0b609dba90d7a/Statement_of_Scope.pdf> (accessed 7 June 2024).
CMA, 'Online Resale Price Maintenance in the Digital Piano and Digital Keyboard Sector' (Case 50565-2) (1 August 2019).
CMA, 'Case 50505—Price Comparison Website: Use of Most Favoured Nation Clauses by BGL' (19 November 2020).
CMA, 'Online Platforms and Digital Advertising' (Market Study—Final Report) (Digital Platforms Report, 1 July 2020).
CMA, 'Online Platforms and Digital Advertising' (Market Study—Final Report) (Digital Platforms Report, 1 July 2020) Appendix E: Ecosystems of Google and Facebook <https://assets.publishing.service.gov.uk/media/5fe49531d3bf7f089e48dec9/Appendix_E_Ecosystems_v.2_WEB.pdf> (accessed 18 August 2023).
CMA, 'Algorithms: How They Can Reduce Competition and Harm Consumers' (2021).
CMA, 'CMA to Investigate Google's "Privacy Sandbox" Browser Changes' (8 January 2021) <https://www.gov.uk/government/news/cmatoinvestigategooglesprivacysandboxbrowserchanges> (accessed 7 June 2024).
CMA, 'The CMA's Digital Markets Strategy: June 2019' (Policy paper, updated 9 February 2021), <https://www.gov.uk/government/publications/competitionandmarketsauthoritysdigitalmarketsstrategy/thecmasdigitalmarketsstrategy> (accessed 17 August 2023).
CMA, 'Merger Assessment Guidelines', CMA 129 (18 March 2021) (CMA MAG).
CMA, 'CMA Investigates Facebook's Use of Ad Data' (Press release, 4 June 2021) <https://www.gov.uk/government/news/cmainvestigatesfacebooksuseofaddata> (accessed 30 September 2024).
CMA, 'Notice of Intention to Accept Commitments Offered by Google in Relation to Its Privacy Sandbox Proposals' (Case No 50972) (11 June 2021) <https://assets.publishing.service.gov.uk/government/uploads/system/uploads/attachment_data/file/992975/Notice_of_intention_to_accept_binding_commitments_offered_by_Google_publication.pdf> (accessed 7 June 2024).
CMA, 'CMA to Scrutinise Apple and Google Mobile Ecosystems' (Press release, 15 June 2021) <https://www.gov.uk/government/news/cma-to-scrutinise-apple-and-google-mobile-ecosystems> (accessed 7 June 2024).
CMA, 'Mobile Ecosystems Market Study—Statement of Scope' (15 June 2021).
CMA, 'CMA to Investigate Amazon and Google over Fake Reviews' (Press release, 25 June 2021) <https://www.gov.uk/government/news/cmatoinvestigateamazonandgoogleoverfakereviews> (accessed 7 June 2024).
CMA, 'Response to the Government's Consultation "A New Pro-Competition Regime for Digital Markets"' (29 September 2021).
CMA, 'CMA Directs Facebook to Sell Giphy' (Press release, 30 November 2021) <https://www.gov.uk/government/news/cmadirectsfacebooktosellgiphy> (accessed 9 June 2024).
CMA, 'Completed Acquisition by Facebook, Inc (Now Meta Platforms, Inc) of Giphy, Inc' (Final Report, 30 November 2021).
CMA, 'Mobile Ecosystems' (Market Study Interim Report, 14 December 2021).
CMA, 'CMA to Keep "Close Eye" on Google as It Secures Final Privacy Sandbox Commitments' (Press release, 11 February 2022) <https://www.gov.uk/government/news/cmatokeepcloseeyeongoogleasitsecuresfinalprivacysandboxcommitments> (accessed 7 June 2024).
CMA, 'CMA Investigates Google and Meta over Ad Tech Concerns' (Press release, 11 March 2022) <https://www.gov.uk/government/news/cmainvestigatesgoogleandmetaoveradtechconcerns> (accessed 7 June 2024).
CMA, 'Online Choice Architecture—How Digital Design Can Harm Competition and Consumers' (Discussion paper, April 2022) <https://assets.publishing.service.gov.uk/gov

ernment/uploads/system/uploads/attachment_data/file/1066524/Online_choice_architecture_discussion_paper.pdf> (accessed 18 August 2023).

CMA, 'Investigation into Suspected Anti-Competitive Conduct by Google in Ad Tech' (25 May 2022) <https://www.gov.uk/cmacases/investigationintosuspectedanticompetitiveconductbygoogleinadtech> (accessed 7 June 2024).

CMA, 'Mobile Ecosystems' (Market Study Final Report, 10 June 2022) <https://assets.publishing.service.gov.uk/government/uploads/system/uploads/attachment_data/file/1138104/Mobile_Ecosystems_Final_Report_amended_2.pdf> (accessed 7 June 2024).

CMA, 'CMA Investigates Amazon over Suspected Anticompetitive Practices' (Press release, 6 July 2022) <https://www.gov.uk/government/news/cmainvestigatesamazonoversuspectedanticompetitivepractices> (accessed 7 June 2024).

CMA, 'CMA Orders Meta to Sell Giphy' (Press release, 18 October 2022) <https://www.gov.uk/government/news/cmaordersmetatosellgiphy> (accessed 16 May 2024).

CMA, 'Completed Acquisition by Facebook, Inc (Now Meta Platforms, Inc) of Giphy, Inc' (Final Report on the case remitted to the CMA by the Competition Appeal Tribunal, 18 October 2022).

CMA, 'Investigation into Suspected Anti-Competitive Agreement between Google and Meta and Behaviour by Google in Relation to Header Bidding' (Press release, 11 March 2023) <https://www.gov.uk/cmacases/investigationintosuspectedanticompetitiveagreementbetweengoogleandmetaandbehaviourbygoogleinrelationtoheaderbidding> (accessed 7 June 2024).

CMA, 'App Developers on Google Play Store Offered Payment Choices Following CMA Probe' (Press release, 19 April 2023) <https://www.gov.uk/government/news/appdevelopersongoogleplaystoreofferedpaymentchoicesfollowingcmaprobe> (accessed 7 June 2024).

CMA, 'Proposed Commitments Regarding Changes to Google Play's Rules to Allow Certain App Developers to Use Alternative Billing Systems for In-App Purchases' (19 April 2023) <https://www.gov.uk/government/consultations/proposedcommitmentsregardingchangestogoogleplaysrulestoallowcertainappdeveloperstousealternativebillingsystemsforinapppurchases> (accessed 7 June 2024).

CMA, 'Anticipated Acquisition by Microsoft of Activision Blizzard, Inc' (Final Report, 26 April 2023) <https://assets.publishing.service.gov.uk/media/644939aa529eda000c3b0525/Microsoft_Activision_Final_Report_.pdf> (accessed 9 June 2024).

CMA, 'Microsoft/Activision Deal Prevented to Protect Innovation and Choice in Cloud Gaming' (Press release, 26 April 2023) <https://www.gov.uk/government/news/microsoftactivisiondealpreventedtoprotectinnovationandchoiceincloudgaming> (accessed 9 June 2024).

CMA, 'AI Foundation Models: Initial Review' (4 May 2023).

CMA, 'Meta Offers to Limit Use of Other Businesses' Ad Data to Address CMA Concerns' (Press release, 26 May 2023) <https://www.gov.uk/government/news/metaofferstolimituseofotherbusinessesaddatatoaddresscmaconcerns> (accessed 7 June 2024).

CMA, 'Amazon's Purchase of Roomba Maker Cleared by CMA' (16 June 2023) <https://www.gov.uk/government/news/amazonspurchaseofroombamakerclearedbycma> (accessed 9 June 2024).

CMA, 'Facebook, Inc (Now Meta Platforms, Inc)/Giphy, Inc Merger Inquiry' (updated 30 June 2023) <https://www.gov.uk/cmacases/facebookincgiphyincmergerinquiry> (accessed 9 June 2024).

CMA, 'Microsoft/Activision Blizzard (Ex-Cloud Streaming Rights) Merger Inquiry' (22 August 2023) <https://www.gov.uk/cmacases/microsoftslashactivisionblizzardexcloudstreamingrightsmergerinquiry> (accessed 9 June 2024).

CMA, 'AI Foundation Models: Initial Report' (18 September 2023).

CMA, 'Decision to Accept Binding Commitments Offered by Meta on Its Use of Data Obtained through Digital Display Advertising' (Case AT.51013) (3 November 2023).

CMA, 'Decision to Accept Binding Commitments under the Competition Act 1998 from Amazon in Relation to Conduct on Its UK Online Marketplace' (Case No 51184) (3 November 2023).

CMA, 'AI Foundation Models: Update Paper' (11 April 2024).

CMA, 'AI Foundation Models: Technical Update Report' (16 April 2024).

CMA, 'CMA Seeks Views on AI Partnerships and Other Arrangements' (Press release, 24 April 2024) <https://www.gov.uk/government/news/cma-seeks-views-on-ai-partnerships-and-other-arrangements> (accessed 2 May 2024).

CMA, 'Investigation into Apple App Store' (updated 21 August 2024) <https://www.gov.uk/cma-cases/investigation-into-apple-appstore> (accessed 9 October 2024).

CMA, Competition Appeal Tribunal, 'Epic Games, Inc. and Others v Alphabet Inc., Google LLC and Others' Case 1378/5/7/20 (29 December 2020) <https://www.catribunal.org.uk/cases/13785720epicgamesincandothers> (accessed 4 July 2020).

CMA, Competition Appeal Tribunal, 'Elizabeth Helen Coll v Alphabet Inc. and Others' Case 1408/7/7/21 (29 July 2021) <https://www.catribunal.org.uk/cases/14087721elizabethhelencoll> (accessed 7 June 2024).

CMA, Competition Appeal Tribunal, 'Ad Tech Collective Action LLP v Alphabet Inc. & Others', Case 1572/7/7/22, 1582/7/7/23 (30 November 2022) <https://www.catribunal.org.uk/cases/1572772215827723adtechcollectiveactionllp> (accessed 4 July 2024).

Coscelli, A, 'Ahead of the Curve' (Bannerman Competition lecture, 9 February 2021) <https://www.gov.uk/government/speeches/andreacoscelliaheadofthecurvebannermancompetitionlecture> (accessed 28 February 2023).

V.3 Office of Fair Trading

OFT (Office of Fair Trading), 'Complete Acquisitions by Motorola Mobility Holding (Google, Inc) of Waze Mobile Limited' (17 December 2013), ME/6167/13.

OFT, 'Joining Up Competition and Consumer Policy', OFT 1151 (December 2009).

OFT, 'Anticipated Acquisition by Facebook Inc of Instagram Inc', ME/5525/12 (14 August 2012).

OFT, 'Roma-Branded Mobility Scooters: Prohibitions on Online Sales and Online Price Advertising', CE/9578-12 (5 August 2013).

OFT, 'Amazon Online Retailer: Investigation into Anti-Competitive Practices', CE/9692/12 (1 October 2013) <https://www.gov.uk/cma-cases/amazon-online-retailer-investigation-into-anti-competitive-practices> (accessed 9 June 2024).

OFT, 'Hotel Online Booking: Decision to Accept Commitments to Remove Certain Discounting Restrictions for Online Travel Agents', OFT1514 (31 January 2014) <https://webarchive.nationalarchives.gov.uk/ukgwa/20140402153926/http://www.oft.gov.uk/shared_oft/ca-and-cartels/oft1514dec.pdf> (accessed 9 June 2024).

OFT, 'Mobility Scooters Supplied by Pride Mobility Products Limited: Prohibition on Online Advertising of Prices below Pride's RRP', Decision (27 March 2014) (Pride).

V.4 French Competition Authority ('Autorité de la Concurrence')

Autoridade da Concorrência, 'Digital Ecosystems, Big Data and Algorithms' (Issue paper, July 2019).

AdC (Autorité de la Concurrence), '30 June 2010: Online Advertising Market' (30 June 2010) <https://www.autoritedelaconcurrence.fr/en/communiquesdepresse/30june2010onlineadvertisingmarket> (accessed 7 June 2024).

AdC, 'Sector Inquiry/Online Advertising' (14 December 2010) <https://www.autoritedelaconcurrence.fr/en/communiquesdepresse/14december2010sectorinquiryonlineadvertising> (accessed 7 June 2024).

AdC, 'Decision 215-D-06 Regarding Practices Implemented by Booking.com B.V., Booking.com France SAS and Booking.com Customer Service France SAS in the Online Hotel Booking Sector' (21 April 2015).

AdC, 'On Data Processing in the Online Advertising Sector' (6 March 2018) <https://www.autoritedelaconcurrence.fr/sites/default/files/integral_texts/2019-10/avis18a03_en_.pdf> (accessed 7 June 2024).

AdC, 'Sector-Specific Investigation into Online Advertising' (6 March 2018) <https://www.autoritedelaconcurrence.fr/en/pressrelease/6march2018sectorspecificinvestigationonlineadvertising> (accessed 7 June 2024).

AdC, 'The Autorité de la Concurrence Has Ordered Interim Measures against Google' (31 January 2019) <https://www.autoritedelaconcurrence.fr/en/communiquesdepresse/31january2019onlineadvertisingdirectoryenquiryservices0> (accessed 7 June 2024).

AdC, 'The Autorité de la Concurrence Hands Down a €150M Fine for Abuse of a Dominant Position' (20 December 2019) <https://www.autoritedelaconcurrence.fr/en/communiquesdepresse/autoritedelaconcurrencehandsdowneu150mfineabusedominantposition> (accessed 7 June 2024).

AdC, 'Fines Handed Down to Apple, Tech Data and Ingram Micro' (16 March 2020) <https://www.autoritedelaconcurrence.fr/en/article/fineshandeddownappletechdataandingrammicro> (accessed 7 June 2024).

AdC, 'Related Rights: The Autorité Has Granted Requests for Urgent Interim Measures Presented by Press Publishers and the News Agency AFP (Agence France Presse)' (9 April 2020) <https://www.autoritedelaconcurrence.fr/en/pressrelease/relatedrightsautoritehasgrantedrequestsurgentinterimmeasurespresentedpress> (accessed 7 June 2024).

AdC, 'Decision 20-D-04 of March 16, 2020 Regarding Practices Implemented in the Apple Products Distribution Sector' (15 June 2020) <https://www.autoritedelaconcurrence.fr/en/decision/regarding-practices-implemented-apple-products-distribution-sector> (accessed 9 January 2023).

AdC, 'In the Context of an Investigation Opened before the Autorité in the Online Advertising Sector, Facebook Proposes Commitments' (3 June 2021) <https://www.autoritedelaconcurrence.fr/en/pressrelease/contextinvestigationopenedautoriteonlineadvertisingsectorfacebookproposes> (accessed 7 June 2024).

AdC, 'The Autorité de la Concurrence Hands Out a €220 Million Fine to Google for Favouring Its Own Services in the Online Advertising Sector' (7 June 2021) <https://www.autoritedelaconcurrence.fr/en/decision/regardingpracticesimplementedonlineadvertisingsector> (accessed 7 June 2024).

AdC, 'Remuneration of Related Rights for Press Publishers and Agencies: The Autorité Fines Google Up to 500 Million Euros for Non-Compliance with Several Injunctions' (13 July 2021) <https://www.autoritedelaconcurrence.fr/en/article/remunerationrelatedrightspresspublishersandagenciesautoritefinesgoogle500million> (accessed 7 June 2024).

AdC, 'Meta Makes Commitments to the Autorité de la Concurrence' (16 June 2022) <https://www.autoritedelaconcurrence.fr/en/communiquesdepresse/metamakescommitmentsautoritedelaconcurrence> (accessed 7 June 2024).

AdC, 'Related Rights: The Autorité Accepts Google's Commitments' (21 June 2022) <https://www.autoritedelaconcurrence.fr/en/pressrelease/relatedrightsautoriteacceptsgooglescommitments> (accessed 7 June 2024).

AdC, 'Online Ad Verification: The Autorité de la Concurrence Issues Interim Measures against Meta' (4 May 2023) <https://www.autoritedelaconcurrence.fr/en/article/onlineadverificationautoritedelaconcurrenceissuesinterimmeasuresagainstmeta> (accessed 7 June 2024).

AdC, 'Advertising on iOS Mobile Applications: The General Rapporteur Confirms Having Notified the Apple Group of an Objection' (27 July 2023) <https://www.autoritedelaconcurrence.fr/en/pressrelease/advertisingiosmobileapplicationsgeneralrapporteurconfirmshavingnotifiedapple> (accessed 7 June 2024).

AdC and Bundeskartellamt, 'Competition Law and Data' (10 May 2016) <https://www.bundeskartellamt.de/SharedDocs/Publikation/DE/Berichte/Big%20Data%20Papier.html;jsessionid=2F34FB1C56475779337616BA96B21934.2_cid381?nn=3591568> (accessed 7 June 2024).

AdC and Bundeskartellamt, 'Algorithms and Competition' (November 2019).

V.5 US Competition Authorities

DoJ (Department of Justice), 'Former E-Commerce Executive Charged with Price Fixing in the Antitrust Division's First Online Marketplace Prosecution' (6 April 2015) <https://www.justice.gov/opa/pr/former-e-commerce-executive-charged-price-fixing-antitrust-divisions-first-online-marketplace> (accessed 24 February 2023).

DoJ, 'Former E-Commerce Executive Pleads Guilty to Price Fixing; Sentenced to Six Months' (28 January 2019) <https://www.justice.gov/opa/pr/former-e-commerce-executive-pleads-guilty-price-fixing-sentenced-six-months> (accessed 24 February 2023).

DoJ, 'Justice Department Sues Monopolist Google for Violating Antitrust Laws' (Press release, 20 October 2020) <https://www.justice.gov/opa/pr/justicedepartmentsuesmonopolistgoogleviolatingantitrustlaws> (accessed 29 September 2024).

DoJ, 'Justice Department Sues Google for Monopolizing Digital Advertising Technologies' (24 January 2023) <https://www.justice.gov/opa/pr/justicedepartmentsuesgooglemonopolizingdigitaladvertisingtechnologies> (accessed 7 June 2024).

FTC (Federal Trade Commission), 'Dissenting Statement of Commissioner Pamela Jones Harbour in the Matter of Google–DoubleClick', FTC File No 071-0170 (20 December 2007) <https://www.ftc.gov/legallibrary/browse/casesproceedings/publicstatements/dissentingstatementcommissionerharbourmattergoogledoubleclick> (accessed 7 June 2024).

FTC, 'Statement of the Federal Trade Commission Regarding Google's Search Practices—in the Matter of Google Inc. FTC File Number 1110163' (3 January 2013).

FTC, '"Sharing" Economy Issues Facing Platforms, Participants and Regulators' (FTC Staff Report, November 2016).

FTC, 'FTC v Facebook', File No 191 0134 (9 December 2020) <https://www.ftc.gov/legallibrary/browse/casesproceedings/1910134facebookincftcv>.

FTC, 'FTC Seeks to Block Virtual Reality Giant Meta's Acquisition of Popular App Creator Within' (Press release, 27 July 2022) <https://www.ftc.gov/newsevents/news/pressreleases/2022/07/ftcseeksblockvirtualrealitygiantmetasacquisitionpopularappcreatorwithin> (accessed 24 February 2023).

FTC, 'Justice Department Obtains Permanent Injunction Blocking Penguin Random House's Proposed Acquisition of Simon & Schuster' (31 October 2022) <https://www.justice.gov/opa/pr/justicedepartmentobtainspermanentinjunctionblockingpenguinrandomhousesproposed> (accessed 7 June 2024).

FTC, '*FTC v Meta*, Order Denying Plaintiff's Motion for Preliminary Injunction (Case No 5:22cv04325EJD) (31 January 2023).

FTC, 'Commission Order Returning Matter to Adjudication and Dismissing the Complaint' (24 February 2023) <https://www.ftc.gov/system/files/ftc_gov/pdf/d09411commorderdismisscomplaint.pdf> (accessed 24 February 2023).

FTC, 'FTC Sues Amazon for Illegally Maintaining Monopoly Power' (Press release, 26 September 2023) <https://www.ftc.gov/newsevents/news/pressreleases/2023/09/ftcsuesamazonillegallymaintainingmonopolypower> (accessed 7 June 2024).

FTC, 'Statement Regarding the Termination of Amazon's Proposed Acquisition of iRobot' (Press release, 31 January 2024) <https://www.ftc.gov/news-events/news/press-releases/2024/01/statement-regarding-termination-amazons-proposed-acquisition-irobot> (accessed 9 June 2024).

V.6 Dutch Competition Authority ('Authority for Consumers and Markets')

ACM (Authority for Consumers and Markets), 'Market Study into Mobile App Stores', Report ACM/18/032693 (2019) (ACM Market Study).

ACM, 'ACM Launches Investigation into Abuse of Dominance by Apple in Its App Store' (11 April 2019) <https://www.acm.nl/en/publications/acmlaunchesinvestigationabusedominanceappleitsappstore> (accessed 7 June 2024).

ACM, 'ACM Launches an Investigation into Users' Freedom of Choice Regarding Payment Apps on Smartphones' (4 December 2020) <https://www.acm.nl/en/publications/acmlaunchesinvestigationusersfreedomchoiceregardingpaymentappssmartphones> (accessed 7 June 2024).

ACM, 'ACM Can Continue Its Investigation into the Apple App Store' (22 June 2021) <https://www.acm.nl/en/publications/acmcancontinueitsinvestigationappleappstore> (accessed 7 June 2024).

ACM, 'Closure of the Investigation into Payment Apps Confirms Need for New Rules' (2 July 2021) <https://www.acm.nl/en/publications/closureinvestigationpaymentappsconfirmsneednewrules> (accessed 7 June 2024).

ACM, 'ACM Launches Market Study into the Platform-to-Business Regulation' (22 October 2021) <https://www.acm.nl/en/publications/acmlaunchesmarketstudyplatformbusinessregulation> (accessed 7 June 2024).

ACM, 'ACM Obliges Apple to Adjust Unreasonable Conditions for Its App Store' (24 December 2021) <https://www.acm.nl/en/publications/acmobligesappleadjustunreasonableconditionsitsappstore> (accessed 7 June 2024).

ACM, 'Apple Changes Unfair Conditions, Allows Alternative Payments Methods in Dating Apps' (11 June 2022) <https://www.acm.nl/en/publications/acmapplechangesunfairconditionsallowsalternativepaymentsmethodsdatingapps> (accessed 7 June 2024).

V.7 Italian Competition Authority

AGCM (Italian Competition Authority), 'A542—ICA: Investigation Opened against Google for an Alleged Abuse of Dominant Position in the Italian Market for Display Advertising' (28 October 2020) <https://en.agcm.it/en/media/pressreleases/2020/10/A542> (accessed 7 June 2024).

AGCM, 'A529—ICA: Google Fined over 100 Million for Abuse of Dominant Position' (13 May 2021) <https://en.agcm.it/en/media/pressreleases/2021/5/A529> (accessed 7 June 2024).

AGCM, 'A528—Italian Competition Authority: Amazon Fined over €1,128 Billion for Abusing Its Dominant Position' (9 December 2021) <https://en.agcm.it/en/media/pressreleases/2021/12/A528> (accessed 7 June 2024).

AGCM, 'I842—Italian Competition Authority: The Fines Applied against Amazon and Apple for Anticompetitive Agreements Have Been Redetermined' (17 December 2021) <https://en.agcm.it/en/media/pressreleases/2021/12/I842> (accessed 7 June 2024).

AGCM, 'PS12585—Italian Competition Authority: A Sanction of EUR 10 Million to Amazon for Unfair Commercial Practice' (24 April 2024) <https://en.agcm.it/en/media/press-releases/2024/4/PS12585> (accessed 7 June 2024).

V.8 Spanish Competition Authority

CNMC (Spanish Competition Authority), 'La CNMC sanciona a las principals empresas fabricantes de tabaco y a Logista por una infracción consistente en unintercambio de información estratégica' (Press release, in Spanish) <https://cnmc.es/node/374435#:~:text=Son%20responsables%20las%20empresas%20Philip%20Morris%20Spain%2C%20Altadis%2C,euros%20JT%20International%20Iberia%3A%2010%20millones%20de%20euros> (accessed 29 December 2022).

CNMC, 'The CNMC Initiates Disciplinary Proceedings against Apple and Amazon for Possible Restrictive Competition Practices' (1 July 2021) <https://www.cnmc.es/sites/default/files/3723098_1000.pdf> (accessed 7 June 2024).

CNMC, 'The CNMC Publishes a Study on the Online Advertising Sector in Spain' (Press release, 26 July 2021) <https://www.cnmc.es/sites/default/files/editor_contenidos/Notas%20de%20prensa/2021/20210726_NP_Estudio_Publicidad_Online_en_GB%20.pdf> (accessed 7 June 2024).

CNMC, 'The CNMC Fines Several Companies EUR 1.25 Million for Imposing Minimum Commissions in the Real Estate Brokerage Market' (Press release, 9 December 2021) <https://www.cnmc.es/sites/default/files/editor_contenidos/Notas%20de%20prensa/2021/20211209_NP_Sancionador_Proptech_eng.pdf> (accessed 8 June 2024).

V.9 Hellenic Competition Commission

Hellenic Competition Commission, 'Computational Competition Law and Economics: Issues, Prospects (Inception Report)' (26 July 2021).

V.10 Australian Competition and Consumer Commission

ACCC (Australian Competition and Consumer Commission), 'Digital Platforms Inquiry—Final Report' (June 2019) <https://www.accc.gov.au/system/files/Digital%20platforms%20inquiry%20%20final%20report.pdf> (accessed 7 June 2024).

ACCC, 'ACCC Rejects Google Behavioural Undertakings for Fitbit Acquisition' (Press release, 22 December 2020) <https://www.accc.gov.au/mediarelease/acccrejectsgooglebehaviouralundertakingsforfitbitacquisition> (accessed 28 February 2023).

ACCC, 'Feedback Sought on Potential New Rules for Large Digital Platforms' (28 February 2022) <https://www.accc.gov.au/mediarelease/feedback-sought-on-potential-new-rules-for-large-digital-platforms> (accessed 7 June 2024).

ACCC, 'Digital Platform Services Inquiry—Interim Report No. 4—General Online Retail Marketplaces' (March 2022) <https://www.accc.gov.au/system/files/DPB%20%20DPSI%20%20March%202022%20%20Full%20interim%20report%20%2031%20March%202022.pdf> (accessed 7 June 2024).

ACCC, 'Digital Platforms Services Inquiry—Interim Report 6: Report on Social Media Services' (March 2023) <https://www.accc.gov.au/system/files/Digital%20platforms%20services%20inquiry%20%20Interim%20report%206%20%20Report%20on%20social%20media%20services_0.pdf> (accessed 7 June 2024).

V.11 Hong Kong Competition Commission

Hong Kong Competition Commission, 'Commitments Given by Trip International Travel (Hong Kong) Limited and Ctrip.com (Hong Kong) Limited to the Competition Commission Pursuant to Section 60 of the Competition Ordinance (Cap. 619)' <https://www.compcomm.hk/tc/enforcement/consultations/past_consultations/files/Proposed_Commitments_Ctrip_HK.pdf> (accessed 7 June 2024).

Hong Kong Competition Commission, 'Notice Issued under Section 2 of Schedule 2 of the Competition Ordinance Regarding the Commission's Proposal to Accept Commitments in Online Travel Agents Case (EC/02NJ)' <https://www.compcomm.hk/en/enforcement/consultations/past_consultations/files/OTA_Notice_ENG.pdf> (accessed 7 June 2024).

Hong Kong Competition Commission, '关于网上旅行社根据《竞争条例》第60条所作出的承诺 [The Commitments Made by Online Travel Agents under Section 60 of the Competition Ordinance]' (13 May 2020) <https://www.compcomm.hk/tc/enforcement/registers/commitments/commitments_online_travel_agents.html> (accessed 4 October 2023).

V.12 Other National Competition Authorities

Austrian Regulatory Authority, 'The Open Internet: OS, Apps and App Stores' (Report—English Summary, 2019).

BWB (Bundeswettbewerbsbehörde), Austrian Federal Competition Authority, 'Merger Control' <https://www.bwb.gv.at/en/merger_control/> (accessed 30 September 2024).

BWB, 'BWB Informs: Amazon Modifies Its Terms and Conditions' (Press release, 17 July 2019) <https://www.bwb.gv.at/en/news/news_2019/detail/bwb-informs-amazon-modifies-its-terms-and-conditions-1> (accessed 7 June 2024).

Danish Competition and Consumer Authority, 'The Danish Competition Council Has Adopted a Decision Finding the Exchange of Information on Prices, Discounts and Quantities in Relation to Future Sales between Retailers of Clothing Items Illegal', (24 June 2020) <https://www.en.kfst.dk/nyheder/kfst/english/decisions/20200624-the-danish-competition-council-has-adopted-a-decision-finding-the-exchange-of-information-on-prices-discounts-and-quantities-in-relation-to-future-sales-between-retailers-of-clothing-items-illegal> (accessed 9 January 2023).

German and Austrian NCAs (National Competent Authorities), 'Guidance on Transaction Value Thresholds for Mandatory Premerger Notification (Section 35(1a) GWB and Section 9(4) KartG)' (January 2022).

Konkurrensverket, 'The Competition on Digital Platform Markets in Sweden—Summary' (2021).

VI Authorities of the People's Republic of China

VI.1 State Administration for Market Regulation

SAMR (State Administration for Market Regluation), '滥用行政权力排除、限制竞争案件 [Cases of Abuse of Administrative Power to Exclude or Restrict Competition] <https://www.samr.gov.cn/jzxts/tzgg/qlpc/index.html> (accessed 10 April 2024).

SAMR, '国家市场监管总局：依据反垄断法及有关规定对滴滴收购优步案件进行调查 [SAMR Investigate the Case of Didi's Acquisition of Uber in Accordance with the Antimonopoly Law and Relevant Regulations]' (16 November 2018) <https://www.samr.gov.cn/xw/xwfbt/art/2023/art_3d552be3060b4f70b62908081a579310.html> (accessed 13 April 2024).

SAMR, '禁止滥用市场支配地位行为暂行规定 [Interim Provisions on Prohibiting Abuse of Dominant Market Position]' (promulgated by the SAMR, 26 June 2019, effective 1 September 2019) <http://www.gov.cn/gongbao/content/2019/content_5430507.htm> (accessed 7 November 2022).

SAMR, '市场监管总局关于附加限制性条件批准英伟达公司收购迈络思科技有限公司股权案反垄断审查决定的公告 [Announcement of Anti-Monopoly Review Decisions Regarding Approval of the SAMR on Additional Restrictive Conditions: Nvidia's Acquisition of Equity of Miloth Technology Co, Ltd]' (16 April 2020) <https://www.samr.gov.cn/zt/qhfldzf/art/2020/art_5062ec6932d8429488e4765c83d2d6ea.html> (accessed 17 April 2024).

SAMR, '市场监管总局关于《关于平台经济领域的反垄断指南（征求意见稿）》公开征求意见的公告 [Guidelines for Anti-Monopoly in the Field of Platform Economy (Draft Proposal for Public Opinion)]' (promulgated by the SAMR, 10 November 2020) <https://www.samr.gov.cn/fldes/tzgg/zqyjgg/art/2023/art_80cfa47c2b9d411c80c036244f3d0d70.html> (accessed 13 April 2024).

SAMR, '市场监管总局联合商务部召开规范社区团购秩序行政指导会 [SAMR and MOFCOM Jointly Held an Administrative Guidance Meeting to Regulate the Order of Community Group Buying]' (22 December 2020) <https://www.gov.cn/xinwen/202012/22/content_5572312.htm> (accessed 27 September 2022).

SAMR,'国家市场监督管理总局行政处罚决定书（国市监处〔2021〕2号）[Administrative Prohibition Decision [2021] No 2]' (27 January 2021) <https://www.samr.gov.cn/jzxts/tzgg/xzcf/art/2023/art_783f995cdfe440eabcdf886a5cd8c97f.html> (accessed 10 April 2024).

SAMR, '市场监管总局依法对互联网领域十起违法实施经营者集中案作出行政处罚决定 [Administrative Prohibition Decisions on Ten Cases of Illegal Mergers in the Field of Digital Economy]' (13 March 2021) <https://www.samr.gov.cn/xw/zj/art/2023/art_1f22ec38ab104caca3b754b5b7b644a6.html> (accessed 2 February 2023).

SAMR, '国家市场监督管理总局行政指导书 [SAMR Administrative Guiding Decision [2021] No 1]' (6 April 2021) <https://www.samr.gov.cn/xw/zj/art/2023/art_4966dda92ab34c398615f5878c10c8f1.html> (accessed 14 April 2024).

SAMR, '国家市场监督管理总局行政处罚决定书（国市监处〔2021〕28号） [SAMR Administrative Prohibition Decision [2021] No 28]' (10 April 2021) <https://www.samr.gov.cn/xw/zj/art/2023/art_4966dda92ab34c398615f5878c10c8f1.html> (accessed 7 November 2022).

SAMR, '市场监管总局发布阿里巴巴集团控股有限公司在中国境内网络零售平台服务市场垄断案行政处罚决定书和行政指导书 [The SAMR Publishes the Decision of an Administrative Penalty and Administrative Guidance for the Case of Alibaba Holdings' Monopolistic Behaviours in the Market of Online Retail Platforms in China' (10 April 2021) <https://www.samr.gov.cn/zt/qhfldzf/art/2021/art_74b2593fd32a432baf3dcbd163935167.html> (accessed 7 June 2024).

SAMR, '互联网平台企业向社会公开《依法合规经营承诺》（第一批）[Internet Platform Enterprises Publicize "Commitment to Operate in Compliance with Law" to Society (First Batch)]' (14 April 2021) <https://mp.weixin.qq.com/s/SlDlWWOcsEt89isAEJKi3Q> (accessed 7 November 2022).

SAMR, '国家市场监督管理总局行政处罚决定书（国市监处〔2021〕38号） [SAMR Administrative Prohibition Decision [2021] No 38]' (27 May 2021) <https://www.samr.gov.cn/xw/zj/art/2023/art_054aa1dab46d4cb8a760e2f46e290d5b.html> (accessed 10 April 2024).

SAMR, '市场监管总局等五部门关于印发《公平竞争审查制度实施细则》的通知 [Detailed Rules for the Implementation of the Fair Competition Review System]' (29 June 2021) <https://www.gov.cn/zhengce/zhengceku/202107/08/content_5623453.htm> (accessed 3 October 2023).

SAMR, '市场监管总局等五部门关于印发《公平竞争审查制度实施细则》的通知 [Detailed Rules for the Implementation of the Fair Competition Review System]' (English translation) (29 June 2021) <https://www.pkulaw.com/en_law/00db3f8e67b71091bdfb.html> (accessed 14 June 2024).

SAMR, '市场监管总局依法对互联网领域二十二起违法实施经营者集中案作出行政处罚决定 [Administrative Prohibition Decisions on Twenty-Two Cases of Illegal Mergers in the Field of Digital Economy]' (7 July 2021) <https://www.samr.gov.cn/xw/mtjj/art/2023/art_7ff4790437fa4d1789b734d95d98168a.html> (accessed 2 February 2023).

SAMR, '市场监管总局关于禁止虎牙公司与斗鱼国际控股有限公司合并案反垄断审查决定的公告 [Announcement of the SAMR on the Antimonopoly Review Decision to Ban the Merger of Huya and DouYu]' (10 July 2021) <https://www.samr.gov.cn/fldes/tzgg/ftj/art/2023/art_47b307e668484e83a598add8793dcdca.html> (accessed 16 April 2024).

SAMR, '市场监管总局关于禁止虎牙公司与斗鱼国际控股有限公司合并案反垄断审查决定的公告 [Announcement of the SAMR on the Antimonopoly Review Decision to Ban the Merger of Huya and DouYu: Index]' (10 July 2021) <https://www.samr.gov.cn/fldes/tzgg/ftj/index.html> (accessed 16 April 2024).

SAMR, '市场监管总局关于禁止虎牙公司与斗鱼国际控股有限公司合并案反垄断审查决定的公告 [Antitrust Review Decision on Prohibiting the Merger of Huya and DouYu]' (10 July 2021) <https://www.samr.gov.cn/fldys/tzgg/ftj/art/2023/art_a04ceb782566465082e165f0a86f5580.html> (accessed 15 April 2021).

SAMR, '关于落实网络餐饮平台责任　切实维护外卖送餐员权益的指导意见 [Guidance Opinion on Implementing Internet Catering Platforms' Responsibilities and Strengthening Protection for Delivery Workers' Rights]' (promulgated by the SAMR,19 July 2021) <https://www.tjxq.gov.cn/zwgk/zfxxgk/zfgbm/scjgj/fdzdgk/zdmsxx/spypjg/202202/W020220210410592915416.pdf> (accessed 14 April 2024).

SAMR, '国家市场监督管理总局行政处罚决定书（国市监处〔2021〕67号）[SAMR Administrative Prohibition Decision [2021] No 67]' (24 July 2021) <https://www.samr.gov.cn/zt/qhfldzf/art/2021/art_61810ad454524ec2b9cb38c78f3d793c.html> (accessed 7 November 2022).

SAMR, '国家市场监督管理总局行政指导书（国市监行指〔2021〕2号） [Administrative Guidance [2021] No 2]' (8 October 2021) <https://www.samr.gov.cn/jzxts/tzgg/xzcf/art/2023/art_e10040bb366242629925685accabfab2.html> (accessed 10 April 2024).

SAMR, '国家市场监督管理总局行政处罚决定书（国市监处罚〔2021〕74号） [SAMR Administrative Prohibition Decision [2021] No 74]' (8 October 2021) <https://www.samr.gov.cn/xw/zj/art/2023/art_31910760066b4f69aa119a20dee250ad.html> (accessed 10 April 2024).

SAMR, '互联网平台分类分级指南（征求意见稿) [Guidelines for Classification and Rating of Internet Platforms (Draft for Public Consultation)]' (29 October 2021) <https://news.cctv.com/2021/10/29/ARTI9KXeKHs4KPZU58VL7GVs211029.shtml> (accessed 7 June 2024).

SAMR, '《互联网平台分类分级指南（征求意见稿）》《互联网平台落实主体责任指南（征求意见稿）》 [Guidelines on Categorization and Classification of Internet Platforms (Draft for Public Opinions), Guidelines on Enforcement of Internet Platform Responsibility (Draft for Public Opinions)]' (29 October 2021) <https://www.samr.gov.cn/hd/zjdc/art/2023/art_c0086d02fcc544ea9506c997b3ac93c1.html> (accessed 14 April 2024).

SAMR, '互联网平台落实主体责任指南（征求意见稿）[Guidelines on Implementing the Main Responsibility of Internet Platforms (Draft for Consultations)]' (promulgated by the SAMR, 29 October 2021) <https://www.samr.gov.cn/hd/zjdc/art/2023/art_c0086d02fcc544ea9506c997b3ac93c1.html> (accessed 10 December 2022).

SAMR, '市场监管总局依法对43起未依法申报违法实施经营者集中案作出行政处罚决定 [Administrative Prohibition Decisions on Forty-Three Cases of Illegal Mergers in the Field of Digital Economy]' (20 November 2021) <https://www.samr.gov.cn/xw/zj/art/2023/art_58890b3964a947438e050bec99133f7e.html> (accessed 2 February 2023).

SAMR, 'The General Administration of Market Supervision Failed to Declare 43 Cases in Accordance with the Law' (20 November 2021) <https://www.samr.gov.cn/xw/zj/art/2023/art_58890b3964a947438e050bec99133f7e.html> (accessed 30 September 2024).

SAMR, '市场监管总局发布腾讯控股有限公司、深圳市红杉煜辰股权投资合伙企业（有限合伙）收购广西叫酒网络科技有限公司股权未依法申报违法实施经营者集中案行政处罚决定书（国市监处罚〔2021〕132号） [SAMR Administrative Prohibition Decision [2021] No 132]' (5 January 2022) <https://www.samr.gov.cn/zt/qhfldzf/art/2022/art_522ef4da559848b78868e5fb618a4050.html> (accessed 13 April 2024).

SAMR, '禁止滥用市场支配地位行为暂行规定 [Interim Provisions on Prohibiting Abuse of Dominant Market Position]' (promulgated by the SAMR, 24 March 2022, effective 1 May 2022) <https://sjfg.samr.gov.cn/law/pageInfo/main.main?order=10&iframe=pageInfo/law_search_new.law_details?lawId=1654ccdf139f45f22da645587e314e6a> (accessed 25 November 2023).

SAMR, '腾讯控股有限公司收购DeepBlue Alpha Inc.股权案行政处罚决定书（国市监处〔2022〕10号） [SAMR Administrative Prohibition Decision [2022] No 10]' (31 March 2022) <https://finance.sina.cn/chanjing/gsxw/2022-07-10/detail-imizmscv0867332.d.html> (accessed 13 April 2024).

SAMR, '腾讯控股有限公司收购奇秦科技（北京）股份有限公司股权案行政处罚决定书（国市监处罚〔2022〕13号）[SAMR Administrative Prohibition Decision [2022] No 13]' (31 March 2022) <https://finance.sina.com.cn/chanjing/gsnews/2022-07-10/doc-imizirav2716388.shtml> (accessed 13 April 2024).

SAMR, '中国反垄断执法年度报告(2021) [Annex of Annual Report of China on Anti-Monopoly Law Enforcement (2021)]' (8 June 2022) <https://www.samr.gov.cn/xw/zj/art/2023/art_bfac0acc333e4bd0be85adf099272047.html> (accessed 27 September 2022).

SAMR, '市场监管总局关于公开征求《国务院关于经营者集中申报标准的规定（修订草案征求意见稿）》意见的公告 [Provisions on Threshold for Merger Notification (Draft of Amended Version for Public Opinions)]' (27 June 2022) <https://www.samr.gov.cn/fldes/tzgg/zqyjgg/art/2023/art_1c119d88523f42ca8bb8bb436f364ecb.html> (accessed 14 April 2024).

SAMR, '禁止滥用市场支配地位行为规定（征求意见稿） [Provisions on Prohibition of Abuse of Market Dominance (Draft for Consultations)]' (promulgated by the SAMR, 27 June 2022) <https://www.samr.gov.cn/hd/zjdc/art/2023/art_6dcdc0b84d0040daad1613ec2a12cc90.html> (accessed 10 December 2022).

SAMR, '市场监管总局发布未依法申报违法实施经营者集中案行政处罚决定书 [The SAMR Issued Decisions on Administrative Prohibition in the Case of Unlawful Implementation of Operator Concentration without Declaring in Accordance with the Law]' (10 July 2022) <https://www.samr.gov.cn/jzxts/tzgg/xzcf/art/2023/art_e938cefc24774f2483b7394abc47bfba.html> (accessed 30 September 2024).

SAMR, '国家市场监督管理总局行政处罚决定书（国市监处罚〔2022〕87号）[SAMR Administrative Prohibition Decision [2022] No 87]' (26 December 2022) <https://www.samr.gov.cn/xw/zj/art/2023/art_0f87ad794f7949e4803dd6c9ce4d2d2a.html> (accessed 16 January 2023).

SAMR, '禁止滥用市场支配地位行为规定 [Provisions on Prohibiting Abuse of Dominant Market Position]' (promulgated by the SAMR, 10 March 2023, effective 15 April 2023) <https://www.gov.cn/gongbao/content/2023/content_5754539.htm> (accessed 16 April 2023).

SAMR, '禁止滥用市场支配地位行为规定 [Provisions on Prohibiting Abuse of Dominant Market Position]' (English translation) (promulgated by the SAMR, 10 March 2023, effective 15 April 2023) <https://pkulaw.com/en_law/4a966fd519ae33cabdfb.html> (accessed 7 July 2024).

SAMR, '经营者集中审查规定 [Provisions on the Review of Concentration of Undertakings]' (promulgated by the SAMR, 10 March 2023, effective 15 April 2023) <https://www.samr.gov.cn/zw/zfxxgk/fdzdgknr/fgs/art/2023/art_4c34a8aa4e62449ab38233bdbba172a7.html> (accessed 16 April 2023).

SAMR, '经营者集中审查规定 [Provisions on the Review of Concentration of Undertakings]' (English translation) (promulgated by the SAMR, 10 March 2023, effective 15 April 2023) <https://pkulaw.com/en_law/4a966fd519ae33cabdfb.html> (accessed 16 April 2023).
SAMR, '市场监管总局关于《公平竞争审查条例（征求意见稿）》公开征求意见的公告 [Announcement of the State Administration for Market Regulation on Requesting Public Comments on the Regulation on Fair Competition Review (Draft for Public Opinions)]' (12 May 2023) <https://www.samr.gov.cn/hd/zjdc/art/2023/art_647feda81bb249a5981a18c7e5efd4d2.html> (accessed 3 October 2023).
SAMR, '市场监管总局关于《公平竞争审查条例（征求意见稿）》公开征求意见的公告 [Announcement of the State Administration for Market Regulation on Requesting Public Comments on the Regulation on Fair Competition Review (Draft for Public Opinions)]' (English translation) (12 May 2023) <https://www.pkulaw.com/en_law/d713af4239291d827ec31f070b8b2980bdfb.html> (accessed 14 June 2024).
SAMR, '年5月15日—5月21日无条件批准经营者集中案件列表 [List of Unconditional Approval of Mergers from 15–21 May 2023]' (30 May 2023) <https://www.samr.gov.cn/fldes/ajgs/wtjjz/art/2023/art_933bfb33968d4799a91c65ac15c9e507.html> (accessed 13 April 2024).
SAMR, '中国反垄断执法年度报告(2022) [Annual Report of China on Anti-Monopoly Law Enforcement (2022)]' (9 June 2023) <https://www.samr.gov.cn/xw/zj/art/2023/art_38056964cf5449daa346237200e24da0.html> (accessed 27 January 2024).
SAMR, '经营者反垄断合规指南（征求意见稿）[Guidelines on Anti-Monopoly Compliance for Business Operators (Draft for Consultations)]', Reference Case No 23 (promulgated by the SAMR, 21 March 2024) <https://www.samr.gov.cn/jzxts/tzgg/zqyj/art/2024/art_3ed68bc139684c7c92487e2e5f12c31e.html> (accessed 1 May 2024).
SAMR, '经营者反垄断合规指南 [Guidelines on Anti-Monopoly Compliance for Business Operators]' (promulgated by the SAMR, 24 April 2024) <https://www.samr.gov.cn/zw/zfxxgk/fdzdgknr/jzzcxds/art/2024/art_2d4b1705febf41c38856dda554e84857.html> (accessed 1 May 2024).
SAMR, Division for Coordination of Competition Policy, '2022年制止滥用行政权力排除、限制竞争执法专项行动案件（第一批）[Typical Cases of Violating the Negative List for Market Access (the First Batch)]' (9 June 2022) <https://www.samr.gov.cn/jzxts/tzgg/qlpc/art/2023/art_abcdf27b28e44dab8d1d3ddf24edb6d9.html> (accessed 9 April 2024).

VI.2 Antimonopoly Commission of the State Council

Antimonopoly Commission of the State Council, '国务院反垄断委员会关于印发《关于相关市场界定的指南》的通知 [Antimonopoly Commission of the State Council's Guidelines on Definition of Relevant Markets]' (promulgated by the Antimonopoly Committee of the State Council, 6 July 2009).
Antimonopoly Commission of the State Council, '国务院反垄断委员会关于平台经济领域的反垄断指南（征求意见稿）[Anti-Monopoly Guidelines on the Platform Economy (Draft for Comments)]' (10 November 2020).
Anti-Monopoly Commission of the State Council, '国务院反垄断委员会关于平台经济领域的反垄断指南（国反垄发〔2021〕1号） [Anti-Monopoly Guidelines on the Platform Economy]' (7 February 2021) <https://www.gov.cn/xinwen/2021-02/07/content_5585758.htm> (accessed 7 November 2022).
Anti-Monopoly Commission of the State Council, '国务院反垄断委员会关于平台经济领域的反垄断指南（国反垄发〔2021〕1号） [Anti-Monopoly Guidelines on the Platform Economy]' (English translation) (7 February 2021) <https://pkulaw.com/en_law/dec522cd66c7b43ebdfb.html> (accessed 9 June 2024).

VI.3 Other Relevant Sources

Central People's Government of the People's Republic of China, 'Guiding Opinions on Promoting the Regulated and Healthy Development of the Platform Economy' (2019) <http://www.gov.cn/gongbao/content/2019/content_5421543.htm> (accessed 7 June 2024).

Central Committee of the Communist Party of China, '中共中央关于坚持和完善中国特色社会主义制度 推进国家治理体系和治理能力现代化若干重大问题的决定 [Decision of the Central Committee of the Communist Party of China on Major Issues Concerning Adherence to and Improvement of the Socialist System with Chinese Characteristics and Advancement of the Modernization of the National Governance System and Capability]' (adopted at the Fourth Plenary Session of the 19th Central Committee of the Communist Party of China, 31 October 2019) <https://www.gov.cn/xinwen/202001/01/content_5465721.htm?eqid=915fb773000307bc0000000264644e94> (accessed 1 June 2024).

Central People's Government of the People's Republic of China, '中共中央、国务院关于构建更加完善的要素市场化配置体制机制的意见 [Opinions of the Central Committee of the Communist Party of China and the State Council on the Construction of a More Improved System Mechanism for the Market-Based Allocation of Factors]' (30 March 2020) <https://www.gov.cn/zhengce/202004/09/content_5500622.htm> (accessed 1 June 2024).

Central Committee of the Communist Party of China, 'Implementation Outline for the Construction of a Rule of Law Society (2020–2025)' (7 December 2020) < https://www.gov.cn/zhengce/2020-12/07/content_5567791.htm > (accessed 27 September 2023).

Central People's Government of the People's Republic of China, '互联网信息服务算法推荐管理规定 [Provisions on the Administration of Algorithmic Recommendation of Internet Information Service]' (1 March 2022) <https://www.gov.cn/zhengce/202211/26/content_5728941.html> (accessed 27 September 2023).

Central People's Government of the People's Republic of China, '李强主持召开国务院常务会议 研究全面推进乡村振兴有关举措等 [Li Qiang Presided over the State Council Executive Meeting to Discuss Measures Related to Comprehensively Promoting Rural Revitalization, Etc.]' (22 January 2024) <https://www.gov.cn/yaowen/liebiao/202401/content_6927581.htm> (accessed 11 April 2024).

China Government Procurement Network, '山东大学知网研学平台单一来源成交公告 [Shandong University CNKI Single-Source Transaction Announcement]' (16 November 2022) <http://www.ccgp.gov.cn/cggg/zygg/cjgg/202211/t20221116_19022783.htm> (accessed 1 May 2024).

China Government Procurement Network, '湖南省市场监督管理局反垄断局滴滴网约平台数据分析技术服务采购项目竞争性磋商 [Competitive Consultations for the Procurement Project of Data Analysis Technology Services for Didi Ride-Hailing Platform by the Anti-Monopoly Bureau of Hunan AMR]' (7 February 2024) <https://www.ccgp.gov.cn/cggg/dfgg/jzxcs/202402/t20240207_21526794.htm> (accessed 14 April 2024).

CNNIC (China Internet Network Information Center), '第41次《中国互联网络发展状况统计报告》 [41st Statistical Report on Internet Development in China]' (31 January 2018) <http://www.cac.gov.cn/201801/31/c_1122347026.htm> (accessed 27 September 2022).

CNNIC, '第42次《中国互联网络发展状况统计报告》 [42nd Statistical Report on Internet Development in China]' (20 August 2018) <https://www.cac.gov.cn/201808/20/c_1123296882.htm> (accessed 27 September 2022).

Ctrip, '供应链及品牌力筑核心壁垒, 国际化布局有望贡献增量 [Supply Chain and Brand Power to Build Core Barriers, International Layout Is Expected to Contribute to the Increase]' (Research Report, 1 October 2023) <https://www.vzkoo.com/read/20231001fc3e5cb1f4b75791873d7f52.html> (accessed 4 October 2023).

Economic and Commercial Office of the Consulate General of the People's Republic of China in Los Angeles, '中华人民共和国外国投资法（草案征求意见稿）[Foreign Investment Law of the People's Republic of China (Draft Proposal for Public Opinion)]' (7 July 2015) <http://losangeles.MOFCOM.gov.cn/article/ddfg/tzzhch/201507/20150701035860.shtml> (accessed 13 April 2024).

General Office of the State Council, '国务院办公厅关于进一步优化营商环境降低市场主体制度性交易成本的意见 [Opinions of the General Office of the State Council on Further Optimizing the Business Environment and Reducing the Institutional Transaction Costs of Market Entities]' (7 September 2022) <https://www.gov.cn/zhengce/content/202209/15/content_5709962.htm> (accessed 9 April 2024).

Hunold, M, R Kesler, and U Laitenberger, 'Hotel Rankings of Online Travel Agents, Channel Pricing and Consumer Protection', ZEW—Centre for European Economic Research, Discussion Paper No 18-059 (2018) <https://papers.ssrn.com/sol3/papers.cfm?abstract_id = 3447828> (accessed 9 June 2024).

Xinhua News Agency, '中共中央办公厅 国务院办公厅关于加快公共数据资源开发利用的意见 [General Office of the CPC Central Committee, General Office of the State Council: Opinions on Accelerating the Development and Utilization of Public Data Resources]' (9 October 2024) <https://www.gov.cn/zhengce/202410/content_6978910.htm> (accessed 9 November 2024).

Haiyan AMR (Administration for Market Regulation), '嘉兴市海盐县市场监督管理局行政处罚决定书（盐市监处字〔2018〕160号）[Haiyan AMR Administrative Prohibition Decision [2018] No 160]' (6 July 2018) <https://lawhtbprolwkinfohtbprolcomhtbprolcn-s.libvpn.zuel.edu.cn/administrative-punishment/detail/MkUwMTI5MDQ0NzM%3D?searchId = 106929513a574a67b39aa90c636629f4&index = 1&q=%E7%9B%90%E5%B8%82%E7%9B%91%E5%A4%84%E5%AD%97%E3%80%942018%E3%80%95160%E5%8F%B7&module=&childModule = all> (accessed 30 May 2024).

Jiangxi Market Supervision Administration, '江西省数字经济领域反垄断合规指引 [Anti-Monopoly Compliance Guidelines in the Field of the Digital Economy in Jiangxi Province]' (promulgated by Jiangxi Market Supervision Administration, 23 November 2023) <http://drc.jiangxi.gov.cn/art/2022/11/23/art_68541_4239578.html> (accessed 13 April 2024).

Jinhua AMR, '金华市市场监督管理局行政处罚决定书（金市监罚字〔2017〕22号） [Jinhua AMR Administrative Prohibition Decision [2017] No 22]' (14 November 2017) <https://lawhtbprolwkinfohtbprolcomhtbprolcn-s.libvpn.zuel.edu.cn/administrative-punishment/detail/MkUwMDM5NDM3MTA%3D?searchId = 0d128d4e58934f51a74937ecac613e34&index = 1&q=%E9%87%91%E5%B8%82%E7%9B%91%E7%BD%9A%E5%AD%97%E3%80%942017%E3%80%9522%E5%8F%B7&module=&childModule = all> (accessed 30 May 2024).

Lanzhou Municipal People's Government, '兰州市人民政府办公厅关于印发兰州市网络预约出租汽车经营服务管理实施细则(试行)的通知 [Announcement of the General Office of the Lanzhou Municipal People's Government on Issuing the Detailed Provisions for the Management of E-Hailing Taxi Operations and Services in Lanzhou (Trial)]' (24 March 2017) <https://www.lawlawing.com/community/380412> (accessed 8 April 2024) (Lanzhou Provisions).

Lishui AMR, '丽水市市场监督管理局行政处罚决定书（丽市监案〔2016〕25号） [Lishui AMR Administrative Prohibition Decision [2016] No 25]' (19 January 2017) <https://lawhtbprolwkinfohtbprolcomhtbprolcn-s.libvpn.zuel.edu.cn/administrative-punishment/detail/MkUwMDE2MTg2NjY%3D?searchId = c84982bf1a71423492a27873eef0ae29&index = 1&q=%E4%B8%BD%E5%B8%82%E7%9B%91%E6%A1%88%E3%80%942016%E3%80%9525%E5%8F%B7&module=&childModule = all> (accessed 30 May 2024).

Ministry of Education of the Central Republic of China, '关于在学位授予工作中加强学术道德和学术规范建设的意见 [Opinions on Strengthening the Construction of Academic Ethics and Academic Norms in the Work of Conferring Degrees]', Degree No 9 [2010] <http://www.moe.gov.cn/jyb_xxgk/xxgk/neirong/fenlei/sxml_gdjy/gdjy_xyzbtxjs/txjs_xgzc/201005/t20100512_87505.html> (accessed 1 May 2024).

Ministry of Transport, '关于鼓励和规范互联网租赁自行车发展的指导意见 [Guiding Opinions on Encouraging and Regulating the Development of Internet Bicycle Rental]' (1 August 2017) <http://www.gov.cn/xinwen/201708/03/content_5215640.htm> (accessed 27 September 2022).

Ministry of Transport, '交通运输部运输服务司司长徐亚华解读《关于鼓励和规范互联网租赁自行车发展的指导意见》 [Interpretation of the Guiding Opinions on Encouraging and Regulating the Development of Internet Bicycle Rental by Yahua Xu, the Director of the Transportation Service Department of the Ministry of Transportation]' (4 August 2017) <www.gov.cn/xinwen/201708/04/content_5215971.htm> (accessed 27 September 2022).

MOFCOM (Ministry of Commerce, People's Republic of China), '商务部公告2012年第9号 关于附加限制性条件批准西部数据收购日立存储经营者集中反垄断审查决定的公告 [Announcement No 9 of 2012 of MOFCOM on the Decision to Approve the Anti-Monopoly Review of Western Data's Acquisition of Hitachi Storage Operators with Additional Restrictive Conditions]' (2 March 2012) < http://m.mofcom.gov.cn/article/zcfb/zcblgg/201203/20120307993792.shtml> (accessed 15 April 2024).

MOFCOM, '商务部公告2015年第64号 关于附加限制性条件批准恩智浦收购飞思卡尔全部股权案经营者集中反垄断审查决定的公告 [Announcement No 64 of 2015 of MOFCOM on the Decision on the Anti-Monopoly Review of the Concentration of Business Operators in the Approval of NXP's Acquisition of All Equity of Freescale with Additional Restrictive Conditions]' (27 November 2015) <http://www.mofcom.gov.cn/article/zcfb/zcdwmy/201511/20151101196189.shtml> (accessed 15 April 2024).

Monti, G, 'The Digital Markets Act—Institutional Design and Suggestions for Improvement', TILEC Discussion Paper DP 2021-004 (2021) <https://papers.ssrn.com/sol3/papers.cfm?abstract_id=3797730>, 1415 (accessed 27 September 2024).

Standing Committee of the National People's Congress, '中华人民共和国电子商务法 [E-Commerce Law of the PRC]' (promulgated by the Standing Committee of the National People's Congress, 31 August 2018, effective 1 January 2019) <http://mg.mofcom.gov.cn/article/policy/201912/20191202923971.shtml> (accessed 7 November 2022).

Standing Committee of the National People's Congress, '中华人民共和国电子商务法 [E-Commerce Law of the PRC]' (English translation) (29 October 2019) <http://mg.mofcom.gov.cn/article/policy/201912/20191202923971.shtml> (accessed 11 October 2024).

Standing Committee of the National People's Congress, '中华人民共和国反垄断法（2022修正）[Anti-Monopoly Law of the PRC (2022 Amendment)]' (promulgated by the Standing Committee of the National People's Congress, 24 June 2022, effective 1 August 2022) <https://www.pkulaw.com/en_law/d3236788421feacfbdfb.html> (accessed 7 November 2022).

National People's Congress of the People's Republic of China, 'Personal Information Protection Law of the People's Republic of China' (updated 29 December 2021) <http://en.npc.gov.cn.cdurl.cn/2021-12/29/c_694559_3.htm> (accessed 6 June 2024).

NDRC (General Office of the National Development and Reform Commission), '国家发展改革委关于建立违背市场准入负面清单案例归集和通报制度的通知 [Notice Circular on the Establishment of a System for Collecting and Notifying Cases of Violation of the Negative List for Market Access]' (19 November 2021) <https://www.gov.cn/zhengce/zhengceku/202112/16/content_5661450.htm> (accessed 9 April 2024).

NDRC, '国家发展改革委办公厅关于违背市场准入负面清单典型案例（第四批）的通报 [Circular of the General Office of the National Development and Reform Commission on Typical Cases of Violation of the Negative List for Market Access (Fourth Batch)]' (28 October 2022) <https://www.gov.cn/zhengce/zhengceku/202211/10/content_5725955.htm> (accessed 9 April 2024).

Office of the Central Cyberspace Affairs Commission, 'Guiding Opinions on Strengthening Overall Governance of Internet Information Service Algorithms?' (17 September 2023) <http://www.cac.gov.cn/202109/29/c_1634507915623047.html> (accessed 27 September 2023).

Office of the Central Cyberspace Affairs Commission, 'Responsible Comrades of the Antimonopoly Bureau of the SAMR Answered Questions on the Guidelines' (8 February 2021) <http://www.cac.gov.cn/202102/08/c_1614358492110420.htm> (accessed 30 July 2023).

Office of the Central Cyberspace Affairs Commission, 'Notice on the Qing-Lang Operation—2022 Algorithmic Comprehensive Management' (8 April 2022) <http://www.cac.gov.cn/202204/08/c_1651028524542025.html> (accessed 27 September 2023).

Office of the Central Cyberspace Affairs Commission, '数字中国发展报告（2021年）[Digital China Development Report (2021)]' (2 August 2022) <https://www.cac.gov.cn/202208/02/c_1661066515613920.htm> (accessed 5 Apr 2024).

Office of Central Cyberspace Affairs Commission, 'Administrative Punishment to CNKI' (6 September 2023) <http://www.cac.gov.cn/202309/06/c_1695654024248502.htm> (accessed 7 June 2024).

Quanzhou City Transportation Commission, '关于印发泉州市网络预约出租汽车经营服务管理实施细则的通知 [Announcement of Issuing the Detailed Provisions on Management of Operations and Services of E-Hailing Taxis of Quanzhou City]' (10 October 2016) <http://jjzd.quanzhou.gov.cn/jtfg/201610/t20161031_408559.htm> (accessed 8 April 2024) (Quanzhou Provisions).

Quanzhou City Transportation Commission, '关于印发调整完善泉州市网络预约出租汽车经营服务管理实施细则的通知 [Announcement of Issuing the Amended Detailed Provisions on Management of Operations and Services of E-Hailing Taxis of Quanzhou City]' (21 September 2017) <http://www.quanzhou.gov.cn/zfb/xxgk/zfxxgkzl/fgwj/sfggz/201709/t20170921_535530.htm> (accessed 9 April 2024) (Amendment of Quanzhou Provisions).

Quanzhou Municipal People's Government, '泉州发放首张网约车平台经营许可证 [Quanzhou Issued the First Online Car-Hailing Platform Business License]' (15 February 2017) <http://www.quanzhou.gov.cn/zfb/xxgk/zfxxgkzl/qzdt/qzyw/201702/t20170215_422995.htm> (accessed 12 October 2022).

Quanzhou City Transportation Commission, '关于印发泉州市网络预约出租汽车经营服务管理实施细则的通知 [Announcement of Issuing the Detailed Provisions on Management of Operations and Services of E-Hailing Taxis of Quanzhou City]' (10 October 2016) <http://jjzd.quanzhou.gov.cn/jtfg/201610/t20161031_408559.htm> (accessed 8 April 2024) (Quanzhou Provisions).

SAIC (Science Applications International Corporation), '国家工商行政管理总局行政处罚决定书（工商竞争案字[2016]1号）[SAIC Administrative Prohibition Decision [2016] No 1]' (9 November 2016) <https://www.samr.gov.cn/zt/qhfldzf/art/2016/art_8ca2ed4b38d842d7b4c363eaac06c103.html> (accessed 7 November 2022).

SAIC, '工商总局依法对利乐滥用市场支配地位案作出行政处罚 [SAIC Imposed Administrative Punishment on Tetra Pak for Abusing Its Dominant Market Position in Accordance with Law]' (16 November 2016) <https://www.gov.cn/xinwen/201611/16/content_5133237.htm> (accessed 3 October 2023).

Shanghai AMR, '上海市市场监督管理局行政处罚决定书（沪市监反垄处〔2020〕06201901001号）[Shanghai AMR Administrative Prohibition Decision [2020] No 06201901001]' (25 December 2020) <https://www.samr.gov.cn/xw/df/art/2023/art_fb84525d385a489db74615d1939883d0.html> (accessed 7 June 2024).

State Council, '关于开展打击《黑车》等非法营运专项整治行动的实施方案 [Enforcement Plan to Punish Illegal Operations Including Unlicensed Taxis]' (23 May 2006) <https://www.gov.cn/govweb/gzdt/2006-05/26/content_292364.htm> (accessed 9 April 2024).

State Council, '国务院关于机构设置的通知 [State Council on the Establishment of Institutions]' (21 March 2008) <https://www.gov.cn/zhengce/content/200804/26/content_7621.htm> (accessed 9 April 2024).

State Council, '国务院关于在市场体系建设中建立公平竞争审查制度的意见 [Opinions of the State Council on Establishing a Fair Competition Examination System in the Building of the Market System]' (1 June 2016) <https://www.gov.cn/zhengce/content/2016-06/14/content_5082066.htm> (accessed 3 October 2023) (accessed 3 October 2023).

State Council, '国务院关于在市场体系建设中建立公平竞争审查制度的意见 [Opinions of the State Council on Establishing a Fair Competition Examination System in the Building of the Market System]' (English translation) (1 June 2016) <https://www.pkulaw.com/en_law/a87136f6ba497fd7bdfb.html> (accessed 14 June 2024).

State Council, '14th Five-Year Plan for the Development of the Digital Economy' (12 December 2021) <https://www.gov.cn/gongbao/content/2022/content_5671108.htm?eqid=c4653e630000247800000000464620cb5> (accessed 27 September 2023).

State Council Standing Committee, '国务院关于开展和保护社会主义竞争的暂行规定 [State Council's Provisional Stipulations on Developing and Preserving Socialism Competition]' (17 October 1980) <https://www.beijing.gov.cn/zhengce/zfwj/zfwj/szfwj/201905/t20190523_70377.html> (accessed 9 April 2024).

Supreme People's Court of China, '最高人民法院关于审理垄断民事纠纷案件适用法律若干问题的规定（公开征求意见稿）[Provisions of the Supreme People's Court on Several

Issues Concerning the Application of Law in Monopoly Civil Disputes (Draft for Public Comments)]' (promulgated by the Supreme People's Court of China, 18 November 2022) <https://www.court.gov.cn/zixun/xiangqing/380101.html> (accessed 2 December 2022).

Tongjiang AMR, '巴中市通江县市场监督管理局行政处罚决定书（通市监管罚字〔2019〕3037号）[Tonghiang AMR Administrative Prohibition Decision [2019] No 3037]' (20 March 2019) <https://finance.sina.com.cn/chanjing/gsnews/2019-04-15/doc-ihvhiewr6055953.shtml> (accessed 30 May 2024).

Wuxi Bureau of Industry and Commerce, '无锡市工商行政管理局行政处罚决定书（锡工商案〔2018〕00097号）[Wuxi Bureau of Industry and Commerce Administrative Prohibition Decision [2018] No 00097]' (1 April 2018) <https://lawhtbprolwkinfohtbprolcomhtbprolcn-s.libvpn.zuel.edu.cn/administrative-punishment/detail/MkUwMDU3MzM0NDI%3D?searchId = 077706718aaa4ca48a2e4d77e57d4c17&index = 1&q=%E9%94%A1%E5%B7%A5%E5%95%86%E6%A1%88%E3%80%942018%E3%80%9500097%E5%8F%B7&module=&childModule = all> (accessed 30 May 2024).

VI.4 Australian Competition and Consumer Commission

ACCC (Australian Competition and Consumer Commission), 'Digital Platforms Inquiry—Final Report' (June 2019) <https://www.accc.gov.au/system/files/Digital%20platforms%20inquiry%20%20final%20report.pdf> (accessed 7 June 2024).

ACCC, 'ACCC Rejects Google Behavioural Undertakings for Fitbit Acquisition' (Press release, 22 December 2020) <https://www.accc.gov.au/mediarelease/acccrejectsgooglebehaviouralundertakingsforfitbitacquisition> (accessed 28 February 2023).

ACCC, 'Feedback Sought on Potential New Rules for Large Digital Platforms' (28 February 2022) <https://www.accc.gov.au/mediarelease/feedback-sought-on-potential-new-rules-for-large-digital-platforms> (accessed 7 June 2024).

ACCC, 'Digital Platform Services Inquiry—Interim Report No. 4—General Online Retail Marketplaces' (March 2022) <https://www.accc.gov.au/system/files/DPB%20%20DPSI%20%20March%202022%20%20Full%20interim%20report%20%2031%20March%202022.pdf> (accessed 7 June 2024).

ACCC, 'Digital Platforms Services Inquiry—Interim Report 6: Report on Social Media Services' (March 2023) <https://www.accc.gov.au/system/files/Digital%20platforms%20services%20inquiry%20%20Interim%20report%206%20%20Report%20on%20social%20media%20services_0.pdf> (accessed 7 June 2024).

VII. Policy Reports

APPG AI (All-Party Parliamentary Group) Artificial Intelligence, 'Ethics and Legal in AI: Data Capitalism' (26 June 2017).

Big Innovation Centre, 'What Is AI?' (Report based on the 1st meeting of the All-Party Parliamentary Group on Artificial Intelligence [APPG AI], 2017).

BRICS (Brazil, Russia, India, China, and South Africa), 'Digital Era Competition: A BRICS View' (BRICS Report, 2019).

Cicilline, DN, 'Investigation of Competition in Digital Markets—Majority Staff Report and Recommendations—Subcommittee on Antitrust, Commercial, and Administrative Law of the Committee on the Judiciary of the House of Representatives' (US Congress Cicilline Report, 2020) <https://www.govinfo.gov/content/pkg/CPRT117HPRT47832/pdf/CPRT117HPRT47832.pdf> (accessed 7 June 2024).

Digital Competition Expert Panel, 'Unlocking Digital Competition' (Report prepared by J Furman, D Coyle, A Fletcher, D McAuley, and P Marsden) (Furman Report, March 2019).

Franck, JU and M Peitz, 'Market Definition and Market Power in the Platform Economy' (CERRE Report, May 2019).

Lear, 'Ex-Post Assessment of Merger Control Decisions in Digital Markets' (Final Report prepared by E Argentesi et al) (Lear Report, 9 May 2019).

Letta, E, 'Much More Than a Market' (April 2024).

OFCOM (Office of Communications), 'Online Nation—2021 Report'.

Petit, N, 'Significant Impediment to Industry Innovation: A Novel Theory of Harm in EU Merger Control?', White Paper 2-17-2 (2017) <https://orbi.uliege.be/bitstream/2268/207345/1/SSRNid2911597.pdf> (accessed 7 June 2024).

Privacy International, 'Personal Data and Competition: Mapping Perspectives, Identifying Challenges and Enhancing Engagement for Competition Regulators and Civil Society' (Report, April 2022).

VIII. Other Resources

SAMR (State Administration for Market Regulation), '禁止垄断协议规定 [Provisions on Prohibiting Anticompetitive Agreements]' (promulgated by the SAMR, 10 March 2023, effective 15 April 2023) <https://www.pkulaw.com/chl/13f8f20ffb8edd3cbdfb.html?keyword=%E7%A6%81%E6%AD%A2%20%E5%8F%8D%E5%9E%84%E6%96%AD%E5%8D%8F%E8%AE%AE&way = listView> (accessed 30 May 2024).

36Kr, 'Retric: 《美团牵手大众点评：一场事先张扬的合并案》 [Retric: Meituan Holds Hands with Dazhong Dianping: Chronicle of a Merger Case Foretold, 36Kr]' (8 October 2015) <https://36kr.com/p/1720945295361> (accessed 7 June 2024).

China Economic Net, 'Main Contents of 2020 Central Economic Work Conference' (December 2020) <http://www.ce.cn/ztpd/xwzt/guonei/2020/ba2018_341986/index.shtml> (accessed 30 October 2022).

Le Maire, B and others, 'Strengthening the Digital Markets Act and Its Enforcement' < https://www.economie.gouv.fr/files/2021-05/1055%20-%20Strengthening%20the%20Digital%20Markets%20Act%20and%20Its%20Enforcement.pdf> (accessed 7 June 2024).

21st Century Business Herald, '滴滴出行或将收购Uber中国垄断问题引关注 [Didi May Acquire Uber China Which Raises Monopoly Concerns]' (1 August 2016) <https://news.sohu.com/20160801/n462031324.shtml> (accessed 2 February 2023).

Academic Degrees Committee of the State Council, '关于在学位授予工作中加强学术道德和学术规范建设的意见 [Opinions on Strengthening the Construction of Academic Ethics and Academic Norms in the Work of Conferring Degrees]', Degree [2010] No 9 (9 February 2010) <http://www.moe.gov.cn/jyb_xxgk/xxgk/neirong/fenlei/sxml_gdjy/gdjy_xyzbtxjs/txjs_xgzc/201005/t20100512_87505.html> (accessed 1 May 2024).

Acemoglu, D et al, 'Too Much Data: Prices and Inefficiencies in Data Markets', National Bureau of Economic Research Working Paper 26296 (2019) <https://www.nber.org/system/files/working_papers/w26296/w26296.pdf> (accessed 18 August 2023).

Administration for Market Regulation of Hebei Province, '河北省市场监督管理局依法查处沧州市城市管理综合行政执法局滥用行政权力排除、限制竞争行为 [Administration for Market Regulation of Hebei Province Instigated and Dealt with Cangzhou Urban Management Bureau's Abuse of Administratie Power to Exclude and Restrict Competition in Accordance with the Law]' (25 October 2021) <https://www.samr.gov.cn/jzxts/tzgg/qlpc/art/2023/art_867f93a53a0f40a2a44994fa6768f56b.html> (accessed 9 April 2024).

Alibaba Group, <https://www.alibabagroup.com/enUS/aboutalibababusinesses> (accessed 7 June 2024).

Alphabet Investor Relations, 'Google Code of Conduct' <https://abc.xyz/investor/other/googlecodeofconduct> (accessed 6 June 2024).

Alphabet Investor Relations, 'G Is for Google' <https://abc.xyz/#> (accessed 3 October 2023).

Amazon, 'Amazon and iRobot Agree to Terminate Pending Acquisition' (Press release, 29 January 2024) <https://press.aboutamazon.com/2024/1/amazonandirobotagreetoterminatependingacquisition> (accessed 9 June 2024).

American Economic Liberties Project, 'Timeline on Internet Advertising Monopoly Lawsuit' <https://www.economicliberties.us/texasvgoogle> (accessed 7 June 2024).

Apple, 'Update on Apps Distributed in the European Union' <https://developer.apple.com/support/dmaandappsintheeu> (accessed 25 January 2024).

Associated Press, 'Chinese Regulator Halts Huya–DouYu Game-Streaming Merger' (Market Watch, 10 July 2021) <https://www.marketwatch.com/story/chineseregulatorhaltshuyadouyugamestreamingmerger01625932174?tesla=y> (accessed 2 February 2023).

Averitt, N, 'Protecting Consumer Choice: Competition and Consumer Protection Together' (30 September 2011).

Baker, LB, J Toonkel, and R Vlastelica, 'Alibaba Surges 38 Percent on Massive Demand in Market Debut' (Reuters, 19 September 2014) <https://www.reuters.com/article/usalibabaipo/alibabasurges38percentonmassivedemandinmarketdebutidUSKBN0HD2CO20140919> (accessed 7 June 2024).

Battelle, J, 'The Birth of Google' (WIRED, 1 August 2005) <https://www.wired.com/2005/08/battelle> (accessed 7 June 2024).

Bazhong AMR Official Site, '巴中市市场监督管理局集中约谈16家驻巴重点电商平台 [Bazhong AMR Interviewed Sixteen Important Ecommerce Platforms Operating in Bazhong at Once]' (7 November 2019) <https://samr.cnbz.gov.cn/xwdt/bjdt/14255821.html> (accessed 22 February 2024).

Beijing Municipal Commission of Transport, '北京市网络预约出租汽车经营服务管理实施细则 [Beijing Network Booking Taxi Service Management Implementation Rules]' (16 August 2022) <https://cz.jtw.beijing.gov.cn/ggl/20161221/1482296745211_1.html> (accessed 9 April 2024).

Beijing Review, 'Is Didi's Dominance Equal to a Monopoly?' (21 October 2016) <http://www.china.org.cn/opinion/201610/21/content_39539886.htm> (accessed 2 May 2024).

BEREC (Body of European Regulators for Electronic Communications), 'BEREC Recommends Clarifying the Scope of the Digital Markets Act in Relation to Number-Independent Interpersonal Communication Services (NIICS)', BoR (21) 97 (11 June 2021) <https://www.berec.europa.eu/en/documentcategories/berec/berecpressreleases/berecrecommendsclarifyingthescopeofthedigitalmarketsactinrelationtonumberindependentinterpersonalcommunicationservicesniics> (accessed 7 June 2024).

Bethell, O, 'Changes to the Android Choice Screen in Europe' (8 June 2021) <https://blog.google/aroundtheglobe/googleeurope/changesandroidchoicescreeneurope> (accessed 7 June 2024).

Bethell, O, 'Our Commitments for the Privacy Sandbox' (11 June 2022) <https://blog.google/aroundtheglobe/googleeurope/ourcommitmentsprivacysandbox> (accessed 7 June 2024).

Biglaiser, G and J Crémer, 'The Value of Incumbency When Platforms Face Heterogeneous Customers' (2019) <https://www.tsefr.eu/sites/default/files/TSE/documents/doc/wp/2016/wp_tse_630.pdf> (accessed 18 August 2023).

Bira (British Independent Retailers Association), 'Bira Leads £1 Billion Damages Claim against Amazon by UK Retailers in Landmark Collective Action' (6 June 2024) <https://www.bira.co.uk/news/biraleads1billiondamagesclaimagainstamazonbyukretailersinlandmarkcollectiveaction> (accessed 28 June 2024).

Bose, S, 'Facebook Acquisitions—The Complete List (2022)!' (TechWyse Blog, 17 February 2022) <https://www.techwyse.com/blog/generalcategory/facebookacquisitionsinfographic> (accessed 7 June 2024).

Bostoen, F, 'Most Favoured Nation Clauses: Towards an Assessment Framework under EU Competition Law', CoRe 223 (2017).

Bourreau, M, 'Some Economics of Digital Ecosystems' (Hearing on Competition Economics of Digital Ecosystems), DAF/COMP/WD(2020)89 (13 November 2020).

Brin, S and L Page, 'The PageRank Citation Ranking: Bringing Order to the Web' <http://ilpubs.stanford.edu:8090/422/1/199966.pdf> (accessed 7 June 2024).

British Academy and Royal Society, 'Data Management and Use: Governance in the 21st Century' (October 2017).

Broadband Search, 'Average Daily Time Spent on Social Media (Latest 2023 Data)' <https://www.broadbandsearch.net/blog/averagedailytimeonsocialmedia> (accessed 18 August 2023).

Brown, I, 'Key Points on DMA Interoperability and Encryption' (1 April 2022) <https://www.ianbrown.tech/2022/04/01/keypointsondmainteroperabilityandencryption> (accessed 7 June 2024).

Browne, R, 'Price Comparison Site Sues Google for $2.4 Billion over Alleged Antitrust Breach' (CNBC, 7 February 2022) <https://www.cnbc.com/2022/02/07/pricerunnersuesgooglefor2point4billionoverallegedantitrustbreach.html> (accessed 7 June 2024).

Brundage, M et al, 'Toward Trustworthy AI Development: Mechanisms for Supporting Verifiable Claims' (ResearchGate, 2020) <https://www.researchgate.net/publication/340662790_Toward_Trustworthy_AI_Development_Mechanisms_for_Supporting_Verifiable_Claims> (accessed 10 April 2024).

Business Wire, 'Fitbit to Be Acquired by Google' (1 November 2019) <https://www.businesswire.com/news/home/20191101005318/en/Fitbit-to-Be-Acquired-by-Google> (accessed 28 February 2023).

Caffarra, C and F Scott Morton, 'The European Commission Digital Markets Act: A Translation' (5 January 2021) <https://voxeu.org/article/europeancommissiondigitalmarketsacttranslation> (accessed 7 June 2024).

CAI Ruoyu, '泉州、兰州率先重订网约车细则，下一个是谁？[Quanzhou and Lanzhou First Amends E-Hailing Provisions, Who's Next?]' (10 November 2017) <https://cj.sina.com.cn/article/detail/5992589948/475742> (accessed 8 April 2024).

Callaham, J, 'Google Made Its Best Acquisition Nearly 17 Years Ago: Can You Guess What It Was?' (13 May 2022) <https://www.androidauthority.com/googleandroidacquisition884194> (accessed 14 February 2023).

Callaham, J, 'The History of Android OS: Its Name, Origin, and More' (Android Authority, 1 December 2023) <https://www.scribd.com/document/377355282/The-History-of-Android-OS-Its-Name-Origin-and-More> (accessed 7 November 2022).

Castillo de la Torre, F, 'Is the Effects-Based Approach Too Cumbersome?: Taking Stock of Recent Practice and Case Law on Article 102 TFEU' (2023) <https://papers.ssrn.com/sol3/papers.cfm?abstract_id=4395401&download=yes> (accessed 7 June 2024).

CB Insights, 'Visualizing Tech Giants' Billion-Dollar Acquisitions' (CB Insights, 24 February 2021) <https://www.cbinsights.com/research/techgiantsbilliondollaracquisitionsinfographic> (accessed 6 October 2023).

CCCS (Competition and Consumer Commission), 'What Are Anti-Competitive Agreements and Why Are They Bad?' (28 February 2019) <https://www.cccs.gov.sg/anticompetitivebehaviour/anticompetitiveagreements> (accessed 27 September 2022).

CCTV Finance, '全国12城市叫停新增投放 共享单车开始骑向海外 [Twelve Cities Stopped the Increase of Shared Bikes, Share Bikes Started to Turn to Overseas Markets]' (21 December 2017) <https://www.nbd.com.cn/articles/20171221/1174097.html> (accessed 27 September 2022).

CCTV News, '商务部：开展滴滴优步合并案反垄断调查 两次约谈滴滴 [MOFCOM: Antimonopoly Investigation into Didi–Uber Merger: Two Interviews with Didi]' (2 September 2016) <https://news.cctv.com/2016/09/02/ARTIJgQdeT2nSZSNETXi5zq8160902.shtml> (accessed 13 October 2023).

CCTV News, '国家市场监管总局：依据反垄断法及有关规定对滴滴收购优步案件进行调查 [SAMR: Ongoing Investigation into Didi–Uber Merger According to the Old AML and Relevant Regulations]' (16 November 2018) <http://news.cctv.com/2018/11/16/ARTIFgxAD8eTn8YU2mY5HJYM181116.shtml> (accessed 13 October 2023).

CCTV News, '人民法院严厉制裁垄断行为，维护市场公平竞争 [People's Court Severely Sanction Monopolistic Behaviour and Maintain Fair Competition in the Market]' (17 November 2022) <https://news.cctv.com/2022/11/17/ARTIu7JF8aBGtAf9Oa7ZNkNP221117.shtml> (accessed 2 December, 2022).

CEIBS (China–Europe International Business School), 'Lessons from the Didi Dache and Kuaidi Dache Taxi App Merger' <https://www.ceibs.edu/lessonsdididacheandkuaididachetaxiappmerger≥ (accessed 2 February 2023).

Changtang, HE, '共享单车应该免押 [Shared Bikes Should Be Free from Deposits]' (18 March 2018) <https://baijiahao.baidu.com/s?id=1595249240416216665&wfr=spider&for=pc> (accessed 27 September 2022).

Changzhou University, '常州大学中国知网（续订）项目成交公告 [Changzhou University CNKI (Renewal) Project Transaction Announcement]' (31 October 2023) <https://zb.cczu.edu.cn/2023/1031/c8598a344317/page.htm> (accessed 1 May 2024).

Chen, C et al, '共享充电宝、共享单车齐涨价引争议，共享经济变贵还是变味？[The Simultaneous Price Increase of Shared Power Banks and Bike-Sharing Services Has Sparked

Controversy: Is the Sharing Economy Getting More Expensive or Has It Taken on a Different Flavour?]' (20 September 2022) <https://new.qq.com/rain/a/20220920A014NS00> (accessed 27 September 2022).

Fang, B and L Ran, '北京治理共享单车的加减法 [Addition and Subtraction in Beijing's Governance of Shared Bikes]' (13 October 2022) <https://baijiahao.baidu.com/s?id=1746509813685238497&wfr=spider&for=pc> (accessed 8 April 2024).

Chen, P and D Wen, '近30家厂商逐鹿共享单车 冬天过后将洗牌 [Nearly 30 Companies Competing in Bike Sharing, There Would Be a Shuffle after the Winter]' (6 January 2017) <http://www.nbd.com.cn/articles/20170106/1067717.html> (accessed 27 September 2022).

Chen, Y, '《滴滴优步合并案》的调查为何这么难 [Why Is It So Difficult to Investigate the Didi–Uber Merger?]' (29 November 2018) <http://m.eeo.com.cn/2018/1129/342209.shtml> (accessed 2 February 2023).

Chen, Y and Y Pan, 'Foreign Investment Crucial for Economic Growth' (*China Daily*, 5 September 2023) <https://www.chinadaily.com.cn/a/202309/05/WS64f660fea310d2dce4bb3d6f.html> (accessed 13 April 2024).

China Daily, '优酷、土豆宣布合并 [Youku's Merger with Tudou]' (13 March 2012) <https://www.chinadaily.com.cn/hqzx/201203/13/content_14824708.htm> (accessed 13 April 2024).

China Daily, '《中华人民共和国外商投资法》（双语对照）[Foreign Investment Law of the People's Republic of China: Bilingual Version]' (22 March 2019) <https://language.chinadaily.com.cn/a/201903/22/WS5c94798ca3104842260b205f.html> (accessed 13 April 2024).

China Daily, 'Tighter Curbs on Monopoly to Ensure Fair Competition' (*China Daily*, 19 November 2021) <http://www.chinadaily.com.cn/a/202111/19/WS6196de0da310cdd39bc762b0.html> (accessed 2 October 2023).

China Development.com, 'The State Anti-Monopoly Bureau Was Formally Established' (19 November 2021) <http://www.chinadevelopment.com.cn/news/zj/2021/11/1753311.shtml> (accessed 30 July 2023).

Cicilline, DN, 'Investigation of Competition in Digital Markets—Majority Staff Report and Recommendations—Subcommittee on Antitrust, Commercial, and Administrative Law of the Committee on the Judiciary of the House of Representatives' (US Congress Cicilline Report, 2020) <https://www.govinfo.gov/content/pkg/CPRT117HPRT47832/pdf/CPRT117HPRT47832.pdf> (accessed 7 June 2024).

Cleary Antitrust Watch, 'The ICA Closes Investigation into Google's Conduct in the Digital Advertising Sector Following the Opening of Proceedings by the European Commission' (Cleary Gottlieb,12 October 2021) <https://www.clearyantitrustwatch.com/2021/10/theicaclosesinvestigationintogooglesconductinthedigitaladvertisingsectorfollowingtheopeningofproceedingsbytheeuropeancommission/#_ftnref2> (accessed 7 June 2024).

CNKI (China National Knowledge Infrastructure), '知网，知网整改方案 [China National Knowledge Infrastructure's Rectification Programme]' (26 December 2022) <https://mp.weixin.qq.com/s/oc0xlh31PViQTf5X8WmcYg> (accessed 30 October 2022).

CCPC (Competition and Consumer Protection Commission), 'Commission Secures 5-Year Commitments from Booking.com' (6 October 2015) <https://www.ccpc.ie/business/commission-secures-5-year-commitments-booking-com/#:~:text = Tuesday%2C%206th%20October%202015%3A%20The,agent%20platform%2C%20Booking.com> (accessed 29 April 2024).

CNIL (National Commission on Informatics and Liberty), 'How Can Humans Keep the Upper Hand? The Ethical Matters Raised by Algorithms and Artificial Intelligence' (December 2017).

Competition Ordinance (Cap. 619), 'Paragraph 3, Commitments Given by Trip International Travel (Hong Kong) Limited and Ctrip.com (Hong Kong) Limited to the Competition Commission Pursuant to Section 60 of the Competition Ordinance (Cap. 619)' <https://www.compcomm.hk/tc/enforcement/consultations/past_consultations/files/Proposed_Commitments_Ctrip_HK.pdf> (accessed 6 June 2024).

Competition Policy International, 'Spain: CNMC Fines Tobacco Companies for 57.7 Million' (15 April 2019) <https://www.competitionpolicyinternational.com/spain-cnmc-fine-to-tobacco-companies-for-57-7-million-euros> (accessed 29 December 2022).

Congress.gov, 'H.R. 5017—Open App Markets Act' <https://www.congress.gov/bill/117th-congress/house-bill/5017> (accessed 7 June 2024).

Congress.gov, 'S. 2992—American Innovation and Choice Online Act (AICOA)' <https://www.congress.gov/bill/117th-congress/senate-bill/2992/text> (accessed 7 June 2024).

Congress.gov, 'S.5339—Platform Accountability and Transparency Act' <https://www.congress.gov/bill/117th-congress/senate-bill/5339> (accessed 7 June 2024).

Council of the European Union, 'Artificial Intelligence Act: Council and Parliament Strike a Deal on the First Rules for AI in the World' (Press release, 9 December 2023) <https://www.consilium.europa.eu/en/press/pressreleases/2023/12/09/artificialintelligenceactcouncilandparliamentstrikeadealonthefirstworldwiderulesforai> (accessed 7 June 2024).

Crouch, E, 'China's Ride Wars: Uber vs. Didi Kuaidi' (Tech in Asia, 30 October 2015) <https://www.techinasia.com/infographicdidikuaidiuber> (accessed 2 February 2023).

Cheng, Z, '泉州调整地方网约车细则 [Quanzhou City Adjusted Detailed Provisions for Online Hailing]' (Fujian Daily, 20 September 2017) <https://jtyst.fujian.gov.cn/zwgk/jtyw/mtsy/201709/t20170928_439039.htm> (accessed 30 October 2024).

Cui, X, '泉州市发布网约车细则，准入车型要求放宽，不再有15万限制！[Quanzhou City Issued Detailed Provisions for Online Hailing, Relaxing the Requirements for Approved Car Models, and There Is No Longer a Price Requirement of ¥150k!]' (19 September 2017) <https://www.dongchedi.com/article/6467436863962481166> (accessed 8 April 2025).

Deutscher, E, 'How to Measure Privacy-Related Consumer Harm in Merger Analysis' (PhD thesis, European University Institute, 2018).

De Corniere, A, 'Should We Break Up Big Tech?' (*The Economist*, 7 November 2019) <https://theteconomist.wordpress.com/2019/11/07/shouldwebreakupbigtech> (accessed 9 June 2024).

DeHeng Law Offices, 'In Brief: Abuse of Dominance in China, DeHeng Law Offices' (Lexology, 19 March 2020) <https://www.lexology.com/library/detail.aspx?g=c6b2314cbc574bfea4e629c8ad04e789> (accessed 7 November 2022).

Ding, J, 'Deciphering China's AI Dream' (Marcg 2018) <https://www.fhi.ox.ac.uk/wpcontent/uploads/Deciphering_Chinas_AIDream.pdf> (accessed 17 August 2023).

Ding, L, 'Merger Control Laws and Regulations China 2024' (12 April 2023) <https://iclg.com/practiceareas/mergercontrollawsandregulations/china> (accessed 2 May 2024).

DNA Web Team, 'China: Didi–Uber Merger Would Lead to Monopoly, Fare Hike?' (updated 2 August 2016) <https://www.dnaindia.com/world/reportchinadidiubermergerwouldleadtomonopolyfarehike2240357> (accessed 2 February 2023).

Ebrun, '二选一再上演：家居家装品牌被迫签保证书 ["Choosing One Out of Two" Again: Furniture Brands Forced to Sign Guarantees]' (11 June 2018) <http://www.ebrun.com/20180611/281442.shtml> (accessed 23 January 2020).

Enberg, J, 'Global Digital Ad Spending 2019: Digital Accounts for Half of Total Medi Ad Spending Worldwide' (EMarketer, 28 March 2019) <https://www.emarketer.com/content/globaldigitaladspending2019> (accessed 6 June 2024).

EPC (European Publishers Council), 'European Publishers Council Files EU Complaint against Google for Anti-Competitive Ad Tech Practices' (11 February 2022) <https://www.epceurope.eu/post/europeanpublisherscouncilfileseucomplaintagainstgoogleforanticompetitiveadtechpractices> (accessed 7 June 2024).

Espinoza, J and E Solomon, 'EU Draft Tech Rules Too "Narrow", Says German Competition Head' (*Financial Times*, 14 July 2021) <http://www.ft.com/content/6cff198792634bc68d8d6426ef303325> (accessed 7 June 2024).

European Competition Network, 'Joint Paper of the Heads of the National Competition Authorities of the European Union: How National Competition Agencies Can Strengthen the DMA' (2021).

Evans, B, 'Tech in 2020: Standing on the Shoulders of Giants' (2020) <https://static1.squarespace.com/static/50363cf324ac8e905e7df861/t/5ed23bd3bdbbdb299cb6aa9f/1590836452410/2020+Benedict+Evans+Shoulders+of+Giants.pdf> (accessed 28 September 2023).

Evans, B, 'The New Gatekeepers' (Presentation, December 2023) <https://www.benevans.com/presentations> (accessed 28 September 2023).

Expert Group for the Observatory on the Online Platform Economy, 'Work Stream on Measurement & Economic Indicators' (Progress Report) <https://platformobservatory.eu/app/uploads/2020/07/ProgressReport_Workstream_on_Measurement_and_Economic_Indicators_2020.pdf> (accessed 7 June 2024).

Fan, J, '新年首批13张反垄断罚单：横跨6年各罚50万，腾讯领9张 [The First 13 Anti-Monopoly Fines in the New Year: Over 6 Years, ¥500 Thousand Each Case, Tencent Responsible for 6' (ThePaper.cn, 5 January 2022), <https://www.thepaper.cn/newsDetail_forward_16151802> (accessed 7 June 2024).

Federal Competition Authority, 'BWB Informs: Amazon Modifies Its Terms and Conditions' (Press release, 17 July 2019) <https://www.bwb.gv.at/en/news/news_2019/detail/bwb-informs-amazon-modifies-its-terms-and-conditions-1> (accessed 7 June 2024).

Field, M, 'Technology Intelligence' (The Telegraph, 26 October 2022).

Fisher, A, 'Google Was Not a Normal Place: Brin, Page, and Mayer on the Accidental Birth of the Company That Changed Everything' (*Vanity Fair*, 10 July 2018) <https://www.vanityfair.com/news/2018/07/valleyofgeniusexcerptgoogle> (accessed 7 June 2024).

Foresight Industry Research Institute, '洞察2022：中国网约车行业竞争格局及市场份额 [Insight 2022: The Online Ride-Hailing Competition Landscape and Market Share in China]' (*Tencent News*, 25 May 2022) <https://new.qq.com/rain/a/20220525A09Z2P00> (accessed 6 June 2024).

Fortune, 'Microsoft in Fortune Rankings'<https://fortune.com/company/microsoft> (accessed 7 June 2024).

Foss Patents, 'Paris Commercial Court Declined to Find Fault in Apple's 30% App Tax, Referred to EU Commission Enforcement of Antitrust Law and DMA: French Government Should Appeal Certain Parts' (20 December 2022) <http://www.fosspatents.com/2022/12/pariscommercialcourtdeclinedtofind.html> (accessed 7 June 2024).

Galston, W and C Hendrickson, 'A Policy at Peace with Itself: Antitrust Remedies for Our Concentrated, Uncompetitive Economy' (Brookings Report, 5 January 2018) <https://www.brookings.edu/research/apolicyatpeacewithitselfantitrustremediesforourconcentrateduncompetitiveeconomy> (accessed 7 June 2024).

Gal, A, 'It's a Feature, Not a Bug: On Learning Algorithms and What They Teach Us', DAF/COMP/WD(2017)50 (OECD, 7 June 2017).

Gennai, P, 'Presenting Search App and Browser Options to Android Users in Europe' (18 April 2019) <https://www.blog.google/aroundtheglobe/googleeurope/presentingsearchappandbrowseroptionsandroiduserseurope> (accessed 7 June 2024).

Gennai, P, 'An Update on Android for Search Providers in Europe' (2 August 2019) <https://www.blog.google/aroundtheglobe/googleeurope/updateandroidsearchproviderseurope> (accessed 7 June 2024).

Geradin Partners, 'Amazon Faces £2.7bn Legal Claim for Its Anticompetitive Conduct to the Detriment of Hundreds of Thousands of Independent UK Sellers' <https://media.licdn.com/dms/document/media/D4E1FAQEEaZRUf6kdnA/feedsharedocumentpdfanalyzed/0/1719474482835?e=1720656000&v=beta&t=kHnr_IUVyMNyEoNjIu3sMoVUqKSHawZn28XJVu792IY> (accessed 28 June 2024).

Goh, B and S Yan, 'In Fresh Regulatory Move, China Tells Tech Giants to Stop Blocking Rivals' Links' (Reuters, 13 September 2021) <https://financialnewsletter.com/infreshregulatorymove> (accessed 10 December 2022).

Grandhi, K, 'China Launches Antimonopoly Investigation into Uber–Didi Deal' (*International Business Times*, 16 February 2009) <https://www.ibtimes.co.uk/chinalaunchesantimonopolyinvestigationintouberdidideal1579350> (accessed 2 February 2023).

Guagming Daily, '光明网评论员：落实公平竞争审查，从网约车细则开始 [Implementing Fair Competition Review, Starting with the Concrete Rules on E-Hailing Cars]' (*Guagming Daily*, 13 November 2017) <https://baijiahao.baidu.com/s?id=1583922156448101294&wfr=spider&for=pc> (accessed 25 August 2022).

Han, W and Y Gao, 'Challenges and Prospects for Merger Control in China in the Digital Economy' (Competition Policy International Antitrust Chronicle, 22 March 2019) <https://

www.pymnts.com/cpiposts/challengesandprospectsformergercontrolinchinainthedigital economy> (accessed 14 April 2024).

Han, W, Y Gao, and A Deng, 'Algorithmic Price Discrimination on Online Platforms and Antitrust Enforcement in China's Digital Economy' (The Antitrust Source, August 2018) <https://www.americanbar.org/content/dam/aba/publications/antitrust/magazine/archived/2018/august/algorithmicpricediscriminationonlineplatforms.pdf> (accessed 11 April 2024).

Hansell, S, 'Yahoo Woos a Social Networking Site' (*New York Times*, 22 September 2006) <https://www.nytimes.com/2006/09/22/technology/22facebook.html> (accessed 15 February 2023).

Harari, Y, 'Yuval Noah Harari on Big Data, Google and the End of Free Will' (*Financial Times*, 26 August 2016) <https://www.ft.com/content/50bb48306a4c11e6ae5ba7cc5dd5a28c> (accessed 20 August 2022).

Heinz, S, 'Bundeskartellamt Ends Abuse Probe after Amazon Agrees to Changing Business Terms for Dealers' (Kluwer Competition Law Blog, 30 July 2019) <http://competitionlawblog.kluwercompetitionlaw.com/2019/07/30/bundeskartellamtendsabuseprobeafteramazonagreestochangingbusinesstermsfordealers> (accessed 7 June 2024).

Heureka Group, 'Heureka Is Suing Google for an Abuse of Dominance That Harms Online Shoppers and Merchants Alike' (30 June 2020) <https://www.politico.eu/wpcontent/uploads/2020/07/Heurekapressrelease.pdf> (accessed 7 June 2024).

Hongxing News, '美团被举报强迫外卖商家独家合作，四川通江代理商遭罚25万 [Meituan Reportedly Forced Takeout Merchants to Work Exclusively with It, and Agents in Tongjiang County, Sichuan Province, Were Fined 250,000 Yuan]' (29 March 2019) <https://baijiahao.baidu.com/s?id=1629318393689842444&wfr=spider&for=pc> (accessed 22 February 2024).

Hornkohl, L, 'Brand Gating: German Competition Authority Once Again Launches an Investigation into Amazon (and Apple)' (Kluwer Competition Law Blog, 6 November 2020) <http://competitionlawblog.kluwercompetitionlaw.com/2020/11/06/brandgatinggermancompetitionauthorityonceagainlaunchesaninvestigationintoamazonandapple> (accessed 7 June 2024).

Hu, S, '腾讯网易回应其关于垄断音乐作品处罚决定：全面接受， 按期整改 [Tencent NetEase Responded to Its Punishment Decision on Monopoly Music Works: Fully Accept and Rectify on Schedule]' (24 July 2021) <https://www.sohu.com/a/479312888_114941> (accessed 14 April 2024).

Hua Sin, J, 'China's Ministry of Commerce Conditionally Clears the Google/Motorola Mobility Deal' (Kluwer Competition Law Blog,19 May 2012) <https://competitionlawblog.kluwercompetitionlaw.com/2012/05/19/chinaconditionallyclearsgooglemotorolamobility> (accessed 7 June 2024).

Huai'an Intermediate People's Court, '淮安中院发布2021年度知识产权司法保护十件典型案例 [Huai'an Intermediate People's Court Release of Ten Typical Cases of Judicial Protection of Intellectual Property Rights for the Year 2021]' (25 April 2022) <http://fy.huaian.gov.cn/col/11895_474188/art/16487424/1650871155464Pq7wSVcr.html> (accessed 22 February 2024).

Huang, L, ''时建中：公共数据取之于民，应该用之于民，惠之于民 [Shi Jianzhong: Public Data, Sourced from the People, Should Be Used for the People's Benefit and Welfare]' (9 November 2023) <https://mp.weixin.qq.com/s/z5nzJJxLiGr65vE5YJp2g> (accessed 30 March 2024).

Huawei and Oxford, 'Digital Spillover: Measuring the True Impact of the Digital Economy' (2017) <https://www.huawei.com/minisite/gci/en/digitalspillover/files/gci_digital_spillover.pdf> (accessed 17 August 2023).

Hubei Daily, '武汉网约车《新政》下周实施 车辆总价要求12万以上 [Wuhan's New Policy on E-Hailing Cars Will Come into Force Next Week, Requiring the Price of the Car Be More Than ¥120k]' (15 April 2017) <https://www.hubei.gov.cn/zxjy/rdhy/201704/t20170415_1764294.shtml> (accessed 8 April 2024).

Hubei Yangtze River Business News, '格兰仕怒怼天猫《二选一》 [A Review of the Chinese Air-Conditioning Industry for 2019: Galanz Accused Tmall for "Choice of One Out of Two"]' (19 June 2019) <https://baijiahao.baidu.com/s?id=1636734728435224012&wfr=spider&for=pc> (accessed 10 February 2020).

Hughes, C, 'It's Time to Break Up Facebook' (Opinion) (*New York Times*, 9 May 2019) <https://www.nytimes.com/2019/05/09/opinion/sunday/chrishughesfacebookzuckerberg.html> (accessed 18 August 2023).

Ibanez Colomo, P, 'The Italian Competition Authority in Enel v Google: Will Bronner and Magill Survive Common Carrier Antitrust?' (27 May 2021) <https://chillingcompetition.com/?s=ENEL+ITALIA> (accessed 7 June 2024).

IMARC (International Mining and Resources Conference), 'Global Online Advertising Market Report and Forecast 2021–2026' <https://www.imarcgroup.com/internetadvertisingmarket> (accessed 7 June 2024).

Investor Insights Asia, 'Tencent Holdings (Part 1): Introducing Tencent' (25 April 2022) <https://www.investorinsights.asia/post/tencentholdingspart1introducingtencent> (accessed 21 September 2023).

iResearch, 'AI Report' <https://report.iresearch.cn/report/202201/3925.shtml> (accessed 21 September 2023).

IT Media Consulting, 'Data Driven Economy—Market Trends and Policy Perspectives' (Executive Summary Research Report, 2017).

Jacobides, M, 'Thoughts about the World & Media—2021–22 Review' <https://www.jacobides.com/202122review> (accessed 7 June 2024).

Jacobs, A, 'Strikes by Taxi Drivers Spread across China' (*New York Times*, 14 January 2015), <https://www.nytimes.com/2015/01/15/world/asia/taxistrikesspreadacrosschina.html> (accessed 6 June 2024).

Jennewine, T, 'Why NVIDIA Will Dominate the Data Center by 2030' (The Motley Fool,10 September 2021) <https://www.fool.com/investing/2021/09/10/whynvidiawilldominatethedatacenterby2030> (accessed 15 October 2023).

Jiang, W, '兰州降低网约车准入门槛 [Lanzhou Lowers Its Thresholds on E-Hailing]' (21 September 2017) <http://it.people.com.cn/n1/2017/0921/c100929550869.html> (accessed 9 April 2024).

Jossen, S, 'The World's Most Valuable Resource Is No Longer Oil, But Data' (*The Economist*, 6 May 2017) <http://www.economist.com/leaders/2017/05/06/theworldsmostvaluableresourceisnolongeroilbutdata> (accessed 7 July 2022).

Katsifis, D, 'The Autorité de la Concurrence Orders Interim Measures against Google in Neighbouring Rights Case' (4 May 2020) <https://theplatformlaw.blog/2020/05/04/theautoritedelaconcurrenceordersinterimmeasuresagainstgoogleinneighbouringrightscase> (accessed 7 June 2024).

Katsifis, D, 'Google Fined € 220 Million by French Autorité de la Concurrence for Breaching Competition Law in Ad Tech; Offers Commitments' (8 June 2021) <https://theplatformlaw.blog/2021/06/08/googlefinede220millionbyfrenchautoritedelaconcurrenceforbreachingcompetitionlawinadtechofferscommitments> (accessed 7 June 2024).

Katsifis, D, 'CMA Publishes Commitments Offered by Google with Respect to Its Privacy Sandbox Proposals, Seeks Comments' (14 June 2021) <https://theplatformlaw.blog/2021/06/14/cmapublishescommitmentsofferedbygooglewithrespecttoitsprivacysandboxproposalsseekscomments> (accessed 7 June 2024).

Katsifis, D, 'The Autorité de la Concurrence Fines Google € 500 Million for Not Complying with Interim Measures in Neighboring Rights Case' (13 July 2021) <https://theplatformlaw.blog/2021/07/13/theautoritedelaconcurrencefinesgooglee500millionfornotcomplyingwithinterimmeasuresinneighboringrightscase> (accessed 7 June 2024).

Kawate, I, 'Foreign Investment in China Falls to Lowest Level on Record' (Nikkei Asia, 12 August 2023) <https://www.radionikkei.jp/podcast/lr/_230823.html> (accessed 13 April 2024).

Keke, '青岛市区出租车百日专项整治 网约车也在整治之列 [The 100-Day Special Rectification of Taxis in Qingdao Urban Area, E-Hailing Cars Included]' (15 February 2019) <https://baijiahao.baidu.com/s?id=1625496685514006418&wfr=spider&for=p> (accessed 17 July 2022).

Kennedy, V, 'Microsoft's Activision Blizzard Bid Provisionally Approved by UK Regulator' (EuroGamer, 22 September 2023) <https://www.eurogamer.net/microsoftsactivisionblizzardbidprovisionallyapprovedbyukregulator> (accessed 13 April 2024).

Kirby, WC et al, 'Uber in China: Driving in the Gray Zone' (Harvard Business School case, January 2016) <https://www.hbs.edu/faculty/Pages/item.aspx?num=50436> (accessed 20 July 2022).

Koc, C, 'Apple Faces Multibillion-Euro Dutch Class Action over App Sales' (29 March 2022) <https://www.bloomberg.com/news/articles/20220329/applefacesmultibillioneurodutchclassactionoverappsales> (accessed 7 June 2024).

Koetsier, J, 'Galloway: Google Is God, Apple Is Sex, Facebook Is Love, and Amazon Is . . . Death?' (Forbes, 10 May 2017) <https://www.forbes.com/sites/johnkoetsier/2017/05/10/gallowaygoogleisgodappleissexfacebookisloveandamazonisdeath> (accessed 7 June 2024).

Koski, H, O Kassi, and F Braesemann, 'Killers on the Road of Emerging Start-Ups—Implications for Market Entry and Venture Capital Financing', Research Institute of the Finnish Economy (ETLA) Working Paper 81 (2020).

Krishna Kamepalli, L, R Raja, and L Zingales, 'Kill Zone', National Bureau of Economic Research Working Paper 27146 (2020) <https://www.nber.org/system/files/working_papers/w27146/w27146.pdf> (accessed 9 June 2024).

Laitenberger, J, 'EU Competition Law in Innovation and Digital Markets: Fairness and the Consumer Welfare Perspective' (Speech, 10 October 2017) <https://ec.europa.eu/competition/speeches/text/sp2017_15_en.pdf> (accessed 17 February 2023).

Legal Weekly, '虎牙斗鱼合并被否 反垄断监管再迎里程碑式进展 [Antitrust Regulation Reaches Another Milestone with the Blocked Merger between Huya and DouYu]' (15 July 2021) <http://m.legalweekly.cn/rdcj/202107/15/content_8551962.html> (accessed 14 October 2023).

Lei, J, '京东与阿里大战再起！ 京东锁定后台强行促销，天猫逼店铺二选一 [War between JD and Ali Again! JD Locked Backend for Forced Promotions, and Tmall forced Operators to Choose One from Two]' (7 June 2017) <http://www.hxnews.com/news/cjpd/cjxw/201706/07/1232138.shtml> (accessed 23 January 2020).

'Letter to Commissioner Vestager by 41 Rival CSS' (28 November 2019) <https://www.hausfeld.com/uploads/documents/final_version_joint_letter_of_css_to_ms_vestager_on_google_shoppingnoncompliance_26.11.2019.pdf> (accessed 12 January 2023).

Li, J, '最高法终审《3Q大战》腾讯奇虎分别回应 [The Supreme People's Court Announces the Final Verdict on Tencent v. Qihu, with Tencent and Qihu Respond Respectively]' (WayBackMachine, 4 March 2016) <https://web.archive.org/web/20160304072357/http://legal.people.com.cn/n/2014/0224/c42510244505 89.html> (accessed 7 June 2024).

Li, X and Y Yin, 'China Fines Meituan $533m for Monopolist Practices, Milder than Alibaba Due to Difference in Rectification Moves' (Global Times, 8 October 2021) <https://www.globaltimes.cn/page/202110/1235798.shtml> (accessed 27 September 2022).

Lithuanian Competition Council, 'Supreme Court Upheld KT Decision on Cartel among Travel Agencies' (Press release, 3 May 2016) <http://kt.gov.lt/en/news/supreme-court-upheld-kt-decision-on-cartel-among-travel-agencies> (accessed 8 June 2024).

Liu, C, A Li, J Yang, and N Torres, King & Wood Mallesons, 'Exploring the Trend of Abuse of Dominance Investigation in China' (China Law Insight, 19 April 2021) <https://www.chinalawinsight.com/2021/04/articles/antitrust/exploringthetrendofabuseofdominanceinvestigationinchina> (accessed 16 March 2023).

Liu, J, '兰州拟限定网约车数量 专家争议政策合理性 [Lanzhou Planning to Limit the Number of E-Hailing Cars, Experts Dispute the Rationality of the Policy]' (CAIXIN, 16 August 2016) <https://china.caixin.com/20160816/100978004.html> (accessed 17 July 2022).

Liu, M, '红星调查：共享单车市场迎来变局, 各地被要求破除垄断 [Red Star Investigation: Bike-Sharing Market Sees Changes as Localities Are Asked to Break Up Monopolies]' (22 November 2022) <https://new.qq.com/rain/a/20221122A0006B00> (accessed 8 April 2024).

Liu, M and M Ke, '刘木木、马可：《各地被要求破除垄断 共享单车市场迎变局》 [Local Governments Demanded to Break Off Monopoly, the Bike-Sharing Business Facing Its Change]' (*China Daily*, 23 November 2022) <https://cnews.chinadaily.com.cn/a/202211/23/WS637d8014a3109bd995a518a6.html> (accessed 7 June 2024).

Liu, Z, 'Kuaidi Marries Didi: End of the Battle or a New Beginning?'(*China Daily*,16 February 2015) <http://www.chinadaily.com.cn/business/tech/201502/16/content_19600016_3.htm> (accessed 2 February 2023).

Lizhi News, '中科院也受不了知网的涨价？没那么简单！[Chinese Academy of Sciences Can't Stand CNKI's Price Hike Either? It's Not That Simple!]' (19 April 2022) <https://baijiahao.baidu.com/s?id=1730511153740211879&wfr=spider&for=pc> (accessed 2 May 2024).

Lockheimer, H, 'Complying with the EC's Android Decision' (16 October 2018) <https://www.blog.google/aroundtheglobe/googleeurope/complyingecsandroiddecision> (accessed 7 June 2024).

Lomas, N, 'Microsoft's $7.2BN Deal to Buy Nokia's Devices Business Gets the Nod in China' (8 April 2014) <https://techcrunch.com/2014/04/08/nokiasoftchinaapproval> (accessed 9 March 2023).

Lomas, N, 'Google's Display Advertising Business Is under Antitrust Probe in Italy' (28 October 2020) <https://techcrunch.com/2020/10/28/googlesdisplayadvertisingbusinessisunderantitrustprobeinitaly> (accessed 7 June 2024).

Lomas, N, 'Google's Adtech Practices Targeted in UK, EU Antitrust Damages Suits' (13 September 2022) <https://techcrunch.com/2022/09/13/googleadtechantitrustdamageslawsuitsuknetherlands> (accessed 7 June 2024).

Lomas, N, 'Beats: Italian Antitrust Fine for Apple and Amazon Cancelled on Appeal' (3 October 2022) <https://techcrunch.com/2022/10/03/italyantitrustamazonapplebeatsfinecancelled> (accessed 7 June 2024).

Long, S, 'Retail MFNs and Online Platforms under EU Competition Law: A Practical Primer' (CPI Antitrust Chronicle, September 2019) <https://euclid-law.eu/wp-content/uploads/2021/09/Retail-MFNs-and-Online-Platforms-under-EU-Competition-Law-A-practical-primer.pdf> (accessed 9 June 2024).

Lu, S, '疫情"重燃"需求，盒马再战社区团购 [Epidemic Rekindles Demand, He Ma Fights Again for Community Group Buying]' (31 May 2022) <https://baijiahao.baidu.com/s?id=1734335845096995123&wfr=spider&for=pc> (accessed 13 October 2023).

Ma, S, 'Ride-hailing giant to delist from NYSE' (China Daily, 4 December 2021) < https://www.chinadaily.com.cn/a/202112/04/WS61aad724a310cdd39bc79532.html > (accessed 12 November 2024).

Ma, X, '《3Q大战》4年长跑落幕：为互联网竞争树司法标杆 ["War between 3Q" Closes after the Four-Year March: Setting a Judicial Benchmark for Internet Competition]' (iFeng Finance, 16 October 2014) <https://finance.ifeng.com/a/20141016/13191381_0.shtml> (accessed 6 June 2024).

Macron, E, 'Europe—It Can Die. A New Paradigm at the Sorbonne' (Groupe d'Études Géopolitiques, Sorbonne 2 speech, 25 April 2024) <https://geopolitique.eu/en/2024/04/26/macroneuropeitcandieanewparadigmatthesorbonne> (accessed 13 May 2024).

Malik, A, 'Amazon Completes $8.5 Billion Acquisition of MGM' (17 March 2022) <https://techcrunch.com/2022/03/17/amazoncompletesits85billionacquisitionofmgm> (accessed 7 June 2024).

McDonald, J, 'China's Tencent Ordered to End Exclusive Music Contracts' (24 July 2021) < https://apnews.com/article/technology-entertainment-business-music-china-bd7e87fdbbce8aad72ae96d8c6c97f07> (accessed 2 February 2023).

Meta, 'About Meta' <https://about.meta.com/company-info> (accessed 13 June 2024).

Meta, 'Founder's Letter' (28 October 2021) <https://about.fb.com/news/2021/10/founderslетter> (accessed 3 October 2023).

Mialki, S, 'Know Before You Spend: The Best Digital Advertising Channels' (28 May 2020) <https://instapage.com/blog/bestdigitaladvertisingchannels> (accessed 7 June 2024).

Ministry of Human Resource and Social Welfare, '关于维护新就业形态劳动者劳动保障权益的指导意见 [Guidance Regarding Safeguarding the Labour Welfare of New Employment Formed Workers]' (16 July 2021) <http://www.gov.cn/zhengce/zhengceku/202107/23/content_5626761.htm> (accessed 14 April 2024).

Misra, N, 'An Analysis on the Increasing Abuse of Dominance in the Digital Market' (Black 'n White Journal, 11 September 2021) <https://bnwjournal.com/2021/09/11/

ananalysisontheincreasingabuseofdominanceinthedigitalmarket> (accessed 7 November 2022).

MLex Staff, 'Alibaba Fined 18.23 Billion Yuan for Abuse of Dominance in China (English translation)' (MLex, 28 April 2021) < https://mlexmarketinsight.com/news/insight/alibaba-fined-18-23-billion-yuan-for-abuse-of-dominance-in-china-english-version > (accessed 10 January 2023).

MLex Staff, 'Digital Tools Highlighted in Enforcement Reports of China's Local Market Supervisors' (MLex, 10 January 2023) <https://mlexmarketinsight.com/news/insight/digitaltoolshighlightedinenforcementreportsofchinaslocalmarketsupervisors> (accessed 3 April 2023).

MLex Staff, 'Horizontal Merger Guidelines Considered by China's SAMR to Boost Review Regime' (MLex,17 January 2023) <https://mlexmarketinsight.com/news/insight/horizontalmergerguidelinesconsideredbychinassamrtoboostreviewregime#:~:text=China%27s%20competition%20authority%20is%20considering%20formulating%20guidelines%20governing,mergercontrol%20regime%2C%20a%20senior%20antitrust%20official%20has%20said> (accessed 3 April 2023).

Modrall, J, 'Google/Fitbit—The EU Commission Misses a Step' (17 June 2021) <https://competitionlawblog.kluwercompetitionlaw.com/2021/06/17/googlefitbittheeucommissionmissesastep> (accessed 3 March 2023).

Moss, S, 'Nvidia's $6.9bn Mellanox Acquisition Closes' (Data Center Dynamics, 28 April 2020) <https://www.datacenterdynamics.com/en/news/nvidias69bnmellanoxacquisitioncloses> (accessed 14 October 2023).

Mukherjee, S and F Yun Chee, 'Exclusive: EU's New Tech Laws Are Working; Small Browsers Gain Market Share (Reuters,10 April 2024) <https://www.reuters.com/technology/eusnewtechlawsareworkingsmallbrowsersgainmarketshare20240410> (accessed 1 May 2024).

Murphy, H and C Criddle, 'Meta Axes Further 10,000 Jobs in Fresh Round of Cuts' (14 March 2023) <https://www.ft.com/content/57d43e90f23e48c48f622b6981e136e4> (accessed 7 June 2024).

National Technical Committee 260 on Cybersecurity of Standardization Administration of China, 'Safety Requirements for Automated Decision-Making of Information Security Technology Based on Personal Information (Draft for Public Opinion)' (16 August 2023) <https://www.tc260.org.cn/front/bzzqyjDetail.html?id=20230818163540&norm_id=20221102151633&recode_id=52619> (accessed 7 June 2024).

NetEase, 'Alibaba Acquires Import ECommerce Platform Kaola from NetEase for Approximately US$2 Billion' (NetEase, 5 September 2019) <https://ir.netease.com/newsreleases/newsreleasedetails/alibabaacquiresimportecommerceplatformkaolanetease> (accessed 6 October 2023).

NetEase Hao, '美团：《二选一》被约谈已成常态, 非法窃取商业机密成行业公敌 [Meituan: Interviewed for "Choose One or the Other" Has Become the Norm, Illegal Theft of Trade Secrets Become the Public Enemy of the Industry]' (19 June 2019) <https://www.163.com/dy/article/EI2L2JRQ05314055.html> (accessed 22 February 2024).

Newman, J, 'Ohio v. American Express: The Good, The Bad, and the Ugly' (Network Law Review, 16 July 2018) <https://www.networklawreview.org/ohiovamex> (accessed 7 June 2024).

Ofgem, 'Infringement by Economy Energy, E (Gas and Electricity) and Dyball Associates of Chapter I of the Competition Act 1998 with Respect to an Anti-Competitive Agreement' (26 July 2019) <https://www.ofgem.gov.uk/system/files/docs/2019/07/decision_on_economy_energy_-_e_gas_and_electricity_-_dyball_associates_infringement_of_chapter_i_ca98_doorstep_sales_redacted_decision_document_26_july_2019.pdf> (accessed 24 February 2023).

Orient Webcasting, '头豹发布2022年中国共享充电宝行业市场研究报告 [2022 Market Research Report on China's Charger-Sharing Industry Released by Toubao]' (5 August 2022) <http://caijing.chinadaily.com.cn/a/202208/05/WS62ecbd71a3101c3ee7ae280e.html> (accessed 27 September 2022).

Orlowski, A, 'Free Market Champions or a Cosy Cartel?' (*The Telegraph*, 5 April 2021).

Palma, S and R Waters, 'US Judge Denies FTC Attempt to Block Microsoft's Activision Deal' (*Financial Times*, 11 July 2023).

Paul, K and D Bartz, 'Meta Battles US Antitrust Agency over Future of Virtual Reality' (Reuters, 9 December 2022) <https://www.reuters.com/technology/metabattlesusantitrustagencyoverfuturevirtualreality20221208> (accessed 24 February 2023).

Pei, Y, '商务部：正在对滴滴和优步中国合并案进行调查 [Ministry of Commerce Claims That the Merger Case of Didi and Uber China Is Currently under Investigation]' (27 July 2017) <https://news.sina.cn/20170727/detailifyinryq6571111.d.html> (accessed 13 April 2024).

Pengpai News, '滴滴快的合并引发垄断质疑, 商务部称未收到相关申报 [Didi Kuaidi Merger Raises Monopoly Questions, MOFCOM Claims No Relevant Notification Was Received]' (ThePaper.cn, 16 February 2015) <https://www.thepaper.cn/newsDetail_forward_1304327> (accessed 6 June 2024).

Pengpai News, '中央网信办、市场监管总局、税务总局联合召开规范线上经济秩序指导会 [SAMR, Cyberspace Administration, and State Taxation Administration Jointly Held an Administrative Guidance Meeting to Regulate Online Economy Order]' (11 November 2020) <https://www.thepaper.cn/newsDetail_forward_9946345> (accessed 7 November 2022).

Pengpai News, '大数据杀熟, 携程被判退一赔三！[Price Discrimination Using Data, Ctrip Is Subject to Full Refund and a Three Times Damage]' (26 July 2021) <https://www.thepaper.cn/newsDetail_forward_13758311> (accessed 6 June 2024).

People's Daily Overseas New Media, 'China's Largest Online Academic Library CNKI Criticized for Monopoly' (20 February 2019) <http://en.people.cn/n3/2019/0220/c900009548124.html> (accessed 7 November 2022).

Petropoulos, G, 'The EU's Digital Markets Act' (CPI Columns, May 2021).

Phillips, T, 'UK MPs Grill Regulator over Microsoft Activision Blizzard Deal Block, Day after EU Grants Approval' (EuroGamer, 16 May 2023) <https://www.eurogamer.net/ukmpsgrillregulatorovermicrosoftactivisionblizzarddealblockdayaftereugrantsapproval> (accessed 13 April 2024).

Podszun, R, 'Facebook: Next Step Europe' (D'Kart, 25 March 2021) <https://www.dkart.de/en/blog/2021/03/25/facebooknextstopeurope> (accessed 2 April 2021).

Quirroz Gutierrez, M, 'Not FAANG But MAMAA: Jim Cramer Reveals New Acronym for the 5 Largest Tech Giants' (29 October 2021) <https://fortune.com/2021/10/29/faangmamaajimcramertechfacebookmeta> (accessed 22 February 2023).

Ram, A, 'European Shopping Sites Sue Google for Abuse of Position' (*Financial Times*, 12 April 2019).

Rana, L and N Nagpal, 'Abuse of Dominant Position in Digital Markets' (Bar and Bench, 2 June 2022) <https://www.barandbench.com/viewpoint/abuseofdominantpositionindigitalmarkets> (accessed 7 November 2022).

Rankdex, 'About Rankdex' <http://www.rankdex.com/about.html> (accessed 3 October 2023).

Rego, AR, 'Google Didn't Abuse Dominance in Ending Navx Ad Deal, Says French Court' (MLex, 27 December 2012).

Reith, N, '10 Biggest Software Companies' (Investopedia, updated 31 October 2023) <https://www.investopedia.com/articles/personalfinance/121714/worldstop10softwarecompanies.asp> (accessed 7 June 2024).

Reuters, 'Chinese Delivery Giant Meituan Handed $527 Million Antitrust Fine' (8 October 2021) <https://www.reuters.com/article/chinaregulationmeituanidUSKBN2GY0U5> (accessed 7 June 2024).

Reuters, '滴滴启动纽交所退市并准备香港上市 [Didi Starts to Delist in NYSE and Prepares to Go Public in HKEX]' (3 December 2021) <https://www.zaobao.com.sg/realtime/china/story202112031219519> (accessed 6 June 2024).

Reuters, 'Google Faces Claim from UK Publishers over Online Advertising' (30 November 2022) <https://www.reuters.com/technology/googlefacesclaimukpublishersoveronlineadvertising20221130> (accessed 7 June 2024).

Reuters, 'Spain's High Court Suspends $209 Million Fines on Apple, Amazon Amid Appeal' (8 February 2024) <https://www.reuters.com/technology/spains-high-court-suspends-209-mln-fines-apple-amazon-amid-appeal-2024-02-08> (accessed 7 June 2024).

Reynolds, A, 'Blizzard Entertainment and NetEase Suspending Game Services in China' (Blizzard Entertainmnet Inc,17 November 2022) <https://investor.activision.com/node/35721/pdf> (accessed 2 May 2024).
Ricker, T, 'Google Will Charge Search Providers to Be the Android Default in Europe' (The Verge, 2 August 2019) <https://www.theverge.com/2019/8/2/20751353/googleauctionandroidsearchchoicescreen> (accessed 7 June 2024).
Røed Steen, J and Fafo Institute for Labour and Social Research, 'Key Technologies in the Digital Transformation: Towards a Social Science Taxonomy of Digital Technology' (Foundation For European Progressive Studies, February 2020).
Rosencrance, L, 'Privacy Groups Say Google–DoubleClick Merger Will Hurt Consumers' (20 December 2007) <https://www.computerworld.com/article/2538252/privacygroupssaygoogledoubleclickmergerwillhurtconsumers.html> (accessed 7 June 2024).
Sago, V, 'Bike Sharing in China—From Bicycle Graveyards to a Regulated Industry' (Georgetown Environmental Law Review, 29 April 2020) <https://www.law.georgetown.edu/environmentallawreview/blog/bikesharinginchinafrombicyclegraveyardstoaregulatedindustry/#_ftn5> (accessed 27 September 2022).
Salinger, MA, 'Self-Preferencing, The Global Antitrust Institute Report on the Digital Economy' (Boston University Questrom School of Business, 2020).
Schwab, K, 'The Fourth Industrial Revolution: What It Means, How to Respond' (World Economic Forum, 14 June 2016) <https://www.weforum.org/agenda/2016/01/thefourthindustrialrevolutionwhatitmeansandhowtorespond> (accessed 17 August 2023).
Shanghai Municipal Transport Commission, '上海市网络预约出租汽车经营服务管理若干规定 [Several Provisions on the Administration of Online Booking Taxi Business Services in Shanghai]' (21 December 2016) <https://jtw.sh.gov.cn/zsk/20210609/0bf46d4e4f514eafb9f0ce2eec3f28e4.html> (accessed 9 April 2024).
Shao, B, '最高涨价50%！ 美团骑行卡也全面开涨, 共享单车还划算吗？ [With the Highest Price Increase of 50%, Meituan Ride Cards Start to Increase in Price. Is Bike Sharing Still a Good Deal?]' (ThePaper.cn, 14 August 2022) <https://www.thepaper.cn/newsDetail_forward_19442011> (accessed 2 May 2024).
Shao, G, '2021年反垄断执法数据分析：滥用市场支配地位 [Analysis of Anti-Monopoly Enforcement Data in 2021: Abuse of Dominance]' (14 March 2022) <https://weibo.com/1794930063/LjIqo3OIh> (accessed 7 November 2022).
Shao, G, '按《反垄断法》拆分美团大众点评, 或将恢复外卖平台市场有效竞争 [Research on Competition Law, Separating Meituan and Dazhong Dianping According to the Anti-Monopoly Law May Restore the Competition in Takeout Delivery Market]' (Sina Weibo, 18 August 2022) <https://weibo.com/ttarticle/p/show?id=2309404803639637311636> (accessed 6 June 2024).
Shao, G, '2021年反垄断执法数据统计（2023年2月9日更新）[Antitrust Law Enforcement Statistics of 2021]' (9 February 2023) <https://zhuanlan.zhihu.com/p/343860381> (accessed 13 April 2024).
Shao, G, '初探：公共数据资源开发利用中应当预防的垄断行为 [A Preliminary Exploration: Monopolistic Practices to be Prevented in the Development and Utilization of Public Data Resources]' (1 November 2024) < https://mp.weixin.qq.com/s/tMM8bm_U2H3Lrth0cubkkg> (accessed 9 November 2024).
Sherman, A and L Feiner, 'Amazon, Microsoft and Alphabet Went on a Buying Spree in 2021 Despite D.C.'s Vow to Take on Big Tech' (CNBC, 22 January 2022) <https://www.cnbc.com/2022/01/22/amazonmicrosoftalphabetsetmoredealsin2021thanlast10years.html> (accessed 14 June 2024).
Shi, J, '加强反垄断监管 促进平台经济在规范中发展 [Strengthen Anti-Monopoly Supervision and Promote the Development of Platform Economy in Regulation]' (10 April 2021) <http://finance.people.com.cn/n1/2021/0410/c100432074571.html> (accessed 3 April 2023).
Shui, P, '垄断就涨价？ 共享充电宝集体涨价，市场监管总局出手遏制 [Monopolies Lead to Price Increases? The Collective Price Hike of Shared Charging Stations Prompts Regulatory

Intervention y the SAMR]' (2 September 2021) <https://www.sohu.com/a/487251053_100082204> (accessed 27 September 2022).

Simpson, I, 'What Exactly Is AdTech?' (2016) <https://clearcode.cc/blog/whatisadtech> (accessed 7 June 2024).

Sina Finance, '立案！ 美团被曝《侵害公共利益》， 地方监管诉苦：多次约谈， 权力有限！ [File a Case! Meituan Was Exposed as "Infringing on the Public Interest", Local Supervision Complained: Repeated Interviews, Limited Power!]' (27 April 2021) <https://finance.sina.com.cn/chanjing/gsnews/20210427/docikmyaawc2098745.shtml> (accessed 22 February 2024).

Sina News, '知网的《权力》从何而来？天下苦知网久矣 [Where Does the "Power" of CNKI Come From? We've Been Suffering for a Long Time]' (14 May 2022) <http://k.sina.com.cn/article_5617133817_14ecea8f900100wysh.html> (accessed 1 May 2024).

Sina Weibo, '竞争法研究：《按〈反垄断法〉拆分美团大众点评， 或将恢复外卖平台市场有效竞争》 [Research on Competition Law, Separating Meituan and Dazhong Dianping According to the Anti-Monopoly Law May Restore the Competition in Takeout Delivery Market]' (*Sina Weibo*, 18 August 2022) <https://weibo.com/ttarticle/p/show?id=2309404803639637311636> (accessed 7 June 2024).

Sitaraman, G, 'Unchecked Power—How Monopolists Have Flourished and Undermined Democracy?' (The New Republic, 29 November 2018) <https://newrepublic.com/article/152294/uncheckedpower> (accessed 7 June 2024).

Smith, T, 'Amazon/iRobot: Does Amazon Have an Incentive to Preference Its Own Products?' (13 July 2023) <https://theplatformlaw.blog/2023/07/13/amazonirobotcma> (accessed 9 June 2024).

Sohu News, '微信为争夺在线办公市场封杀钉钉 [WeChat Blocked the Ding Talk for the Online Office Market]' (4 March 2020) <https://www.sohu.com/a/377641393_120003738> (accessed 10 December 2022).

Sohu Technology, '中国出租汽车产业联盟呼吁继续对滴滴优步合并案展开反垄断调查 [China Taxi Industry Alliance Calls for Continued Anti-Monopoly Investigation of Didi and Uber]' (19 December 2020) <https://www.sohu.com/a/439234215_115565> (accessed 16 March 2023).

Southern Metropolis Daily, '京东唯品会炮轰天猫垄断 天猫回应称对方误导公众 [JD and Vipshop Accuse Tmall of Monopoly, and Tmall Responded That They Misled the Public]' (13 July 2017) <http://finance.sina.com.cn/chanjing/gsnews/20170713/docifyiakwa3982343.shtml> (accessed 23 January 2020).

Spagnolo, G et al, 'Google/Fitbit Will Monetise Health Data and Harm Consumers' (30 September 2020) <https://cepr.org/voxeu/columns/googlefitbitwillmonetisehealthdataandharmconsumers> (accessed 6 March 2023).

Statista, 'Banner Advertising—China' (April 2023) <https://www.statista.com/outlook/dmo/digitaladvertising/banneradvertising/china> (accessed 7 June 2024).

Statista, 'Search Advertising—China' (April 2023) <https://www.statista.com/outlook/dmo/digitaladvertising/searchadvertising/china> (accessed 7 June 2024).

Statista, 'Social Media Advertising—China' (April 2023) <https://www.statista.com/outlook/dmo/digitaladvertising/socialmediaadvertising/china> (accessed 7 June 2024).

Statista, 'Video Advertising—China' (April 2023) <https://www.statista.com/outlook/dmo/digitaladvertising/videoadvertising/china#keyplayers> (accessed 7 June 2024).

Stigler Committee on Digital Platforms, 'Final Report' (Stigler Report, 2019) <https://www.sipotra.it/wpcontent/uploads/2020/02/StiglerCommitteeonDigitalPlatformsFinalReport.pdf> (accessed 9 June 2024).

Stoller, M, 'The First Big Antitrust Trial of the Century Is About to Start' (BIG, 6 August 2023) <https://www.thebignewsletter.com/p/the-first-big-antitrust-trial-of> (accessed 3 October 2023).

Stolton, S, 'EU Negotiators Agree New Rules to Rein in Tech Giants' (Politico, 24 March 2022) <https://www.politico.eu/article/eusdigitalmarketsactadopted> (accessed 7 June 2024).

Su, N, Y Fang, and Y Yang, 'Main Case Didi Kuaidi' (Harvard Business Publishing Education, 12 April 2016) <https://hbsp.harvard.edu/product/W16197PDFENG?Ntt=Main%20case%20Didi%20Kuaidi> (accessed 15 April 2024).

Sweeney, M, 'The Colourful History of Advertising Technology in Just 63 Slides' (2015) <https://clearcode.cc/blog/thecolorfulhistoryofadvertisingtechnologyinjust63slides> (accessed 7 June 2024).

Sweeney, M, 'The Rise of TikTok: Why Facebook Is Worried about the Booming Social App' (*The Guardian*, 9 April 2022) <https://www.theguardian.com/technology/2022/apr/09/riseoftiktokwhyfacebookisworriedboomingsocialapp?CMP=Share_iOSApp_Other> (accessed 7 June 2024).

Swift, M, 'Khan Not Ready to Ease Off Throttle at US FTC as She Marks First Year at Helm' (MLex comment, 9 June 2022).

Tai, T, 'Didi Kuaidi & China's Car-Hailing Market' (Harvard Business School, 4 December 2015) <https://d3.harvard.edu/platformrctom/submission/didikuaidichinascarhailingmarket> (accessed 2 February 2023).

Taufen, '数字经济领域经营者集中审查制度的现状与完善 [Present Situation and Perfection of Merger Review System for Operators in Digital Markets]' (5 October 2021) <https://zhuanlan.zhihu.com/p/417320348> (accessed 2 February 2023).

Tencent, '致广大QQ用户的一封信 [A Letter to QQ Users]' (6 November 2010) <https://web.archive.org/web/20101106123940/http://im.qq.com/qq.shtml> (accessed 6 June 2024).

Tencent News, '洞察2022：中国网约车行业竞争格局及市场份额 [Insight 2022: The Online Ride-Hailing Competition Landscape and Market Share in China]' (Tencent News, 25 May 2022) <https://new.qq.com/rain/a/20220525A09Z2P00> (accessed 7 June 2024).

The China Project, 'Angela Zhang on Why the West Should Pay More Attention to Chinese Antitrust Law' (24 October 2023) <https://thechinaproject.com/2023/10/24/angelazhangonwhythewestshouldpaymoreattentiontochineseantitrustlaw> (accessed 7 June 2024).

ThePaper.cn, '滴滴快的合并引发垄断质疑，商务部称未收到相关申报 [Didi Kuaidi Merger Raises Monopoly Questions, MOFCOM Claims no Relevant Notification Was Received]' (ThePaper.cn, 16 February 2015) <https://www.thepaper.cn/newsDetail_forward_1304327> (accessed 7 June 2024).

ThePaper.cn, '大数据杀熟，携程被判退一赔三！ [Price Discrimination Using Data, Ctrip Is Subject to Full Refund and a Three Times Damage]' (ThePaper.cn, 26 July 2021) <https://www.thepaper.cn/newsDetail_forward_13758311> (accessed 7 June 2024).

The Privacy Sandbox, 'Protecting Your Privacy Online' <https://www.privacysandbox.com> (accessed 7 June 2024).

Thompson, B, 'Antitrust and Aggregation' (Stratechery, 26 April 2016) <https://stratechery.com/2016/antitrustandaggregation> (accessed 18 August 2023).

Thompson, B, 'Defining Aggregators' (Stratechery, 26 September 2017) <https://stratechery.com/2017/definingaggregators> (accessed 18 August 2023).

Thompson, B, 'Aggregation Theory' (Stratechery, 21 July 2022) <https://stratechery.com/2015/aggregationtheory> (accessed 18 August 2023).

Tiku, N, 'Do Not Mistake Orrin Hatch for #HipsterAntitrust' (WIRED, 3 August 2017) <https://www.wired.com/story/orrinhatchantitrusthipsterantitrust> (accessed 7 June 2024).

US Association for Computational Mechanics (USACM), 'Statement on Algorithmic Transparency and Accountability' (12 January 2017) <http://www.acm.org/binaries/content/assets/public-policy/2017_usacm_statement_algorithms.pdf> (accessed 14 February 2023).

US Consolidation Guide, '4.1 Determining Whether an Entity Is a VIE' (PWC Viewpoint, 31 December 2022) <https://viewpoint.pwc.com/dt/us/en/pwc/accounting_guides/consolidation_and_eq/consolidation_and_eq_US/chapter_4_equity_met_US/41_determining.html#pwctopic.dita_4a8ec6fd32794ffd8f7258907d6ae2fd> (accessed 13 April 2024).

Valentine, R, 'China Approves Microsoft's Acquisition of Activision Blizzard' (Imagine Games Network, 23 May 2023) <https://www.ign.com/articles/chinaapprovesmicrosoftsacquisitionofactivisionblizzard> (accessed 13 April 2024).

Valletti, T, '"An Offer We Can't Refuse": How We Gave Away Our Data and Made Big Tech What It Is Today' (18 January 2021) <https://www.promarket.org/2021/01/18/facebookwhatsapptermsofserviceadsdataprivacy> (accessed 7 June 2024).

Valletti, T, 'How to Tame the Tech Giants: Reverse the Burden of Proof in Merger Reviews' (Promarket, 28 June 2021) <https://www.promarket.org/2021/06/28/techblockmergerreviewenforcementregulators> (accessed 9 June 2024).

Van Wamel, D, 'In Search of Clarity: Amsterdam Court Refers Preliminary Questions on Parity Clauses to CJEU' (Kluwer Competition Law Blog, 20 April 2023) <https://competitionlawblog.kluwercompetitionlaw.com/2023/04/20/in-search-of-clarity-amsterdam-court-refers-preliminary-questions-on-parity-clauses-to-cjeu> (accessed 9 June 2024).

Vestager, M, 'A Healthy Democracy in a Social Media Age' (Democrazy—Democracy in Crisis?, 7 June 2017).

Vestager, M, 'The Future of EU Merger Control' (Speech, International Bar Association 24th Annual Competition Conference, 11 September 2020).

Vestager, M, 'Algorithms and Democracy' (Speech, Algorithm Watch Online Policy Dialogue, 30 October 2020).

Wang, B, 'China Taxi Industry Alliance Calls for Antitrust Probe into Didi–Uber Merger' (PINGWEST, 31 December 2020) <https://en.pingwest.com/a/8195> (accessed 2 February 2023).

Wang, F, '工信部叫停网络通话 影响的可不只是钉钉和微信 [The Ministry of Industry and Information Technology Suspending Voice Calls, Affecting More Than Just Dingding and WeChat]' (25 June 2016) <https://www.jiemian.com/article/713764.html> (accessed 8 April 2024).

Wang, F, '腾讯市值首度超过中国移动 成亚洲市值最高公司 [Tencent's Market Value Exceeds China Mobile for the First Time and Becomes the Most Valuable Company in Asia]' (3 October 2018), <https://web.archive.org/web/20181003101012/http://tech.163.com/16/0905/14/C075PMN400097U7R.html> (accessed 6 June 2024).

WayBackMachine, '腾讯市值首度超过中国移动 成亚洲市值最高公司 [Tencent's Market Value Exceeds China Mobile for the First Time and Becomes the Most Valuable Company in Asia]' (WayBackMachine, 3 October 2018) <https://web.archive.org/web/20181003101012/http://tech.163.com/16/0905/14/C075PMN400097U7R.html> (accessed 7 June 2024).

WeChat Security Center, '针对第三方违规导流链接的治理公告 [On the Handling of Third-Party Illegal Infusion Links]' (11 December 2020) <https://mp.weixin.qq.com/s/wrzynlw92rRGo528hZItVg> (accessed 11 March 2023).

Weck, T, 'The New Abuse Rules in the German Competition Act—What's in It for the EU?' (Competition Policy International, 14 April 2020) <www.competitionpolicyinternational.com/thenewabuserulesinthegermancompetitionactwhatsinitfortheeu> (accessed 7 June 2024).

Wei, S, 'Huya, DouYu Abandon Game-Streaming Merger after Regulators Block Deal' (Tech Node, 13 July 2021) <https://technode.com/2021/07/13/huyadouyuabandongamestreamingmergerafterregulatorsblockdeal> (accessed 2 February 2023).

Weiwen, '专家激辩交通部专车新规, 交通部官员回应质疑 [Experts Debate the Ministry of Transport Special Car New Regulations: Ministry of Transport Officials Respond to Questions]' (16 October 2015) <https://www.sohu.com/a/35904982_115250> (accessed 17 July 2022).

Wenzel Bulst, F and S De Vinck, 'DG COMP: Understanding the Metaverse—a Competition Perspective' (17 October 2022) <http://dg-comp-understanding-the-metaverse-a-competition-perspective> (accessed 11 April 2023).

Werner, S and S Du, 'China Increases the Threshold for Merger Control Filing' (Bird&Bird, 2 February 2024) <https://www.twobirds.com/en/insights/2024/china/chinaincreasesthethresholdformergercontrolfiling> (accessed 2 May 2024).

Whish, R, 'New Competition Tool: Legal Comparative Study of Existing Competition Tools Aimed at Addressing Structural Competition Problems with a Particular Focus on the UK's

Market Investigation Tool' (Expert study, 2020) <https://ec.europa.eu/competition/consultations/2020_new_comp_tool/kd0420573enn.pdf> (accessed 2 December 2022).

Wohlsen, M, 'Uber Boss Says Surging Prices Rescue People from the Snow'(WIRED, 17 December 2013) <https://www.wired.com/2013/12/uber-surge-pricing> (accessed 8 June 2024).

Woitier, C, 'France: Google condamné à une amende de 2 millions d'euros pour son magasin d'applications' (*Le Figaro*, 29 March 2022) <https://www.lefigaro.fr/secteur/high-tech/france-google-condamne-a-une-amende-de-2-millions-d-euros-pour-son-magasin-d-applications-20220329> (accessed 7 June 2024).

Liu, Z, 'Kuaidi Marries Didi: End of the Battle or a New Beginning?'(*China Daily*,16 February 2015) <http://www.chinadaily.com.cn/business/tech/201502/16/content_19600016_3.htm> (accessed 2 February 2023).

Woiter, C, 'France: Google condamné à une amende de 2 millions d'euros pour son magasin d'applications' (*Le Figaro*, 29 March 2022) <https://www.lefigaro.fr/secteur/hightech/france googlecondamneauneamendede2millionsdeurospoursonmagasindapplications20220329> (accessed 7 June 2024).

World Economic Forum, 'Competition Policy in a Globalized, Digitalized Economy Report' (2019).

Wu, D, '没有本地户籍开不了出租车？ 属于就业歧视！ 全国人大出手纠正 [Can't Drive a Taxi without a Local Household Registration? It Is Employment Discrimination! National People's Congress Should Correct]' (20 January 2021) <https://news.southcn.com/node_179d29f1ce/68e99e9c25.shtml> (accessed 17 July 2022).

Wu, X, '同程、艺龙合并， 携程的资本收割机是如何炼成的？ [Tongcheng Merged with Yilong, How Was the Ctrip Capital Built?]' (iFeng Finance, 8 January 2018) <https://finance.ifeng.com/a/20180108/15914472_0.shtml> (accessed 7 June 2024).

Wu, Y, '43张反垄断罚单腾讯和阿里系领走25张， 为何罚金仅50万 [25 Out of 43 Antitrust Fines on Tencent and Alibaba Group, Why the Fine Is Only ¥500,000 Yuan] (20 November 2021) <https://www.thepaper.cn/newsDetail_forward_15476991> (accessed 9 October 2023).

Wu, T and S Thompson, 'The Roots of Big Tech Run Disturbingly Deep' (*New York Times*, 7 June 2019).

Wu, P, K Dong, and R Long, '互联网平台企业的市场支配地位认定 [Determination of Market Dominance of Internet Platform Enterprises]' (Beijing Zhonglun Law Firm, 10 May 2021) <https://www.sohu.com/a/465629816_221481> (accessed 7 November 2022).

Xin, H, '中央经济工作会议举行 习近平李克强作重要讲话 [The Central Economic Work Meeting Was Held, Xi Jinping and Li Keqiang Made Important Remarks]' (18 December 2020) <https://www.gov.cn/xinwen/202012/18/content_5571002.htm> (accessed 13 April 2024).

Xin, M, '携程参与《互联网旅游服务行业自律公约》制定 用服务和技术为行业赋能 [Ctrip Participated in the Formulation of the "Internet Travel Service Industry Self-Discipline Convention" to Empower the Industry with Services and Technology]' (27 October 2020) <https://baijiahao.baidu.com/s?id=1681674965693421580&wfr=spider&for=pc> (accessed 4 October 2023).

Xinhua, 'China Establishes Anti-Monopoly Bureau to Secure Fair Competition' (*China Daily*, 19 November 2021) <https://www.chinadaily.com.cn/a/202111/19/WS61973a37a310cdd39bc765f5.html> (accessed 30 July 2023).

Xinhua Net, 'Explanation of the State Council's Institutional Reform Plan at the First Meeting of the 13th National People's Congress on March 13th, 2018' (14 March 2018) <http://www.xinhuanet.com/politics/2018lh/201803/14/c_1122533011.htm> (accessed 30 July 2023).

Xinhua Net, '《竞争法视野下的平台自我优待》学术研讨会召开 [Seminar on "Self-Preferencing of Platforms in the Perspective of Competition Law" Was Successfully Held]' (28 January 2021) <https://baijiahao.baidu.com/s?id=1690123772257090597&wfr=spider&for=pc> (accessed 10 December 2022).

Xu, Z (ed), '互联网平台《二选一》研讨会观点综述 [Summary of the Views of the Seminar on "Either–Or Choice" by Platforms]' (25 April 2019) <https://www.imsilkroad.com/news/p/363138.html> (accessed 7 November 2022).

Yang, X, '大众点评和美团《相杀到相爱》全过程解密：资本意志助推 [Dianping and Meituan's "Killing Each Other to Falling in Love" Whole Process Decryption: The Will of Capital Boosts]' (8 October 2015) <https://www.thepaper.cn/newsDetail_forward_1382928> (accessed 14 April 2024).

Yen, A, 'Apple's DMA Compliance Plan Is a Trap and a Slap in the Face for the European Commission' (Proton Blog, 5 February 2024) <https://proton.me/blog/appledmacompliianceplantrap> (accessed 5 February 2024).

Yi, X and G Tian, 'China Responding to Regulatory Challenges of IT Industry Competition: A Quick Guide to the Antimonopoly Guidelines for Platform Economy (Draft for Comment)' (Zhong Lun Law Firm, 16 November 2020) <https://www.lexology.com/library/detail.aspx?g=7b929b9aa51e4dc593dd2e0ea6b42d88> (accessed 4 October 2023).

Yu, J, '上海出租车非沪籍司机或超三成 主管部门正研究适度放宽属地限制 [The Number of Non-Shanghainese Taxi Drivers May Exceed 30 Per Cent in Shanghai, the Competent Authorities Studying to Moderately Relax Territorial Restrictions]' (*China News*, 24 June 2019) <https://baijiahao.baidu.com/s?id=1637212786052313659&wfr=spider&for=pc > (accessed 17 July 2022).

Yuan, A, 'Didi and Uber China's Merger from an AML Perspective' (In-House Community, 14 March 2017) <https://www.inhousecommunity.com/article/didiuberchinasmergerantimonopolylawperspective> (accessed 2 February 2023).

Yn House, '云南房网：昆明公交垄断呈贡共享单车业务被叫停， 另一霸王合同也得解除 [Kunming Transit Monopoly in Chenggong Bike-Sharing Business Was Called Off, and Another Overbearing Contract Got Rescinded]' (18 November 2022) <https://www.ynhouse.com/news/view252554.html> (accessed 8 April 2024).

Yun Chee, F, 'Exclusive: Apple Offers to Let Rivals Access Tap-and-Go Tech in EU Antitrust Case' (Reuters, 12 December 2023) <https://www.reuters.com/technology/apple-offers-settle-eu-antitrust-charges-apple-pay-sources-say-2023-12-12> (accessed 7 June 2024).

Yun Chee, F, 'EU Regulators Assess Apple's Plan for Complying with Music Streaming Order' (Reuters, 8 April 2024) <https://www.reuters.com/technology/eu-regulators-assess-apples-plan-complying-with-music-streaming-order-2024-04-08> (accessed 27 May 2024).

Yun Chee, F, 'Google Offers to Settle EU Antitrust Probe into Digital Advertising—Source' (Reuters, 23 September 2021) <https://www.reuters.com/technology/exclusivegoogleseekingsettleeuantitrustprobeintoadtechsource20210923> (accessed 7 June 2024).

Zhang, A, 'How Antitrust Facilitates China's Goal to Achieve Technological Self-Sufficiency' (Centre for International Governance Innovation, 27 June 2022) <https://www.cigionline.org/articles/howantitrustfacilitateschinasgoaltoachievetechnologicalselfsufficiency> (accessed 7 June 2024).

Zhang, N, '滴滴有没有垄断市场？ 合并优步中国反垄断调查为何两年无果 [Does Didi Qualify as Monopoly Power? Why There's No Result for the Merger Control Case of Uber China]' (30 August 2018) <https://www.thepaper.cn/newsDetail_forward_2390607> (accessed 13 April 2024).

Zhang, S, '中国批准微软收购暴雪， 魔兽却回不了中国 [China Clears M&A between Microsoft and Activision Blizzard, But Activision Blizzard Can No Longer Return to China]' (31 May 2023) <https://www.thepaper.cn/newsDetail_forward_23294031?commTag=true> (accessed 13 April 2024).

Zhang, X, '携程和去哪儿宣布合并，百度将成携程第一大股东 [Ctrip and Qunar Announce Merger, Baidu Will Become Ctrip's Largest Shareholder]' (26 October 2015) <https://www.thepaper.cn/newsDetail_forward_1389317> (accessed 14 April 2024).

Zheng, S, 'JD Wins $140 Million Damages from Alibaba in Antitrust Suit' (Bloomberg News, 29 December 2023) <https://news.bloomberglaw.com/antitrust/jdwins1byuanindamagesinantimonopolycaseagainstalibaba> (accessed 25 January 2024).

Zhong, R, 'China Fines Alibaba $2.8 Billion in Landmark Antitrust Case' (*New York Times*, 9 April 2021) <https://www.nytimes.com/2021/04/09/technology/chinaalibabamonopolyfine.html> (accessed 7 June 2024).

Zhou, W, '阿里被罚182亿 互联网平台反垄断破局 [Alibaba Fined for 18.2 bn Yuan, a Breakthrough of Platform Antitrust]' (19 April 2019) <https://www.spp.gov.cn/spp/zdgz/202104/t20210419_516009.shtml> (accessed 10 April 2024).

Zhou, X, '北京知识产权法院正式受理抖音诉腾讯垄断纠纷案 [Beijing Intellectual Property Court Formally Accepts ByteDance v. Tencent in Terms of Monopoly Dispute]' (7 February 2021) <http://www.techweb.com.cn/it/20210207/2825270.shtml> (accessed 11 March 2023).

Ziady, H, 'UK Blocks Microsoft Takeover of Activision Blizzard' (CNN News, 26 April 2023) <https://edition.cnn.com/2023/04/26/tech/microsoftactivisionblizzard/index.html> (accessed 2 May 2024).

Zou, J, '拼多多上线《48小时保供套餐》，到达集单数量需求即可下单 [Pinduoduo Online "48 Hours Guarantee Package" Orders Can Be Placed When Arriving at the Set Single Number of Demand]' (8 April 2022) <https://www.thepaper.cn/newsDetail_forward_17519276> (accessed 13 October 2023).

Index

For the benefit of digital users, indexed terms that span two pages (e.g., 52–53) may, on occasion, appear on only one of those pages.

Tables and figures are indicated by an italic *t* and *f* following the page number.